Scene Reconstruction, Pose Estimation and Tracking

Edited by
Rustam Stolkin

Scene Reconstruction, Pose Estimation and Tracking,
Edited by Rustam Stolkin

Republished by InTech
Janeza Trdine 9, 51000 Rijeka, Croatia

Technical Editor Teodora Smiljanic

Cover Designer Dino Smrekar

Additional hard copies can be obtained from orders@intechopen.com

Scene Reconstruction, Pose Estimation and Tracking,, Edited by Rustam Stolkin
p. cm.
ISBN 978-3-902613-06-6

For EU product safety concerns:
IN TECH d.o.o., Prolaz Marije Krucifikse Kozulić 3, 51000 Rijeka, Croatia,
info@intechopen.com or visit our website at intechopen.com.

Meet the editor

Rustam Stolkin is a Research Assistant Professor at the Center for Maritime Systems, Stevens Institute of Technology. He received a MEng degree in Engineering from Oxford University and a PhD in Robot Vision from London University. His research interests include robotics, computer vision, machine intelligence and sensor Systems.

Preface

This volume, in the ITECH Vision Systems series of books, reports recent advances in the use of pattern recognition techniques for computer and robot vision. The sciences of pattern recognition and computational vision have been inextricably intertwined since their early days, some four decades ago with the emergence of fast digital computing. All computer vision techniques could be regarded as a form of pattern recognition, in the broadest sense of the term. Conversely, if one looks through the contents of a typical international pattern recognition conference proceedings, it appears that the large majority (perhaps 70-80%) of all pattern recognition papers are concerned with the analysis of images. In particular, these sciences overlap in areas of low-level vision such as segmentation, edge detection and other kinds of feature extraction and region identification, which are the focus of this book.

Those who were research students in the 1980s may recall struggling to find enough example images in digital form with which to work. In contrast, since the 1990s there has been an explosive increase in the capture, storage and transmission of digital images. This growth is continuing apace, with the proliferation of cheap (even disposable) digital cameras, large scale efforts to digitally scan the world's written texts, increasing use of imaging in medicine, increasing use of visual surveillance systems and the display and transmission of images over the internet.

This growth is driving an acute demand for techniques for automatically managing and exploiting this vast resource of data. Intelligent machinery is needed which can search, recognize, sort and interpret the contents of images. Additionally, vision systems offer the potential to be the most powerful sensory inputs to robotic devices and are thus set to revolutionize industrial automation, surgery and other medical interventions, the security and military sectors, exploration of our oceans and outer space, transportation and many aspects of our daily lives. Computational intelligence, of which intelligent imaging is a central part, is also driving and driven by our inner search to understand the workings of the human brain, through the emerging interdisciplinary field of computational neuroscience.

Not surprisingly, there is now a large worldwide community of researchers who publish a huge number of new discoveries and techniques each year. There are several excellent texts on vision and pattern recognition available to the reader. However, while these classic texts serve as fine introductions and references to the core mathematical ideas, they cannot hope to keep pace with the vast and diverse outpouring of new research papers. In contrast, this volume is intended to gather together the most recent advances in many aspects of visual pattern recognition, from all over the world. An exceptionally international and interdisci-

plinary collection of authors have come together to write these book chapters. Some of these chapters provide detailed expositions of a specific technique and others provide a useful tutorial style overview of some emerging aspect of the field not normally covered in introductory texts.
The book will be useful and stimulating to academic researchers and their students and also industrial vision engineers who need to keep abreast of research developments. This book also provides a particularly good way for experts in one aspect of the field to learn about advances made by their colleagues with different research interests. When browsing through this volume, insights into one's own work are frequently found within a chapter from a different research area. Thus, one aim of this book is to help stimulate cross-fertilization between the multiplying and increasingly disparate branches of the sciences of computer vision and pattern recognition.
I wish to thank the many authors and editors who have volunteered their time and material to make this book possible. On this basis, Advanced Robotic Systems International has been able to make this book entirely available to the community as open access. As well as being available on library shelves, any of these chapters can be downloaded free of charge by any researcher, anywhere in the world. We believe that immediate, world-wide, barrier-free, open access to the full text of research articles is in the best interests of the scientific community.

Editor

Rustam Stolkin
Stevens Institute of Technology
USA

Contents

1

Real-Time Object Segmentation of the Disparity Map Using Projection-Based Region Merging

Dongil Han
Vision and Image Processing Lab.
Sejong University 98 Kunja-dong, Kwagjin-gu, Seoul
Korea

1. Introduction

Robots have been mostly used in industrial environment, but modern developments of household robot-cleaner suggest the necessity of household robots as becoming in reality. Most industrial robots have been used for factory automation that perform simple and iterative tasks at high speed, whereas household robots need various interfaces with a man while moving in indoor environment like a household robot-cleaner does.

Robots activate in indoor environment using various sensors such as vision, laser, ultrasonic sensor, or voice sensor to detect indoor circumstance. Especially robot's routing plan and collision avoidance need three-dimensional information of robot's surrounding environment. This can be obtained by using a stereo vision camera which provides a general and huge amount of 3-D information. But this computation is too big to solve in real-time with the existing microprocessor when using a stereo vision camera for capturing 3-D image information.

High-level computer vision tasks, such as robot navigation and collision avoidance, require 3-D depth information of the surrounding environment at video rate. Current general-purpose microprocessors are too slow to perform stereo vision at video rate. For example, it takes several seconds to execute a medium-sized stereo vision algorithm for a single pair of images using one 1 GHz general-purpose microprocessor.

To overcome this limitation, designers in the last decade have built reprogrammable chips called FPGA(Field-Programmable Gate Arrays) hardware systems to accelerate the performance of the vision systems. These devices consist of programmable logic gates and routing which can be re-configured to implement practically any hardware function. Hardware implementations allow one to apply the parallelism that is common in image processing and vision algorithms, and to build systems to perform specific calculations quickly compared to software implementations.

A number of methods of finding depth information in video-rate have been reported. Among others, multi-baseline stereo theory is developed and the video-rate stereo machine has the capability of generating a dense depth map of 256x240 pixels at the frame rate of 30 frames/sec in [1-2]. An algorithm proposed from *parallel relaxation algorithm for disparity computation* [3] results reduction of error rate and enhancement of computational complexity of problems. Also, an algorithm proposed from *depth discontinuities by pixel-to pixel stereo* [4] is concentrated on the calculation speed and rapidly changing disparity map. It is not possible to search for the exact depth of the discontinuities when there is no change in lightness of boundary. Also the high-accuracy stereo technique [5] mentioned the difficulty of drawing sharp line between intricate occlusion situations and some highly-slanted surfaces (cylinder etc.), complex surface shapes and textureless shapes. Nevertheless, for algorithm suggested in this chapter, we can use the post-processing as first half of process to get more neat disparity map produced by other many stereo matching algorithms, which can be used for the object segmentation.

To embody object segmentation, we used hardware-oriented technology which reduces tasks of the software, contrary to conventional software-oriented method. Also, it has great effectiveness that reduces software processing time by the help of real-time region data support, which containing various kinds of object information, that reduces total area of search process such as object or face recognition. Use of embedded software based on low-cost embedded processor, compare to use of high-tech processor, to conduct tasks of object recognition, object tracking, etc in real-time provides a suggestion of a household robot application.

This chapter is organized as follows: Section 2 describes a brief review of proposed algorithm. Section 3 explains refinement block while Section 4 explains segmentation. At the conclusion, the experimental results including results of depth computation and labeling are discussed in Section. 5

2. Algorithm Overview

In this chapter, we attempted to make clearer object segmentation using projection-based region merging of disparity map produced by applied trellis-based parallel stereo matching algorithm described in [6]. Throughout this experiment, we verified the performance. Necessity of post-processing algorithm application for many different characterized stereo matching has been ascertained through various experiment performed in this chapter.

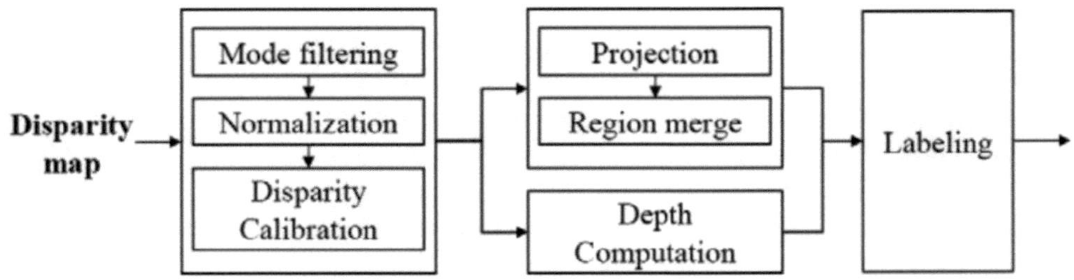

Figure 1. Block diagram of the post processing algorithm

The block diagram of the proposed post-processing algorithm is shown in figure 1. The post-processing algorithm is progressed in three big stages. The first stage is the refinement block, which carries normalization referenced from filtering and disparity max value, and elimination of noise using histogram consecutively. In second stage, the depth computation which helps to find out the distance between camera and original objects on disparity map and the image segmentation which takes responsibility of object partition are accomplished

in a row. Finally in the last stage, information of object existed in original image is gathered and integrated with all information proposed in second stage.
The cause of noise in disparity map can be textureless object, background video, or occlusion etc. In stereo matching algorithm, possibility of textureless object and occluded area must be necessarily considered, but even through consideration has been applied, precise result may not be processed. Therefore, refinement stage like filtering must be included on the first half of post-processing to be able to segment the object with much more clear disparity map.

3. Refinement

In this stage, we try to obtain purified disparity map by the utilization of disparity calibration algorithm which used for mode filtering of disparity map out of trellis-based parallel stereo matching algorithm, with the normalization, and disparity calibration.

3.1 Mode filtering

The noise removal techniques in image and video include several kinds of linear and nonlinear filtering techniques. Through out the experiment, we adopted the mode filter technique for preserving boundary of image and effective removal of noise. The window size used for filtering has been fixed to 7x7, considering the complexity and performance of hardware when it is implemented. The numerical equation used for mode filtering is as follow:

$$C_i = \begin{cases} C_i + 1 & \left(D_{ij} = 0\right), 0 \le j < k \\ C_i & (D_{ij} \ne 0), 0 \le j < k \end{cases} \tag{1}$$

Here,

$$D_{ij} = x_i - x_j (0 \le i < k, 0 \le j < k) \tag{2}$$

And then, we can get

$$X_m = \begin{cases} x_i \; for \max_i(\forall C_i) & (\forall C_i \ne 1) \\ x_{center} & (\forall C_i = 1) \end{cases} \tag{3}$$

In equation (1) and (2), the value of k represents the window size. In this chapter, 7x7=49 is used. From equation (2), with given disparity map input x_i , and only changing the argument of pixel value j in the 7x7 window, we can calculate the difference between two pixel values. When D_{ij} value is 0 in equation (1), we increase the C_i value by one. If we can find the largest value of C_i, then the mode value X_m can be decided. If all the values of x_i are different, we can not find the maximum value of C_i. In this case, we select and decide on the center value of window, x_{center}(window size 7x7 has been used in this chapter, thus x_{24} should be utilized).

3.2 Normalization

After the mode filtering, noise removed disparity map can be obtained. Then by using the disparity max value used for getting the stereo matching image, the disparity values of mode filtered image are mapped out new normalized values with regular and discrete intervals.

The disparity max value can be decided in the stereo matching stage, which is the value to decide the maximum displacement of matching pixels which can be calculated from the left image to right image. In normalization stage, disparity map pixels, composed of 0~255 gradation values, is divided into 0~disparity max range (in barn1 image, disparity max value is 32). This process removes unnecessary disparity map. The value of 0~disparity max range is again multiplied to the pixel values calculated before, and finally restored to 0~255 gradation values.

3.3 Disparity Calibration

In disparity calibration stage, which is the final stage of refinement, the normalized disparity value is accumulated to form a histogram of each frame. During accumulation process, we ignore the disparity value under the given threshold value to remove the noise in dark area.

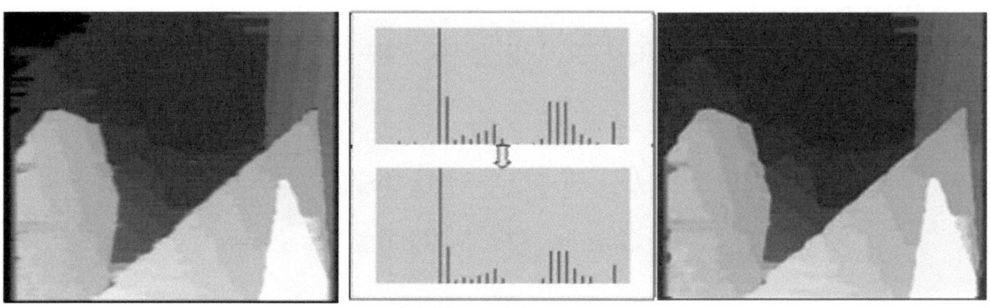

(a) Barn1 image

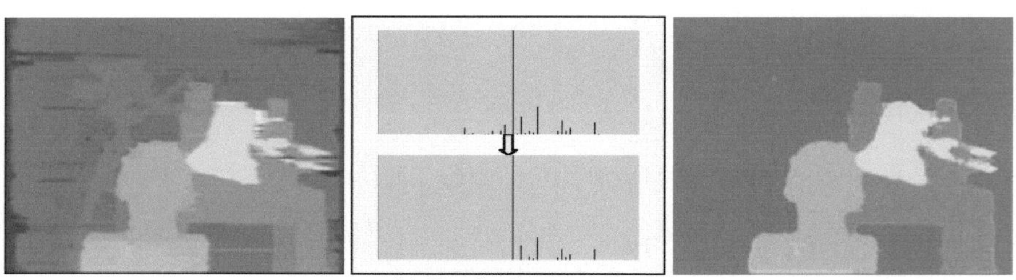

(b) Tsukuba image

Figure 2. The result of disparity calibration (*left: stereo matching result, middle: histogram comparison, right: calibrated disparity map*)

And in this histogram, the data under the predetermined frequency level can also be considered as noise. Thus, after the formation of the histogram, the accumulated pixel data are sorted out according to the frequency. The upper part of the histogram which consists of approximately 90% of total histogram area holds their pixel values. About the pixel frequency which does not reach the given specific threshold, the nearest value is selected among the accumulated pixel values which belong to the upper part of the sorted histogram. The center part of figure 2 (a) and (b) shows the histogram data before and after the disparity calibration. And the right part of figure 2 (a) and (b) shows the tsukuba and barn1 image after the disparity calibration stage.

4. Segmentation

The objective of this block is to separate objects from the disparity map and to partition slanted objects to other objects. In this chapter, to achieve the objectives, we conducted the horizontal and vertical projection for each level of disparity map and sequential region merging with projection results.

4.1 Projection

The task to separate object from the distance information is completed by processing horizontal and vertical projection of each disparity map. The results of specific projections are shown in figure 3.

Using the horizontal and vertical projection for each disparity level, the region data for all level of disparity map could be obtained, and the horizontal position information of a region data is expressed by starting and ending point of vertical direction projection $P_x(n)=(X_s(n), X_e(n))$, while the vertical position information of a region data is expressed by starting and ending point of horizontal direction projection $P_y(n)=((n), Y_e(n))$. Also a region data is represented as $R(n)=(P_x(n), P_y(n))$.

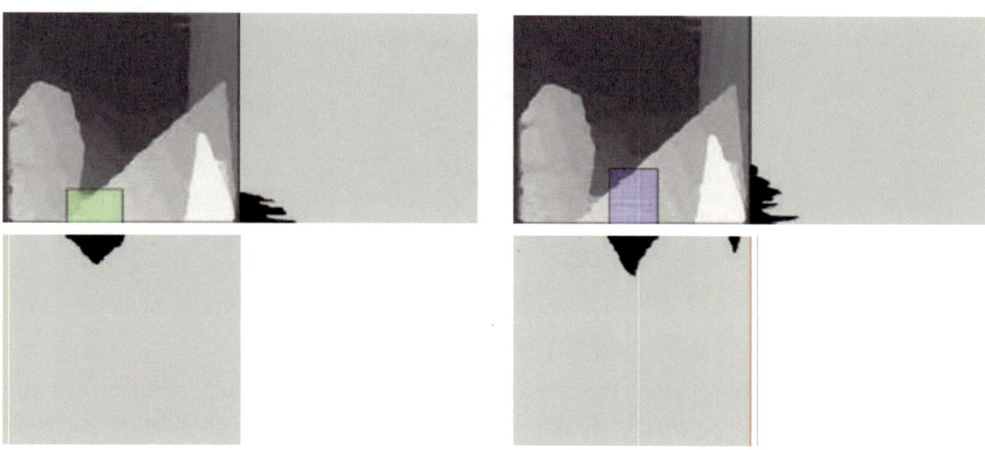

(a) Second level (b) Third level

Figure 3. The projection examples about each disparity level

4.2 Region Merge

Whether to merge the region or not can be decided after all of the region information about each depth level is obtained. In the case of flat or slanted object, which produce wide range of distances from camera, the objects need to be recognized as one object. Therefore, regular rule is necessary to be applied on the merging algorithm.

In this chapter, the merging algorithm is such that the two region of depth level is overlapped and its difference of depth level is just one level, merging the regional information of two depth level. And this procedure is conducted until there are no remaining depth levels to merging. The above description is summarized as follows:

$$\begin{aligned} P_x(n) &= \{X_s(n), X_e(n)\} \\ P_y(n) &= \{Y_s(n), Y_e(n)\} \\ R(n) &= \{P_x(n), P_y(n)\} \quad n = r, \ldots, 3, 2, 1 \end{aligned} \tag{4}$$

$$\begin{aligned} P_X(n) &= (\min(X_s(n), X_s(n-1)), \max(X_e(n), X_e(n-1))) \\ P_Y(n) &= (\min(Y_s(n), Y_s(n-1)), \max(Y_e(n), Y_e(n-1))) \end{aligned} \tag{5}$$

$$R^{merge}(n) = \begin{cases} R'(n) = [P_X(n), P_Y(n)] & R(n) \in R(n-1) \\ R\ (n) = [P_x(n), P_y(n)] & R(n) \notin R(n-1) \end{cases} \tag{6}$$

The r value in equation (4) represents the number of all separated region in each disparity depth level, and n in equation (4)~(6) is the level of disparity map. $P_x(n)$, $P_y(n)$, $R(n)$ in equation (4) represents the obtained region data in projection block.

When the adjacent two regions are overlap each other, we regard two regions as one object, and merge two regional information by using the equation (5). The final region merging rule is described in equation (6).

Figure 4. Disparity map after region merging (*barn1 image*)

Figure 4 shows disparity map after the region merging process. When considering the implementation of hardware, the result of this chapter shows the possibility of easy hardware implementation.

5 Experimental Results

5.1 Experimental environment

In this chapter, we proved the validity of proposed algorithm with C-language level implementation. And, after that, we implemented the proposed algorithms with VHDL level and we were able to get result of hardware simulation using Modelsim. Finally, the proposed post-processing algorithm is implemented in FPGA. We used 320x240 resolution and frame rates of 60 fps, 1/3" CMOS stereo camera, and the full logic is tested with Xilinx

Virtex-4 Series XC4VLX200. Figure 5 shows experimental environment. The stereo camera takes images to embedded system and the display monitor shows processed result in real-time. Control PC is linked to embedded system and to hub to conduct control task.

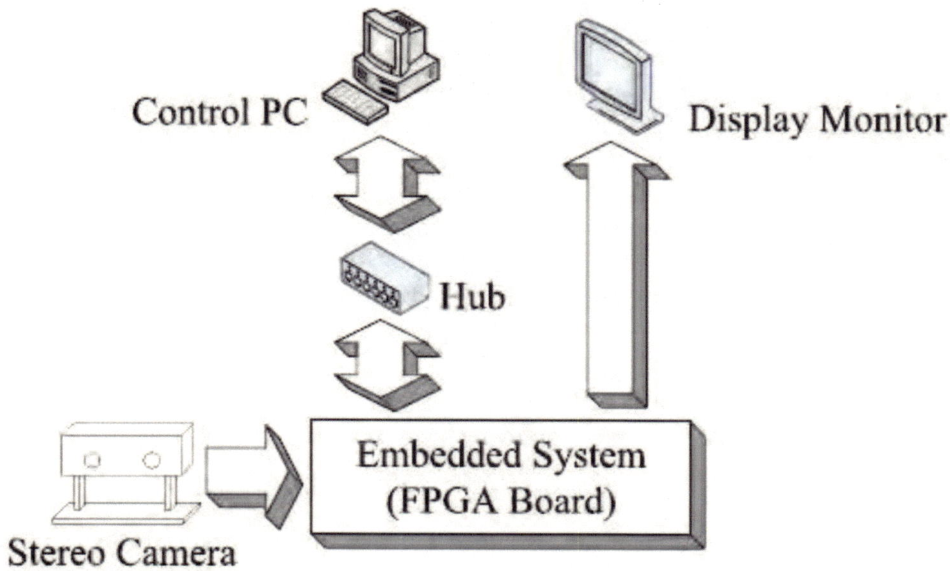

Figure 5. Experimental environment

5.2 stereo matching post processing FPGA logic simulation

Figure 6 shows the result of VHDL simulation to activate *stereo matching post processing* (SMPP) module. When Vactive sync is in high region, it takes 320x240-sized stereo image and shows it on the screen after post processing in real time. Also the control pc in Figure 5 can choose an object to be shown. Table 1 explains signals used in simulation established with FPGA.

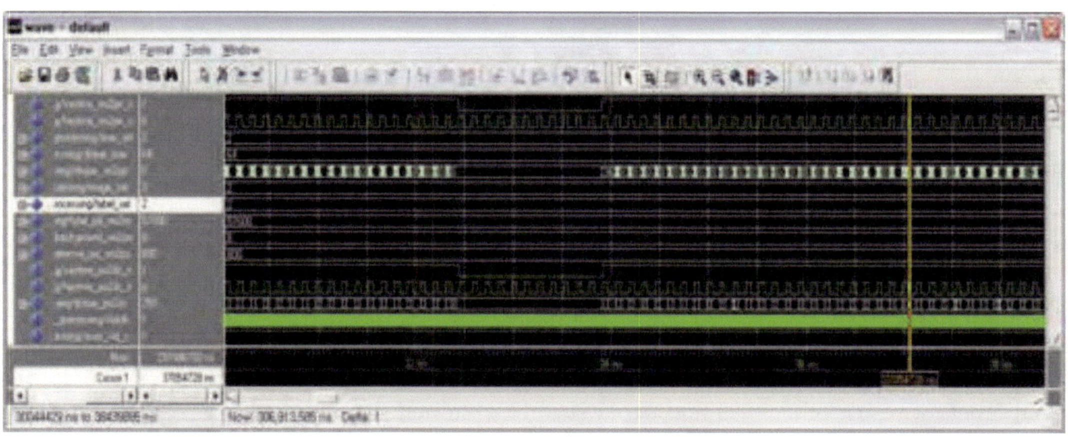

Figure 6. The result of VHDL simulation to activate SMPP module

Vactive_sm2po_n	Input vactive signal of SMPP
Hactive_sm2po_n	Input hactive signal of SMPP
Dispar_sm2po	Input disparity map signal of SMPP
Max_sel	Input register for selecting gray value about object
Dispar_max	Input register about Maximum disparity
Image_sel	Input register for selecting image
Label_sel	Input register for selecting label order
Total_pxl_se2re	Input register about total pixel number of threshold of histogram
Background_sm2po	Input register about background value
Remove_pxl_sm2po	Input register about noise threshold of histogram
Heighte_lb2dp_info	Output register about Height end point of segment object
Vactive_po2ds_n	Output vactive signal of SMPP
Hactive_po2ds_n	Output hactive signal of SMPP
Dispar_po2ds`	Output Disparity map signal of SMPP
CLK	Active clock of FPGA
RESET	Active reset of FPGA

Table. 1. Simulation signal

5.3 Result

This chapter examined the algorithms using various images within stereo matching database for first step and secured its validity. As shown in figure 4, we obtained perfect result with *barn1* image. We performed another experiment using *tsukuba* image and proved that the equal result can be gained. Also, in the result of applying post-processing algorithm in several other stereo images, we are able to obtain similar image as figure 4.

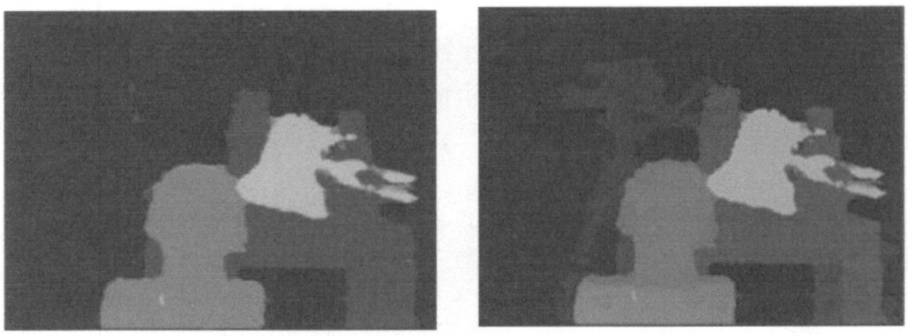

Figure 7. Disparity map after region merging (tsukuba image) (left: C simulation result, right: VHDL simulation result)

The proposed post-processing algorithm is also implemented in fixed-point C and VHDL code. The C and VHDL code test result about the *tsukuba* image is shown in figure 7 and we obtained same results. This result is passed onto labeling stage, with the depth information of camera extracted from depth calculation block. Synthesizing region information and depth information of segmented object is processed in labeling stage. Figure 8 shows the final labeling result of *tsukuba* and *barn1* images obtained from VHDL simulation. Figure 9 shows the BMP (Bad Map Percentage) and PSNR test results with *barn1*, *barn2* and *tsukuba* images.

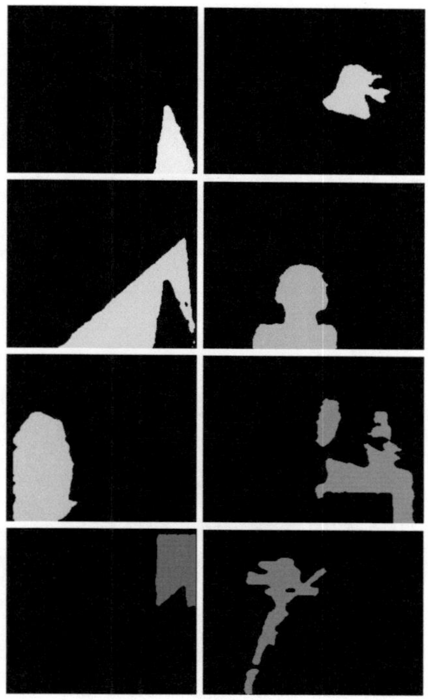

Figure 8. Labeling results (left: barn1 image, right: tsukuba image)

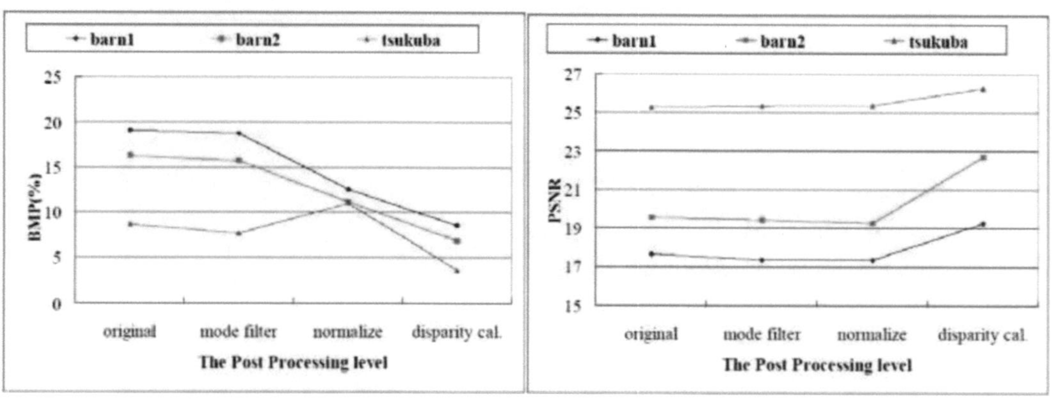

(a) BMP test results (b) PSNR test results

Figure 9. Image quality comparison with intermediate result images

We have designed unified FPGA board module for stereo camera interface, stereo matching, stereo matching post processing, host interface and display. And we also implemented embedded system software by constructing necessary device driver with MX21 350MHz microprocessor environment. Table 2 shows the logic gates of proposed SMPP module when retargeting FPGA. Figure 10 ~13 show real time captured images of stereo camera input and the results of SMPP modules using control pc.

	Virtex4 Available	**Unified module**	**SM module**	***SMPP module***
Number of Slice Flip Flops	178,176	38,658	11,583	17,369
Number of 4 input LUTs	178,176	71,442	25,124	40,957
Number of occupied Slices	89,088	55,531	19,917	29,507

Table 2. The logic gates for implementing the FPGA board

(a) Left camera input

(b) Right camera input

(c) Stereo matching result

(d) Nearest object segment result

Figure 10. Real-time test example 1

(a) Left camera input

(b) Right camera input

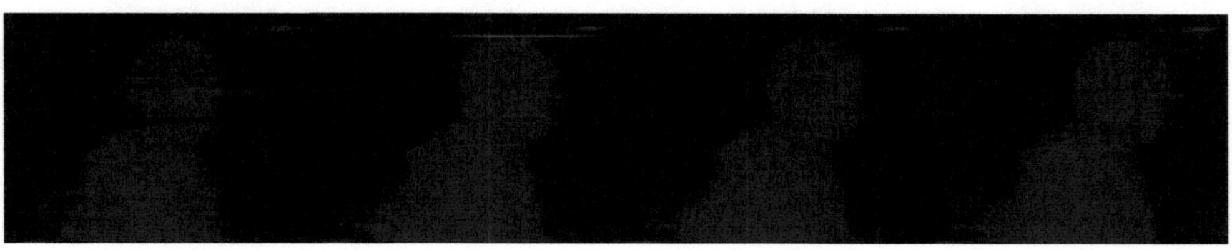

(c) Stereo matching result

(d) Nearest object segment result

Figure 11. Real-time test example 2

(a) Left camera input

(b) Right camera input

(c) Stereo matching result

(d) Nearest object segment result

Figure 12. Real-time test example 3

(a) Left camera input

(b) Right camera input

(c) Stereo matching result

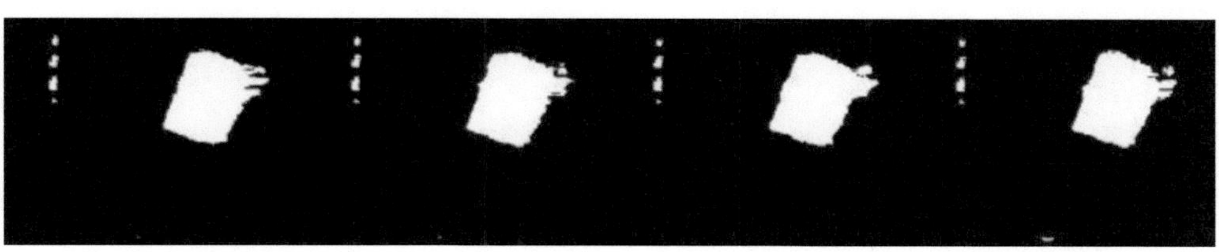

(d) Nearest object segment result

Figure 13. Real-time test example 4

Figure 14 shows control application program operated on control pc. This application program communicates to board and hub to calibrate camera and to modify registry of each modules. Also it can capture images on the screen which can be useful for debug jobs. Figure 15 shows image collecting stereo camera. Figure 16 shows implemented embedded system and unified FPGA board module.

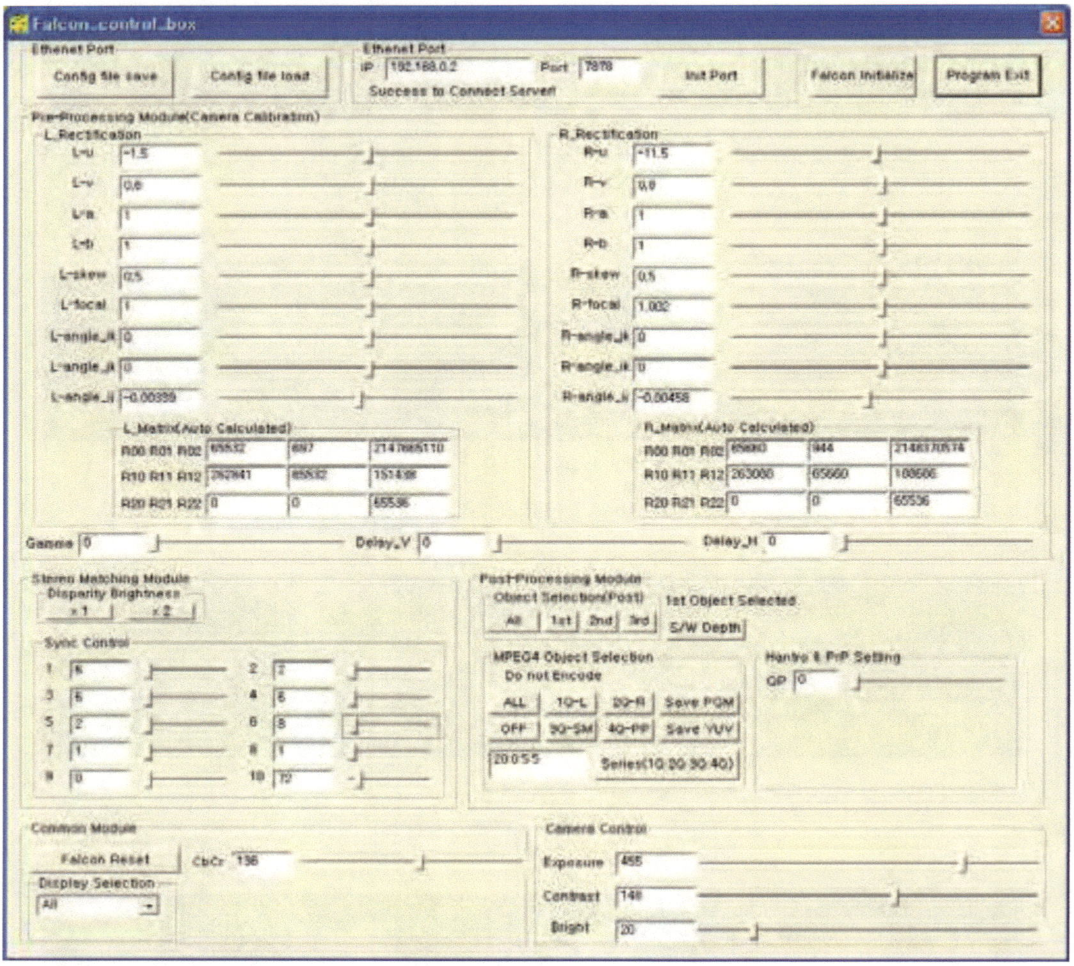

Figure 14. The control applications operated on control pc

Figure 15. The stereo camera.

Figure 16. Embedded System and unified FPGA board module

5.4 Software application

A household robot has to perform actions like obstacle avoidance or human recognition activity. One of systems used widely can recognize human by extracting possible human-like areas among those with motions within the screen. However, the system can have performance drops when human doesn't move or the robot moves.
The algorithm suggested in this chapter extracts human shapes on depth map using stereo matching to get relative distances between camera and other objects in real-time, as it also can separate each area in real-time, which keeps performance regardless of human's or robot's motions mentioned above.

A. Application to human recognition

The followings are description of the human recognition method using results of our study.

- ***Step. 1.*** Extract edge of screen in 80x60 size from the labeled image (Fig 17.(a),320x240).
- ***Step. 2.*** Recognize Ω/A pattern (Fig. 17. (c)) among extracted edges.
- ***Step. 3.*** Determine possibility of human exist considering face size (a,b), height of face (c), width of shoulders, distances, or etc with edges of Ω/A pattern.

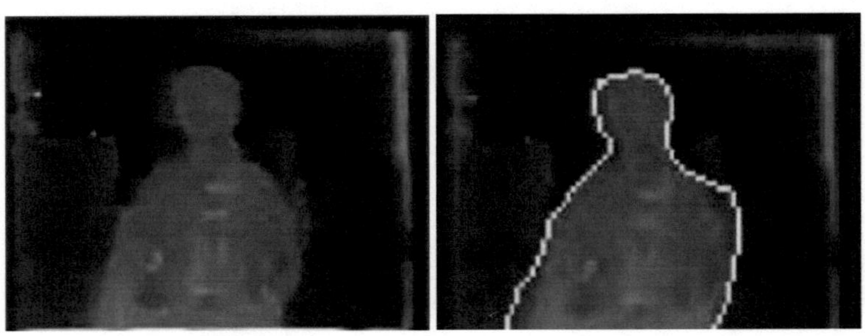

(a) Labeled image (b) Extracted edges

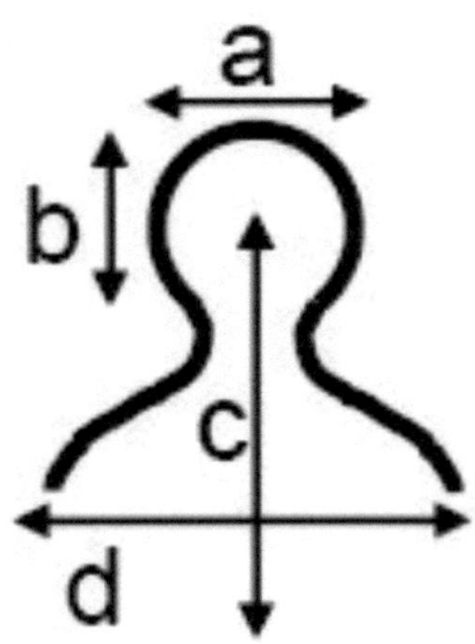

(c) Ω/A type pattern

Figure 17. Example of human recognition with software application

B. Application to face recognition

Figure 18 shows an application of our study to face recognition issue. Figure 18 (a) is an input image, and (b) is an area of object segmentation produced by the algorithm suggested in this chapter. Figure 18 (c) is an overlapped image that has an advantage of faster processing speed by focusing target area to possible human position using segmentation information , compare to total search for face recognition.

(a) Input image

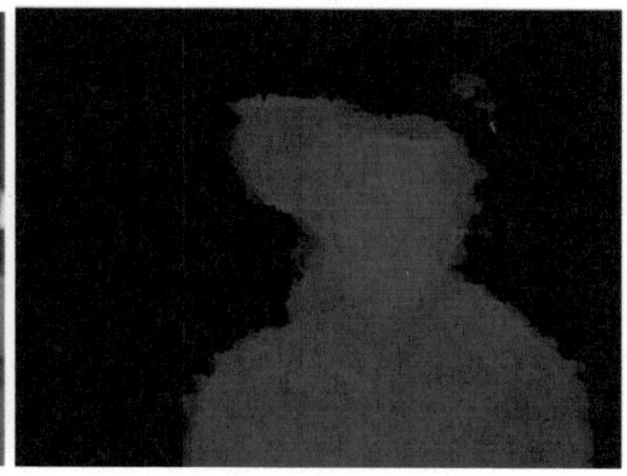

(b) Labeling image

(c) Overlap image

Figure 18. Application to face recognition

6. Conclusion

If we can get more accurate result than the conventional stereo vision system, performance of object recognition and collision avoidance will be improved in robot vision applications. So, we used the process of stereo matching algorithm with post processing in this chapter.
The problems such as lack of texture and existence of occlusion area must be carefully considered in matching algorithm and accurate dividing objects must be processed. Also post processing module is necessary as removal of remaining noise. Thus, this chapter developed stereo matching post process algorithm that is able to provide distance between robot and the object regarding trellis-based parallel stereo matching result and to provide the object's area data in real time and examined it by real time FPGA test.
The developed stereo matching post process algorithm is considering possibility of hardware implementation and implemented it using C-algorithm for first step. Then we examined it with various images registered in stereo matching database to secure validity. Also we have developed VHDL and on-boarded it to unified FPGA board module to examine various real time tests using stereo camera on various indoor environments for

second step. As the result of many experiments, we were able to confirm quality improvement of stereo matching images.
To embody object segmentation, we used hardware-oriented technology which reduces tasks of the software. Also, it has great effectiveness that reduces software processing time by the help of real-time region data support, which containing size and distance information of various kinds of objects, that reduces total area of search process for face or object recognition. Use of embedded software based on low-cost embedded processor to conduct tasks of object recognition, object tracking, etc in real-time provides a suggestion of a household robot application.

7. Acknowledgments

This work is supported by ETRI. The hardware verification tools are support by the NEXTEYE Co., Ltd and the IC Design Education Centre.

8. References

1. Takeo Kanade, Atsushi Yoshida, Kazuo Oda, Hiroshi Kano and Masaya Tanaka: A Stereo Machine for Video-rate Dense Depth Mapping and Its New applications. Proceeding of IEEE Computer Society Conference on Computer Vision and Pattern Recognition. 18–20 June (1996) 196–220
2. Dongil Han, and Dae-Hwan Hwang: A Novel Stereo Matching Method for Wide Disparity Range Detection. Proceeding of LNCS 3656 (Image analysis and Recognition). Sep. –Oct. (2005) 643–650
3. Jung-Gu Kim, Hong Jeong: Parallel relaxation algorithm for disparity computation. IEEE Electronics Letters, Vol. 33, Issue 16. 31 July (1997) 1367–1368
4. Birchfield S. Tomasi C: Depth discontinuities by pixel-to-pixel stereo. Proceeding of Computer Vision, 1998. Sixth International Conference on 4–7. Jan. (1998) 1073–1080
5. Scharstein D. Szeliski R: High-accuracy stereo depth maps using structured light. Proceeding of Computer Vision and Pattern Recognition, 2003. IEEE Computer Society Conference, Vol. 1. 18–20 June (2003) 195–202, Vol. 1. Digital Object Identifier 10.1109/CVPR.2003. 1211354.
6. Yuns Oh, Hong Jeong: Trellis-based Parallel Stereo Matching. Proceeding of Acoustics, Speech, and Signal Processing, 2000. ICASSP '00. 2000 IEEE International Conference, Vol. 6. June (2000) 2143–2146

2

A Novel Omnidirectional Stereo Vision System via a Single Camera[1]

Chuanjiang Luo, Liancheng Su & Feng Zhu
Shenyang Institute of Automation, Chinese Academy of Sciences
P.R. China

1. Introduction

Obtaining panoramic 3D map information for mobile robots is essential for navigation and action planning. Although there are other ways to fulfill this task, such as ultrasonic sensors or laser range finders, stereo vision system excels them in its precision and real-time speed without energy emission.

But the conventional stereo vision systems are limited in their fields of view (FOV). An effective way to enhance FOV is to construct an omnidirectional vision system using mirrors in conjunction with perspective cameras. These systems are normally referred to as catadioptric and have been applied to robot localization and navigation by several researchers (Bunschoten & Krose, 2002; Menegatti et al., 2004). A common constraint upon the omnidirectional sensors modeling requires that all the imaged rays pass through a unique point called single viewpoint (SVP) (Baker & Nayar, 1999). The reason a single viewpoint is so desirable is that it is a requirement for the generation of pure perspective images from the sensed images. These perspective images can subsequently be processed using the vast array of techniques developed in the field of computer vision that assume perspective projection. The mirrors popularly used to construct wide FOV catadioptric are hyperbolic or parabolic. But the latter must be coupled with expensive telecentric optics which restricts them to limited applications in panoramic vision.

Mobile robot navigation using binocular omnidirectional stereo vision has been reported in (Menegatti et al., 2004; Yagi, 2002; Zhu, 2001). Such two-camera stereo systems can be classified as horizontal stereo systems and vertical stereo systems according to their cameras' configuration. In (Ma, 2003), the cameras are configured horizontally and the baseline of triangulation is in the horizontal plane. This configuration brings two problems: one is that the epiploar line becomes curved line leading to increasing computational cost; the other is that the accuracy of the 3D measurement depends on the direction of a landmark. In the omnidirectional stereo vision system (Gluckman et al., 1998; Koyasu et al., 2002; Koyasu et al., 2003), two omnidirectional cameras are vertically arranged. Such configuration escapes the shortcomings brought by horizontal stereo system, but the power cable and data bus introduce occlusion to the images captured by this configuration. In

[1] This work is supported by National Science Foundation of P.R. China (60575024).

addition, two-camera stereo systems are costly and complicated besides having the problem of requiring precise positioning of the cameras.

Single camera stereo has several advantages over two-camera stereo. Because only a single camera and digitizer are used, system parameters such as spectral response, gain, and offset are identical for the stereo pair. In addition, only a single set of intrinsic parameters needs to be determined. The prominent advantage of single camera stereo over two-camera configuration is that it does not need data synchronization. Omnidirectional stereo based on a double lobed mirror and a single camera was developed in (Southwell et al., 1996; Conroy & Moore, 1999; Cabral et al., 2004). A double lobed mirror is a coaxial mirror pair, where the centers of both mirrors are collinear with the camera axis, and the mirrors have a profile radially symmetric around this axis. This arrangement has the advantage to produce two panoramic views of the scene in a single image. But the disadvantage of this method is the relatively small baseline it provides. Since the two mirrors are so close together, the effective baseline for stereo calculation is quite small.

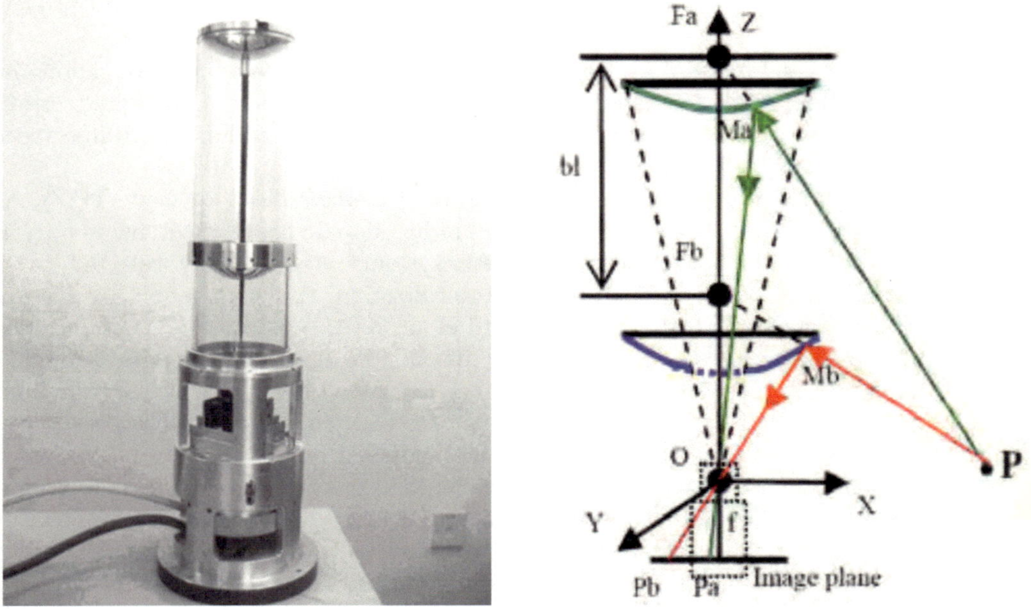

a) b)

Figure 1. a) The appearance of the stereo vision system. b) The configuration of the system

To overcome this drawback, we have proposed a novel large baseline panoramic vision system in this chapter. We will describe in detail how to use this vision system to obtain reliable 3D depth maps of surrounding environment. In the subsequent arrangement of this chapter, Section 2 is dedicated to describe the principle of our catadioptric stereo vision system. Following that, a full model of calibrating the system including the rotation and translation between the camera and mirrors is presented in Section 3. In Section 4, a three-step method that combines the merit of feature matching and dense global matching is proposed to get a fast and reliable matching result and eventually the 3D depth map. Finally, we will give a brief evaluation of our system and some ideas for our future work in the summary.

2. Principle of Our Vision System

The system we have developed (Su & Zhu, 2005) is based on a common perspective camera coupled with two hyperbolic mirrors, which are separately fixed inside a glass cylinder (Fig.1a). The two hyperbolic mirrors share one focus which coincides with the camera center. A hole in the below mirror permits imaging via the mirror above. As the separation between the two mirrors provides much enlarged baseline, the precision of the system has been improved correspondingly. The coaxial configuration of the camera and the two hyperbolic mirrors makes the epipolar line radially collinear, thus making the system free of the search process for complex epiploar curve in stereo matching (Fig. 3).
To describe the triangulation for computing 3D coordinates of space points, we define the focal point C as the origin of our reference frame, z-axis parallel to the optical axis pointing above. Then mirrors can be represented as:

$$\frac{(z-c_i)^2}{a^2}-\frac{(x^2+y^2)}{b^2}=1, \quad (i=1,2) \tag{1}$$

Only the incident rays pointing to the focus $F_a(0,0,2c_a)$, $F_b(0,0,2c_b)$ will be reflected by the mirrors to pass through the focal point of the camera. The incident ray passing the space point $P(x,y,z)$ reaches the mirrors at points M_a and M_b, being projected onto the image at points $P_a(u_a,v_a,-f)$ and $P_b(u_b,v_b,-f)$ respectively. As P_a and P_b are known, M_a and M_b can be represented by:

$$\frac{x_{M_i}}{u_i}=\frac{y_{M_i}}{v_i}=\frac{z_{M_i}}{-f}, \quad (i=1,2) \tag{2}$$

Since point M_a and M_b are on the mirrors, they satisfy the equation of the mirrors. Their coordinates can be solved from equation group (1) and (2). Then the equation of rays F_aP and F_bP are:

$$\frac{x_p}{x_i}=\frac{y_p}{y_i}=\frac{z_p-2c_i}{z_i-2c_i}, \quad (i=1,2) \tag{3}$$

We can finally figure out coordinate of the space point P by solving the equation (3).

3. System Calibration

3.1 Overview

In using the omnidirectional stereo vision system, its calibration is important, as in the case of conventional stereo systems (Luong & Faugeras, 1996; Zhang & Faugeras, 1997). We present a full model of the imaging process, which includes the rotation and translation between the camera and mirror, and an algorithm to determine this relative position from observations of known points in a single image.
There have been many works on the calibration of omnidirectional cameras. Some of them are for estimating intrinsic parameters (Ying & Hu, 2004; Geyer & Daniilidis, 1999; Geyer Daniilidis, 2000; Kang, 2000). In (Geyer & Daniilidis, 1999; Geyer Daniilidis, 2000), Geyer & Daniilidis presented a geometric method using two or more sets of parallel lines in one

image to determine the camera aspect ratio, a scale factor that is the product of the camera and mirror focal lengths, and the principal point. Kang (Kang, 2000) describes two methods. The first recovers the image center and mirror parabolic parameter from the image of the mirror's circular boundary in one image; of course, this method requires that the mirror's boundary be visible in the image. The second method uses minimization to recover skew in addition to Geyer's parameters. In this method the image measurements are point correspondences in multiple image pairs. Miousik & Pajdla developed methods of calibrating both intrinsic and extrinsic parameters (Miousik & Pajdla, 2003a; Miousik & Pajdla, 2003b). In (Geyer & Daniilidis, 2003), Geyer & Daniilidis developed a method for rectifying omnidirectional image pairs, generating a rectified pair of normal perspective images.

Because the advantages of single viewpoint cameras are only achieved if the mirror axis is aligned with the camera axis, these methods mentioned above all assume that these axes are parallel rather than determining the relative rotation between the mirror and camera. A more complete calibration procedure for a catadioptric camera which estimates the intrinsic camera parameters and the pose of the mirror related to the camera appeared at (Fabrizio et al., 2002), the author used the images of two known radius circles at two different planes in an omnidirectional camera structure to calibrate the intrinsic camera parameters and the camera pose with respect to the mirror. But this proposed technique cannot be easily generalized to all kinds of catadioptric sensors for it requires the two circles be visible on the mirror. Meanwhile, this technique calibrated the intrinsic parameters combined to extrinsic parameters, so there are eleven parameters (five intrinsic parameters and six extrinsic parameters) need to be determined. As the model of projection is nonlinear the computation of the system is so complex that the parameters cannot be determined with good precision.

Our calibration is performed within a general minimization framework, and easily accommodates any combination of mirror and camera. For single viewpoint combinations, the advantages of the single viewpoint can be exploited only if the camera and mirror are assumed to be properly aligned. So for these combinations, the simpler single viewpoint projection model, rather than the full model described here, should be adopted only if the misalignment between the mirror and camera is sufficiently small. In this case, the calibration algorithm that we describe is useful as a software verification of the alignment accuracy.

Our projection model and calibration algorithm separate the conventional camera intrinsics (e.g., focal length, principal point) from the relative position between the mirrors and the camera (i.e., the camera-to-mirrors coordinate transformation) to reduce computational complexity and improve the calibration precision. The conventional camera intrinsics can be determined using any existing method. For the experiments described here, we have used the method implemented in http://www.vision.caltech.edu/bouguetj/calib_doc/. Once the camera intrinsics are known, the camera-to-mirrors transformation can be determined by obtaining an image of calibration targets whose three-dimensional positions are known, and then minimizing the difference between coordinates of the targets and the locations calculated from the targets' images through the projection model. Fig. 3 shows one example of calibration image used in our experiments. The locations of the three dimensional points have been surveyed with an accuracy of about one millimeter. If the inaccuracy of image point due to discrete distribution of pixels is taken into account, the total measuring error is about five millimeters.

3.2 Projection Model

Fig. 2 depicts the full imaging model of a perspective camera with two hyperbolic mirrors. There are three essentially coordinate systems.

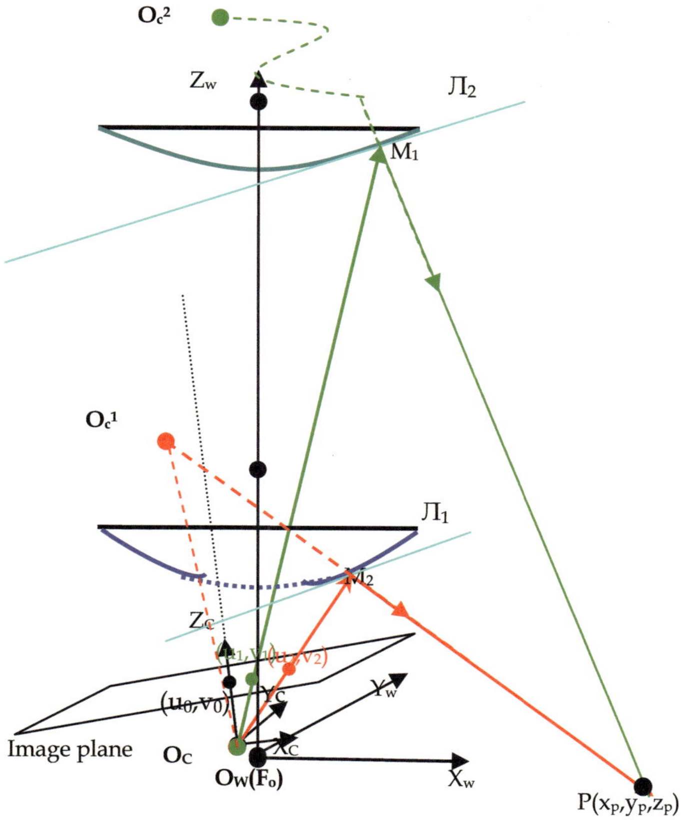

Figure 2. The projection model of the omnidirectional stereo vision system. There are transformations between the camera coordinate system and the mirror (or world) coordinate system

1. The camera coordinate system centered at the camera center O_c, the optical axis is aligned with the z-axis of the camera coordinate system;
2. The mirror system centered at common foci of the hyperbolic mirrors F_o, the mirrors axes is aligned with the z-axis of the mirror coordinate system (We assume that the axes of the mirrors are aligned well, and the common foci are coincident, from the mirrors manufacturing sheet we know it is reasonable);
3. The world system centered at O_w. The omnidirectional stereo vision system was placed on a plane desk. As both the base of vision system and desk surface are plane, the axis of the mirror is perpendicular to the base of the system and the surface of the desk feckly. We make the mirror system coincide with the world system to simplify the model and computations.

So the equations of hyperboloid of two sheets in the system centered at O_w are the same as equation (1). For a known world point $P(x_w, y_w, z_w)$ in the world (or mirror) coordinate system whose projected points in the image plane are also known, $q_1(u_1, v_1)$ and $q_2(u_2, v_2)$ are respectively projected by the upper mirror and bellow mirror. Then we get their coordinates in the camera coordinate system:

$$\begin{bmatrix} x_i^c \\ y_i^c \\ z_i^c \end{bmatrix} = \begin{bmatrix} (u_i - u_0)k_u \\ (v_0 - v_i)k_v \\ f \end{bmatrix}, \quad (i = 1,2) \tag{4}$$

Where f is the focal length; k_u and k_v are the pixel scale factors; u_0 and v_0 are the coordinates of the principal point, where the optical axis intersects the projection plane. They are intrinsic parameters of the perspective camera.
So the image points $P_c(x_i^c, y_i^c, z_i^c)$ of the camera coordinate system can be expressed relative to the mirror coordinate system as:

$$\begin{bmatrix} x_i^m \\ y_i^m \\ z_i^m \end{bmatrix} = R \begin{bmatrix} x_i^c \\ y_i^c \\ z_i^c \end{bmatrix} + t, \quad (i = 1,2) \tag{5}$$

Where R is a 3×3 rotation matrix with three rotation angles around the x-axis (pitch α), y-axis (yaw β) and z-axis (title χ) of the mirror coordinate system respectively; $t = [t_x, t_y, t_z]$ is the translation vector. So the origin $O_c = [0,0,0]^T$ of the camera coordinate system can be expressed in the world coordinate system $O_m = [t_x, t_y, t_z]^T$, so the equations of lines $O_c M_1$ and $O_c M_2$ which intersect with the upper mirror and bellow mirror respectively at points M_1 and M_2, can be determined by solving simultaneous equations of the line $O_c M_1$ or $O_c M_2$ and the hyperboloid. Once the coordinates of the point M_1 and M_2 have been worked out, we can write out the equations of the tangent plane л1 and л2 which passes the upper and the bellow mirror at point M_1 and M_2 respectively. Then the symmetric points O_c^1 and O_c^2 of the origin of the camera coordinate system O_c relative to tangent plane л1 and л2 in the world coordinate system can be solved from the following simultaneous equations:

$$\begin{cases} \dfrac{x_{o_c^i} - tx}{a_i^2 x_{M_i}} = \dfrac{y_{o_c^i} - ty}{a_i^2 y_{M_i}} = \dfrac{z_{o_c^i} - tz}{-b_i^2 z_{M_i} + b_i^2 c_i} \\ a_i^2 x_{M_i}(tx + x_{o_c^i}) + a_i^2 y_{M_i}(ty + y_{o_c^i}) - (-b_i^2 z_{M_i} + b_i^2 c_i)(tz + z_{o_c^i}) \\ + 2[-a_i^2 x_{M_i}^2 - a_i^2 y_{M_i}^2 - z_{M_i}(-b_i^2 z_{M_i} + b_i^2 c_i)] = 0 \end{cases}, \quad (i = 1,2) \tag{6}$$

Hitherto the incident ray $O_c^1 M_2$ and $O_c^2 M_1$ can be written out to determine the world point $P(x_w, y_w, z_w)$. Generally, the two lines are non-co-plane due to various parameter errors and measuring errors, we solve out the midpoint $G=(\hat{x}_w,\hat{y}_w,\hat{z}_w)^T$ of the common perpendicular of the two lines by

$$\left.\begin{cases}[\overrightarrow{O_c^{\,1}M_2}\times(\overrightarrow{O_c^{\,1}M_2}\times\overrightarrow{O_c^{\,2}M_1})]\bullet\overrightarrow{G_1M_2}=0\\ \overrightarrow{G_1M_1}=t\overrightarrow{G_1O_c^{\,2}}\end{cases}\Rightarrow\overrightarrow{OG_1}\quad\begin{cases}[\overrightarrow{O_c^{\,2}M_1}\times(\overrightarrow{O_c^{\,1}M_2}\times\overrightarrow{O_c^{\,2}M_1})]\bullet\overrightarrow{G_2M_1}=0\\ \overrightarrow{G_2M_2}=t\overrightarrow{G_2O_c^{\,1}}\end{cases}\Rightarrow\overrightarrow{OG_2}\right\}\quad\overrightarrow{OG}=(\overrightarrow{OG_1}+\overrightarrow{OG_2})/2 \tag{7}$$

From all of them above, we finally come to the total expression to figure out the world point $G=(\hat{x}_w,\hat{y}_w,\hat{z}_w)^T$ from two image points respectively projected by the upper mirror and bellow mirror and six camera pose parameters left to be determined.

$$G(\alpha,\beta,\chi,t_x,t_y,t_z,u_1,v_1,u_2,v_2)=\begin{bmatrix}\hat{x}_w\\ \hat{y}_w\\ \hat{z}_w\end{bmatrix} \tag{8}$$

Equation (8) is a very complex nonlinear equation with high power and six unknown parameters to determine. The artificial neural network trained with sets of image points of the calibration targets is used to estimate the camera-to-mirror transformation.

Taking advantage of the ANN capability, which adjusts the initial input camera-to-mirror transformations step by step to minimize the error function, the real transformations parameters of the camera-to-mirror can be identified precisely.

3.3 Error Function

Considering the world points with known coordinates, placed onto a calibration pattern, at the same time, their coordinates can be calculated using the equation (8) from back-projection of their image points. The difference between the positions of the real world coordinates and the calculated coordinates is the calibration error of the model. Minimizing the above error by means of an iterative algorithm such as Levenberg-Marquardt BP algorithm, the camera-to-mirror transformation is calibrated. The initial values for such algorithm are of consequence. In our system, we could assume the transformation between cameras and mirrors is quite small, as the calculation error without considering the camera-to-mirror transformation is not significant thus using R=I and T=0 as the initial values is a reasonable choice.

We minimize the following squared error ε^2:

$$\varepsilon^2=\sum_{i=1}^{n}\left\|P_i-G_i(\alpha,\beta,\chi,t_x,t_y,t_z,u_1^i,v_1^i,u_2^i,v_2^i)\right\|^2 \tag{9}$$

Where n is the number of the calibration points.

Because $G_i(\alpha,\beta,\chi,t_x,t_y,t_z,u_1^i,v_1^i,u_2^i,v_2^i)$ depends on the camera-to-mirror transformation, (9) is optimized with respect to the six camera-to-mirror parameters.

3.4 Calibration Result

The calibration was performed using a set of 81 points equally distributed on a desk with different heights from 0 to 122mm around the vision system.

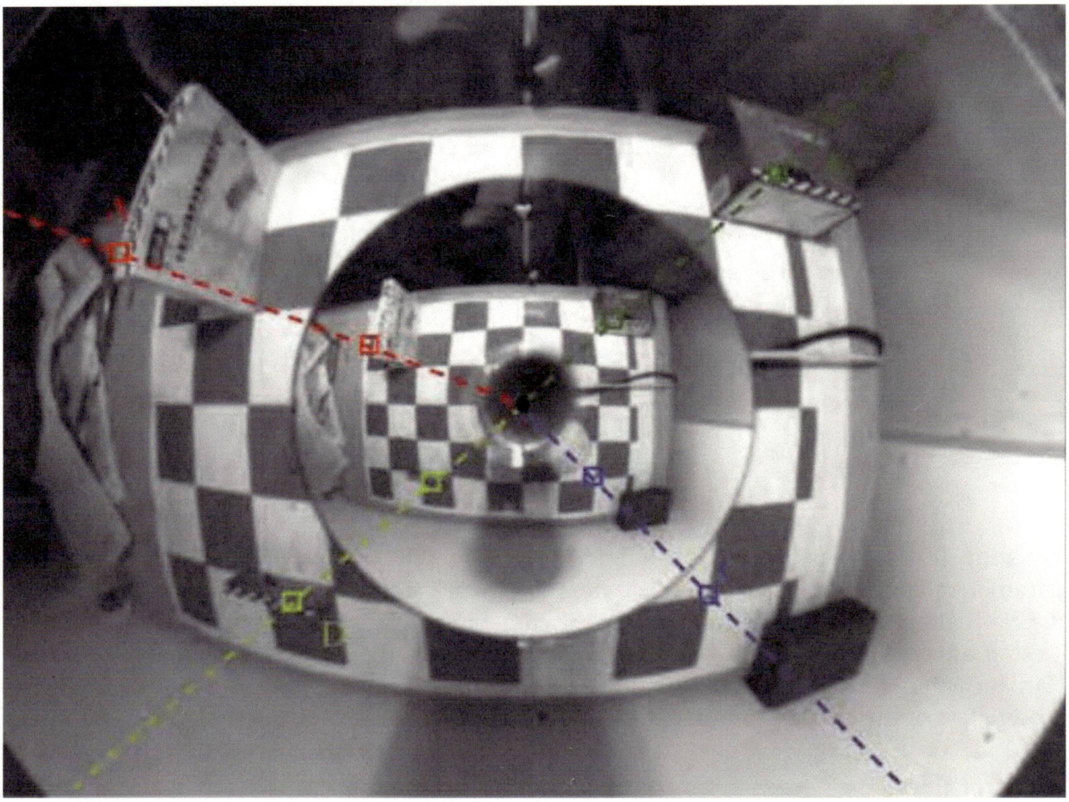

Figure 3. A calibration image used in our experiments. The coaxial configuration of the camera and the two hyperbolic mirrors makes the epipolar line radially collinear, which makes the system free of the search process for complex epipolar curve in stereo matching

The calibration results with real data are listed in Table 1.

	α	β	χ	t_x	t_y	t_z
value	-0.9539°	0.1366°	0.1436°	-0.0553mm	-0.1993mm	1.8717mm

Table 1. Calibration result with real data

The calibration error was estimated using a new set of 40 untrained points, the average square error of the set points is 34.24mm without considering the camera-to-mirror transformation. Then we calculate the error with the transformation values listed in Table 1, the average square error decrease to 12.57mm.

4. Stereo Matching

4.1 Overview

To build a depth map for mobile robot navigation, the most important and difficult process is omnidirectional stereo matching. Once two image points respectively projected by upper mirror and bellow mirror are matched, the 3D coordinate of the corresponding space point can be obtained by triangulation. State of the art algorithms for dense stereo matching can be divided into two categories:

Figure 4. Real indoor scene captured by our vision system for depth map generation

1. Local method: These algorithms calculate some kind of similarity measure over an area (Devernay & Faugeras, 1994). They work well in relatively textured areas in a very fast speed, while they cannot gain correct disparity map in textureless areas and areas with repetitive textures, which is a unavoidable problem in most situations. In (Sara, 2002) a method of finding the largest unambiguous component has been proposed, but the density of the disparity map varies greatly depend on the discriminability of the similarity measure in a given situation.
2. Global method: These methods make explicit smoothness assumptions and try to find a global optimized solution of a predefined energy function that take into account both the matching similarities and smoothness assumptions. The energy function is always in the form of $E(d) = E_{data}(d) + \lambda \bullet E_{smooth}(d)$, where λ is a parameter controlling the proportion of smoothness and image data. Most recent

algorithms belong to this category (Lee et al., 2004; Bobick, 1999; Sun & Peleg, 2004; Felzenszwalb & Huttenlocher, 2006). Among them belief propagation (Felzenszwalb & Huttenlocher, 2006) ranked high in the evaluation methodology of Middlebury College. It is based on three coupled Markov Random Fields that model smoothness, depth discontinuities and occlusions respectively and produces good result. The biggest problem of global method is that the data term and the smoothness term represent two processes competing against each other, resulting in incorrect matches in areas of weak texture and areas where prior model is violated.

Although numerous methods exist for stereo matching, they are designed towards ordinary stereo vision purpose. The images acquired by our system (Fig. 4) have some particularities in contrast to normal stereo pairs as follows, which may lead to poor result using traditional stereo matching methods:

1. The upper mirror and bellow mirror have different focal length that the camera focal length has to compromise with the two, thus causing defocusing effect, resulting in much less discriminable similarity measures. A partial solution is to reduce the aperture size at the cost of decreasing the intensity and contrast of the image.
2. Indoor scene has much more weak textured and textureless areas than outdoor scene. There are more distortions in our images, including spherical distortions and perspective distortions due to close quarters of the target areas and the large baseline.
3. The resolution gets lower when moving away from the image center. The result is the farther off the center, the more unreliable the matching result is.

To solve problem (1), we propose a three-step method that allows matching distinctive feature points first and breaks down the matching task into smaller and separate subproblems. For (2) we design a specific energy function used in the third step DTW, in which different weights and penalty items are assigned to points of different texture level and matching confidence; and throw away the matching result of the most indiscrminable points, replacing it with interpolation. For (3), we regard points farther than the most farthest matched feature point off the center as unreliable, leaving them as unknown areas. This is also required by DTW.

Epipolar geometry makes the stereo matching easier by reducing the 2D search to a 1D search along the same epipolar line in both images. To handle epipolar property conveniently, we unwrapped the raw image to two panoramic images which corresponding to images via bellow and upper mirrors respectively (Fig. 9, a, b). The matching process is done on every epipolar pair respectively. The red lines labeled in the two panoramic images are the same epipolar line for the subsequent illustration of our proposed method, of which the one above has 190 pixels and the one below 275 pixels.

4.2 Similarity Measure and Defined Texture Level

The similarity measure we choose here is zero-mean normalized cross correlation (ZNCC), since it is invariant to intensity and contrast between two images. But directly using this measure would result in low discriminability as two templates with great difference in average gray-level or standard deviation which cannot be deemed as matched pair may have high ZNCC value. To avoid this possibility, we modified ZNCC (called MZNCC) by multiplying a window function as follows:

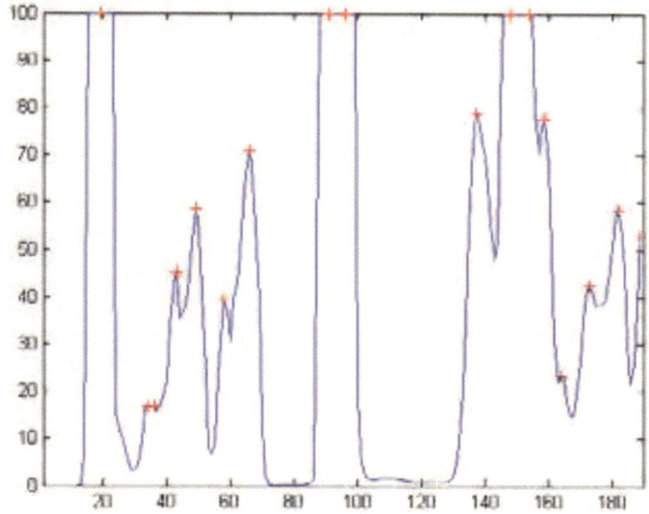

a)

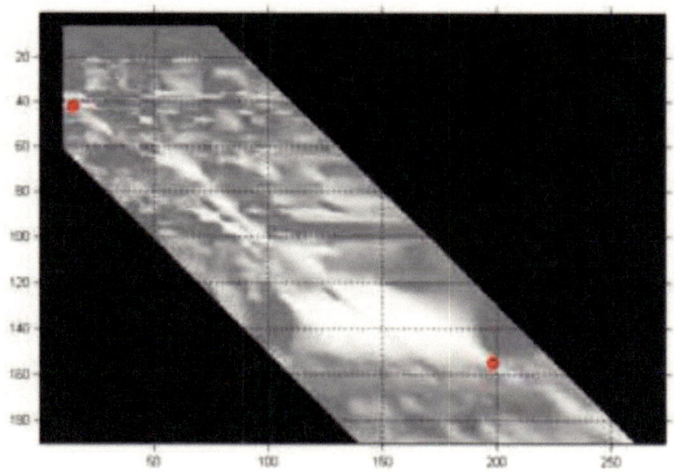

b)

Figure 5. a) The curve of texture intensity along the epipolar line. To show it clearly, we removed the part where the curve is higher than 100 and only labeled the detected feature points. b) Detected reliable FX-dominant matching result in the MZNCC matrix. The black region of the matrix is formed since it is out of the disparity search range

$$MZNCC(p,d)=\frac{\sum(I_a(i,j+d)-\mu_a)\bullet(I_b(i,j)-\mu_b)}{\sigma_a\bullet\sigma_b}\bullet w(|\mu_a-\mu_b)\bullet w(\frac{\max(\sigma_a,\sigma_b)}{\min(\sigma_a,\sigma_b)}-1) \quad (10)$$

where $w(x)=\begin{cases}1, & x<\lambda \\ 1-(x-\lambda), & x\geq\lambda\end{cases}$, μ_a and μ_b are the average grey-level of matching window, σ_a and σ_b are the standard deviation. For every epipolar line, all MZNCC values are stored as a matrix (Fig. 5b) to be used in the next step. The y-axis represents the pixel number in the epipolar of Fig. 9a, while x-axis represents the number in Fig. 9b.

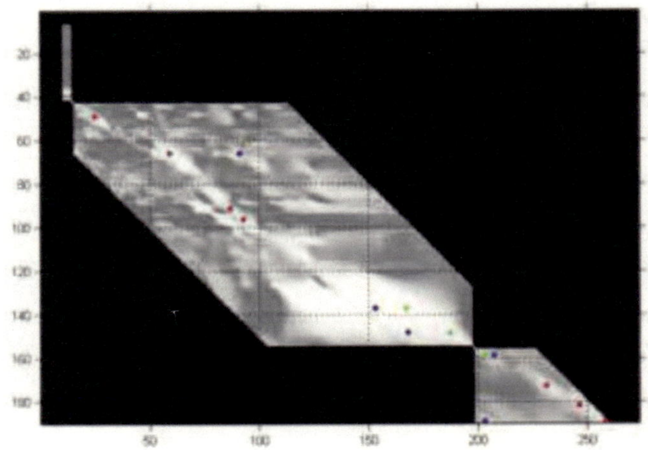

a)

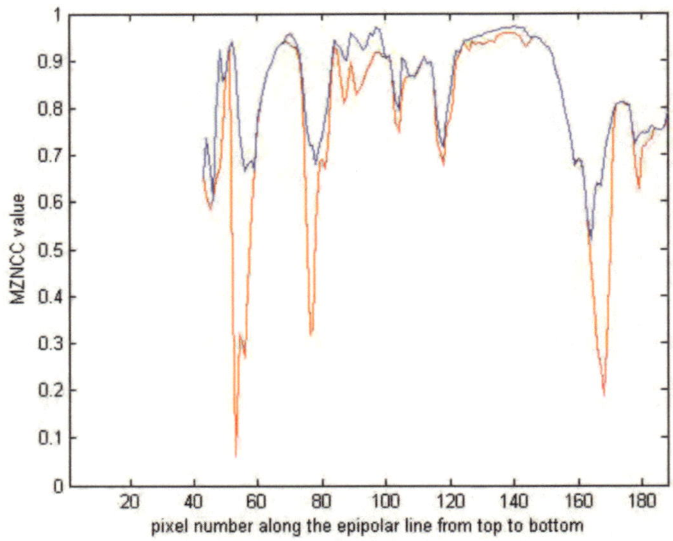

b)

Figure 6. a) Result of feature matching. All points labeled in the graph mean candidate match for detected features, of which red and green are the result chosen by maximization of sum of MZNCC and then green are removed for being ambiguous. b) the global maximum MZNCC value for each point in this epipolar (blue) and MZNCC value along the matching route chosen by our algorithm (red)

We define our texture level of each point following the notion of bandwidth of the bandpass filter. For a given pixel and a given template centred in the pixel, we slide the template one pixel at a time in the two opposite directions along the epipolar line and stop at the location the MZNCC value of the shifted template with the primary one decrease below a certain threshold for the first time. Let l be the distance between the two stop points, which is inverse proportional the texture level. The definition of texture intensity can be formalized as:

$$T(u,v) = \sum_{-r\le(i,j)\le r} (I(u+i,v+j)-\bar{I})^2 \Big/ l^2 \tag{11}$$

where r is the radius of the template. The texture intensity curve of the red labelled epipolar line is shown in Fig. 5a. With the use of this defined texture intensity and two thresholds, the whole image can be divided into three regions: strong textured, weak textured and textureless regions.

4.3 Reliable FX-dominant Matching

This step follows the notion of FX-dominant defined by Sara (Sara, 2001). The key of this notion is the uniqueness constraint which means each point may be matched with at most one point in another image, and the ordering constraint which states the order of the matched points in the two epipolar line is the same. The latter one is not always true, but it is reasonable for most cases, especially indoor scene. The FX-region of a certain matched pair (i,j) in the MZNCC matrix is defined as the set of pairs that cannot coexist with (i,j) without violating these two constraints:

$$FX(p) = \{q=(k,l) \mid (k\ge i \wedge l\le j) \vee (k\le i \wedge l\ge j) \wedge q\ne p\} \tag{12}$$

It is formed by two opposite quadrants around (i,j) in the MZNCC matrix. And FX-dominant matching is to find pairs that have higher value than any pair in the FX-region.
However, due to noise and distortion, the selected FX-dominant pairs still can not ensure its reliability. We only choose pairs from the FX-dominant results which satisfy the condition that the difference of the MZNCC value of the pair and the second local maximum MZNCC of $FX(p)\cup p$ is higher than a threshold (we choose 0.15). The number of pairs chosen by such strategy is quite small (2--8 in our case), but it does make sense because FX-region of these pairs can be removed that the matching problem is divided into subproblems. Without this step, the next step of feature matching will find much less number of reliable matched features. The result of reliable FX-dominant matching is shown in Fig. 5b, and the matrix with FX-region cut is shown in Fig. 6a.

4.4 Feature Matching and Ambiguous Removal

In this step, firstly we plot the curve of the texture intensity for a given epipolar line and choose all local maximum as feature points (Fig. 5a all points labelled red cross). For every feature point every matching pair with local maximum MZNCC higher than 0.7 is labelled as a candidate match (Fig. 6a all labelled points). Then we select a combination of candidate matching pairs that obeys uniqueness constraint and ordering constraint and has the highest sum of MZNCC (A feature point can be left unmatched with a zero contribution to the sum of MZNCC). The selected combination of illustrating epipolar shown in Fig. 6a is labelled red and green. In this selected combination, still some ambiguous match candidates exist. We mean a selected candidate is unambiguous if it is the only choice without altering other matched feature points under uniqueness and ordering constraint, otherwise it is ambiguous. We will then remove all ambiguous feature points until no matched feature is ambiguous. In Fig. 6a, the ambiguous match candidates are labelled green and they are to be removed from the feature matching result.

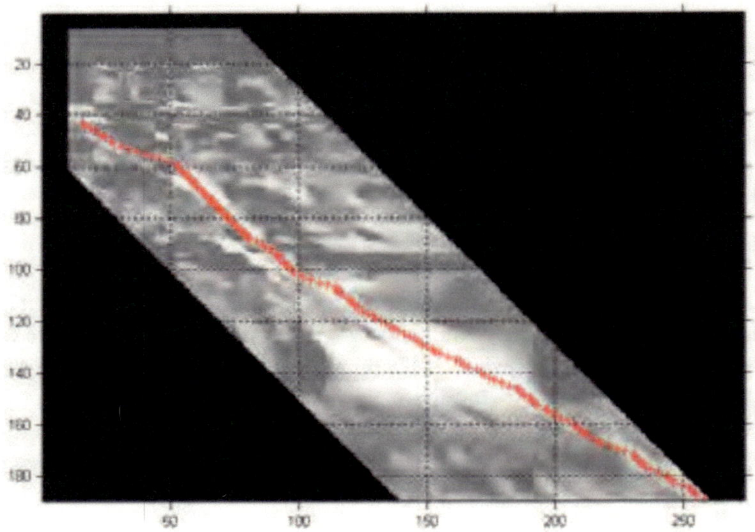

a)

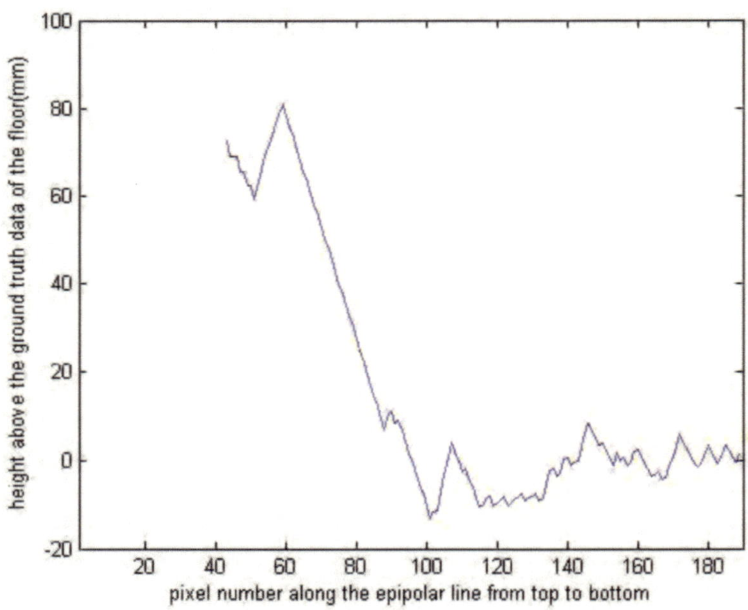

b)

Figure 7. a) Matching route in the MZNCC matrix via DTW. b) computed depth curve for this epipolar line

4.5 Dense Matching via DTW

The remaining correspondences can be determined by dynamic time warping (DTW) (Lee et al., 2004). A starting and an ending point should be known at first to use DTW. The matched feature points in the last step can naturally perform this role. Therefore, DTW can be applied to every range between adjacent matched feature points. This objective of DTW is achieved by finding a path with optimized energy function in a search space defined by the search range and restricted by the starting and ending point as well as the uniqueness and ordering constraint, using dynamic programming technique. The most important part is the definition of the energy function. Unlike others straightforwardly use sum of intensity difference (Lee et al., 2004) or define the energy function with smoothness item (this can hardly be implemented in our case as the assumption that flat areas correspond to constant disparity route usually does not hold due to the large baseline), we define our energy function in the form of sum of MZNCC value plus a penalty item aim to assign different weights to different points based on the texture level and matching confidence:

$$E = \sum MZNCC(i,j) + \sum penalty(i,j) \tag{13}$$

where (i,j) is in the matching route. To define the penalty item, we make another classification of all points. A point is belong to Class A (high confidence) if the global maximum MZNCC value is higher than 0.7, Class B (low confidence) if the global maximum MZNCC is between 0.5 and 0.7, otherwise Class C (noise). Then the penalty item is defined as Table 2,

	strong textured	weak textured	textureless
A	$-\lambda \bullet \mu \bullet \max((0.7 - MZNCC),0)$	$-\mu \bullet \max((0.7 - MZNCC),0)$	0
B	$-\sigma \bullet \lambda \bullet \mu \bullet \max((0.5 - MZNCC),0)$	$-\sigma \bullet \mu \bullet \max((0.5 - MZNCC),0)$	$-MZNCC$
C	$-MZNCC$	$-MZNCC$	$-MZNCC$

Table 2. The penalty item

where λ is the strong texture weight, μ is penalty level and σ low confidence weight (in our case, λ =4, μ =4, σ =0.4).

The result of DTW performed in the red labelled epipolar is shown in Fig. 7a, the computed depth curve in Fig. 7b. Fig. 6b shows the MZNCC curve along the matching route and the global maximum MZNCC curve for the epipolar. From Fig. 5a and Fig. 6b, we can see that the result route only deflects the global maximum MZNCC curve in textureless points and points belonging to low confidence or noise, which is an ideal result.

4.6 Postpocessing

A postprocessing step replacing textureless match with interpolation is applied to get smooth surfaces. As in the textureless areas, the similarity value is very ambiguous that the matching route can vary greatly with very small energy variation. The result is that the maximization of energy function does not necessarily correspond to the correct match, causing jagged depth map (Fig. 7b) Easily observed, the textureless areas almost correspond to a plane (as the threshold of textureless area is set so low that uneven areas will be categorized as weak textured areas due to slightly different illumination), we use two nearest textured (strong or weak) match to interpolate the textureless point. After that, a medium filter is applied to ensure the smoothness of depth map. Fig. 8 shows the result of matching route and the depth curve after postprocessing.

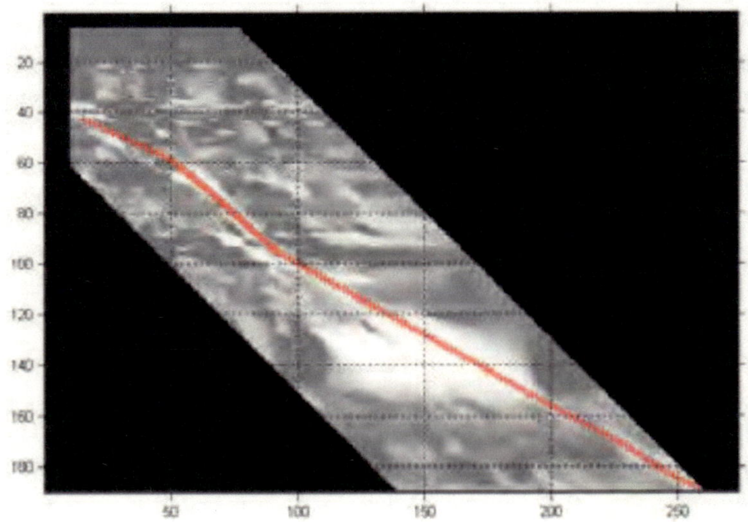

a)

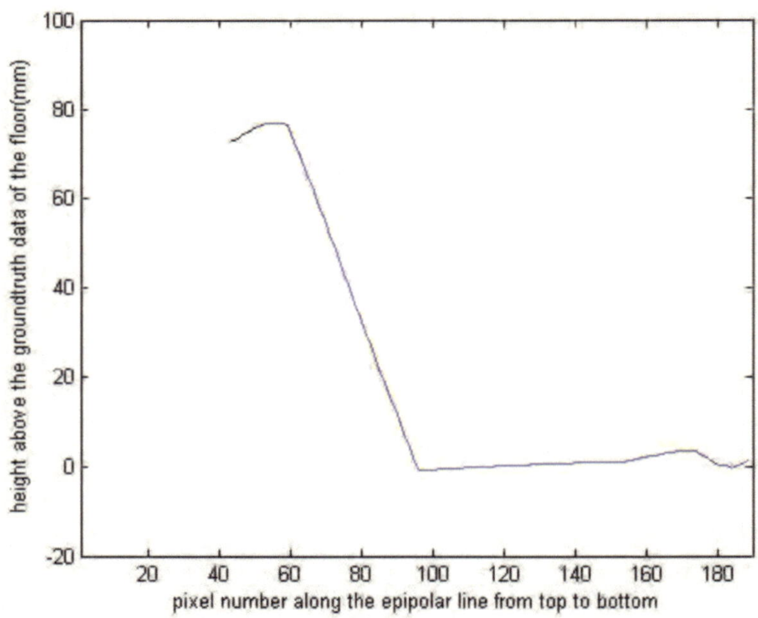

b)

Figure 8. a) Final matching route in the MZNCC matrix after post-processing. b) computed depth curve for this epipolar line

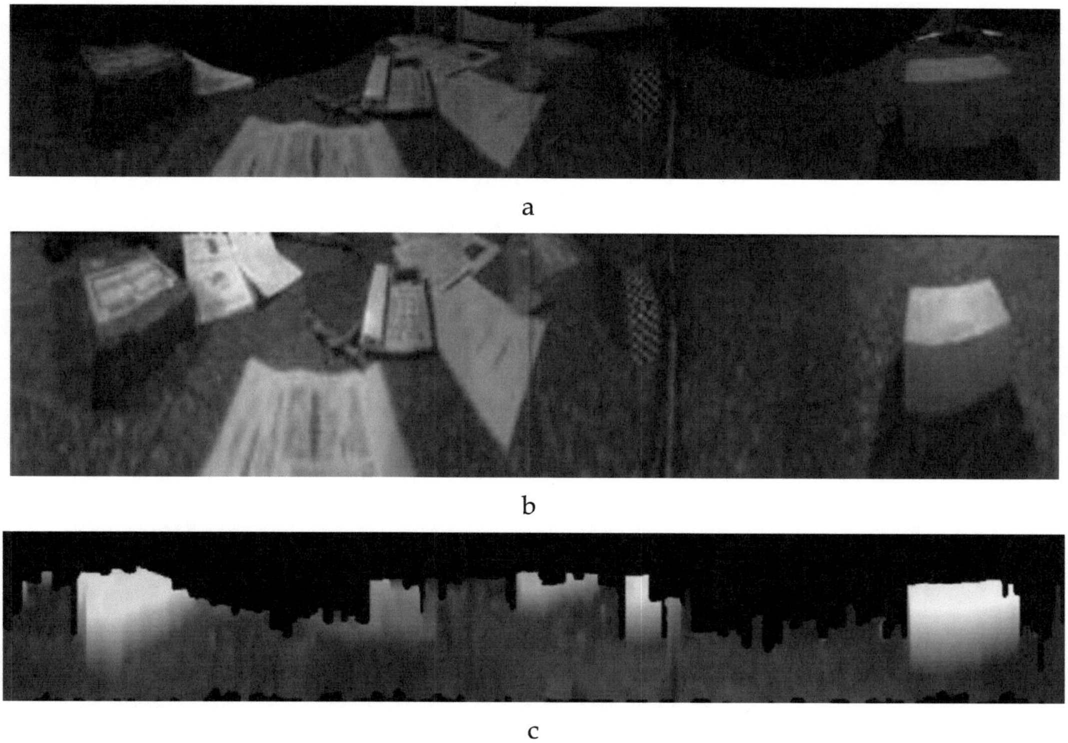

Figure 9. Panoramic images unwrapped from the raw images of Fig.4 (a and b are converted by images via the bellow and upper mirrors respectively) and the detected depth map (c) corresponding to a

4.7 Result

Fig. 9c shows the result of the generated depth map via the proposed method. This depth map measures the height above the floor. The brightness of the map is proportional to the height, while black represents unknown areas. Although the ground truth map is unavailable, the real height can be surveyed accurately for most points. We randomly selected hundreds of points and checked the error, finding that most are smaller than 15mm, only slightly higher than the calibration error. We set the threshold of navigable areas as 25mm above the floor and get the navigable map in Fig. 10.

5. Summary

We have developed a complete framework of automatically generating omnidirectional depth maps around a mobile robot using a novel designed panoramic vision sensor. Compared to previous vision systems, our system has such significant advantages as its geometry calculating easy and fast and simultaneous acquisition of precise range information without high cost or system complexity. And as the separation between the two hyperbolic mirrors provides a large baseline, the range information obtained from this method has much improved precision. We have proposed an imaging model for omnidirectional cameras that accounts for the full rotation and translation between the camera and mirrors, and a LMBP method for recovering the relative position form back-projection the images points. The method is general in that any combination of camera and mirrors can be calibrated, including non-single-viewpoint combinations. For SVP cameras, where the merit of a single viewpoint can be exploited only if the camera and mirrors are assumed to be perfectly aligned, this algorithm can be used to verify the alignment accuracy. We also have presented a three-step method for stereo matching of our vision system, which combines the advantage of feature matching and global matching. This method basically solved the three major difficulties faced by our vision system. The experimental result is quite convincing. Although this method uses some thresholds and parameters, the matching result does change in case of small variation of parameters.

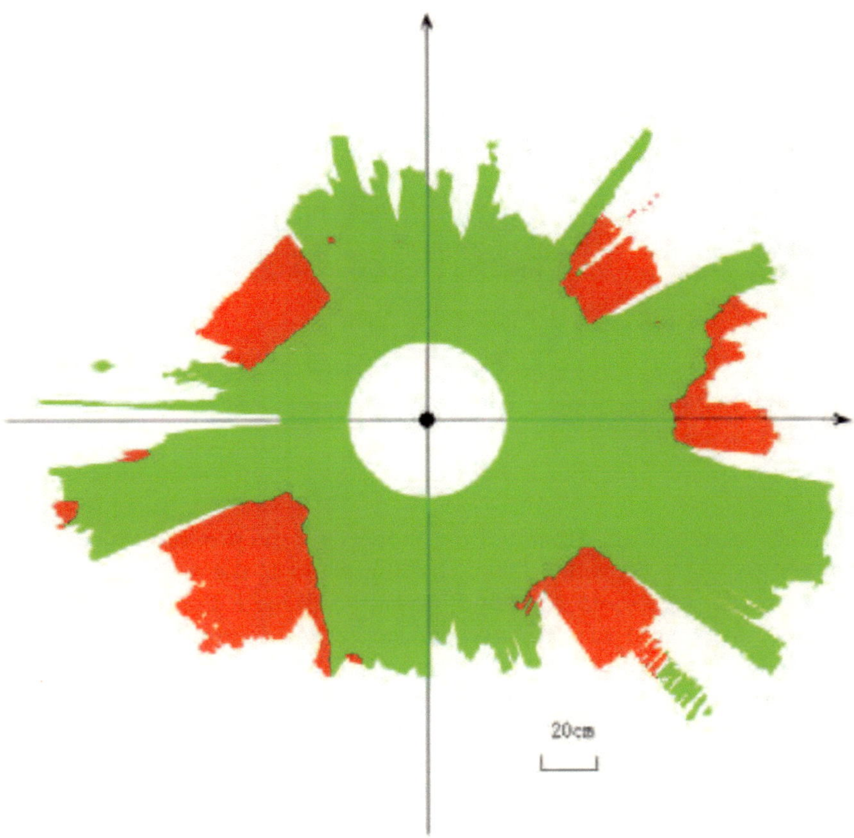

Figure 10. Omnidirectional scene information obtained by our system, of which green represents navigable areas, red detected obstacle areas

However, the proportion of detected areas is a bit small in a few epipolar lines. To solve this problem, one way is to impose inter-epipolar consistency in the stereo matching method. Another is to use multibaseline stereo, that is, we can first estimate relative pose between different shooting positions, and then depth map can be generated more reliably with more virtual cameras. Our future work will focus on these aspects. Also, we found that some techniques to deal with the defocusing effect have been proposed to improve the image quality. We will also investigate the possibility to get a better method with some pre-processing techniques.

6. References

Baker, S. & Nayar, S.K. (1999). A Theory of Single-Viewpoint Catadioptric Image Formation, *International Journal of Computer Vision*, Vol. 35, No. 2, pp. 1 - 22

Bobick, A. (1999). Large Occlusion Stereo, International Journal of Computer Vision, Vol. 33, No. 3, pp. 181-200

Bunschoten, R. & Kröse, B. (2002). Robust Scene Reconstruction from an Omnidirectional Vision System, *IEEE Transaction on Robotics and Automation*, Vol. 19, No. 2, pp. 351-357

Cabral, E.L.L.; de Souza Jr., J.C. & Hunold, M.C. (2004). Omnidirectional Stereo Vision with a Hiperbolic Double Lobed Mirror, *Proceedings of International Conference on Pattern Recognition*, pp. 1-4, Vol. 1, Cambridge, England, Aug 2004

Conroy, T.L. & Moore, J.B. (1999). Resolution Invariant Surfaces for Panoramic Vision Systems, *Proceedings of International Conference on Computer Vision*, pp. 392-397, Kerkyra, Greece, Sep 1999

Devernay, F. & Faugeras, O. (1994). Computing Differential Properties of 3-D Shapes from Stereoscopic Images without 3-D Models, *Proceedings of IEEE Conf. on Computer Vision and Pattern Recognition*, pp. 208-213, Seattle, Washington, Jun 1994

Fabrizio, J.; Tarel, J. & Benosman, R. (2002). Calibration of Panoramic Catadioptric Sensors Made Easier, *Proceedings of Workshop on Omnidirectional Vision*, pp. 45-52, Copenhagen, Denmark, Jun 2002

Felzenszwalb, P.F. & Huttenlocher, D.P. (2006). Efficient Belief Propagation for Early Vision, *International Journal of Computer Vision*, Vol. 70, No. 1, pp. 41-54

Geyer, C. & Daniilidis, K.(1999). Catadioptric Camera Calibration, *Proceedings of International Conference on Computer Vision*, Vol. 1, pp. 398-404, Kerkyra, Greece, Sep 1999

Geyer, C. & Daniilidis, K. (2000). Paracatadiopric Camera Calibration, *IEEE Trans. on Pattern Analysis and Machine Intelligence*, Vol. 24, No. 5, pp. 687-695

Geyer, C. & Daniilidis, K. (2003). Conformal Rectification of Omnidirectional Stereo Pairs, *Proceedings of IEEE Workshop on Omnidirectional Vision and Camera Networks*, pp. St. Louis, USA, Jun 2003

Gluckman, J.; Nayar, S.K. & Thoresz, K.J. (1998). Real-time Omnidirectional and Panoramic Stereo, *Proceedings of the DARPA Image Understanding Workshop*, pp. 299-303, Monterey, California, Nov 1998

Kang, S.B. (2000). Catadioptric Self-calibration, *Proceedings of IEEE Conf. on Computer Vision and Pattern Recognition*, pp. 201-207, Hilton Head Island, South Carolina, Jun 2000

Koyasu, H.; Miura, J. & Shirai, Y. (2002). Recognizing Moving Obstacles for Robot Navigation Using Real-time Omnidirectional Stereo Vision, *Journal of Robotics and Mechatronics*, Vol. 14, No. 2, pp. 147-156

Koyasu, H.; Miura, J. & Shirai, Y. (2003). Mobile Robot Navigation in Dynamic Environments Using Omnidirectional Stereo, *Proceedings of IEEE Int. Conf. on Robotics and Automation*, pp. 893-898, Taipei, May 2003

Lee, Y.; Kim, D. & Chung, M. (2004). Feature Matching in Omnidirectional Images with a Large Sensor Motion for Map Generation of a Mobile Robot, *Pattern Recognition Letters*, Vol. 25, No. 4, pp. 413-427

Luong, Q.T. & Faugeras, O.D. (1996). The Fundamental Matrix: Theory, Algorithms, and Stability Analysis. *Int. J. of Computer Vision*, Vol. 17, No. 1, pp. 43-76

Ma, J. (2003). Omnidirectional Vision Based Localization and Path Planning for Mobile Robots, *Doctor Thesis of Beijing Institute of Technology*, 2003

Menegatti, E.; Maeda, T. & Ishiguro, H. (2004). Image-Based Memory for Robot Navigation Using Properties of Omnidirectional Images, *Robotics and Autonomous Systems*, 47 (4), pp. 251-267

Miousik, B. & Pajdla, T. (2003a). Estimation of Omnidirectional Camera Model from Epipolar Geometry, *Proceedings of 2003 IEEE Conf. on Computer Vision and Pattern Recognition*, Vol. 1, pp. 485-490, Madison, USA, Jun 2003

Miousik, B. & Pajdla, T. (2003b). Omnidirectional Camera Model and Epipolar Geometry Estimation by RANSAC with Bucketing, *Proceedings of Scandinavian Conf. on Image Analysis*, pp. 83-90, Goteborg, Sweden, Jun 2003

Nayar, S.K. (1997). Catadioptric Omnidirectional Camera, *Proceedings of IEEE Conf. on Computer Vision and Pattern Recognition*, pp. 482-488, San Juan, Puerto Rico, Jun 1997

Sara, R. (2001). The Class of Stable Matchings for Computational Stereo, *Research Report*, CTU-CMP-1999-22, Center for Machine Perception, Czech Technical University, 2001

Sara, R. (2002). Finding the Largest Unambiguous Component of Stereo Matching, *Proceedings of European Conf. on Computer Vision*, Vol. 2, pp. 900-914, Copenhagen, Denmark, May 2002

Southwell, M.F.D.; Basu, A. & Reyda, J. (1996). Panoramic Stereo, *Proceedings of IEEE Conf. on Computer Vision and Pattern Recognition*, pp. 378-382, Vienna, Austria, Aug 1996

Su, L. & Zhu, F. (2005). Design of a Novel Stereo Vision Navigation System for Mobile Robots, *Proceedings of IEEE Conference on Robotics and Biomimetics*, No. 1, pp. 611-614, Hong Kong, Jun 2005

Sun, C. & Peleg, S. (2004). Fast Panormaic Stereo Matching Using Cylindrical Maximum Surfaces, *IEEE Trans. on Systems, Man and Cybernetics*, Part B, Vol. 34 No. 1, pp. 760-765

Yagi, Y. (2002). Real-time Omnidirectional Image Sensor for Mobile Robot Navigation, *Proceedings of IEEE International Symposium on Intelligent Control*, pp. 702-708, Vancouver, Canada, Oct 2002

Ying, X. & Hu, Z. (2004). Catadioptric Camera Calibration Using Geometric Invariants, *IEEE Trans. on Pattern Analysis and Machine Intelligence*, Vol. 26, No. 10, pp. 1260-1271

Zhang, Z. & Faugeras, O. (1997). An Effective Technique for Calibrating a Bincular Stereo Through Projective Reconstruction Using Both a Calibration Object and the Environment, *Journal of Computer Vision Research*, Vol. 1, No. 1, pp. 58-68

Zhu, Z. (2001). Omnidirectional Stereo Vision, *Proceedings of Workshop on Omnidirectional Vision in the 10th IEEE ICAR*, pp. 1-12, Budapest, Hungary, Aug 2001

3

Stereo Vision Camera Pose Estimation for On-Board Applications

Sappa A.*, Gerónimo D.*, Dornaika F.* , and López A.* ‡
*Computer Vision Center and ‡Autonomous University of Barcelona
08193 Bellaterra, Barcelona,
Spain

1. Introduction

Traffic accidents have become an important cause of fatality in modern countries. For instance, in 2002, motor vehicle accidents represented the half of non-natural death in the United States (National Center of Health Statistics, 2002); while in 2003 there were reported almost 150,000 injured and 7,000 killed in pedestrian accidents only in the European Union (United Nations Economic Commission for Europe, 2005). In order to improve safety, the industry has progressively developed different elements of increasing complexity and performance: from turn signals and seat belts to Anti-lock Braking Systems (ABS) and internal Airbags. Recently, research has moved towards even more intelligent on-board systems that aim to anticipate and prevent the accidents, or at least, minimize their effects when unavoidable. They are referred as Advanced Driver Assistance Systems (ADAS), in the sense that they assist the driver to take decisions, provide warnings in dangerous driving situations, and even at taking automatic evasive actions in extreme cases.
One of the most prominent components of ADAS are the vision systems (monocular or stereo), which capture in a single snapshot all the surrounding information. Although monocular vision systems allow higher acquisition/processing rates, the use of on-board stereo vision heads is gaining popularity in ADAS applications. Stereo rigs are able to provide 3D information useful for facing up problems that can not be tackled with monocular systems (e.g., reliable distance estimation). Furthermore, the current technology is producing more and more inexpensive and compact stereo vision systems that let us think on a promising future.
Accurate and real time camera pose estimation is one of the common difficulties of on-board vision systems. Applications such as obstacle avoidance, pedestrian detection, or traffic signal recognition, could both speed up the whole process and make use of additional information by a precise estimation of the current camera extrinsic parameters, related to the

---

This work has been partially supported by the Spanish Ministry of Education and Science under project TRA2004-06702/AUT. First and third authors were supported by The Ramón y Cajal Program. Second author was supported by Spanish Ministry of Education and Science grant BES-2005-8864.

road. Most of recent works (e.g., Bertozzi et al., 2003b; Coulombeau & Laurgeau, 2002; Liang et al., 2003; Ponsa et al., 2005; Labayrade & Aubert, 2003) assume, or impose, a scene prior knowledge to simplify the problem. Although prior knowledge has been extensively used to tackle the driver assistance problem, it should be carefully used since it may lead to wrong results. Unlike previous works, this chapter presents an approach to estimate in real time stereo vision camera pose by using raw 3D data points.

This chapter is organized as follows. Section 2 summarizes some of the approaches proposed in the literature to compute on-board vision system pose. The proposed approach is described in section 3. Section 4 presents experimental results on urban scenes, together with comparisons with (Sappa et al., 2006). Finally, conclusions and further improvements are given in section 5.

2. Previous Approaches

In this work, since we only have a road plane equation, the camera pose will refer to two independent angles plus a translational distance. Several techniques have been proposed in the literature for robust vision system pose estimation. They can be classified into two different categories: *monocular* or *stereo*. In general, monocular systems are used on an off-line pose estimation basis. To this end, the car should be at rest and should face a flat road; once the camera pose is estimated its values are assumed to keep constant, or vary within a predefined range, during the on-line process (e.g., Ponsa et al., 2005; Bertozzi et al., 2003b). Although useful in most of highway scenarios, constant camera position and orientation is not a valid assumption to be used in urban scenarios since in general, vehicle pose is easily affected by road imperfections or artifacts (e.g., rough road, speed bumps), car's accelerations, uphill/downhill driving, to mention a few. Notice that since the vision system is rigidly attached to the vehicle, camera pose and vehicle pose are indistinctly used through this work.

In order to tackle urban scenarios, some monocular systems have been proposed to automatically compute camera pose by using the prior knowledge of the environment (e.g., Franke et al., 1998; Bertozzi et al., 2003a; Suttorp & Bücher, 2006). However, scene prior-knowledge not always can help to solve problems, in particular when cluttered and changing environment are considered, since visual features are not always available.

On the contrary to monocular approaches, stereo based systems in general are used on an on-line pose estimation basis. Since 3D data points are computed from every stereo pair, the corresponding vision system pose can be directly estimated related to these data whenever required. Broadly speaking, two different stereo matching schemes are used to compute 3D data points, either matching edges and producing sparse depth maps or matching all pixels in the images and producing dense depth maps (Faugeras & Luong, 2001). The final application is used to define whether preference is given to edge-based correspondences or to dense stereo correspondences. In general, for a successful reconstruction of the whole environment it is essential to compute dense disparity maps defined for every pixel in the entire image. However, the constraint of having a reduced computational complexity some times prevents the use of dense disparity maps. This very challenging problem has been usually tackled by making assumptions regarding the scene or by imposing constraints on the motion of the on-board stereo system. Furthermore, several solutions are proposed in order to compute 3D data points in a fast way based on ad hoc or application-oriented stereo vision systems. Although attractive, from the point of view of reduced processing

time, the use of ad hoc stereo vision systems is limited since no other approaches could take advantage of those application-oriented 3D data points.
Different techniques relying on stereo vision systems have been proposed in the literature for driver assistance applications. For instance, the edge based *v*-disparity approach proposed in (Labayrade et al., 2002), for an automatic estimation of horizon lines and later on used for applications such as obstacle or pedestrian detection (e.g., Bertozzi et al., 2005; Broggi et al., 2003; Hu & Uchimura, 2005); it only computes 3D information over local maxima of the image gradient. A sparse disparity map is computed in order to obtain a real time performance. This *v*-disparity approach has been extended to a *u*-*v*-disparity concept in (Hu & Uchimura, 2005). In this new proposal, dense disparity maps are used instead of only relying on edge based disparity maps. Working in the disparity space is an interesting idea that is gaining popularity in on-board stereo vision applications, since planes in the original Euclidean space become straight lines in the disparity space. Up to our knowledge, all the approaches proposed to work on *v*-disparity space are based on Hough transform algorithm for extracting straight lines.
In this chapter a real time approach able to handle the whole 3D data points of a scene is presented. Hence, while the proposed technique is intended to estimate the stereo vision camera pose parameters, collision avoidance algorithms or pedestrian detection could make use of the same 3D data together with the estimated camera pose. In other words, the underlying idea of the proposed approach is to develop a standalone application that runs independently from others applications or hardware systems. In this sense, a commercial stereo pair is used, instead of relying on an ad hoc technology. This will allow us in the future to upgrade our current stereo vision sensor without changing the proposed technique.

3. Proposed Approach

The proposed approach consists of two stages. Initially, 3D data are mapped onto YZ plane (see Fig. 1), where a set of *candidate points* are selected—candidates to belong to the road. The main objective of this first stage is to take advantage of the 2D structured information before applying more expensive processing algorithms working with raw 3D data. Secondly, a RANSAC based least squares fitting is used to estimate the parameters of a plane (i.e., road plane) fitting to those candidate points. Finally, camera position and orientation are directly computed, referred to the fitted plane. Similarly to (Sappa et al., 2006), the provided results could be understood as a piecewise planar approximation, due to the fact that road and camera parameters are continuously computed and updated. Note that since on-board vision system pose is related to the current 3D road plane, camera position and orientation are equivalent to the 3D road plane parameters—3D plane parameters are expressed in the camera coordinate system. The proposed technique could be indistinctly used for urban or highway environments, since it is not based on a specific visual traffic feature extraction but on raw 3D data points. Before going into details about the proposed approach, the on-board stereo vision system is briefly introduced.

3.1 Stereovision System

A commercial stereo vision system (Bumblebee from Point Grey[1]) was used. It consists of two Sony ICX084 colour CCDs with 6mm focal length lenses. Bumblebee is a pre-calibrated system that does not require in-field calibration. The baseline of the stereo head is 12cm and it is connected to the computer by a IEEE-1394 connector. Right and left colour images were captured at a resolution of 640×480 pixels and a frame rate near to 30 fps. After capturing these right and left images, 3D data were computed by using the provided 3D reconstruction software. Fig. 1 shows an illustration of the on board stereo vision system.

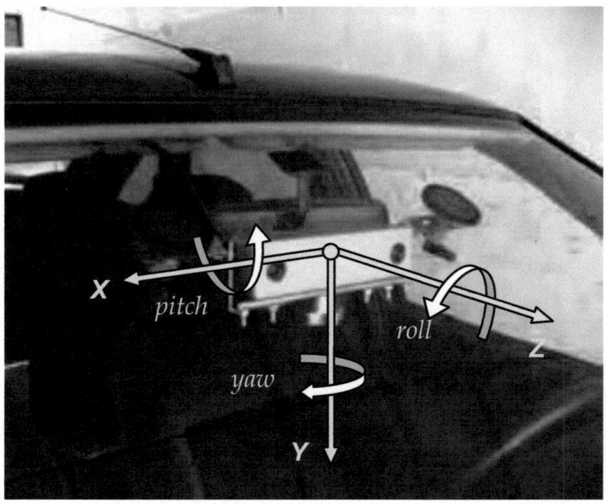

Figure 1. On-board stereo vision sensor with its corresponding coordinate system

3.2 3D data point projection and noisy data filtering

Let *S(r,c)* be a stereo image with *R* rows and *C* columns, where each array element *(r,c)* ($r \in [0,(R-1)]$ and $c \in [0,(C-1)]$) is a scalar that represents a surface point of coordinates (x,y,z), referred to the sensor coordinate system. Fig. 1 depicts the sensor coordinate system attached to the vehicle's windshield. Notice that vertical variations between consecutive frames—due to road imperfections, car accelerations, changes in the road slope: *flat/uphill/downhill* driving, etc—will mainly produce changes on camera height and pitch angle (camera height is defined as the distance between the origin of the coordinate system and the road plane). In other words, yaw and roll angles are not so affected by those variations. Even though the roll angle is not plotted in this paper, its value is easily retrieved from the plane equation. The estimation of yaw angle is not considered in this work.
The aim at this stage is to find a compact subset of points, ζ, containing most of the road points. Additionally, noisy data points should be reduced as much as possible in order to avoid both a very time consuming processing and a wrong plane fitting.
Original 3D data points (x_i, y_i, z_i) are mapped onto a 2D discrete representation $P(u,v)$; where $u = \lfloor (y_i \cdot \sigma \rfloor$ and $v = \lfloor (z_i \cdot \sigma \rfloor$. σ represents a scale factor defined as: $\sigma=((R+C)/2)/((\Delta X+\Delta Y+\Delta Z)/3)$; R, C are the image's rows and columns respectively, and

[1] www.ptgrey.com

(ΔX, ΔY, ΔZ) is the working range in every dimension—on average (34×12×50) meters. Every cell of $P(u,v)$ keeps a pointer to the original 3D data point projected onto that position, as well as a counter with the number of mapped points. Fig. 2(*top-right*) shows the 2D representation obtained after mapping the 3D cloud presented in Fig. 2(*left*)—every black point represents a cell with at least one mapped 3D point.

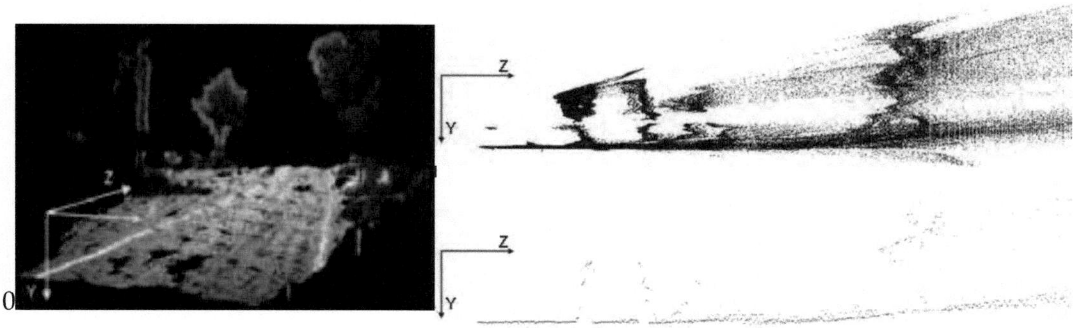

Figure 2. (*left*) 3D data points from the stereo rig. (*top-right*) Points projected to the YZ plane. (*bottom-right*) Cells finally selected to be used during the plane fitting stage (notice that one cell per column has been selected using the dynamic threshold)

Finally, points defining the ζ subset are selected by picking up one cell per column. This selection process is based on the assumption that the road surface is the predominant geometry in the given scene—urban or highway scenarios. Hence, it goes bottom-up, in the 2D representation, through every column, and picks the first cell with more points than an adaptive threshold, τ. Cells containing less mapped points than τ are filtered by setting to zero its corresponding counter—points mapped onto those cells are considered as noisy data. The value of τ is defined for every column as 80% of the maximum amount of points mapped onto the cells of that column. It avoids the use of a fixed threshold value for all columns. Recall that the density of points decreases with the distance to the sensor, hence the threshold value should depend on the depth—the column position in the 2D mapping. This is one of the differences with respect to (Sappa et al., 2006), where a constant threshold value was defined. Fig. 2(*bottom-right*) depicts cells finally selected. The ζ subset of points gathers all the 3D points mapped onto those cells.

3.3 RANSAC based plane fitting

The outcome of the previous stage is a subset of points, ζ, where most of them belong to the road. In the current stage a RANSAC based technique (Fischler & Bolles, 1981) is used for fitting a plane to those data[2], $ax+by+cz=1$. In order to speed up the process, a predefined threshold value for inliers/outliers detection has been defined (a band of ±5cm was enough for taking into account both 3D data point accuracy and road planarity). An automatic threshold could be computed for inliers/outliers detection following robust estimation of standard deviation of residual errors (Rousseeuw & Leroy, 1987).

[2] Notice that the general expression $ax+by+cz+d=0$ has been simplified dividing by $(-d)$, since we already know that $(d \neq 0)$.

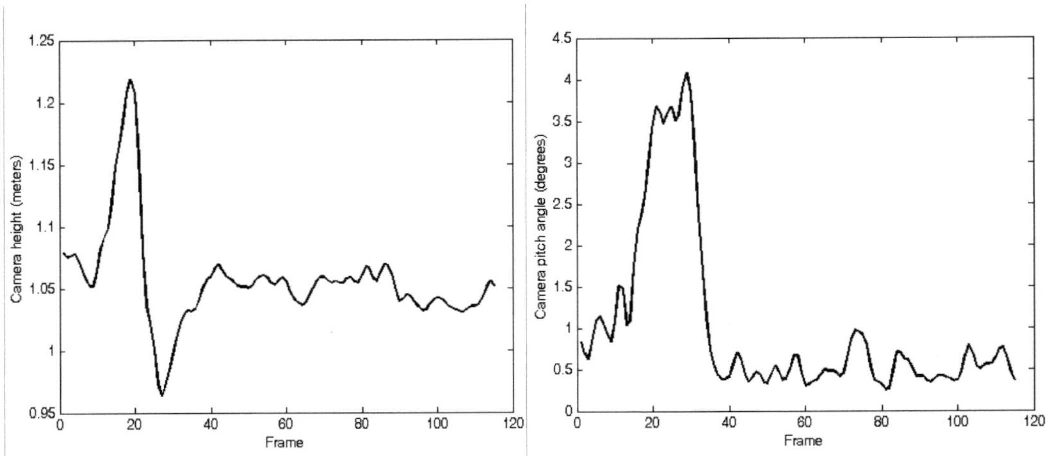

Figure 3. Results from a short video sequence: (*left*) Camera height; (*right*) Camera pitch angle

The proposed plane fitting works as follows.

Random sampling: *Repeat the following three steps K times (in our experiments K=100)*
1. Draw a random subsample of 3 different 3D points from ζ.
2. For this subsample, indexed by k $(k = 1, \ldots, K)$, compute the plane parameters (a,b,c).
3. For this solution $(a,b,c)_k$, compute the number of inliers among the entire set of 3D points contained in ζ, as mentioned above using ±5cm as a fixed threshold value.

Solution:
1. Choose the solution that has the highest number of inliers. Let $(a,b,c)_i$, be this solution.
2. Refine $(a,b,c)_i$ considering its corresponding inliers, by using the least squares fitting approach (Wang et al., 2001), which minimize the square residual error $(1-ax-by-cz)^2$.
3. In case the number of inliers is smaller than 10% of the total amount of points contained in ζ, those plane parameters are discarded and the ones corresponding to the previous frame are used as the correct ones. In general, this happens when 3D road data are not correctly recovered since occlusion or other external factor appears.

Finally, camera height (h) and orientation (Θ), referred to the fitted plane (a,b,c), are easily computed. Camera height is given by: $h = 1/\sqrt{a^2+b^2+c^2}$. Camera orientation—pitch angle—is directly computed from the current plane orientation: $\Theta = \arctan(c/b)$. Both values can be represented as a single one by means of the horizon line (e.g., Zhaoxue & Pengfei, 2004; Rasmussen, 2004a; Rasmussen, 2004b), in particular this compact representation will be used in the next section for comparisons. The horizon line position (v_i) for a given frame (i) is computed by back-projecting into the image plane a point lying over the plane, far away from the camera reference frame, $P_i(x, y, z)$. Let $(y_i = (1 - cz_i)/b)$ be the y coordinate of P_i by assuming $x_i=0$. The corresponding y_i back-projection into the image plane, which define the row position of the sought horizon line, is obtained as $v_i = v_0 + f y_i / z_i = v_0 + f/(z_i b) - f c/b$; where, f denotes the focal length in pixels; v_0 represents the vertical coordinate of the principal point; and z_i is the depth value of P_i (in the experiments $z_i = 10{,}000$).

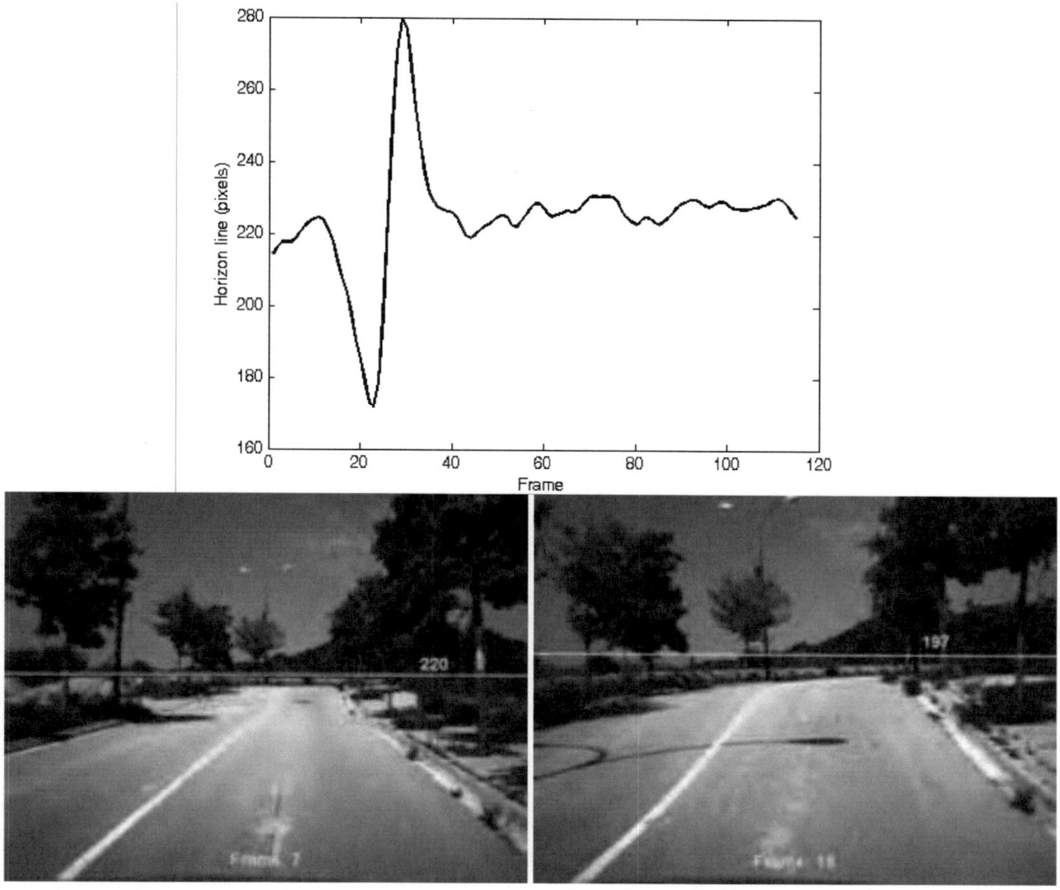

Figure 4. (*top*) Horizon line for the video sequence presented in Fig. 3. (*bottom*) Two single frames with their corresponding horizon line

4. Experimental Results

The proposed technique has been tested on different urban environments. The proposed algorithm took, on average, 350 ms per frame on a 3.2 GHz Pentium IV PC with a non-optimized C++ code.

Fig. 3 presents variations in the camera height and pitch angle during a sequence of about one minute long—only variations in the camera height position and pitch angle are plotted, both related to the current fitted plane. Notice that, although short, this video sequence contains downhill/uphill/flat scenarios (see Fig. 4 (*bottom*)). This illustration shows that variations in the camera position and orientation cannot be neglected, since they can change considerably in a short trajectory (something that does not happen on highways scenarios). These variations can be easily appreciated on the horizon line representation presented in Fig. 4 (*top*).

A comparison between the proposed technique and (Sappa et al., 2006) has been performed using a 100 frame-long-video sequence. The main difference between these techniques lies on the way cells to be fitted are selected, section 3.2. Fig. 5 presents camera height and pitch angle of both approaches. Fig. 6 depicts the corresponding horizon line position, computed with both approaches, as a function of the sequence frames. Although both approaches give similar results, values obtained with the new proposal are more reliable and fit better the current road geometry, since not only cells near to the sensor but the whole set of point on the direction of the camera optical axis is used. Finally, Fig. 7 presents four single frames of this video sequence together with their corresponding horizon line.

The proposed technique is already being used on a shape-based pedestrian detection algorithm (Gerónimo et al., 2006) in order to speed up the searching process. Although out of the scope of this paper, Fig. 8 presents illustrations of two different scenarios showing the importance of having the right estimation of camera position and orientation. In these illustrations, *(a)*, *(b)* and *(c)* columns show results by using three different, but constant, horizon line positions, while *(d)* column depicts the corresponding results obtained by using a horizon line position automatically computed by the proposed technique. Following the algorithm presented in (Ponsa et al., 2005), a 3D grid, sampling the road plane, is projected on the 2D image. The projected grid nodes are used as references to define the bottom-left corners of pedestrian sized searching windows. These windows, which have a different size according to their corresponding 3D depth, move backward and forward over the assumed plane looking for a pedestrian-like shape. Therefore, a wrong road plane orientation—i.e., horizon line—drives to a wrong searching space, so that the efficiency of the whole algorithm decreases. A few searching bounding boxes are highlighted in Fig. 8 to show their changes in size according to the distance to the camera.

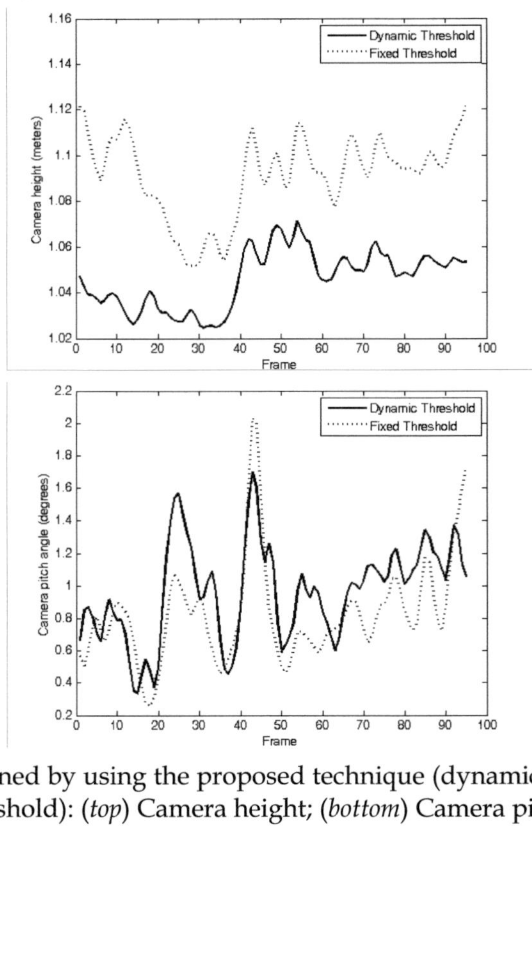

Figure 5. Results obtained by using the proposed technique (dynamic threshold) and (Sappa et al., 2006) (fixed threshold): (*top*) Camera height; (*bottom*) Camera pitch angle

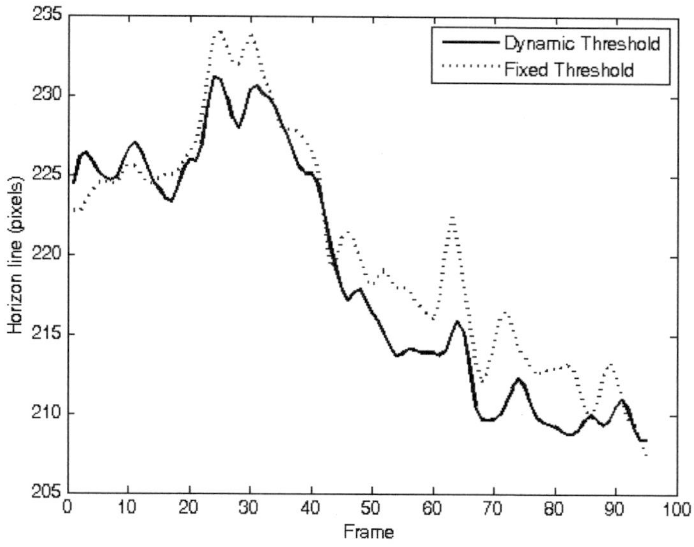

Figure 6. Horizon line position corresponding to the sequence presented in Figure 5.

Figure 7. Horizon line for four different frames of the sequence presented in Figure 5.

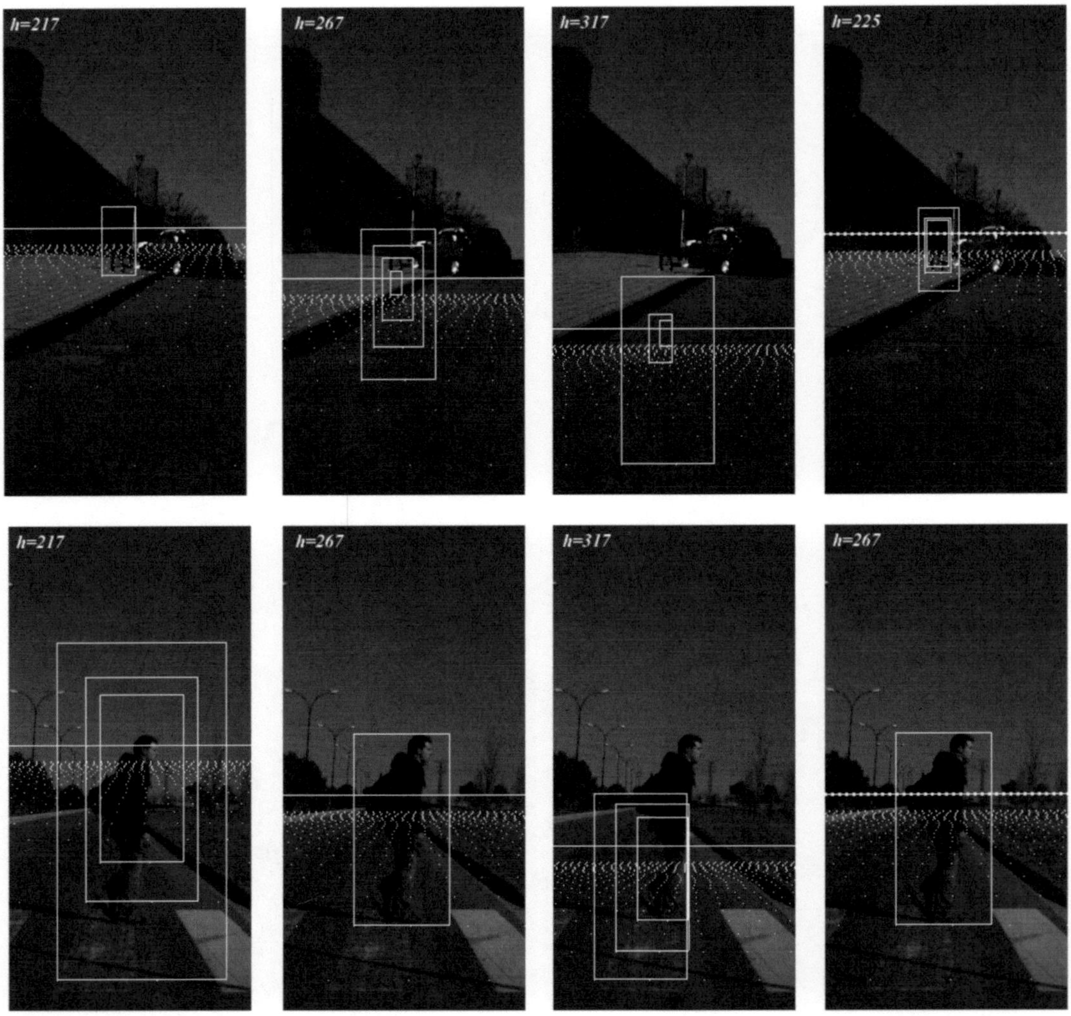

(a) *(b)* *(c)* *(d)*

Figure 8. Searching bounding boxes using fixed and automatically computed horizon lines. In all the cases only very few bounding boxes are highlighted. Fixed horizon line ASSUMING: *(a)* an uphill road; *(b)* a flat road; *(c)* a downhill road. *(d)* Automatically computed horizon line by using the proposed technique. Notice that, only in the latter case, the horizon line position is correctly placed in both scenarios.

5. Conclusions and Further Improvements

An efficient technique for a real time pose estimation of an on-board camera has been presented. It improves a previous proposal (Sappa et al., 2006) by defining a dynamic threshold for selecting points to be fitted. After an initial mapping and filtering process, a

compact set of points is chosen for fitting a plane to the road. The proposed technique can fit very well to different road geometries, since plane parameters are continuously computed and updated. A good performance has been shown in several scenarios—uphill, downhill and flat roads. Furthermore, critical situations such as car's accelerations or speed bumps were also considered. Although it has been tested on urban environments, it could be also useful on highways scenarios.
Further work will be focused on developing new strategies in order to reduce the initially chosen subset of points; for instance by using a non-constant cell size for mapping the 3D world to 2D space (through the optical axis). A reduced set of points will help to reduce the whole CPU time. Furthermore, the use of Kalman filtering techniques and other geometries for fitting road points will be explored.

6. References

Bertozzi, M.; Broggi, A.; Carletti, M.; Fascioli, A.; Graf, F.; Grisleri, P. & Meinecke, M. (2003a). IR pedestrian detection for advaned driver assistance systems, *Proceedings of 25th. Pattern Recognition Symposium*, pp. 582–590, Magdeburg, Germany, September 2003.

Bertozzi, M.; Broggi, A.; Chapuis, R.; Chausse, F.; Fascioli, A. & Tibaldi, A. (2003b). Shape-based pedestrian detection and localization, *Proceedings of IEEE Int. Conf. on Intelligent Transportation Systems*, pp. 328–333, Shangai, China, October 2003.

Bertozzi, M.; Binelli, E.; Broggi, A. & Del Rose, M. (2005). Stereo vision-based approaches for pedestrian detection, *Proceedings of IEEE Int. Conf. on Computer Vision and Pattern Recognition*, pp. 23–28, San Diego, USA, June 2005.

Broggi, A.; Fascioli, A.; Fedriga, I.; Tibaldi, A. & Del Rose, M. (2003). Stereo-based preprocessing for human shape localization in unstructured environments, *Proceedings of IEEE Intelligent Vehicles Symposium*, pp. 410–415, Columbus, OH, USA, June 2003.

Coulombeau P. & Laurgeau, C. (2002). Vehicle yaw, pitch, roll and 3D lane shape recovery by vision, *Proceedings of IEEE Intelligent Vehicles Symposium*, pp. 619–625, Versailles, France, June 2002.

Faugeras, O. & Luong, Q. (2001). The Geometry of Multiple Images: the Laws that Govern the Formation of Multiple Images of a Scene and Some of their Applications, MIT, 2001.

Fischler M. & Bolles, R. (1981). Random sample consensus: A paradigm for model fitting with applications to image analysis and automated cartography, *Graphics and Image Processing*, vol. 24, no. 6, pp. 381-395, June 1981.

Franke, U.; Gavrila, D.; Görzig, S.; Lindner, F.; Paetzold, F. & Wöhler, C. (1998). Autonomous driving goes downtown, *IEEE Intelligent Systems and Their Applications*, pp. 40–48, January 1998.

Gerónimo, D.; Sappa, A.; López, A. & Ponsa, D. (2006). Pedestrian detection using adaboost learning of features and vehicle pitch estimation, *Proceedings of Int. Conf. on Visualization, Imaging, and Image Processing*, pp. 400–405, Palma de Mallorca, Spain, August 2006.

Hu, Z. & Uchimura, K. (2005). U-V-Disparity: an efficient algorithm for stereovision based scene analysis, *Proceedings of IEEE Intelligent Vehicles Symposium*, pp. 48–54, Las Vegas, USA, June 2005.

Labayrade, R.; Aubert, D. & Tarel, J. (2002). Real time obstacle detection in stereovision on non flat road geometry through 'V-disparity' representation, *Proceedings of IEEE Intelligent Vehicles Symposium*, pp. 646–651, Versailles, France, June 2002.

Labayrade, R. & Aubert, D. (2003)., In-vehicle obstacles detection and characterization by stereovision, *Proceedings of 1st. Int. Workshop In-Vehicle Cognitive Computer Vision Systems*, pp. 13–19, Graz, Austria, April 2003.

Liang, Y.; Tyan, H.; Liao, H. & Chen, S. (2003). Stabilizing image sequences taken by the camcorder mounted on a moving vehicle, *Proceedings of IEEE Int. Conf. on Intelligent Transportation Systems*, pp. 90–95, Shangai, China, October 2003.

National Center of Health Statistics. (2002). National vital statistics report.

Ponsa, D.; López, A.; Lumbreras, F.; Serrat, J. & Graf, T. (2005). 3D vehicle sensor based on monocular vision, *Proceedings of IEEE Int. Conf. on Intelligent Transportation Systems*, pp. 1096–1101, Vienna, Austria, September 2005.

Rasmussen, C. (2004a). Grouping dominant orientations for ill-structured road following, *Proceedings of IEEE Int. Conf. on Computer Vision and Pattern Recognition*, pp. 470–477, Washington, USA, June 2004.

Rasmussen, C. (2004b). Texture-based vanishing point voting for road shape estimation, *Proceedings of British Machine Vision Conference*, London, UK, September 2004.

Rousseeuw P. & Leroy, A. (1987). Robust Regression and Outlier Detection, John Wiley & Sons, New York, 1987.

Sappa, A. ; Gerónimo, D.; Dornaika, F. & López, A. (2006). Real time vehicle pose using on-board stereo vision system, *Proceedings of Int. Conf. on Image Analysis and Recognition*, LNCS Vol. 4142, Springer Verlag, pp. 205–216, Póvoa de Varzim, Portugal, September 2006.

Suttorp, T. & Bücher, T. (2006). Robust vanishing point estimation for driver assistance, *Proceedings of IEEE Intelligent Transportation Systems*, pp. 1550–1555, Toronto, Canada, September 2006.

United Nations Economic Commission for Europe. (2005). Statistics of road traffic accidents in Europe and North America.

Wang, C.; Tanahashi, H.; Hirayu, H.; Niwa, Y. & Yamamoto, K. (2001). Comparison of local plane fitting methods for range data, *Proceedings of IEEE Computer Vision and Pattern Recognition*, pp. 663–669, Hawaii, December 2001.

Zhaoxue, C. & Pengfei, S. (2004). Efficient method for camera calibration in traffic scenes, *Electronics Letters*, vol. 40, no. 6, pp. 368–369, March 2004.

4

Correcting Radial Distortion of Cameras with Wide Angle Lens Using Point Correspondences

Leonardo Romero and Cuauhtemoc Gomez
División de Estudios de Postgrado, Facultad de Ingeniería Eléctrica
Universidad Michoacana de San Nicolás de Hidalgo
Morelia, Michoacán, México

1. Introduction

Most algorithms in 3-D Computer Vision rely on the pinhole camera model because of its simplicity, whereas video optics, especially wide-angle lens, generates a lot of non-linear distortion. In some applications, for instance in stereo vision systems and robotic systems, this distortion can be critical.

Camera calibration consists of finding the mapping between the 3-D space and the camera plane. This mapping can be separated in two different transformations: first, the relation between the origin of 3-D space (the global coordinate system) and the camera coordinate system, which forms the external calibration parameters (3-D rotation and translation), and second the mapping between 3-D points in space (using the camera coordinate system) and 2-D points on the camera plane, which forms the internal calibration parameters (Devernay & Faugeras, 1995).

Fig. 1 shows two types of distortion due to lens: barrel and pincushion distortions and a rectangle without any distortion like reference (e.g. the image taken by an ideal pinhole camera) (Weng et al. 1992). The pincushion distortion is due to zoom lens and the barrel distortion is due to wide angle lens. In commercial cameras with wide angle lens the most important component of the barrel distortion is the radial distortion and this chapter introduces a method to find the internal calibration parameters of a camera, specifically those parameters required to correct the radial distortion due to wide-angle lens.

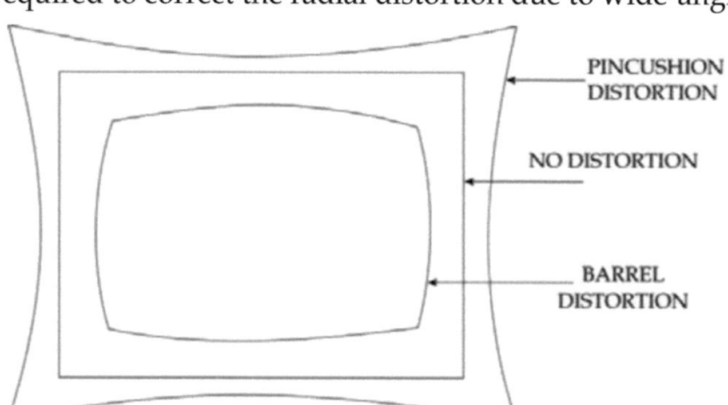

Figure 1. Types of distortion

The method works with two images, one from the camera and one from a calibration pattern (without distortion) and it is based on a non-linear optimization method to match feature points of both images, given a parametric distortion model. The image from the calibration pattern can be a scanned image, an image taken by a high quality digital camera (without lens distortion), or even the binary image of the pattern (which printed becomes the pattern).

First, a set of feature point correspondences between both images are computed automatically. The next step is to find the best distortion model that maps the feature points from the distorted image to the calibration pattern. This search is guided by analytical derivatives with respect to the set of calibration parameters. The final result is the set of parameters of the best distortion model.

The rest of this chapter is organized as follows. Section 2 describes the problem to compute transformed images and it presents the Bilinear Interpolation as a solution to that problem. Sections 3 and 4 describe the distortion and projective model that we are using. Section 5 presents the method to match pairs of points. A brief comparison with previous calibration methods is found in section 6. Here we show the problems associated with cameras using wide angle lens and why some previous methods fail or require a human operator. Experimental results are shown in Section 7. Finally, some conclusions are given in Section 8.

2. Computing Transformed Images

For integer coordinates (i,j), let $I(i,j)$ gives the intensity value of the pixel associated to position (i,j) in image I. Let I_d and I_t be the original (distorted image taken from the camera) and the transformed image, respectively. A geometric transformation, considering a set Θ of parameters, computes pixels of the new image, $I_t(i,j)$ in the following way:

$$I_t(i,j) = I_d(x(\Theta,i,j),y(\Theta,i,j)) \tag{1}$$

If $x(\Theta,i,j)$ and $y(\Theta,i,j)$ are outside of the image I_0, a common strategy is to assign zero value which represents a black pixel. But, What happen when $x(\Theta,i,j)$ and $y(\Theta,i,j)$ have real values instead of integer values? Remember that image $I_d(x,y)$ have only valid values when x and y have integer values. An inaccurate method to solve this problem is to use their nearest integer values, but next section presents the bilinear interpolation, a much better method to interpolate a pixel with real coordinates (x,y) in an image.

From other point of view, pixel $I_d(x,y)$ moves to the position $I_t(i,j)$. However, most transformations define points in the new image given points in the original image. In that case, to apply the bilinear transformation, we need to compute the inverse transformation that maps new points (or coordinates) to points (or coordinates) in the original image.

2.1 Bilinear Interpolation

If x_i and x_f are the integer and fractional part of x, respectively, and y_i and y_f the integer and fractional part of y, Figure 2 illustrates the bilinear interpolation method (Faugeras, 1993) to find $I(x_i+x_f,\ y_i+y_f)$, given the four nearest pixels to position $(x_i+x_f,\ y_i+y_f)$: $I(x_i,y_i)$, $I(x_i+1,\ y_i)$, $I(x_i,y_i+1)$, $I(x_i+1,y_i+1)$ (image values at particular positions are represented by vertical bars in Figure 2). First two linear interpolations are used to compute two new values $I(x_i,y_i+y_f)$ and

$I(x_i+1,y_i+y_f)$ and then another linear interpolation is used to compute the desired value $I(x_i+x_f,y_i+y_f)$ from the new computed values:

$$
\begin{aligned}
I(x_i, y_i+y_f) &= (1-y_f)I(x_i,y_i)+y_f I(x_i,y_i+1) \\
I(x_i+1, y_i+y_f) &= (1-y_f)I(x_i+1,y_i)+y_f I(x_i+1,y_i+1) \\
I(x_i+x_f, y_i+y_f) &= (1-x_f)I(x_i,y_i+y_f)+x_f I(x_i+1,y_i+y_f)
\end{aligned}
\quad (2)
$$

Using the bilinear interpolation, a smooth transformed image is computed. Now we are able to deal with the transformation associated with cameras. In section 5.3 we describe the process to build new images from distorted images and the set of parameters of the distortion and projection model.

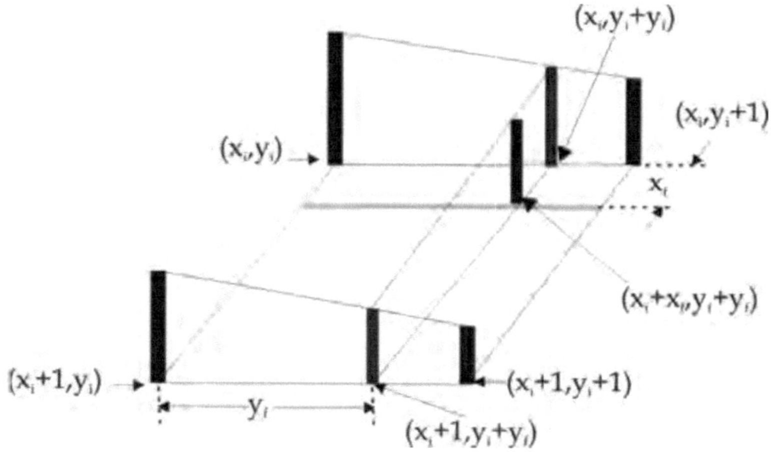

Figure 2. Using the bilinear interpolation

3. The Distortion Model

The radial distortion process due to wide-angle lens is illustrated in Figure 3. Figure 3 (b) shows an image taken from the camera when the pattern shown in Figure 3 (a) is in front of the camera. Note the effect of lens, the image is distorted, specially in those parts far away from the center of the image.

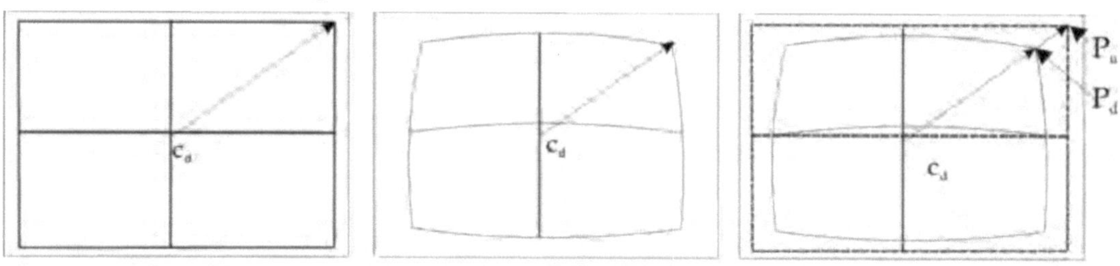

(a) Pattern in front of the camera

(b) Image captured by the camera

(c) Both Images

Figure 3. The distortion process due to wide angle lens

Figure 3 (c) shows the radial distortion in detail, supposing that the center of distortion is the point C_d with coordinates (c_x, c_y) (no necessarily the center of the image). Let I_d be the distorted image captured by the camera and I_u the undistorted image associated to I_d.
In order to correct the distorted image, the distorted point at position P_d with coordinates (x_d, y_d) in I_d should move to point P_u with coordinates (x_u, y_u). Let r_d and r_u be the Euclidian distance between P_d and C_d, and between P_u and C_d, respectively. The relationship between radial distances r_d and r_u can be modeled in two ways:

$$r_d = r_u f_1(r_u^2) \tag{3}$$

$$r_u = r_d f_2(r_d^2) \tag{4}$$

Approximations to arbitrary function f_1 and f_2 may be given by a Taylor expansion: $(f_1(r_u^2) = 1+k_1 r_u^2+k_2 r_u^4+\ldots)$ and $(f_2(r_d^2) = 1+k_1 r_d^2+k_2 r_d^4+\ldots)$. Figure 4 helps to see the difference between f_1 and f_2 considering only k_1 for a typical distortion in a wide-angle lens. f_1 models a compression while f_2 models an expansion.

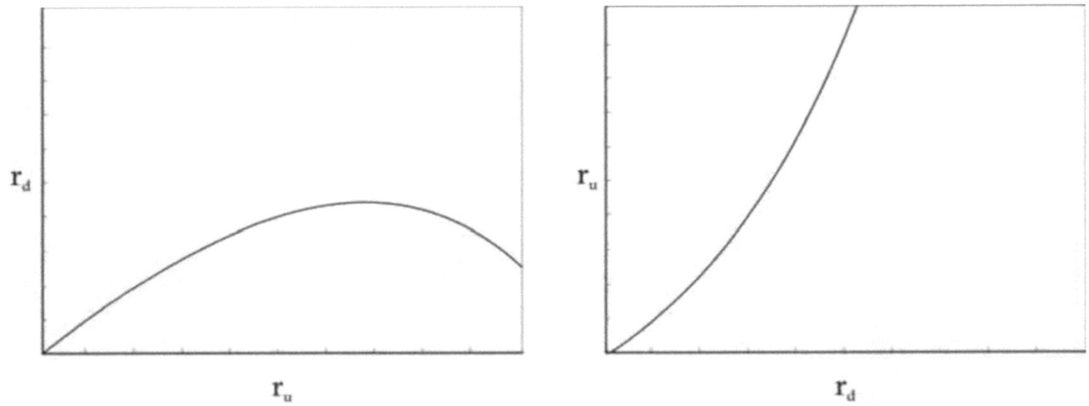

(a) $r_d = r_u f_1(r_u^2)$, $f_1 = 1 - 3 \times 10^{-6} r_u^2$ (b) $r_u = r_d f_2(r_d^2)$, $f_2 = 1 + 3 \times 1.3x10^{-5} r_d^2$

Figure 4. Two different functions to model the distortion of images

The problem with f_1 is that there is the possibility to get the same r_d for two different values of r_u (see Fig. 5).

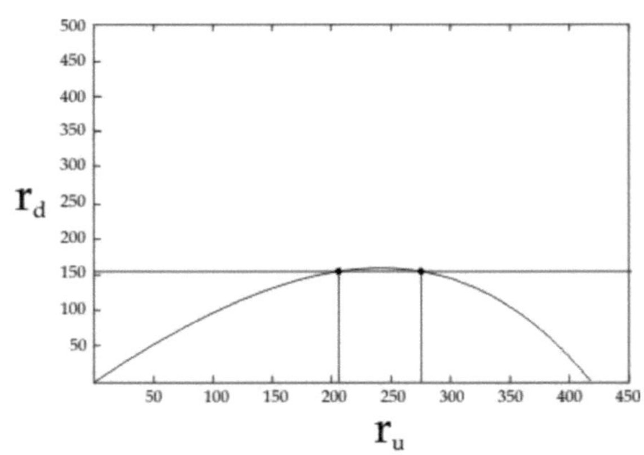

Figure 5. Problem using f_1. A single r_d is related with two different r_u

In fact, this behavior was found experimentally when we use f_1. Figure 6 shows an example. Borders of the corrected image duplicate parts of the image (see the top corners in Figure 6(b)). However f_2 does not have this problem.

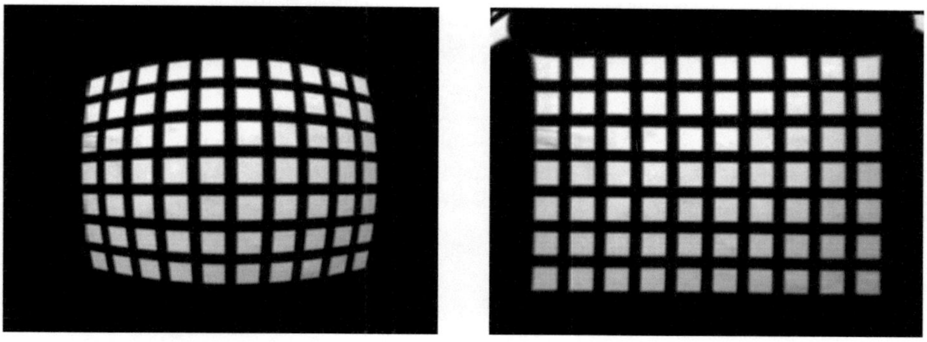

(a) Original image (b) Corrected image

Figure 6. An example of a wrong correction using f_1

From now on, we consider only eq. 4. Experimentally we found that we need to consider four terms for f_2, to remove the distortion due to wide-angle lens. Then, the coordinates (x_u, y_u) of P_u can be computed by:

$$\begin{aligned} x_u &= c_x + (x_d - c_x)\, f_2(r_d^2) \\ &= c_x + (x_d - c_x)(1 + k_1 r_d^2 + k_2 r_d^4 + k_3 r_d^6) \\ y_u &= c_y + (y_d - c_y)\, f_2(r_d^2) \\ &= c_y + (y_d - c_y)(1 + k_1 r_d^2 + k_2 r_d^4 + k_3 r_d^6) \\ r_d^2 &= (x_d - c_x)^2 + (y_d - c_y)^2 \end{aligned} \tag{5}$$

where (c_x, c_y) are the coordinates of the center of radial distortion. So, this distortion model have a set of five parameters $\Theta^d = \{c_x, c_y, k_1, k_2, k_3\}$. This model works fine if the camera have square pixel, but if not, we need another parameter, s_x, called aspect ratio that divide the term $(x_d - c_x)$. Since most cameras have square pixels, we consider $s_x = 1$.

Figure 7 helps to understand the process to transform the image taken from the camera, I_d, to a new image, I_d, similar to the reference image. A point P_i in image I_d with coordinates (x_d, y_d) maps to an undistorted point (x_u, y_u). Figure 7(b) illustrates the image without radial distortion and the transformation T_u that maps the point with coordinates (x_d, y_d) to new coordinates (x_u, y_u). This new image is bigger than I_d because the compression due to the wide angle lens has been removed, lines in the environment maps to lines in this image.

In a second step, the point with coordinates (x_u, y_u) is projected to a new point (x_p, y_p) in image I_t,. Next section focuses in this projection step.

4. The Projection Model

Figure 3 shows and ideal case, where the plane of the pattern is parallel to the camera plane and center of the pattern coincides with the optical axis of the camera. A more realistic case is illustrated in Figure 7. Conceptually we can assume that a pinhole camera captures the undistorted image (a planar image) into the new image I_t. Since cameras are projective devices, a projective transformation is involved. A projective transformation is the most general transformation that maps lines into lines (Hartley & Zisserman, 2004).

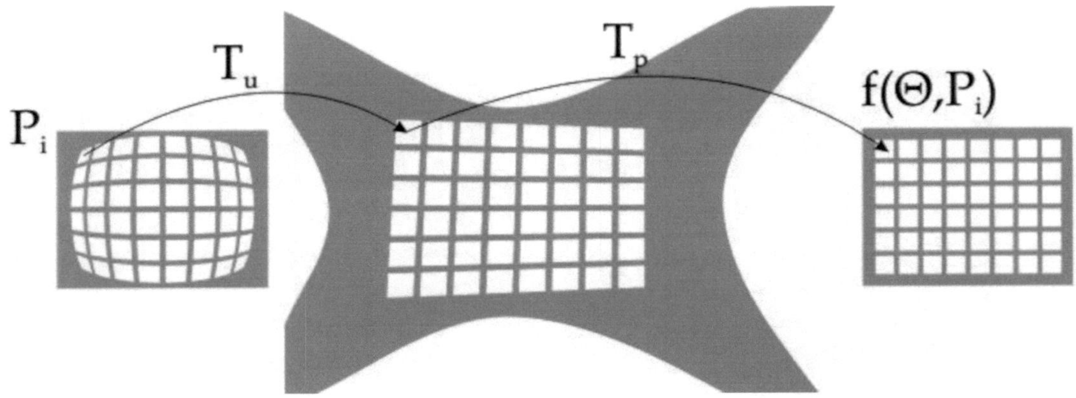

(a) Input image I_d b) Image I_u without radial distortion (c) New image I_t

Figure 7. Transforming the input image

Using homogeneous coordinates, the class of 2-D planar projective transformations between the camera plane and the plane of the undistorted image is given by (Szeliski, 1996) (Hartley & Zisserman, 2004) $[x_p', y_p', w_p']^t = M[x_u', y_u', w_u']^t$, where matrix M is called an homography and it has eight degrees of freedom. For our calibration application, M has the form:

$$M = \begin{bmatrix} m_0 & m_1 & m_2 \\ m_3 & m_4 & m_5 \\ m_6 & m_7 & 1 \end{bmatrix}$$

Plane and homogeneous coordinates are related by $(x_p = x_p'/w_p', y_p = y_p'/w_p')$ and $(x_u = x_u'/w_u', y_u = y_u'/w_u')$. So, a point $P_u(x_u, y_u)$ in image I_u moves to $P_p(x_p, y_p)$ in the new projected image I_t. Assigning $w_u' = 1$, the new coordinates of P_p are given by:

$$x_p = \frac{m_0 x_u + m_1 y_u + m_2}{m_6 x_u + m_7 y_u + 1}$$

$$y_p = \frac{m_3 x_u + m_4 y_u + m_5}{m_6 x_u + m_7 y_u + 1} \qquad (6)$$

And now the projection parameters are $\Theta^p = \{m_0, m_1, m_2, m_3, m_4, m_5, m_6, m_7\}$.

5. The Point Correspondences Method

The goal is to find a set of parameters Θ^d and Θ^p that transform the distorted image captured by the camera, I_d, into a new projected image, I_t, that match the image, I_r, of the calibration pattern put in front of the camera. To do that, a set of point correspondences are extracted from I_d and I_r (see section 5.2 for details).

Let n be the number of features, (x_{rk},y_{rk}) be the coordinates of the k-th feature $(k=1,\ldots,n)$ in I_r and (x_{dk},y_{dk}) be its correspondence point in I_d. From (x_{dk},y_{dk}) and using eq. 5, we can compute (x_{uk},y_{uk}) and using eq. 6, we can get the coordinates (x_{pk},y_{pk}) of the projected feature. So we have a set of pairs of points $C = \{<(x_{r1},y_{r1}),(x_{p1},y_{p1})>,\ldots,<(x_{rn},y_{rn}),(x_{pn},y_{pn})>\}$.

We formulate the goal of the calibration as to find a set of parameters $\Theta = \Theta^d \cup \Theta^p$ such the sum, E, of square distances between projected points and reference points is a minimum,

$$
\begin{aligned}
e_{xk} &= x_p(\Theta,x_{dk},y_{dk}) - x_{rk} \\
e_{yk} &= y_p(\Theta,x_{dk},y_{dk}) - y_{rk} \\
E(\Theta) &= \sum_{k=1}^{n}\left(e_{xk}^{\;2} + e_{yk}^{\;2}\right) \\
\Theta &= \operatorname{argmin} E(\Theta)
\end{aligned}
\tag{7}
$$

5.1 Non-Linear Optimization

The Gauss-Newton-Levenberg-Marquardt method (GNLM) (Press et al., 1986) is a non-linear iterative technique specifically designated for minimizing functions which has the form of sum of square functions, like E. At each iteration the increment of parameters, vector $\delta\Theta$, is computed solving the following linear matrix equation:

$$[A+\lambda I]\delta\Theta=B \tag{8}$$

If there is n point correspondences and q parameters in Θ, A is a matrix of dimension qxq and matrix B has dimension $qx1$ and $\delta\Theta=[\,\delta\theta_1, \delta\theta_1,\ldots, \delta\theta_q\,]^t$. λ is a parameter which is allowed to vary at each iteration. After a little algebra, the elements of A and B can be computed using the following formulas,

$$
\begin{aligned}
a_{i,j} &= \sum_{k=1}^{n}\left(\frac{\partial x_{pk}}{\partial\theta_i}\frac{\partial x_{pk}}{\partial\theta_j} + \frac{\partial y_{pk}}{\partial\theta_i}\frac{\partial y_{pk}}{\partial\theta_j}\right) \\
b_i &= -\sum_{k=1}^{n}\left(\frac{\partial x_{pk}}{\partial\theta_i}e_{xk} + \frac{\partial y_{pk}}{\partial\theta_i}e_{yk}\right)
\end{aligned}
\tag{9}
$$

In order to simplify the notation, we use x_p instead of x_{pk} and y_p instead of y_{pk}. Then, $\partial x_p / \partial\theta_i$ and $\partial y_p / \partial\theta_i$ for $(\theta_i \in \Theta^p)$ can be derived from eq. 6,

$$
\begin{aligned}
&\frac{\partial x_p}{\partial m_0} = \frac{x_u}{D} && \frac{\partial y_p}{\partial m_0} = 0 \\
&\frac{\partial x_p}{\partial m_1} = \frac{y_u}{D} && \frac{\partial y_p}{\partial m_1} = 0 \\
&\frac{\partial x_p}{\partial m_2} = \frac{1}{D} && \frac{\partial y_p}{\partial m_2} = 0 \\
&\frac{\partial x_p}{\partial m_3} = 0 && \frac{\partial y_p}{\partial m_3} = \frac{x_u}{D} \\
&\frac{\partial x_p}{\partial m_4} = 0 && \frac{\partial y_p}{\partial m_4} = \frac{y_u}{D} \\
&\frac{\partial x_p}{\partial m_5} = 0 && \frac{\partial y_p}{\partial m_5} = \frac{1}{D} \\
&\frac{\partial x_p}{\partial m_6} = \frac{-x_u x_p}{D} && \frac{\partial y_p}{\partial m_6} = \frac{-x_u y_p}{D} \\
&\frac{\partial x_p}{\partial m_7} = \frac{-y_u x_p}{D} && \frac{\partial y_p}{\partial m_7} = \frac{-y_u y_p}{D}
\end{aligned}
\tag{10}
$$

Where $D = m_6 x_u + m_7 y_u + 1$. Partial derivatives of distortion parameters are derived from eq. 5 and two applications of the chain rule,

$$
\begin{aligned}
&\frac{\partial x_p}{\partial \theta_i} = \frac{\partial x_p}{\partial x_u}\frac{\partial x_u}{\partial \theta_i} + \frac{\partial x_p}{\partial y_u}\frac{\partial y_u}{\partial \theta_i} \qquad \theta_i \in \{c_x, c_y, k_1, k_2, k_3\} \\
&\frac{\partial y_p}{\partial \theta_i} = \frac{\partial y_p}{\partial x_u}\frac{\partial x_u}{\partial \theta_i} + \frac{\partial y_p}{\partial y_u}\frac{\partial y_u}{\partial \theta_i} \qquad \theta_i \in \{c_x, c_y, k_1, k_2, k_3\}
\end{aligned}
\tag{11}
$$

$$
\begin{aligned}
\frac{\partial x_p}{\partial x_u} &= \frac{Dm_0 - (m_0 x_u + m_1 y_u + m_2) m_6}{D^2} \\
\frac{\partial y_p}{\partial x_u} &= \frac{Dm_3 - (m_3 x_u + m_4 y_u + m_5) m_6}{D^2} \\
\frac{\partial x_p}{\partial y_u} &= \frac{Dm - (m_0 x_u + m_1 y_u + m_2) m_7}{D^2} \\
\frac{\partial y_p}{\partial y_u} &= \frac{Dm_4 - (m_3 x_u + m_4 y_u + m_5) m_7}{D^2}
\end{aligned}
\tag{12}
$$

Finally, the last set of formulas are derived from eq. 5,

$$
\begin{aligned}
\frac{\partial x_u}{\partial k_1} &= r_d^2 (x_d - c_x) \\
\frac{\partial y_u}{\partial k_1} &= r_d^2 (y_d - c_y) \\
\frac{\partial x_u}{\partial k_2} &= r_d^4 (x_d - c_x) \\
\frac{\partial y_u}{\partial k_2} &= r_d^4 (y_d - c_y) \\
\frac{\partial x_u}{\partial k_3} &= r_d^6 (x_d - c_x) \\
\frac{\partial y_u}{\partial k_3} &= r_d^6 (y_d - c_y) \\
\frac{\partial x_u}{\partial c_x} &= -(k_1 r_d^2 + k_2 r_d^4 + k_3 r_d^6) - 2(k_1 + 2k_2 r_d^2 + 3k_3 r_d^4)(x_d - c_x)^2 \\
\frac{\partial y_u}{\partial c_x} &= -2(k_1 + 2k_2 r_d^2 + 3k_3 r_d^4)(x_d - c_x)(y_d - c_y) \\
\frac{\partial x_u}{\partial c_y} &= -2(k_1 + 2k_2 r_d^2 + 3k_3 r_d^4)(x_d - c_x)(y_d - c_y) \\
\frac{\partial y_u}{\partial c_y} &= -(k_1 r_d^2 + k_2 r_d^4 + k_3 r_d^6) - 2(y_d - c_y)^2 (k_1 + 2k_2 r_d^2 + 3k_3 r_d^4)
\end{aligned}
\tag{13}
$$

Where r_d was defined previously in eq. 5.

Next section describes how to compute feature points from each image, as well as their correspondences automatically.

5.2 Selecting Feature Points

As we can see in Figure 6(a), the image has white squares over a black background. As robust feature points we select the *center of mass* of each one of the white squares (or distorted white squares) of both images. The mass of each pixel is its gray level in the range [0-255] (0 for black pixels and 255 for white pixels).
In the implementation, once a white pixel is found (considering a given threshold), its cluster is identified visiting its neighbours recursively, and the center of mass is computed from all pixels in the cluster.
To compute automatically point correspondences, we assume that the array of white squares in each image is centered, specially in the case of the image from the camera. In this way, bad clusters (for instance when the camera capture some white areas outside of the calibration pattern) can be eliminated because the good clusters are closer to the image center. This is not a problem with the reference pattern, because we use the perfect graphic file of the image and there are no bad clusters of white pixels.
We also assume that the image from the camera does not have a significant rotation, relative to the reference image, so relative positions of white squares hold in both images. For instance, the top left-most white square is the closest square to the top-left corner of the image.

5.3 Computing Corrected Images

If we compute a set of parameters Θ we are able to map a point (x_d,y_d) into a new projected point (x_p,y_p). But to compute a new image I_t we need the inverse mapping: to set the pixel value with integer coordinates (x_p,y_p) in I_t, we need to compute the pixel value with coordinates (x_d,y_d) in the distorted image I_d.
It is easy to compute (x_u,y_u) given (x_p,y_p) and the homography M. In homogeneous coordinates, $[x_u',y_u',w_u']^t = M^{-1}[x_p',y_p',w_p']^t$.
However, it is harder to compute (x_d,y_d) given (x_u,y_u). There is no a direct way to solve this problem. To solve it, we use the binary search algorithm. Our goal is to find r_d given $r_u^2 = (x_u-c_x)^2+(y_u-c_y)^2$, k_1, k_2 and k_3. Once r_d has been found, x_d and y_d are easily computed using eq. 5. ($x_d = (x_u-c_x) / f_2(r_d^{\,2}) + c_x$ and $y_d = (y_u-c_y) / f_2(r_d^{\,2}) + c_y$). From eq. 4, we formulate a new function f:

$$f(r_d) = r_u - r_d f_2(r_d^2) = r_u - r_d(1+k_1r_d^2+k_2r_d^4+k_3r_d^6) \tag{14}$$

If $x_u=c_x$ and $y_u=c_y$, from eq. 5 we have $x_d = x_u$ and $y_d=y_u$. If $x_u \neq c_x$ and $y_u \neq c_y$, we need to find a low limit, r_{d0}, and high limit, r_{d1}, such that $f(r_{d0}) > 0$ and $f(r_{d1}) < 0$. With these limits, the binary search algorithm is able to find the right r_d such that $f(r_d)=0$ (or very close to zero) and then $r_u = r_d f_2(r_d^{\,2})$.
If $x_u \neq c_x$ and $y_u \neq c_y$ then $r_u>0$ and $f(0) > 0$, so we have the low limit $r_{d1}= 0$. To find the high limit r_{d1} we iteratively increment r_d until $f(r_d) < 0$.

5.4 The Calibration Process

The calibration process starts with one image from the camera, I_d, another image from the calibration pattern, I_r, and initial values for parameters Θ. In the following algorithm, Θ and $\delta\Theta$ are considered as vectors. We start with (c_x,c_y) at the center of the image, $k_1=k_2=k_3=0$ and the identity matrix for M. The calibration algorithm is as follows:

1. From the reference image, compute the reference feature points (x_{rk},y_{rk}), $(k=1,...n)$.
2. From Θ and the distorted image, compute a corrected image.
3. From the corrected image compute the set of feature points (x_{pk},y_{pk}), $(k=1,...n)$.
4. From $(x_{pk},y_{pk})(k=1,...n)$ and Θ compute $(x_{dk},y_{dk})(k=1,...n)$.
5. Find the best Θ that minimize E using the GNLM algorithm:
   (a) Compute the total error, $E(\Theta)$ (eq. 7).
   (b) Pick a modest value for λ, say $\lambda=0.001$.
   (c) Solve the linear system of equations (8), and calculate $E(\Theta+\delta\Theta)$.
   (d) If $E(\Theta+\delta\Theta) >= E(\Theta)$, increase λ by a factor of 10, and go to the previous step. If λ grows very large, it means that there is no way to improve the solution Θ.
   (e) If $E(\Theta+\delta\Theta) < E(\Theta)$, decrease λ by a factor of 10, replace Θ by $\Theta+\delta\Theta$, and go to step 5a.
6. Repeat steps 2-5 until $E(\Theta)$ does not decrease.

When $\lambda=0$, the GNLM method is a Gauss-Newton method, and when λ tends to infinity, $\delta\Theta$ turns to so called steepest descent direction and the size of $\delta\theta_i$ tends to zero.
The calibration algorithm apply several times the GNLM algorithm to get better solutions. At the beginning, the clusters of the distorted image are not perfect squares and so point features can not match exactly the feature points computed using the reference image. Once a corrected image is ready, point features can be better estimated.

6. Related Approaches

There are two kinds of calibration methods. The first kind is the one that uses a calibration pattern or grid with features whose world coordinates are known. The second family of methods use geometric invariants of the image features like parallel lines, spheres, circles, etc. (Devernay & Faugeras, 2001).
The method described in this paper is in the first family of methods. Feature point correspondences are computed automatically. Some other methods require a human operator (with a lot of patience) to find such correspondences (Tamaki et al., 2001). Some other registration methods use all pixels of images as features, instead of a small set of point correspondences. However these methods need an initial set of parameters close enough to the right one and also have problems due to non uniform illumination (Tamaki et al., 2001).
The main problem when we have a high radial distortion is the accurate detection of features. Detect white clusters of pixels is easier than detect lines or corners. Some other methods apply the function f_1 of eq. (3), computing r_d directly from r_u. But they tend to fail when there is a high radial distortion, as shown in Figure 6. Also, in order to correct images, we have to introduce more terms in the distortion model (k_1,k_2,k_3). Other methods use only k_1 and find a direct solution for r_d. However they also fail to model higher radial distortions. Other methods (Ma et al. 2003) use a Taylor expansion of r_d instead of r_d^2. Experimentally we found better results using r_d^2 instead of r_d for wide angle lens.
Once a set of parameters was found using our method, computing each pixel of the new image is slow (due to the binary search method). However, in order to process many images

from the same camera, that process of finding correspondences between I_t (the new image) and I_d (the distorted image) should be done only once. Given such correspondences, the bilinear interpolation process is very fast and a new corrected image is computed quickly.
We have described a calibration method based on the Gauss-Newton-Levenberg-Marquardt non-linear optimization method using analytical derivatives. Other approaches compute numerical derivatives (Devernay, 1995; Sten, 1997; Devernay 2001), so we have faster calculations and better convergence properties.

7. Experimental results

We test a MDCS2, ½" format CMOS, Firewire color camera from Videre Design with a 3.5mm C-mount lens. This camera acquire 15fps with resolution of 1280 x 960 pixels.
The pattern calibration (image I_r), showed in Figure 8(a), was made using the program xfig under Linux. The image taken by the camera is shown in Figure 8(b). The corrected and projected image, using our point correspondences method, is shown in Figure 8(c), a very good result. The GNLM process was applied twice, requiring 6 iterations in the first case and *108* iterations in the second case. The error E after the first GNLM search was $1.706x10^5$ and at the end of the second search it was $1.572x10^5$. It is interesting to compute the maximum individual distance between points $\left(d_i = \sqrt{e_{x_i}^2 + e_{y_i}^2}\right)$ to see the maximum individual error. Using this criteria, at the end of the process we got d_i^{max} = 1.86 pixels. The final parameters found are listed in Table 1.

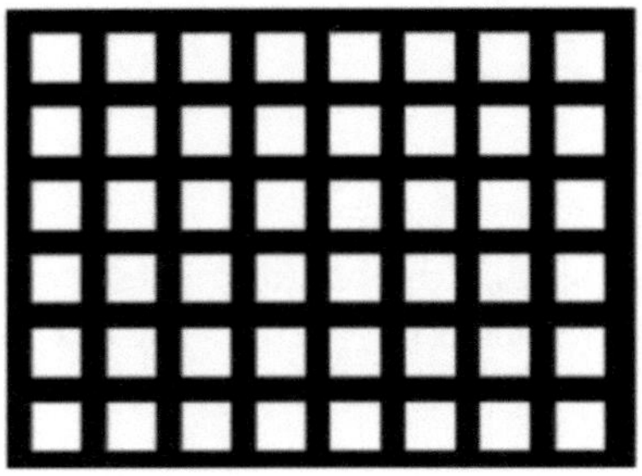

(a) Calibration Pattern

(b) Image from camera

(c) New image

Figure 8. The calibration process

Finally, Figure 9 shows an example of removing distortion using an image of our Laboratory.

Figure 9. Original and corrected images

m_0	m_1	m_2	m_3	m_4	m_5	m_6	m_7
.0752	.0146	131.0073	-.0132	.0788	115.4594	-.00002	-.000036
m_8	k_1	k_2	k_3	c_x	c_y	s_x	
-.000048	1.2026E-6	-4.2812E-13	6.6317E-18	508.936	625.977	1	

Table 1. Final set of parameters

8. Conclusions

We propose a robust method to remove radial distortion from images using a reference image as a guide. It is based on point correspondences between the acquired image from the

camera (with wide-angle lens) and the reference image. This method is faster than image registration methods and it is able to model high radial distortions. Also the selection of the center of mass of clusters of white pixels within images, as point features, are easier to detect than lines or corners. Another advantage of this method is its good convergence properties even starting with a set of parameters that no introduces any distortion.
This method was implemented in Linux and it is available online[1], using the C language and standard routines from the Free Gnu Scientific library (GSL) to solve the linear system of equations and to find the inverse of matrix *M*.

9. References

Devernay, F & Faugeras, O. (1995). Automatic calibration and removal of distortion from scenes of structured environments, *SPIE*, 2567;62-72

Devernay, F & Faugeras, O.D. (2001), *Straight lines have to be straight. MVA*, 13(1);14-24

Faugeras, O. (1993). *Three-Dimensional Computer Vision*, The MIT Press

Hartley, R. I. & Zisserman A. (2004) *Multiple View Geometry in Computer Vision*, .Camdbrige University Press, ISBN: 0521540518, second edition

Ma, Lili; Chen, YangQuan & Moore, Kevin L. (2003), A new analytical radial distortion model for camera calibration. http://www.citebase.org/abstract?id=oai:arXiv.org:cs/0307046.

Press, W.; Flannery, S.; Teukolsky & Vetterling, W. (1986), *Numerical Recipes, the art of scientific computing*, Cambridge University Press

Stein, G. P., (1996) Lens distortion calibration using point correspondences. In Proc. *Conference on Computer Vision and Pattern Recognition (CVPR '97)*

Szeliski, R. (1996), Video mosaic for virtual environments. *IEICE Computer Graphics and Applications*, 16(2):22-30

Tamaki, T.; Yamamura, T. & Ohnish, N. (2001), A method for compensation of image distortion with image registration technique. *IEICE Trans. Inf. and Sys*, E84-D(8):990-998

Weng, J.; Cohen, P. & Herniou, M. (1992), Camera calibration with distortion models and accuracy evaluation. *IEEE Trans. Pattern Analysis and Machine Intelligence.*, 14(10):965-980. ISSN 0162-8828.

[1] http://faraday.fie.umich.mx/~lromero/calibrate.html

5

Soft Computing Applications in Robotic Vision Systems

Victor Ayala-Ramirez, Raul E. Sanchez-Yanez, Carlos H. Garcia-Capulin and Francisco J. Montecillo-Puente
Universidad de Guanajuato FIMEE
Mexico

1. Introduction

1.1 Soft Computing

Soft computing is a collection of intelligent techniques working in a complementary way to build robust systems at low cost. Soft computing includes techniques such as neural networks, fuzzy logic, evolutionary computation (including genetic algorithms) and probabilistic reasoning (Wang and Tang, 1997). These techniques are capable of dealing with imprecision, uncertainty, ambiguity, partial truth, machine learning and optimization issues we usually face in real world problems.

Soft computing addresses problem solving tasks in a complementary approach more than in a competitive one. Main advantages of soft computing are: i) its rich knowledge representation (both at signal and pattern level), ii) its flexible knowledge acquisition process (including machine learning and learning from human experts) and iii) its flexible knowledge processing. These advantages let us to build intelligent systems with a high machine intelligence quotient at low cost. Soft computing systems have already been applied in industrial sectors like aerospace, communications systems, robotics and automation and transport systems (Dote and Ovaska, 2001).

1.2 Robotic Vision

Vision, as an exteroceptive sensor, enables autonomous systems to complete complex tasks where environment information is needed. Robotic vision is used in a set of robotic tasks like local and global map building, reactive navigation, topological navigation, object tracking, visual servoing and active sensing among others (de Souza and Kak, 2002). Most of these tasks include a pattern recognition component. In each of these tasks the robot needs to process large amounts of data at a fast rate in order to satisfy real time operation constraints (Barnes and Liu, 2002). Another fact to take into account is the presence of different perturbations in the signals acquired by the robot. At each run, the robot acquires essentially different information even if real life test conditions are very similar. For example, in outdoor environments, sun and clouds can provoke very significant illumination changes in the images, difficulting then to achieve the expected performance of the vision algorithms. To cope with these uncertainties, soft computing techniques have been used because its robustness when facing this kind of scenarios.

1.3 Soft Computing Applications in Robotics and Vision

Soft computing has been widely used in robotics and vision applications. Fuzzy logic is mainly used in robot control and in the pattern recognition issues arising from robotic tasks. Robot control is particularly addressed by fuzzy logic because we can specify the desired behavior for a system in terms of rules. For example (Saffioti, 1997) presents how to apply fuzzy logic in robot navigation. Another example of fuzzy logic for autonomous vehicle navigation is the FUZZY-NAV project (Pan et al., 1995). Fuzzy pattern recognition uses patterns and models where a given degree of uncertainty, imprecision and inaccuracy is included in the form of associative rules. For example, in human robot interaction, gesture and faces need to be recognized. These kinds of objects are very difficult to characterize in terms of features or relations in a statistical way. That is what makes interesting to use fuzzy systems to incorporate uncertainty handling. (Buschka et al., 2000) have proposed the detection of fuzzy landmarks for map construction. Similar applications have been also proposed by (Bloch and Saffioti, 2002; Gasós and Saffioti, 1999) where map building is addressed.

Neural networks are useful when we have only some examples of the behavior we want to incorporate on a system. In robotics, NAVLAB is a project where neural networks were used to steer an autonomous vehicle (Pomerleau, 1994). Another application for neural networks in robotics concerns denoising techniques for images or even in control applications where, from a set of input-output pairs, neural networks are capable of approximating control surfaces whose behavior we try to emulate.

Genetic algorithms are well suited for optimization problems where we have some cues about desired performance that we can encode in a fitness function. This kind of scenario arises when detecting landmarks or artificial shapes in the robot environment. Another application for genetic algorithms in the robotics domain concerns the path planification issues where the trajectory search space can be verified faster than by brute force approaches or randomized searches.

Detailed discussions on soft computing approaches are given in a number of texts. Neuro-fuzzy algorithms are presented in (Pal and Mitra, 1999), (Mitra and Hayashi, 2000) and (Buckley and Hayashi, 1994). (Herrera and Verdegay, 1996) also include the GA and their relation with other soft computing algorithms. The intelligent systems development is covered in (Ovaska, 2004) and (Abraham et al., 2002).

In this work, we present three robotic vision applications where soft computing techniques are a crucial component for the success of our application. Firstly, we will present a fuzzy color tracking system where color is represented by means of membership functions and fuzzy rules to aggregate color information in the CIELab space. A second system presented here concerns a genetic algorithm based approach for the detection of parametric shapes in images acquired by a mobile robot. A third example includes the hybridization of two soft computing techniques, we present a geno-fuzzy controller used for the servo-control of a pan and tilt camera. For all three methods we present the specific soft computing aspects of their implementation both in simulation platforms and in a robotic platform named XidooBot, a P3AT robot (Fig. 1.).

Fig. 1. XidooBot, a Pioneer P3AT robot used as our experimental test bed.

2. Fuzzy Color Tracking

2.1 Tracking System Components

A high level task for autonomous robot navigation is visual object tracking. This capability is used to avoid collisions or to self-localize by using visual landmarks. Almost all visual tracking systems follow the block diagram shown in Fig. 2. These systems process the visual information acquired by a camera in order to locate a target in the image.

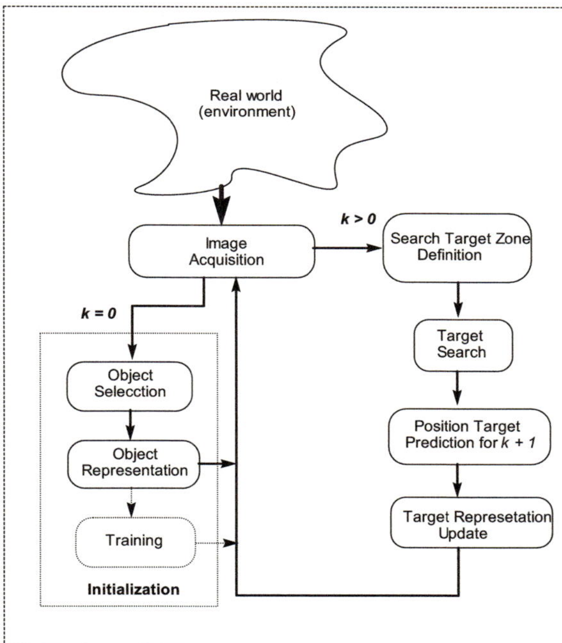

Fig. 2. Block diagram for a general system for target tracking. We use a fuzzy logic-based approach to model the color of the target.

The initialization phase requires using a model to represent the target. The search step requires defining similarity measures to detect it along the visual sequence. Generally, the target representation defines the way in which the comparisons are made. There are several cues to represent the target, among them color is one that has been successfully used on real time applications (Nummiaro et al., 2003; Argyros and Louriakis, 2004). Robustness of a visual object tracking system relies in the target representation. In this way, we have combined color and fuzzy logic to represent targets (Vertan et al., 2000; Montecillo-Puente et al., 2003), and here we present a fuzzy color tracking system. We use fuzzy logic in order to separate color components and color attributes, like illumination (Keller and Matsakis, 1999). Our main concern is to solve the illumination problems because in real applications illumination changes very often and that appears as if the target was changing its visual appearance.

2.2 Fuzzy Color for Object Representation

Color is one of the features most oftenly used to represent objects. But this feature has some inherent problems, mainly the representation of color in an optimal way. By optimal way we mean to be capable of distinguish between different and similar colors, i.e. red and blue or light red and dark red, respectively. Due to changes in illumination it is possible that a color passes from a light one to dark one, so in real time tracking it is necessary to update the actual representation for color. In this way, the well known problem of saturation also arises due to illumination conditions. These are the topics covered in this section. First we define the fuzzy color and then we describe the procedure to update the fuzzy color.

2.2.1 Fuzzy Color

In order to represent a target by color, we assume that it is monochromatic, that is, it is composed by a set of visually homogeneous pixels, i.e. the target appearance is composed of pixel with intensity values very close in a given color space. The goal is to represent this set of color pixels visually homogeneous, in some way. That is a common situation in real applications due to illumination sources and video cameras noise. In order to represent these color pixels, it is necessary to select a color space. We have selected the *CIELab* color space because in such model visually similar colors have close color coordinates; additionally it possesses a luminance component. The two chromatic components of this space are named, a and b, and the luminance component, L (Braum et al., 1998). Fuzzy color is the assignation of convenient fuzzy sets to each color component. The procedure to define them is as follows:

1. Assume we have a set of visually homogeneous pixels in the RGB color space, p_i with color components p_i^R, p_i^G and p_i^B.
2. Convert all pixels, p_i, to the *CIELab* color space obtaining color components p_i^L, p_i^a and p_i^b.
3. Compute the normalized histogram to each component.
4. Adjust a membership function to each histogram. We may use triangular, trapezoidal or Gaussian ones.
5. The membership functions define the fuzzy sets attached to the set of pixels. That is μ_L, μ_a and μ_b are the membership functions for the components L, a and b

The fuzzy representation of the set of color pixels is given by these membership functions. For deciding if a particular pixel p belongs to the set of pixels (or target) we evaluate the following fuzzy rule

$$\text{if } (R_L \text{ and } R_a \text{ and } R_b) \text{ then } p \text{ is the target} \quad (1)$$

where R_L, R_a and R_b are defined as

$$R_L : L_p \text{ belongs to color component } L \text{ of the target}$$
$$R_a : a_p \text{ belongs to color component } a \text{ of the target} \quad (2)$$
$$R_b : b_p \text{ belongs to color component } b \text{ of the target}$$

and L_p, a_p and b_p are the *CIELab* components of the pixel p. Let be C_L, C_a and C_b the membership values of R_L, R_a and R_b for the pixel p, respectively. That is, $C_L = \mu_L(L_p)$, $C_a = \mu_a(a_p)$ and $C_b = \mu_b(b_p)$. Finally, we define truth value for the rule (1), $C_{p,}$, which expresses how much the pixel p belongs to the set of pixels (or target), as

$$C_p = \min(C_L, C_a, C_b) \quad (3)$$

For the case in which the target is non-monochromatic, e.g. the target is composed by dark red and yellow, we apply the above procedure for defining fuzzy sets to each set of colored pixels. That is a problem because, in general, we do not know how many colors there are and obviously we do not know also the set of colored pixels corresponding to them. We can use in this case some method for determining the number of colors and the set of pixels attached to it, i.e. the Mean Shift procedure (Comaniciu et al., 2000). Once we have the number of colors and the corresponding set of pixels attached to each of them. We apply the above procedure for each color. So we define, for a non-monochromatic target composed by k different colors, its representation as follows:

$$\begin{aligned} &if\ (R_L^1 \ and\ R_a^1 \ and\ R_b^1) \\ &or\ ...\ or\ (R_L^i \ and\ R_a^i \ and\ R_b^i) \\ &or\ ...\ or\ (R_L^k \ and\ R_a^k \ and\ R_b^k) \end{aligned} \quad (4)$$

where R^i_L, R^i_a and R^i_b are defined as (2) for the color i.
So the truth value for a pixel p, with L_p, a_p and b_p *CIELab* components, now is given by

$$C_p = \max(\min(C_L^1, C_a^1, C_b^1), ..., \min(C_L^i, C_a^i, C_b^i), ..., \min(C_L^k, C_a^k, C_b^k)) \quad (5)$$

where the expression $\min(C^i_L, C^i_a, C^i_b)$ represents the truth value of the pixel p for the color i. Then, we define on C_p a fuzzy set with a triangular membership function spanned over [0, 1]. Finally, we form the region of the object by applying an α-cut to all pixels into the search region.

2.2.2 Fuzzy Color Update

In real conditions the target changes its color components, mainly due to illumination variations. Some times it is not a crucial problem because the fuzzy representation of color absorbs them, for example in indoor environments. But some times there are big changes in color components what makes impossible to detect the target, specifically in outdoor environments. Generally, a big change does not occur instantaneously. So we can use these gradual changes to update the membership functions of the color components.

To update the membership functions we illustrate our procedure by using triangular ones as in Fig. 3. These functions are determined by three parameters p_0, p_1, and p_2. These parameters are known after target color modelling. Now we focus only on p_1, assuming that distances from p_1 to p_o and from p_1 to p_2 are constants. Let be R_α the set of pixels which are classified as the target, with $p_i \in R_\alpha$. We could compute the mean of the color components on this set, that is

$$\bar{I}_L = \frac{1}{N_{R_\alpha}} \sum_{p_i \in R_\alpha} p_i^L \tag{6}$$

$$\bar{I}_a = \frac{1}{N_{R_\alpha}} \sum_{p_i \in R_\alpha} p_i^a \tag{7}$$

$$\bar{I}_b = \frac{1}{N_{R_\alpha}} \sum_{p_i \in R_\alpha} p_i^b \tag{8}$$

where N_{R_α} is the cardinality of R_α. We change the centers of the memberships by adding

$$\Delta p_1^L = \gamma(p_1^L - \bar{I}_L) \tag{9}$$

$$\Delta p_1^a = \gamma(p_1^a - \bar{I}_a) \tag{10}$$

$$\Delta p_1^b = \gamma(p_1^b - \bar{I}_b) \tag{11}$$

with p_1^L, p_1^a and p_1^b being the membership centers for the L, a and b components, respectively and γ is a smoothing constant.

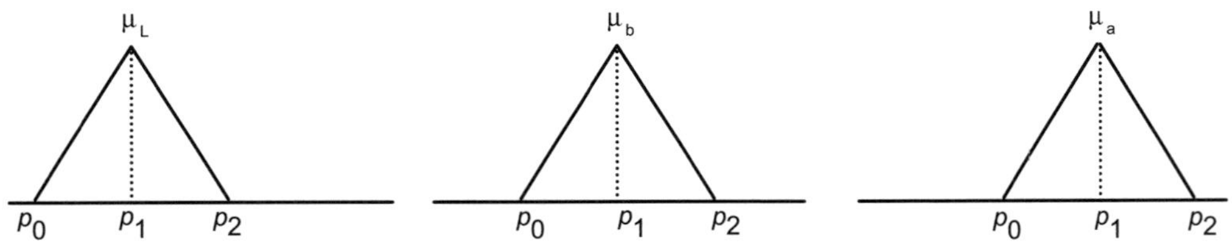

Fig. 3. Triangular membership functions.

2.3 Performance Evaluation

In order to evaluate the fuzzy representation we have performed the following test: In an OpenGL environment simulator, we have set a red ball with a varying light source, then we have moved the ball along a circular path and we have made controlled illumination changes in our environment. In this test we know the ground truth of the center position of the ball in each image. We save an image sequence and the ball position at each image of this sequence. If the error position in each image is small and the number of pixels composing the detected object is almost constant, we can say that our fuzzy color representation is good. In order to show that, we apply a fuzzy color tracking having the test image sequence described previously as input. In Fig. 4, we present an image and the corresponding detected color blob. In Fig. 5, some frames of the sequence are shown and also the detected blob that satisfies the fuzzy color model. In Fig. 6, we present the position error between the exact ball position in the test image and the position detected by our color tracking system. We observe that maximum error is between 4 pixels. We can consider this error as a low one, that is, our tracking method has a good accuracy.

Fig. 4. A pair of images showing the ball in the simulated environment and the region where the object is detected by our tracking system satisfying the fuzzy color constraints.

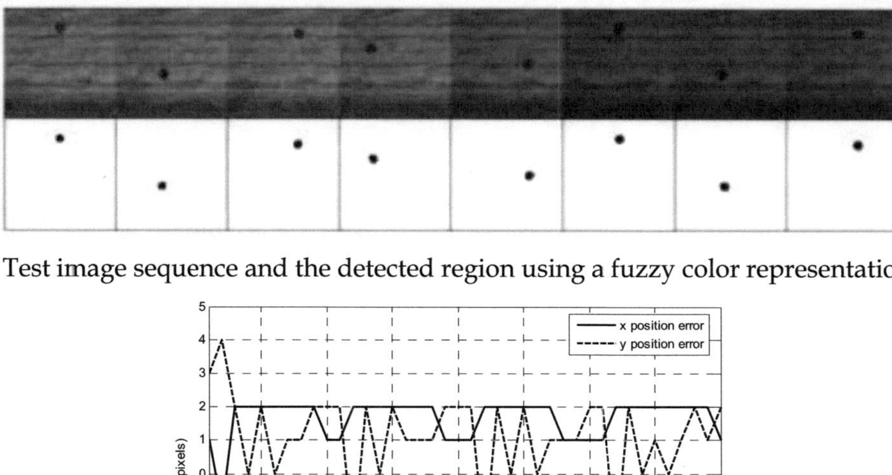

Fig. 5. Test image sequence and the detected region using a fuzzy color representation.

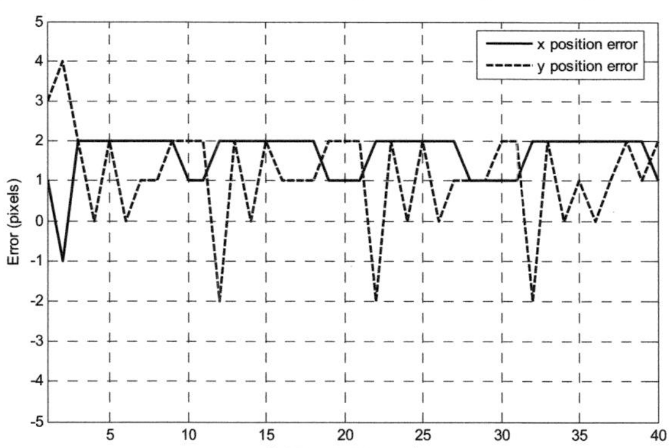

Fig. 6. Graph of the error position between the ground truth image position for the target and the detected position by the fuzzy color tracking system.

In Fig. 7, we show a graph of the number of pixels correctly detected along the frames of the sequence. We can observe that, between frames 30 and 40, there is a transient in the number of pixel detected as belonging to the object. That is caused by the fuzzy color adaptation. An explanation for this behavior is related to the edges of the ball. When the image is lighter, the ball has a good contrast against the background. In the other hand, when light turns dark that effect diminishes. An outdoor sequence taken from the described system implemented in XidooBot, our robotic platform is shown in Fig. 8. The computing time for a tracking cycle is 0.08 seg, that results in a 12.5 Hz frame rate.

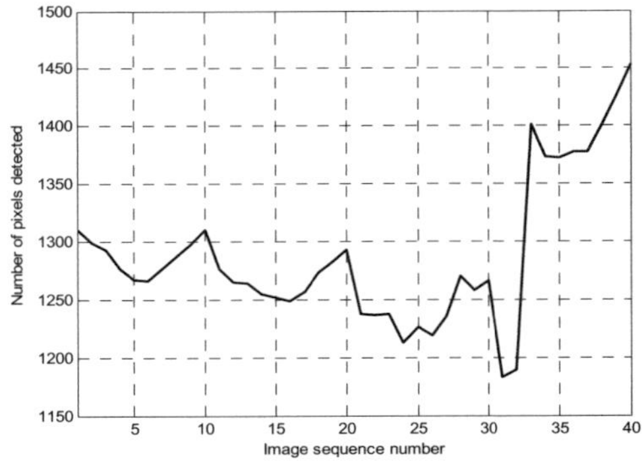

Fig. 7. Graph of number of pixels detected.

Fig. 8. Some frames of an outdoor image sequence where a girl is kicking a yellow soccer ball.

3. Object Recognition using Genetic Algorithms

Genetic algorithms (GA) are pseudo-random search techniques inspired from evolutionary processes. We start from an initial set of feasible solutions for a problem and by mimicking natural evolution, best solution individuals survive and they are the basis of new populations of solutions. This evolutionary cycle is repeated until a solution satisfying problem constraints emerge. GAs are optimization methods; they are useful when we need to search through a large number of feasible solutions. Solutions are evaluated to determine which ones are the best suited to the problem by using a fitness function that encodes the knowledge we have about the nature of the solution of our problem. In robotics, GA have found application in path planning problems for a robotic arm (Ahuactzin et al., 1993), path planning for mobile robots (Gerke, 1999) and for estimating the position of a mobile robots (Kang et al. 1995). Specifically, genetic algorithms are useful to find a good solution in large search spaces because they can avoid local minima by using genetic operators like mutation, that help the GA to probe in practically every region of the search space. Other GA-based applications in robotics are in visual landmark detection tasks (Hao and Yang, 2003, Mata et al., 2003).

In our work, we present a GA-based circle detector. Our system uses a three edge point circle representation that enables the system to reduce the search space by eliminating unfeasible circle locations in our image. This approach results in a sub-pixellic circle detector that can detect circles in real images even when the circular object has a significative occluded portion. For robotic applications, these circles could be issued from circular landmarks or even being a part of the landmark. After benchmarking our algorithm with synthetic images, we have tested our algorithm on real world images. We present the results of both cases. The latter implementation has been tested on a mobile robot platform XidooBot for circular landmarks detection on the robot environment.

3.1 Circle Detection using GAs

Shape detection is needed in robotic vision tasks like object tracking, visual servoing or landmark recognition. In addition to color and texture, shape is an important cue for modelling objects in scenes of the robot workspace. Object location techniques are solved using two types of methods: i) deterministic methods like Hough transform, e.g. (Yuen et al., 1990), geometric hashing and template or model matching, e.g. (Iivarinen et al., 1997; Jones et al., 1990) and ii) stochastic tecniques, including RANSAC (Fischer and Bolles, 1981), simulated annealing and genetic algorithms (Roth and Levine, 1994).

Using GAs to detect shapes in an image involves mainly the making of design choices for the solution elements in a genetic algorithms framework. We work on images containing one or several circles. The circles are searched through the edge image obtained from an image pre-processing step. A classical Sobel edge detector was used for this purpose. In the following paragraphs we show how to pose the circle detection problem in terms of a genetic algorithm approach.

3.1.1 Individual Representation

Each individual C uses three edge points as chromosomes. Edge points are represented by their relative index in a list V of all the edge points resulting from the edge extraction step. Each individual represents then a feasible circle where their (x_0, y_0, r) parameters are defined as follows:

$$(x - x_0)^2 + (y - y_0)^2 = r^2 \tag{12}$$

with:

$$x_0 = \frac{\begin{vmatrix} x_j^2 + y_j^2 - (x_i^2 + y_i^2) & 2(y_j - y_i) \\ x_k^2 + y_k^2 - (x_i^2 + y_i^2) & 2(y_k - y_i) \end{vmatrix}}{4((x_j - x_i)(y_k - y_i) - (x_k - x_i)(y_j - y_i))} \tag{13}$$

$$y_0 = \frac{\begin{vmatrix} 2(x_j - x_i) & x_j^2 + y_j^2 - (x_i^2 + y_i^2) \\ 2(x_k - x_i) & x_k^2 + y_k^2 - (x_i^2 + y_i^2) \end{vmatrix}}{4((x_j - x_i)(y_k - y_i) - (x_k - x_i)(y_j - y_i))} \tag{14}$$

and

$$r = \sqrt{(x - x_0) + (y - y_0)} \tag{15}$$

We can then represent the shape parameters (for the circle, $[x_0, y_0, r]$) as a transformation T of the edge vector indexes *i, j, k*.

$$[x_0, y_0, r] = T(i, j, k) \tag{16}$$

This approach enables us to sweep a continuous space for the shape parameters while keeping a binary string for the GA individual. We can then reduce the search space by eliminating unfeasible solutions.

3.1.2 Fitness Evaluation

Each individual has a fitness proportional to the number of actual edge points matching the locus generated by the parameters of the shape (x_0, y_0, r). In our practical implementation, we can not test for every point in the feasible circle so we perform a uniform sampling along the circumference. If we take N_s points, we construct an array of points $S_i = (x_i, y_i)$. Their coordinates are given by:

$$x_i = x_0 + r \cdot \cos \frac{2\pi\, i}{N_s} \tag{17}$$

$$y_i = y_0 + r \cdot \sin \frac{2\pi\, i}{N_s} \tag{18}$$

Fitness function *F(C)* accumulates the number of expected edge points (i.e. the points in the set S) that actually are present in the edge image. That is:

$$F(C) = \frac{\sum_{i=0}^{N_s - 1} E(x_i, y_i)}{N_s} \tag{19}$$

We use also some other factors to favor the context of specific applications for detection, including completeness of the circumference or a given size for the circles.

3.2 Performance Evaluation

We have carried up three tests to evaluate the performance of our approach to circle detection. Firstly, we have generated 10 synthetic grayscale images with only one circle in them and where the ground truth of the circle parameters was known *a priori*. Our method has been run 100 times on each image and the results were recorded in Table 1. We can see that our algorithm detects the circle parameters with sub-pixellic accuracy (lower than 0.194 pixels for the center coordinates and radius length). Our method is robust with respect to translation and scale. Average elapsed time to detect a circle in an image containing exactly one circle is 5 ms.

We have also studied the behavior of the elapsed time for detection of our algorithm with respect to the circle radius. As expected, time seems to grow at a quadratic rate with respect to the radius of the circle. That can be seen in Fig. 9.

Img.	Time	Position	$\overline{x}$	$\overline{y}$	$\overline{r}$	Error	$\lvert e_x \rvert$	$\lvert e_y \rvert$	$\lvert e_r \rvert$
1	0.003	Real	90.00	198.00	10.00	avg	0.046	0.023	0.023
		Detected	89.95	197.98	10.02	max	0.046	0.023	0.023
2	0.001	Real	35.00	28.00	17.00	avg	0.052	0.042	0.052
		Detected	34.95	27.96	17.05	max	0.056	0.056	0.056
3	0.000	Real	167.00	14.00	10.00	avg	0.069	0.023	0.069
		Detected	167.07	13.98	10.07	max	0.103	0.035	0.104
4	0.004	Real	38.00	221.00	28.00	avg	0.003	0.005	0.013
		Detected	38.00	220.99	28.01	max	0.005	0.009	0.018
5	0.025	Real	76.00	44.00	28.00	avg	0.001	0.005	0.013
		Detected	76.00	44.01	28.01	max	0.009	0.022	0.018
6	0.000	Real	184.00	82.00	24.00	avg	0.110	0.077	0.118
		Detected	184.11	81.92	23.88	max	0.144	0.126	0.126
7	0.001	Real	133.00	38.00	10.00	avg	0.014	0.018	0.035
		Detected	133.01	38.02	10.03	max	0.044	0.059	0.050
8	0.001	Real	233.00	108.00	11.00	avg	0.101	0.117	0.171
		Detected	233.10	107.88	11.17	max	0.194	0.160	0.194
9	0.484	Real	120.00	126.00	69.00	avg	0.001	0.001	0.009
		Detected	120.00	126.00	69.01	max	0.029	0.009	0.019
10	0.001	Real	217.00	82.00	20.00	avg	0.068	0.150	0.086
		Detected	216.93	81.85	20.09	Max	0.068	0.150	0.086

Table 1. Circle detection results on synthetic images containing a single circle.

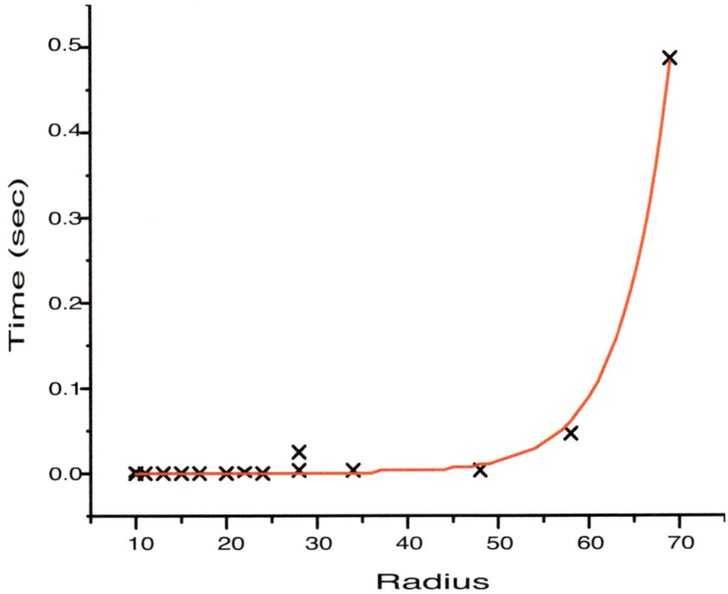

Fig. 9. Time needed to find a single circle in an image against its radius.

3.3 Application to Robotic Vision Tasks

We applied the circle detection method for a robotic task. We have used it for the detection of artificial landmarks containing circular forms. Our interest is to develop a system that uses elliptical shapes (now only covering circular shapes) for using them as landmarks in a topological navigation task. Such a system will be similar to other systems that use quadrangular planar landmarks (essentially posters) for the same task. We consider only quadrangular and circular shapes as structurally salient in a semi-estructured environment. The entire circular landmark recognition process uses two processing loops. The circle detection task achieves a processing rate of about 5 Hz and it interacts with the color tracking system already described that runs at about 13 Hz. The circle detection is launched at the beginning of the navigation task and then it is relaunched only when the robot fails to perceive the detected landmark. This situation arises when the robot is in transit from a topological place to another. Fig. 10 shows some typical images acquired by our mobile robot with circular landmarks on them. An example of an image with multiple circles and the results of the detection process are shown in Fig. 11.

(a) (b) (c) (d)

Fig. 10. Typical scenarios where circular landmarks are useful.

4. Geno-Fuzzy Visual Servoing

We present a genetic algorithm optimization approach for a visual servoing system using a fuzzy controller for an active camera. Visual task for the camera is to center an object with a known model in the field of view of the camera. Our system implements the two-dimensional controller by multiplexing a fuzzy controller for only one motion axis of the camera. We have simulated our system and obtained the controller response to different inputs. We have studied four cases for comparison purposes: a proportional controller, a trial and error tuned fuzzy controller, a fuzzy controller using a genetically-optimized rule base and another one with a database optimization using genetic algorithms.

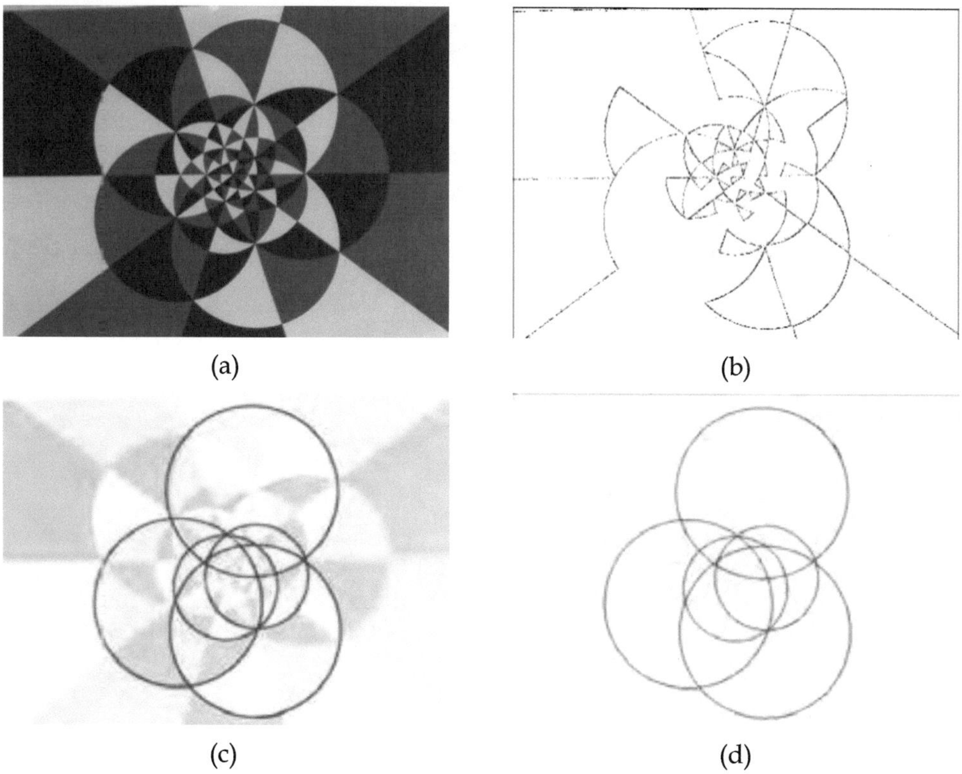

Fig. 11. Results of the circle detection process in a poster with several circles: (a) the original image, b) the edge image of (a), (c) the best 5 circles found by our algorithm overlaid on (a), and (d) the detection results overlaid on the edge image.

We take advantage of the collaborative approach of soft computing for problem solving by combining genetic algorithms and fuzzy logic in a visual servoing controller. In the following paragraphs, we will describe current approaches and applications for hybridization of fuzzy and genetic techniques (so named geno-fuzzy techniques) and some of their applications.

4.1 Visual Servoing

Visual servoing is a maturing approach for controlling robots. It uses a visual task specification instead of using a Cartesian coordinate system previously taught to the robot

(Corke and Hutchinson, 2000). Most robotic systems are instructed interactively to reach some important points for a particular task. Robot task consists in the optimization of the path for all the points not already taught. Using visual servoing, information acquired by the visual sensors of the robot is used to control robot motion in manipulators or mobile robots. Flexibility of robot use is increased in this way, in particular when the robot has to interact with some other objects in its workspace (parts to handle, obstacles to avoid, etc.) A visual servoing system includes techniques from computer vision, robotics and control, and could be considered as a fusion of these disciplines.
According to Corke and Hutchinson, visual servoing systems can be classified in two types: i) image-based visual servoing (IBVS), where error is measured directly on the image and mapped into actuator control signals, and ii) position-based visual servoing (PBVS), where vision techniques are used to reconstruct the 3D environment where the robot evolves and then an actuator control is computed from the error obtained from such an information.
For the PBVS systems, a calibration step needing vision techniques and geometric models is required. In IBVS systems, control computations involve computation of the system Jacobian matrix $\mathbf{J}_v$, a linear transformation that maps the end effector velocity $\dot{\mathbf{r}}$ into the motion of some image feature $\dot{\mathbf{f}}$:

$$\dot{\mathbf{f}} = \mathbf{J}_v(\mathbf{r})\dot{\mathbf{r}} \tag{20}$$

Simplest approach to visual servoing uses the control law that assumes a square and non-singular Jacobian matrix:

$$\mathbf{u} = \mathbf{J}_v^{-1}(\mathbf{r})\dot{\mathbf{f}} \tag{21}$$

A soft computing approach has been the use of fuzzy logic and neural networks to avoid the computation of the Jacobian matrix, as done in (Suh and Kim, 2000) (Stanley et al., 2001), where a fuzzy rule optimization is performed by training a neural network. In this work, we propose to use geno-fuzzy learning techniques to optimize an image-based fuzzy visual servocontroller.

4.2 Geno-Fuzzy Techniques

A highly useful soft computing technique for implementing controllers is fuzzy logic. As pointed out in (Klir and Yuan, 1995), fuzzy logic controllers have advantages over traditional controllers when i) the system to be controlled is complex, ii) the system has been traditionally controlled by human experts, or iii) when human input is needed in the controller model. A fuzzy controller is composed of several basic elements. The fuzzifier translates numerical input into fuzzy values for linguistic input variables. A fuzzy knowledge base is composed of two parts: i) a database, where information about fuzzy membership functions for the input and output linguistic variables used by the system are stored and, ii) a rule base, where rules that determine the controller behavior are stored. This knowledge is used by the fuzzy inference engine to compute a fuzzy output at each instant. Fuzzy output is converted into a numerical output value by means of a defuzziffier.
It is also known that the main drawback of fuzzy controllers is their need of a more complex tuning procedure than for conventional controllers. Building the knowledge base of a fuzzy

system can be done by four methods (McNeill and Thro, 1994; Cordón and Herrera, 1995): i) Synthesis of expert knowledge, ii) trial and error synthesis procedures, used in this work for obtaining an initial or primitive model, iii) synthesis from numerical evidence, and iv) use of machine learning techniques. In this work, a genetic algorithm-based approach is used for tuning the primitive model of the fuzzy visual servocontroller.

Genetic programming, particularly, genetic algorithms, are used to optimize a fitness function by mimicking natural evolution for organisms. Individuals for this evolution are computational representations of potential solutions for the problem to be solved. Each individual is represented as a binary string also known as a computational chromosome. The entire set of individuals examined at a time is called the population.

Geno-fuzzy systems, as is called the combination of genetic algorithms and fuzzy logic controllers, are feasible because in one hand, the behavior of a fuzzy controller is determined by a set of parameters included in the controller knowledge base. Optimal parameter search for the fuzzy controller defines a complex search space. In the other hand, this type of search spaces can be handled efficiently using genetic algorithms. Therefore, fuzzy logic and genetic algorithms could be used to design and optimize fuzzy controllers by formulating optimal parameter search as a genetic algorithm problem.

Pioneering work on geno-fuzzy systems has been done by Karr. He has been the first one to propose fuzzy set parameter tuning for a fuzzy controller (Karr, 1991). (Herrera and Cordón, 1997) have proposed another methodology for genetic algorithm based optimization of a fuzzy controller and its application to the inverted pendulum problem. In robotics, geno-fuzzy techniques have been applied for the control of manipulators as in the work of (Jin, 1998) and a hierarchical fuzzy controller for the navigation of an outdoor mobile robot proposed by (Hagras et al., 2001). Geno-fuzzy systems enable us to develop automatic design methods for fuzzy controllers. This procedure can be applied for automatic design or optimization methods.

4.3. Fuzzy Visual Servoing

We have implemented a visual servoing system using a fuzzy controller to map image features into camera control commands. In a first step, we have synthesized the controller by trial and error and we have compared its performance against a proportional controller for a target recentering task. In order to cope with complexity in the fuzzy controller rule set, we propose a multiplexed fuzzy controller. Secondly, we have optimized the fuzzy controller by using genetic algorithms. We have analyzed two cases: i) Adaptation of the fuzzy rule set, and ii) scaling of a constant gain in inputs and output of the fuzzy controller.

We consider a recentering task for an active camera to follow a given target with a known model moving on a vertical plane. Visual servoing is needed to perform this task. Fig. 12 depicts the implemented system.

In such an IBVS system, the position estimation is computed directly from the last image acquired by the robot. Position error is then computed from the comparison of the reference image I_r and the current image I_c. We also compute an estimate for target velocity. These variables are then fuzzified and input to a fuzzy controller. The controller computes actual commands to be sent to the camera in order to center the target in the camera image. Inputs to our fuzzy controller are positioning error $\mathbf{e}$ and current target velocity $\mathbf{v}$. Both variables are vector quantities with x and y components. Output variable for our controller is the velocity correction V_o. The components of this velocity vector are pan displacement velocity

V_{ox} and tilt velocity V_{oy} for the camera. The structure selected for our controller implementation was a multiplexed one. We have chosen to decouple the x-y controller into an x-controller and a y-controller. Each of them controls only one degree of freedom of the active camera. At each iteration of the control loop, we compute the x-controller output and then the y-controller output. By making this design choice, we have reduced complexity without sacrifying too much accuracy in the controller performance. Structure for our fuzzy controller is shown in Fig. 13.

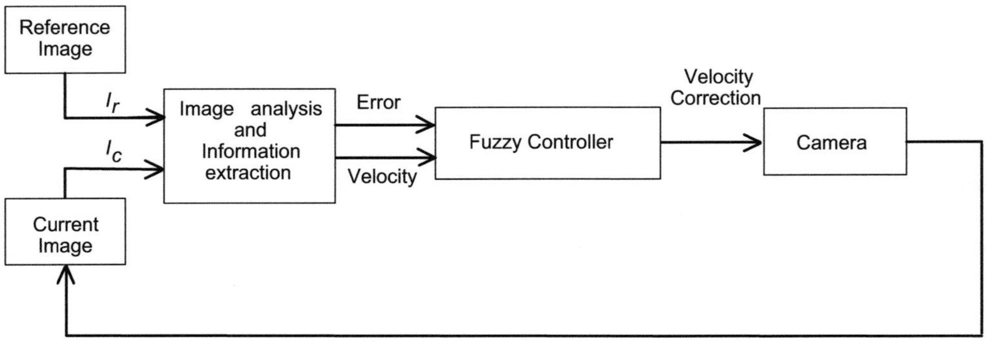

Fig. 12. Fuzzy visual servoing loop.

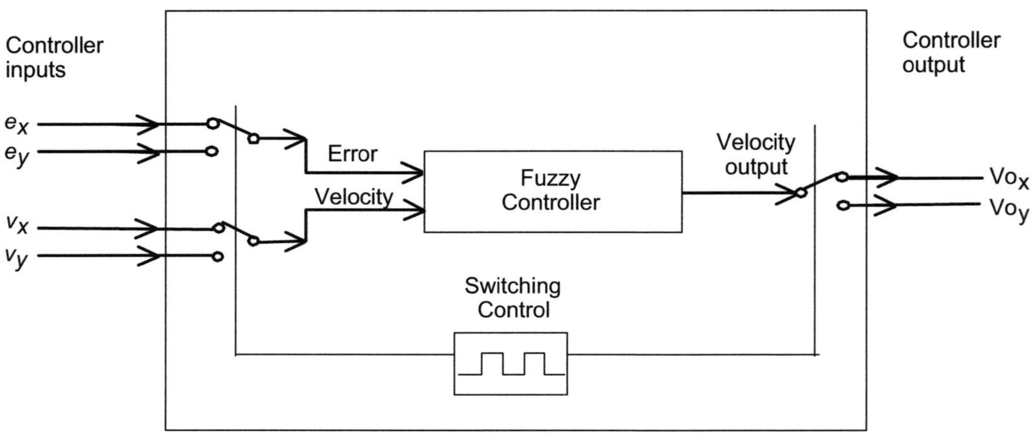

Fig. 13. Multiplexed fuzzy visual servocontroller.

Our system is modelled by a fuzzy logic controller with input universe U, output universe V, and a set of IF-THEN rules that determine a mapping $U \in R^n \to V \in R$. Every rule of this set has the form:

$$R_i :: \text{IF } (x_1 \text{ is } F_{1i}) \text{ and } (x_2 \text{ is } F_{2i}) \text{ THEN } (y \text{ is } G_i) \quad (22)$$

where F_{ji} and G_i are fuzzy sets of the input and output linguistic variables, respectively (Wang, 1994). We use the singleton fuzzifier and the COA (Center Of Average) method for the defuzzification step. We code the knowledge into a BIOFAM (Binary Input-Output Fuzzy Associative Memory) matrix where the inputs are the error between the center coordinate of the camera image and the position of the center of the object, and the velocity of the object being tracked for a given direction, and the output is the correction needed on the camera position.

4.4 Hybridization Approaches for Geno-Fuzzy Controllers

Learning strategies for fuzzy controllers by using genetic algorithms are classified using three main approaches (Cordón et al., 2001): i) Michigan approach, where optimization is carried on particular elements of the fuzzy controller specification, ii) Pittsburgh approach, when the system as a whole is optimized, and iii) Iterative Rule Learning (IRL) approach, where the system is synthesized by optimizing independent rules that combine fuzzy sets from a given rule repository, defined either explicitly or implicitly.

Michigan approach encodes each rule in a complete chromosome. Only best rules are kept at each iteration as elite members of the genetic algorithm population. As pointed out by (Ishibuchi et al., 20000), the optimization of the fuzzy rule-based system is indirectly performed by searching for good fuzzy rules. Fuzzy rules have generally a pre-defined structure and a pre-defined set of fuzzy concepts to be used in these rules.

Pittsburgh approach (Ishibuchi et al., 1999) involves encoding a complete or partial rule set into one computational individual. Optimization by using genetic algorithms is equivalent then to find fuzzy rule-based systems with high performance indexes.

In the IRL approach (Cordón et al., 2001), knowledge acquisition is done by acquiring concepts from a repository of fuzzy sets related with input and output linguistic variables. Structure is not pre-defined for these rules and even fuzzy sets associated with the linguistic labels can be chosen in a flexible way from a repository of known fuzzy sets.

A common strategy for all three approaches described above is to adapt the fuzzy controller database. In this technique, fuzzy membership functions (shape and parameters) are individually adapted. In this work, we have tested the database adaptation of a fuzzy controller and the Pittsburgh approach for learning a complete rule base as described below.

In order to optimize our controller, we need to define a fitness function. This fitness function usually consists in the evaluation of the controller performance for an interval of time. Fig. 14 shows a block diagram of the optimization procedure. In our implementation, the fitness function is a measure of the controller performance.

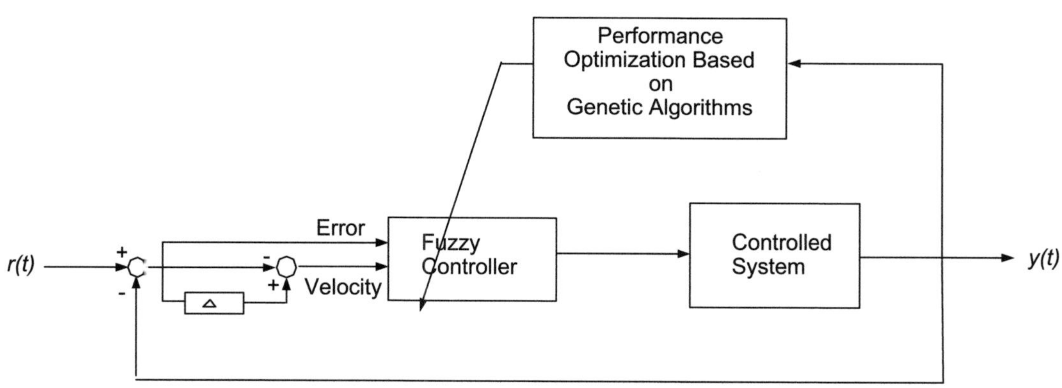

Fig. 14. Optimization of a fuzzy visual servocontroller by using genetic algorithms.

Several performance criteria can be applied in this context. A fitness function that takes into account several parameters at the same time according to the controller characteristics to be improved can be suggested. Some authors (Zhimin et al., 2000) have been concerned with proposing methods for tuning multiple characteristics of the controller. In conformity with the nature of our problem, our controller performance is measured using the difference between the position of the center of the object to be tracked and the center of the image frame, during an interval of time. In order to measure this performance, we use a least square method to compute a figure of merit q as follows:

$$q = \sqrt{\sum_{t=1}^{t_{\max}} \sum_{i=1}^{2} (X_i(t) - X_{d,i}(t))^2} \tag{23}$$

where $X_1(t)$ is the x coordinate of the camera at instant t, $X_2(t)$ is the y coordinate of the camera at same instant and $X_{d,i}(t)$ is the true target position for X_i at instant t.

Another issue to be considered is the length of the chromosome in use. For example, this length is critical for the execution time of the computer implementation for the mutation operation. In this work, we propose two optimization strategies using genetic algorithms: i) Genetic adaptation of the rule base, and ii) genetic adaptation of the database by means of the scaling functions.

Pittsburgh approach for complete rule base adaptation

We specify our fuzzy controller by using a decision table approach. This approach enables the entire rule base to be encoded in a single entity or chromosome. Coding takes place as follows. We start at the BIOFAM position (1, 1) and each row in the matrix is scanned from left to right. Then, the rows are linked together. In order to avoid the generation of a larger chromosome each rule is coded into a genetic alphabet using positive integer numbers in the [0, n-1] range, where n is the number of fuzzy sets of the output variable. The coding process is shown in Fig. 15.

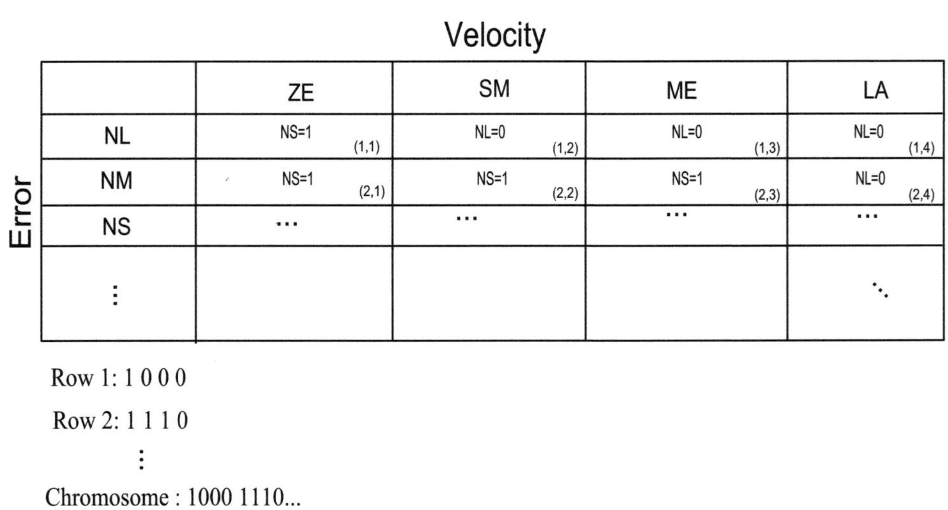

Fig. 15. Rule base encoding scheme.

Genetic database adaptation approach

The second optimization method proposed is the coding of the database using scaling functions. This method was chosen because the controller behavior can be completely modified with just three real numbers. These numbers are a scaling factor for the input variables or, from the control point of view, a gain. An integer representation for each data is used for coding these real numbers. Each number is mapped into an integer value range from -32768 to 32767. The gain range is [0, 2], therefore, the precision for mapping into an integer representation is 3.0517578×10^{-5}. In this form, each real number represents a specific gain for each section of the controller. Thus, each gain value is coded into an integer interval, coded in a binary form. Any real number is then represented by a binary string with 16 bits. There exist 6 possible gain constants to be modified in the controller. Choosing the values to be modified or grouped is an important decision to make. Working with the 6 gains will lead to a larger chromosome and as a consequence, to a more complex search space, and accordingly, the algorithm will take a longer time to find a good solution.

4.5 Tests and Results

We have developed a graphical simulation environment in C language. In this environment, we simulate the x-y plane where the target moves and the field of view of the camera. The visual task is to center an object in the field of view of the camera. In our work, this object is a ball of uniform intensity. We have already developed some libraries to manage fuzzy models. We use these libraries to implement the closed loop simulation of our controllers. The fuzzy visual servoing algorithm is executed for all the duration of the time interval to be simulated. Simulation will be stopped also if the tracked object goes beyond the limits of our world simulation.

We have studied four different controllers for the visual servoing task, namely:

Case I: A proportional controller, used only for comparison purposes, implemented as proposed by (Corke, 1996).

Case II: A fuzzy controller tuned by hand (Perez-Garcia et al., 2003) using a self-developed integrated development environment for fuzzy models.

Case III: A genetically-optimized fuzzy controller, using a controller rule base adaptation approach (Pittsburgh approach).

Case IV: A genetically-optimized fuzzy controller, using a controller database adaptation approach.

We simulated different motion patterns for the target on the simulation environment. For each controller, we have applied some motion patterns for the target to be recentered. Results for all different cases will be compared in order to evaluate the controller performance when different design strategies are used.

Case I: Proportional controller.

Some authors, like (Corke, 1996), have studied problems arising in visual servoing. He has pointed out that a proportional controller will exhibit poor performance when used for visual servoing tasks. Main problem is originated by the sampling frequency rate that is too low. For a real time system, target tracking frequency rates are between 2.5 and 12 Hz. When we use a personal computer, tracking execution loop runs at about 4.0 Hz. In order to make the simulation more realistic, we have modelled our camera plant as a first-order system including some time delay T and some inertia a. The camera model used is:

$$C(s) = \frac{1}{Ts + a} \tag{24}$$

According to control theory, K, the proportional gain has to be large enough to compensate system errors. In a servo-controller, there is a conflict because a large value for K can cause the target to get out of the camera view. When dealing with dynamic systems, Corke proposes to use small values for K in order to avoid system instabilities. We have computed the response for a proportional controller with K =0.15, a common value in visual servoing implementations.

Case II: Fuzzy controller tuned by trial and error.

In this section, we will present simulation results when a fuzzy controller is used for the visual servoing task. We have tuned the fuzzy visual servocontroller by a trial and error process. We tested different configuration parameters for all the components of our system and different motion laws for the target. We have reached a final configuration where position error of the target with respect to the center of the acquired image is minimized. Input and output ranges were chosen taking into account specification of a Sony EVI-D30 pan and tilt camera to make a realistic simulation.

We show the final configuration for input and output variables in Fig. 16. We can see that the input variable Error has seven linguistic variables. This fact enables us to achieve a better accuracy in the controller output without having a big number of rules in the BIOFAM for the controller shown in Table 2. Labels are as follows: NL= Negative Large, NM= Negative Medium, NS= Negative Small, ZE= Zero, PS= Positive Small, PM= Positive Medium, PL= Positive Large, SM= Small, ME= Medium and LA= Large.

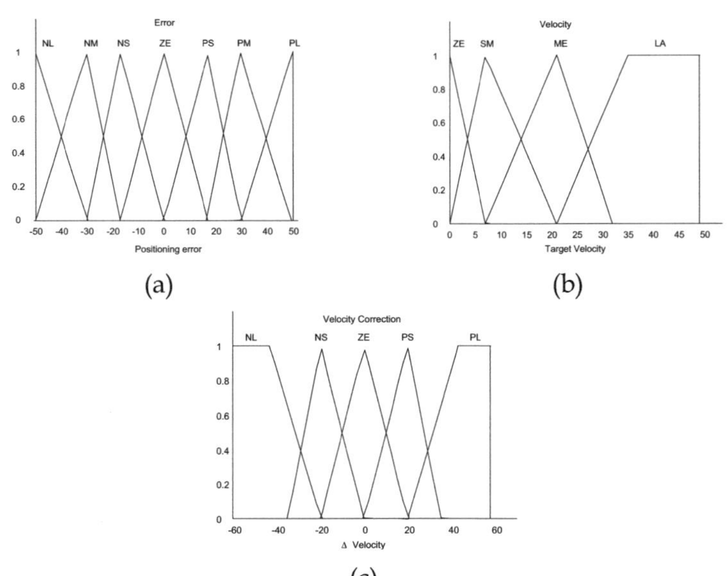

Fig. 16. Membership functions for input and output linguistic variables of the fuzzy controller tuned by trial and error.

Velocity Error	ZE	SM	ME	LA
NL	NS	NL	NL	NL
NM	NS	NS	NS	NL
NS	NS	NS	NL	NL
ZE	ZE	ZE	ZE	ZE
PS	PS	PS	PL	PL
PM	PS	PS	PS	PL
PL	PS	PL	PL	PL

Table 2. BICFAM matrix for the fuzzy controller. See text for labels meaning.

We have obtained the controller response to step and ramp inputs. These responses were computed when the controller was using the BIOFAM shown in Table 2 and the input and output variables defined as in Fig. 16. Results are shown in Table 3. We can see that the fuzzy controller outperforms the proportional controller for step input. The fuzzy servocontroller presents an underdamped response and a shorter transient time than the proportional controller. The former presents an overdamped response. When a ramp input signal is used, the proportional controller presents a classical delayed action of the input signal. Otherwise, the fuzzy controller shows an almost zero error. This behavior can be explained by the fact that we have some prediction step because object velocity is an input to the fuzzy controller. This fact enables us to estimate the new positions where the target features could appear.

Case III: Genetically optimized fuzzy controller using Pittsburgh approach

Here we present our results for a fuzzy visual servocontroller optimized by using the Pittsburgh approach over the complete rule set. Figs. 17 (a) and (c) show the error response to step and ramp inputs of the fuzzy visual servocontroller after the rule set had been optimized. Genetic optimization of the rule base slightly improves the response of the fuzzy visual servoing system originally tuned by trial and error. The optimized rule set has a better performance when a similar input to the learned one is fed to the controller but it degrades its performance when a different type of input signal is used.

Case IV: Database adaptation by using a linear scaling function

For this kind of optimization, we have used a gain constant for each input and another for the output of the fuzzy visual controller. As we have only one multiplexed controller for both x and y axes, we have decided to optimize in parallel the same controller. As for the others cases, the optimized servocontroller has been fed with step and ramp inputs. Error responses to these inputs are shown in Figs. 17 (b) and (d), respectively. As we can note there, there are significant improvements in the visual servocontroller response when compared with the other cases. Transient response to step inputs is shorter than for the other cases and the static error for ramp input vanishes, something very difficult to achieve using conventional techniques as pointed out by (Corke, 1996).

Performance evaluation comparison for visual servocontrollers

We have compared the four controllers and the results are summarized in Table 3. We have computed maximum error in pixels for step and ramp inputs. In the case of step input, we have also computed the settling time in seconds and for the ramp, we have computed the steady state static error. We can see that the non optimized fuzzy controller clearly outperforms the proportional controller when both standard inputs are applied. Comparing the fuzzy controller performance to the rule base-optimized one, we find that maximum error for the last decreases for step input. In the ramp input case, optimized controller maximum error increases slightly but steady state static error is negligible. The fuzzy visual servocontroller optimized by using data-base adaptation outperforms all other controllers in all cases except for the settling time when a step input is applied. In this case, the non-optimized fuzzy controller takes the same time to settle.

Functional performance evaluation on a robotic platform

We have tested our fuzzy visual servocontroller on a real time robotic platform. We aim to center an object in the image acquired by the vision system of a robot. The target was detected by using Hausdorff distance as the similarity metric on the edge image of a sequence. Our system process images up to a frame rate of about 10 frames/sec. Obviously, this rate depends largely on the complexity for the edge model of the target. We have optimized the frame rate for the visual servoing task by implementing a Monte Carlo version of the Hausdorff distance (Perez-Garcia et al., 2006).

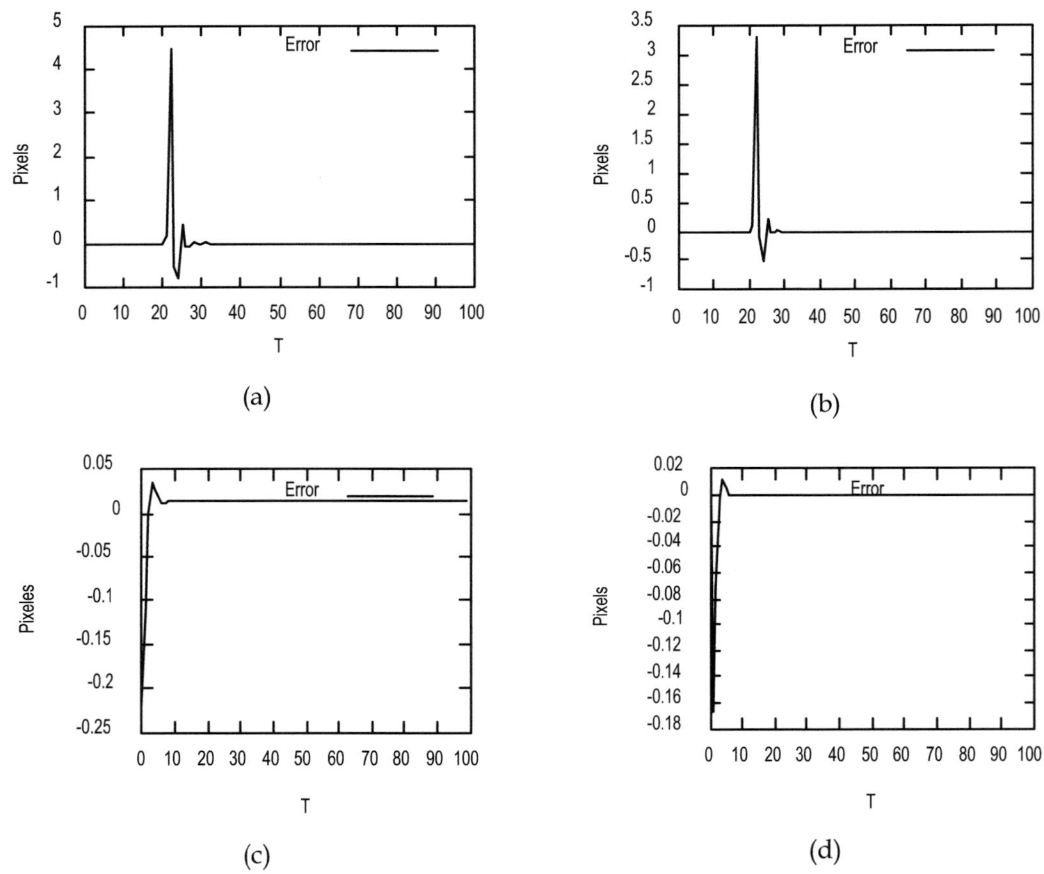

Fig. 17. (a),(b) Step error response for case III and case IV controllers respectively. (c),(d) Ramp error response for case III and case IV controllers respectively.

Controller type	Input Signal			
	Step input		Ramp input	
	Maximum Error (in pixels)	Settling time (in s)	Maximum Error (in pixels)	Steady state static error (in pixels)
Case I: Proportional	16.40	5.25	11.12	11.12
Case II: Fuzzy	12.00	1.50	0.18	0.17
Case III: Geno-fuzzy with rule base adaptation	4.48	2.00	0.22	0.01
Case IV: Geno-fuzzy with data base adaptation	3.31	1.50	0.16	0.00

Table 3. Controller performance comparison using different design methodologies for step and ramp inputs

5. Conclusion

Several conclusions arise from our experience applying soft computing (specifically fuzzy logic and genetic algorithms) to develop robotic vision applications. Fuzzy logic is well suited for problems where uncertainty representation is a critical issue. We already applied fuzzy logic to cope with illumination changes when tracking objects in a visual sequence. Another domain for application of fuzzy logic in robotic vision is to use it where only qualitative experience is available to perform a function. We have applied it on the implementation of a fuzzy visual servocontroller. Genetic algorithms are useful in optimization related tasks in robotic vision. For example, we have used this methodology to optimize the match between a parametric shape (a circle) and an observed set of edge points in an image. Another example of application was the tuning of the fuzzy servocontroller cited above by using a least squares criterion over a time frame.

From a systems perspective, we have used simulation as a tool to benchmark our algorithms before implementation on real platforms. We have also used composition of different modules to integrate more complex systems. This modular system approach has been essential to develop succesful real world applications.

Concerning our applications, we have proposed three methods to use soft computing technologies in robotic vision applications. We address a visual tracking system based on a fuzzy color description of the target, a parametric shape detection task using a genetic algorithm and a geno-fuzzy visual servoing task. The first two methods are developed using a single soft computing technique and the third one uses a hybrid approach by combining genetic algorithms and fuzzy logic as the basis of a robotic vision application. For these applications, we have developed the main aspects of the systems, their implementations and the tests we have carried out to evaluate their performance. Our systems are implemented on board of an experimetal robotics platform, namely a Pioneer P3AT robot. We show experimental results for all of them in real time applications.

Of course, soft computing applications on robotic vision tasks could include other approaches like artificial neural networks not included in the applications presented here. Such methods and a numer of hybrid techniques in soft computing must be taken into account before deciding a particular implementation.

6. Acknowledgements

This work has been partially supported by the CONCYTEG project "Herramientas Mecatrónicas para la Implementación de Entornos Virtuales" and by the UG project "Modelado difuso para la segmentación de imágenes y el reconocimiento de elementos de escenas naturales".

7. References

Abraham, A.; Ruiz-del-Solar; J. & Koppen, M. (Eds.)(2002). *Soft computing systems: Design, management and applications*, IOS Press, Amsterdam.

Ahuactzin, J.M.; Talbi, E.G.; Bessiere, P. & Mazer, E. (1993). Using genetic algorithms for robot motion planning, In: *Geometric Reasoning for Perception and Action*, Springer Verlag, Berlin.

Argyros, A. & Lourakis, M. (2004). Real time tracking of multiple skin-colored objects with a possibly moving camera, *Proc. of the European Conf. on Computer Vision (ECCV'2004)*, Vol. 3, pp. 368.

Barnes, N. & Liu, Z.Q. (2002). *Knowledge-based vision guided robots*, Physica-Verlag, New York.

Bloch, I & Saffioti, A. (2002). On the representation of fuzzy spatial relations in robot maps, *Proc. of the 9th Int. Conf. on Information Processing and the Management of Uncertainty (IPMU)*, pp. 1587-1594.

Braum, G.; Fairchild, M. & Ebner, F. (1998). Color gamut mapping in a Hue-linearized CIELAB color space, *Proc. of the 6th Color Imaging Conf.*, pp. 163-168.

Buckley, J.J. & Hayashi, Y. (1994). Fuzzy neural networks: A survey, *Fuzzy Sets Syst.*, Vol. 66, pp. 1-13, 1994.

Buschka, P.; Saffioti, A. & Wasik, Z. (2000). Fuzzy landmark-based localization for legged robots, *Proc. of the IEEE/RSJ Int. Conf. on Intelligent Robots and Systems (IROS'2000)*, pp. 1205-1210.

Chiang, C. K.; Chung, H. Y. & Lin, J. J. (1997). A self-learning fuzzy logic controller using genetic algorithms with reinforcements, *IEEE Trans. on Syst. Man Cybern.*, Vol. 5, No. 3, pp. 460-467.

Comaniciu, D.; Ramesh, V. & Meer P. (2000). Mean Shift: A robust approach toward feature space analysis, *IEEE Trans. on Pattern Anal. Mach. Intell.*, Vol. 24, No. 5, pp. 603-619.

Cordón, O. & Herrera, F. (1995). A general study in genetic fuzzy systems, In: *Genetic algorithms in engineering and computer science*, John Wiley & Sons, pp 33-57.

Cordón, O.; Herrera, F. Magdalena, L. & Hoffman, F. (2001). *Genetic Fuzzy Systems: evolutionary tuning and learning of fuzzy knowledge bases*, World Scientific, Singapore.

Corke, P. I. (1996). Dynamic Issues in Robot Visual-Servo Systems, In: *Robotics Research*, pp. 488-498.

Corke, P. & Hutchinson, S. (2000). Real time vision, tracking and control, *Proc. of the Int. Conf. Robot. Automat. (ICRA 2000)*, Vol. 1, pp. 622-629.

de Sousa, G. & Kak, A. (2002). Vision for mobile robot navigation: a survey, *IEEE Trans. Pattern Anal. Mach. Intell.*, Vol. 24, No. 2, pp. 237-267.

Dote, Y. & Ovaska, S. J. (2001). Industrial applications of soft computing: A review, *Proc. IEEE*, Vol. 89, pp. 1243-1265.

Fischer, M., Bolles, R., 1981. Random sample consensus: A paradigm to model fitting with applications to image analysis and automated cartography, *Comm. ACM*, Vol. 24, No. 6, pp. 381–395.

Gasós, J. & Saffioti, A. (1999). Integrating fuzzy geometric maps and topological maps for robot navigation, *Proc. of the 3rd Int. Symposium on Soft Computing (SOCO)*, pp. 754-760.

Gerke, M. (1999). Genetic path planning for mobile robots. *Proc. of the 1999 American Control Conf.*, Vol. 4, pp. 2424-2429.

Hao, L. & Yang, S.X. (2003). A behavior-based mobile robot with a visual landmark-recognition system, *IEEE/ASME Trans. On Mechatronics*, Vol. 8, No. 3, pp. 390-400.

Hagras, H.; Callaghan, V. & Colley, M. (2001). Outdoor mobile robot learning and adaptation, *IEEE Robot. Automat. Mag.*, Vol. 8, No. 3, pp. 53-69.

Herrera, F. & Verdegay, J.L. (Eds.) (1996). *Genetic algorithms and soft computing*, Physica-Verlag, New York.

Herrera, F. & Cordón, O. (1997). A three-stage evolutionary process for learning descriptive and approximative fuzzy logic controller knowledge bases from examples, *Int. J. Approximate Reasoning*, Vol. 17, No. 4, pp. 369-407.

Iivarinen, J.; Peura, M.; Sarela,J. & Visa, A. (1997). Comparison of combined shape descriptors for irregular objects, *Proc. 8th British Machine Vision Conf.*, pp. 430–439.

Ishibuchi, H.; Nakashima, T. & Kuroda, T. (1999). A hybrid fuzzy-genetics based machine learning algorithm: Hybridization of Michigan approach and Pittsburg approach, *Proc. of IEEE Int. Conf. on Systems, Man and Cybernetics (SMC)*, Vol. 1, pp. 296-301.

Ishibuchi, H.; Nakashima, T. & Kuroda, T. (2000). A hybrid fuzzy GBML algorithm for designing compact rule-based classification systems, *Proc. of the 9th Int. Conf. Fuzzy Syst. (FUZZ-IEEE 2000)*, Vol. 2, pp. 706-711.

Jin, Y. (1998). Decentralized adaptive fuzzy control of robot manipulators, *IEEE Trans. Syst. Man Cybern. B*, Vol. 28, No. 1, pp. 47-57.

Jones, G.; Princen, J.; Illingworth, J. & Kittler, J. (1990). Robust estimation of shape parameters. *Proc. British Machine Vision Conf.*, pp. 43–48.

Kang, D. ; Hashimoto, H. & Harshima, F. (1995). Position estimation for mobile robot using sensor fusion. *Proc. of IEEE/RSJ Int. Conf. on Intelligent Robots and Systems (IROS'95)*, Vol. 1, pp. 271-276.

Karr, C. L. (1991). Genetic algorithms for fuzzy controllers, *AI Expert*, Vol. 6, No. 2. pp. 26-33.

Keller, M. & Matsakis, P. (1999). Aspects of high level computer vision using fuzzy sets, *Proc. of IEEE Int. Conf. on Fuzzy Systems*, pp. 847-852.

Klir, G. J. & Yuan B. (1995). *Fuzzy sets and fuzzy logic: theory and applications*, Prentice Hall PTR, New Jersey.

Mata, M; Armingol, J.M.; de la Escalera, A. & Salichs, M.A. (2003). Using learned visual landmarks for intelligent topological navigation of mobile robots, *Proc. IEEE Int. Conf. on Robotics and Automation (ICRA'03)*, Vol. 1, pp. 1324-1329.

McNeill, F. M. & Thro, E. (1994). *Fuzzy logic: a practical approach*, Academic Press, New Jersey.

Mitra, S. & Hayashi, Y. (2000), Neuro-fuzzy rule generation: survey in soft computing framework, *IEEE Trans. Neural Networks*, Vol. 11, No. 3, pp. 748-768.

Montecillo-Puente, F.; Ayala-Ramirez, V.; Perez-Garcia, A. & Sanchez-Yanez R. E. (2003). Fuzzy color tracking for robotic tasks, *Proc. IEEE Int. Conf. on Systems, Man Cybernetics*, Vol. 3, pp. 2769-2773.

Nummiaro, K.; Koller-Meier, E. & Gool, L. V. (2003). Color features for tracking non-rigid objects, *Chinese Journal on Automation*, Vol. 29, No. 3, pp. 345-355.

Ovaska, S.J. (Ed.)(2004). *Computationally intelligent hybrid systems*, Wiley-IEEE Press.

Pal, S.K. & Mitra, S. (1999) *Neuro-fuzzy pattern recognition: Methods in soft computing*, Wiley, New York.

Pan, J.; Pack, D.J.; Kosaka, A. & Kak, A.C. (1995). FUZZY-NAV: A vision-based robot navigation architecture ussing fuzzy inference for uncertainty reasoning, *Proc. IEEE World Congress Neural Networks*, Vol. 2, pp. 602-607.

Pérez-García, A; Ayala-Ramírez, V. & Jaime-Rivas, J. (2003). Fuzzy visual servoing for an active camera, *Proc. 21st Int. Conf. Applied Informatics (AI'2003)*, pp. 292-296.

Pérez-García, A; Ayala-Ramírez, V.; Sanchez-Yanez, R.E. & Avina-Cervantes, J.G., Monte Carlo evaluation of the Hausdorff distance for shape matching, *Lecture Notes in Computer Science*, Vol. 4225, pp. 686-695.

Pomerleau, D.A. (1994). Reliability estimation for neural network based autonomous driving, *Robotics and Autonomous Systems*, Vol. 12, pp. 113-119.

Roth, G. & Levine, M.D. (1994). Geometric primitive extraction using a genetic algorithm., *IEEE Trans. Pattern Anal. Mach. Intell.*, Vol. 16, No. 9, pp. 901–905.

Saffioti, A. (1997). The uses of fuzzy logic in autonomous robot navigation, *Soft Computing*, Vol. 1, No. 4, pp. 180-197.

Stanley, K.; Wu, J. & Gruver, G. (2001). A hybrid neural network based visual servoing robotic system, *Proc. Int. Conf. IFSA-NAFIPS*.

Suh, I. & Kim, T. (2000). A visual servoing algorithm using fuzzy logic and fuzzy neural networks, *Mechatronics Journal*, Vol. 10, pp. 1-18.

Tan, K. C.; Lee, T. H. & Khor, E. F. (2002). Evolutionary algorithms for multi-objective optimization: Performance assessments and comparisons, *Artif. Intell. Rev.*, Vol. 17, No. 4, pp. 251-290.

Vertan, C.; Boujemma, N. & Buzuloiu, V. (2000). A fuzzy color credibility approach to color image filtering, *Proc. IEEE Int. Conf. on Image Processing*, Vol. 2, pp. 808-811.

Yuen, H.; Princen, J.; Illingworth, J. & Kittler, J. (1990). Comparative study of Hough transform methods for circle finding, *Image Vision Comput.*, Vol. 8, No. 1, pp. 71–77.

Wang, L. X. (1994). *Adaptive fuzzy systems and control: design and stability analysis*, Prentice Hall, Eglewoog Cliffs, NJ.

Wang, P.H. & Tan, S. (1997). Soft computing and fuzzy logic, *Soft Computing*, Vol. 1, No. 1, pp. 35-41.

Zhimin, Y.; WangXu & Xianyi, Z. (2000). Multi-criteria Control Systems Parameters Optimization Based on Genetic Algorithm, *Proc. 3rd World Congress on Intelligent Control and Automation*, pp. 651-655.

6

Analysis of Video-Based 3D Tracking Accuracy by Using Electromagnetic Tracker as a Reference

Matjaž Divjak, Damjan Zazula
University of Maribor
Slovenia

1. Introduction

In recent years video-based tracking systems have been gaining widespread attention in several application fields. They are often used in military or surveillance applications (Ellis & Black, 2003; Collins et al, 2000; Cupillard et al., 2003; Fischer et al.,2004; Safeguards, 2007), in medicine (Grimson et al., 1998; Bornik et al, 2003; Pandya & Siadat, 2001; Tang et al., 1998; Bernd & Seibert, 2004), entertainment industry (Stapleton et al., 2002; Wren et al., 1997; Huang & Yan, 2002; Collomosse et al., 2003; Fua & Plankers, 2003) or sport (Qiu et al., 2004; Gueziec, 2002; Kristan et al., 2006), for research on human-computer interaction (Sato et al., 2004; Bradley & Roth, 2005; Polat et al., 2003), intelligent environments (Krumm et al., 2000) and similar. Continuous technological development and increasing competition among vendors have led to a great selection of tracking systems that are available on the market today with a variety of capabilities.

To compare them, several factors have to be considered. While price, speed or technical limitations may be very important for initial selection, the tracking accuracy is usually the most important property. To assess a tracking system and its precision, we need a reliable measure which allows for comparison of tracking system performance, provides estimates of tracking errors and indicates how to optimize the tracking system parameters.

The natural way to analyze the accuracy of any tracking system is to compare it to some reliable reference data. While a selection of comparison methods is readily available to the research community (Needham & Boyle, 2003), a reliable reference data (ground truth) can be hard to obtain, especially if greater accuracy is desired. Publicly available collections of video recordings with registered 3D ground truth information can be helpful, but are very scarce and with limited selection (Scharstein & Szeliski, 2003; CVTI, 2007). Such collections can be very useful in the development and testing of tracking algorithms, but are not enough for evaluation of a complex video tracking system in its actual operating environment.

Instead, one of the most popular approaches to obtain the reference data is to resort to an electromagnetic tracking device. These devices offer fast and accurate measurements and are insensitive to the line-of-sight requirements of optical motion trackers, which makes them ideally suited for tracking free-moving objects.

In this chapter we describe a general framework for assessing the 3D accuracy of video-based tracker by comparing it to an electromagnetic tracking device. Since both devices record data within their local coordinate systems, the data needs to be aligned accordingly before any comparison. This transformation between the coordinate systems of a video camera and the reference tracker is crucial for reliable and unbiased analysis of the optical tracking algorithm performance.

We analyze three possible models for the coordinate system alignment, based on measuring the position and orientation of video camera inside the reference coordinate frame. We also derive methods and metrics for comparing the models and their sensitivity. The transformation error is analytically and statistically separated from the tracking error of the algorithm, making it possible to compare 3D tracking accuracy of different algorithms in the same experimental setting.

The last part of the chapter demonstrates the applied value of the introduced models by a real-world experiment. The accuracy of a stereo camera-based face and hand tracker is analyzed by comparing the simultaneous measurements from the Polhemus 3Space Fastrak electromagnetic tracker (Polhemus, 1998). Three various transformation models are tested and compared using the derived metrics. Finally, the algorithm's tracking error is estimated by statistically separating it from the transformation-induced error.

2. Survey of the performance characterization of optical 3D tracking systems

Performance characterization of 2D tracking systems is a well developed field. Its maturity is confirmed by the growing success of conferences such as IEEE *Performance Evaluation of Tracking and Surveillance – PETS* (PETS, 2005), along with other workshops and specialised conference sections. The European project *Performance Characterization in Computer Vision – PCCV* (PCCV, 2007) also boosted the growing awareness and interest in the scientific community. A comprehensive review of the field can be found in (Christensen & Förstner, 1997; Gavrila, 1999; Black et al., 2003; Bashir & Porikli, 2006; Georis et al., 2003). In (Needham & Boyle, 2003), several metrics are presented for comparing the tracked trajectories, but they are still limited to 2D. The paper also describes an example of how to generate ground truth data by manually marking the video sequence. This approach is often used, despite the fact that it is very labour intensive, time demanding and unreliable. To make the process easier, several authors developed semi-automatic procedures that use existing collections of ground truth data to generate new reference data (Jaynes et al., 2002; Doermann & Mihalcik, 2000; Black et al., 2003; Georis et al., 2004).

Performance characterization of 3D optical trackers is faced with a serious obstacle, since reliable ground truth data is much harder to obtain than for 2D trackers. Manual and semi-automatic annotation of video streams with 3D reference information still have all the drawbacks of 2D approaches, and are even less precise due to difficulties in estimating the depth, which makes it generally unsuitable for such tasks. The best approach is to measure ground truth using a second 3D tracking or measuring device with significantly better accuracy than the tested device. Electromagnetic tracking devices, marker-based optical systems and laser scanners are all frequently used for this purpose.

Electromagnetic trackers such as (Polhemus, 1998) and (Ascension, 2007) are examples of the most popular solutions, and have been in use for more than 30 years. The latest models can produce measurements of a sensor's position and orientation (6 DOF) with sample rates up to 240 Hz and static accuracy of 0.8 mm RMS for position and 0.15° RMS for orientation.

They are insensitive to occlusions, which makes them very suitable for tracking free-moving targets, such as humans and their body parts in movement. The majority of products use wired sensors which can be cumbersome to wear and may interfere with the free movement of the object. However, newer devices solve this problem by using wireless, battery-powered sensors. A bigger concern is electromagnetic interference which greatly affects the actual device's precision and is very hard to avoid in any urban environment. Precision also decreases rapidly once the distance from the transmitter crosses a certain limit. Therefore, appropriate means should be taken to reduce the effect of environment prior to performing any experiments (Kindarenko, 2000; La Cascia et al., 2000). Recent reports on the usage of a magnetic tracker for tracking the position of head movements were published in (Xiao et al., 2003; La Cascia & Sclaroff, 1999), while (Rehg & Kanade, 1994) reports using it for tracking the hand movements. In (Bernd & Seibert, 2004) a specially designed magnetic sensor was implemented to guide an augmented reality system during minimally invasive surgery.

Marker-based optical systems mean another attractive solution. To ensure the accuracy which is required for a reliable ground truth, the reference optical trackers usually depend on active or passive markers that are attached to the target. The NDI Optotrak Certus system (NDI, 2007) uses up to 512 markers at distances up to 2.25 m. Markers are scanned at 1500 Hz with accuracy of 0.15 mm RMS. NaturalPoint (NP, 2007) and ARTracking (ART, 2007) also supply various marker-based trackers. Besides their speed and reasonably good accuracy, optical trackers have another advantage. To calibrate them, a specially designed target is usually shown to the camera (Bornik et al, 2003). This same target can also be used to calibrate the optical tracker whose accuracy is being measured, so the same coordinate system is used, which greatly simplifies the data comparison. However, the main obstacle remains their sensitivity to occlusions, which is undesired when tracking the complex movements. It also hinders a reliable performance evaluation of the video-based tracker. Recent examples of application include tracking the position of the head (Vogt et al., 2006), the body (Herda et al., 2001), person tracking (Balan et al., 2005), in medicine (Keemink et al., 1991; Bornik et al, 2003), etc.

While the electromagnetic devices and marker-based optical trackers can only provide measurements for a limited number of 3D points, laser scanners can scan the whole scene and obtain dense range measurements with great accuracy. For example, the systems (Optix, 2007) and (VIVID, 2007) achieve the resolution of 0.05 mm at 100 mm distance and 0.5 mm at 900 mm distance. Dense range information is very useful for a number of applications, but comes at a price: the scene is usually scanned through a lens by a single laser and this operation typically takes a couple of seconds on modern devices. This currently makes laser trackers inappropriate for tracking any reasonably fast movement, but they can provide an excellent reference for static scenes. A combination of laser and optical tracking system for neuro-surgery application is described in (Grimson et al., 1998).

Unfortunately, a surprisingly low number of papers can be found on general evaluation of 3D tracking accuracy. Some authors (Yao & Li, 2004; La Cascia et al., 2000; Kindarenko, 2000) inspect this issue in more detail, but they ignore the relationship between the two coordinate systems, i.e. of the verified system and of the reference, and usually align the two sets of measurements by only looking for an optimal fit (Needham & Boyle, 2003). Such performance analysis is insufficient, as it masks possible tracker alignment errors and doesn't give real accuracy information. To clarify this issue the next chapter focuses on electromagnetic tracking device as an example of a ground truth for video-based tracking evaluation. We also explain the necessary coordinate system transformation and evaluate the factors involved in it.

3. Electromagnetic tracker as a reference for video-based tracking

In this section we describe the general framework for assessing the 3D accuracy of video-based tracker by comparing it to an electromagnetic tracking device. Fig. 1 depicts the usual approach. In order to compare the tracking performance, the target's position must be measured by both systems simultaneously. The magnetic sensor is firmly attached to the target object. Each time a frame of the scene is captured by the camera, the sensor's position is read and stored into a file, thus forming a motion trajectory of the target as detected by the magnetic tracker (a reference trajectory). Afterwards, the video is processed by a tracking algorithm to reconstruct the vision-based trajectory. Each trajectory is expressed in its own coordinate system (CS). In order to compare them, they need to be transformed into a common CS. Without loss of generality we select the coordinate system of magnetic tracker as the common CS in this discussion.

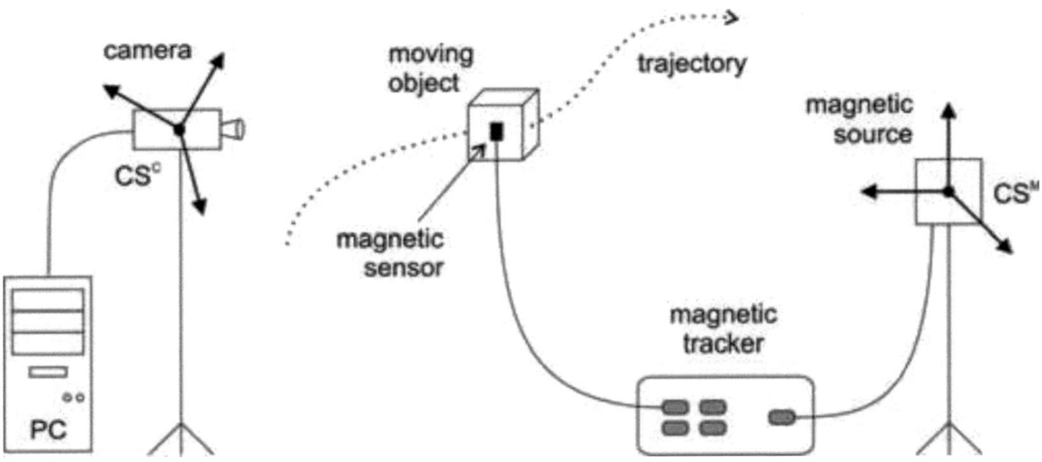

Figure 1. A general approach to analyzing the accuracy of video-based tracking with an electromagnetic tracking device. Suitable alignment of coordinate systems is necessary for comparison of detected motion trajectories

This transformation between the coordinate systems is crucial for a reliable and unbiased analysis of the optical tracking algorithm performance. Once the tracking data is properly aligned, it can be compared using any standard metrics, such as Root Mean Square (RMS) for example. The most frequently used method for aligning two trajectories uses optimization that minimizes the distances between them. Such a solution completely ignores possible bias errors and gives little information on how well the tracking algorithm follows the actual movement of the object. For example, if an algorithm consistently provides overestimated depths, the aligned trajectories can still show a close match. Another solution to this problem is aligning of the two coordinate systems physically by carefully positioning the camera and the magnetic tracker. Although this might seem a fast and simple procedure, such alignment is never perfect and results in considerable transformation errors. A quick calculation shows that an orientation error of 1° results in the position error of 3.5 cm at a distance of 2 meters from the camera.

A better approach to align the coordinate systems is by measuring the position and orientation of video camera using the magnetic tracker's sensors. This gives us enough information to derive a mathematical transformation between the CS of video camera (CS^C) and magnetic tracker (CS^M). Such alignment enables more thorough study of the transformation and its parameters, as well as comparison between the errors caused by the transformation and by the tested tracking algorithm. Although the idea seems straightforward, its implementation must be carefully considered, as will be explained in the next subsections.

3.1 Transformation models for coordinate systems

Assume we have a point in 3D space that needs to be expressed in two coordinate systems simultaneously. In CS^C we denote it by $\mathbf{p}^C = (p_1^C, p_2^C, p_3^C, 1)^T$ and in CS^M by $\mathbf{p}^M = (p_1^M, p_2^M, p_3^M, 1)^T$, respectively (using homogenous coordinates and denoting the transposition of vectors by ^{T}). Since both vectors $\mathbf{p}^M$ and $\mathbf{p}^C$ represent the same point in space, the following equation holds:

$$\mathbf{p}^M = \mathbf{A}\mathbf{p}^C . \tag{1}$$

Transformation matrix **A** contains the information about translation and rotation of CS^C with regards to CS^M. The position of camera's origin can be described by point $\mathbf{o}^C = (o_1, o_2, o_3)^T$, while base vectors $\mathbf{i}^C = (i_1, i_2, i_3)^T$, $\mathbf{j}^C = (j_1, j_2, j_3)^T$ and $\mathbf{k}^C = (k_1, k_2, k_3)^T$ describe its orientation. If homogenous coordinates are used, matrix **A** has the following structure:

$$\mathbf{A} = \begin{bmatrix} i_1 & j_1 & k_1 & o_1 \\ i_2 & j_2 & k_2 & o_2 \\ i_3 & j_3 & k_3 & o_3 \\ 0 & 0 & 0 & 1 \end{bmatrix} . \tag{2}$$

Vectors $\mathbf{i}^C$, $\mathbf{j}^C$, $\mathbf{k}^C$ and $\mathbf{o}^C$ that define **A** depend on a set of parameters $\mathbf{\Theta}$, $\mathbf{\Theta} = \{\Theta_l\}$, $l = 1, \ldots, N$. The exact number of parameters, N, depends on the procedure selected for building the transformation model. One of the most important parameters is the exact camera position. Of course, this information is usually not readily available, but it can be measured by placing one of the magnetic sensors on the camera and reading its position and orientation data. This simple approach has several shortcomings:

- The origin of CS^C is usually located inside the camera body and is impossible to be measured directly.
- The camera housing is usually metallic and therefore distorts the sensor's electromagnetic field.
- While inaccurate measurements of camera position have a relatively small effect on the overall accuracy, the erroneous camera orientation can cause significant deviations in results.

To address the abovementioned problems we present three different models for transformation of CS^C into CS^M. In all three models, the magnetic tracker is used to measure only the position of a number of control points around the camera that are used to calculate its position and orientation. Positional information shows significantly lower level of signal distortion than the information about orientation, as we have indicated. For a unique solution at least three control points in space are needed. They can be selected in a number of ways, but due to physical limitations of the used equipment (presence of ferromagnetic materials, camera range) this selection can affect the quality of transformation. The following options will be examined:

- All three control points are measured away from the camera (model A).
- Two points are measured on the camera and one away from it (model B).
- One point is measured on the camera and the other two away from it (model C).

Model A

To ensure that the camera body does not interfere with measuring magnetic sensor, all three control points are measured at a certain distance from it. The camera housing is fixed to a flat wooden board and accurately aligned with the board's sides (Fig. 2). Three corners of the board are selected and their coordinates are measured by magnetic sensor to obtain three control points $\mathbf{T}_1$, $\mathbf{T}_2$ and $\mathbf{T}_3$. Since it is assumed that camera's coordinate axes are completely aligned with the board, the base vector $\mathbf{i}^C$ can be expressed by $\overline{\mathbf{T}_3\mathbf{T}_1}$, the base vector $\mathbf{k}^C$ by $\overline{\mathbf{T}_2\mathbf{T}_1}$ and the base vector $\mathbf{j}^C$ is determined by the cross product (Fig. 2):

$$\mathbf{i}^C = \frac{\overline{\mathbf{T}_3\mathbf{T}_1}}{\left\|\overline{\mathbf{T}_3\mathbf{T}_1}\right\|},\ \mathbf{k}^C = \frac{\overline{\mathbf{T}_2\mathbf{T}_1}}{\left\|\overline{\mathbf{T}_2\mathbf{T}_1}\right\|},\ \mathbf{j}^C = \mathbf{k}^C \times \mathbf{i}^C\ . \tag{3}$$

The position of the camera's CS origin, $\mathbf{o}^C$, is expressed in CS^M by manually measuring the relative distances d_1 and d_2 between control point $\mathbf{T}_1$ and $\mathbf{o}^C$ (Fig. 2):

$$\mathbf{o}^C = \mathbf{T}_1 - d_1\mathbf{i}^C - d_2\mathbf{j}^C\ . \tag{4}$$

This way the transformation model A can be completely described by 11 parameters $\mathbf{\Theta}_A = \{x_1, y_1, z_1, x_2, y_2, z_2, x_3, y_3, z_3, d_1, d_2\}$, where $\mathbf{T}_1 = (x_1, y_1, z_1)$, $\mathbf{T}_2 = (x_2, y_2, z_2)$ and $\mathbf{T}_3 = (x_3, y_3, z_3)$.

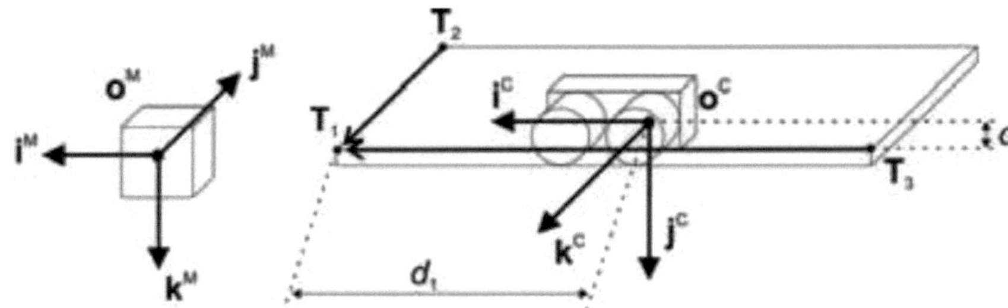

Figure 2. The setup of the magnetic tracker (left) and the camera (right) for model A. Vectors $\mathbf{i}^M$, $\mathbf{j}^M$, $\mathbf{k}^M$ denote base vectors of CS^M, while $\mathbf{i}^C$, $\mathbf{j}^C$, $\mathbf{k}^C$ denote base vectors of CS^C. $\mathbf{T}_1$, $\mathbf{T}_2$ and $\mathbf{T}_3$ mark the control point positions, while d_1 and d_2 mark manual measurements

Model B

The second transformation model neglects the fact that the camera housing disturbs the measurements, but it can be implemented only if those disturbances are proven very small compared to the errors caused by false orientation data. If the magnetic sensor is placed on the camera lens' face (Fig. 3), the disturbances caused by the camera housing are reduced to a minimum. This model also considers a stereoscopic (Jain et al., 1995) camera setup with two lenses that are used as two acceptable position measuring spots. The proposed model could be extended to a single camera, but the second measured point on the camera, $\mathbf{T}_3$, would be more problematic. This is why we are developing only the stereoscopic setup here.

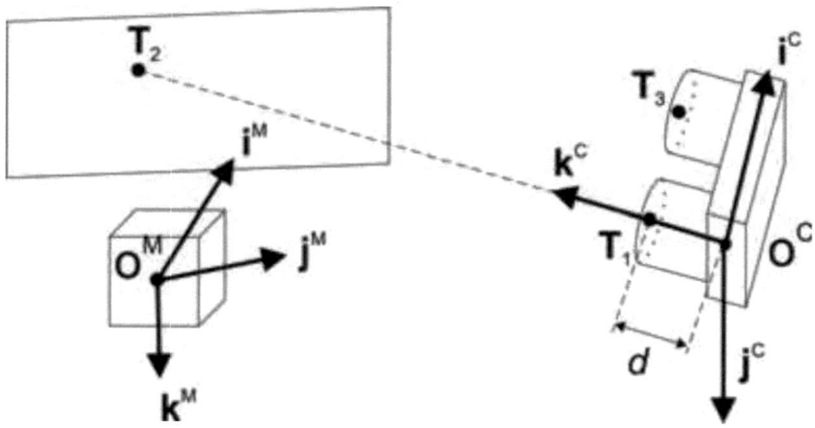

Figure 3. The setup of the magnetic tracker and the camera for model B. Vectors $\mathbf{i}^M$, $\mathbf{j}^M$, $\mathbf{k}^M$ denote base vectors of CS^M, while $\mathbf{i}^C$, $\mathbf{j}^C$, $\mathbf{k}^C$ denote base vectors of CS^C. $\mathbf{T}_1$, $\mathbf{T}_2$ and $\mathbf{T}_3$ mark the control point positions, while d marks the lens' focal length

First, the position of control point $\mathbf{T}_1$ on the face of the left camera lens (Fig. 3) is measured. Next, the magnetic sensor is attached to an arbitrary flat screen in front of the camera (control point $\mathbf{T}_2$ in Fig. 3) and the camera is aligned in such a way that the sensor is visible exactly in the centre of the left image. This step insures that the point $\mathbf{T}_2$ lies on the camera's (i.e. the lens') left optical axis. Since base vector $\mathbf{k}^C$ has the same direction as this optical axis, we calculate it from $\mathbf{T}_1$ and $\mathbf{T}_2$. The base vector $\mathbf{i}^C$ is obtained by measuring the coordinates of the third control point $\mathbf{T}_3$ on the face of the right camera lens (Fig. 3):

$$\mathbf{k}^C = \frac{\overline{\mathbf{T}_1\mathbf{T}_2}}{\left\| \overline{\mathbf{T}_1\mathbf{T}_2} \right\|}, \quad \mathbf{i}^C = \frac{\overline{\mathbf{T}_1\mathbf{T}_3}}{\left\| \overline{\mathbf{T}_1\mathbf{T}_3} \right\|}. \tag{5}$$

Base vector $\mathbf{j}^C$ is calculated from Eq. (3). The origin of CS^C lies on the camera's left optical axis and is determined by displacing the point $\mathbf{T}_1$ by d, i.e. the camera's focal length (Fig. 3):

$$\mathbf{o}^C = \mathbf{T}_1 - d\mathbf{k}^C. \tag{6}$$

The transformation model B is therefore described by 10 parameters:

$$\mathbf{\Theta}_B = \{x_1, y_1, z_1, x_2, y_2, z_2, x_3, y_3, z_3, d\},$$

where the initial 9 parameters have the same meaning as with $\mathbf{\Theta}_A$, and d is the focal length. When aligning $\mathbf{T}_2$ with the centre of left image, a quantization error of at least ½ pixel is unavoidable. This error causes a displacement of $\mathbf{T}_2$ from the optical axis by r_H in horizontal direction and r_V in vertical direction (relative to camera's left optical axis). At distance h from the screen, camera's field of view measures equal $u_H \times u_V$ (Fig. 4). At the same time, this area is represented in the image by $v_H \times v_V$ pixels. Therefore, an error of 1 pixel (± 0.5 pixel) causes a displacement of point $\mathbf{T}_2$ by

$$r_H = \frac{u_H}{v_H} = \frac{2h\,\mathrm{tg}\left(\frac{\varphi_H}{2}\right)}{v_H}, r_V = \frac{u_V}{v_V} = \frac{2h\,\mathrm{tg}\left(\frac{\varphi_V}{2}\right)}{v_V}, \tag{7}$$

where φ_H and φ_V mark the camera's horizontal and vertical view angles (Jain et al, 1995). Other parameters of model B are not affected by the image quantization error.

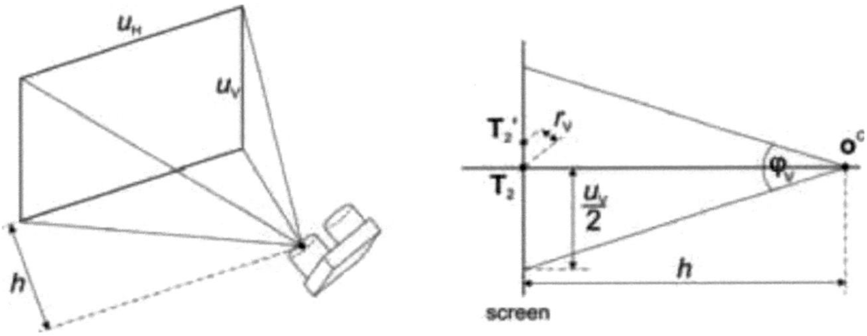

Figure 4. Left: stereo camera's field of view. Right: vertical displacement r_V of point $\mathbf{T}_2$ due to 1 pixel of error when aligning it with the centre of the left image

Model C

This model is similar to model B, except that control point $\mathbf{T}_3$ is also measured on the screen in front of the camera (Fig. 5). The camera should be aligned so that its left image displays $\mathbf{T}_2$ in the centre, while $\mathbf{T}_3$ is displaced from the image centre by m_H pixels horizontally and m_V pixels vertically. Therefore, base vectors $\mathbf{k}^C$ and $\mathbf{j}^C$ are obtained by using the same procedure as with model B.

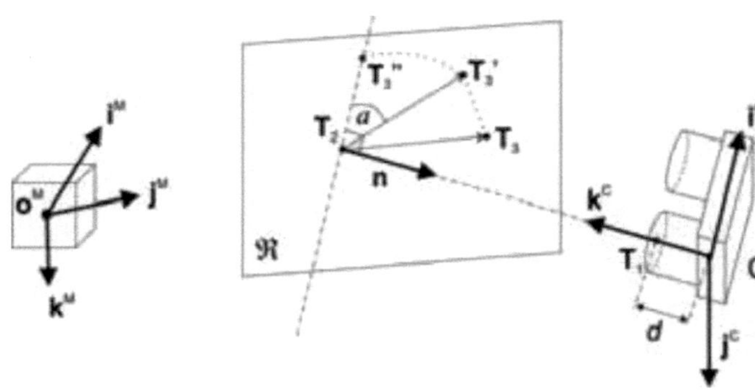

Figure 5. The setup of the magnetic tracker and the camera for model C. Vectors $\mathbf{i}^M$, $\mathbf{j}^M$, $\mathbf{k}^M$ denote base vectors of CS^M, while $\mathbf{i}^C$, $\mathbf{j}^C$, $\mathbf{k}^C$ denote base vectors of CS^C. $\mathbf{T}_1$, $\mathbf{T}_2$ and $\mathbf{T}_3$ mark the original control point positions, $\mathbf{T}_3'$ and $\mathbf{T}_3''$ mark recalculated position of $\mathbf{T}_3$, while d denotes the lens' focal length. Plane $\Re$ is perpendicular to the left optical axis

Base vector $\mathbf{i}^C$ could be determined by $\mathbf{T}_2$ and $\mathbf{T}_3$, but since the camera's optical axis is, in general, not perpendicular to the screen, the point $\mathbf{T}_3$ position must be recalculated accordingly. Imagine a plane $\Re$ which is perpendicular to the optical axis and intersects it in

$\mathbf{T}_2$. Point $\mathbf{T}_3' \in \mathfrak{R}$ can be determined by the intersection of $\mathfrak{R}$ and a line that is passing through $\mathbf{T}_3$ and is perpendicular to $\mathfrak{R}$ (Fig. 5). The new vector $\overrightarrow{\mathbf{T}_2\mathbf{T}_3'}$ is coplanar with $\mathbf{i}^{\mathrm{C}}$, but needs to be rotated around the camera's left optical axis to get parallel with $\mathbf{i}^{\mathrm{C}}$. The required angle of rotation α is determined by m_{H} and m_{V}:

$$\alpha = \mathrm{arctg}\frac{m_{\mathrm{V}}}{m_{\mathrm{H}}}. \tag{8}$$

The new point $\mathbf{T}_3''$, obtained after the rotation, is finally used to calculate the base vector $\mathbf{i}^{\mathrm{C}}$:

$$\mathbf{i}^{\mathrm{C}} = \frac{\overrightarrow{\mathbf{T}_2\mathbf{T}_3''}}{\left\|\overrightarrow{\mathbf{T}_2\mathbf{T}_3''}\right\|}. \tag{9}$$

The origin of CS^{C} is determined by focal length d, as in Eq. (6). The third transformation model is therefore described by 12 parameters:

$$\mathbf{\Theta}_{\mathrm{C}} = \{x_1, y_1, z_1, x_2, y_2, z_2, x_3, y_3, z_3, d, m_{\mathrm{H}}, m_{\mathrm{V}}\}.$$

3.2 Sensitivity of transformation models and their parameters

Inaccuracies in matrix **A** (Eq. (2)) cause erroneous transformations of coordinate systems, that depend also on the measurement model applied. To assess the appropriateness of a particular model, a measure for comparing the transformations and their parameters is needed. When parameter values are measured, the inherent measurement error can be statistically estimated using standard techniques (Stoodley, 1984). However, the effect of each parameter on the final transformation error depends also on its sensitivity. To determine the sensitivity of transformation matrix **A** to the parameter set $\mathbf{\Theta}$, each element $a_{u,v} \in \mathbf{A},\ \forall u,v \in [1,2,3,4]$, will be described as a function of parameters $\Theta_l \in \mathbf{\Theta}$:

$$a_{u,v} = f_{u,v}(\Theta_1, \Theta_2, \ldots, \Theta_N). \tag{10}$$

Sensitivity of transformation matrix **A** can be expressed by derivatives:

$$\frac{\partial \mathbf{A}}{\partial \Theta_l} = \frac{\partial a_{u,v}}{\partial \Theta_l} = \frac{\partial f_{u,v}(\Theta_1, \Theta_2, \ldots, \Theta_N)}{\partial \Theta_l}, \text{ for } \forall u,v \in [1,2,3,4], \forall l \in [1,\ldots,N]. \tag{11}$$

Unfortunately, the resulting mathematical expressions in Eq. (11) are too complex for direct comparison. Instead, the derivatives can be compared numerically by using real parameter values obtained from experiments (Section 4). This procedure gives an estimate on the largest contributor to the transformation error.

The effect of a mutual interaction of parameter errors on the sensitivity of matrix **A** is generally too complex to determine, but the overall upper error bound of each transformation model can still be estimated. The magnitude of error amplification for a certain parameter can be expressed if Eq. (1) is differentiated:

$$\left\|\frac{\partial \mathbf{p}^{\mathrm{M}}}{\partial \Theta_l}\right\| = \left\|\frac{\partial \mathbf{A}}{\partial \Theta_l}\mathbf{p}^{\mathrm{C}}\right\| \le \left\|\frac{\partial \mathbf{A}}{\partial \Theta_l}\right\| \cdot \left\|\mathbf{p}^{\mathrm{C}}\right\|, \tag{12}$$

$$S_l = \frac{\left\| \frac{\partial \mathbf{p}^{\mathrm{M}}}{\partial \Theta_l} \right\|}{\left\| \mathbf{p}^{\mathrm{M}} \right\|} \le \frac{\left\| \frac{\partial \mathbf{A}}{\partial \Theta_l} \right\| \cdot \left\| \mathbf{p}^{\mathrm{C}} \right\|}{\left\| \mathbf{p}^{\mathrm{M}} \right\|}, \text{for } \forall l = 1,\dots,N \,. \tag{13}$$

Expression (13) describes the relative sensitivity S_l of point $\mathbf{p}^{\mathrm{M}}$ with regards to parameter Θ_l. For matrix norm calculation, a spectral norm $\|\mathbf{A}\|_2$ is suggested (Meyer, 2001). Replacing $\mathbf{p}^{\mathrm{C}}$ in (13) by relationship from Eq. (1), an expression for calculating the relative sensitivity for individual parameters yields:

$$S_l = \frac{\left\| \frac{\partial \mathbf{p}^{\mathrm{M}}}{\partial \Theta_l} \right\|}{\left\| \mathbf{p}^{\mathrm{M}} \right\|} \le \frac{\left\| \frac{\partial \mathbf{A}}{\partial \Theta_l} \right\| \cdot \left\| \mathbf{A}^{-1}\mathbf{p}^{\mathrm{M}} \right\|}{\left\| \mathbf{p}^{\mathrm{M}} \right\|} \le \frac{\left\| \frac{\partial \mathbf{A}}{\partial \Theta_l} \right\| \cdot \left\| \mathbf{A}^{-1} \right\| \cdot \left\| \mathbf{p}^{\mathrm{M}} \right\|}{\left\| \mathbf{p}^{\mathrm{M}} \right\|} = \left\| \frac{\partial \mathbf{A}}{\partial \Theta_l} \right\| \cdot \left\| \mathbf{A}^{-1} \right\|, \text{for } \forall l = 1,\dots,N \,. \tag{14}$$

Finally, the upper relative sensitivity limit of the whole model (S^{MAX}) equals the sum of individual sensitivities:

$$S^{\mathrm{MAX}} = \frac{\left\| \frac{\partial \mathbf{p}^{\mathrm{M}}}{\partial \mathbf{\Theta}} \right\|}{\left\| \mathbf{p}^{\mathrm{M}} \right\|} \le \left(\left\| \frac{\partial \mathbf{A}}{\partial \Theta_1} \right\| + \left\| \frac{\partial \mathbf{A}}{\partial \Theta_2} \right\| + \dots + \left\| \frac{\partial \mathbf{A}}{\partial \Theta_N} \right\| \right) \cdot \left\| \mathbf{A}^{-1} \right\| . \tag{15}$$

Sensitivity of a certain model, S^{MAX}, shows how much the inaccuracies of measured model parameters destroy the correct coordinate system's alignment. It can serve as a model robustness measure. On the other hand, the transformation sensitivities related to the individual parameters, S_l, indicate how much uncertain parameter measurements can ruin a good alignment. Thus, they rank the parameters according to their devastating influence on the correct alignment and point out those whose measurements must be done most accurately.

3.3 Decomposition of vision-based tracking error

With a suitable reference, such as a magnetic tracker, the tracking error of a vision-based system can always be assessed. However, as we showed in previous sections, this error consists of two contributions: the error which emerges from the tracking algorithm and the error caused by inaccurate coordinate system transformation. The latter depends on the combination of parameter values, and can be made in favour for any of the models A, B or C from Subsection 3.1 just with adequate choice of parameter values. It is therefore important that any comparison of the models respect the same specific set of parameters, related to one specific setup of the camera and magnetic tracker. All comparison results and conclusions are thus valid for this selected setup only.

Performance of transformation models can be most realistically evaluated by comparing the actual motion trajectories obtained by the magnetic tracker with the aligned trajectories from the tracking algorithm. The RMS difference of matching coordinate pairs reveals the average deviation of the algorithm results from the magnetic tracker's reference. However, this error does not reveal the true accuracy of the tracking algorithm, because the transformation errors caused by inaccurate parameter values also contribute to the difference between trajectories. For detailed analysis, the transformation error needs to be separated from the tracking error of the algorithm. In the sequel, we describe two possible approaches.

Analytical approach

Eq. (1) explains the transformation of a 3D point from CS^C into CS^M under ideal circumstances. In reality, the measurements of control point positions $\mathbf{T}_1$, $\mathbf{T}_2$ and $\mathbf{T}_3$ contain inaccuracies. As a result, the transformation matrix $\mathbf{A}$ is determined corrupted. Denote it by $\mathbf{A}_e$:

$$\mathbf{A}_e = \mathbf{A} \cdot \Delta\mathbf{A}, \tag{16}$$

where $\Delta\mathbf{A}$ is a 4×4 matrix representing the transformation errors. Any vision-based tracking algorithm is also incapable of estimating the exact location of a target $\mathbf{p}^C$, but instead reports corrupted coordinate position $\mathbf{p}_e^C$:

$$\mathbf{p}_e^C = \Delta\mathbf{P}^C \cdot \mathbf{p}^C. \tag{17}$$

Error matrix $\Delta\mathbf{P}^C$ contains unknown coordinate errors dp_1, dp_2 and dp_3 that are added to $\mathbf{p}^C$:

$$\Delta\mathbf{P}^C = \begin{bmatrix} 1 & 0 & 0 & dp_1 \\ 0 & 1 & 0 & dp_2 \\ 0 & 0 & 1 & dp_3 \\ 0 & 0 & 0 & 1 \end{bmatrix}, \tag{18}$$

The errors of magnetic tracker are considered significantly smaller than algorithm-based errors, so points $\mathbf{p}^M$ are considered exact in this derivation. Finally, the transformation from CS^C into CS^M can, under realistic circumstances, be expressed by

$$\mathbf{p}^M = \mathbf{A}_e \cdot \mathbf{C} \cdot \mathbf{p}_e^C, \tag{19}$$

where matrix $\mathbf{C}$ compensates the errors of both the algorithm and the transformation. Eq. (19) is valid for any pair of points $\mathbf{p}^M$ and $\mathbf{p}^C$. So, we can observe more of them together. If four points are selected, they together can be described by a matrix $\mathbf{P}^C = \begin{bmatrix}\mathbf{p}_1^C & \mathbf{p}_2^C & \mathbf{p}_3^C & \mathbf{p}_4^C\end{bmatrix}$. This matrix contains ideal homogenous coordinates of four arbitrary points. Analogously, the corresponding error-corrupted points can be joint in matrix $\mathbf{P}_e^C$ and related magnetic measurements in matrix $\mathbf{P}^M$. If we can find four points whose coordinate errors dp_1, dp_2 and dp_3 are the same, Eq. (17) can be extended to all four points together. Although this condition is hard to verify in practice, four measurements with the most similar error can still be found by searching through all the combinations of the observed points. A criterion for the error similarity will be presented at the end of this section. At this point, we suppose that $\Delta\mathbf{P}^C$ contains the identical error of four selected points.

By substitution of Eq. (1) in Eq. (17), the following relationship is obtained:

$$\mathbf{P}^M \cdot \left(\mathbf{P}_e^C\right)^{-1} = \mathbf{A} \cdot \mathbf{P}^C \cdot \left(\mathbf{P}^C\right)^{-1} \cdot \left(\Delta\mathbf{P}^C\right)^{-1} = \mathbf{A} \cdot \left(\Delta\mathbf{P}^C\right)^{-1}. \tag{20}$$

Since the left-hand side of (20) is known and $\Delta\mathbf{P}^C$ has a specific structure, the contents of the ideal matrix $\mathbf{A}$ can be reconstructed as:

$$\mathbf{A}\cdot\left(\Delta\mathbf{P}^{\mathrm{C}}\right)^{-1}=\begin{bmatrix} i_1 & j_1 & k_1 & o_1 \\ i_2 & j_2 & k_2 & o_2 \\ i_3 & j_3 & k_3 & o_3 \\ 0 & 0 & 0 & 1 \end{bmatrix}\cdot\begin{bmatrix} 1 & 0 & 0 & -dp_1 \\ 0 & 1 & 0 & -dp_2 \\ 0 & 0 & 1 & -dp_3 \\ 0 & 0 & 0 & 1 \end{bmatrix}=\begin{bmatrix} i_1 & j_1 & k_1 & -i_1dp_1-j_1dp_2-k_1dp_3+o_1 \\ i_2 & j_2 & k_2 & -i_2dp_1-j_2dp_2-k_2dp_3+o_2 \\ i_3 & j_3 & k_3 & -i_3dp_1-j_3dp_2-k_3dp_3+o_3 \\ 0 & 0 & 0 & 1 \end{bmatrix}. \quad (21)$$

First three columns of the resulting matrix in (21) represent the rotational part of ideal transformation matrix **A**, only the translation part (the fourth column) cannot be directly determined. However, new base vectors **i**, **j**, **k**, that are more reliable, can be computed and used to construct new transformation matrix $\hat{\mathbf{A}}$. This matrix represents the best estimate of ideal matrix **A**. If $\hat{\mathbf{A}}$ is used in Eq. (16) instead of **A**, the estimated transformation error $\Delta\mathbf{A}$ can be obtained:

$$\Delta\mathbf{A}=\left(\hat{\mathbf{A}}\right)^{-1}\cdot\mathbf{A}_{\mathrm{e}}. \quad (22)$$

Using Eqs. (1) and (17), Eq. (19) can be rearranged into

$$\mathbf{p}^{\mathrm{C}}=\Delta\mathbf{A}\cdot\mathbf{C}\cdot\Delta\mathbf{P}^{\mathrm{C}}\cdot\mathbf{p}^{\mathrm{C}}, \quad (23)$$

which proves that

$$\Delta\mathbf{A}\cdot\mathbf{C}\cdot\Delta\mathbf{P}^{\mathrm{C}}=\mathbf{I}, \quad (24)$$

where **I** stands for identity matrix.
Since matrix **C** can be calculated from Eq. (19), the error matrix $\Delta\mathbf{P}^{\mathrm{C}}$ can also be determined, giving also the matrix $\mathbf{P}^{\mathrm{C}}$ afterwards:

$$\begin{aligned}\Delta\mathbf{P}^{\mathrm{C}}&=(\mathbf{C})^{-1}\cdot(\Delta\mathbf{A})^{-1},\\ \mathbf{P}^{\mathrm{C}}&=\left(\Delta\mathbf{P}^{\mathrm{C}}\right)^{-1}\cdot\mathbf{P}_{\mathrm{e}}^{\mathrm{C}}.\end{aligned} \quad (25)$$

Finally, the exact vision-based points $\mathbf{P}^{\mathrm{C}}$ can be compared to magnetic tracker reference data, which results in a reliable tracking accuracy analysis.
Of course, this conclusion is based on the assumptions that four point vectors joint in matrix $\mathbf{P}_{\mathrm{e}}^{\mathrm{C}}$ contain the same error $\Delta\mathbf{P}^{\mathrm{C}}$ and that the magnetic tracker can be considered error-free. If such a set of four points can be found that the reconstructed rotation vectors (denoted by $\hat{\mathbf{A}}_{\mathrm{ROT}}$) are orthonormal to each other, then both assumptions are satisfied. This property can be used as a criterion function when searching for a suitable set of points:

$$f_{\mathrm{ORTO}}\left(\hat{\mathbf{A}}_{\mathrm{ROT}}\right)=\sum_{\forall a\in\hat{\mathbf{A}}_{\mathrm{ROT}}}\left|\left(\hat{\mathbf{A}}_{\mathrm{ROT}}\right)^{\mathrm{T}}\cdot\hat{\mathbf{A}}_{\mathrm{ROT}}-\mathbf{I}\right|. \quad (26)$$

Four points obtained by tracking algorithm that generate the matrix $\hat{\mathbf{A}}_{\mathrm{ROT}}$ (using Eq. (20)) with the lowest f_{ORTO} value are the ones that best satisfy the assumptions.

Statistical approach

Another approach to separate the coordinate-system transformation error from the tracking-algorithm error is based on statistics. It can always be implemented, which makes it preferred to the analytical approach with four selected trajectory points whose proper choice is not always guaranteed in practice. Eq. (1) can again serve as a starting point, but instead of grouping four camera-based trajectory points with similar errors, we express the transformation of each point separately. Same as before, the ideal values of **A** and $\mathbf{p}^C$ are unknown, only error-contaminated $\mathbf{A}_e$ and $\mathbf{p}_e^C$ are available:

$$\begin{gathered}\mathbf{A}_e = \mathbf{A} + \Delta\mathbf{A}, \mathbf{p}_e^C = \mathbf{p}^C + \Delta\mathbf{p}^C, \\ \mathbf{p}^M + \mathbf{e} = \mathbf{A}_e \mathbf{p}_e^C\end{gathered} \tag{27}$$

Note that the transformation error $\Delta\mathbf{A}$ and algorithm-based error $\Delta\mathbf{p}^C$ are handled differently than in previous approach, although the same notation is adopted. Instead of multiplicative error model, an additive error model is used here. Vector **e** denotes the total deviation of each transformed point $\mathbf{A}_e\mathbf{p}_e^C$ from its magnetic reference position $\mathbf{p}^M$. The error of magnetic tracker is considered to be insignificant compared to other errors, so the tracker's measurements are considered exact.

Using Eq. (27), the total tracking error can be expressed by

$$\begin{gathered}\mathbf{e} = -\mathbf{p}^M + (\mathbf{A} + \Delta\mathbf{A})(\mathbf{p}^C + \Delta\mathbf{p}^C), \\ \mathbf{e} = \mathbf{A}\Delta\mathbf{p}^C + \Delta\mathbf{A}\mathbf{p}_e^C.\end{gathered} \tag{28}$$

Since the actual value of **e** can be calculated for each point, only **A**, $\Delta\mathbf{A}$, and $\Delta\mathbf{p}^C$ remain unknown. Matrices **A** and $\Delta\mathbf{A}$ remain constant throughout the analysis. Consequently, some estimates about their value can be made using statistical methods. First, the maximum expected error of each transformation parameter Θ_l must be realistically estimated. Then, a set of random, normally distributed errors is generated and added to the measured parameter values of a selected coordinate-system transformation model, resulting in a transformation matrix $\mathbf{A}_{SIM}$ whose coefficients are influenced by additional errors introduced artificially and, thus, exactly known. This matrix is used to transform the points $\mathbf{p}_e^C$, recognized by vision-based algorithm. A new trajectory is obtained which is a variation of the proper camera-tracked trajectory in CS^M. By repeating this process and generating a large set of possible transformation matrices, their mean transformation error $m_{RMS}(\mathbf{A}_{SIM})$ can be calculated. Due to the averaging properties of the RMS metrics, this error is expected to approximate the actual mean transformation error $m_{RMS}(\mathbf{A}_e)$. Experiments confirm this, provided that $\mathbf{A}_e$ is sufficiently close to ideal **A**.

If a large enough set of errors is simulated, one or more of the resulting trajectories may closely resemble the ideal transformation. Unfortunately, it cannot be specifically identified since the initial measurement error of $\mathbf{A}_e$ remains unknown. The best we can do is to find the simulated trajectories that minimally or maximally deviate from the $m_{RMS}(\mathbf{A}_{SIM})$ and use them as estimates of minimal and maximal expected transformation error, $\Delta\mathbf{A}_{SIM}^{MIN}$ and $\Delta\mathbf{A}_{SIM}^{MAX}$. When those values are entered into Eq. (28) together with matching $\mathbf{A}_{SIM}$ and **e** values, the estimated $\Delta\mathbf{p}_{SIM}^C$ can be calculated, and consequently the estimated $\mathbf{p}_{SIM}^C$ as well (Eq. (27)). Those simulation-based estimates can be used to statistically compare individual factors involved in the presented tracking accuracy analysis.

4. A practical example: stereo video tracking compared to the Polhemus Fastrak magnetic tracker

To illustrate the presented ideas on a practical example, we describe an experiment in which the Polhemus 3Space Fastrak magnetic tracker (Polhemus, 1998) is used as a reference for analysis of 3D tracking algorithm based on images from the Videre Design's STH-MD1-C stereo head (Videre, 2001). The obtained motion trajectories are aligned using all three presented transformation models and analyzed according to procedures explained in Section 3.

The Fastrak tracker uses four wired sensors and produces measurements with static resolution of 0.8 mm RMS for position and 0.15° RMS for orientation. This accuracy is only achieved when the sensor is less than 75 cm away from magnetic transmitter. We adapted the experiment to this requirement and took several measures to ensure that electromagnetic interference was minimal.

The digital STH-MD1-C stereo head uses two synchronized CMOS sensors with 9 cm of baseline distance and was in our case equipped with f = 48 mm lenses. At maximum resolution of 1288 × 1032 pixels the camera captures only 7.5 frames per second (fps), but if the frame size is reduced to 320 × 240 pixels, the frame rate increases to 110 fps. During all our experiments the camera was positioned approximately 1 meter away from the test subject. Detailed schematics of camera, Fastrak and test object are depicted in Fig. 6.

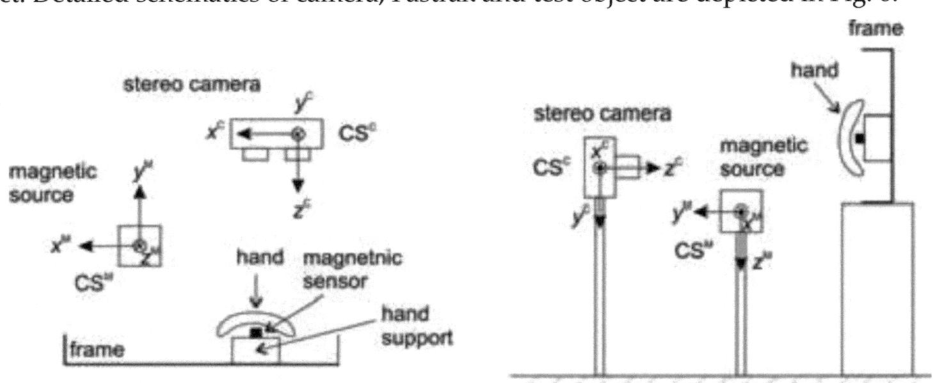

Figure 6. Schematics of the experiment setup including a stereo camera (CS^C), a source of magnetic pulses (CS^M), magnetic sensor and a frame for limiting the movement of the user's hand. Left side shows top view of the setup, right side shows side view

Video data was processed by our algorithm for detection of human hands and faces (Divjak, 2005). The algorithm uses bimodal colour and range information to detect consistent skin coloured regions. 3D centroids of those regions are tracked temporally by a Kalman filter-based prediction algorithm, resulting in smooth 3D motion trajectories of the tracked objects (Fig. 7).

The positions of all control points and other transformation model parameters were measured before conducting the experiment (Tables 1 and 2). Then, one of Fastrak's sensors was attached to the back of the test subject's right hand. The test subject moved his hand along a predefined, physically limited path so that the movement remained practically the same during all the experiments. Every time the stereo camera captured a pair of images, the position of magnetic sensor was read and stored. Three different video sequences were captured, each consisting of 120 - 200 colour image pairs with 320 × 240 pixels, and, in parallel, also the magnetic tracker reference data.

Figure 7. A few frames of the captured video overlaid with the object region borders (in white), as detected by the stereo tracking algorithm

Parameter	d_1	d_2	d	m_H	m_V
Value	490 mm	14 mm	48 mm	85 pixels	9 pixels

Table 1. Manually measured transformation parameter values for models A, B and C

Parameter	x_1	y_1	z_1	x_2	y_2	z_2	x_3	y_3	z_3
Model A (mm)	201.4	241.9	91.3	211.2	522.2	100.2	-68.1	266.0	124.5
Model B (mm)	-83.7	204.8	88.9	-62.4	-99.4	-41.7	-97.4	198.8	84.8
Model C (mm)	-83.7	204.8	88.9	-62.4	-99.4	-41.7	107.4	-17.7	-10.6

Table 2. Coordinates of control point T_1, T_2, T_3 for models A, B and C as determined by the Polhemus magnetic tracker

4.1 Comparison of transformation models

Using parameter values from Table 1 and Table 2 the base vectors $\mathbf{i}^C$, $\mathbf{j}^C$, $\mathbf{k}^C$ and coordinate system origin $\mathbf{o}^C$ were calculated for each model (Table 3). Those vectors can be used to construct transformation matrix $\mathbf{A}$ by Eq. (2). Relative sensitivity of model parameters is presented in Table 4. Finally, the upper sensitivity limit S^{MAX} of each transformation model is compared in Table 5. With our selection of parameter values, the model A turned out to be the most sensitive.

Model	Calculated CS^C base vector values
A	$\mathbf{i}^C = \begin{bmatrix} 0.999 \\ -0.028 \\ -0.038 \end{bmatrix}, \mathbf{j}^C = \begin{bmatrix} 0.037 \\ -0.033 \\ 0.999 \end{bmatrix}, \mathbf{k}^C = \begin{bmatrix} -0.035 \\ -0.999 \\ -0.032 \end{bmatrix}, \mathbf{o}^C = \begin{bmatrix} -288.6 \\ 255.9 \\ 96.0 \end{bmatrix}$
B	$\mathbf{i}^C = \begin{bmatrix} 0.999 \\ -0.028 \\ -0.038 \end{bmatrix}, \mathbf{j}^C = \begin{bmatrix} 0.037 \\ -0.038 \\ 0.999 \end{bmatrix}, \mathbf{k}^C = \begin{bmatrix} -0.027 \\ -0.999 \\ -0.037 \end{bmatrix}, \mathbf{o}^C = \begin{bmatrix} -289.2 \\ 250.0 \\ 96.1 \end{bmatrix}$
C	$\mathbf{i}^C = \begin{bmatrix} 0.998 \\ -0.045 \\ -0.040 \end{bmatrix}, \mathbf{j}^C = \begin{bmatrix} 0.038 \\ -0.038 \\ 0.998 \end{bmatrix}, \mathbf{k}^C = \begin{bmatrix} -0.027 \\ -0.999 \\ -0.037 \end{bmatrix}, \mathbf{o}^C = \begin{bmatrix} -289.2 \\ 250.0 \\ 96.1 \end{bmatrix}$

Table 3. Base vectors of CS^C and its origin (expressed in CS^M), as defined by measured parameter values

Model A		Model B		Model C	
Parameter	S_l value	Parameter	S_l value	Parameter	S_l value
x_1	398.5	x_1	410.4	x_1	408.8
y_1	175.2	y_1	390.7	y_1	389.1
z_1	174.8	z_1	410.2	z_1	408.5
x_2	1.4	x_2	20.4	x_2	20.3
y_2	0.7	y_2	3.4	y_2	3.4
z_2	19.9	z_2	20.3	z_2	20.2
x_3	10.6	x_3	0.4	x_3	0.1
y_3	224.3	y_3	6.9	y_3	0.1
z_3	224.3	z_3	4.5	z_3	0.8
d_1	398.6	d	390.1	d	388.5
d_2	398.6			m_H	0.5
				m_V	4.6

Table 4. Numerical relative sensitivity values S_l for all parameters of models A, B and C

Model	A	B	C
S^{MAX}	2026.9	1661.1	1651.2

Table 5. The upper sensitivity limit (S^{MAX}) of models A, B and C for our experimental setup

4.2 Trajectory comparison

Fig. 7 shows an example of how the algorithm detected the image regions that represent the tracked objects. However, it doesn't give us any clue about how accurate is matching between the reconstructed and the reference 3D position. To obtain this information, all captured trajectories were transformed from CS^C into CS^M (using constructed matrices **A**) and their deviation from the magnetic reference was estimated. Table 6 reports RMS differences for all three transformation models. An example of the aligned trajectories is depicted in Fig. 8. We experimented with 3 trajectories consisting of 500 3D points all together.

Model	X RMS difference (mm)	Y RMS difference (mm)	Z RMS difference (mm)	Total RMS difference (mm)
A	$16.1 \pm 6{,}1$	5.8 ± 1.2	10.7 ± 1.7	20.5 ± 4.9
B	14.8 ± 2.9	12.7 ± 0.7	72.5 ± 6.4	75.1 ± 6.8
C	34.7 ± 3.2	12.7 ± 0.4	55.1 ± 6.7	66.4 ± 6.9

Table 6. The RMS difference between the coordinates of video-based and magnetic-based trajectories, as aligned by each transformation model. Mean values plus standard deviation for all captured trajectories are shown

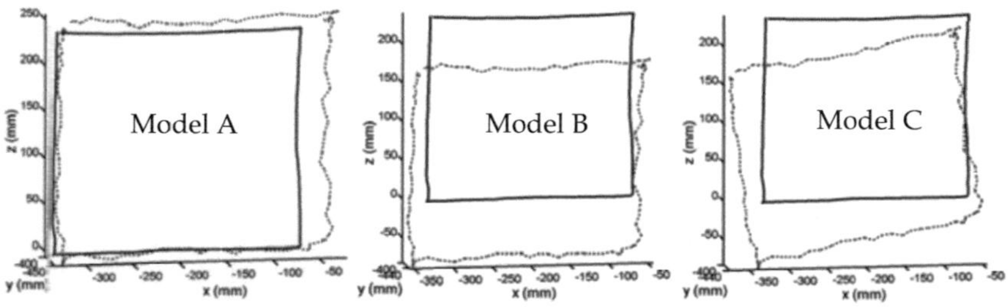

Figure 8. An example of transformation of vision-based trajectories from CS^C to CS^M, for each transformation model. The magnetic tracker data is depicted by solid lines, the video-based tracking algorithm data is depicted by dotted lines

4.3 Error analysis

The total tracking error (Table 6) origins in the transformation error and algorithm error, as described in Section 3.3. We tried to decompose the total error into its constituent components by the proposed statistical approach. First, we empirically estimated maximal expected errors of all model parameters. For Fastrak measurements, its factory specified accuracy of ± 0.8 mm was used, while for manual measurements with a tape measure we estimated accuracy of ± 0.5 mm. For measurements in pixels we estimated an error of ± 0.5 pixel, which according to our setup (the camera was 1 m away from the object) is equivalent to ± 4 mm. Using those values we generated a set of random, normally distributed measurement errors (zero mean, 1000 Monte-Carlo runs) that were added to actual measured parameter values, simulating the effect of error matrix $\Delta\mathbf{A}$. Mean values of vectors of the simulated matrix $\mathbf{A}_{SIM}$ are shown in Table 7.

Model	Simulated CS^C base vector values
A	$\mathbf{i}^C = \begin{bmatrix} 0{,}999 \pm 0{,}000 \\ -0{,}028 \pm 0{,}001 \\ -0{,}038 \pm 0{,}001 \end{bmatrix}, \mathbf{j}^C = \begin{bmatrix} 0{,}037 \pm 0{,}001 \\ -0{,}033 \pm 0{,}004 \\ 0{,}999 \pm 0{,}000 \end{bmatrix}, \mathbf{k}^C = \begin{bmatrix} -0{,}035 \pm 0{,}004 \\ -0{,}999 \pm 0{,}000 \\ -0{,}032 \pm 0{,}004 \end{bmatrix}, \mathbf{o}^C = \begin{bmatrix} -288{,}7 \pm 0{,}8 \\ 249{,}9 \pm 0{,}6 \\ 95{,}8 \pm 0{,}7 \end{bmatrix}$
B	$\mathbf{i}^C = \begin{bmatrix} 0{,}999 \pm 0{,}001 \\ -0{,}028 \pm 0{,}011 \\ -0{,}038 \pm 0{,}011 \end{bmatrix}, \mathbf{j}^C = \begin{bmatrix} 0{,}037 \pm 0{,}011 \\ -0{,}038 \pm 0{,}003 \\ 0{,}999 \pm 0{,}000 \end{bmatrix}, \mathbf{k}^C = \begin{bmatrix} -0{,}027 \pm 0{,}003 \\ -0{,}999 \pm 0{,}000 \\ -0{,}037 \pm 0{,}003 \end{bmatrix}, \mathbf{o}^C = \begin{bmatrix} -289{,}2 \pm 0{,}7 \\ 249{,}9 \pm 0{,}8 \\ 96{,}1 \pm 0{,}7 \end{bmatrix}$
C	$\mathbf{i}^C = \begin{bmatrix} 0{,}999 \pm 0{,}000 \\ -0{,}025 \pm 0{,}003 \\ -0{,}038 \pm 0{,}011 \end{bmatrix}, \mathbf{j}^C = \begin{bmatrix} 0{,}038 \pm 0{,}007 \\ -0{,}038 \pm 0{,}003 \\ 0{,}999 \pm 0{,}000 \end{bmatrix}, \mathbf{k}^C = \begin{bmatrix} -0{,}027 \pm 0{,}003 \\ -0{,}999 \pm 0{,}000 \\ -0{,}037 \pm 0{,}003 \end{bmatrix}, \mathbf{o}^C = \begin{bmatrix} -289{,}2 \pm 0{,}8 \\ 249{,}9 \pm 0{,}8 \\ 96{,}1 \pm 0{,}8 \end{bmatrix}$

Table 7. Base vectors of CS^C and its origin (expressed in CS^M), obtained by a simulated matrix $\mathbf{A}_{SIM}$. Mean values and standard deviations were estimated by 1000 iterations

The effect of transformation errors was evaluated on all available trajectories, detected by the tracking algorithm during our experiments. Each trajectory was transformed into CS^M using matrix $\mathbf{A}_{SIM}$ and compared to the magnetic reference. Trajectories with minimal and maximal deviation from the mean simulated value were identified and the resulting transformation errors $\Delta\mathbf{A}_{SIM}^{MIN}$ and $\Delta\mathbf{A}_{SIM}^{MAX}$ were used to calculate the lower and upper bounds of estimated tracking errors, separating the transformation error from the error of the tracking video-based algorithm (Table 8).

Model	Min. transformation error (mm RMS)	Max. transformation error (mm RMS)	Min. algorithm error (mm RMS)	Max. algorithm error (mm RMS)
A	2.5 ± 0.002	11.6 ± 0.02	17.1	20.5
B	2.3 ± 0.02	9.5 ± 0.23	20.9	22.8
C	1.7 ± 0.01	6.3 ± 0.08	21.4	22.2

Table 8. Separation of total tracking error into transformation-induced error and algorithm-induced error. Values shown are mean estimates based on $\Delta\mathbf{A}_{\mathrm{SIM}}^{\mathrm{MIN}}$ and $\Delta\mathbf{A}_{\mathrm{SIM}}^{\mathrm{MAX}}$, for all captured trajectories

4.4 Discussion

Our experiment demonstrates the importance of trajectory transformation models and their effects on the estimated tracking error. The main difference between the presented models was the placement and the way of measuring the control point positions. In model A, control points $\mathbf{T}_1$, $\mathbf{T}_2$, $\mathbf{T}_3$ are measured at a safe distance from the stereo camera and its coordinate system centre (approximately 50 cm). When a measurement error is made, its effect on the calculation of camera orientation is much smaller than if the same measurement error is made at close distance to the coordinate origin. In models B and C the metal body of the camera distorted the measurements slightly, but close to the CS^C origin the prevailing errors appear again.

It is important to notice that an imprecise physical alignment of the stereo camera's two image sensors significantly corrupts the trajectory comparison. This is particularly obvious for models B and C, because they require manual alignment of control point $\mathbf{T}_2$ with the left optical axis. Any displacement of the optical axis can be verified during the calibration of the camera and should be corrected accordingly.

Relative sensitivity values in Table 4 show which parameters amplify the measurement errors the most, possibly causing a significant transformation error. In model A, such parameters are $\mathbf{T}_1$, $\mathbf{T}_3$, d_1 and d_2. In models B and C, parameters $\mathbf{T}_1$ and d are the most sensitive. Comparison of the upper relative sensitivity limits S^{MAX} (Table 5) also confirms that model A is the most sensitive, while model C is the least. But, we need to consider the fact that a highly sensitive parameter with low actual numerical value can have less impact on the transformation than a parameter with low sensitivity and large numerical value. For example, if a measurement error of a few millimetres is made at close distance to the camera (like control point $\mathbf{T}_3$ in model B), it would greatly distort the trajectory comparison, even if the parameter in question has very low sensitivity.

Consequently, the trajectory comparison results cannot be matched directly with the estimated S^{MAX}. In our experiments, the real parameter values generated such coordinate system transformations that model A produced the lowest tracking error, while model B performed the worst (Table 6, Fig. 8). On the other hand, the simulation of the transformation errors $\Delta\mathbf{A}$ determined the trajectories with the minimum and maximum errors (Table 8). In this context, model C corresponds to the lowest expected error, while model A to the biggest, which is consistent with the S^{MAX} predictions. Thus, a conclusion based on the model sensitivity about the accuracy of the proposed coordinate-system transformation is that model C is theoretically the least error-prone, while model A is the most.

Since the identical tracking algorithm data was used in all comparisons, the error of the tracking algorithm should appear the same for all three transformation models. Our best estimate of the total tracking error is 20.5 mm RMS, as obtained by model A (Table 6). The minimal and the maximal transformation errors of individual models can be used to decompose the total tracking error, resulting in estimates of the lower and upper bound of the algorithm error. For model A, the transformation error is estimated between 2.5 and 11.6 mm RMS, while the algorithm video-based error is between 17.1 and 20.5 mm RMS (Table 8).

Reference measurements of the Fastrak tracker also contain certain inaccuracies, but since their magnitude is significantly lower than transformation error or algorithm error, they are ignored and Fastrak measurements are considered error-free. However, in experiments where the magnetic sensor is more than 75 cm away from the magnetic transmitter, those errors should be considered and compensated accordingly.

5. Conclusion

When a magnetic tracker is used as a reference for vision-based tracking, a reliable transformation of their coordinate systems is crucial for proper tracking accuracy estimation. To address this issue in more detail, three different models of coordinate system alignment were developed. By analyzing the worst-case sensitivity of transformation models a limited comparison of those models is possible. The most influential model parameters are easy to identify and should be measured with special care. However, the actual parameter values used also have a significant effect on the final transformation error. With appropriate selection of parameter values, any model can be manipulated to produce the most accurate transformation. Therefore, such comparisons are only reasonable if the parameters are fixed to a certain setup of a camera and a magnetic tracker.

In our experiment the transformation model A resulted in the lowest total trajectory difference, despite being the most sensitive. Statistical separation of this error into estimates of the tracking algorithm's error and the transformation-induced error provides more detailed discrepancy analysis.

The presented approach is applicable to any setup where the performance of video-based tracking is to be estimated by a reference device with its separate coordinate system. Experimentally determined parameter values and conclusions are valid only for the specific setup, but the proposed methodology can be applied to any similar problem.

6. References

Ascension (2007). *Ascension Technology Corporation,* Burlington, USA, http://www.ascension-tech.com/.

ART (2007). *Advanced Realtime Tracking GmbH,* Munich, Germany, http://www.ar-tracking.de/.

Balan, A.O.; Sigal, L.; Black, M.J. (2005). A Quantitative Evaluation of Video-based 3D Person Tracking. *The Second Joint IEEE International Workshop on Visual Surveillance and Performance Evaluation of Tracking and Surveillance,* Beijing, China, October 15-16, pp. 349-356.

Bashir, F. & Porikli, F. (2006). Performance Evaluation of Object Detection and Tracking Systems. *IEEE International Workshop on Performance Evaluation of Tracking and Surveillance*, June.

Black, J.; Ellis, T.; Rosin, P. (2003). A Novel Method for Video Tracking Performance Evaluation. *The Joint IEEE International Workshop on Visual Surveillance and Performance Evaluation of Tracking and Surveillance*, Nice, France, pp. 125-132.

Bornik, A.; Beichel, R.; Reitinger, B.; Gotschuli, G.; Sorantin, E.; Leberl, F.; Sonka, M. (2003). Computer Aided Liver Surgery Planning Based on Augmented Reality Techniques. *Workshop Bildverarbeitung für die Medizin*, Springer Verlag, pp. 249-253.

Bradley, D. & Roth, G. (2005). *Proceedings of the ACM SIGCHI International Conference on Advances in Computer Entertainment Technology*. Valencia, Spain, pp. 19 - 26.

Christensen, H.I. & Förstner, W. (1997). Performance characteristics of vision algorithms. *Machine Vision and Applications*, Springer-Verlag, Vol. 9, No. 5-6, pp. 215-218.

Collins, R.T.; Lipton, A.J.; Kanade, T. (2000). Introduction to the Special Section on Video Surveillance. *IEEE Transactions on PAMI*, Vol. 22, No. 8, pp. 745 - 746.

Collomosse, J.P.; Rowntree D.; Hall, P.M. (2003). Video Analysis for Cartoon-like Special Effects. *14th British Machine Vision Conference*, UK.

Cupillard, F.; Bremond, F.; Thonnat, M. (2003). Behaviour recognition for individuals, groups of people and crowd. *IEE Proceedings of the IDSS Symposium Intelligent Distributed Surveillance Systems*, February, London.

CVTI (2007). *Computer Vision Test Images (on-line collection)*. Calibrated Imaging Lab, Carnegie Mellon University, USA, http://www.cs.cmu.edu/~cil/v-images.html.

Divjak, M. (2005). *Evaluation of models and procedures for 3D tracking of human body using a stereocamera*. PhD Dissertation, Faculty of Electrical Engineering and Computer Science, University of Maribor, Slovenia.

Doermann, D. & Mihalcik, D. (2000). Tools and Techniques for Video Performance Evaluation. *Proceedings of the International Conference on Pattern Recognition*, Barcelona, Spain, September, pp. 4167–4170.

Ellis, T.J.; Black, J. (2003). A Multi-view surveillance system. *IEE Intelligent Distributed Surveillance Systems*, London, UK, February.

Fischer, J.; Neff, M.; Freudenstein, D.; Bartz. D. (2004). Medical Augmented Reality based on Commercial Image Guided Surgery. *Eurographics Symposium on Virtual Environments*, The Eurographics Association, Germany.

Fua, P. & Plankers, R. (2003). Articulated Soft Objects for Multiview Shape and Motion Capture. *IEEE Transactions on Pattern Analysis and Machine Intelligence*, Vol. 25, No. 9, pp. 1182 - 1187.

Gavrila, D.M. (1999). The visual analysis of human movement: A survey. *Computer Vision and Image Understanding*, Vol. 73, No. 1, pp. 82-98, Academic Press.

Georis, B.; Brémond, F.; Thonnat, M.; Macq, B. (2003). Use of an Evaluation and Diagnosis Method to Improve Tracking Performances. *The 3rd IASTED International Conference on Visualization, Imaging and Image Proceeding*, September 8-10, Benalmadena, Spain.

Grimson, E.; Leventon, M.; Ettinger, G.; Chabrerie, A.; Ozlen, F.; Nakajima, S.; Atsumi, H.; Kikinis, R.; Black, P. (1998). Clinical Experience with a High Precision Image-Guided Neurosurgery System. *Lecture Notes In Computer Science*, Springer-Verlag, London, UK, Vol. 1496, pp. 63 - 73.

Gueziec, A. (2002). Tracking pitches for broadcast television, *Computer*, IEEE, March, Vol. 35, No. 3, pp. 38-43.

Herda, L.; Fua, P.; Plankers, R.; Boulic, D.R.; Thalmann D. (2001). Using skeleton-based tracking to increase the reliability of optical motion capture. *Human Movement Science*, No. 20, pp. 313—341.

Huang, D. & Yan, H. (2002). Modeling and animation of human expressions using NURBS curves based on facial anatomy. *Proceedings of the 6th International Computer Science Conference*, Hong Kong, China, December 18-20, No. 17, pp. 457-465.

Jain, R.; Kasturi, R.; Schunck, B.G. (1995). *Machine Vision*, International Edition, McGraw-Hill Inc., 1995.

Jaynes, C.; Webb, S.; Steele, R.; Xiong, Q. (2002). An Open Development Environment for Evaluation of Video Surveillance Systems. *Proceedings of the Third International Workshop on Performance Evaluation of Tracking and Surveillance*, Copenhagen, June.

Keemink, C.J.; Hoek van Dijkel, G.A.; Snijders, C.J. (1991). Upgrading of efficiency in the tracking of body markers with video techniques. *Medical and Biological Engineering and Computing*, Vol. 29, No. 1, January.

Kindarenko, V. (2000). A Survey of Electromagnetic Position Tracker Calibration Techniques. *Virtual Reality*, Vol. 5, No. 3, September, pp. 169–182.

Kristan, M.; Perš, J.; Perše, M.; Kovačič, S. (2006). Towards fast and efficient methods for tracking players in sports. *Proceedings of the ECCV Workshop on Computer Vision Based Analysis in Sport Environments*, May, pp. 14-25.

Krumm, J.; Harris, S.; Meyers, B.; Brumitt, B.; Hale, M.; Shafer S. (2000). Multi-Camera Multi-Person Tracking for EasyLiving. *Third IEEE International Workshop on Visual Surveillance*, IEEE Computer Society, Washington, DC, USA, pp. 3.

La Cascia, M.; Sclaroff, S.; Athitsos, V. (2000). Fast, Reliable Head Tracking under Varying Illumination: An Approach Based on Registration of Texture-Mapped 3D Models. *IEEE Transactions on Pattern Analysis and Machine Intelligence*, Vol. 22, No. 4, pp. 322 - 336.

La Cascia, M. & Sclaroff, S. (1999). Fast, reliable head tracking under varying illumination. *Proceedings of IEEE Conference on Computer Vision and Pattern Recognition*, pp. 604-610.

Meyer, C. D. (2001). *Matrix Analysis and Applied Linear Algebra*. Society for Industrial and Applied Mathematics, Philadelphia, USA.

Needham, C.J.; Boyle, R.D. (2003). Performance Evaluation Metrics and Statistics for Positional Tracker Evaluation. *International Conference on Computer Vision Systems*, Graz, Austria, April, pp. 278-289.

NDI (2007) *NDI Optotrak Certus System*, NDI International, Waterloo, Canada, http://www.ndigital.com/.

NP (2007). *NaturalPoint Inc.*, Corvallis, Oregon, USA, http://www.naturalpoint.com/.

Optix (2007). *Optix 400 Series Laser Scanner*, 3D Digital Corp., USA, http://www.3ddigitalcorp.com/products.htm.

Pandya, A. & Siadat, M. (2001). Tracking Methods for Medical Augmented Reality. *Proceedings of Medical Image Computing and Computer-Assisted Intervention*, Utrecht, The Netherlands, October 14-17 Springer Berlin, pp. 1404-1405.

PCCV (2007). *Performance Characterization in Computer Vision*. PEIPA - Pilot European Image Processing Archive, http://peipa.essex.ac.uk/index.html.

PETS (2005). *IEEE International Workshop on Performance Evaluation of Tracking and Surveillance*, IEEE Winter Vision Multi-Meeting, Breckenridge, Colorado, USA, http://pets2005.visualsurveillance.org/.

Polat, E.; Yeasin, M.; Sharma, R. (2003). Robust tracking of human body parts for collaborative human computer interaction. *Computer Vision and Image Understanding*, Vol. 89, No. 1, pp. 44-69.

Polhemus (1998). *3Space Fastrak User's Manual*. Polhemus Inc., USA, http://www.polhemus.com.

Qiu, X.; Wang, Z.; Xia S. (2004). A Novel Computer Vision Technique Used on Sport Video, *Proceedings of International Conference on Signal Processing*, Vol. 2, No. 31 pp. 1296 - 1300.

Rehg, J.M. & Kanade, T. (1994). Visual Tracking of High DOF Articulated Structures: an Application to Human Hand Tracking. *3rd European Conference on Computer Vision*, Stockholm, Sweden, pp. 35-46.

Safeguards (2007). *Safeguards Technology Inc.*, Hackensack, USA, http://www.safeguards.com/.

Sato, Y; Oka, K.; Koike, H.; Nakanishi, Y. (2004). Video-based tracking of user's motion for augmented desk interface. *Proceedings of Sixth IEEE International Conference on Automatic Face and Gesture Recognition*, May 17-19, pp. 805- 809.

Scharstein, D. & Szeliski, R. (2003). High-accuracy stereo depth maps using structured light. *IEEE Computer Society Conference on Computer Vision and Pattern Recognition*, Vol. 1, pp. 195-202, Madison, WI, USA.

Stapleton, C.; Hughes, C.; Moshell, M.; Micikevicius, P.; Altman, M. (2002). Applying mixed reality to entertainment. *Computer*, IEEE, Vol. 35, No. 12, pp. 122 - 124.

Stoodley, K.D.C. (1984). *Applied and Computational Statistics: A First Course*. Ellis Horwood Ltd.

Tang, S.L.; Kwoh, C.K.; Teo, M.Y.; Sing, N.W.; Ling, K.V. (1998). Augmented reality systems for medical applications. *Engineering in Medicine and Biology Magazine*, IEEE, May/June, Vol. 17, No. 3, pp. 49-58.

Videre (2001). *STH-MD1/-C Stereo Head*. User's Manual, Videre Design Inc., USA, http://www.videredesign.com.

VIVID (2007). *VIVID 910 Series 3D Digitizer*, Konica Minolta Holdings, http://konicaminolta.com/.

Vogt, S.; Khamene, A.; Sauer, F. (2006). Reality Augmentation for Medical Procedures: System Architecture, Single Camera Marker Tracking, and System Evaluation. *International Journal of Computer Vision*, Springer Netherlands, Vol. 70, No. 2, November, pp. 179-190.

Wren, C.R. et al. (1997). Perceptive Spaces for Performance and Entertainment: Untethered Interaction using Computer Vision and Audition. *Applied Artificial Intelligence*, Taylor & Francis, Vol. 11, No. 4, pp. 267 - 284.

Xiao, J.; Moriyama, T.; Kanade, T.; Cohn, J. F. (2003). Robust full-motion recovery of head by dynamic templates and re-registration techniques. *International Journal of Imaging Systems and Technology*, No. 13, pp. 85-94.

Yao, Z. & Li, H. (2004). Is A Magnetic Sensor Capable of Evaluating A Vision-Based Face Tracking System? *Conference on Computer Vision and Pattern Recognition Workshop*, Vol. 5, Washington, USA.

7

Photorealistic 3D Model Reconstruction based on the Consistency of Object Surface Reflectance Measured by the Voxel Mask

K. K. Chiang, K. L. Chan and H. Y. Ip
City University of Hong Kong
China

1. Introduction

To create three-dimensional (3D) models of real scenes and objects is an old and challenging computer vision problem. Systems that can reconstruct the 3D model of object, for instances the human head or cultural artefacts, have found many applications such as virtual character animation and interactive museum exhibition. Real object models can be reconstructed automatically using active and passive methods. Object range scanning by laser or structured light are typical examples of the active methods. They often demand expensive equipment and special skill to operate. Moreover, they are not very good in modeling very glossy objects. The passive methods can acquire images of the object at different viewpoints using off-the-shelf CCD cameras (Chang & Chen, 2002). The camera is usually calibrated by taking pictures of a specially designed calibration pattern or object. The camera viewpoints can be arbitrarily selected and the camera model is adjustable. For instance, Niem (Niem, 1999) proposes a 3D object reconstruction method using a mobile camera to capture image of the object and calibration pattern simultaneously.

Our system of 3D object model reconstruction consists of four major steps: camera calibration, volumetric model reconstruction, polygonal model formation and texture mapping. An overview of our system is shown in Figure 1. The camera calibration is to obtain the intrinsic and extrinsic parameters defining the internal camera properties and the viewpoint orientation with respect to the object. The object and the calibration patterns can be captured simultaneously. Therefore, the camera can be placed anywhere and each view can be calibrated independently. One of the popular approaches for volumetric modeling is shape from silhouette (SFS), which is to recover the shape of object from its contours. However, reconstruction of a complex rigid object from its images is a challenging computer vision problem, especially when the object exhibits large textureless surface or concave surface. Previously, we enhance the SFS-based volumetric modeling algorithm by imposing the photo-consistency in neighboring views and the aggregation of evidence in volume space via the use of voxel mask (Wong & Chan, 2004; Chiang & Chan, 2006). Although the algorithm is very good in tackling textureless as well as concave surface, it is still unable to model non-Lambertian object surface accurately. In the present investigation, we propose a novel volumetric modeling algorithm that further improves the shape reconstruction by explicitly taking into account the object surface specularity. Then the polygonal model is formed by the marching cubes algorithm (Lorensen & Cline, 1987). Various operations are applied to refine the polygonal model. Finally, a texture map is created from the original image sequence and mapped onto the polygonal model to give it a realistic appearance. Computer graphics techniques are adopted for the synthesis of missing or unseen texture.

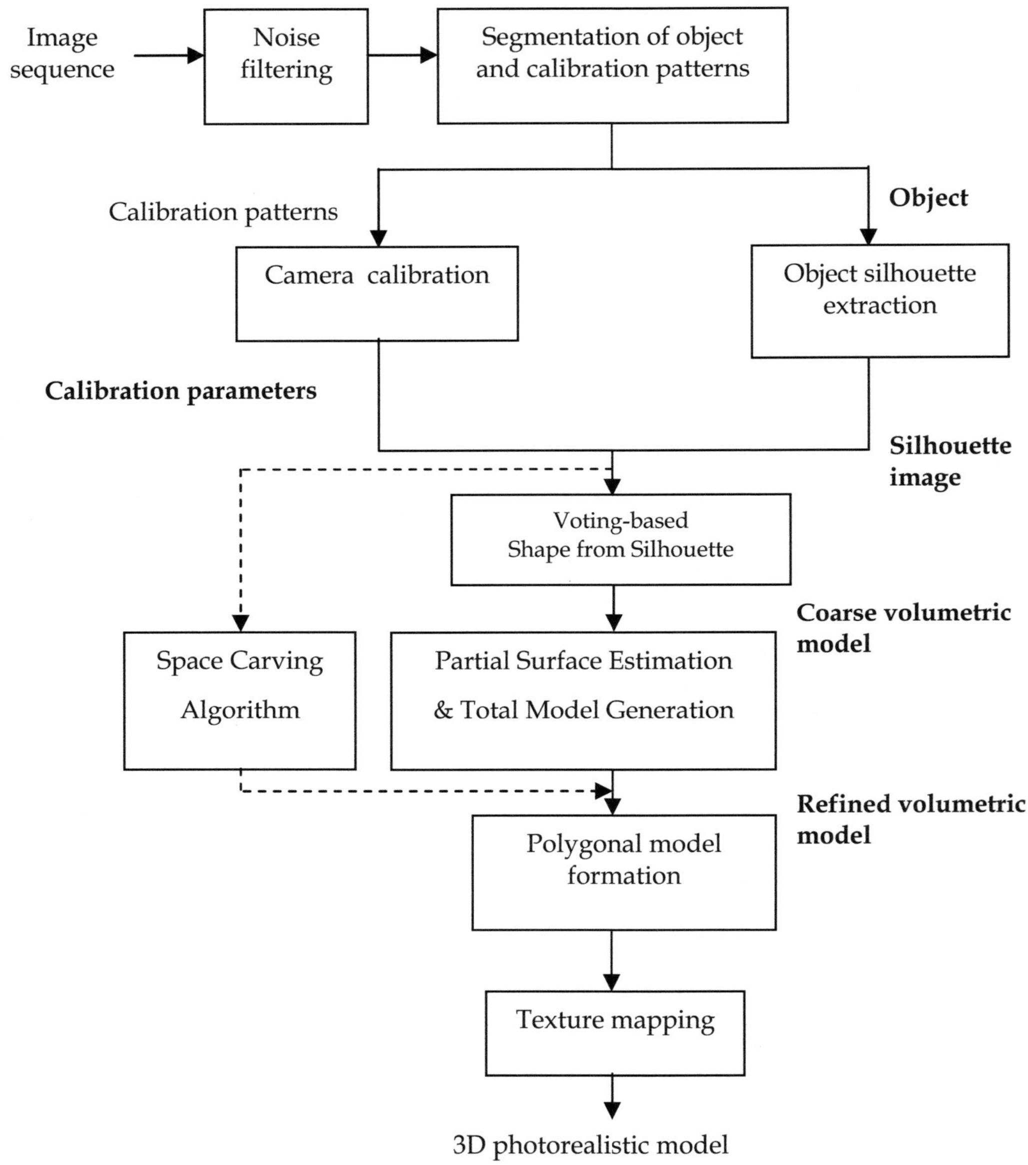

Figure 1. Overview of 3D model reconstruction system

2. Volumetric model reconstruction

Volumetric modeling is an important part of 3D model reconstruction. Conceptually, it is based on computations in 3D volume space in order to construct the object volume in the

world coordinate system that is consistent with the input images. Image-based volumetric modeling methods generally assume that the object or scene is Lambertian. Ideally, only matte surface exhibiting purely diffuse reflection satisfies Lambert's Law. Many real objects are moderately glossy, e.g. plastic and ceramic objects. They exhibit both diffuse and specular reflections. The model reconstructed by conventional volumetric modeling algorithms contains many errors due to violation of this assumption. Therefore a lot of post-processing effort is needed before the 3D model can be used in practical applications.
In our system, the topology of the object is first obtained by a voting-based SFS technique. Detail object shape is reconstructed in two steps: partial surface estimation and total model generation. In our first attempt, partial surface is estimated by exploiting color-consistency and the aggregation of evidence in volume space. A novel 3D voxel mask is used for measuring the color dispersion, instead of using the conventional image block matching technique. To tackle real glossy objects, we further enhance the 3D model reconstruction system by proposing a novel partial surface estimation algorithm that can handle the co-existence of both diffuse and specular surfaces. Based on the dichromatic reflection model, we derive an explicit relation characterizing the specular reflection. Voxel mask is employed for measuring either photo-consistency or surface specularity during the volumetric modeling.

2.1 Shape from silhouette/photo-consistency

The volumetric modeling assumes that there is a bounded volume (V) within which contains the object of interest. This volume is often assumed to be a cube and the most common approach to representing it is a regular tessellation of cubes called voxels (v). SFS reconstructs the volumetric model using a sequence of images. Each viewpoint location can be estimated from the camera calibration process. Our first volumetric model reconstruction method, called shape from silhouette/photo-consistency (SFSPC), uses the voting-based SFS firstly to reproject the object silhouettes onto the 3D voxel space to obtain the topology of object. Partial surface estimation and total model generation are then used to refine the volumetric model which will be explained later.
In our system, the contour of the object is simply extracted from each of the input images with the use of a monochromatic background during image acquisition. The reason why we set up the system in front of a monochromatic background is to save the computation time. Object silhouette can be extracted easily and subsequent computation can be confined to the object region. It should be mentioned that a relaxation of the acquisition environment is possible at the cost of longer computation time. That will not affect the reconstructed model as the background voxels can still be carved away by the partial surface estimation algorithm, no matter it exploits photo-consistency or surface specularity.
Each silhouette image is represented in binary form. SFS recovers the volumetric description of the object from multiple silhouette images by volume intersection. Firstly, a bounding cone is constructed, using the camera focal point and the corresponding object silhouette. If a point of the voxel is back-projected onto the inside the object silhouette, that voxel may be occupied by the object. Otherwise, the voxel is outside the object. To make the estimation of the object in 3D space more accurate, multiple silhouette images taken at various viewpoints can be used. Then, a visual hull (VH) is constructed by intersecting all the bounding cones formed by the object silhouettes (Laurentini, 1994).

Many SFS-based methods assume that the silhouette images are errorless. However, in real situation, silhouette images may contain errors which can affect the accuracy of the reconstructed model. Therefore, an extension of conventional SFS, such as the voting-based SFS, is implemented such that silhouette image error does not seriously affect the reconstructed object shape. First, the volume space V is set up and the score of each voxel is initialized to zero. Based on the voting-localizing scheme, a score of the voxel is incremented each time if the voxel is projected onto the silhouette image region, that is the projected color is not the background color. An accumulated value is obtained until all images are visited. The voxel is considered as visible only and is included in the visual hull VH if its accumulated score is larger than a pre-defined threshold as shown in the following pseudo-code.

```
For each voxel v in V
   v.score = 0
End For
VH = ϕ
For each voxel v in V
   For each silhouette image i, where i = 1…NumOfImages
      Color = ProjectVoxelOnImage(v, i)
      If Color != BackgroundColor
      Then v.score = v.score + 1
      End If
   End For
End For
For each voxel v in V
   If v.score ≥ Threshold
   Then VH = VH ∪ v
   End If
End For
```

The voting-based SFS can be treated as a generalization of SFS, by which setting the threshold as the total number of views becomes the conventional SFS. The advantage of the voting-based SFS over the conventional SFS is to minimize the adverse effect of the artefact in silhouette images to the resultant model.

It is well known that SFS is not guaranteed to reconstruct a correct 3D shape of the target object, especially when the object has concave surface. To cope with this problem, it is necessary to incorporate other technique to detect and recover the shape concavity. Shape from photo-consistency is one of the choices. For a greyscale or color image, the photometric information does give improvement in volumetric reconstruction. If a voxel corresponds to the surface of an object, the texture and color properties of its projection points on the images, from which it can be seen, must be nearly the same. There is an assumption made in any color-consistency method: surface of the object is assumed to satisfy the Lambertian reflectance model, so that every surface appears equally bright in all directions regardless of the illumination. The shape from photo-consistency algorithm consists of two steps: (i) partial surface estimation, and (ii) total model generation. The basic idea of partial surface estimation is that if a voxel corresponds to the surface of the object, the color of its projection point on each image is similar to each other. Due to lighting fluctuation and image noise, the ideal color-consistency (or zero color dispersion) is not possibly achieved using the whole set of images. However, it is much easier to estimate a fairly good partial surface from a small set of neighboring images by relaxing the color dispersion to a small value. As there are as many partial surfaces as the images and each partial surface may still have error, a merging step that can integrate the partial surfaces and at the same time reduce error is needed.

For the estimation of partial surface for each viewpoint, the color dispersion for each voxel must be calculated first. Color dispersion is to measure the difference of color values for a voxel projected to a number of consecutive images. The visible voxels with minimum color dispersion are chosen and regarded as the partial surface for that viewpoint. Equation (1) is used to calculate the color dispersion:

$$D(v,i) = \sum_{j=i-m}^{i+m} \sum_{block\ size} \{C(p(v,i)) - C(p(v,j))\}^2 \tag{1}$$

where the number of consecutive images is $2m+1$, *block size* is the block area in the image for pixel-by-pixel comparison, and $C(p(v, i))$ is the color value of the projection point of voxel v on image i. The partial surface for the ith viewpoint is referred as V_{sp}^{i}. Then, for each viewpoint i, v in the visual hull VH is projected onto the consecutive images from view $i-m$ to $i+m$ for calculating the color dispersion. After the color dispersion calculation is finished, a set of voxels V_r^i along a ray from the focal point of i through v is obtained. Assign v to V_{sp}^{i} if its color dispersion is the minimum among the voxels in V_r^i. These operations are performed for all voxels and repeatedly for all viewpoints. To ensure that the voxels of each partial surface are photo-consistent, only a small number of consecutive viewpoints in the neighborhood of the partial surface viewpoint are examined instead of examining the whole sequence of camera views. If the voxel is occluded in one or more examining viewpoints, the color dispersion is high and that voxel will very unlikely be selected as partial surface.

To generate the complete 3D volumetric model, the partial surfaces have to be integrated. However, error may still occur in each partial surface. For instance, variation of the color value of a surface point between two captured images due to environmental lighting can lead to false detection of the surface voxel. Therefore, a relaxation is allowed in integrating the partial surfaces by the voting-localizing scheme such that the error is rounded to construct a high precision model. The total model generation algorithm is as follow.

1. Set the score of all voxels in VH as zero.

2. For each voxel v, increment the score using the following scheme:
   a. Calculate the distance between the focal point of i and v, $L(v, i)$, and the distance between the focal point of i and voxel v', $L(v', i)$, where v' is the intersection of a set of voxels along a ray (from the focal point of i to v) and the partial surface V_{sp}^{i}.
   b. Both distances are measured in the Euclidean space. If $L(v, i)$ is greater than or equal to $L(v', i)$, that means v is behind or lying on V_{sp}^{i}. Then increment the score of v by 1.
3. After looping all the viewpoints, if the total score is greater than a given threshold, v is appended to the final volumetric model.
4. The process is repeated for all voxels.

2.2 3D voxel mask

The common practice of conventional shape from photo-consistency, or methods based on the color-consistency, is to project 'one' voxel into consecutive image views and threshold the variance of the color values. This makes the algorithm heavily rely on the image quality. Even in the multi-hypothesis testing (Eisert et al. 1999), only one voxel is used to measure the photo-consistency which is insufficient. On the other hand, the use of image-based pixel-by-pixel comparison in a block area for measuring the color dispersion cannot guarantee a correct volumetric model. Therefore, the formulation of color dispersion should be re-defined. Instead of using image-based comparison and multi-hypothesis testing of one-voxel projection, a novel 3D voxel mask for evaluating the photo-consistency is proposed. Voxels in the mask are used to measure the photo-consistency among the consecutive images.

The idea of voxel mask is somewhat similar to the image filter kernel. The voxel mask is oriented in three orthogonal directions with respect to the camera viewpoint. The line joining the camera and the examining voxel - centre of voxel mask, is called the axial direction. The other two directions are called coronal and sagittal. Each voxel in the 3D voxel mask is denoted as v_{vm}. The structure of the voxel mask and the generation procedure are shown in Figures 2 and 3 respectively.

Figure 2. 3D voxel mask

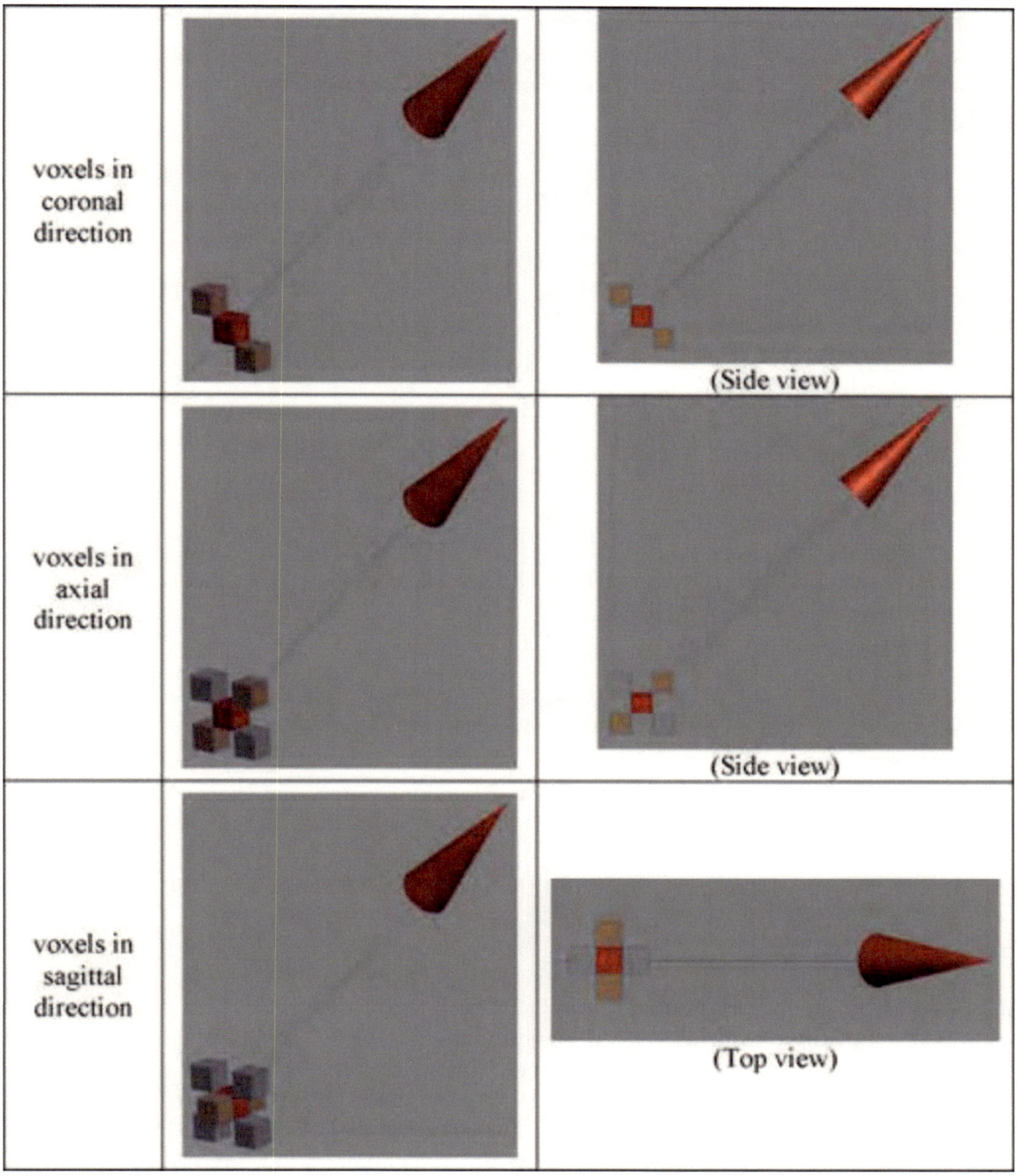

Figure 3. Generation of 3D voxel mask (cone: camera viewpoint, red voxel: centre of mask, brown voxels: voxels in a particular direction)

The mask for each examining voxel is generated independently. The structure of mask is symmetric and invariant in the voxel space. This ensures that the same mask structure is used to evaluate the color dispersion among the neighboring images. However, not all voxels in the mask will be used to evaluate the color dispersion. In each direction, if any component v_{vm} is not in the visual hull, all voxels in this direction are excluded from the color dispersion calculation. This mechanism can prevent the surface voxels from erroneously removed from the volumetric model. As the number of voxels in the mask used to evaluate the color dispersion may be different, the accumulated color dispersion value is averaged by the actual number of comparisons. The new function for color dispersion evaluation is re-defined as:

$$D(v_{vm},i) = \sum_{j=i-m}^{i+m} \{C(p(v_{vm},i)) - C(p(v_{vm},j))\}^2 \tag{2}$$

The modified partial surface estimation using 3D voxel mask in our SFSPC algorithm is shown in the following pseudo-code.

```
For each camera viewpoint i
    V^i_sp = ϕ
    For each voxel v in VH
        v.NoOfComparison = 0
        v.ColorDispersion = 0
        Form voxel mask for v
        For each voxel v_vm in voxel mask
            v.ColorDispersion += D(v_vm, i)
            v.NoOfComparison++
        End For
        v.ColorDispersion = v.ColorDispersion / v.NoOfComparison
    End For
    For each voxel v in VH
        If v.ColorDispersion = MIN_{V_r^i}(v.ColorDispersion)
        Then V^i_sp = V^i_sp ∪ v
        EndIf
    End For
End For
```

2.3 Shape from specularity consistency

Volumetric modeling methods generally assume that the object surface is Lambertian. Real objects and scenes may have specular surfaces. Today, the visual quality of models becomes the main point of attention due to the increasing demand for 3D models in various areas such as virtual reality and product design. The presence of specular reflection hinders the accurate reconstruction of the model but it is this phenomenon that gives the 3D model a true sense of realism. It is therefore important to have sophisticated volumetric modeling methods that can handle non-Lambertian surfaces.

The image pixel represents the reflection of light incident on a microfacet of the surface. The dichromatic reflection model (Shafer, 1985) describes the surface reflection as the sum of diffuse and specular reflections. The diffuse reflection is characterized by subsurface scattering and represents the shape of surface. The specular reflection occurs at the air/material interface and is only observed at some locations on the surface. We propose to model the non-Lambertian surface in our multi-view volumetric modeling framework.

Figure 4 shows the relationship between incident light, specular reflection, and camera viewpoints. The surface reflection R is modeled as $R = R_d + R_s$, where R_d and R_s are the diffuse and specular reflections respectively. R_d is proportional to $cos(\theta_i)$ where θ_i is the angle between the surface normal and the incident light direction. R_s can be decomposed into $R_{sc} + R_{sv}$. R_{sc} depends on surface material properties and θ_i. R_{sv} is modeled as a cosine function $R_{sv} = k \cdot cos(\theta_v - \theta_r)$ where θ_r is the angle between the surface normal and the specular reflection, θ_v is the angle between the surface normal and the viewpoint direction, and k depends on surface material properties. For a surface point illuminated by a fixed light source, R_d and R_{sc} are both constant and is represented as $R_c = R_d + R_{sc}$. Without using the polarizer, we cannot separate R_d and R_{sc}. But we do not need to eliminate R_{sc} as we have already stated that specularity gives the model a true sense of realism. We only need to exploit R_{sv} which varies with the change in viewpoint orientation, and devise volumetric modeling method that can accurately identify the specular surface voxels. Assume that R_i is the color of the surface voxel observed in viewpoint i. R_{i+1} is the color of the same surface voxel observed in adjacent viewpoint $i+1$. These two adjacent viewpoints are separated by an angle $\Delta\theta$. Therefore,

$$R_i = R_c + R_{svi} = R_c + k \cdot \cos(\theta_{vi} - \theta_r) = R_c + k \cdot \cos(\theta)\ , \tag{3}$$

$$R_{i+1} = R_c + k \cdot \cos(\theta - \Delta\theta)\ . \tag{4}$$

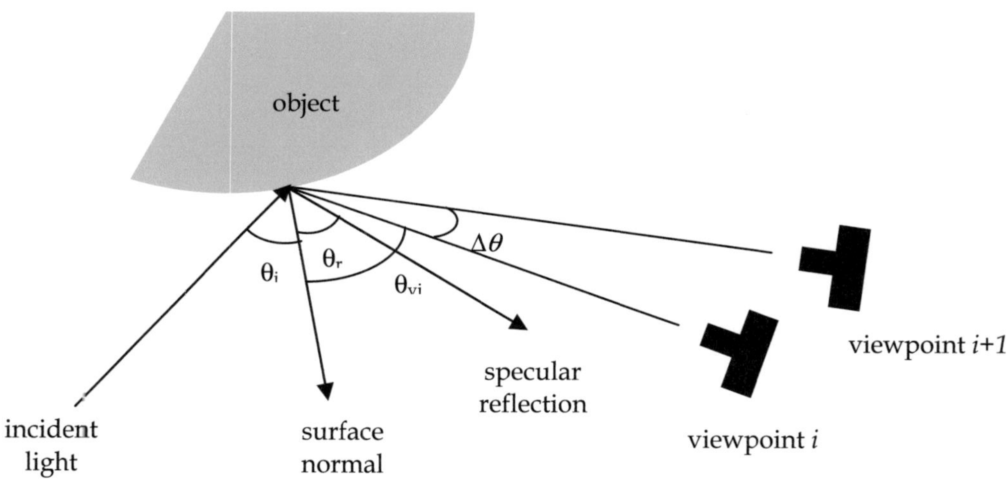

Figure 4. Relationship between incident light, specular reflection and camera viewpoints

If $\Delta\theta$ is small,

$$R_{i+1} = R_c + k\,[\cos(\theta) \cdot \cos(\Delta\theta) + \sin(\theta) \cdot \sin(\Delta\theta)] \cong R_c + k \cdot \cos(\theta) \cdot \cos(\Delta\theta)\ , \tag{5}$$

$$R_{i+1} - R_i = k \cdot \cos(\theta)[\cos(\Delta\theta) - 1] = R_{svi}[\cos(\Delta\theta) - 1]\ . \tag{6}$$

This relation still holds for positive or negative $\Delta\theta$ or θ. To evaluate the similarity in specularity among neighboring voxels, a planar voxel mask is used. A small size voxel mask is good enough to analyze the surface specularity in a local object surface. Voxels in the mask are used to measure the R_{sv} in consecutive images. The generation of a voxel mask for each examining voxel is based on the camera viewpoint. The mask is oriented in three orthogonal directions with respect to the viewpoint as shown in Figure 5. The mask for each examining voxel is generated independently. The structure of mask is invariant in the voxel space. This ensures that the same mask structure is used to evaluate the specularity among the neighboring images. Again, the size of the voxel mask can be reduced when any voxel in the voxel mask (v_{vm}) is not in the visual hull. As the number of voxels in the mask used in the evaluation may be different, the accumulated surface specularity (v.SpecularityDispersion) is averaged by the actual number of comparisons involved. If the examining voxel is a surface voxel, all the specularities measured by the voxel mask are small and similar. The accumulated (normalized) surface specularity is minimum.

When there is sufficient texture information or the object surface exhibits inhomogeneity, the partial surface estimation can easily define the surface voxels. However, if the object contains a large, flat area in homogeneous color, accurate partial surface is difficult to obtain as the true color of that surface is almost the same in neighboring views. Considering the existing of image noise, the voxel with the color or specularity very similar to neighboring voxels may not be a real surface voxel. Based on our observation, the dispersion between the voxel near to the camera along the ray v_{near} and the minimum dispersion is checked. If the difference is smaller than the pre-defined threshold, v_{near} is assigned as the surface voxel. Otherwise, the examining voxel is the surface voxel. This measure ensures the reconstructed volumetric model is conservative rather than carves away true object voxels. The partial surface estimation, denoted as shape from specularity consistency (SFSC), is shown in the following pseudo-code.

For each camera viewpoint i
    $V_{sp}{}^i = \phi$
    For each voxel v in VH
        v.TotalNumOfComparison = 0
        v.SpecularityDispersion = 0
        Form planar voxel mask for v
        For each voxel v_{vm} in voxel mask
            v.SpecularityDispersion += R_{svi}
            v.TotalNumOfComparison += 1
        End For
        v.SpecularityDispersion = v.SpecularityDispersion / v.TotalNumOfComparison
    End For
    For each voxel v in VH
        If v.SpecularityDispersion = $\text{MIN}_{V_r{}^i}$ (v.SpecularityDispersion)
            If v_{near}.SpecularityDispersion – v.SpecularityDispersion $\leq$ Threshold
            Then $V_{sp}{}^i = V_{sp}{}^i \cup v_{near}$
            Else $V_{sp}{}^i = V_{sp}{}^i \cup v$
            End If
        End If
    End For
End For

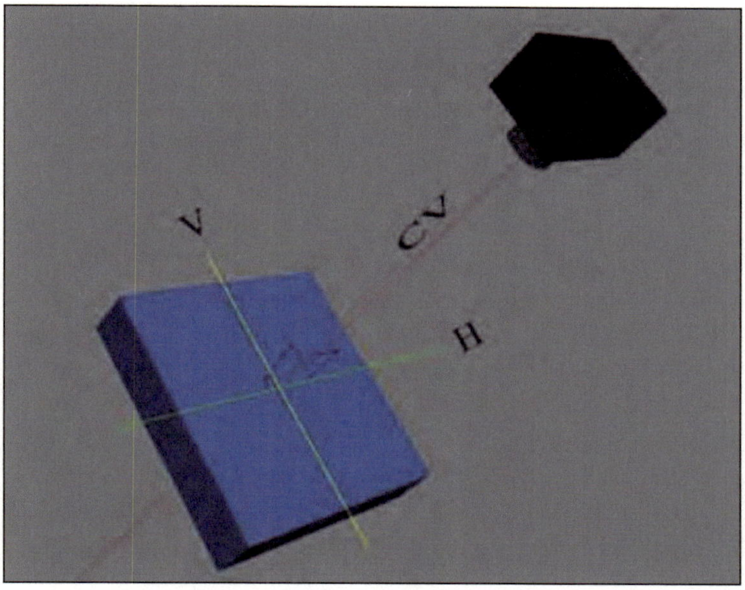

Figure 5. Planar voxel mask and its orientation – V: vertical axis, H: horizontal axis, CV: camera viewpoint axis

3. Result

Three objects (tiger, flower, square rubber) have been used to test our first volumetric model reconstruction algorithm SFSPC. The images are captured by a consumer-type digital camera at the resolution of 1024 × 768 pixel. The program is run on a 1.2GHz PC with Microsoft Windows 2000 and 512 MB RAM. 44 images are used to reconstruct the tiger model while models of flower and square rubber use 36 images. The resolution of the voxel space is 256 × 256 × 256 for all models. For the generation of partial surfaces, the number of consecutive views is set to be five (2 preceding views, the current view and 2 successive views). Figure 6 shows image views of the objects (top row), the corresponding partial surfaces (middle row), and partial surfaces at another view (bottom row). Figure 7 shows the volumetric models of the three objects. The voting-based SFS takes from 5 minutes to 12 minutes. The partial surface estimation plus total model generation takes from 32 minutes to 129 minutes

The square rubber is used to test the robustness of the SFSPC algorithm. Comparison is made between SFSPC and shape from silhouette/stereo (SFS^2) (Matsumoto et al., 1999). We select SFS^2 as the reference because SFSPC follows the concept of SFS^2 while we enhance the shape from photo-consistency step by the use of 3D voxel mask. Also, SFS^2 has demonstrated a better shape reconstruction than various existing techniques. The square rubber is used as it exhibits convex, flat, as well as deeply concave surfaces. The number of consecutive images is set to be five and the threshold for total model generation is 0.85. Different views of the reconstructed model are shown in Figure 8. It can be seen that SFSPC always generates a better volumetric model than SFS^2. Figure 9 shows several rendered views of texture mapped models at arbitrary viewing positions.

Figure 6. Image views and partial surfaces of three test objects reconstructed using SFSPC

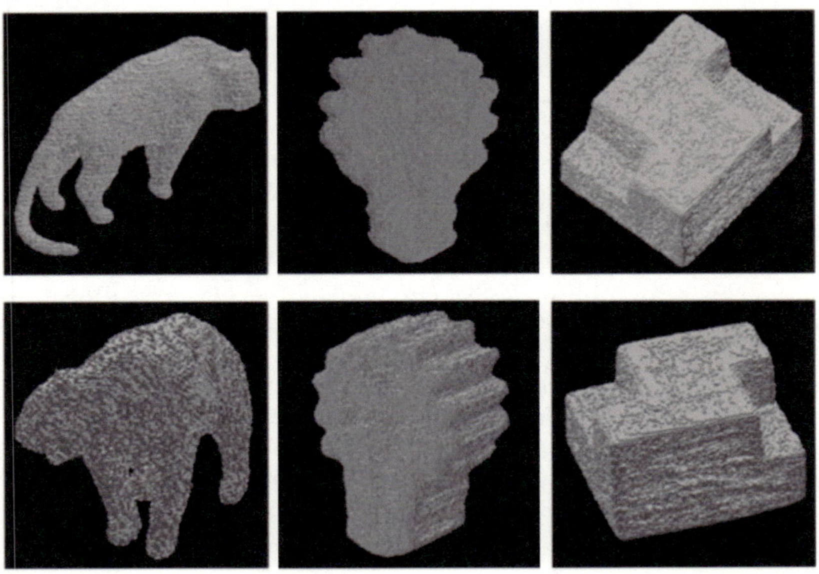

(a) Tiger (b) Flower (c) Square rubber

Figure 7. Different views of volumetric models of three test objects

SFS² SFSPC

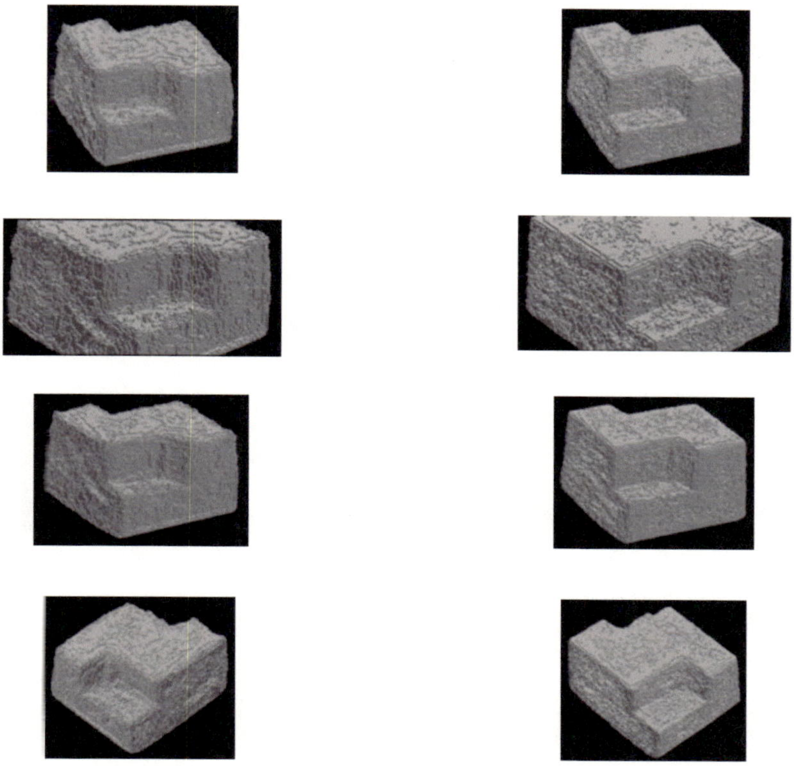

Figure 8. Comparison of SFS² and SFSPC

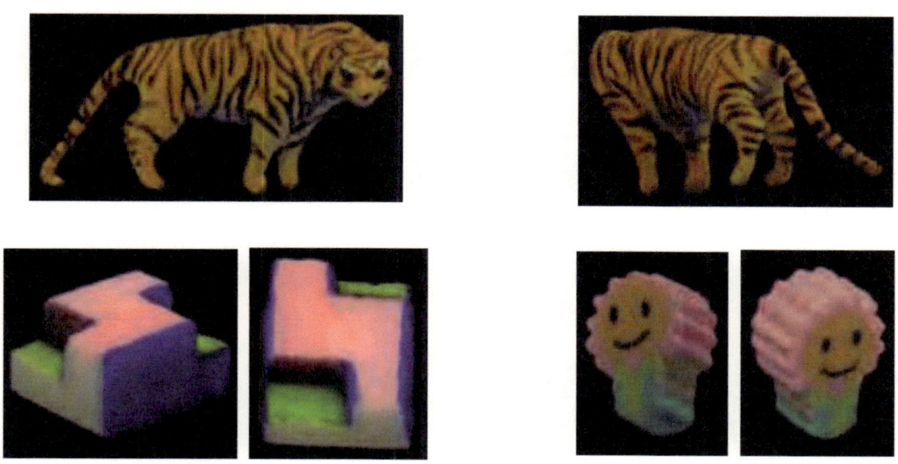

Figure 9. Synthetic views of texture mapped models of tiger, flower and square rubber

Next, we test our second volumetric model reconstruction algorithm SFSC using three plastic head objects and two ceramic teapots. The objects exhibit variety in topology (there is a hole in teapot handle) and also different degrees of concavity. They all exhibit moderately specular reflection. Each image sequence is captured by a consumer-type digital camera with a 2,048 x 1,536 CCD sensor. The target object and the calibration box are placed on a computer controlled turntable in front of the stationary camera. With neighboring views separated by 10 degrees, each image sequence contains 36 images. Photographs of the head objects and teapots are shown in Figure 10. The 3D model reconstruction system is run on an ACPI Multiprocessor x64-based PC with two Intel Xeon CPUs running at 3.6 GHz and 2 GB RAM. Each volumetric model is reconstructed in a volume space of 128 x 128 x 128.

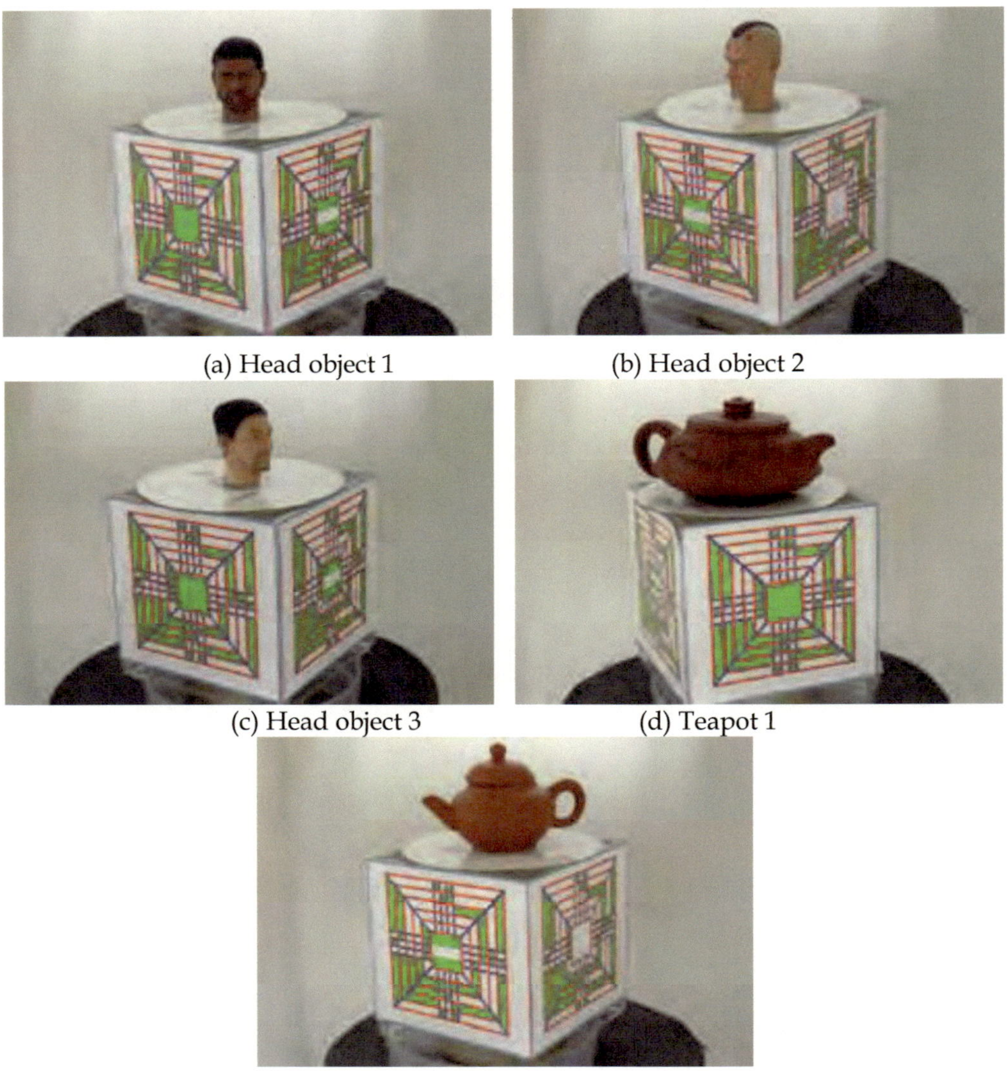

(a) Head object 1 (b) Head object 2

(c) Head object 3 (d) Teapot 1

(e) Teapot 2

Figure 10. Photographs of the head objects and teapots

We also implement the well-known Space Carving algorithm (Kutulakos & Seitz, 2000) for comparison purpose. The volume space (128 x 128 x 128) is carved in four directions, with a group of 9 views allocated for each carving direction. Variance of pure color region is estimated in the background of the scene. Figure 11 shows the reconstructed models of head object 1. Figure 12 shows the reconstructed models of teapot 2. Figure 13 shows the texture mapped models of the objects which are reconstructed by SFSC.

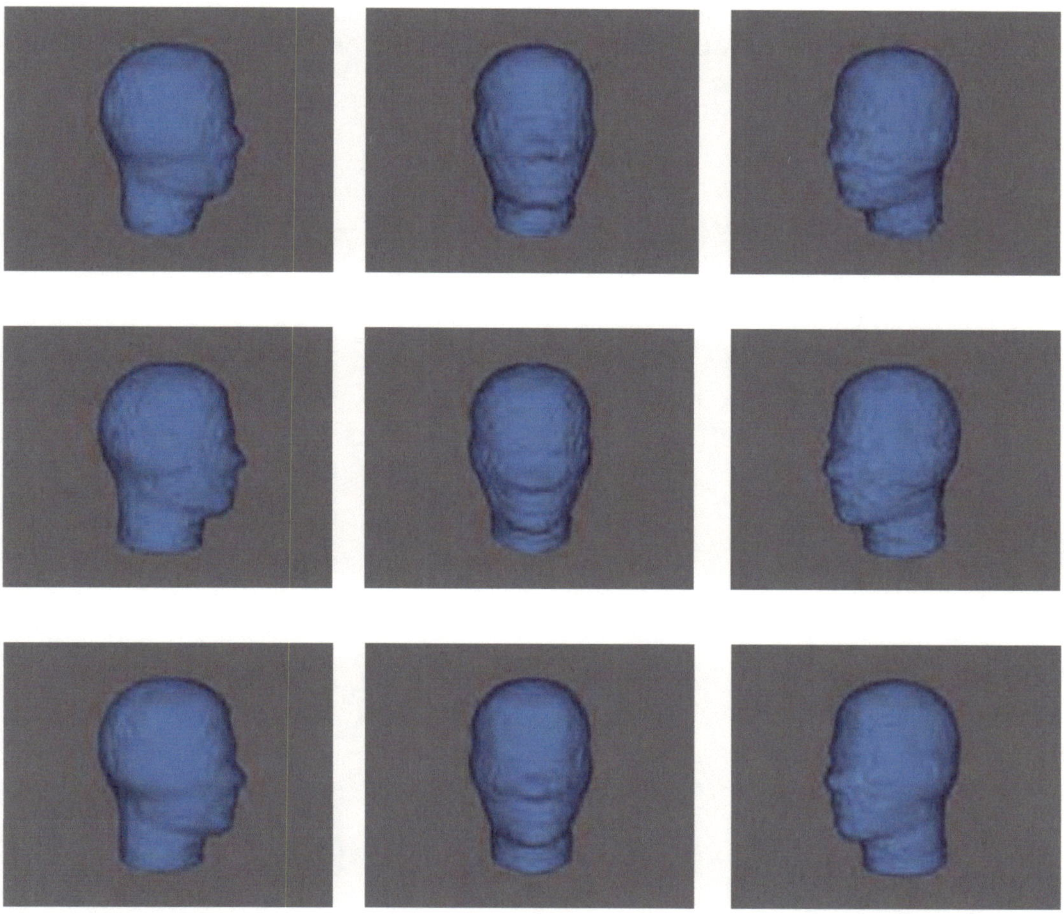

Figure 11. Reconstructed models of head object 1 using: (top row) SFSPC; (middle row) Space Carving Algorithm; (bottom row) SFSC

We also compare the performance of these volumetric model reconstruction methods quantitatively. The reprojection correctness is the ratio of the number of pixels correctly reprojected from the volume space into the object and background regions to the total number of pixels of the acquired image. In principle, this measure only indicates the accuracy of the model silhouette in the acquisition viewpoints. The quality of the reconstructed model in arbitrary viewpoints should better be judged visually than comparing the reprojection accuracy. Ideally, the reprojection correctness should be 100%.

The accuracy is lowered due to erroneous removal of model voxels and non-removal of background voxels in the refinement of the volumetric model. Therefore, the reprojection accuracy values among the three comparing algorithms are very close. Theoretically, the closer the reprojection accuracy to 100%, the better is the volumetric modeling algorithm. Figure 14 shows the reprojection correctness of head object 1. Figure 15 shows the reprojection correctness of teapot 2. For head object 1, SFSC achieves higher reprojection correctness than the Space Carving Algorithm in all image views, while the average reprojection correctness is comparably with SFSPC. For teapot 2, SFSC scores higher reprojection correctness than the Space Carving Algorithm in 34 image views, while the average reprojection correctness is slightly lower than SFSPC.

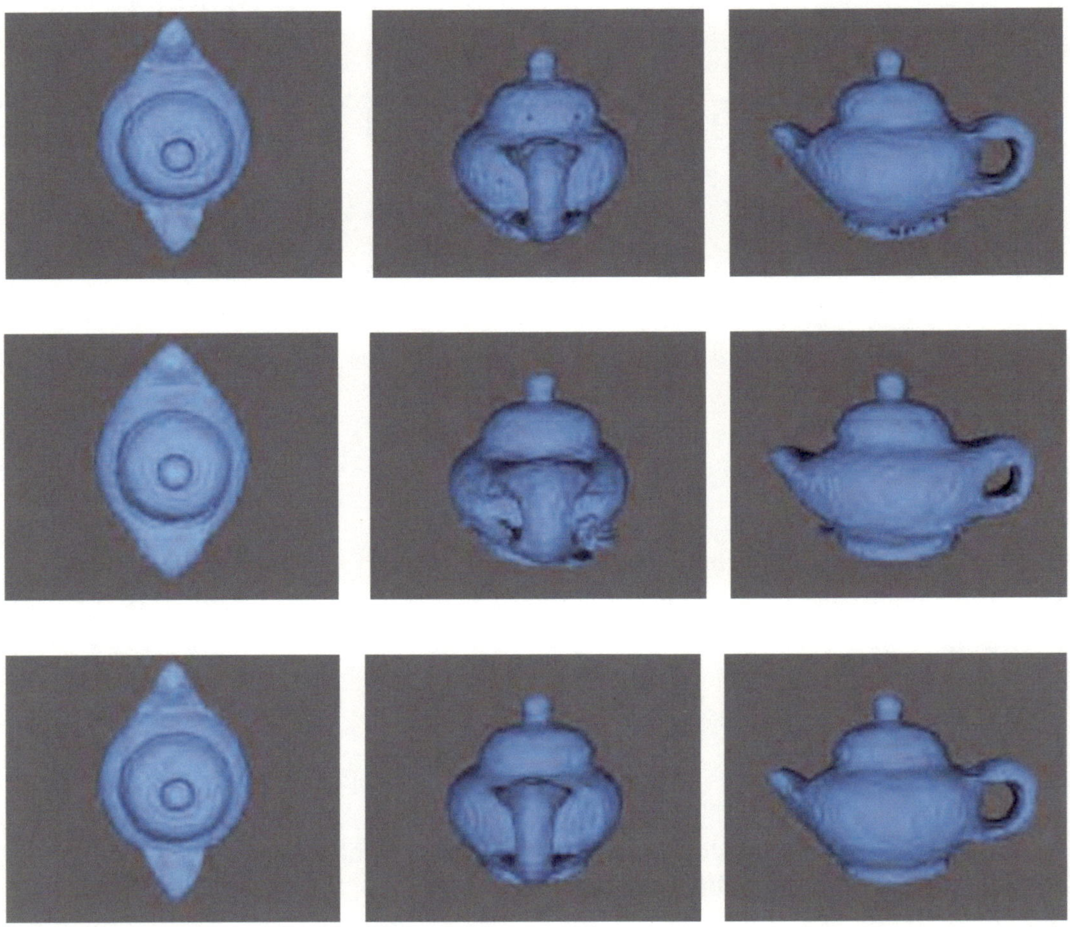

Figure 12. Reconstructed models of teapot 2 using: (top row) SFSPC; (middle row) Space Carving Algorithm; (bottom row) SFSC

4. Discussion

SFSPC works well to model objects with more color inhomogeneity or sufficient texture information. It can quite accurately carve the concave regions. However, if the object contains a large, flat area in homogeneous color, partial surface estimation may not truly identify the real surface voxels. Besides, the computational time is still a problem. The higher the resolution is set, the more accurate and finer reconstructed model is generated. However, as the number of voxels in the volumetric model increases, more computation is needed to process the entire model. As for SFSPC, most of the time is spent on the partial surface estimation process. The computational time is directly proportional to the number of remaining voxels after the voting-based SFS. It is the trade-off between the computational time and quality of the model. Methods based on color-consistency evaluation depend on the quality and consistency of the input images, which are in turn sensitive to the lighting condition in the image capturing environment. This factor also affects SFSPC. It is the reason why the Lambertian reflectance model is assumed during the generation of the volumetric model. However, this assumption does not always apply in practical situations.

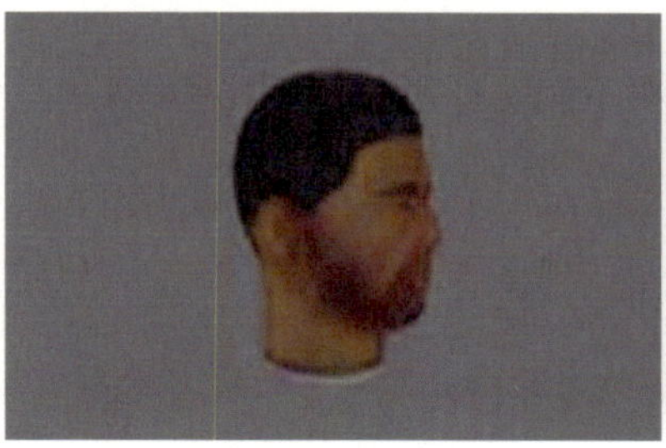

(a) Head object 1

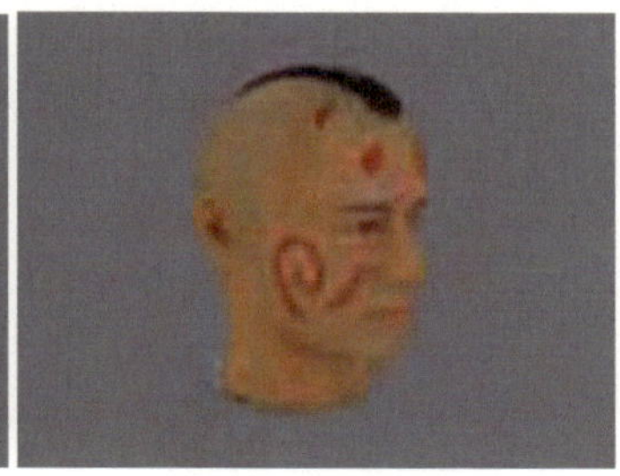

(b) Head object 2

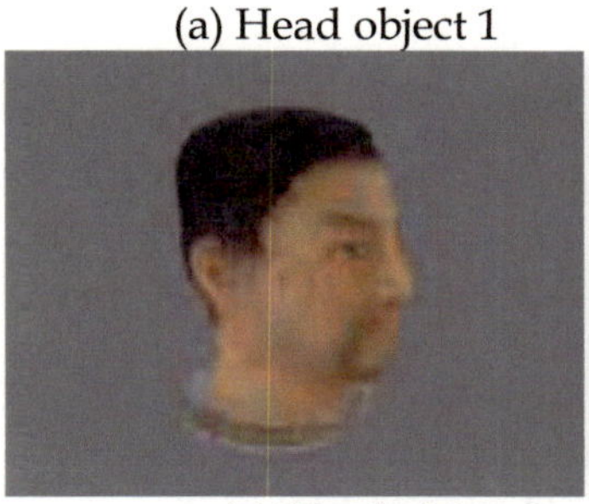

(c) Head object 3

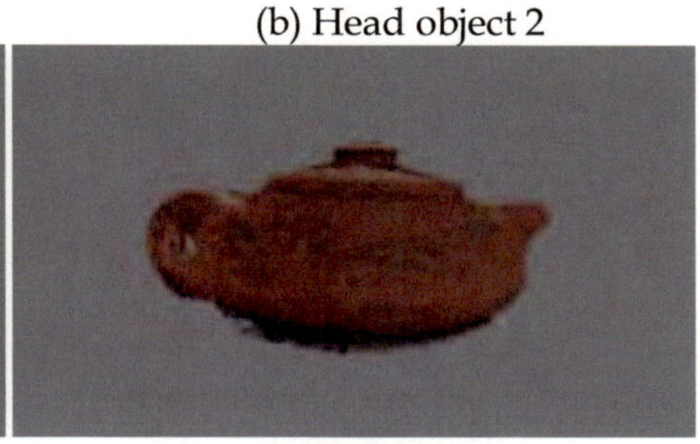

(d) Teapot 1

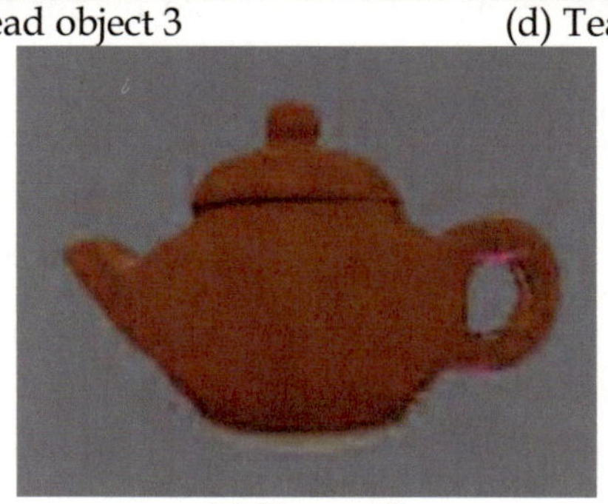

(e) Teapot 2

Figure 13. Texture mapped models of head objects and teapots

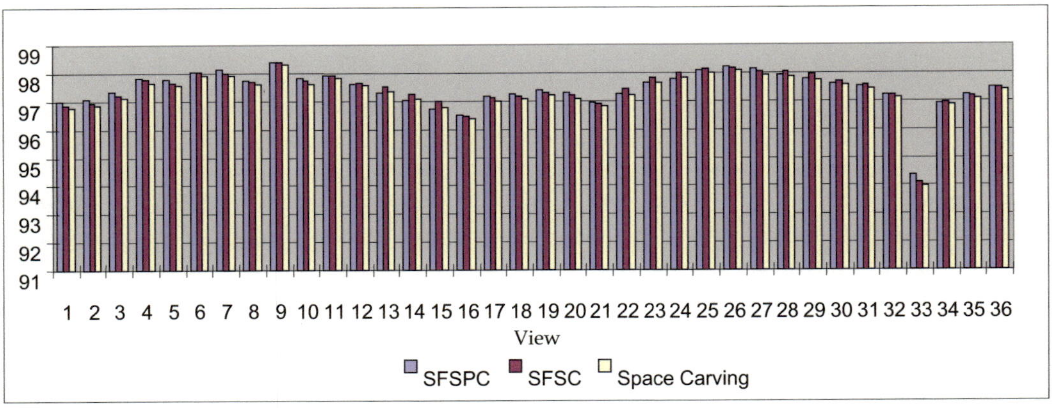

Figure 14. Reprojection correctness of head object 1

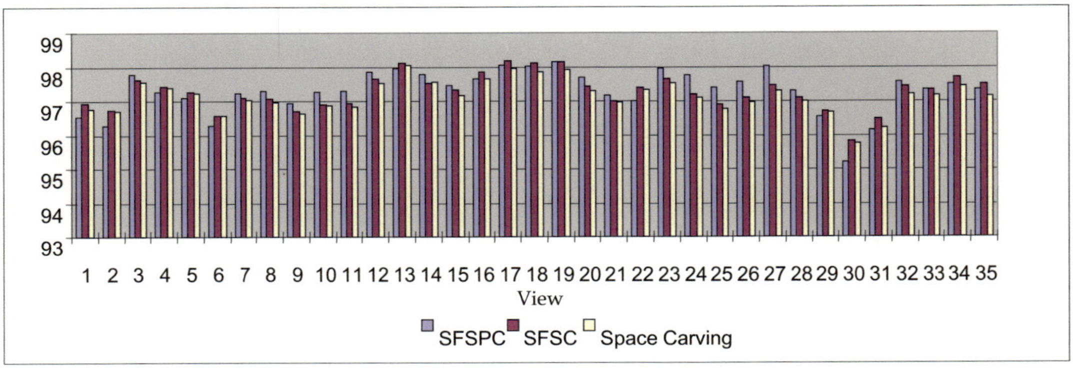

Figure 15. Reprojection correctness of teapot 2

Our second volumetric modeling method SFSC works well on the objects not only with sufficient texture information but also with color homogeneity. Moreover, it can nicely reconstruct the concavity regions. It can be seen that the new algorithm, which explicitly takes into account surface specularity, can produce better results particularly in the reconstruction of frontal face, ears and top of the head object. The SFSPC can erroneously carve away many voxels (see the volumetric model of teapot 2). This is due to the Lambertian surface reflection assumption adopted in this method. The Space Carving Algorithm produces models which are very smooth with insufficient detail structure (see the facial features of head object 1). This is a very conservative method and many background voxels are still preserved in the volumetric model as shown in the volumetric model of teapot 2. Although there is no top view in our image sequence, SFSC can produce more accurate model than the other two methods (see the first column of Figure 12).

5. Conclusion

In summary, we develop a system that can reconstruct the photorealistic 3D object model from a set of photographs. This image-based modeling system can create realistic models without requiring expensive hardware. The volumetric modeling is an important step in the system. We adopt the shape from silhouette approach to obtain the topology of the object. Detail object shape is reconstructed based on the constraint of photo-consistency. Meanwhile, a 3D voxel mask is introduced to check the photo-consistency of voxel, instead of using the conventional pixel-by-pixel block matching technique. However, the problem caused by non-Lambertian object surface is outstanding. To solve this problem, we propose a new algorithm that explicitly measures surface specularity during partial surface estimation. Meanwhile, a planar voxel mask is introduced for checking the consistency of specularities obtained from neighboring voxels in order to confirm the validity of a surface voxel. All these changes can enhance the performance of the volumetric model generation and solve the problem caused by non-Lambertian object surface. Our results show that the new volumetric modeling algorithm can produce better models than the Space Carving Algorithm and the concept of surface specularity is significant in generating high quality object model.

Future research will be focused on further improvement of the quality of the model and the speed of the reconstruction process. New calibration pattern can be designed that can facilitate more accurate camera calibration. The research in volumetric modeling is still an on-going problem. The accuracy of the volumetric modeling also depends on the volume space resolution. However, the computational time is increased with higher volumetric resolution. Future work should be done in optimizing the modeling algorithm.

6. Acknowledgement

The work described was fully supported by a grant from City University of Hong Kong (Project No. 7001857).

7. References

Chang, Y.J. & Chen, Y.C. (2002). Facial model adaptation from a monocular image sequence using a textured polygonal model. *Signal Processing: Image Communication*, Vol. 17, 373-392

Chiang, K.K. & Chan, K.L. (2006). Volumetric model reconstruction from unrestricted camera views based on the photo-consistency of 3D voxel mask. *Machine Vision and Applications*, Vol. 17, No. 4, 229-250

Eisert, P.; Steinbach, E. & Girod, B. (1999). Multi-hypothesis, volumetric reconstruction of 3-D objects from multiple calibrated camera views. *Proceedings of the International Conference on Acoustics, Speech, and Signal Processing*, pp. 3509–3512, ISBN 0-7803-5041-3, Phoenix, USA, March 1999, IEEE

Kutulakos, K.N. & Seitz, S.M. (2000). A theory of shape by space carving. *International Journal of Computer Vision*, Vol. 38, No. 3, 199-218

Laurentini, A. (1994). The visual hull concept for silhouette-based image understanding. *IEEE Transactions on Pattern Analysis and Machine Intelligence*, Vol. 16, No. 2, 150-162

Lorensen, W.E. & Cline, H.E. (1987). Marching cubes: a high resolution 3D surface construction algorithm. *Computer Graphics*, Vol. 21, No. 4, 163-169

Matsumoto, Y.; Fujimura, K. & Kitamura, T. (1999). Shape-from-silhouette/stereo and its application to 3-D digitizer. *Proceedings of the 8th International Conference on Discrete Geometry for Computer Imagery*, pp. 177-188, ISSN 0302-9743, Marne-la-Vallée, France, March 1999, Springer-Verlag

Niem, W. (1999). Automatic reconstruction of 3D object using a mobile camera. *Image and Vision Computing*, Vol. 17, 125-134

Shafer, S. (1985). Using color to separate reflection components. *Color Research and Applications*, Vol. 10, 210-218

Wong, S.S. & Chan, K.L. (2004). Multi-view 3D model reconstruction: exploitation of color homogeneity in voxel mask. *Proceedings of the 3rd International Conference on Image and Graphics*, pp. 142-145, ISBN 0-7695-2244-0, Hong Kong, December 2004, IEEE

8

Collaborative MR Workspace with Shared 3D Vision Based on Stereo Video Transmission

Shengjin Wang , Yaolin Tan , Jun Zhou, Tao Wu, and Wei Lin
Tsinghua University
P.R.China

1. Introduction

Mixed reality (MR) research aims to develop technologies that inputting or mixing the real world objects into computer generated three dimensional (3D) virtual space. The mixed reality, including augmented reality (AR) and augmented virtuality (AV), produces an environment in which the real objects are superimposed on user's view of the virtual environment or the virtual objects are superimposed on user's view of the real environment. Mixed reality has received a great deal of attention as a new method for displaying information or increasing the reality of virtual environments. Many research results have been reported and demonstrated [P. Biermann and B. Jung, 2004 - Shintaro Ono et al., 2005]. Recently, some new assessments have been developed that such new model of virtual systems which are different from traditional form is efficient for exciting user's sense [Yi Cai et al., 1997 - Raphael Grasset, 2005]. However, most of such large-scale assessments still remain at the level of viewing computer graphics (CG)-generated virtual objects. It has revealed that such model of virtual system is no longer functional or fascinate based on virtual reality techniques only. The new, innovative, and mixed reality based approaches are required for operation or exhibition in 21st century. That means the new virtual reality model is focusing on cooperation-centred, real object-based operation. The features of such operation are mainly real or mixed, natural interactive, three dimensional with stereo vision, and collaborative.

Mixed reality environments are defined by Milgram as those in which real world and virtual world objects are presented together on a single display [Milgram P. and Kishino, 1994]. The single user based mixed reality interfaces have been developed for computer aided instruction [S. Feiner et al., 1993], manufacture [Cruz-Neira et al., 1992] and medical visualization [Bajura et al., 1992]. Recently, Seon-Min et al. [Seon-Min et al., 2006] presents a method for merging a live video stream of multiple users into a shared virtual space. These applications have shown that mixed reality interfaces can enable users to interact with the real world in ways never before possible.

Furthermore, the combination of mixed reality and network communication is becoming a more interesting research subject. Although mixed reality techniques have proven enough valuable in single user applications, there has been less research on group collaborative applications. We believe that mixed reality is ideal for collaborative interfaces because it addresses two major issues in three dimensional computer supported collaborative work:

seamlessness and enhancing reality. In this paper we mainly describe a framework of our proposed collaborative system based on stereo vision for a shared mixed reality application and report the development experimental results. This research is sponsored by the national project of demonstrative application of China Next Generation Internet (CNGI2006).

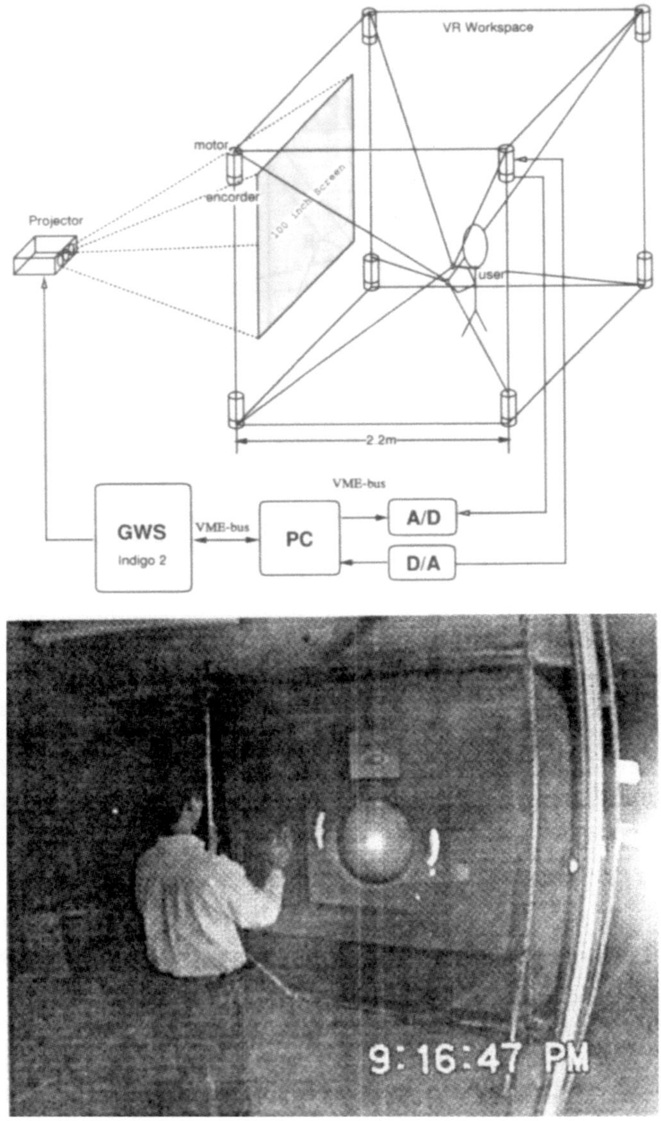

Figure 1. A human-scale direct motion instruction system of virtual reality[Yi Cai et al., 1997]

There are several different approaches for facilitating three dimensional collaborative operations. The most obvious is adding collaborative capability to existing screen-based three dimensional packages. The CAVE Automatic Virtual Environment (CAVE™) -like systems [Cruz-Neira et al., 1992] allow a number of users to view stereoscopic three dimensional images by wearing LCD-shutter glasses. These images are projected on multiple large screen projection walls in the case of the CAVE™. Li-Shu [Li-Shu et al., 1994] developed a workstation based collaborative computer-aided design (CAD) package but users found it difficult to visualize the different viewpoints of the collaborators making communication difficult. Alternative ways include using large parabolic stereo projection screens or holographic optical systems to project a three dimensional virtual image into space. We had developed a human-scale direct motion instruction system for education and training shown in Fig.1 [Yi Cai et al., 1997]. However the system mainly emphasizes the haptic senses by way of virtual objects. Unfortunately in these cases there is still no suitable interface way for multi-users to communicate their view intension each other in three dimensional environment.

Multi-user immersive virtual environments provide an extremely natural medium for three dimensional system. In this case computers provide the same type of collaborative information that people have in face-to-face interactions, such as communication by object manipulation and gesture [Wexelblat, 1993]. Work on the DIVE project [Carlson et al., 1993], GreenSpace [Ishii H. and Miyake, 1991] and other fully immersive multi-participant virtual environments has shown that collaborative work is indeed intuitive in such surroundings. Gesture, voice and graphical information can all be communicated seamlessly between the users.

The mixed reality can superimpose real world objects into the virtual world. This allows the creation of mixed reality that combines the advantages of both virtual environment and seamless cooperation. Information overlay may be used by remote collaborators to annotate the user's view, or may enhance face-to-face conversation by producing shared interactive object models. In this way mixed reality techniques can be used to enhance communication regardless of proximity. There are few examples of multi-user mixed reality systems. Amselen [Amselen, 1995] and Rekimoto [Rekimoto and J. Transvision, 1996] have explored the use of tracked hand held LCD displays in a multi-user environment. Klaus et. al. [Klaus et al., 1995] also use video compositing techniques to superimpose virtual image over a real world view. Ogi et al. [Ogi et al., 2003] take the basis of segmentation by stereo cameras to a further step and generate video avatars. S. Wuemlin et al. generate a 3D video of a user in virtual world [S. Wuemlin et al., 2004]. Vorozcovs et al. present an optical tracking approach for a spatially immersive display [Vorozcovs et al., 2005].

Our collaborative operation system presents a framework to use stereo video and 3D CG model with combination form for showing and indicating a real world object in a shared collaborative virtual workspace. These types of MR interfaces allow multiple users in the different location to see a shared stereo vision simultaneously. This approach is most closely related to that of image-based rendering and efficiently to allow users to collaboratively view and discuss the real world arts and products in stereoscopic types.

The purpose of this research is to develop a platform for group user cooperation with stereo video and shared three dimensional vision. This paper presents a novel framework of collaborative MR workspace with shared three dimensional vision based on stereo video transmission. Our approach combines techniques of stereo video capturing, image/CG fusion and combination, and data transmission for shared stereo vision.

The remainder of this paper is organized as follows. Section 2 introduces the distributed virtual environment. Section 3 discusses the framework of the proposed collaborative operation system. Section 4 describes the development of video based stereo vision system.

Collaborative operation in distributed virtual environment is shown in Section 5, and communication of collaborative workspace is drawn in Section 6.

2. Shared Vision of Collaborative Environment

With the development of mixed reality techniques, a group cooperation system for on-line distributed application, instead of an individual user system, becomes more and more eager. That means a world wide workspace environment via IP network needs to be considered. Such applications likes scientific discussion, product design, indoor virtual tourist, and etc.. In virtual reality (VR) system, it is called distributed virtual environment (DVE). Generally, the distributed virtual environments consist of computer graphics, virtual reality, and distributed servers. In such environments, multiple users can do collaborative operations and view shared interactive scenes. Each participant can indicate object and change status in the scene or change viewpoints to walk-through the virtual space. The scenes are transmitted to all of other participants connecting to the distributed system via network and all of other participants can see the object or scenes change in real time. This framework guarantees that all users can see the same scene representation.

For the early stage of research work on distributed virtual environments, the most of researchers focus their efforts on the use of function simulation, of which the almost of the scenes are generated by computer graphics. However, recent years the development of virtual reality and mixed reality requires the researchers to exploit new technologies satisfying many increasing interesting applications, including:

- Scientific discussion. Scientific discussion based on distributed VR/MR system requires a collaborative scientific visualization environments. Such environments can be regarded as physical extensions of the model based discussion space. In such three dimensional virtual spaces, researchers can represent a data-driven model, view an image being captured from a real world object by a desk top camera, or show a dynamic module test to the participants in real time. The researchers can meet in a shared vision of three dimensional scenes and furthermore they can talk and write within such visual space.
- Product design. Recently number of product designs are entrusted to special designing companies. Whether in the stage of CG-based three dimensional model design or in the stage of prototype module fabrication, the product design should be shown to consigners with frequently discussion. For this application we intend to extend the use of DVE to facilitate computer-supported collaborative working (CSCW) space between two separated physical locations.
- Indoor virtual tour. A new application may come to our daily life soon, called indoor virtual tour. Actually the application does not view video at home alone only. It is a group indoor virtual tour which shares a common vision, may be three dimensional vision, among connected physical locations. With the shared vision each viewer can see the same scenes simultaneously and share his knowledge to the touring fancy community. DVE is a logical prototype of indoor virtual tours and can provide a rich framework for advanced touring applications.

- Arts appreciation. Supposing that you and your friends want to appreciate a cultural relic located in British Museum, without going to spot there. A shared vision of collaborative environment may provide such applications. This means the system has the ability to enable participants to navigate through a cultural relic around and to appreciate it based on video sequences captured by a network video camera. Such shared vision environments hold great promise for a broad range of arts appreciation and so far as to e-commerce applications.
- Demonstration lecture of medical operation. Another interesting application of shared vision is demonstration lecture. Typical one is demonstration lecture of medical operation. A video based, not CG based or image base, scene capture system delivers sequences operation scenes to the physical separated demonstration hall. The participants view and learn from demonstration lecture of medical operation and the teacher can interpreter each operation procedure simultaneously.

The technologies concerned with above applications include, but are certainly not limited to, image/video capturing, CG based modelling for the accurate and realistic real-time representation of scenes, fusion of image and CG modelling, natural user interface, group communications via network for updating the shared consistent scenes by transmitting streamed combination data of CG model, image and audio into the shared vision system.

In order to provide the visual realism for such high demands on the underlying distributed systems and enable DVE to accomplish such applications within highly presence feeling for distributed systems, two essential factors play an important roles in their domain which are listed below.

Vision of real scenes. For shared visual spaces of DVE, especially those used for existed objects, they are often required to provide lifelike scenes not only the CG generated model. The desire for visual realism has driven different visual medias, for example, the use of arts appreciation based on a group still images which are captured from objects or natural landscape around and well arranged in visual spaces is an typical instance. Furthermore, the scenes generated from CG based model have already no any fascination for those of real arts appreciators and the pioneered information techniques should take up the mission for exploiting a novel medium in the shared space. To realize such DVE system, several of the media data need to be applied to three dimensional visions, including image, video, audio, and CG models, in any scene updates. Thus, the lifelike scenes of vision can be obtained. Especially, in this occasion, the effects of data fusion on illumination, position, and scaling principally determine the scene presence.

Real time communications. To support a group of users simultaneously with large shared scenes, audio, and operating commands in DVE causes a heavy load of data transmission. Therefore two main problems cannot be neglected, real time response (no delay) and media data synchronism, since either of them may obviously affect the specific of the shared vision systems. To guarantee the update of multiple viewers of a particular scene at the right moment, for example the operation happened or object moved, requires that such updates should be propagated quickly. However, the scene changes from any one viewer side usually cause quantity data updates that are sent to the network for data transmission. Several techniques are used to minimize the transmission amount, including the use of media data combinations, image/video compressions, operation detection, and simplex data transmissions in particular updates to reduce actual information traffic. An efficient approach to reduce the traffic is to partition updates to related objects or users of a scene in general group communications, despite of P2P or multicast types.

3. System Framework

In this section, we will briefly describe our system framework, device setup for stereo video, and shared collaborative MR environment. The main process in our system is also explained here, including stereo video capture, operation detection, image/CG model combination, and media transmission for stereo video streams of group users.

3.1 Stereo Video and Shared Mixed Reality Cooperation

Recent developed VR and MR system do provide an alternative medium that allows people to share the same object in communication space. However, most of these system are within CG model based workspace. When people talk to one another on discussing an object, the object is usually the CG-generated model, shape-like but no sense of reality, and with insipid texture status, let alone the complex CG modeling of the object. Actually, people do likely appreciate real world arts and products, as well as CG models in a shared common three dimensional environments even by applying a commentator instructions. To construct a real scene vision system, the scenes of real world and real world objects need to be obtained by image/video capture devices and inputted into the virtual environment.

As mentioned above, our research is the part of the project of exemplary application of China Next Generation Internet (CNGI). This research project is aiming at a shared collaborative environment based on high performance video transmission for the increasing demands on developed VR and MR application, including man-machine interfaces, IP network communication, real world stereo vision, and collaborative operation.

To achieve the goal of developing a platform for stereo vision of real scenes, it needs to develop a stereo video capture deveice with two cameras. The device can capture image sequences in dual video channels. For doing fusion of images and CG models, it needs to generate an assigned CG model and further more to determine the corresponding position within right and left images; then using compression algrithm to form video streams again for network transmission. Also, each user's operation in the connected group should be detected for scenes updates. Finally, in the physical receiver side of the DVE system, decompression process is applied and a stereo display device is used for stereo vision which is active and real based on video streams. The parts above are the principal descriptions of our DVE concepts, which focuses on stereo video-based collaborative environment.

In our system there are several subjects need to be solved. Firstly, stereo video based vision system needs to be developed, including stereo video cameras (see Fig. 5) and left and right channel image sequences processing, media fusion, data compressing, and stereo video display. Secondly, operation interface with model based vision indicator is required for collaborative workspace. Thirdly, a key subject, media data transmission via network either for IPv4 or IPv6 environment needs to be established. For each part we will explain detail in the following.

3.2 System Structure

Now we briefly describe the structure of the system. Though in this paper we focus on a P2P application platform it is easily to extend it to server-client type. Figure 2 shows the flow diagram of our video based collaborative operation system. The system mainly consists of four functional modules which can be described as side of user A (as teacher), side of user B (as student), dotted line block 1, and dotted line block 2 in Fig. 2. Actually, the fact that we regard as user A as a teacher and user B as a student is just for system flow explaining and they certainly can exchange their status freely in the system. In this P2P collaborative platform user A and user B locate separately in physical location and are connected with IP network. The system may contain more users with user C, user D, and etc. by extension. Here, the side of user A is assigned as a teacher side, in where the real object is captured, an indicator is operated, and the combined image/CG sequences are transmitted to the side of user B. User B is assigned as a student who can see stereo video scenes of the interested object and the generated indicator which tracks the surface of the real object.

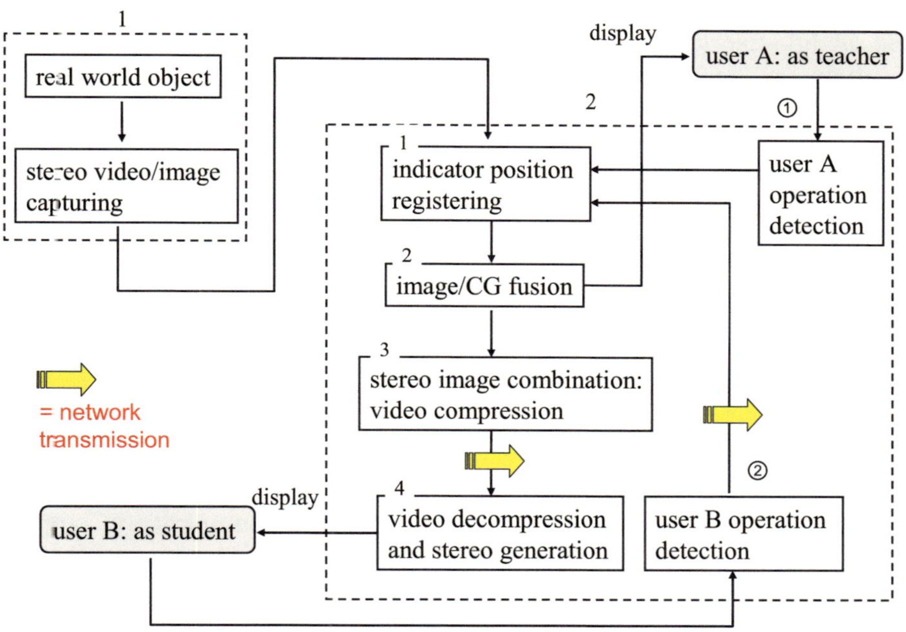

Figure 2. Flow diagram of MR based collaborative operation system

Meanwhile, user B can also operate the indicator which is already displayed within the scenes. The system limits that only one operation is permitted at the same moment, either user A or user B. That means when user A operates the indicator the operation of user B is locked and contrariwise, user A side is the same status when user B do operation since these two possess identity status. This guarantees the identical vision of the system. Here, in side of user B, the system does not transmit video streams to side of user A, in where the side of user B is just a receiver for visual media. In side of user B, the system only transmits audio and operation information to side of user A. This mechanism can reduce the transmission complexity of the collaborative operation system. The procedure of scene updates according to the operation of user B will be illustrated in the following description.

The dotted line frame 1 in Fig. 2 describes the module of stereo video/image capturing. The output of the module block is stereo video sequences of real object or real world scene.

Moreover the capture device consists of two cameras for capturing two channel image sequences which is shown in Fig. 5. Figure 3 is the structures of two channel image capture and process diagram in outgoing system. The central processing module is based on DirectShow® framework where handles capturing image sequences in buffer, three dimensional indicator model generation, indicator position registration, and stereo video stream combination. The corresponding outputs of the central processing module are then delivered to stereo display and network transmission modules.

The dotted line frame 2 in Fig. 2 describes the main function of the video based collaborative environment. In order to reduce the complexity of computation in this paper only indicator model is used and is regarded as a CG model for image/CG model fusion. By that as it may, it is easily to add other CG models if there are demands. The dotted line frame 2 contains the four modules of processing unit, besides user operation detection modules being described below:

The first module (block 1) processes indicator position registration. When two images are read from image buffer captured from two cameras, the right indicator position is determined at once by, for example, user A operation detection which is shown by circle 1 in Fig. 2. The operation detection can be mouse movement distance checking (in this paper) or other natural interface detection by some other special devices. Next, in order to get the left indicator position image registration technique is used to find the suitable matching position in left image.

The second module (block 2) takes image/CG model combination processing. When position of the indicator in left image is found two CG models within right and left two images will be generated, respectively. The process includes generation of right eye indicator CG model and left eye CG model, shading with illumination, and image /CG model fusion of stereo image based on the determined indicator positions. As a result, two image/CG model fusion images are obtained.

The third module (block 3) does stereo image combination and data compression. Since there are two channel images, right and left eye image, two video streams are necessary to be transmitted. This transmission pattern will cause communication complexity and encoding/decoding loads. To simplify system transmission we try to combine two images sequences into one combined image sequence which has the same size in width and double size in height comparing to the original single image. After that, the compression algorithm of mpeg4 is used to execute data compression for the combined image sequences to obtain one video stream. For audio communication mp3 is used for audio compression.

The fourth module (block 4) accomplishes video stream decompression and stereo image generation. By decompressing the video streams received via IP network each combined image, having the same size in width and double size in height of the original one, is obtained sequentially. Followed up with decompression each combined image is then parted into right eye image and left eye image, respectively. Moreover the indicator modelled by CG is simultaneously shown in the vision scenes of user B. Though the description above is based on the operation in side of user A, the procedure is the same when system detects user B operation which is shown by circle 2 in Fig. 2. The difference is only that the sending engine in side of user B will send user B's operation information to the receiving engine in side of user A via network transmission.

The collaborative workspace works via network environment and adapts to IPv4 connections. To establish the system connection between user A and user B the receiving engine in side of user B needs to start up firstly. When receiving engine runs, the side of user B is in waiting call status. When user B's IP address is known by user A, the sending engine in side of user A then calls user B according to the IP address to establish the P2P connection. We stress that though the network connection of the collaborative workspace above adapts IPv4 environment it also works within IPv6 protocols, just needs to change the protocol module and setting interface of sending engine.

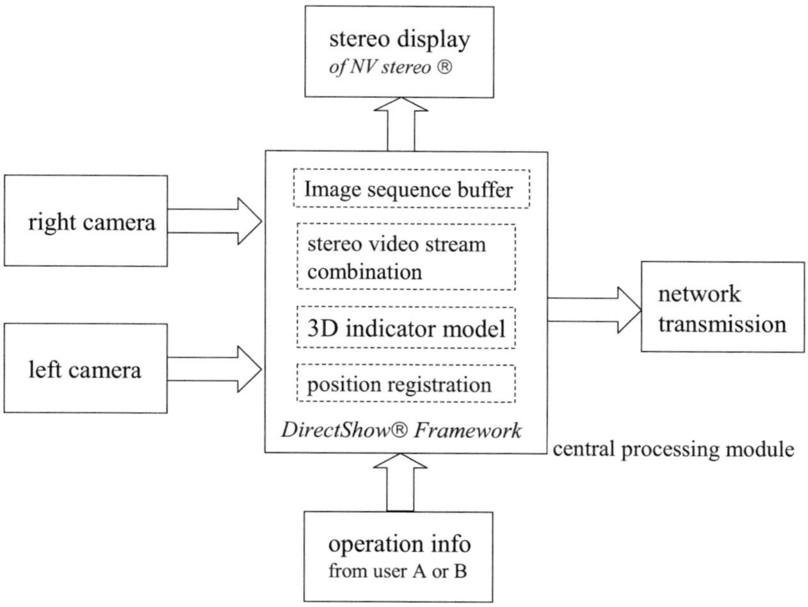

Figure 3. Capture of two channels and process diagram in outgoing system

4. Video Based Stereo Vision

Since the collaborative operation system is a stereo video based MR system we need to develop a video based stereo vision framework, including stereo video capture device, stereo video stream transmission, and stereo video display installation, which enable users view stereo scenes at their separated locations. In this section we mainly describe the component parts of stereo video capture device, stereo video image combination, and stereo video display installation.

4.1 Stereo Video Capture

The sketch of the stereo video capture system is shown in Fig. 4. The stereo video capture device consists of two video cameras, where has 6cm-7cm interval between their optical axises. Figure 5 shows one of our develped stereo camera device. In order to simplify the stereo capture device the usb interface cameras are used in this paper. Each usb camera has high performance in its capture features. It can get 30frame/sec within 640*480 pixels resulution.

The capture process is based on DirectShow® framework shown in Fig. 3. DirectShow® is an important part of DirectX®, which is provided by Microsoft® and is a high performance API to develop graphics, stream media, and audio applications on Windows® platform. The right and left eye images coming from right and left camera of the stereo video device are captured into image buffer sequentially under DirectShow® capture framework. Then the image sequences are delivered to fusion/combination module for the processing of image/CG model fusion, data compression and local side stereo diaplay.

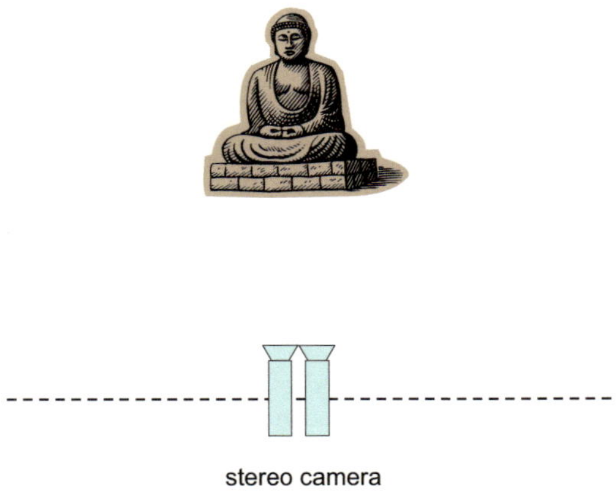

Figure 4. Capture system of video based stereo vision in the collaborative system

Figure 5. The developed stereo camera for capturing image sequences of stereo video

4.2 Display of Stereo Vision

With regard to the stereo display in local side the fused right eye image and left eye image generated respectively by the fusion of image/CG model are directly delivered to 3D stereo display buffer of NV stereo®. Meanwhile, in order to obtain a smooth display for video based stereo vision for far apart side in a DVE system we propose a combination approach to handle the stereo image sequence, named as stereo video stream combination module (see Fig. 2 or Fig. 3). Fig. 6 shows the proposed combination approach, of where image 1 and image 2 is assigned as the fused right eye and left eye image, respectively. To piece the two images, 1 and 2, together in up and down relation a combined image shown in Fig. 6 right side can be obtained. By doing data compression on such image sequence a mpeg4 formatted video streams are generated and then transmitted to the other users via IP network transmission.

In the receiving side of DVE system the video streams received via IP network are decompressed and each combined image, having the same size in width and double size in height of the original one, is obtained sequentially. Then each combined image in the image sequence is then split into the two original image 1 and 2 and afterwards delivered to 3D stereo display buffer of NV stereo®, respectively. Figure 7 shows an example display of stereo vision of the collaborative operation system.

Figure 6. The combination of right and left images and the appearance of combined image

Figure 7. The display of stereo vision with fused (image/CG model) right and left eye images

In our system an active infrared control stereo display device is used for stereo vision in collaborative workspace. The stereo display device consists of an infrared control unit and pairs of liquid crystal eyeglasses, which are shown in Fig. 8. The liquid crystal eyeglasses have an optical shutter, which controls the right and left optical lens opens and closes alternatively in an appropriate frequency. Usually the optical shutter frequency is concerned with field frequency of display device. According to human being's visual response in order to avoid the feeling of scintillation, the frequency of each optical shutter should be more than 30Hz. Since the infrared control unit needs to control two optical shutters open and close for right and left eye, the field frequency of display device should at least be more than 60Hz. In our stereo vision system the field frequency of display device is set to 100Hz. By this means when users wear the liquid crystal eyeglasses and view screen in front of display device the fascinating stereo scenes then really come to their eyes.

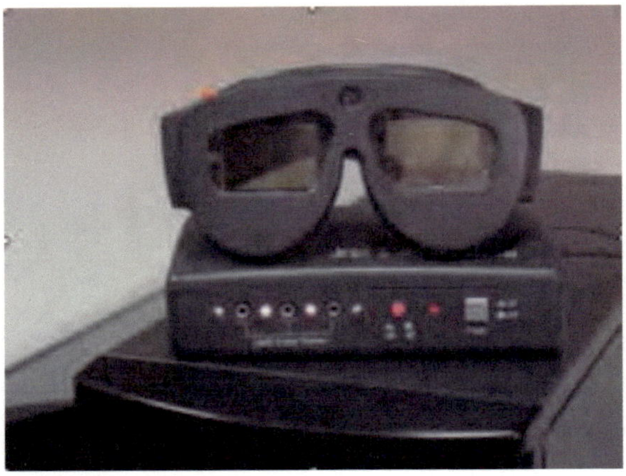

Figure 8. An active infrared control stereo display device and a pair of liquid crystal eyeglasses

5. Collaborative Operation of DVE

As mentioned above in this paper, to be an example of fusion application, a 3D indicator is regarded as a 3D CG model for accomplishing the fusion of image and CG model. The other CG models, if it is necessary, can be easily generated and fused in the same way. In this section, we mainly describe the capture of 3D indicator motion, indicator generation and image/CG model fusion, and collaborative operation control.

5.1 Capture of 3D Indicator Motion

The operation interface of our collaborative operation system provides co-located users to interact with shared virtual space while viewing the video based inputted real world objects simultaneously. There are two proposals being presented for collaborative operation in DVE system, complex one with natural interface and smiple one with mouse operation. Though both of the two methods will be mentioned in the following, in order to reduce the sytem complexity and costs the mouse operation method is employed in our collaborative operation sysetm. Therefor, when people construct such collaborative operation system they can select ones between these two interface methods acording to their purpose, space, and research outlay.

A natural interface framework, within camera based detection and tracking of indicator in three dimensional space, is shown in Fig. 9. The configuration of the prototype of natural indicating interface consists of two video based detecting cameras for indicator position detection. The upper camera in Fig. 9 detects the movement of the indicator in a height-based horizontal plane and the front-upper camera detects the shifts information in height for indicator operation, respectively. Using the two detecting cameras, the position of indicator in three dimensional space can be obtained. The indicator being used can be a lightened spot device or a specially colour markered marker and user uses it to indicate the position on the video based stereo object. If there needs to detect user's viewpoint for follow-up scene changing, we prefer to employ an approach of human face detection and tracking rather than body detection and tracking. Both of face detection and body detection have ripe and efficient algorithms developed in motion capture resreach field which can be employed for natural man-machine interface of such collaborative operation systems.

As illustrated above for simplifying the scale of the collaborative operation system a 2D mouse operation style is used in our operation interface. Since the optical axises of the stereo cameras are generally set to pass through the shape center of a real world object, the relations of 3D indicator movement and mouse operation can be assigned as follows for simulation of 3D movement:

- mouse movement in desk plane simulates in a height-based horizontal plane movement of the indicator in three dimensional space.
- The size of indicator scales smaller and larger corresponding to the movement of going in and out in the horizontal plane.
- The movement of mouse contact roller controls up and down movement of the indicator in height in three dimensional space.
- The indicator maintains the size of its shape when user operates mouse contact roller alone.

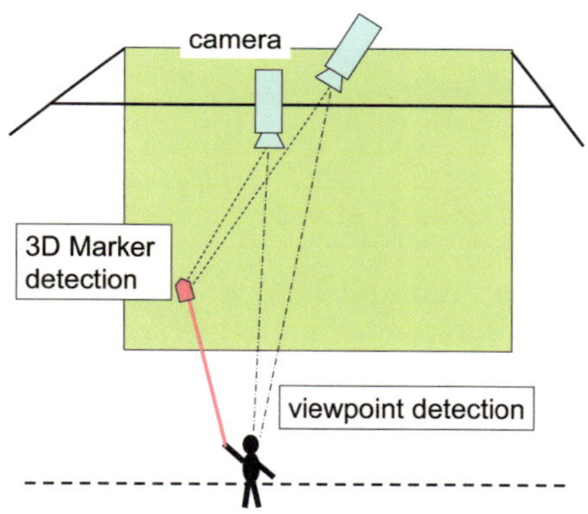

Figure 9. Camera based detection and tracking of indicator in three dimensional space

5.2 Indicator Generation and Image/CG model Fusion

The 3D indicator is employed to indicate a 3D virtual object in three dimensional space. The way of 3D indicator generation is to overlay 2D geometric figures of indicator into right and left eye images, respectively. There is a certain interval between the two geometric figures of indicator, of where the interval is the same as the displacement of 3D object in right and left eye images in screen. More exactly to say the displacement of the 3D object is the distance between the same point on the object surface in right and left eye images. This guarantees an effect that the 3D indicator adjoins closely to the surface of the 3D object. In order to obtain a ideal visual effect the 3D indicator is better to be a solid geometry possessing volume sense and shading effect.

Being with a part of collaborative operation system we adopt the method of addition class and DLL to realize 3D indicator, in which C3DCursor class realizes the modelling and rendering and a Match.DLL we developed realizes the registration (sometimes being regarded as matching) of the corresponding point (actually a block area) in right and left eye images. Using block area to execute the registration rather than a point is for avoiding noise disturbing. Moreover, in order to update the registration algorithm easily a DLL driven type is used in our program. There are two registration algorithm we suggest which are shown in formula (1) and (2), one is based on block histogram and another is based on block vector of grey values.

For formula (1) [Swain M and Ballard D, 1991], the colour space of each [0, 255] are quantified into feature colour V=v×v×v. The size of block area is set to level L (L is set to 3) for calculating block histogram , $\boldsymbol{H}=\{H(l, i) \mid l=0, \ldots, L\text{-}1, i=0, \ldots V\text{-}1\}$. Here v is set to 16. Therefore the similarity value of S varies in [0,1], where 1 means the feature of two blocks is total same and 0 means no similar pixel values in the two registration blocks. $\boldsymbol{H}_1$ and $\boldsymbol{H}_2$ indicate the block histogram corresponding to right eye and left eye image, respectively.

$$S = \{\sum_{l=0}^{L-1}\sum_{i=0}^{V-1} \min[\boldsymbol{H}_1(l,i),\ \boldsymbol{H}_2(l,i)]\} / L \quad (1)$$

The normalized correlation function C shown in formula (2) [David A and Jean Ponce, 2002] is vector of grey value based computation, easier than the algorithm above, where d is a shift distance of a block in left eye image, and w and w′ are the vector formed by scanning grey value of the corresponding blocks sequentially in right eye and left eye image, respectively. Moreover $\overline{w}$ and $\overline{w}'$ are their averages.

$$C(d) = \frac{1}{|\boldsymbol{w}-\overline{\boldsymbol{w}}|}\frac{1}{|\boldsymbol{w}'-\overline{\boldsymbol{w}}'|}[(\boldsymbol{w}-\overline{\boldsymbol{w}})\bullet(\boldsymbol{w}'-\overline{\boldsymbol{w}}')] \quad (2)$$

There are several approaches to accomplishing a 3Dindicator modelling and rendering. Though OpenGL® or Direct3D® can easily be used to construct more complex 3D indicator and more real illumination and rendering can be obtained, the construction of modelling system is rather complicated and moreover, as for our experience OpenGL® and Direct3D® may occasionally emerge conflict with some modules in main program and cause an unstable system. For this reason in our system we adopt a way that drawing geometric figure directly by assigning values to an image matrix to generate a 3D indicator. An example of generated 3D indicator model is shown in Fig. 10. Figure 11 shows a rendering 3D indicator and the fusion of image and the rendering indicator CG model in the collaborative operation system.

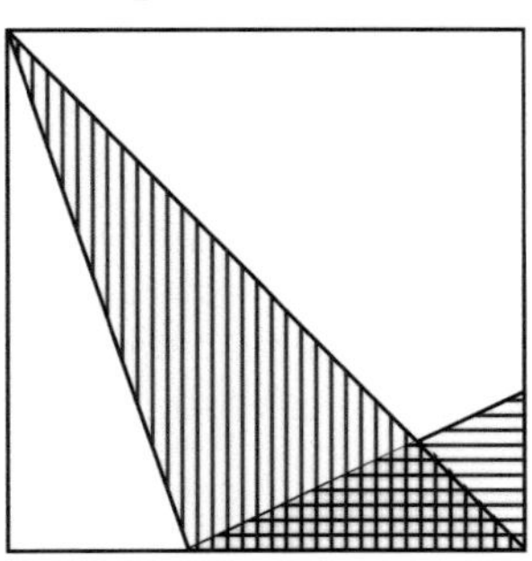

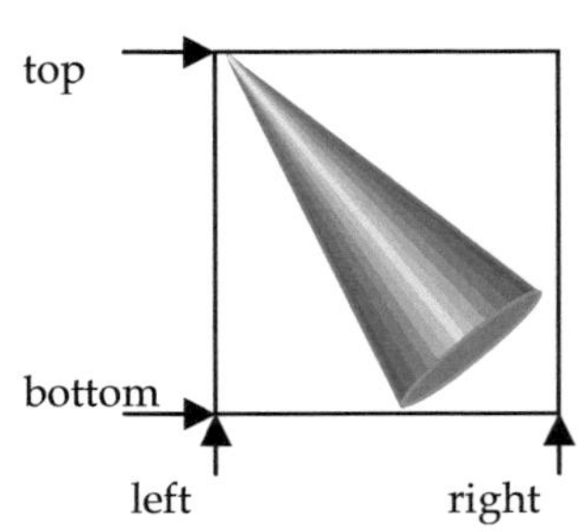

(a) (b)

Figure 10. An example of generated 3D indicator model

After four vertexes of the square in Fig. 10(a) are defined the shape of a circular cone is constructed by following loop statement :

$$\text{shape a}=\{(x,y)\mid bottom<y<top,\ left+top/3-y/3<x<right+bottom-y\},$$
$$\text{shape b}=\{(x,y)\mid bottom<y<top,\ 3*(y-bottom)+left+(right-left)/3<x<right\}, \tag{3}$$

where x and y are coordinates in the square, shape a and shape b are described by vertical line and horizontal line, respectively. Then circular cone can be get from a-b which is shown in Fig. 10(a).

The illumination effect can be simulated by following function of grey values :

$$f(x,y)=255-K*|A| \tag{4}$$

where

$$A=(left+top/3-y/3+right+bottom-y)/2-x \tag{5}$$

controls the variance of grey scale of each row pixels, and

$$K=360.0/(right+bottom-y-left-top/3+y/3) \tag{6}$$

controls the variance of two extremity sizes of circular cone. After assigning the pixel values according to the algorithm above, the circular cone is then possess a stereoscopic visual effect which is shown in Fig. 10(b).

5.3 Collaborative Operation Control on 3D Indicator

For the collaborative operation system the operation control among group users separated in physical location is also a key subject that cannot be ignored. In this paper we adopt two techniques to execute the control of collaborative operation, priority operation and simplex combined image transmission. The priority operation means if one user moves mouse to shift the indicator position the indicator changes in the stereo scenes being caused by operations of other users connected via network are restricted till that user releases the priority by stopping his operation.

Figure 11. The generated indicator and the fusion of image and indicator CG model

The simplex combined image transmission is a mechanism to reduce the system complexity. By employing this mechanism the all mouse move information, despite of user B's or user C's if there is, will be delivered to side of user A. When their sending engines send their operation information to the receiving engine in the side of user A via network transmission the indicator CG model is then generated and set to the corresponding position for the follow-up manipulation of fusion and combination. This mechanism guarantees that an unique CG model generation engine and stereo video streams transmission engine can support system running which greatly cuts down the complexity of the collaborative operation system.

6. Communication of Collaborative Workspace

In order to construct a shared virtual workspace for users separated in real locations the collaborative operation system needs to preserve a real time communications for enjoying in face-to-face meeting, operation, and arts appreciation. All of the connected users can view and indicate the inputted real world objects in such virtual workspace with no bearing time delay. In this collaborative operation system a transmission module based on either IPv4 or IPv6 stereo video has been accomplished for the formed mpeg4 video and mp3 audio streams transmission.

6.1 Data Transmission via IP Network

To interact with shared virtual workspace the system needs to preserve real time communications to enable users separated in real world enjoying in face-to-face liked meetings, leanings, and arts appreciations with inputting real world object into MR based DVE systems. The media data for communication includes human voice, video based stereo sequences, and indicator position. Figure 12 shows the configuration of the collaborative environment with a shared MR workspace via IP network. Based on the applications of the system, the network for communication in this prototype prefers an Internet based distributed network rather than a special-use distributed network. For this purposes all protocols for command and stream media transmission are Internet Protocols with IPv4 and IPv6. We have tested successfully the data transmission in both IPv4 LAN and over three layers of node point with IPv6 environment. The program below shows part of socket communication sour code. The interface of IPv4/v6 network communication in sending side (user A) is shown in Fig. 13 and 14, respectively. Figure 15 is the interface of IPv4/v6 network communication in receiving side (user B). The right figure shows the waiting call status. Noticing that the receiving engine should be starts before sending engine.

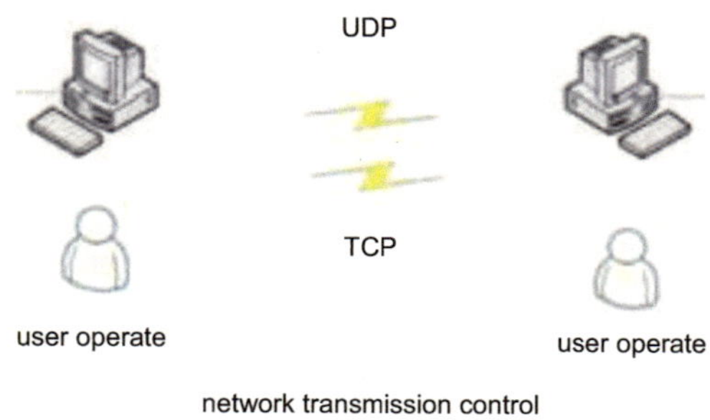

Figure 12. configuration of collaborative environment via IP network

```
mSocket = socket(AF_INET, SOCK_STREAM, IPPROTO_TCP);
if (mSocket != INVALID_SOCKET){
        BOOL sopt = TRUE;
        setsockopt(mSocket, IPPROTO_TCP, TCP_NODELAY,
                (char *)&sopt, sizeof(BOOL));
        setsockopt(mSocket, SOL_SOCKET, SO_DONTLINGER,
                (char *)&sopt, sizeof(BOOL));
        SOCKADDR_IN   saddr;
        memset(&saddr, 0, sizeof(SOCKADDR_IN));
        saddr.sin_addr.S_un.S_addr = htonl(inTargetIP);
        saddr.sin_family        = AF_INET;
        saddr.sin_port          = htons((WORD)inPort);
        if (connect(mSocket, (SOCKADDR *)&saddr, sizeof(SOCKADDR_IN)) != 0) {
                Detach();
                return FALSE;
        }
        mIsConnected = TRUE;
        return TRUE;
}
return FALSE;
```

6.2 Collaborative Workspace Based on Shared Stereo Video

The proposed stereo video based collaborative operation MR system shown in Fig. 16 can be widely used in many applications. Figure 17 and 18 shows the experiment scenes of the system. The video of object scenes are captured into centre computer in side of user A which serves as a server to implement video capturing, video delivering, and operating command exchanging. The computer in both side of user A and B serves the stereo video sequences displaying.

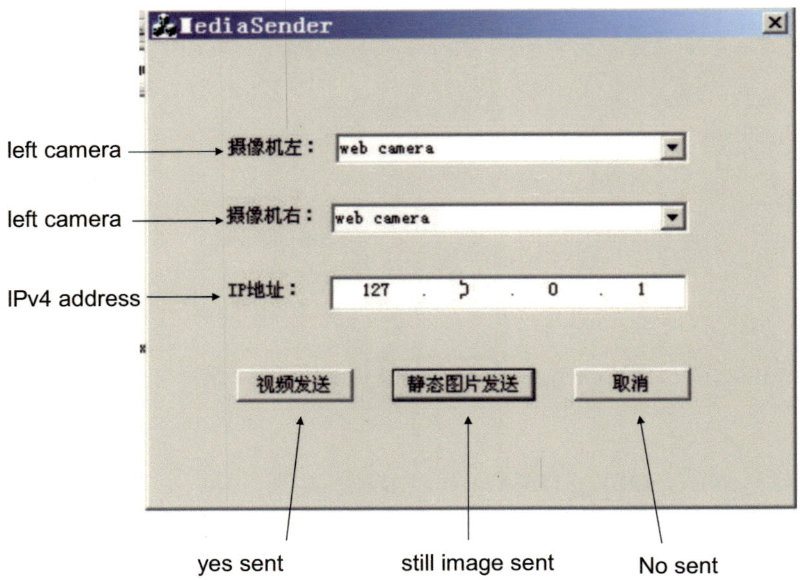

Figure 13. The interface of IPv4 network communication in sending side (user A)

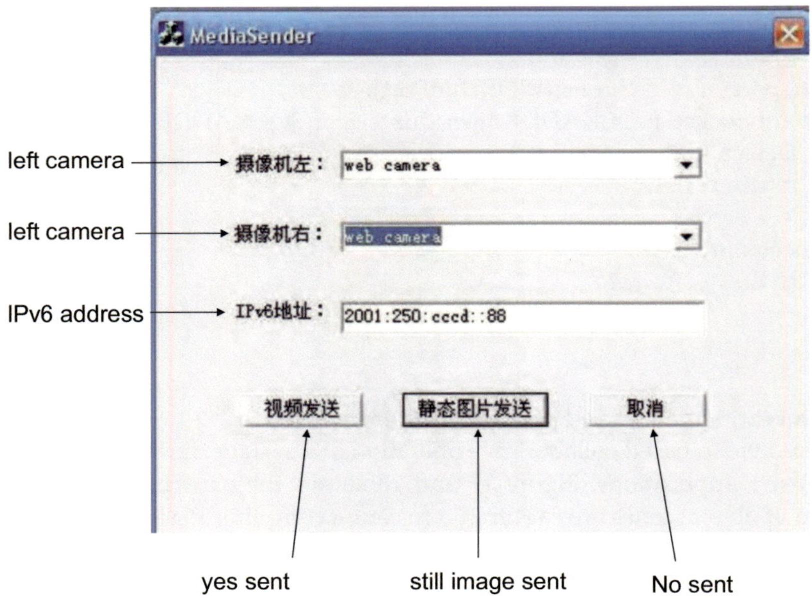

Figure 14. The interface of IPv6 network communication in sending side (user A)

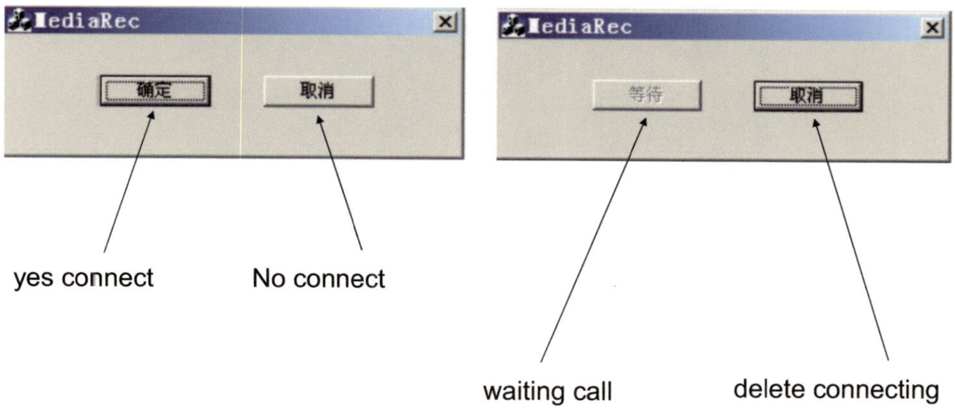

Figure 15. The interface of IPv4/v6 network communication in receiving side (user B). The right figure shows the waiting call status

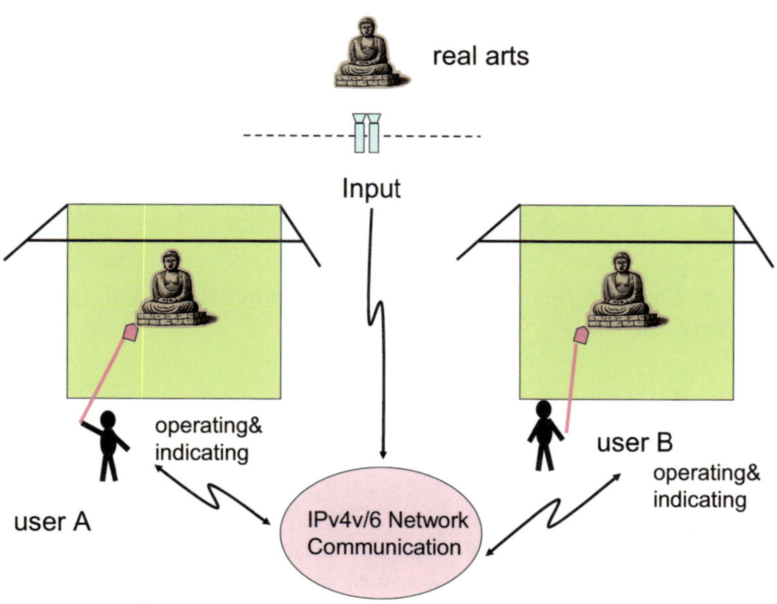

Figure 16. Collaborative operation framework of shared mixed reality via IP network

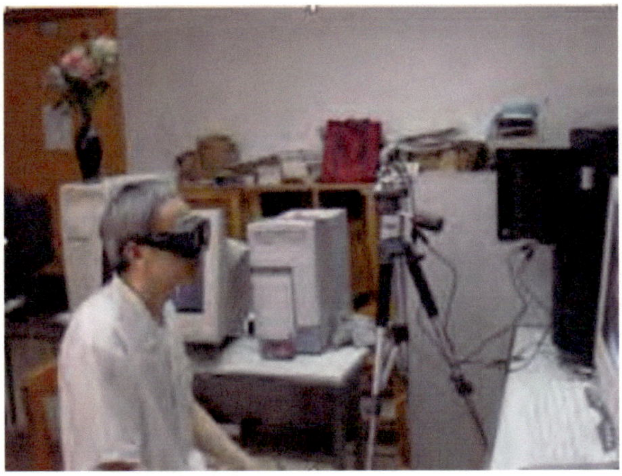

Figure 17. The experiment scene of collaborative operation MR system

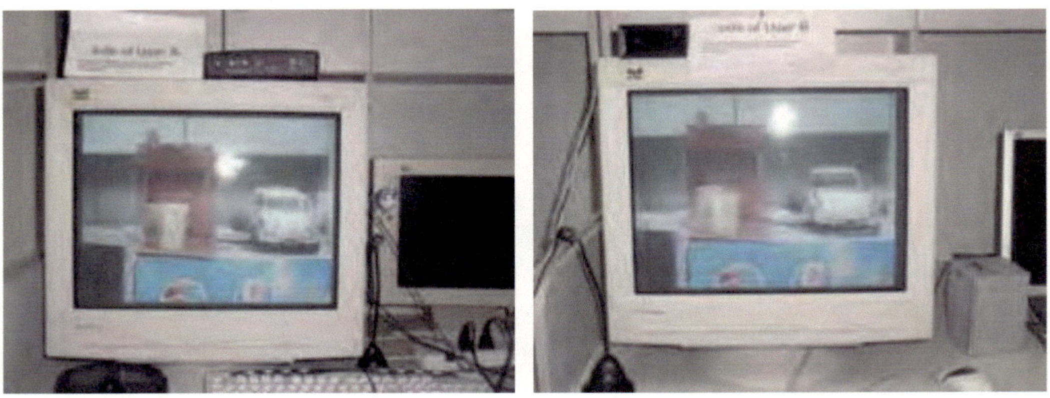

(a) (b)

Figure 18. The experiment scene of collaborative operation MR system. (a) is in side of user A and (b) is in side of user B

7. Conclusion and Future work

We have presented a framework of collaborative MR workspace with shared three dimensional vision based on stereo video transmission, established and experimented for collaborative operation. The system provide a 3D-like operating interface by a CG indicator. Though the system is tested successfully for the data transmission in both IPv4 LAN and over three layers of node point with IPv6 environment there still several tasks need to be accomplished in future work. The one is although we regard a CG indicator as 3D CG models now, for a widely use more 3D CG may need to be added into virtual space and operated in shift, rotate, and spin, as an extended function in future. The second is that

though the size of video frame used in now system is 640*480 pixels we plan to test more larger image, such as high resolution image, in the collaborative operation system both for testing its performance and for more wide use. Moreover in future work the performance evaluation for both operation feeling and time response is also an important task which is should be done. Moreover our future work will try to focus on realizing more desired dreams, including multi-stereo vision construction, natural indicating operation, and viewpoint detection, in addition to the ones mentioned above.
Thanks again for sponsoring this research by the national project of demonstrative application of China Next Generation Internet (CNGI).

8. References

Shintaro Ono, Koichi Ogawara, and et.al. A Photo-Realistic Driving Simulation System for Mixed-Reality Traffic Experiment Space. IEEE Intelligent Vehicles Symposium (IV2005), June 2005

S. Feiner, B. Maclntyre, and D. Seligmann. Knowledge-based Augmented Reality. In Commun. of the ACM, volume 36(7), pages 53–62, 1993

T. Ohshima, K. Satoh, H. Yamamoto, and H. Tamura. AR Hockey: A Case Study of Collaborative Augmented Reality. In Proc. VRAIS'98, pages 14–18, 1998

Andreas Pomi and Philipp Slusallek. Interactive Mixed Reality Rendering in a Distributed Ray Tracing Framework. IEEE and ACM International Symposium on Mixed and Augmented Reality (ISMAR) USA, November, 2004

P. Biermann and B. Jung. Variant Design in Immersive Virtual Reality: A Markup Language for Scalable CSG Parts. Proceedings AMDO-2004, Palma de Mallorca, Spain, Springer (LNCS 3179), pp.123-133, 2004

Raphael Grasset, Julian Looser, Mark Billinghurst. A Step Towards a Multimodal AR Interface: A New Handheld Device for three dimensional Interaction, ISMAR2005, pp.206-207, 2005

A. Orimoto, T. Matsuyama, R. Shizaki, R.Masuda, and M. Masuda. Development of education system for handicapped children. 11th Symposium on Human Interface, pp.209-214, 1995

Y. Hirata and M. Sato. 3-D interface device for virtual work space. Proc. 1992 IEEE/RSJ International Conference on Intelligent Robots and Systems, pp.889-896, July 1992

Yi Cai, Shengjin Wang, and Makoto Sato. A Human-Scale Direct Motion Instruction System Device for Education Systems. IEICE Transactions on Information and Systems, vol E80-D, no.2, pp.212-217, Feb. 1997

Milgram, P., and Kishino, F. A taxonomy of mixed reality visual displays, IEICE Transactions on Information and Systems, Special issue on Networked Reality, Dec. 1994

Cruz-Neira, C., Sandin, D. J., Defanti, T. A., Kentyon, R. V., and Hart, J. C. The CAVE: Audio Visual Experience Automatic Virtual Environment. Communications of the ACM, vol. 35 (6), pp. 65, 1992

Bajura, M., Fuchs, H., Ohbuchi, R. Merging Virtual Objects with the Real World: Seeing Ultrasound Imagery Within the Patient. In Proceedings of SIGGRAPH '92, New York: ACM Press, pp. 203-210, 1992

Li-Shu, Flowers, W. Teledesign: Groupware User Experiments in Three-Dimensional Computer Aided Design. Collaborative Computing, vol. 1(1), pp. 1-14, 1994

Wexelblat, A. The Reality of Cooperation: Virtual Reality and CSCW, in Virtual Reality: Applications and Explorations. Edited by A. Wexelblat. Boston, Academic Publishers, 1993

Carlson, C., and Hagsand, O. (1993) DIVE - A Platform for Multi-User Virtual Environments. Computers and Graphics. Nov/Dec, vol. 17(6), pp. 663-669, 1993

Ishii, H., Miyake, N., Toward an Open WorkSpace: Computer and Video Fusion Approach of TeamWorksation. Communications of the ACM, vol 34, No. 12, pp. 37-50, Dec 1991

Amselen, D. A Window on Shared Virtual Environments. Presence, vol. 4(2), pp. 130-145, 1995

Rekimoto, J. Transvision: A Hand-held Augmented Reality System for Collaborative Design. In Proceeding of Virtual Systems and Multimedia '96 (VSMM '96), Gifu, Japan, 18-20 Sept., 1996

Klaus, A., Kramer, A., Breen, D., Chevalier, P., Crampton, C., Rose, E., Tuceryan, M., Whitaker, R., Greer, D. Distributed Augmented Reality for Collaborative Design Applications. In Proceedings of Eurographics '95. pp. C-03-C-14, September 1995

Seon-Min Rhee, Jiyoung Park, and Myoung-Hee Kim (2006). Multi-user Live Video in a Shared Virtual World for Enhanced Group Cooperation, *Proceedings of International conference Edutainment 2006*, pp.1131-1140, LNCS 3942, Hangzhou China, April 2006, Springer, New York

T. Ogi, T. Yamada, Y. Hattori, Y. Kurita, and M. Hirose, Usage of video avatar technology for immersive communication. In *Proc. First Intl Workshop on Language Understanding and Agents for Real World Interaction 2003*, 2003.

S. Wuemlin, E. Lamboray, and M. Gross. 3D video fragments: Dynamic point samples for real time free viewpoint video. *Computers and Graphics*, 28(1):3-14, 2004.

A. Vorozcovs, A. Hogue, and W. Stuerzlinger. The hedgehog: a novel optical tracking method for spatially immersive displays. In *Proc. IEEE VR 2005*. IEEE Computer Society press, 2005.

Swain M J, and Ballard D H. Color indexing. *International Journal of Computer Vision*, 1991, 7: 11-32.

David A Forsyth and Jean Ponce, Computer Vision: A Modern Approach , *Prentice Hall; US Ed edition (August 14, 2002)*, English ISBN-10: 0130851981 ISBN-13: 978-0130851987

9

Multiple Omnidirectional Vision System and Multilayered Fuzzy Behavior Control for Autonomous Mobile Robot

Yoichiro Maeda
University of Fukui
Japan

1. Introduction

In the research on multiple autonomous mobile robots such as RoboCup, some methods for obtaining the environmental information over all circumferences used an omnidirectional vision sensor, were proposed. In case of the research using the omnidirectional camera (called omni-camera), only one camera is almost used in general. However, the object image in the mirror is compressed according to the distance. If the height of the object is uncertain, the accurate distance measurement is generally impossible.

To solve these problems, some researches for the stereo vision system used two omni-cameras were also proposed. For example, the research for the stereo vision system which two omni-cameras are vertically fixed was proposed by J.Gluckman (Gluckman; Nayar & Thoresz, 1998), H.Koyasu (Koyasu; Miura & Shirai, 2002) and T.Matsuoka (Matsuoka; Motomura & Hasegawa, 2003). The other approach which two omni-cameras are horizontally fixed is proposed by R.Miki (Miki et al., 1999).

In our laboratory, we have developed a multiple omnidirectional vision system (called MOVIS) which three omnidirectional cameras are arranged on an autonomous soccer robot like as a horizontal and equilateral triangle (Shimizuhira & Maeda, 2003). As a result, the stereo-vision system by the principle of the triangulation is made by each two cameras. The purpose of this research is to realize the object recognition and the position measurement of the robot accurately in real time. Furthermore, we propose the real-time object position measurement and the self-localization method for the autonomous soccer robot with MOVIS.

On the other hand, there are some researches for the autonomous behavior under the complicated environment by using fuzzy reasoning. In the research of the behavior control in the RoboCup middle-size league, a control system based on the fuzzy potential method was proposed by R.Tsuzaki (Tsuzaki & Yosida, 2003), a multi-layered learning system was proposed by Y.Takahashi (Takahashi; Hikita & Asada, 2003). Generally, it is well known that an operator is easy to express his control knowledge by using fuzzy reasoning. We have already proposed a multi-layered fuzzy behavior control method that element behaviors of the robot are individually controlled with the behavior decision fuzzy rule in lower-layer, and combined them with the behavior selection fuzzy rule in higher-layer (Shimizuhira; Fujii & Maeda, 2004) (Maeda & Shimizuhira, 2005).

The goal of our work is to acquire the surrounding environment information overall circumferences under the complicated environment, and to realize the omnidirectional adaptive behavior in an autonomous mobile robot. In this paper, we propose the useful self-localization method for MOVIS in any environment. To confirm the efficiency of the proposed method and system, we performed the measurement and self-localization experiment by MOVIS carried on an actual autonomous soccer robot.

2. Multiple Omnidirectional Vision System

To acquire the surrounding information in dynamic environment, we developed the multiple omnidirectional vision system (MOVIS). Measurement of the distance and direction to an object by only vision sensor without active sensors (sonar, infrared sensor, etc.) becomes possible by using MOVIS.

2.1 Hardware of MOVIS

Three omnidirectional cameras (M_1, M_2, and M_3) with same performances respectively are used in MOVIS. In this system, the omni-cameras are horizontally arranged in the equilateral triangle on a soccer robot as shown in Fig.1. Sample images of three omni-cameras are shown in Fig.2. The center of gravity of the robot and the equilateral triangle vertically exist in the same point.

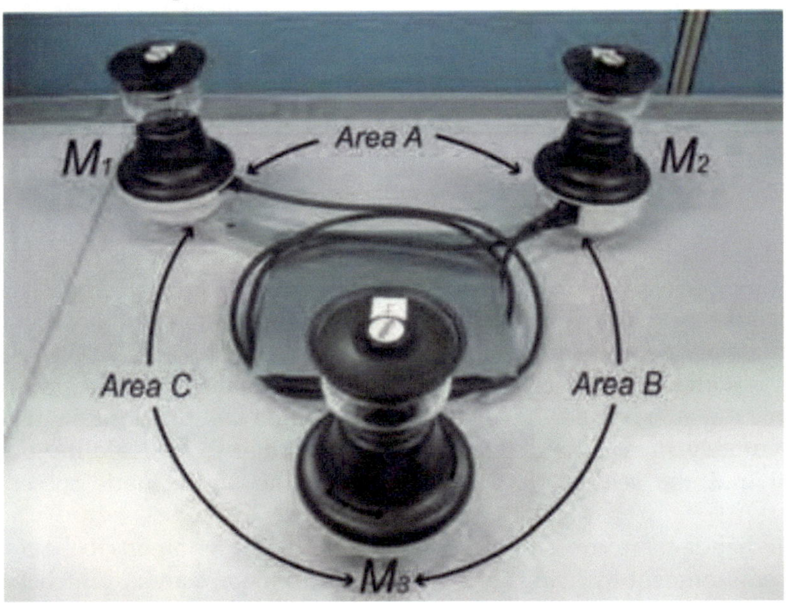

Figure 1. Overview of MOVIS

By the line extended from the center of gravity of the equilateral triangle to each vertex point, the range of the acquisition of images are divided into three areas which each two cameras perform as the stereo vision within 120 degrees (Area A, B and C in Fig.1). Stereo visions in each area provide the precise distance information by the principle of triangulation.

a) Camera M_1 b) Camera M_2 c) Camera M_3

Figure 2. Camera Images of MOVIS

2.2 Scanning Method of Omni-directional Camera

In general, the extraction of the selection area in an image is performed after making a binary format image and saving an array. The scanning process on Cartesian coordinates includes some useless searches out of an image in the omni-directional camera, but scanning on Polar coordinates has the efficient search performance because of its circular image (see Fig.3). In this method, after scanning process on Polar coordinates, the color information in Cartesian coordinates is obtained by the following transformation. In this equation, θ and r show the parameters in Polar coordinates and x and y in Cartesian coordinates.

$$x = r \cdot cos\theta \tag{1}$$

$$y = r \cdot sin\theta \tag{2}$$

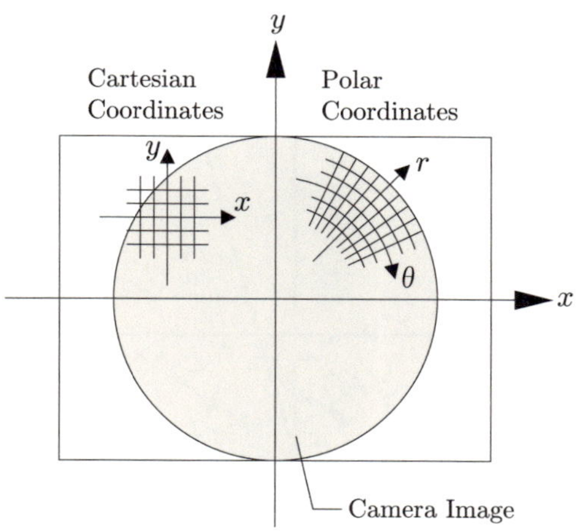

Figure 3. Scanning Method of Omni-directional Camera

2.3 Object Recognition by MOVIS

In our method, we adopted the scanning method based on Polar coordinates for the efficient image processing. At first, we count the number of extracted selection pixels in the binary format image in Polar coordinates and save it to the array arranged according to the orientation angle. Next, the panorama information for objects is obtained from the histogram made by the extracted pixel number in the array. By setting up the threshold value of pixel number, we are able to find the desired object. Fig.4 shows a histogram example in Polar coordinates for three omni-directional cameras.

Generally, we must reduce noises in the preprocess of image by compressing and enlarging. However, by using this histogram, we easily recognize the object tuning the threshold adaptively except the noise reduction process. By this method, the load of image processing is decreased.

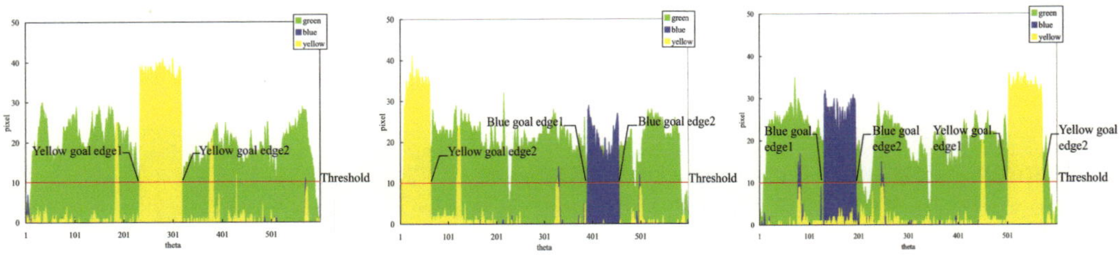

(a) Camera M_1 (b) Camera M_2 (c) Camera M_3

Figure 4. Extracted Pixel Histogram of Camera Image

2.4 Position Measurement by MOVIS

Outline of the overall measurement process of MOVIS is shown as below. The measurement process of the object position and the self-localization used in MOVIS has four main processes.

1. Object Position Measurement in Robot Coordinates
2. Self-Localization in Absolute Coordinates
3. Self-Localization after Measurement Error Correction
4. Modification of Absolute Object Position

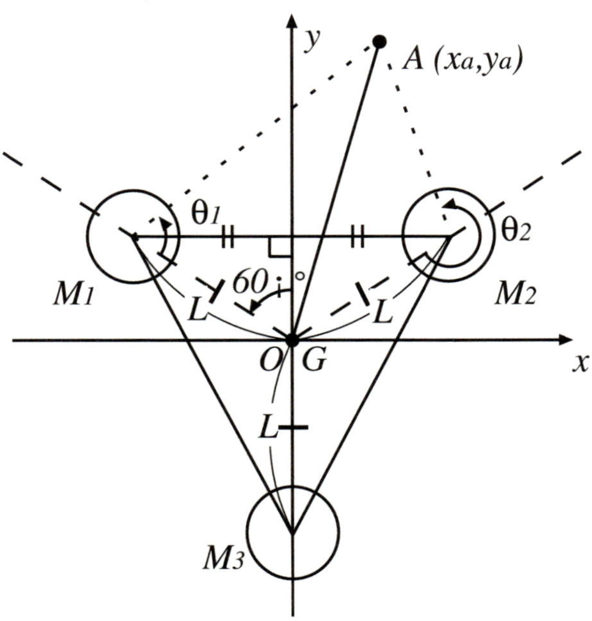

Figure 5. Structure of MOVIS

In the position measurement, an object position $A(x_a, y_a)$ in Fig.5 is obtained by using omni-camera M_1 and M_2 in the robot coordinates. In the view point of $\overline{M_1M_2}$, a slant angle of $\overline{AM_1}$ is $(\theta_1 - \pi/6)[=\lambda_1]$, that of $\overline{AM_2}$ is $(\theta_2 - 5\pi/6)[=\lambda_2]$. The distance between the center of gravity of the robot and the center of camera is assumed as L. As a result, a position (x_a, y_a) of the object A in the robot coordinates is calculated by the following equations.

$$x_a = \frac{\sqrt{3}}{2}L \cdot \frac{\tan\lambda_2 + \tan\lambda_1}{\tan\lambda_2 - \tan\lambda_1} \tag{3}$$

$$y_a = \frac{1}{2}L + \sqrt{3}L \cdot \frac{\tan\lambda_2 \cdot \tan\lambda_1}{\tan\lambda_2 - \tan\lambda_1} \tag{4}$$

3. Self-Localization by MOVIS

In this research, a half field of RoboCup middle-size robot league was constructed for the measurement experiment. The center and the corner of soccer goals were used as a landmark for the self-localization in this experiment. In this section, we propose two different measurement methods for the self-localization of a soccer robot and the mixed criterion of these methods.

3.1 Method1

Method 1 is the measurement method used the center of both goals as the landmark. The coordinate axis in the absolute coordinates is shown in Fig.6. The origin point is fixed in the center of the soccer field. P and Q show the center of goals, and P_1, P_2, Q_1, and Q_2 show the edge of goals with the width F_w and the depth F_d from the origin of the field. These absolute positions are used as landmarks in the proposed method.

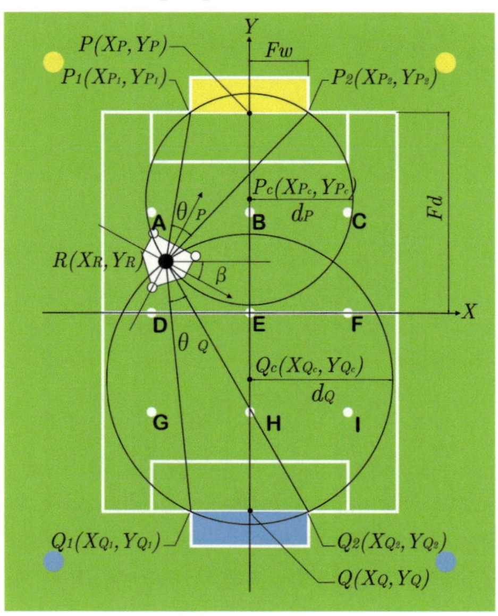

Figure 6. Self-Localization in Absolute Coordinates

Moreover, the absolute position of the center of gravity of the robot R is assumed as (X_R, Y_R) and the slant angle of x axis of the robot coordinates in the absolute coordinates is assumed as β.

In the robot coordinates, assuming that relative positions of the landmark P and Q obtained from the position measurement are $p(x_P, y_P)$ and $q(x_q, y_q)$ respectively, the landmark's absolute positions (X_P, Y_P) and (Y_Q, Y_Q) are described as the following equations.

$$\begin{pmatrix} X_P \\ Y_P \\ 1 \end{pmatrix} = \begin{pmatrix} \cos\beta & -\sin\beta & X_R \\ \sin\beta & \cos\beta & Y_R \\ 0 & 0 & 1 \end{pmatrix} \begin{pmatrix} x_p \\ y_p \\ 1 \end{pmatrix} \tag{5}$$

$$\begin{pmatrix} X_Q \\ Y_Q \\ 1 \end{pmatrix} = \begin{pmatrix} \cos\beta & -\sin\beta & X_R \\ \sin\beta & \cos\beta & Y_R \\ 0 & 0 & 1 \end{pmatrix} \begin{pmatrix} x_q \\ y_q \\ 1 \end{pmatrix} \tag{6}$$

where the yellow and blue goal are used as the landmark $P(X_P, Y_P)$ and $Q(X_Q, Y_Q)$ in the experiment respectively.

The center of the gravity position (X_R, Y_R) of a robot in the absolute coordinates is calculated by these equations as the following equations.

$$X_R = y_p \sin\beta - x_p \cos\beta \tag{7}$$

$$Y_R = Fd - x_p \sin\beta - y_p \cos\beta \tag{8}$$

$$X_R = y_q \sin\beta - x_q \cos\beta \tag{9}$$

$$Y_R = -Fd - x_q \sin\beta - y_q \cos\beta \tag{10}$$

$$\beta = \arctan\frac{x_p - x_q}{y_p - y_q} \tag{11}$$

By our experimental results, we confirmed that the self-localization performance in X axis orientation is relatively good in the accuracy of the position estimation, but the measurement in Y axis has some errors because the distance data error of MOVIS has quite larger than the direction data error.

3.2 Method2

Method 2 is the measurement method used the corners of both goals as the landmark. As Fig.6, after the robot measures the corner edge of both goals, θ_P (=angle of P_1RP_2) as the parallax angle for both edges of a goal P and θ_Q (=angle of Q_1RQ_2) as that of a goal Q are obtained. The radius of a circumscribed circle for triangles of ΔP_1P_2R and ΔQ_1Q_2R are shown in the following equations.

$$d_P = \frac{Fw}{sin\theta_P} \tag{12}$$

$$d_Q = \frac{Fw}{sin\theta_Q} \tag{13}$$

where F_w means the distance between a center and each corner edge of a goal.

Next, the absolute position of the center of each circumscribed circle $P_C(X_{PC},Y_{PC})$ and $Q_C(X_{QC},Y_{QC})$ is calculated as follows.

$$X_{P_C} = X_{Q_C} = 0 \tag{14}$$

$$\begin{aligned} Y_{P_C} &= Fd - \sqrt{d_P^2 - Fw^2} \qquad \left(0 < \theta_P < \frac{\pi}{2}\right) \\ &= Fd + \sqrt{d_P^2 - Fw^2} \qquad \left(\frac{\pi}{2} \le \theta_P < \pi\right) \end{aligned} \tag{15}$$

$$\begin{aligned} Y_{P_C} &= Fd - \sqrt{d_P^2 - Fw^2} \qquad \left(0 < \theta_P < \frac{\pi}{2}\right) \\ &= Fd + \sqrt{d_P^2 - Fw^2} \qquad \left(\frac{\pi}{2} \le \theta_P < \pi\right) \end{aligned} \tag{16}$$

where F_d means the distance between a center line and a goal line.
Therefore, the intersection of these circumscribed circles shows the robot position. The self-position of the robot $R(X_R,Y_R)$ is decided by the following equations.

$$\begin{aligned} X_R &= -\sqrt{r_P^2 - (Y_R - Y_{P_C})^2} \qquad (x_{P_1}^2 + y_{P_1}^2 \le x_{P_2}^2 + y_{P_2}^2) \\ &= \sqrt{r_P^2 - (Y_R - Y_{P_C})^2} \qquad (x_{P_1}^2 + y_{P_1}^2 > x_{P_2}^2 + y_{P_2}^2) \end{aligned} \tag{17}$$

$$Y_R = \frac{(r_P^2 - Y_{P_C}^2) - (r_Q^2 - Y_{Q_C}^2)}{2 \cdot (Y_{Q_C} - Y_{P_C})} \tag{18}$$

This method has relatively high performance of the self-localization for the Y axis orientation, but the measurement for X axis orientation includes some errors. As this reason, we consider that larger errors are generated in X axis orientation rather than Y axis orientation in the calculation for the intersection of these circumscribed circles.

3.2 Self-Localization Method

Two above-mentioned methods have merits and demerits. Therefore, we proposed a composed method with each merit in this research. By composing two method, the self-localization method with better performance in all measurement area is constructed. In this

method, we compose Method 1 with better performance in X axis orientation and Method 2 with better performance in Y axis orientation.
In the estimation of X position, we adopt Equation (7) and (9). For the improvement of the measurement accuracy, the absolute robot position in X axis is calculated with the average of these equations.
In the estimation of Y position, we adopt Equation (18) with better performance in Y axis orientation. Finally, the self-localization position of the robot is calculated by the following equation.

$$X_R = \frac{y_p sin\beta - x_p cos\beta + y_q sin\beta - x_q cos\beta}{2} \tag{19}$$

$$Y_R = \frac{(r_P^2 - Y_{P_C}^2) - (r_Q^2 - Y_{Q_C}^2)}{2 \cdot (Y_{Q_C} - Y_{P_C})} \tag{20}$$

4. Experiments

We actually performed the measurement experiment by MOVIS and the shoot experiment by a soccer robot with the multi-layered fuzzy behavior control method. The experiment was executed by using three IEEE1394 digital omni-cameras and a notebook PC with Celeron 600A MHz CPU and Vine Linux 3.0.

4.1 Experiment for Performance of MOVIS

In order to confirm the precision of MOVIS, we carried out the measurement experiment of the ball direction and distance from the robot with MOVIS. This experiment was performed at the wide space with a uniform light source. We used an orange soccer ball regulated in the RoboCup middle-size league as the measurement object. The origin of the absolute coordinates is a center of the measurement space within 800cm square and the measurement place are 289 lattice points at each 50cm interval from -400cm to 400cm. Omni-cameras were fixed at 25cm height from the floor during the experiment.
Fig.7 shows measurement results for the distance and direction error in polar coordinates. Results for a single omni-vision are shown in Fig.7a),b), the vertical stereo omni-vision (Koyasu, Miura & Shirai, 2002) in Fig.7c),d) and MOVIS with the error correction in Fig.7e),f). In the measurement experiment of the single omni-vision, large particular errors were found in the area around (-400, -400). We confirmed a single omni-vision has an individual difference such as this type of error. The absolute average of the distance error was 92.63 cm in this experiment. On the other hand, we confirmed the omni-vision has an ability of the precise measurement for the direction by the result that the absolute average of the direction error was 0.61 degrees.
In Fig.7c) to f), the absolute average of the direction error in the vertical stereo omni-vision and MOVIS was relatively small within -1.5 to 1.5 degrees as same as a single omni-vision. Moreover, the absolute average of the distance error in MOVIS was remarkably smaller than that of the vertical stereo omni-vision. By this results, we could confirm the performance of the precise distance measurement of MOVIS.

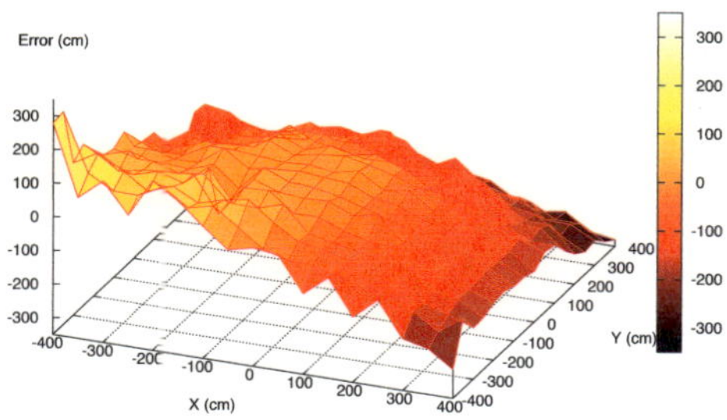

a) Single Omni-Vision (Distance Error)

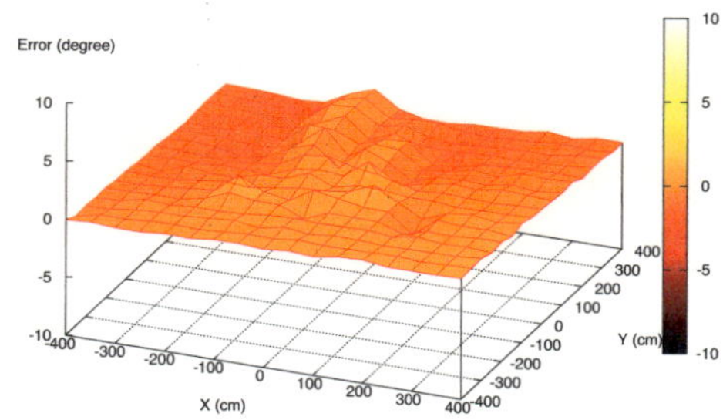

b) Single Omni-Vision (Direction Error)

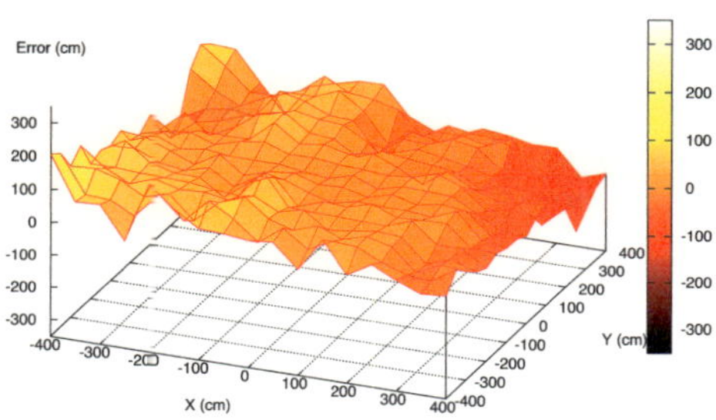

c) Stereo Omni-Vision (Distance Error)

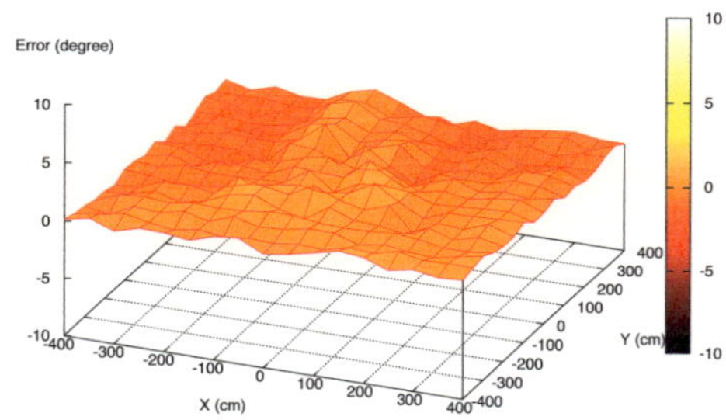

d) Stereo Omni-Vision (Direction Error)

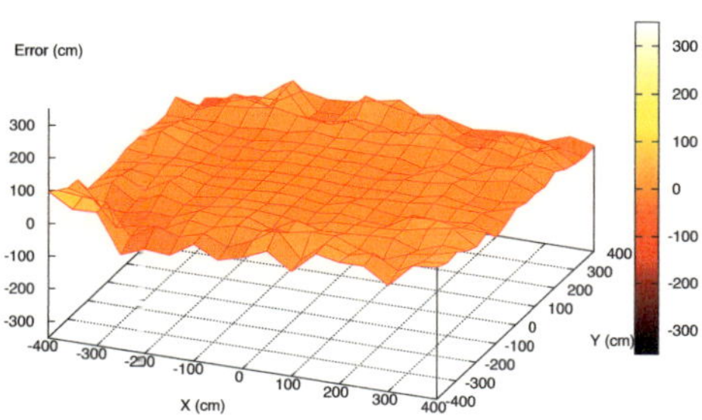

e) MOVIS (Distance Error)

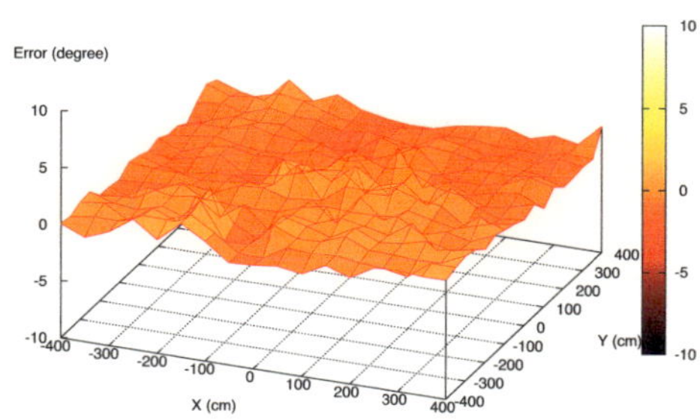

f) MOVIS (Direction Error)

Figure 7. Results of Measurement Experiment

4.1 Experiment for Self-Localization

Furthermore, Fig.8 to 16 shows the results for the measurement error of the self-localization. These results show the self-localization error measured on nine spots A to I in miniature field with 3.5m width and 4m depth while a robot rotates on a spot. In these figures, for example, Position A means the self-localization experimental result executed in place of point A in Fig.6. Left graph shows the position error estimated by the proposed self-localization method and right figure shows the real position plotted in the field.

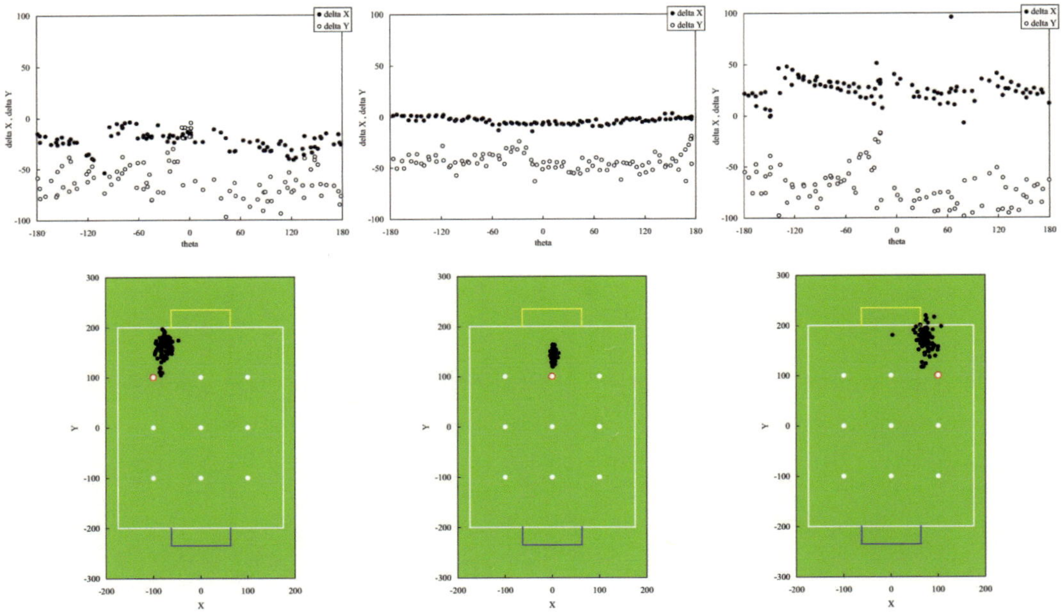

a) Spot A b) Spot B c) Spot C

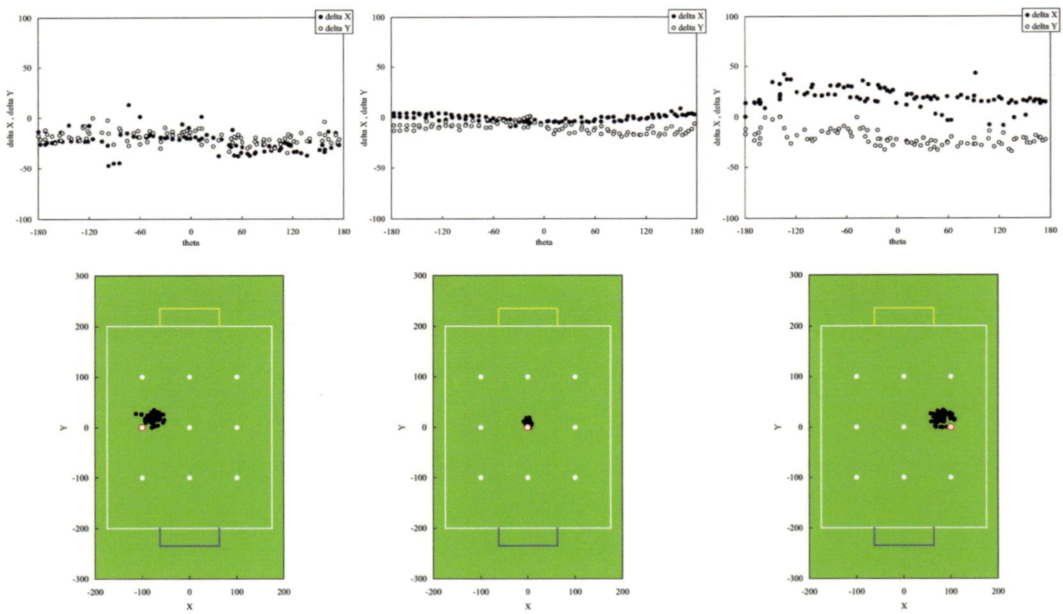

d) Spot D e) Spot E f) Spot F

Figure 8. Experimental Result of Self-Localization (1)

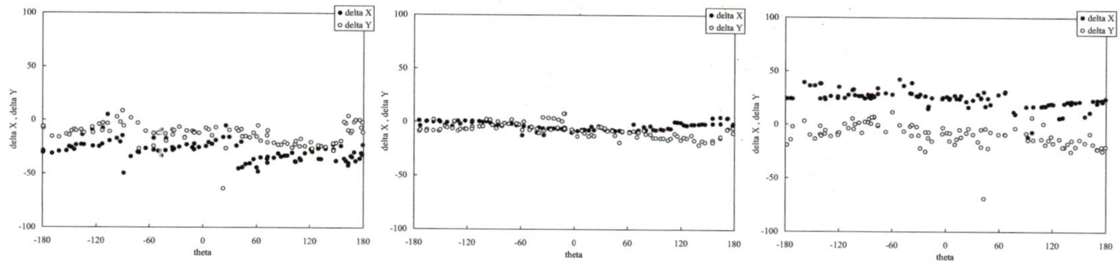

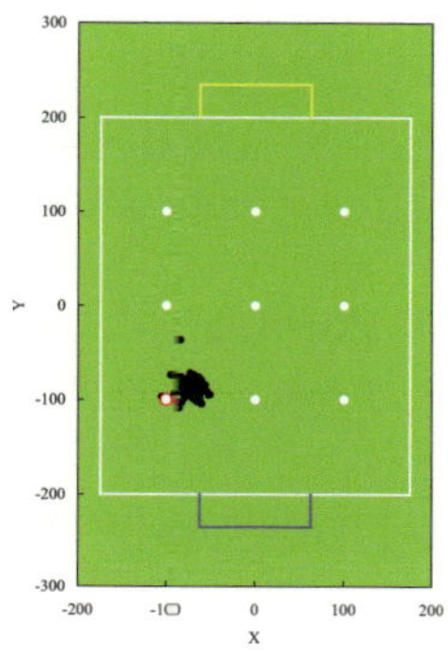

g) Spot G

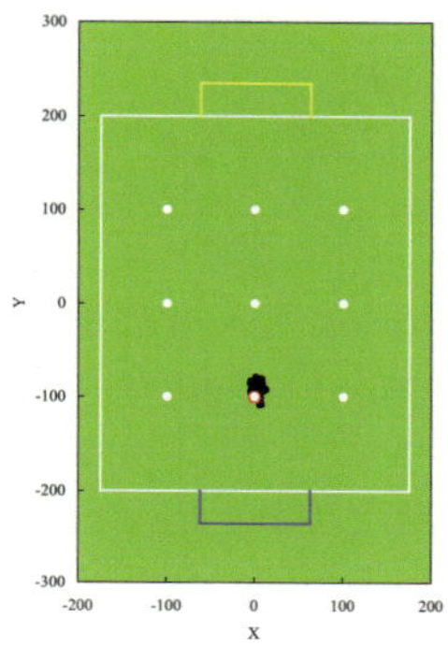

h) Spot H

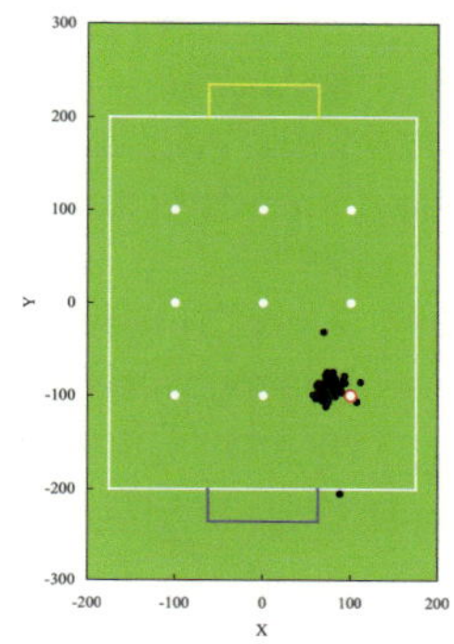

i) Spot I

Figure 8. Experimental Result of Self-Localization (2)

As a result, we confirmed that the proposed method is useful for the self-localization. Especially, the performance of self-localization on Y axis (spot B, E, and H) was better than that on the other spots. Maybe we consider that the reason is caused by the measurement error of the distance in far area. In all results, the result on the spot A and C was the worse because the robot could not successfully execute the color extraction of blue goal near the yellow goal area. We think that we are able to make better the performance of these areas by improvement of lighting environment.

5. Conclusions

The multiple omnidirectional vision system (MOVIS) with three omni-cameras and its self-localization method for the autonomous mobile robot were proposed in this paper. Moreover, the experiment of the measurement performance and self-localization by MOVIS on the real miniature soccer field was carried out by using the proposed method. As a result, we confirmed that the measurement of MOVIS is remarkably more accurate than that of a single omni-vision and the vertical stereo omni-vision, and the self-localization performance is relatively useful in all area of soccer field. In the near future, we would like to develop the real soccer robot with MOVIS and the proposed self-localization method.

6. References

Koyasu, H.; Miura, J. & Shirai, Y. (2002). Estimation of Ego-Motion and Its Uncertainty for a Mobile Robot Using Omnidirectional Stereo, *Proceedings of* the 20th Annual Conference of the Robotics Society of Japan, CD-ROM, 3A24 [in Japanese]

Matsuoka, T.; Motomura, A. & Hasegawa, T. (2003). Real-time Self-Localization Method in a Dynamically Changing Environment, *Proceedings of* the 2003 IEEE/RSJ International Conference on Intelligent Robots and Systems, 1234-1239

Gluckman, J.; Nayar, K. & Thoresz, J. (1998). Real-Time Omnidirectional and Panoramic Stereo, *Proceedings of* Image Understanding Workshop, 299-303

Miki, R.; Yamazawa, K.; Takemura, H. & Yokoya, N. (1999). A Remote Surveillance System Using Omnidirectional Sensors, Technical Report of IEICE, PRMU98-177, 7-14 [in Japanese]

Shimizuhira, W. & Maeda, Y. (2003). Self-Localization Method Used Multiple Omnidirectional Vision System, *Proceedings of* SICE Annual Conference 2003, 2796-2799

Tsuzaki, R. & Yosida, K. (2003). Motion Control Based on Fuzzy Potential Method for Autonomous Mobile Robot with Omnidirectional Vision, *Proceedings of* the Robotics Society of Japan, Vol.21, No.6, 656-662 [in Japanese]

Takahashi, Y.; Hikita, K. & Asada, M. (2003). Incremental Purposive Behavior Acquisition based on Self-Interpretation of Instructions by Coach, *Proceedings of* the 2003 IEEE/RSJ International Conference on Intelligent Robots and Systems, 686-693

Shimizuhira, W.; Fujii, K. & Maeda, Y. (2004). Fuzzy Behavior Control for Autonomous Mobile Robot in Dynamic Environment with Multiple Omnidirectional Vision System, *Proceedings of* IEEE/RSJ International Conference on Intelligent Robots and Systems (IROS 2004), CD-ROM, SA2-M3

Maeda, M. & Shimizuhira, W. (2005). Omnidirectional Adaptive Behavior Control for Autonomous Mobile Robot, *Proceedings of* Second International Conference on Modeling Decisions for Artificial Intelligence (MDAI 2005), 252-263

10

A Tutorial on Parametric Image Registration

Leonardo Romero and Félix Calderón
División de Estudios de Postgrado, Facultad de Ingeniería Eléctrica
Universidad Michoacana de San Nicolás de Hidalgo
Morelia, Michoacán, México

1. Resume

This chapter introduces the reader to the area of parametric image registration, from a beginner's point of view. Given a model, an input image and a reference image, the parametric registration task is to find a set of parameters (of the model) that transform the input image into the reference image. This chapter reviews models of the general projective, affine, similarity and Euclidean transformations of images, and develop a full example for affine and projective transformation. It also describes two new methods of computing the set of image derivatives needed, besides the classical method reported in the literature. The new methods for computing derivatives are faster and more accurate than the classical method.

2. Introduction

Image registration is the process of overlaying two or more images of the same scene taken at different times, from different viewpoints or by different sensors [Zitova and Flusser, 2003]. In this chapter, only two images are considered: a reference image and an input image. The idea is to find a way to convert the input image into another image, similar to the reference image. If the model, that transforms the input image, has a small set of parameters, the task is called parametric image registration. Otherwise, the task it is called non-parametric registration [Calderon and Marroquin, 2003] (e.g. a set of parameters for each pixel of the image).
The literature is plenty of parametric registration techniques. Some of them are based on Spatiotemporal Energy [Adelson and Bergen, 1986], [Barman et al., 1986] and [Heeger, 1987], other methods are based on correlation [Kaneko et al., 2002] [Kaneko et al., 2003], others are based on the minimization of the Sum of Squared Differences (SSD) [Lai and Vemuri, 98], [Szeliski and Coughlan, 1994] (also named radial basis function in [Zitova and Flusser, 2003]), and others are based on optical Flow [Barron et al., 1994].
This tutorial describes in detail a SSD technique which can be extended easily to the M Estimators (for different M estimators see [Huber, Peter J. 2003]). The literature on parametric images registration often reports only advanced applications of this technique, but research papers do not address details of the implementation of these kinds of methods. Also surveys have been writing for experts (e.g. [Zitova and Flusser, 2003]) and this area is not fully covered in computer vision books. To our knowledge there is not a tutorial of

parametric image registration and this chapter tries to introduce beginners in computer vision into this area.
The rest of this chapter is organized as follows. Section 3 describes the registration problem as an optimization problem and Section 4 introduces the bilinear interpolation to compute accurate transformations of images. Section 5 introduces some basic transformations, from Euclidean to general projective transformations. Section 6 shows three methods to compute the set of derivatives of images needed, two new methods and the classical method reported in the literature. The first new method is a fast method based on interpolation of derivatives of the input image. The second method is the classical method based on derivatives of the transformed image. The third method is a new one and it is a more accurate and complete method than the classical method. Section 7, gives minimization details for an error function and subsection 7.1 presents the well known Levenberg-Marquard non-linear optimization method [Nocedal and Wright, 1999], commonly used in many computer vision problems. Experimental results are shown in section 8 using the three methods of computing derivatives. Results confirm the accuracy of the third method of computing derivatives. Finally, some conclusions are given in Section 9.

3. Parametric Registration Problem

Let $I(i,j)$ denote a gray level image (typically an integer value from 0 to 255), for integer coordinates $<i,j>$, $I(i,j)$ gives the intensity value of the pixel associated to position $<i,j>$ (see Figure 1), and $I_r(i,j)$ denotes the reference image.
If the set of parameters is denoted by Θ, the parametric registration problem is to find a set Θ that minimizes an error function E, between the transformed input image $I_t(i,j)$ and the reference image. Considering the SSD, E can be expressed in the following way:

$$E(\Theta) = \sum\nolimits_{\forall <i,j> \in I_r} \left(I(x(\Theta,i,j), y(\Theta,i,j)) - I_r(i,j) \right)^2 \tag{1}$$

For instance, given a position $x=i+1$ and $y=j$, one pixel $I_r(i,j)$ is going to be compared with pixel $I(i+1,j)$. This situation is equivalent to have a transformed input image, $I_t(i,j)=I(i+1,j)$, where all pixels of the input image, have moved to the next position upwards (see Figure 1). The error E compares each pixel, between I_t and I_r, at the same position $<i,j>$. With the right Θ^*, image I_t and I_r should be very similar and E should reach a minimum value. The new image I_t (i,j) can be computed by

$$I_t(i,j) = I(x(\Theta,i,j), y(\Theta,i,j)) \tag{2}$$

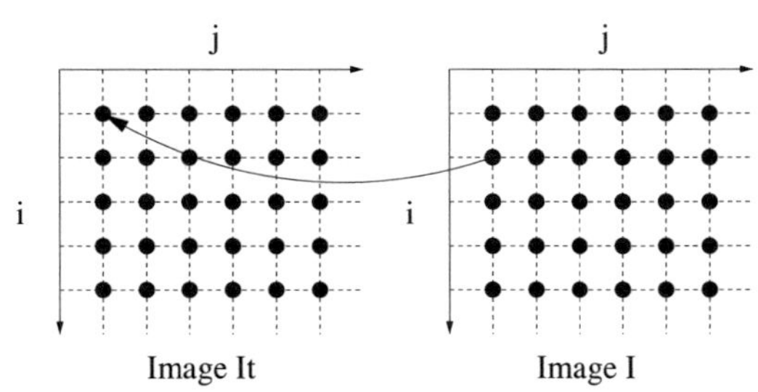

Figure 1. Computing transformed image I_t from I

If $x(\Theta,i,j)$ and $y(\Theta,i,j)$ are outside of the image I, a common strategy is to assign zero value which represents a black pixel. But, What happen when $x(\Theta,i,j)$ and $y(\Theta,i,j)$ have real values instead of integer values?. Remember that image $I(x,y)$ have only valid values when x and y are integer values. An inaccurate method to solve this problem is to use their nearest integer values. Next section presents a much better method to solve this problem.

4. Bilinear Interpolation

If x_i and x_f are the integer and fractional part of x ($x = x_i+x_f$), and y_i and y_f the integer and fractional part of y ($y = y_i+y_f$), Figure 2 illustrates the bilinear interpolation method [Faugeras, 1993] to find $I(x_i+x_f, y_i+y_f)$, given the four nearest pixels to position $<x_i+x_f, y_i+y_f>$: $I(x_i, y_i)$, $I(x_i+1, y_i)$, $I(x_i, y_i+1)$ and $I(x_i+1, y_i+1)$ (image values at particular positions are represented by vertical bars in Figure 2). First two linear interpolations are used to compute two new values ($I_{new}(x_i, y_i+y_f)$ and $I_{new}(x_i+1, y_i+y_f)$) and then another linear interpolation is used to compute the desired value $I(x_i+x_f, y_i+y_f)$ from the new computed values:

$$
\begin{aligned}
I_{new}(x_i, y_i + y_f) &= (1-y_f)I(x_i, y_i) + y_f I(x_i, y_i+1) \\
I_{new}(x_i+1, y_i + y_f) &= (1-y_f)I(x_i+1, y_i) + y_f I(x_i+1, y_i+1) \\
I(x_i+x_f, y_i + y_f) &= (1-x_f)I_{new}(x_i, y_i+y_f) + x_f I_{new}(x_i+1, y_i+y_f)
\end{aligned}
\tag{3}
$$

Using the bilinear interpolation, a smooth transformed image is computed. Next section introduces a hierarchy of transformations that maps lines, in the input image, to lines in the transformed image [Hartley and Zisserman, 2000].

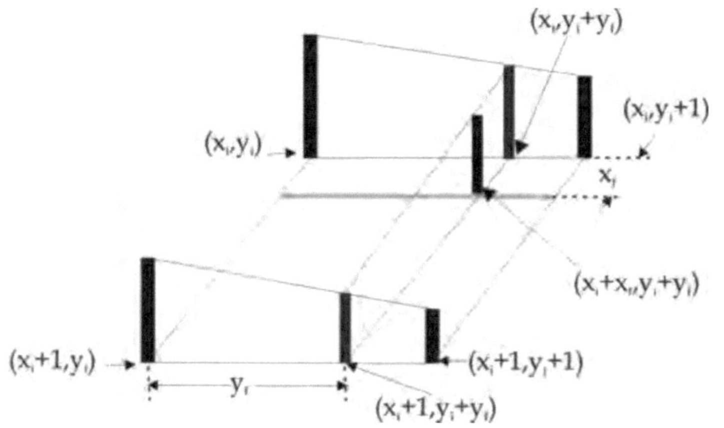

Figure 2. Using the Bilinear Interpolation

5. Basic Transformations

In this section Euclidean, Similarity, Affine and Projective transformations are reviewed briefly. In order to have a uniform frame of reference for these transformations, homogeneous coordinates are going to be used [Hartley and Zisserman, 2000]. A point $<x,y>$ in a plane is represented in homogeneous coordinates (HC) by a vector of 3 coordinates, $[x_h, y_h, w_h]^T$, and both coordinates are related by $x=x_h/w_h$ and $y=y_h/w_h$. In HC, a vector v and $\kappa\, v$ ($\kappa \in \Re$) represent the same point, an important advantage of using homogeneous coordinates is that original and transformed positions, as well as composition of transformations, are related by matrix multiplications [Hartley and Zisserman, 2000]. Figure 3, illustrates the Euclidian, Similarity, Affine and Projective transformation.

(a) (b) (c) (d) (e)

Figure 3. Linear Transformations in Homogeneous Coordinates: (a) Original, (b) Euclidean, (c) Similarity, (d) Affine and (e) Projective

5.1 Euclidean Transformations

In the case of Euclidian Transformation, angles and length of line segments are preserved, and only translations and rotations are allowed (see Figure 3(b)). This transformation have three parameters, $\Theta = \{\phi, t_i, t_j\}$, where ϕ is the rotation angle, and t_i, t_j are translation in directions i and j respectively. Using HC, $x(\Theta,i,j)=x_h/w_h$ and $y(\Theta,i,j)=y_h/w_h$, can be represented by:

$$[x_h, y_h, w_h]^T = H_e[i, j, 1]^T$$
$$H_e = \begin{bmatrix} \cos\phi & -\sin\phi & t_i \\ \sin\phi & \cos\phi & t_j \\ 0 & 0 & 1 \end{bmatrix} \tag{4}$$

5.2 Similarity Transformations

Besides translations and rotations, an isotropic scaling given by s is allowed (the same in both directions). Under this transformation, objects can be bigger or smaller, but their original shape is preserved (see Figure 3 (c)). The matrix representation, H_s, for this transformation is given by

$$[x_h, y_h, w_h]^T = H_s[i, j, 1]^T$$
$$H_s = \begin{bmatrix} s\cos\phi & -s\sin\phi & st_i \\ s\,\sin\phi & s\cos\phi & st_j \\ 0 & 0 & 1 \end{bmatrix} \tag{5}$$

5.3 Affine Transformations

An affine transformation is the most general transformation that preserves parallelism between lines (see Figure 3 (d)). This case is represented by H_a and has six parameters,

$$[x_h, y_h, w_h]^T = H_a[i, j, 1]^T$$
$$H_a = \begin{bmatrix} \theta_0 & \theta_1 & \theta_2 \\ \theta_3 & \theta_4 & \theta_5 \\ 0 & 0 & 1 \end{bmatrix} \tag{6}$$

Where θ_2 and θ_5 represent the translation in both directions. This transformation allows rotation, scaling, shearing, translation or combinations of these transformations.

5.4 Projective Transformations

This is the most general transformation that maps lines into lines, and it generalizes an affine transformation. The matrix H_p for this transformation has nine elements (actually only eight independent ratios among the nine elements of H_p, because in HC proportional vectors represent the same vector). An example of this transformation where parallelism is not preserved is shown in Figure 3(e). In most interesting cases, projective transformations H_p, has the form:

$$[x_h, y_h, w_h]^T = H_p[i, j, 1]^T$$
$$H_p = \begin{bmatrix} \theta_0 & \theta_1 & \theta_2 \\ \theta_3 & \theta_4 & \theta_5 \\ \theta_6 & \theta_7 & 1 \end{bmatrix} \tag{7}$$

Next section develops examples of finding the set of parameter for affine and projective transformations.

6. Finding the Set of Parameters

In order to compute a set of parameter Θ, equation (1), can be rewritten as follows

$$E(I(\Theta), I_r) = \sum_{\forall < i,j > \in I_r} \rho(e_{ij})$$
$$e_{ij} = I(x(\Theta, i, j), y(\Theta, i, j)) - I_r(i, j) \tag{8}$$

$\rho(e)$ is an error function which could be a quadratic function or any M-estimator (see [Huber, Peter J. 2003]). In case of a quadratic function the solution is known as Least Squares. Given a set $\Theta = \{\theta_0, \dots, \theta_k, \dots, \theta_K\}$ of K parameters, E will have a minimum value when $\partial E / \partial \theta_k = 0$ for all k. The k-th element of the gradient value $G_k = \partial E / \partial \theta_k$, can be computed as

$$G_k(\Theta) = \frac{\partial E}{\partial \theta_k} = \sum_{\forall <i,j> \in I_r} \frac{\partial \rho(e_{ij})}{\partial e_{ij}} \frac{\partial e_{ij}}{\partial \theta_k} \quad k=0,1,\ldots K \tag{9}$$

In the literature, the derivative $\partial\rho(e_{ij})/\partial e_{ij}$ is called the influence function [Huber, Peter J. 2003] and it is represented by $\varphi(e_{ij})$. In the case of a quadratic error function $\varphi(e_{ij}) = 2e_{ij}$. If we introduced the gradient vector $G(\Theta)=[G_0(\Theta), G_1(\Theta), \ldots G_K(\Theta)]^T$ and the vector $J_{ij}(\Theta)$ as

$$J_{ij}(\Theta) = \left[\frac{\partial e_{ij}}{\partial \theta_0}, \frac{\partial e_{ij}}{\partial \theta_1}, \ldots, \frac{\partial e_{ij}}{\partial \theta_K}\right]^T \tag{10}$$

$G(\Theta)$ can be written in a single one :

$$G(\Theta) = \sum_{\forall <i,j> \in I_r} \varphi_{ij}(\Theta) J_{ij}(\Theta) \tag{11}$$

Let's develop an expression for each term of the vector $J_{ij}(\Theta)=[J_{ij0}(\Theta), J_{ij1}(\Theta), \ldots J_{ijK}(\Theta)]^T$ from equation (8) so an expression for $J_{ijk}(\Theta)$ can be derived as:

$$J_{ijk}(\Theta) = \frac{\partial e_{ij}}{\partial \theta_k} = \frac{\partial I(x(\Theta,i,j), y(\Theta,i,j))}{\partial \theta_k} \tag{12}$$

Using the chain rule from the differential calculus, the desired value can be computed as follows,

$$J_{ijk}(\Theta) = \frac{\partial I(x(\Theta,i,j), y(\Theta,i,j))}{\partial x(\Theta,i,j)} \frac{\partial x(\Theta,i,j)}{\partial \theta_k} + \frac{\partial I(x(\Theta,i,j), y(\Theta,i,j))}{\partial y(\Theta,i,j)} \frac{\partial y(\Theta,i,j)}{\partial \theta_k} \tag{13}$$

Using matrix notation $J_{ij}(\Theta) = M(\Theta,i,j)\nabla I(x,y)$ with

$$M(\Theta,i,j) = \begin{bmatrix} \frac{\partial x(\Theta,i,j)}{\partial \theta_0} & \frac{\partial y(\Theta,i,j)}{\partial \theta_0} \\ \vdots & \vdots \\ \frac{\partial x(\Theta,i,j)}{\partial \theta_K} & \frac{\partial y(\Theta,i,j)}{\partial \theta_K} \end{bmatrix} \tag{14}$$

$$\nabla I(x,y) = \begin{bmatrix} \dfrac{\partial I(x(\Theta,i,j), y(\Theta,i,j))}{\partial x(\Theta,i,j)} \\ \dfrac{\partial I(x(\Theta,i,j), y(\Theta,i,j))}{\partial y(\Theta,i,j)} \end{bmatrix} \tag{15}$$

M will called the Coordinate Matrix Model (CMM) which depends of the characteristics of the model and $\nabla I(x,y)$ the gradient vector respect to x and y (remember that the image only have integer coordinates values). Subsection 6.1 presents the CMM for affine and projective transformations and subsection 6.2 presents three methods of computing the gradient vector $\nabla I(x,y)$.

6.1 Coordinate Matrix Model

An affine transformation given by equation (6) can be rewritten as follows.

$$\begin{aligned} x(\Theta,i,j) &= \theta_0 i + \theta_1 j + \theta_2 \\ y(\Theta,i,j) &= \theta_3 i + \theta_4 j + \theta_5 \end{aligned} \tag{16}$$

By definition of CMM given by equation (14), the CMM, for affine transformation, has a simple form given by equation (17).

$$M(\Theta,i,j) = \begin{bmatrix} \dfrac{\partial x}{\partial \theta_0} & \dfrac{\partial y}{\partial \theta_0} \\ \dfrac{\partial x}{\partial \theta_1} & \dfrac{\partial y}{\partial \theta_1} \\ \dfrac{\partial x}{\partial \theta_2} & \dfrac{\partial y}{\partial \theta_2} \\ \dfrac{\partial x}{\partial \theta_3} & \dfrac{\partial y}{\partial \theta_3} \\ \dfrac{\partial x}{\partial \theta_4} & \dfrac{\partial y}{\partial \theta_4} \\ \dfrac{\partial x}{\partial \theta_5} & \dfrac{\partial y}{\partial \theta_5} \end{bmatrix} = \begin{bmatrix} i & 0 \\ j & 0 \\ 1 & 0 \\ 0 & i \\ 0 & j \\ 0 & 1 \end{bmatrix} \tag{17}$$

In a similar way, the projective transformation (eq. (7)), can be rewritten as

$$
\begin{aligned}
x(\Theta,i,j) &= \frac{\theta_0 i + \theta_1 j + \theta_2}{w(\Theta,i,j)} \\
y(\Theta,i,j) &= \frac{\theta_3 i + \theta_4 j + \theta_5}{w(\Theta,i,j)} \\
w(\Theta,i,j) &= \theta_6 i + \theta_7 j + 1
\end{aligned}
\tag{18}
$$

The CMM, in this case, is given by equation (19)

$$
M(\Theta,i,j) = \frac{1}{w}\begin{bmatrix} i & 0 \\ j & 0 \\ 1 & 0 \\ 0 & i \\ 0 & j \\ 0 & 1 \\ -ix & -iy \\ -jx & -jy \end{bmatrix}
\tag{19}
$$

6.2 Computing Derivatives of Images

Here we present three methods to compute the terms not previously described in eq. (14). In all the three methods, derivative of images are needed which can be approximated by the following central-difference approximations [Trucco and Verri, 1998]:

$$
\begin{aligned}
\frac{\partial I(i,j)}{\partial i} &= \frac{I(i+1,j) - I(i-1,j)}{2} \\
\frac{\partial I(i,j)}{\partial j} &= \frac{I(i,j+1) - I(i,j-1)}{2}
\end{aligned}
\tag{20}
$$

More accurate approximations consider more pixels in the neighborhood [Trucco and Verri, 1998]:

$$
\begin{aligned}
\frac{\partial I(i,j)}{\partial i} &= \frac{-I(i+2,j) + 8I(i+1,j) - 8I(i-1,j) + I(i-2,j)}{12} \\
\frac{\partial I(i,j)}{\partial j} &= \frac{-I(i,j+2) + 8I(i,j+1) - 8I(i,j-1) + I(i,j-2)}{12}
\end{aligned}
\tag{21}
$$

An even better method is called derivative of Gaussian Filters [Ma et al., 2004] [Romeny, 1994], and it computes much smaller noise responses, compared with the previous ones. The Gaussian function and its derivative are given, respectively, by

$$
\begin{aligned}
g(t) &= \frac{1}{\sqrt{2\pi\sigma}} e^{\frac{-t^2}{2\sigma^2}} \\
g'(t) &= \frac{dg(t)}{dt} = \frac{-t}{\sigma^3\sqrt{2\pi}} e^{\frac{-t^2}{2\sigma^2}}
\end{aligned}
\tag{22}
$$

The computation of image derivatives is accomplished as a pair of 1-D convolutions with filters obtained by sampling the continuous Gaussian function and its derivative,

$$
\begin{aligned}
\frac{\partial I(i,j)}{\partial i} &= I(i,j) * g'(i) * g(j) = \sum_{k=-w/2}^{w/2} \sum_{l=-w/2}^{w/2} \left[I(i,j) g'(i-k) g(j-l) \right] \\
\frac{\partial I(i,j)}{\partial j} &= I(i,j) * g(i) * g'(j) = \sum_{k=-w/2}^{w/2} \sum_{l=-w/2}^{w/2} \left[I(i,j) g(i-k) g'(j-l) \right]
\end{aligned}
\tag{23}
$$

σ (in pixels units) controls the Gaussian form, and usually $w = 3\sigma$. If the window defined by w is bigger, then more pixels in the neighborhood are considered. In equation (23), the operator (*) represents convolution.
Now three methods, to compute the gradient vector of the input image, ($\nabla I(x,y)$ in eq. (15)) are presented in next section. Remember that x and y in general can be real numbers.

6.2.1 Method 1: Using derivatives of the input image

Considering that $<i,j> \in N^2$ and $<x,y> \in R^2$, if $\partial I(i,j)/\partial i$ and $\partial I(i,j)/\partial j$ are computed using one of the previous methods, a simple and fast method to compute $\partial I(x,y)/\partial x$ is to use bilinear interpolation from $\partial I(i,j)/\partial i$ to get an approximate value. In a similar way, $\partial I(x,y)/\partial y$ can be estimated from $\partial I(i,j)/\partial j$.

6.2.2 Method 2: Using approximate derivatives of the transformed image

Considering the transformed image I_t and from equation (2), another approximation is given by

$$
\begin{aligned}
\frac{\partial I(x(\Theta,i,j), y(\Theta,i,j))}{\partial x(\Theta,i,j)} &= \frac{\partial I_t(i,j)}{\partial i} \\
\frac{\partial I(x(\Theta,i,j), y(\Theta,i,j))}{\partial y(\Theta,i,j)} &= \frac{\partial I_t(i,j)}{\partial j}
\end{aligned}
\tag{24}
$$

Because this approximation is reported in many papers, we named it the classical method.

6.2.3 Method 3: Using derivatives of the transformed image

Method 2 considers $I_t(i,j) = I(x(\Theta,i,j), y(\Theta,i,j))$, and also considers derivatives given by equation (24). The first one is correct, but not the second one, because increments in x does not necessarily correspond to the same increments of i (and the same argument with y and j). The right derivatives can be computed using the chain rule, as follows:

$$\begin{aligned}\frac{\partial I(x,y)}{\partial x} &= \frac{\partial I_t(i,j)}{\partial i}\frac{\partial i}{\partial x} + \frac{\partial I_t(i,j)}{\partial j}\frac{\partial j}{\partial x} \\ \frac{\partial I(x,y)}{\partial y} &= \frac{\partial I_t(i,j)}{\partial i}\frac{\partial i}{\partial y} + \frac{\partial I_t(i,j)}{\partial j}\frac{\partial j}{\partial y}\end{aligned} \tag{25}$$

Using matrix notation equation (25) can be rewritten as

$$\begin{aligned}\begin{bmatrix} \dfrac{\partial I(x,y)}{\partial x} \\ \dfrac{\partial I(x,y)}{\partial y} \end{bmatrix} &= \begin{bmatrix} \dfrac{\partial i}{\partial x} & \dfrac{\partial j}{\partial x} \\ \dfrac{\partial i}{\partial y} & \dfrac{\partial j}{\partial y} \end{bmatrix} \begin{bmatrix} \dfrac{\partial I_t(i,j)}{\partial i} \\ \dfrac{\partial I_t(i,j)}{\partial j} \end{bmatrix} \\ \nabla I(x,y) &= N(\Theta,x,y)\nabla I_i(i,j)\end{aligned} \tag{26}$$

Lets define $N(\Theta,x,y)$ as the Derivative Correction Matrix (DCM) and $\nabla I_t(i,j)$ as the gradient vector image of Image I_t and it can be computed using, for instance, the derivative of Gaussian Filter previously mentioned.

Now a closed expression for the matrix N, in case of a projective transformation, is developed. To compute the elements of DCM matrix, explicit formulas for i and j are needed, for this reason equation (18) is rewritten as follows:

$$\begin{aligned}(x\theta_6-\theta_0)i+(x\theta_7-\theta_1)j &= (\theta_2-x) \\ (y\theta_6-\theta_3)i+(y\theta_7-\theta_4)j &= (\theta_5-y)\end{aligned} \tag{27}$$

Then the system of equation given by (27) is solved using the well known Cramer's rule from linear algebra and its solution for i and j are given as:

$$\begin{aligned}i &= \frac{(\theta_4-\theta_5\theta_7)x+(\theta_2\theta_7-\theta_1)y+(\theta_1\theta_5-\theta_2\theta_4)}{(\theta_3\theta_7-\theta_4\theta_6)x+(\theta_1\theta_6-\theta_0\theta_7)y+(\theta_0\theta_4-\theta_1\theta_3)} \\ j &= \frac{(\theta_5\theta_6-\theta_3)x+(\theta_0-\theta_2\theta_6)y+(\theta_2\theta_3-\theta_0\theta_5)}{(\theta_3\theta_7-\theta_4\theta_6)x+(\theta_1\theta_6-\theta_0\theta_7)y+(\theta_0\theta_4-\theta_1\theta_3)}\end{aligned} \tag{28}$$

From equation (28) the elements of matrix N are derived by definition given in equation (26) and after a little algebra the DCM matrix is given as:

$$N(\Theta,x,y) = F\begin{bmatrix} -(\theta_7 y-\theta_4) & (\theta_6 y-\theta_3) \\ (\theta_7 x-\theta_1) & -(\theta_6 x-\theta_0) \end{bmatrix} \tag{29}$$

With

$$F = \frac{\theta_0(\theta_4 - \theta_5\theta_7) - \theta_1(\theta_3 - \theta_5\theta_6) + \theta_2(\theta_3\theta_7 - \theta_4\theta_6)}{[(\theta_3\theta_7 - \theta_4\theta_6)x + (\theta_1\theta_6 - \theta_0\theta_7)y + (\theta_0\theta_4 - \theta_1\theta_3)]^2} \tag{30}$$

When the projective transformation is only an affine transformation the vector parameter can be written as $\Theta = [\theta_0, \theta_1, \theta_2, \theta_3, \theta_4, \theta_5, 0, 0]$ and the DCM, in this case, is

$$N(\Theta, x, y) = \frac{1}{\theta_0\theta_4 - \theta_1\theta_3}\begin{bmatrix} \theta_4 & -\theta_3 \\ -\theta_1 & \theta_0 \end{bmatrix} \tag{31}$$

In the translation transformation case, the parameter vector can be written as $\Theta = [1, 0, \theta_2, 0, 1, \theta_5, 0, 0]$ and its DCM is

$$N(\Theta, x, y) = \begin{bmatrix} 1 & 0 \\ 0 & 1 \end{bmatrix} \tag{32}$$

Note, that only for translation model, this method and method 2 are the same.

7. Minimization procedure

Let $G_k(\Theta^n) = \partial E / \partial \theta_k$, ($k$=0, …, K), Θ^n be an initial set of parameter values, and Θ^{n+1} an improved set of parameter values, where $\theta_k^{n+1} = \theta_k^n + \delta\theta_k^n$. The condition to reach an optimum Θ^{n+1} is to find a set of increments $\delta\theta_k^n, (k = 0, \dots K)$, such that the $G_k(\Theta^{n+1}) = 0$ (for all k). To compute the set of increments, functions G_k can be approximate using the Taylor expansion using only first order derivatives:

$$G_k(\Theta^{n+1}) = G_k(\Theta^n) + \frac{\partial G_k(\Theta^n)}{\partial \theta_0}\delta\theta_0^n + \frac{\partial G_k(\Theta^n)}{\partial \theta_1}\delta\theta_1^n + \dots + \frac{\partial G_k(\Theta^n)}{\partial \theta_K}\delta\theta_K^n$$

$$k=0, 1, ..K \tag{33}$$

Next we can compute the set of increments, doing $G_k(\Theta^{n+1}) = 0$ and solving the system of K equations of the form:

$$\frac{\partial G_k(\Theta^n)}{\partial \theta_0}\delta\theta_0^n + \frac{\partial G_k(\Theta^n)}{\partial \theta_1}\delta\theta_1^n + \dots + \frac{\partial G_k(\Theta^n)}{\partial \theta_K}\delta\theta_K^n = -G_k(\Theta^n)$$

$$k=0, 1, ..K \tag{34}$$

In matrix form we have,

$$H\Delta\Theta = G \tag{35}$$

Where

$$H(\Theta^n)=\begin{bmatrix} \frac{\partial G_0(\Theta^n)}{\partial \theta_0} & \frac{\partial G_0(\Theta^n)}{\partial \theta_1} & \cdots & \frac{\partial G_0(\Theta^n)}{\partial \theta_K} \\ \frac{\partial G_1(\Theta^n)}{\partial \theta_0} & \frac{\partial G_1(\Theta^n)}{\partial \theta_1} & \cdots & \frac{\partial G_1(\Theta^n)}{\partial \theta_K} \\ \cdots & \cdots & \cdots & \cdots \\ \frac{\partial G_K(\Theta^n)}{\partial \theta_0} & \frac{\partial G_K(\Theta^n)}{\partial \theta_1} & \cdots & \frac{\partial G_K(\Theta^n)}{\partial \theta_K} \end{bmatrix}$$
$$\Delta\Theta = \left[\delta\theta_0^n, \delta\theta_1^n, \cdots, \delta\theta_K^n\right]^T$$
$$G=\left[-G_0(\Theta^n), -G_1(\Theta^n), \cdots, -G_K(\Theta^n)\right]^T \tag{36}$$

Once this system of equation is solved, a new set of parameter Θ^{n+1} can be computed, and using the same procedure another set of parameter Θ^{n+2} is estimated, and so on. The iterative process ends when all the increments are very small.
In the literature matrix H is known like the Hessian matrix. If full derivatives for the elements $H_{rc}(\Theta^n)=\partial G_r(\Theta^n)/\partial\theta_c$ of the Hessian matrix (where r and c represents the row and column of H) are computed from equation (9), then results the Newton's method [Nocedal and Wright, 1999]. But, if we discard second order derivatives, the method is called Gauss-Newton (GN) [Nocedal and Wright, 1999], and it is commonly used due to its simple form and because it warranties to have a semi positive defined matrix H. The Matrix H for the GN method is presented in equation (37)

$$H_{rc}(\Theta^n)=\frac{\partial^2 E(\Theta^n)}{\partial\theta_r \partial\theta_c}=\sum_{\forall<i,j>\in I_r}\psi(e_{ij})\frac{\partial e_{ij}}{\partial\theta_r}\frac{\partial e_{ij}}{\partial\theta_c} \tag{37}$$

Where $\psi(e_{ij})=\partial^2\rho(e_{ij})/\partial^2 e_{ij}$ and for a quadratic error function $\psi(e_{ij})=2$. In matrix form, the equation (37) can be rewritten as

$$H(\Theta^n)=\sum_{\forall<i,j>\in I_r}\psi(e_{ij})\left[J_{ij}(\Theta^n)\right]\left[J_{ij}(\Theta^n)\right]^T \tag{38}$$

Unfortunately, the Newton or Gauss-Newton not always reaches a minimum value for the error E, because only first order derivatives in the Taylor Expansion are used. More robust and better methods, like the one presented in subsection 0, expand the Newton or Gauss-Newton to avoid the case when $E(\Theta^{n+1}) > E(\Theta^n)$.

7.1 The Levenberg-Marquard Method

The Levenberg-Marquard method (LM) [Nocedal and Wright, 1999] is a non-linear iterative technique specifically designated for minimizing functions which has the form of Sum of Square functions, like E. At each iteration, the increment of parameters $\Delta\Theta$, is computed solving the following linear matrix equation:

$$(H + \Lambda)\Delta\Theta = G \tag{39}$$

Where G and H are defined by equation (11) and (38) respectively for GN, Λ is a diagonal matrix $\Lambda = diag(\lambda, \lambda, ..., \lambda)$, and λ is a variable parameter at each iteration.
The process starts with the input image, I, and the reference image, I_r, and initial values for parameters Θ^0. The
Algorithm 1 describes the LM method.

1. Pick a small value for λ (say $\lambda = 0.001$), an initial value for Θ^0, an error function (for instance $\rho(e) = e^2$) and set $n=0$.
2. For a given Θ^n, compute the transformed image I_t^n (eq. (2)) applying bilinear interpolation to improve the quality of the image using equation (3).
3. Compute the total error, $E(\Theta^n)$ using equation (1).
4. Compute a new set of parameter using the following steps
   a. Compute $M(\Theta^n,i,j)$ and $N(\Theta^n,x,y)$ using, the equation (19) and (29) for projective transformation or the equation (17) and (31) for affine transformation, respectively.
   b. Compute the Gradient vector image $\nabla I_t^n(i,j)$ applying a derivative of Gaussian Filter (eq. (23))
   c. Compute the matrix $J_{ij}(\Theta^n) = M(\Theta^n, i, j) N(\Theta^n, x, y) \nabla I_t^n(i, j)$
   d. Compute the Gradient vector $G(\Theta^n)$ and Hessian matrix $H(\Theta^n)$ by equation (11) and (38) respectively.
   e. Solve the linear system of equations given by (39) for $\Delta\Theta$, and then calculate $E(\Theta^n + \Delta\Theta)$
5. If $E(\Theta^n + \Delta\Theta) >= E(\Theta^n)$, increase λ by a factor of 10, and go to step 4. If λ grows very large, it means that there is no way to improve the solution Θ^n and the algorithm ends with this solution $\Theta^* = \Theta^n$.
6. If $E(\Theta^n + \Delta\Theta) < E(\Theta^n)$, decrease λ by a factor of 10. Set $\Theta^{n+1} = \Theta^n + \Delta\Theta$, $n=n+1$ and go to the step 2.

Algorithm 1. The Levenberg-Marquard Method

Note when $\lambda = 0$, the LM method is a Gauss-Newton method, and when λ tends to infinity, $\Delta\Theta$ turns to so called steepest descent direction and the size of increments in $\Delta\Theta$ tends to zero.

8. Experimental results

To test the methods previously described, a computer program was built under the Redhat 9 Linux operating System, using the C language. All the experiments were running in a PC Pentium 4, 2.26 Ghz. and we use standard routines from the Free Gnu Scientific library

(GSL) to solve the linear system of equations. The error function was defined as a quadratic function ($\rho(e) = e^2$ with $\varphi(e) = 2e$ and $\psi(e) = 2$).
The PGM image format was selected because its simplicity to load and save gray level images with 256 gray levels, from 0 to 255. The PGM format is as follows,

```
P5 {nl}
# CREATOR: The GIMP's PNM Filter Version 1.0 {nl}
640 480 {nl}
255
<I(0,0)><I(0,1)>...<I(0,639)><I(1,0)><I(1,1)> ...
```

Where P5 means gray level images (P6 is reserved for color images), # starts a comment, 640 and 480 is the width and height of the image respectively, and {nl} is the new line character. <I(i,j)> is a single byte (an unsigned char in C) and they are ordered from left to right of the first row of pixels, then the second row of pixels, and so on.
Figure 4 shows two binary input images (Figure 4 (a) and Figure 4 (b)) and the associated reference image (Figure 4 (c)). Sequences of images for the three methods, to compute derivatives, are shown in Figures 5, 6 and 7; the number, below each Figure, indicates the number of iteration for Algorithm 1. In these cases the input image was the image shown in Figure 4 (a) and derivative of Gaussian Filter with $\sigma = 6$ was used. The numerical results for Algorithm 1, are presented in Table 1. The results of this Table show us, that methods 1 and 3 find the right transformation (a very low error), method 2 have the highest error and method 1 is the fastest.

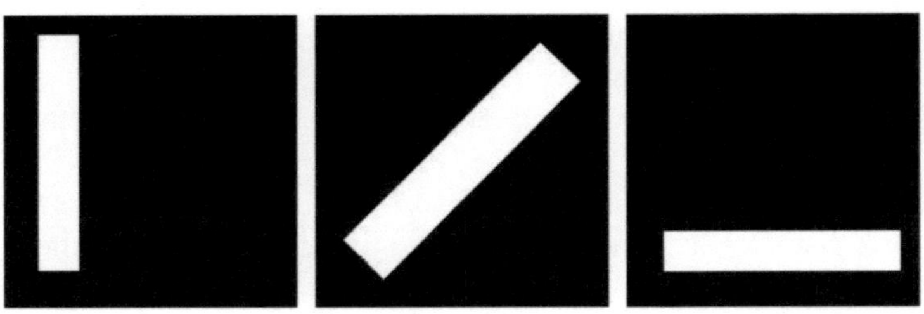

(a) I_1 (b) I_2 (c) I_r

Figure 4. Input images (I_1 and I_2) and the reference image I_r. Images are of dimension *300 X 300*

Method	Time (seconds)	Iteration	Error
1	11	88	3.78 E-9
2	18	41	1902.6
3	18	49	3.22 E-9

Table 1. Comparing the three derivative methods for the test case of Figure 4(a) and (c)

(a) 15 (b) 30 (c) 45 (d) 60 (e) 75

Figure 5. Comparing method 1, sequence a-b-c-d-e. The number of iteration of each image is shown

(a) 8 (b) 16 (c) 24 (d) 32 (e) 42

Figure 6. Comparing method 2, sequence a-b-c-d-e. The number of iteration of each image is shown

(a) 8 (b) 16 (c) 24 (d) 32 (e) 40

Figure 7. Comparing method 3, sequence a-b-c-d-e. The number of iteration of each image is shown

Numerical results for images of Figure 4 (b) and (c) are shown in Table 2. Again Methods 1 and 3 find the right transformation (a low error), but Method 2 have a higher error. In this case Method 1 is also the fastest.

Method	Time (seconds)	Iteration	Error
1	12	70	1.59
2	26	59	51.51
3	27	44	1.59

Table 2. Comparing the three derivative methods for the test case of Figure 4(b) and (c)

Figure 8(a) and 8(b) shown an input image and the associated reference image respectively, with dimensions *256 X 256*. In this case, the case, the Algorithm 1, was applied two times; at first with derivatives of a Gaussian function with $\sigma = 10$ and then with $\sigma = 1$. In the first case with $\sigma = 10$, derivatives include information of a big window around the desired pixel value and so the derivatives are good enough to guide the search near to the right set of parameters. In the second, with $\sigma = 1$, derivatives are more accurate, given the previous set of parameters, and the final error, *E*, gets smaller values than in the first case. Final results for the three methods are shown in Figure 9. In this case only method 3 was able to find the right transformation.

(a)

(b)

Figure 8. Another case of test. a) Input image and b) Image Reference

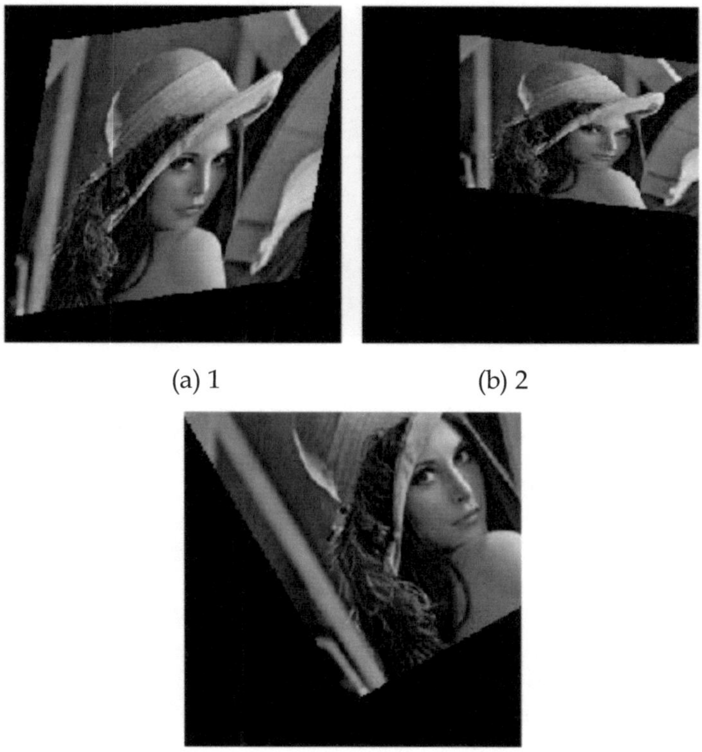

(a) 1 (b) 2

(c) 3

Figure 9. Final results of the three methods for image of Figure 8

9. Conclusions

A tutorial, with all the details related to the parametric image registration task, has been presented. Also two new methods (Method 1 and Method 3) are presented besides the classical method to compute derivatives of images.

Method 1 computes the image derivatives faster than the other two methods, but it does not give accurate estimations. Methods 2 and 3 take more time because they compute derivatives of the transformed image (at each iteration) while method 1 computes derivatives of the input image only once.

Method 3 is an improved version of method 2 because it takes into account the exact derivatives needed. However the classical method 2, reported in the literature is the same as the method 3 under translations. Experiments confirm the poor estimation computed by method 2 when rotations, scaling, or an affine transformation are involved.

In general, derivatives of images with big σ values are recommended when the right transformation is far away from identity, in other words, when big translations, rotations, scaling, etc , are involved. In contrast, small values of σ are recommended to get more accurate results. In fact, we mixed both strategies, big values at first and then small values.

10. References

[Adelson and Bergen, 1986] Adelson, E. and Bergen, J. R. (1986). The extraction of spatiotemporal energy in human and machine vision. *In IEEE, editor, IEEE Workshop on Visual Motion*, pp. 151-156, Charleston USA.

[Barman et al., 1986] Barman, H., Haglund, L., Knutsson, H., and Beauchemin, S. S. (1986). Estimation of velocity, acceleration and disparity in time sequences. *In Princeton, editor, IEEE Workshop on Visual Motion*, pp. 151-156, USA.

[Barron et al., 1994] Barron, J. L., Fleet, D. J., and Beauchemin, S. S. (1994). Performance of optical flow techniques. *International Journal of Computer vision*, 12(1): pp.43-47.

[Calderon and Marroquin, 2003] Calderon, F. and Marroquin, J. L. (2003). A new algorithm for computing optical flow and his application to image registration. *Computacion y Sistemas*, 6 (3) pp.213-226.

[Faugeras, 1993] Faugeras, O. (Nov 19 1993). *Three-Dimensional Computer Vision.* The MIT Press.

[Hartley and Zisserman, 2000] Hartley, R. and Zisserman, A. (2000). *Multiple View Geometry in Computer Vision.* Cambridge, University Press, second edition.

[Heeger, 1987] Heeger, D. (1987). Model for the extraction of image flow. *J. Opt. Soc Am*, 4: pp. 1455--1471.

[Huber, Peter J. 2003] Huber, Peter J. (Dec 23, 2003). *Robust Statistics.* Wiley Series in Probability and Statistics

[Kaneko et al., 2002] Kaneko, S., Murase, I., and Igarashi, S. (2002). Robust image registration by increment sign correlation. *Pattern Recognition*, 35: pp. 2223-2234.

[Kaneko et al., 2003] Kaneko, S., Satoh, Y., and Igarashi, S. (2003). Using selective correlation coefficient for robust image registration. *Pattern Recognition*, 29: pp. 1165-1173.

[Lai and Vemuri, 98] Lai, S. H. and Vemuri, B. C. (98). Reliable and efficient computation of optical flow. *International Journal of Computer vision*, 29(2) pp.87--105.

[Ma et al., 2004] Ma, Y., Soatto, S., Kosecka, J., and Sastry, S.S. (2004). *An Invitation to 3-D Vision From Images to Geometric Models.* Springer.

[Nocedal and Wright, 1999] Nocedal, J. and Wright, S. J. (1999). *Numerical Optimization.* Springer.

[Szeliski and Coughlan, 1994] Szeliski R. and Coughlan, J. (1994). Spline-based image registration. *Technical Report, Harvard University, Departmet of Physics,* Cambridge, Ma 02138.

[Romeny, 1994] Romeny, Bar ter Haar, editor (1994). *Geometry-Driven Diffusion in Computer Vision.* Kluwer Academic Publishers.

[Trucco and Verri, 1998] Trucco, E. and Verri, A. (1998). *Introductory techniques for 3-D Computer Vision.* Prentice Hall.

[Zitova and Flusser, 2003] Zitova, B. and Flusser, J. (2003). Image registration methods: A survey. *Image and vision Computing.* 21 pp. 977-1000

11

A Pseudo Stereo Vision Method using Asynchronous Multiple Cameras

Shoichi Shimizu, Hironobu Fujiyoshi, Yasunori Nagasaka and Tomoichi Takahashi
Chubu University & Meijo University
Japan

1. Introduction

Systems of multiple baseline stereo vision (Okutomi & Kanade, 1993 and Kanade et al., 1997) have been proposed and used in various fields. They require cameras to synchronize with one another to track objects accurately to measure depth. However, inexpensive cameras such as Web-cams do not have synchronous systems.

A system of tracking human motion (Mori et al., 2001) and a method of recovering depth dynamically (Zhou & Tao, 2003) from unsynchronized video streams have been reported as approaches to measuring depth using asynchronous cameras. In the former, the system can obtain the 2D position of a contact point between a human and the floor, and the cycle of visual feedback is 5 fps on average. In the latter, the method creates a non-existing image, which is used for stereo triangulation. The non-existing image is created from the estimated time delay between unsynchronized cameras and optical flow fields computed in each view. This method can output a depth map at the moment of frame *t*-1 (one frame before the current one), not the current frame.

We propose a method of pseudo-stereo vision using asynchronous multiple cameras. Timing the shutters of cameras asynchronously has an advantage in that it can output more 3D positions than a synchronous camera system. The 3D position of an object is measured as a crossing point of lines in 3D space through the observation position on the last frame and the estimated 3D position using the previous two frames. This makes it possible for the vision system to consist of asynchronous multiple cameras. Since the 3D position is calculated at the shutter timing of each camera, the 3D position can be obtained from the number of cameras x 30 points.

This chapter is organized as follows. Section 2 describes a method of measuring the 3D position using asynchronous multiple cameras. Section 3 reports experimental result on the recovery of motion when an object is moved in virtual 3D space, and discusses the effectiveness of the proposed method. Section 4 describes some experimental setups and reports experimental results using real images of an object moving at high speed. Section 5 discusses the processing time and enhancement of n cameras. Finally, Section 6 summarizes the method of pseudo-stereo vision.

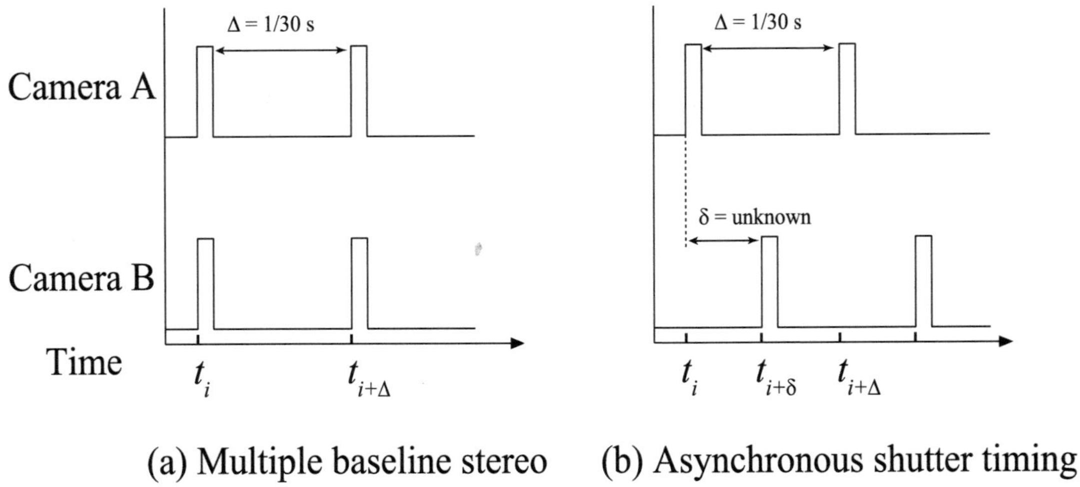

Figure 1. Two possible combinations of shutter timings

2. 3D position measurement with multiple cameras

The method of stereo vision, which measures the 3D position of an object, requires two images to be captured at the same time to reduce errors in measurement. We investigated a method of pseudo-stereo vision taking advantage of the time delay between the shutter timings of two asynchronous cameras to calculate the 3D positions of objects.

2.1 Shutter timings of two cameras

Two possible combinations of shutter timings by two cameras are outlined in Fig. 1. The first (a) is the same shutter timings, which is used in multiple baseline stereo vision, synchronized by a synchronous signal generator. In a conventional stereo vision system, the 3D positions can be obtained at a maximum of 30 fps using a normal camera with a fast vision algorithm (J. Bruce et al., 2000).

Figure 1 (b) outlines the other type of shutter timing using asynchronous cameras where there is a time delay of δ. When an object moves fast, the stereo vision with this shutter timing calculates the 3D position from corresponding points with the time delay. Therefore, the estimated 3D position, $\hat{,P}_{t+1}$ has error, as shown in Fig. 2. This chapter focuses on this kind of shutter timing, and proposes a method of calculating the 3D position taking time delay δ into account, which is unknown. Since our method calculates the 3D position at each shutter timing, it is possible to output the 3D position from the number of cameras x 30 points per second.

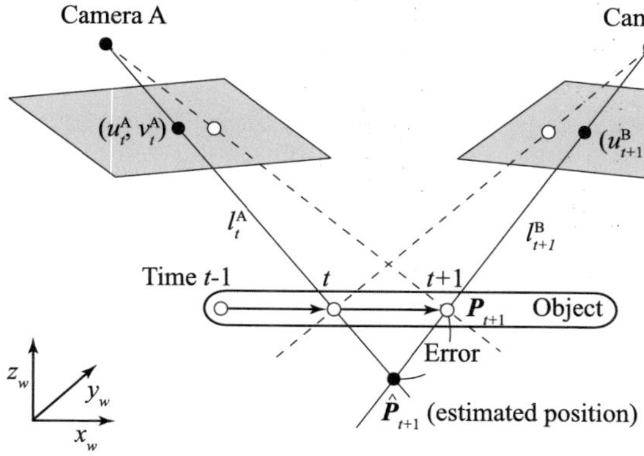

Figure 2. Error in stereo vision with time delay

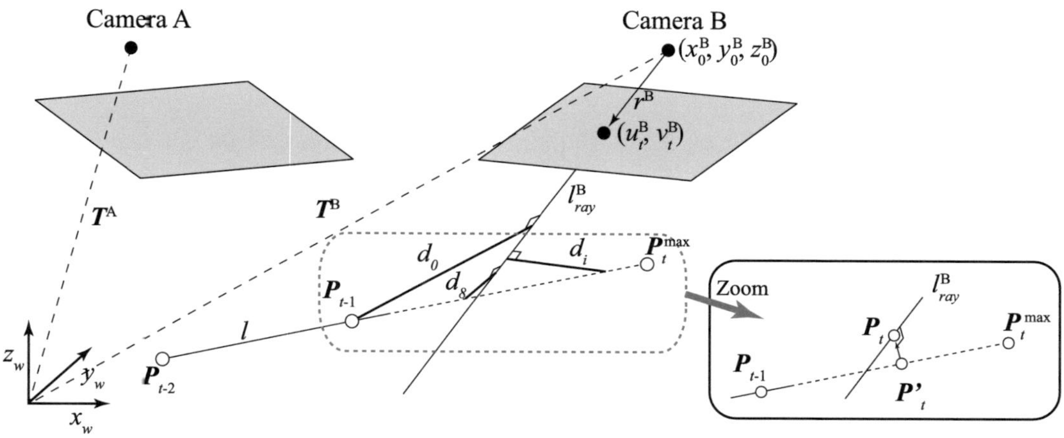

Figure 3. Estimate of 3D position of last frame

2.2 Estimate 3D position of last frame

The 3D position, $P_t = [x_t, y_t, z_t]$, of the last frame, t, is estimated from positions P_{t-1} and P_{t-2} in the previous two frames as shown in Fig. 3. Where the image in last frame t is captured by camera B, the algorithm to calculate the 3D position in last frame t is described as follows:

1. Given the 3D positions in the previous two frames, $P_{t-1} = [x_{t-1}, y_{t-1}, z_{t-1}]$ and $P_{t-2} = [x_{t-2}, y_{t-2}, z_{t-2}]$, straight line l is calculated by:

$$l = \frac{x - x_{t-1}}{x_{t-2} - x_{t-1}} = \frac{y - y_{t-1}}{y_{t-2} - y_{t-1}} = \frac{z - z_{t-1}}{z_{t-2} - z_{t-1}}. \tag{1}$$

2. The instant in time when the images are captured to estimate the 3D positions $\boldsymbol{P}_{t-1}$ and $\boldsymbol{P}_{t-2}$, are unknown due to asynchronous cameras being used. The maximum number of frames for a normal camera is generally 30 fps. Since the maximum time delay is assumed to be 1/30 s, the range of locations in 3D position can be estimated by:

$$\begin{aligned}\boldsymbol{P}_t^{\max} &= \max_{(0<\delta<1/30)}\left(\frac{\left(\boldsymbol{P}_{t-1}-\boldsymbol{P}_{t-2}\right)}{\delta}(\Delta-\delta)+\boldsymbol{P}_{t-1}\right)\\ &= \max_{(0<\delta<1/30)}\left(\frac{\left(\boldsymbol{P}_{t-1}-\boldsymbol{P}_{t-2}\right)\Delta}{\delta}-\left(2\boldsymbol{P}_{t-1}-\boldsymbol{P}_{t-2}\right)\right),\end{aligned} \tag{2}$$

where Δ is the frame rate (1/30 s).

3. Let $\boldsymbol{T}^{\mathrm{B}}=[T_x^{\mathrm{B}}\ T_y^{\mathrm{B}}\ T_z^{\mathrm{B}}]$ be the translation vector from the origin of the world coordinate to the focus point of camera B, and $\boldsymbol{r}^{\mathrm{B}}=[\lambda\ \mu\ \nu]^T$ be the vector that denotes the direction of the viewing ray, l_{ray}^{B}, passing through the position on image coordinate $(u_t^{\mathrm{B}}, v_t^{\mathrm{B}})$ and the focus point of the camera B. Then, viewing ray l_{ray}^{B} is defined by

$$l_{ray}^{\mathrm{B}}=\frac{x-T_x^{\mathrm{B}}}{\lambda}=\frac{y-T_y^{\mathrm{B}}}{\mu}=\frac{z-T_z^{\mathrm{B}}}{\nu}. \tag{3}$$

The distance, d, is calculated between points $\boldsymbol{P}_i=[x_i, y_i, z_i]$ on straight line l and viewing ray l_{ray}^{B} using:

$$d(x_i,y_i,z_i)=\sqrt{\left\{\mu\left(x_i-T_z^{\mathrm{B}}\right)-\lambda\left(y_i-T_y^{\mathrm{B}}\right)\right\}^2+\left\{\nu\left(y_i-T_y^{\mathrm{B}}\right)-\mu\left(z_i-T_z^{\mathrm{B}}\right)\right\}^2+\left\{\lambda\left(z_i-T_z^{\mathrm{B}}\right)-\nu\left(x_i-T_z^{\mathrm{B}}\right)\right\}^2}\,. \tag{4}$$

Then, the 3D position, $\boldsymbol{P}_i$, which produces the minimum distance, is selected as $\boldsymbol{P}'_t$ by calculating:

$$\boldsymbol{P}'_t=\underset{(\boldsymbol{P}_{t-1}\le \boldsymbol{P}_i\le \boldsymbol{P}_t^{max})}{\arg\min}\left[d(\boldsymbol{P}_i)\right]. \tag{5}$$

4. The 3D position may not exist on the viewing ray l_{ray}^{B}, as shown in Fig. 3, because of prediction error. To solve this problem, 3D position $\boldsymbol{P}_t$ is calculated as the nearest point on viewing ray l_{ray}^{B} by:

$$\boldsymbol{P}_t=\frac{\left(\boldsymbol{P}'_t-\boldsymbol{T}^{\mathrm{B}}\right)\cdot\boldsymbol{r}^{\mathrm{B}}}{\left|\boldsymbol{r}^{\mathrm{B}}\right|^2}\boldsymbol{r}^{\mathrm{B}}+\boldsymbol{T}^{\mathrm{B}}. \tag{6}$$

If the last frame is camera A, 3D position $\boldsymbol{P}_t$ can be calculated by changing the suffix.

2.3 Calculation of 3D positions of previous two frames

It is necessary to calculate the previous 3D positions, $\boldsymbol{P}_{t-1}$ and $\boldsymbol{P}_{t-2}$, accurately to obtain the current frame using the method described in section 2.2. Where frame *t*-1 is camera B, the position of an object using the image coordinates from camera A at frame *t* does not have a corresponding point from camera B at the same time, which is needed to calculate the 3D position using stereo vision. The predicted point of camera B, $(u'^{B}_{t-1}, v'^{B}_{t-1})$, corresponding to observed point $(u^{A}_{t-1}, v^{A}_{t-1})$ is generated by a basic interpolation technique, as shown in Fig.4. The 3D position can be measured by stereo vision using observed point $(u^{A}_{t-1}, v^{A}_{t-1})$ and pseudo-corresponding point $(u'^{B}_{t-1}, v'^{B}_{t-1})$. The algorithm to calculate the 3D position at $t-1$ is described as follows:

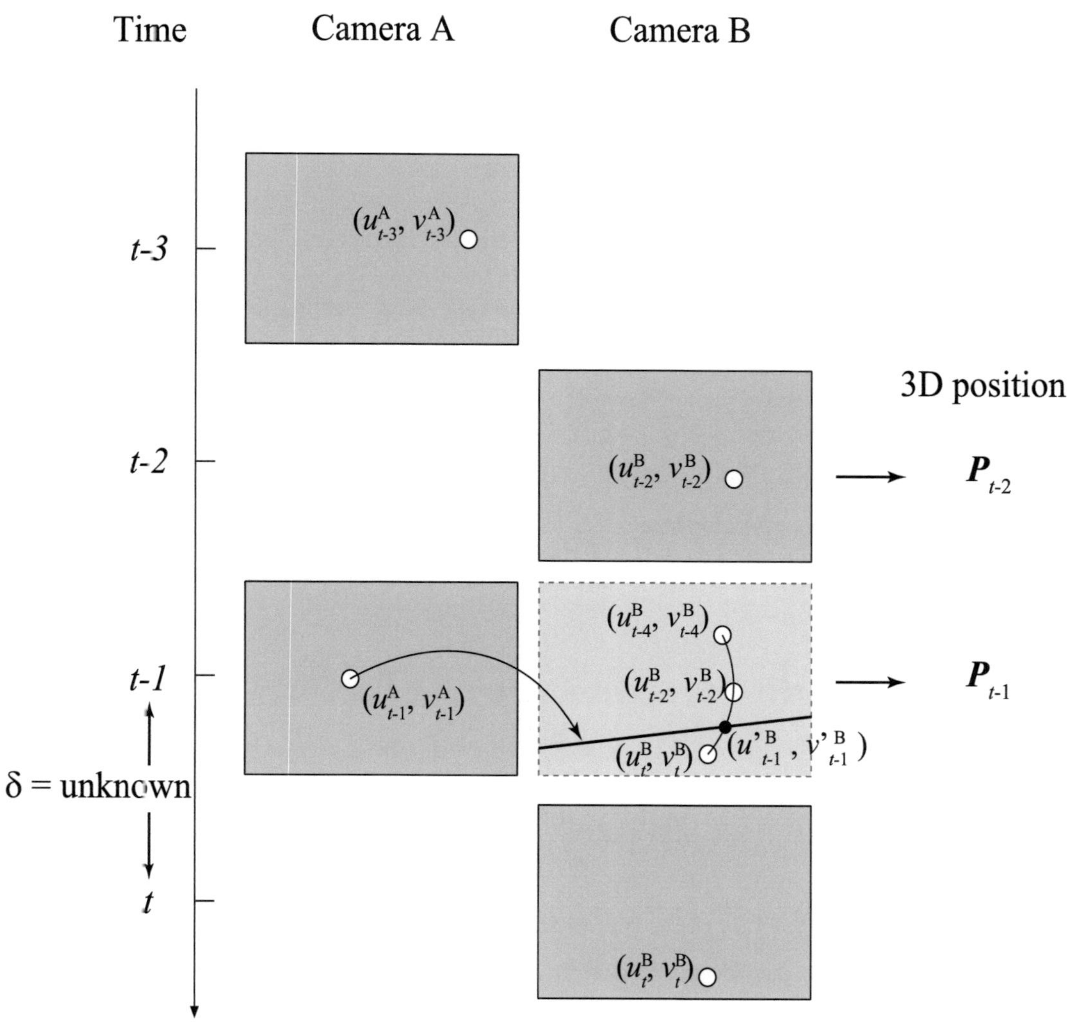

Figure 4. 3D position is estimated using spline curve

Estimation of 3D position using spline curve

The object's trajectory is estimated by spline-curve fitting (de Boor, 1978). The pseudo-corresponding point is obtained as the intersection between the trajectory and epipolar line, as shown in Fig. 4. The spline curve on the camera image can be calculated from three observed points, (u_t^B, v_t^B), (u_{t-2}^B, v_{t-2}^B), and (u_{t-4}^B, v_{t-4}^B) by:

$$u(s) = \sum_{i=0}^{N-1} \alpha_i B_{i,K}(s), \quad v(s) = \sum_{i=0}^{N-1} \beta_i B_{i,K}(s)\,, \tag{7}$$

where s is a parameter uniquely determined by (u, v), $u = u(s)$ and $v = v(s)$ are determined by s, and $B_{i,K}$ means the $(K - 1)$ dimensional B spline. Here, parameters α and β are solved from some input point (u, v). The spline curve can be constructed using parameters α and β. Then, the epipolar line (Faugeras, 1993) on camera B is calculated from observation point (u_{t-1}^A, v_{t-1}^A) on camera A. Let $\boldsymbol{F}$ denote a fundamental matrix of 3x3 which is defined by:

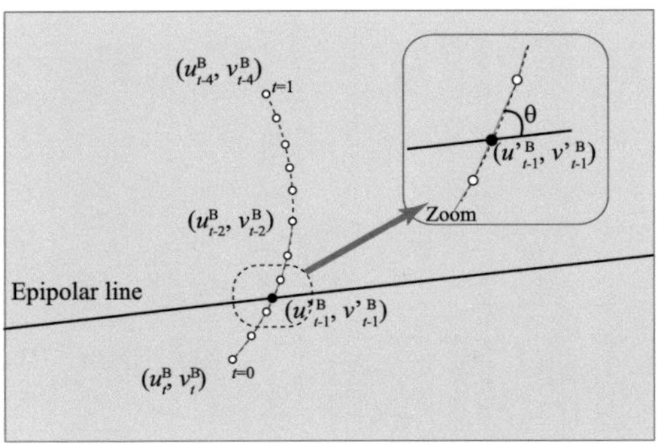

Figure 5. Calculate intersecting point of spline curve and epipolar line

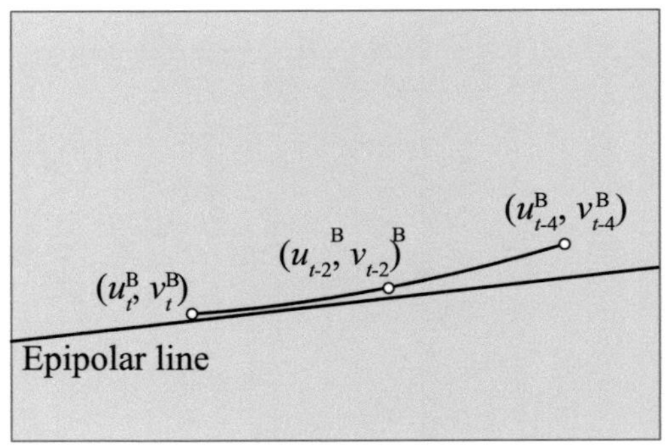

Figure 6. Error in the intersecting point

$$\boldsymbol{m}_1 \, \boldsymbol{F} \, \boldsymbol{m}_2^T = 0\,, \tag{8}$$

where $\boldsymbol{m}_1 = \begin{bmatrix} u^A{}_{t-1} & v^A{}_{t-1} & 1 \end{bmatrix}$, $\boldsymbol{m}_2 = \begin{bmatrix} u'^B_{t-1} & v'^B_{t-1} & 1 \end{bmatrix}$, $F = \begin{bmatrix} f_1 & f_2 & f_3 \\ f_4 & f_5 & f_6 \\ f_7 & f_8 & f_9 \end{bmatrix}$. The epipolar line on camera B is given by:

$$v = -\frac{\boldsymbol{m}_1 \begin{bmatrix} f_1 & f_4 & f_7 \end{bmatrix}^T u + \boldsymbol{m}_1 \begin{bmatrix} f_3 & f_6 & f_9 \end{bmatrix}^T}{\boldsymbol{m}_1 \begin{bmatrix} f_2 & f_5 & f_8 \end{bmatrix}^T}\,. \tag{9}$$

The spline curve has various node points from (u_t^B, v_t^B) to (u_{t-4}^B, v_{t-4}^B), and the intersecting point is determined as pseudo-corresponding point (u'^B_{t-1}, v'^B_{t-1}) on camera B as shown in Fig. 5. Then, the 3D position $\boldsymbol{P}_{t-1}$ is calculated from pseudo-corresponding point (u'^B_{t-1}, v'^B_{t-1}) and observation point (u_{t-1}^A, v_{t-1}^A) on camera A using stereo vision.

3D position P_{t-2} at frame *t*-2 is calculated in the same way as above, i.e., as the intersecting point of the spline curve of *t*-1, *t*-3, *t*-5 frames, and the epipolar line from image coordinate (u^B_{t-2}, v^B_{t-2}) of camera B.

Reliability of estimated position

Angle θ of the intersecting position Fig. 5 is calculated to measure how reliable the intersecting position is. There is a case where the spline curve becomes parallel to the epipolar line, as shown in Fig. 6. For this reason, the object moves along the epipolar plane. Here, the estimated 3D position includes a large amount of error. Therefore, it is necessary to reject the outlier causing the error in the 3D position using angle θ.

3. Simulation experiments

3.1 Recovery of object motions

We evaluated the method we propose by simulating the recovery of object's movement with uniform and non-uniform motion in 3D space (3,000 x 2,000 x 2,000 mm). In the experiment, we assumed that n (n= 2, 3) cameras would be mounted at a height of 3,000 [mm]. The conventional approach and the proposed method were evaluated using two kinds of motion.

- Uniform motion (spiral) : An object moves in a spiral with a radius of 620 mm at a velocity of 3,000 mm/s at center (x, y) = (1,000, 1,000)
- Non-uniform motion : An object falls from a height of 2,000 mm, then describes a parabola (gravitational acceleration: g = 9.8 m/s^2)

The trajectory of the object is projected to the virtual image planes of each camera. A 3D position is estimated with the proposed method described in Section 2 using the point projected on the virtual image plane (u, v) of each camera.

3.2 Simulation results

Table 1 lists the averages for estimation error in the simulation experiments, and Fig. 7 has examples of the recovery of spiral and non-uniform motion using three cameras. The "constant" in Table 1 means the time delay of the shutter timing is the same (δ = 1/60 s when there are two cameras, and 1/90 sec when there are three), and "random" in Table 1 means the time delays at every frame are not the same (0 < δ < 1/30 s). The "stereo (asynchronous)" shows the results for general stereo vision with time delay. It is clear that the proposed method provides more accurate estimates than stereo vision. This is because it can estimate the 3D position using the pseudo-corresponding points at the same time. Using three cameras provides more accurate results than using two cameras. This is why time delay δ is short, and the accuracy of a linear prediction is improved.

Motion	Camera	Proposed method	Stereo(asynchronous)

		Constant	Random	Constant	Random
Spiral	2	0.86	2.89	13.68	13.68
	3	0.32	2.17	12.54	13.72
Non-uniform	2	2.30	3.61	11.07	11.92
	3	1.23	2.51	9.87	12.54

Table 1. Average of absolute errors in 3D positions [mm]

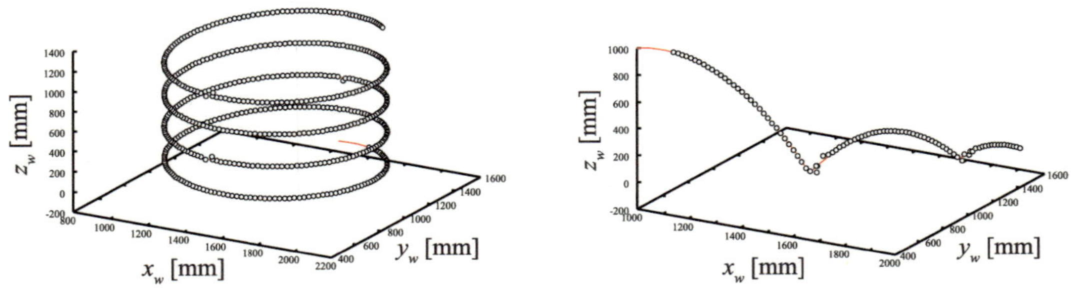

(a) Proposed method (left: spiral, right: non-uniform motion)

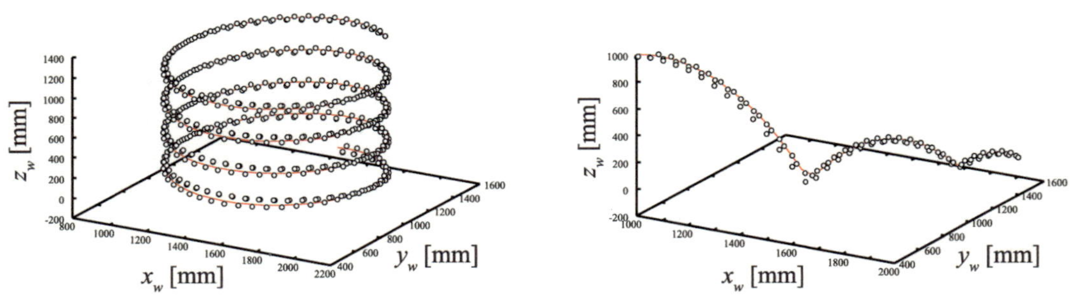

(b) Stereo vision (left: spiral, right: non-uniform motion)

Figure 7. Example of recovery of 3D position

4 Experiments using real cameras

4.1 Configuration of vision system

Figure 8 shows how we placed the three cameras in our vision system. They were mounted at a height of 2,800 mm, and each viewed an area of 2,000 x 3,000 mm. Each was calibrated using corresponding points of world coordinates (x_w, y_w, z_w) and image coordinate (u, v) based on Tsai's camera model (Tsai, 1987). The shutter timing for all three cameras was controlled by a TV-signal generator. Three frame grabbers for the three cameras were installed on a PC. Our hardware specifications were:

<Hardware Specifications>
- PC (DELL PRECISION 530)
    - ■ CPU (XEON DUAL PROCESSOR 2.2 GHz)
    - ■ MEMORY (1.0 GB)
- CAMERA (SONY XC-003) x 3
- FRAME GRABBER (ViewCast Osprey-100) x 3
- TV SIGNAL GENERATOR (TG700 + BG7)

Process-1, process-2, and process-3 in Fig. 8 analyze images from camera A, camera B, and camera C every 1/30 s. Analyzed results such as object position in image coordinate (u_t, v_t) and the instant at which the analyzed image is captured are sent via the UDP interface to process-4, which outputs the 3D positions of the object using the procedure described in Section 2. There is negligible delay due to communications between processes because this work is done on the same computer.

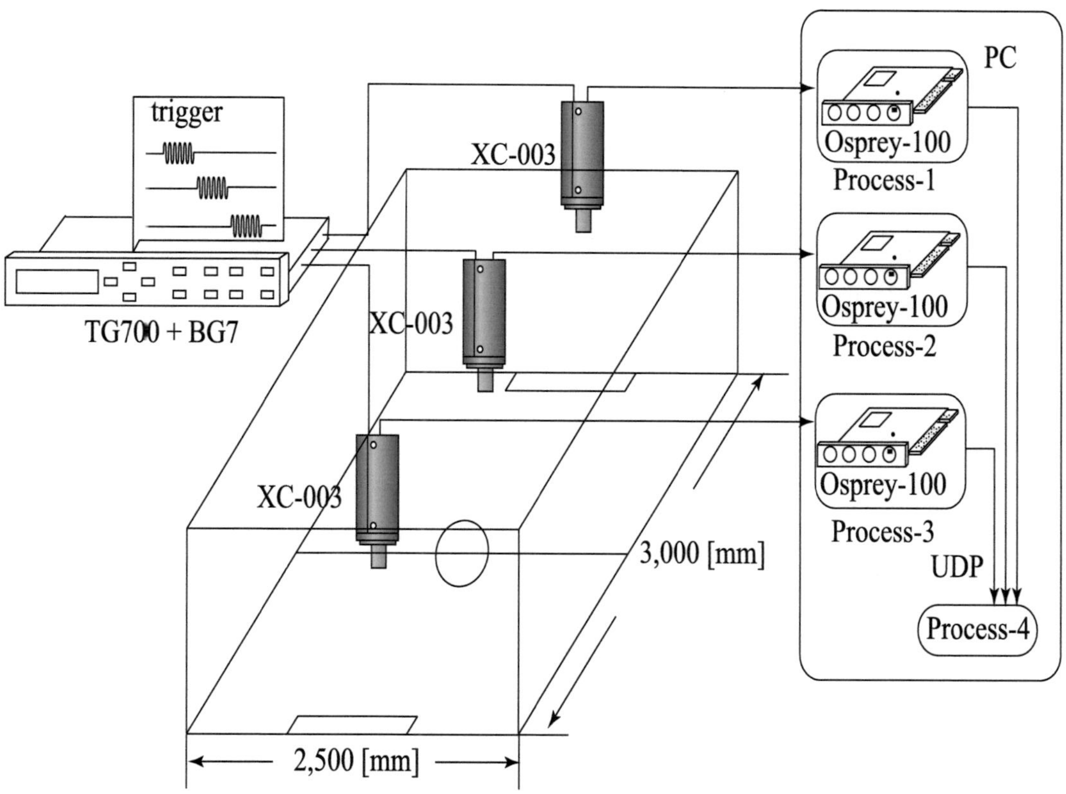

Figure 8. Overview of our vision system

4.2 Recovery of uniform circular motion

We used a turntable and a ball, as shown in Fig. 9, to evaluate the accuracy of the estimated 3D positions. A ball attached to the edge of a ruler (1,000 mm in length) makes a uniform circular motion with a radius of 500 mm. The turntable is placed on a box at a height of 500 mm, and the ball is 660 mm above the floor. The turntable rotates at a speed of 45 rpm, and its rotation speed per second is (45x2)/60 = 0.478 radian.

Table 2 lists the averages for estimation error. The pixel resolution at the floor is 4 mm. The average of the positions using stereo vision with synchronous cameras was measured within 4 mm; this error is an appropriately result from the viewpoint of resolution. It is clear that our method is better than the stereo vision with asynchronous shutter timing. However, the error with our method is approximately 6 mm larger than with stereo vision with synchronous shutter timing. This is because the pseudo-corresponding points have the error. However, it is possible to reject 3D positions using angle θ, which was described in Section 2.3.

Proposed method	Stereo	
	Synchronous	Asynchronous
9.2	3.7	266.0

Table 2. Average and variance in estimation error [mm]

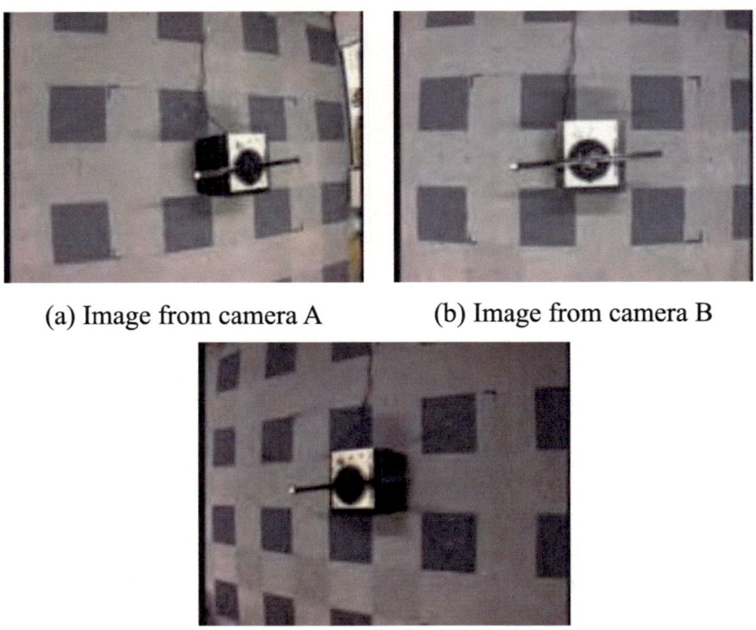

(c) Image from camera C

Figure 9. Captured images of turntable and ball

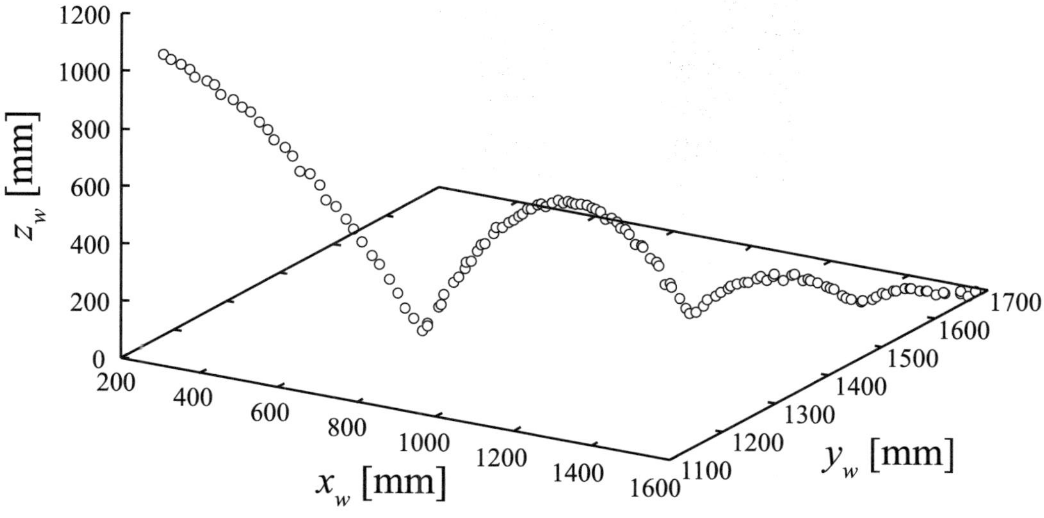

Figure 10. Recovery of bounding motion

4.3 Recovery of bounding ball

We performed an experiment to recover a bounding object to evaluate the proposed method since the recovery of uniform circular motion was at a constant speed. Figure 10 has an example of the motion of a hand-thrown ball bounced for about 1.5 s. We can see 135 plotted points. This indicates that the speed is the same as a 90 fps camera. Therefore, the proposed method can obtain the 3D position at 90 fps, when we use three normal cameras (30 fps) when the time delay of each shutter timing is 1/90 s.

5. Processing time

Our vision system was implemented on a PC with dual Xeon processors 2.2 GHz dual Xeon processors. It took 2.7 ms for the vision process to calculate the positions of colored objects from an image, and 1.8 ms for the transmission process via UDP with one PC in our implementation. Therefore, this system can determine the 3D positions of an object in 4.5 ms from the time the analyzed image was captured. It is possible to use n cameras with our system when the time delay from each of them is δ, if $\delta > n \times$ (processing time) is satisfied.

6. Discussion and Conclusion

We proposed a method of pseudo-stereo vision method using cameras with different shutter timings, where the previous two frames were calculated using a spline curve. The method can output a 3D position at 90 fps using three cameras, and using multiple cameras is expected to enhance the output of the 3D positions.

We confirmed that our method was better than stereo vision with the time delay in simulation experiments. The error was 9.2 mm in experiments using real cameras. However, the error was within a useful range, because the object's radius was 20 mm. Moreover, it is clear that our method is better than the stereo vision with asynchronous shutter timing.

7. References

M. Okutomi.; & T. Kanade. (1993). A Multiple Baseline Stereo, IEEE Trans. PAMI, Vol.15, No. 4, pp. 353-363, 1993.

T. Kanade.; H. Kano.; S. Kimura.; E. Kawamura; A. Yoshida.; & K. Oda. (1997). Development of a Video-Rate Stereo Machine, Journal of the Robotics Society of Japan, Vol. 15, No.2, pp.261-267, 1997

H. Mori.; A. Utsumi.; J. Ohya. & M. Yachida. (2001). Human Motion Tracking Using Non-synchronous Multiple Observations. In the IEICE, Vol.J84-D-II, Num. 1, pp. 102-110, 2001.

C. Zhou. & H. Tao. (2003). Dynamic Depth Recovery from Unsynchronized Video Streams. In Proc. IEEE Computer Society Conference on Computer Vision and Pattern Recognition, pp. 351-358, 2003.

J. Bruce.; T. Balch. & M. Veloso. (2000). Fast and Inexpensive Color Image Segmentation for Interactive Robots, IROS-2000, Vol. 3, pp. 2061-2066, 2000.

O.D. Faugeras. (1993). Three-Dimensional Computer Vision: A Geometric Viewpoint. MIT Press, Cambridge, MA, 1993.

de. Boor. (1978). A Practical Guide to Splines. Splinger-Verlag, New York, 1978.

R. Y. Tsai. (1987). A versatile Camera Calibration Technique for High-Accuracy 3D Machine Vision Metrology Using Off-the-Shelf TV Cameras and Lenses, In IEEE Journal of Robotics and Automation, Vol.RA-3, Num.4, pp.323-344, 1987.

12

Real-Time 3-D Environment Capture Systems

Jens Kaszubiak, Robert Kuhn, Michael Tornow, Bernd Michaelis
Otto-von-Guericke-University of Magdeburg
Germany

1. Introduction

Real-time environment capture systems provide autonomous robotic machines and vehicles with vital information for interacting with their environments. Navigation and obstacle detection are key features of these systems. The systems are designed to capture objects, and establish their locations and approximate dimensions. These system capabilities are described in detail in this chapter. The ability to identify objects to facilitate manipulation or interaction is not the primary subject of investigation.

Environment capture systems can be designed with a number of sensors. However, information provided by many sensors is very limited. Very large amounts of information can be obtained with systems comprising cameras and a few sensors, as camera images can be processed in a great variety of ways. These systems have some issues, namely – very complex algorithms, high memory requirements for images, and limited real-time capabilities. However, rapid advances in micro-electronics are quickly addressing these issues.

In this chapter, we show how measurement methods based on stereophotogrammetry can be adapted and optimized for embedded systems. We will also deal in detail with key challenges and issues encountered in designing the systems. We provide experimental results for a number of typical applications.

2. 3-D Environment Capture Procedures

There is a host of sensor systems available that are suited for environment capture. They can be combined to compensate for different subsystem deficiencies and weaknesses. By combining a number of sensors, extensive information can be obtained from the surroundings.

Among the many environment capture systems available for vehicles are:

- radar systems
- ultrasonic devices
- laser systems
- active and passive optical measurement methods

Some measurement systems are based on the principle of the active propagation delay of an emitted signal. Ultrasonic sensors are suitable for short distance targets. These systems are useful indoors for measurement ranges of a few meters. Distances to objects can be measured very accurately (see Uhler et al., 2003). Ultrasound measurements taken outdoors can be disturbed by bad weather conditions – with the result that the detection range is

restricted and the reliability is impaired. Due to the narrow aperture angles many sensors are needed for fully comprehensive environment capture.
Radar sensors are deployed for objects at close range (24 GHz), and for objects at long distances (76 GHz). The aperture angle is very small. The surroundings can only be completely scanned and surveyed by panning the radar antenna (as in aeronautics), or by deploying a bank of radar sensors. Devices for ground-based vehicles are offered at this time for distances to objects ranging from a few meters to many hundred meters. However, these systems interfere with other equipment and pose a risk to living organisms. They are also expensive (Venhovens & Naab, 2000).
More recently, laser scanners are being adopted for use in environment capture systems. They also work on the propagation delay principle and scan and range a 3-d point at a particular point in time. These systems are quite accurate. For complete environment capture, a mechanically moveable deflection mirror is needed (Fuerstenberg et al., 2003). Distances to objects are of the order of a few meters and go up to some hundred meters. Object distances are limited in outdoor public areas by laser radiation and the risk of serious damage to biological eyes.
Active optical propagation delay techniques (Lange & Seitz, 2001; Tyrrel, 2004) have been under investigation for some years now. These techniques produce an extensive depth image with a single sensor. The Photonic Mixer Device (PMD) is one such system. In this system, a modulated optical signal is transmitted to a scene and reflections from the scene are captured by the elements of a matrix (preferably a CMOS sensor). This is similar to the way ultrasonic sensors work. The advantage of this system is that only one camera is needed. Quite dense disparity maps are generated, and they can be processed in real-time. One drawback with this technique is the high processing power needed. The maximum object distance is a function of the wavelength of the modulated signal, the optical transmit capacity brought to bear on the scene, and sensor characteristics. This method of measurement is a very recent innovation and has a lot of potential.
Images are processed directly in many optical systems. The texture of the object is overlaid with additional information in active imaging systems. Distance and surface information can be determined to a high degree of accuracy with the help of fringe projection.
Accuracies on the order of μm can be achieved for limited observation spaces with active systems comprising a number of cameras. Numerous applications for these techniques can be found in the fields of automation, quality assurance, medical systems, and, to a lesser extent, security systems. They are not widely deployed for environment capture.
When a number of active systems are deployed together there is always a risk that they will interfere with each other. Systems with large aperture angles, or systems designed to range over great distances, sometimes emit very powerful light. This restricts their use.
3-d data can also be acquired with the help of passive optical systems in systems comprising more than one camera. The simplest case of multi-camera systems, i.e. stereophotogrammetry, comprises two cameras. This dual-camera constellation generates depth images.
Environment capture systems do not need to be very accurate. However, a large observation space has to be scanned and surveyed rapidly. Passive systems, such as stereophotogrammetric measuring systems, are suited for these types of applications (Knoeppel et al., 2000). The images provide information on the entire scene being scanned.

The camera system is the key to adapting a stereophotogrammetric system for different applications. The arrangement of the cameras, the base, aperture angle, and the resolution of the cameras determine the measurement range. The normal case of stereophotogrammetry, whereby the cameras are arranged parallel to each other, is suited for environment capture over large distances.
In the next section we describe what we consider to be the key algorithms and parameters needed for a compact 3-d environment capture solution based on a stereo camera system.

3. Function and Setup of Stereo Camera Systems for Generating 3-D Depth Information

The coordinates of a point in 3-d space are determined using a stereo camera system by mapping the object point in two camera images taken from different angles. When a point has been detected in both camera images, the 3-d coordinates of the point are calculated using basic geometrical functions.

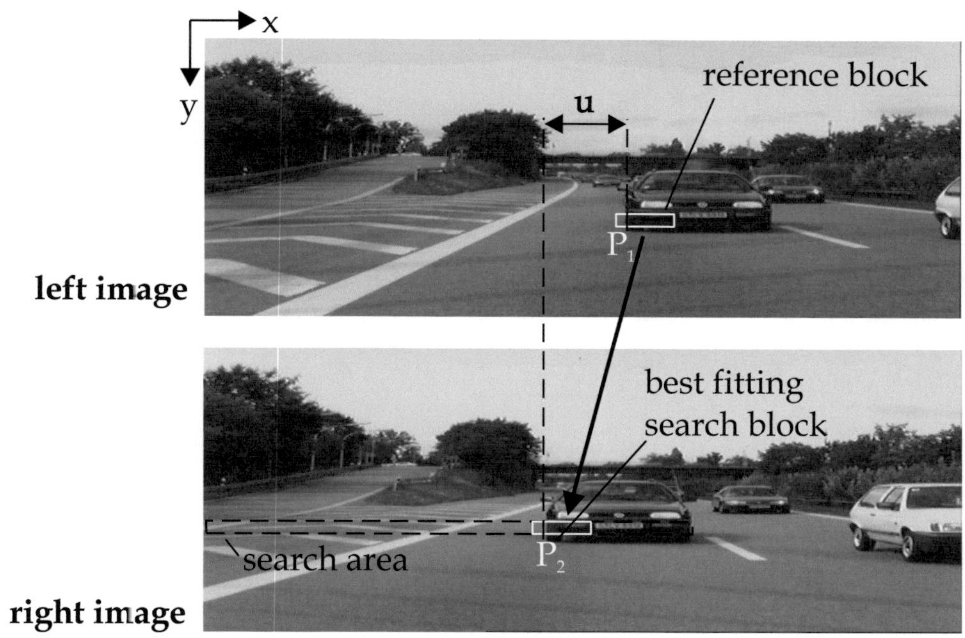

Figure 1. Basic principles of block matching

Typically, a 3-d stereo camera system consists of two calibrated cameras connected together rigidly, whereby the clearance between them is the base.
The detection of the object point in the two images (generally known as the correspondence search) is typically nontrivial. There are a number of detection solutions available.
One option is to attach suitable indicator marks to the target. These marks are detected in the image by segmenting and measuring punctiform patterns. It is normally impossible or impracticable to attach separate markers to targets in the applications at hand. Typically one has to use the object texture instead.

In correspondence analysis, a section of the first image (reference block, position P_1 in fig. 1) and a block of the same size (search block, position P_2 in fig. 1) in the second image are isolated. The similarity between these two blocks is then calculated (see fig. 1). Due to the geometry of the shot (the two projection centers and the object point form a plane that can be intersected by the image plane – also known as the epipolar line), the corresponding point can only be located on a specific line in the search image. The similarity for every point along this line is then determined (see fig. 2). The location of the extremum (= offset u of the features with respect to each other) is the position of the corresponding point.

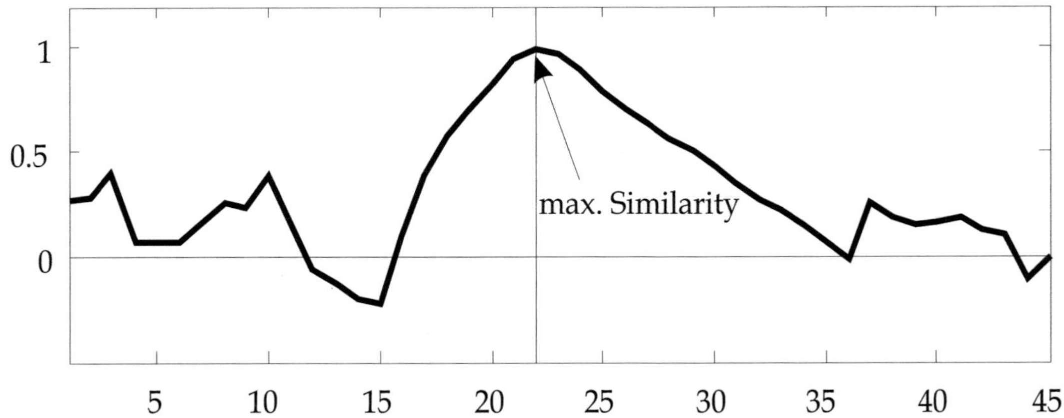

Figure 2. A typical correlation function (NCCF)

Standard correlation functions such as the Sum of Absolute Differences (SAD; eq. 1) or the Normalized Cross Correlation Function (NCCF; eq. 2) can be invoked to calculate the similarity. The quality of the results provided by these two functions differs; the numerical overheads also differ. The SAD is calculated for each pixel in the search window by computing the correlation value using

$$SAD(\xi,\eta)=\sum_{i=0}^{m-1}\sum_{j=0}^{n-1}\left|F(i,j)-P(\xi+i,\eta+j)\right| \tag{1}$$

$F(j,i)$ *- pixel in the search block*

$P(j,i)$ *- pixel in reference block*

M, n - window size

ξ,η *- displacement in x, y- direction*

F and P represent $m\times n$ large image cut-outs from the reference and search images. The SAD function is very sensitive to brightness variations and does not always give useful results. The NCCF function produces better results but they are numerically more complex to compute :

$$NCCF(\xi,\eta) = \frac{\sum_{j=0}^{n-1}\sum_{i=0}^{m-1}\left(\overline{F(i,j)} \cdot \overline{P_r(\xi+i,\eta+j)}\right)}{\sqrt{\sum_{j=0}^{n-1}\sum_{i=0}^{m-1}\overline{F(i,j)}^2 \cdot \sum_{j=0}^{n-1}\sum_{i=0}^{m-1}\overline{P_r(\xi+i,\eta+j)}^2}} \quad (2)$$

$\overline{F(j,i)}$ - *zero-mean pixel in search block*

$\overline{P(j,i)}$ - *zero-mean pixel in reference block*

It is difficult to analyze the correspondence for objects such as white walls with little or no texture of their own. In these cases a preliminary search should be made for edges or image sections that have sufficient texture. The correspondence search should only be made at these locations. Other areas are removed or interpolated. This can also be beneficial, because it thins out the 3-d point cloud.

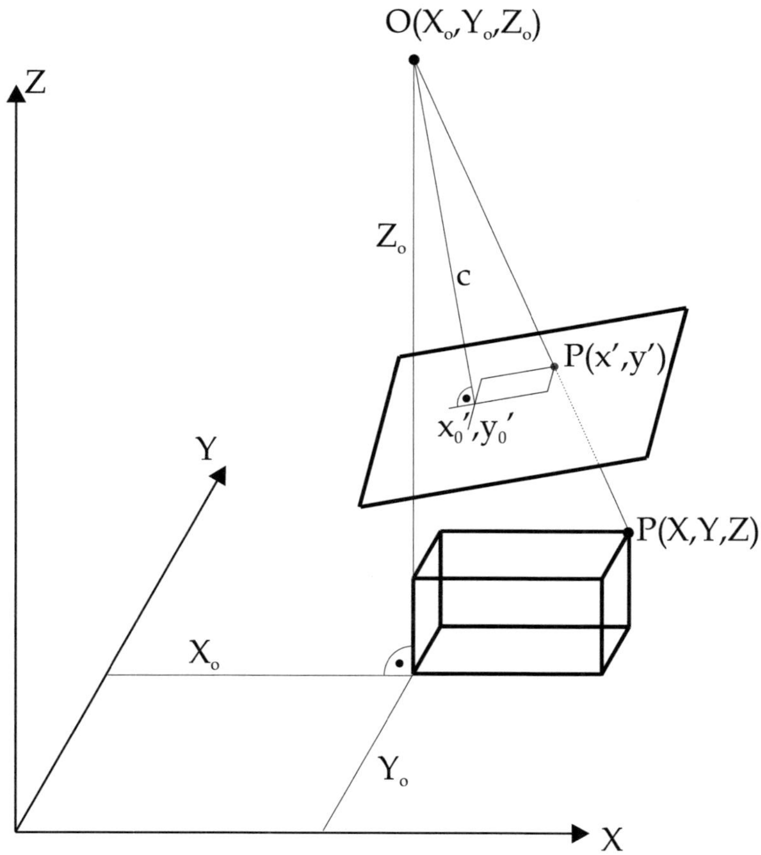

Figure 3. Elements of a camera orientation

When the object point has been detected in both images, the 3-d coordinates of the point are calculated using the collinearity equations (Schenk, 1999) (see also fig. 3):

$$x' = x'_0 - c_k \frac{a_{11}(X - X_0) + a_{21}(Y - Y_0) + a_{31}(Z - Z_0)}{a_{13}(X - X_0) + a_{23}(Y - Y_0) + a_{33}(Z - Z_0)} \tag{3}$$

$$y' = y'_0 - c_k \frac{a_{12}(X - X_0) + a_{22}(Y - Y_0) + a_{32}(Z - Z_0)}{a_{13}(X - X_0) + a_{23}(Y - Y_0) + a_{33}(Z - Z_0)} \tag{4}$$

The coordinates x' and y' are the image coordinates, and X, Y and Z are the object coordinates of the observed point (see fig. 3). The other elements in the equation define the internal and external orientation of the camera. The constant c_k is the calibrated focal length, and x_0' and y_0' the principal point. This point is defined as the point of intersection of the optical axis and the image plane. Terms for the radial and tangential distortion are examples of other elements in the internal orientation. The six elements in the external orientation describe the location of the camera (X_0, Y_0, Z_0) and its viewing angle (a_{xx} are the elements of the rotation matrix). Camera calibration is complete once these values have been determined.

Typically, the calibration data is produced using a bundle block adjustment. A calibration plate with known points is required for this procedure. The nine unknown parameters for eq. 3 and eq. 4 are then determined by adjusting the intermediate observations. The relationship between observations (image coordinates) and unknowns (calibration) is nonlinear. Approximate values need to be assigned to the unknowns. This is often a very difficult and time-consuming exercise! Once the calibration data are known, the mapped object point can be calculated from the image coordinates by re-arranging eq. 3 and eq. 4.

The normal case of stereophotogrammetry is a special case of a stereo system. The cameras are arranged so that both image planes are in the same plane, and the camera axes run parallel to one another. Determining the object coordinates is then simplified to a beam intersection problem and is thus more straightforward than the general case. The formulas for calculating the 3-d coordinates then become:

$$X = x' \cdot \frac{B}{u}; \quad Y = y' \cdot \frac{B}{u}; \quad Z = c_k \cdot \frac{B}{u} \tag{5}$$

The base (i.e. the clearance between the two cameras) is represented by B. The disparity u is the offset of the same object point in the two camera image planes (fig. 1). The image coordinates of the point in the reference image are x' and y'.

Another advantage of the normal case is the simplified correspondence analysis. This can be restricted to the pixel line in the search image, without having to calculate the epipolar line separately (see also fig.1). The systematic errors in the camera system can be compensated by using the standard camera model (eq. 3 and eq. 4). The corrections ΔZ and ΔX can be calculated with $\Delta Z = d \cdot Z^2 + e \cdot Z + f$ and $\Delta X = g \cdot Z + h \cdot X + i$ $(d,...,i \in \Re)$. Combining ΔZ *and* ΔX *with* eq. 1 yields

$$Z = \frac{k}{u^2} + \frac{l}{u} + m \quad (k,l,m \in \Re) \tag{6}$$

Coefficients *k*, *l* and *m* only have to be acquired for eq. 6 during calibration. There is no need to determine base and focal length. The derivations for X and Y are similar (see Albertz & Kreiling, 1989).
Rectification has to be performed in order to apply the algorithms from the normal case of stereophotogrammetry to a general camera set-up. The original images taken by the camera in the general camera set-up are transformed so that they are the same as an image in the normal stereo case. A virtual image plane, in the same location as the normal case, is calculated. The original images are then converted to this plane. We can derive the transformation from the calibration parameters. The conversion can be carried out on special image processing hardware during imaging.
The accuracy of a stereo camera system is a function of the geometry of the imaging configuration and the image processing accuracy. System accuracy can often be estimated successfully by applying the laws of error propagation to the formulas for the normal case (eq. 5). The mean error σ_Z in the typically predominant Z direction then becomes

$$\sigma_z = \frac{Z^2}{c \cdot B}\sigma_u \tag{7}$$

Better accuracies are achieved the shorter the distance to the object, the larger the camera constant, the wider the camera base, and the more accurate the image coordinate calculations are.
The resolution of the cameras yields a quasi quantization of the measurable distance. The disparity is less than a pixel width at a distance to the object that is greater than a specific threshold. The resolution can also be improved with a subpixel interpolation function. The optics – and thus system accuracy – are also affected by air. Camera aperture angles determine the system viewing range. However, large aperture angles give rise to distortions, that have to be corrected by non-linear correction terms in eq. 3 and 4 (El-Melegy & Farag, 2003). This is always necessary with precision measurements.
The above image processing algorithms have to be implemented and evaluated. The various implementations are described in the next section.

4. Designing an Embedded Stereo System

4.1 Hardware Architectures for Information Processing

Image processing algorithms may be implemented on standard PCs or PC clusters. This option is very common due to the good availability of state-of-the-art high performance PCs. These computer systems can be deployed universally in a range of applications due to their considerable computing power.
They are not so useful in mobile applications because of the low space and performance requirements of these applications. Specially developed embedded systems are favored in these situations. The embedded hardware is often only suited for specific applications. Often, PCs or embedded processors are not powerful enough for real-time image processing due to their architecture and bus systems. A number of processor elements, connected in parallel or in a pipeline is a more suitable arrangement. Processor elements can be complete processors or special hardware elements. Options for different hardware structures are shown in fig. 4.

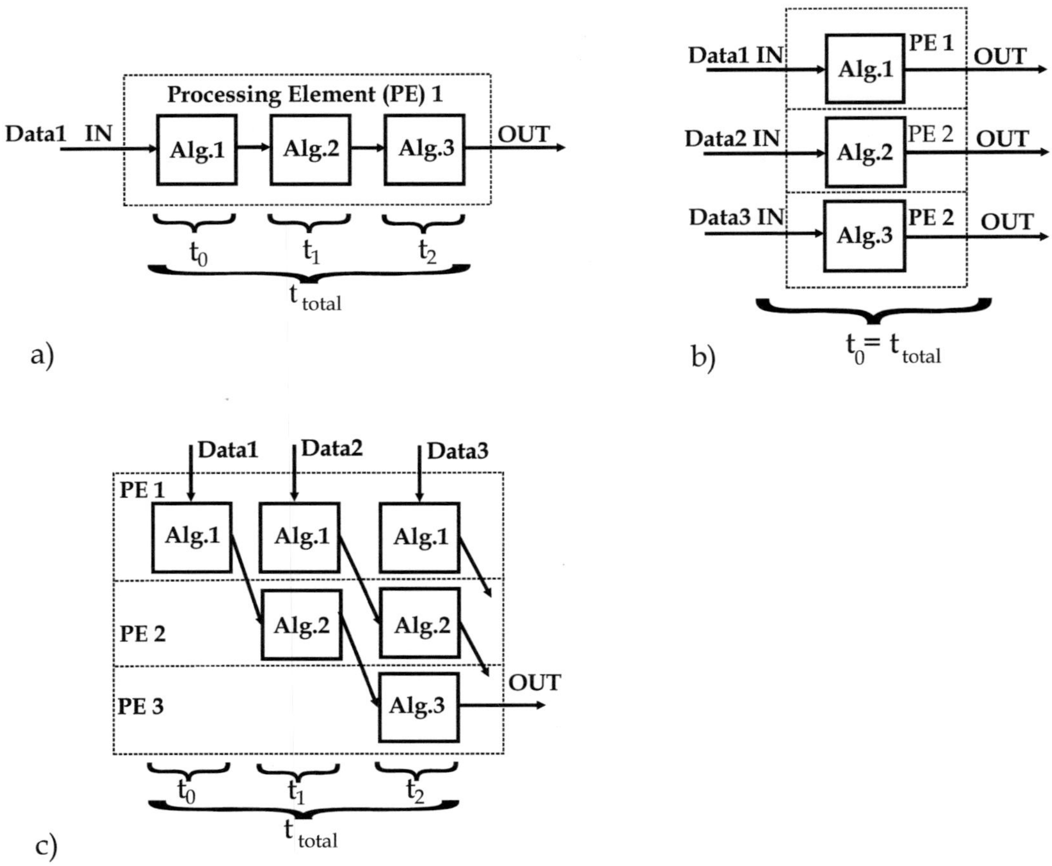

Figure 4. Processing principles a) Serial b) Parallel c) Pipeline

A single processor system is shown in fig 4 a). The algorithms are processed chronologically and in series by a single processor. This processing model is called Computing in Time. The data throughput per unit time is increased in comparison to fig. 4 a) by the parallel processing in fig. 4 b) and c). The processing elements may be fully fledged processors, or specially developed hardware. FPGAs are available for hardware development in low-volume production. FPGAs are programmable logic chips. They may also be described as special processors, where a program may be implemented and executed in hardware.

A number of processing operations may be executed simultaneously in a single processing step in the hardware logic. The algorithm is data-flow oriented, i.e. it is continuously compiled and executed as a single instruction in structured logic. This programming model is distributed spatially and is known as Computing in Space (fig. 4 b) and 4 c)).

Data-flow oriented algorithms are best implemented in hardware, whereas control-flow oriented algorithms run better on a single processor or processor system. Data-flow oriented algorithms can process high data rates. They consist of basic operations and there are few logic branches in the data flow. On the other hand, control-flow oriented algorithms can process small quantities of data only, but with a very complex data flow.

4.2 Data Flow in the Image Processing System

The standard data flow model of an image processing algorithm (Noelle, 1996) is shown in fig. 5. There is a tendency to use data-flow oriented algorithms for preprocessing, and control-flow oriented algorithms for feature extraction, and interpretation & classification.

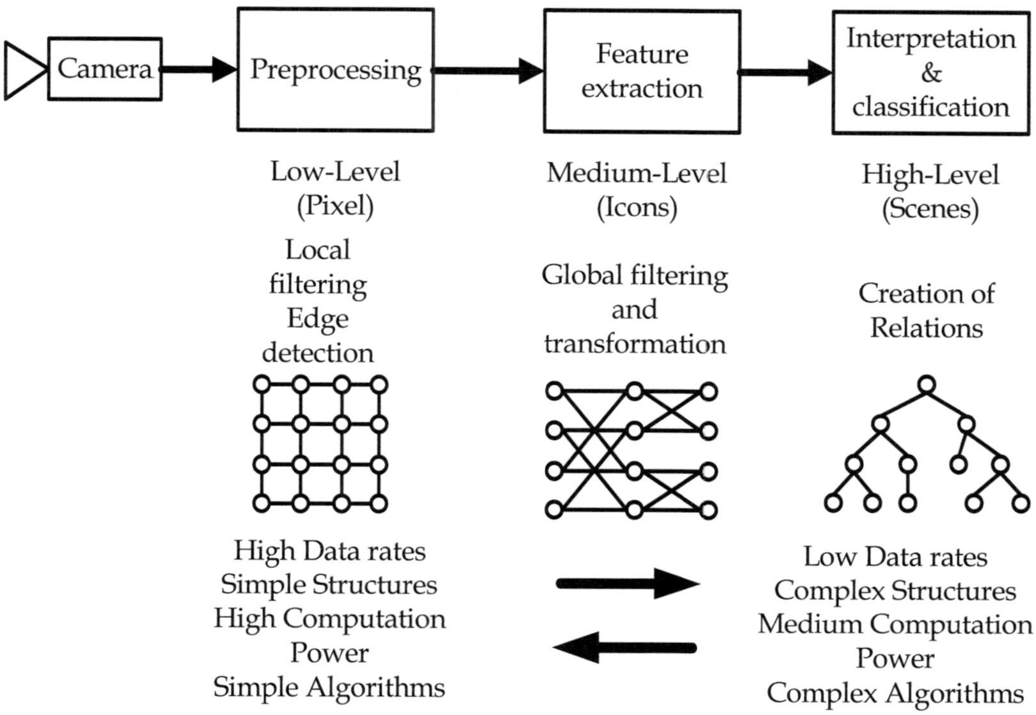

Figure 5. Data flow model of image processing algorithms (Noelle, 1996)

Preprocessing is often implemented in hardware logic. Interpretation & classification is typically run on processors as shown in fig. 5. This system of hardware logic and processors is also referred to as hardware-software co-design (Gupta & Rajesh, 1995). The developer decides which algorithms to implement in hardware and which in software, or the structure of the hardware-software co-design is automatically selected by a separate algorithm.

A typical image processing algorithm implemented as a hardware-software co-design for a stereo system is shown in fig. 6 (Kaszubiak et al., 2005). The preprocessing stage comprising the correlation and edge detection functions, and the subpixel interpolation function are implemented in hardware. The implementation on a single processor is not efficient enough, due to the architecture of the data bus systems which cause bottlenecks when images are read in real time. Knoeppel (Knoeppel et al., 2000) presented this type of system. Implementation in hardware requires that a data-flow oriented solution is developed for real-time data processing.

The object detection step using a depth histogram (see section 4.4) can also be viewed as a data-flow oriented algorithm. It is therefore also implemented in the FPGA hardware. The downstream stages in the processing chain are implemented as a pipeline on three processors, because of the many control-flow oriented structures.

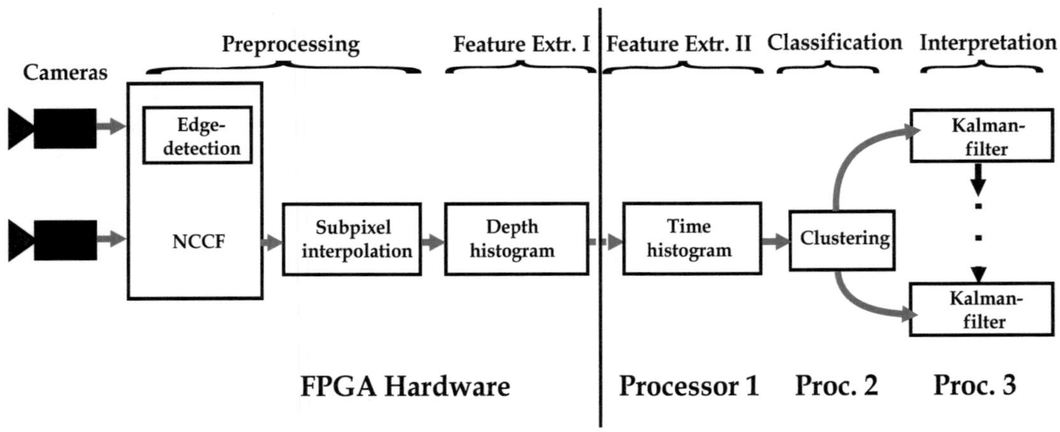

Figure 6. Algorithm as a hardware-software co-design

We can achieve real-time processing conditions for a stereo image processing system as shown in fig. 6 with a 1024x500 pixel resolution and a 25 Hz image rate by implementing the hardware-software co-design in an embedded system. We will now describe how the different parts of the algorithm are adapted and implemented as an embedded system as shown in fig. 6.

To detect objects with the very limited resources of an embedded system, a data reduction stage with a straightforward algorithm is needed. The first step is to acquire the 3-d points/disparity map with the help of stereo image analysis. We will discuss the implementation of these algorithms in hardware in the next section.

4.3 Optimizing and Implementing the Algorithms for Generating the 3-D Disparity Map in Hardware

4.3.1 Steps for Reducing Computation Costs

The input data for generating the 3-d disparity map is a sequence of stereo images containing a lot of information that is not vital for the application.

The strategy for system optimization and thus the reduction in computation costs for determining the disparity map consists of the application of a suitable similarity criterion, the pre-selection of relevant image sections, data organization and flow, and improving the input data.

When the lighting conditions are good, simple similarity criteria are used. The simple structure of the SAD function (eq. 1) and its simple mathematical elements make it the function of choice for many applications. It is also processed at a higher speed than the NCCF (eq. 2). However, since the SAD is not very reliable, a preprocessing step or extra criteria are needed for reliable results. The benefits of speed in some applications compensates for some of the disadvantages of the SAD function. Nevertheless, the NCCF has proven itself to be a reliable criterion for many cases of environment capture.

By rectifying the images, image data processing could be simplified, but the rectification task has the disadvantage of high computation costs. To save computation costs we can avoid fully rectifying the images to produce the epipolar condition by applying correction equations (eq. 6) as described in section 3, especially if we can align the cameras accurately. The objects being captured are mainly other vehicles, houses, bridges, and people; and they all have long vertical edges, which allows a number of lines to be averaged in the vertical direction – thus keeping system calibration work to a minimum. A slight rotation of the camera can be compensated for by averaging 2-4 lines and combining them to a single new line.

We can perform the correction step and the step for calculating the 3-d coordinates in different parts of the system. We can optimize the computation costs by determining the 3-d coordinates for the center point of scanned objects only. In order to reduce computational overheads the correction step is run for the necessary points only.

The computation power needed to fully compute all blocks in a line is very high. This is, however, necessary for continuous image processing over a longer period.

Environment capture systems can be divided into two major groups according to their detection ranges:

- imaging systems with a wide aperture angle for objects at close range
- systems with a narrow aperture angle for objects at greater distances (as needed for a lane change assistant (see section 5.2))

We have developed an optimized algorithm for this latter case.

4.3.2 Hierarchical Search Algorithm

We used the error characteristic (eq. 7) in determining the location over the detection range in this algorithm. It is desirable to have a constant relative error over the entire detection range in many environment capture applications. We optimize the area correlation algorithm by means of an image pyramid (Tornow et al. 2003) for implementation in hardware. We make use of the fact that the maximum camera resolution is only needed at the greatest object distance, whereas the available resolution at close range is more a hindrance than a benefit due to the large disparity.

We reduce computation costs by producing image layers with different resolutions. The layers in the pyramids are ranked by factor 2 (see fig. 7). We have to adapt the accuracy for locating distant objects, as the error in determining the distance is a function of the square of the distance. This means that there is considerable redundancy available for the measurement accuracy for objects at close range. We generate each layer by replacing two pixels by their mean value. L_0 is the image taken with the original resolution. The individual layers are arranged so that the correlation method described in section 3 can be applied in all resolution layers in the same manner.

We can thus achieve a large detection range with an approximately constant relative error using a very small search block in each layer. Only one specific distance range is represented by each layer in the pyramid. We can cover the entire detection range by summarizing the data from all layers, as shown in fig. 8.

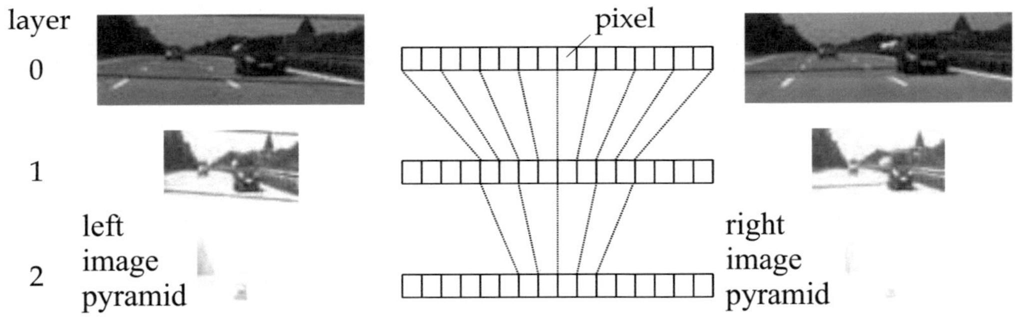

Figure 7. Generating the layers

Calculating the root of NCCF (eq. 2) poses problems in the hardware implementation. The squared NCCF can be used as an alternative, as only the position of the extremum is relevant. All negative values are set to zero.

We now establish the locations of the maxima above a predefined threshold in the resulting search block. Only maxima corresponding with object features (object edges) are processed. The disparity with the greatest weighted correlation value is then selected for the reference block from all layers (see below). Disparities from layers with reduced resolution have to be recalculated to the original resolution.

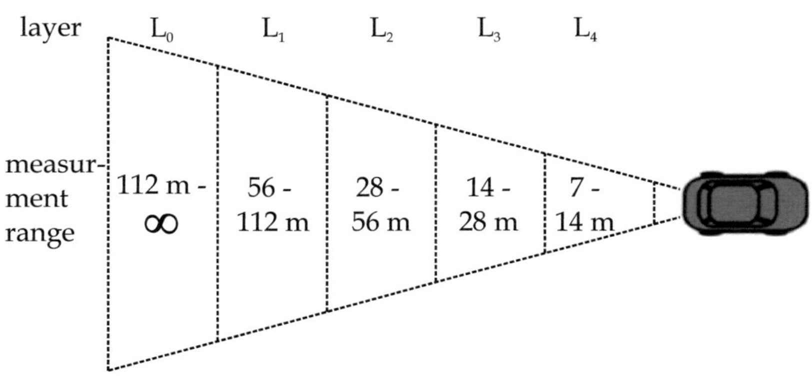

Figure 8. Distribution of the entire range for the application in section 5.2

Having created a disparity map for each layer, we append this information to the resulting disparity map. We now select the significant layer for each 16-pixel block in the original resolution. We search for the extremum of the correlation values in the stacked blocks (fig. 9) in the layers.

Objects that are very close only produce a response that is above the threshold in the layer with the lowest resolution. The further away the objects are, the more layers respond. Different layer resolutions generate results with different accuracies. We have to introduce a penalty to ensure the best result is always selected. Thus, the higher resolution layer always wins.

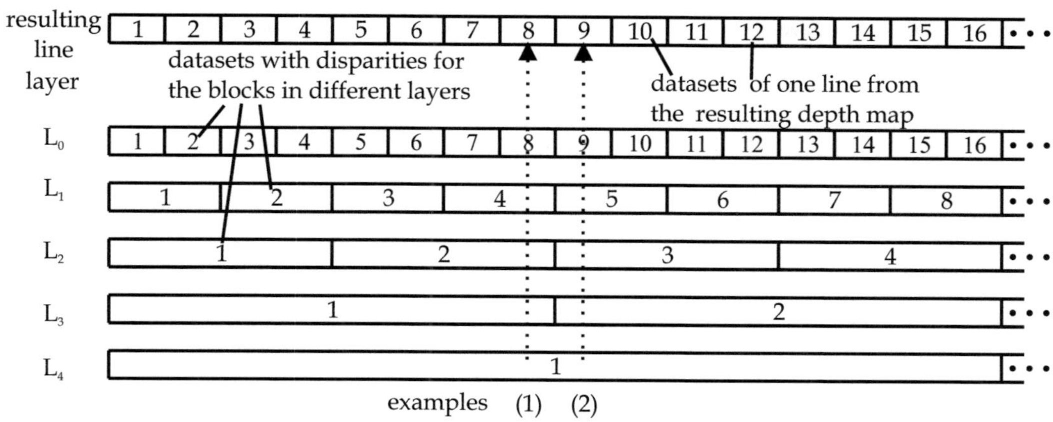

Figure 9. Assembling the layers

Disparities u_{layer} and x-coordinates x_{layer} in the disparity map are only valid for the layer they were calculated in. Disparities u and coordinates x′ in the original resolution in the stereo images are needed for calculating the object coordinates from the disparity and the image coordinates with eq. 5. They can be calculated with eq. 9 and eq. 10. The index or the exponent layer is the associated number. The value s, the difference between the center points of two neighboring reference blocks, and v_{layer}, the position-related number of the reference block in the layer, are needed to calculate x_{layer}. The following relationship applies:

$$x_{layer} = v_{layer} \cdot s \tag{8}$$

The window size for the reference and search blocks is defined in section 3 by m x n. Thus the middle of the reference block is represented by m/2. Thus

$$x' = (x_{layer} + \frac{m}{2}) \cdot 2^{layer} \tag{9}$$

and

$$u = (u_{layer} + u_{\min}) \cdot 2^{layer} \tag{10}$$

u_{min} is an offset in eq. 10 and it represents the minimum disparity. All values except v_{layer} are measured in pixels.

The maximum effect of implementing this procedure in hardware is achieved when the size of the reference block m is equal to the search block. In this case the costly methods for loading the output data for the correspondence analysis are no longer needed, and the maximum clock rate can be lowered significantly. This yields 16 correlation results for the 16x1 pixel block size in our application. We were able to remove disparities smaller than 8 pixels in all layers to reduce the data further, as we are only dealing with objects at distances up to 150 m.

The disparity is then calculated to subpixel accuracy by means of quadratic interpolation (Tornow et al., 2006). We then determine the 3-d coordinates using eq. 5 and add them to the resulting disparity map.
If a standard area correlation based on the epipolar geometry up to a maximum disparity of 256 pixels is executed, then the processed data volume and thus the necessary clock rate are increased sixteen times due to the great number of block combinations. By running the hierarchical algorithm with 5 layers and meeting the same requirements the data volume is only doubled. Thus, the correlator only runs at double the pixel clock for continuous real-time processing. This optimization means that a 3-d disparity map (fig. 10.) is calculated quasi simultaneously with the image acquisition from the stereo image pairs.
We must now extract the necessary information from the disparity map. The information we need to take from the disparity map differs from application to application. We discuss some typical applications in section 5.

4.4 High-Level Processing

4.4.1 Object Detection

Objects with closed contours are detected and an attempt is made to classify them.
We search for points belonging to an object and assign them to an object cluster. We will briefly explain selected clustering algorithms and present a typical application. 3-d points can be clustered in accordance with their spatial relationships (segmenting algorithm). We can also represent in a histogram the relationship between the points in the disparity map (condensation algorithm). There is another algorithm that finds the collinear points (Hough transform) belonging to an object (see section 4.4.3).
Segmenting algorithm (Knoeppel et al., 2000)**:** There is a nonlinear relationship between the disparity map coordinates x′,y′ and u, and the real coordinates X,Y,Z according to eq. 5. All image coordinates have to be converted to real coordinates for the geometrical algorithm. The different 3-d points can then be correlated spatially with one another, thus locating 3-d points that are spatially related. Many different criteria may apply, namely target shape (triangle, square, circle) or distance to an object. Features are detected using a feature space, where the features are entered for every point. 3-d points are clustered in the feature space. These points can be assigned to a specific object. Very good a-priori knowledge is often needed to segment objects. It can be a very difficult task to span a unique feature space. The segmenting algorithms are therefore only suited for a small number of different objects that can be uniquely identified, such as traffic signs (Fang et al., 2003).
Condensation algorithm (Dellaert et al., 1999): The condensation algorithm may be better suited than the segmenting algorithm for detecting raised objects or edges. This is the case when objects and edges that are fixed on a plane have to be located (see also 4.1.1. 4.1.2). However, one cannot differentiate between the objects of a given category. The vehicle category can be detected very well on a road with this algorithm. The different car models cannot be separated into subcategories with the condensation algorithm, as too few features are processed. This algorithm is based on a histogram that allows the vertical edges for the objects contained in the image to be located, as the 3-d points on an edge are located at the same distance away.

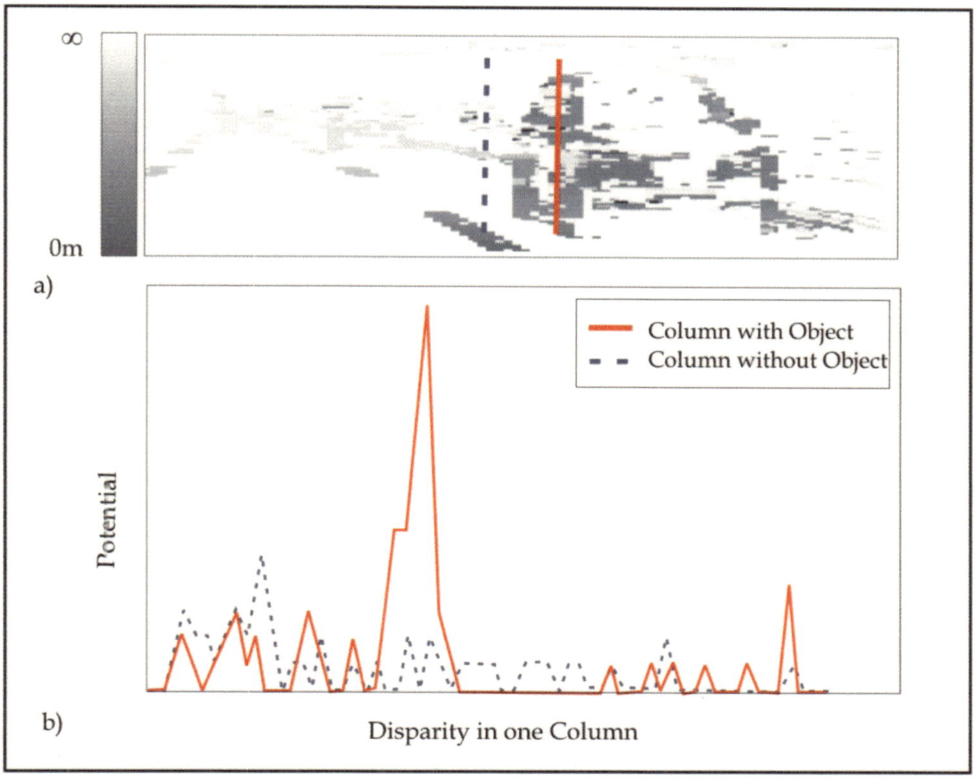

Figure 10. Condensation algorithm a) Depth map b) Potential view along the column

A detected 3-d point produces a potential on the plane. If another 3-d point is found at the same distance (vertical edge), the potential increases accordingly. Fig. 10 a) shows a disparity map, and fig. 10 b) a section view of the generated histogram along the columns in fig. 10 a).

A raised object is detected when the potential reaches a predefined threshold. The potential only indicates the height and location of a detected object, but gives no detailed information on its shape. The advantage of the condensation algorithm is the rapid speed at which it processes the 3-d points (it uses only the distance and potential of a specific position to process the scene).

We will describe a typical condensation algorithm and discuss its benefits and advantages in an embedded system. Approaching objects are detected on a plane and their speed is determined. The camera system itself is also moving. Examples of this type of application are vehicle detection (Kaszubiak et. al., 2005) and the detection of pedestrians (Gavrila, 2004). Complex search operations are executed by the clustering and tracking algorithms – making them control-flow oriented algorithms. They run on processors.

The condensation algorithm is deployed as a clustering algorithm to detect raised objects on a plane. Raised objects on this plane are not only approaching objects, but can also be objects that are not moving or objects that are moving in the opposite direction. These objects are filtered out with the help of two histograms (fig. 11).

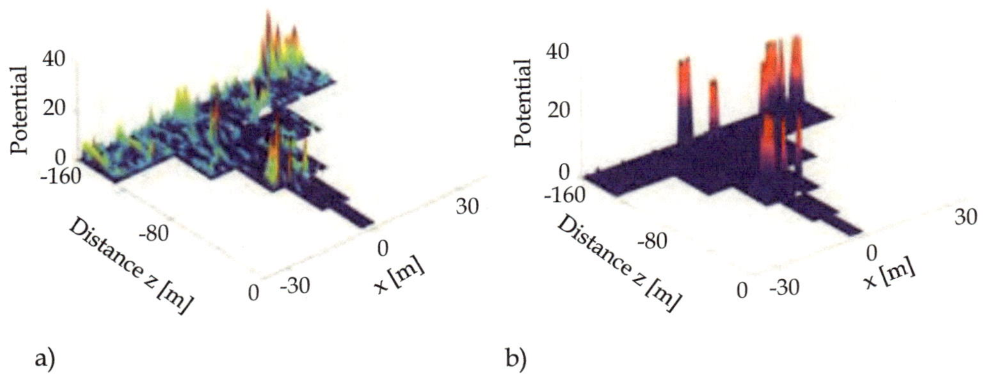

Figure 11. a) Depth histogram b) Time histogram

The depth histogram is generated from the disparity map. 3-d points at the same distance and lateral position (vertical edge) are accumulated. The non-linear relationship from eq. 5 is not invoked for generating the depth histogram, as we are dealing with vertical edges only. This means that we can generate the depth histogram solely with the image coordinates (x',y',u). Thus we can avoid using a large number of calculations to generate the 3-d points. The variables x' and u serve also as addresses for a memory cell in the histogram. The memory cell is an accumulator that totals the number of accesses to this memory cell per image. Fig. 11 a) shows the depth histogram for the disparity map in fig. 10 a). One depth histogram is generated per image. Raised objects in the depth histogram are found with a threshold.

The time histogram (fig. 11 b) is structurally the same as the depth histogram. Vertical edges found in the depth histogram are tracked in the time histogram. The current depth histogram is compared with the time histogram. A search is made in the time histogram for a maximum at the location of a maximum in the depth histogram, or in a search area in the vicinity of this location in the previous image.

The accumulator entry at this position indicates the age of the edge. If an edge is found in the search block, the accumulator entry is set at the location of the point in the current depth histogram and incremented. Raised objects only are detected with this search box if they are objects that are located at the same distance from the observer's vehicle in a number of images, or if they are objects that are approaching the observer's vehicle. If the point in the previous image belonged to a cluster, the number of this cluster is also stored in the new image. The age of entries in the time histogram that have no corresponding maxima in the current depth histogram is decremented. Thus previously detected objects can disappear from the time histogram.

Clustering is based on the time histogram. Values in the time histogram that are greater than a specific threshold are assigned to different object clusters. The closer the objects are to the cameras, the larger they appear in the image sensor. This means that distances between left and right vehicle edges increase in the image.

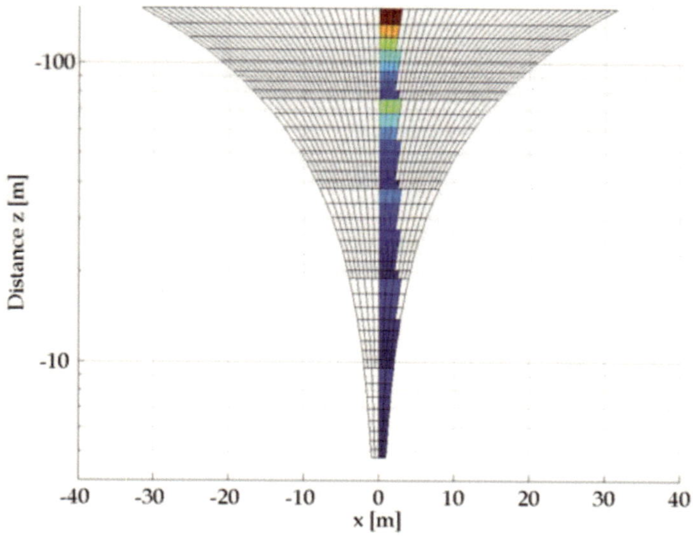

Figure 12. Mapped width of an object in the histogram as a function of the distance

We distribute the depths in a hierarchy and generate the layers as described in section 4.3.2. This allows us to keep the clearances between object edges within an almost constant range. Fig. 12 shows the range for a 1.80 m wide object in the histogram. We can see from the figure that the lateral spread of the object over the entire depth is effectively constant. By reducing the resolution we keep object edges very close together so they can be detected easily.
We do not need to calculate the 3-d edge coordinates because we cluster the objects in the histogram. We calculate one 3-d edge only for every detected and clustered object. This 3-d edge is the center point of the object cluster. Thus we reduce considerably the number of calculations needed. This straightforward clustering technique, based on the hierarchical depth map, also reduces the number of computations. This type of algorithm is very suitable for implementation in an embedded system.

4.4.2 Tracking

Disturbances during image acquisition and quantization of the hierarchical depth (section 4.3.2) cause jumps in the distance measurements. These jumps have to be smoothed in order to determine object speeds. A Kalman filter is used to smooth the jumps (S. Lee & Y. Kay, 1990). The Kalman filter is an ideal, recursive data processing algorithm that allows us to determine object speeds without delay and after an initial settling period. Let us consider an object at a distance of 150m behind the camera system as an example. We wish to detect this object and track it to a distance of 10m. The object is traveling at a uniform speed of 45km/h. It accelerates to 65km/h at a distance of 100m. The Kalman filter algorithm smoothes and estimates the speed as shown in fig. 13. Distance and speed are plotted as negative values, as the object moves toward the camera system from behind.

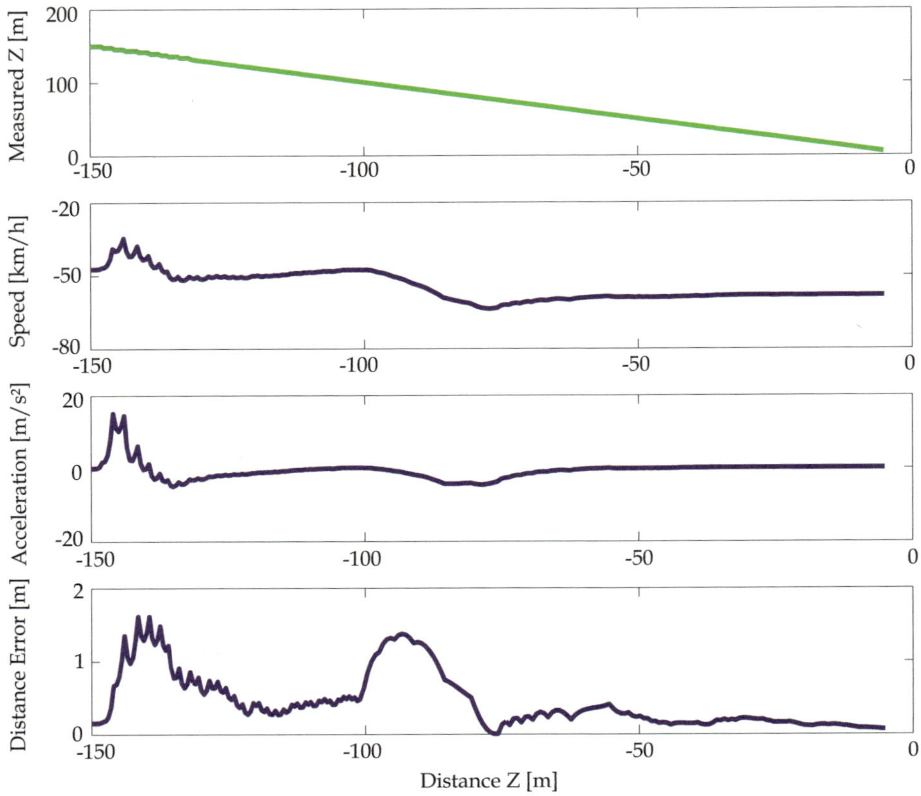

Figure 13. Speed and distance estimation with the Kalman filter

4.4.3 Detecting Boundaries

We often need to detect the boundaries of the planes on which the objects move. We tackle this task using the **Hough transform** (Kluge & Lakshmanan, 1995). It enables us to find straight lines located at different angles in the image, e.g. plane boundaries. Among the items we are looking for are lane markings, skirting boards, markings on playing fields, and the like.

The Hough transform typically executes in the camera image. However, in some applications it can be run inside the disparity map, the depth histogram or the 3-d space. A basic element of the Hough transform is the description of a straight line in the Hessian normal form (eq. 11)

$$r = X \cdot \cos\varphi + Y \cdot \sin\varphi \tag{11}$$

A line bundle is placed on the point (fig. 14). A radius r and an angle φ are associated with each line. The (r,φ)-coordinates points to the accumulator cells in a (r,φ) histogram. All points on the same line in the (X,Y) space have one line in their line bundle with the same (r,φ) coordinates. These lines are then accumulated in the (r,φ) space and a histogram is generated (this procedure is the same as for the condensation algorithm). High histogram entries indicate a line at this location in the image. We can search for the associated points along these lines by executing an inverse transformation in the (X,Y) space.

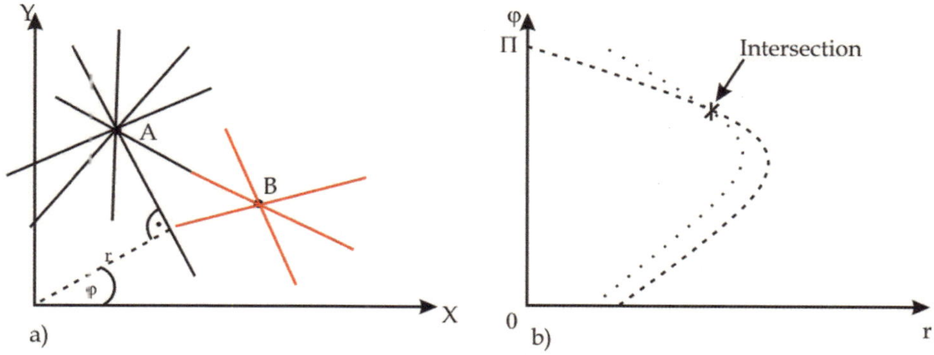

Figure 14. Hough transform a) Line bundle in the X, Y system b) Line bundle in the r,φ system

Again here we can reduce the computation overhead by running the Hough transform in the depth histogram. We only need to generate the line bundle in a specific area because lines that are parallel with the line of viewing only appear in the image.
For example, we could then restrict the angles of the generated line bundle to a 0° to 50° range for lines to the left of the camera system and to a 310° to 360° range for lines to the right of the camera system. This would produce the histogram in the Hough space as shown in fig. 15.

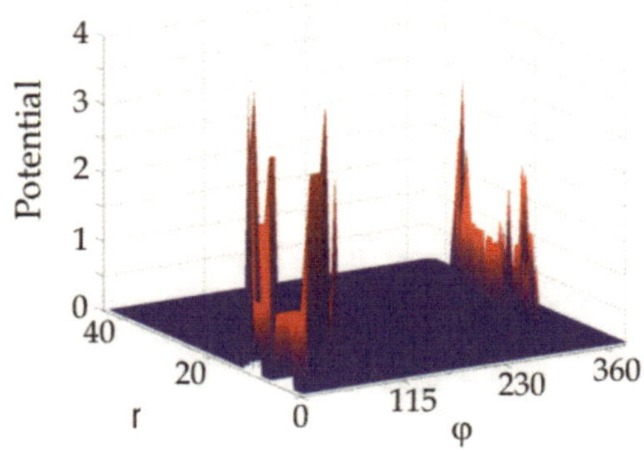

Figure 15. Accumulator in the Hough space

The algorithms outlined above are all suited for numerous applications in robotics, autonomous vehicles, and in road traffic situations. We now present a number of examples.

5. Typical Applications

5.1 Stereo Applications in Road Traffic

Stereo-image analysis is deployed on roads for a variety of purposes. The algorithms encountered here can be divided into two main categories:

- feature-based algorithms (direct triangulation of special features)
- correlation algorithms for determining corresponding points in the images

Combinations of these two categories also exist. There is a wide spectrum of different quality criteria, that differ greatly in computational costs and sensitivity to image information (see also section 3). Recent research in graph theory is producing very promising techniques for highly structured scenes. The optical flow is also applied in some cases. Great care needs to be taken in selecting the right methods. Many examples are to be found in the literature.

[Saneyoshi, 1996] detects vehicles with a stereo camera system using a SAD criterion implemented in hardware. The maximum object distance is very restricted due to the low camera resolution. The system does not run in real time despite fast processing speeds. Lane and road intersection detection at close range in software is presented.

A stereo system is described for detection and tracking in urban traffic in [Franke et al., 1997]. He deploys detected information on the surroundings for route planning for autonomous vehicles. Franke detects small features (that are restricted to corners and edges) in the image for the correspondence search. Each feature is marked with a typical code word that indicates, for example, whether a feature is a bottom left corner or top right corner etc. Code words only are compared to save CPU time during the correspondence search.

[Stiller et al., 1998] introduces special correspondence hypotheses to improve the recognition capability of vehicles in real road traffic situations. A number of quality scores and road parameters are assigned to each correspondence hypothesis.

[Yoshika et al., 1999] deploys a low resolution stereo camera module (16x46 pixels) for detecting vehicles in the blind spot area. The system has special hardware for the correspondence search. The stereo module produces a 3-d point for every pixel. No details are given as to how the correspondences are determined.

Subaru has offered a stereo-camera-based Adaptive Cruise Control (ACC) system since 2000. A 4x4 correlation is calculated in a special hardware. The size of the control unit is 35x20 cm without cameras. The camera is a 640x256 pixel CCD camera. The cycle time is 100ms.

The Acadia vision processor from a company called Sarnoff is another solution. It has a special integral stereo unit on chip. The system is available as a PC development environment. Camera integration is not part of the offering.

The company called 3-d-IP (www.3d-ip.com) offers an FPGA implementation of a stereo image analysis based on artificial neural networks along with a stereo head.

The Point Grey Research company has very recently launched the Bumblebee system with continuous hardware-supported stereo image analysis on the market. The system consists of a very compact module with an integral camera system with a fixed base. The CCD camera resolution is low. The system is very suited for close-range work indoors. However, it is only of limited use outdoors due to the integrated CCD cameras.

We will now present the experimental results of our investigations, based on our brief summary of global state-of-the-art technology, and the description of our own in-house design and development work in sections two to four.

5.2 Experimental Results for Embedded Solutions

The focus of our investigations is a driver assistance system which is a lane change assistant that observes the area behind the vehicle and determines the speed of, and distance to, observed vehicles with reference to the speed of the observer vehicle. The system also checks whether the drivers of the observer vehicles has sufficient time to change lanes, and alerts him if there is a risk of collision.

The detection range of 10-150m was choosen to match driver reaction times and the high speeds encountered on highways. The field of vision is small. Lenses with a 30° aperture angle and a 25mm focal length are used. It was possible to apply the normal case of stereophotogrammetry.
CMOS cameras are better suited than CCD cameras for outdoor applications — they have a wide dynamic range for brightness, and are not unduly affected by glare. The application requires a very high line resolution. The column resolution may be relatively low. Color is in fact more of a hindrance than a benefit for detecting vehicles, as the results from a simple algorithm can be corrupted by a multitude of color information. More complex algorithms use up more computation power. We had only CMOS cameras with a resolution of 1024x1024 at our disposal. This forced us to increase the base of the measuring system to 70cm. This allowed us to achieve a 1% relative error for the static case. An error of this order of magnitude is satisfactory for the lane change assistant.
High speeds and very short reaction times mean very challenging real-time requirements. The system must be able to detect and locate a number of objects in the range of sight in a fraction of a second, i.e. approximately 5-8 images at 25 images/s. We deployed a hardware solution implemented in Altera FPGAs to calculate the distance. The system is based on the hierarchical algorithm described above and applies the NCCF. The system can cover a large detection range and provides approximately constant relative accuracy over the entire detection range. The calculations are performed during image acquisition and are completed approximately 70µs after image acquisition.
A disparity map is generated and passed to the object detection and tracking stages with the help of embedded software. By skillfully distributing the algorithmic logic on a number of softcore processors (this can also be implemented in FPGAs), this step is also completed within one image acquisition time. The condensation algorithm is applied for object detection, and tracking is by Kalman filter. The Kalman filter needs a few images to settle when new objects enter the viewing range, and when there are periods when data drop-outs occur. If the environment capture time needs to be decreased significantly, faster cameras are needed. We only consider objects moving towards the vehicle or remaining at the same relative distance from the camera system. Finally, object locations, approximate object dimensions, and object speed are transferred to the master system. Experimental results for object imaging on a highway are shown in fig. 16 a.

5.3 Robotics and Autonomous Vehicles

The detection and tracking of objects both at a distance and at close range is common in road traffic scenes, environment capture systems for autonomous vehicles or robotic machines deal primarily with close-range objects. Key features of these close-range systems are:

- a large field of vision
- outstanding accuracy
- the ability to capture all objects in the vehicle/robot surroundings

Some systems are designed to detect and track obstacles in a narrow driving lane only, or all objects in the surroundings that are needed to select alternative routes or to establish a free passageway. Detected objects could be identified with the help of image processing algorithms in very complex systems. Examples of such objects are signs and landmarks.

The Götting KG, FOX GmbH companies have joined together to produce autonomous vehicles based on conventional trucks. The speed of the vehicles fitted with standard, traditional detection and tracking systems based on laser scanners is very restricted at this time due to stringent safety requirements on company sites. Magdeburg University is involved in a project to develop a system consisting of a combination of stereophotogrammetric algorithms and a laser scanner that will capture all objects in the vehicle surroundings, and increase the approved speed. The vehicle in question is shown in fig. 16 b.
A large aperture angle is needed for the relatively large field of vision. Should cameras with lenses smaller than 8 mm be deployed, then we recommend a rectification stage. The base of the stereo camera system can be reduced to 5-10 cm as the specified object distances are quite small (20-30m with typically moderate error specifications).
We will not normally need the hierarchical algorithm to calculate the depth values described in section 4 because of the restricted detection range. We may be able to utilize simplified criteria such as the SAD function, as we may be operating under more favorable lighting conditions.

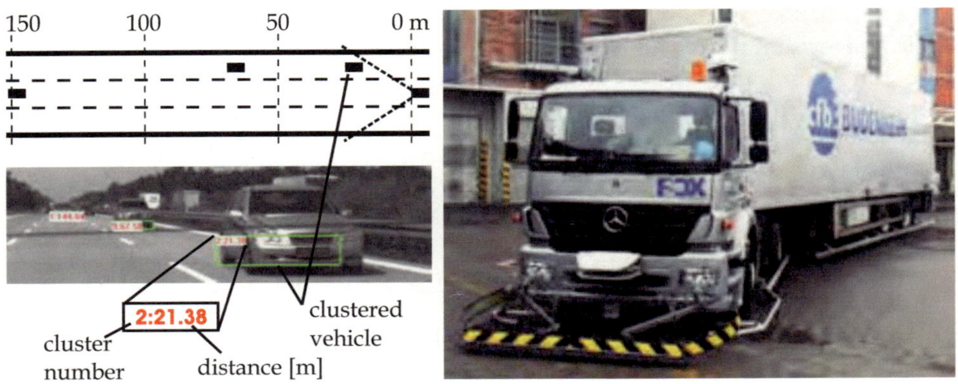

(a) (b)

Figure 16. a) Driver assistance system, b) Autonomous vehicle (FOX GmbH & Götting KG)

Object detection and tracking is more difficult compared to section 5.2, as the objects are significantly more complex and can vary to a greater degree than with the driver assistance system described above. We can still apply the condensation algorithm and the stereo image analysis for gray value cameras for the simple case of obstacle detection. However, we recommend a color image processing system combined with complex signal processing for the capturing and possible identification of all objects.

6. Conclusion

The field of environment capture technology is vast: a wide range of different measured variables are processed. A complete picture of the surroundings can be provided by deploying very many sensors. In other words we can gain comprehensive information on the surroundings. Optical sensors and camera systems can be deployed in a variety of ways, so that massive amounts of varied information can be acquired with few sensors.

Image processing is the key technology applied for processing information from optical image sensors. Typical applications for image sensors include driver assistance systems, autonomous vehicles, and robotic machines. Stereo camera systems supply the necessary 3-d information for environment capture and have crucial advantages. Image processing algorithms can be very complex and with high computation overheads.
Robust solutions are needed for the applications cited. Challenging real-time requirements are often specified for robotic machines and driver assistance systems.
We often have to modify signal processing algorithms very extensively in order to implement them in hardware. This is very challenging for continuous real-time processing at high speed. Thus, we present a hardware-software co-design for an algorithm for locating multiple objects in a variety of applications in section 4.
The measurement technique is based on algorithms from stereophotogrammetry. We implemented an optimized algorithm in conjunction with image pyramids in an FPGA as a parallel structure in hardware that would cover a large detection range as required in driver assistance systems. The algorithm implemented in hardware consists of the NCCF calculation, subpixel interpolation, and depth histogram generation (condensation algorithm).
Other object detection tasks (time histogram, clustering) and tracking system run on three processors, operating in a pipeline configuration in real time. We applied a Kalman filter to track captured objects – this was to smooth out jumps and invalid detections, and to successfully and accurately estimate distance and speed.
There are a number of different approaches out there for generating disparity maps in hardware. Each of these approaches is suited for different applications. Many of these algorithms are established and well known. Much of the global research effort focuses on effective real-time hardware or software implementations.
The standard of global research on higher-level processing techniques for analyzing the disparity map and image information is very high indeed. The development of reliable, robust, and real-time algorithms continues to be the prerequisite for a broad application base.

7. References

Albertz, J. & Kreiling, W. (1989) , Photogrammetric Guide, *Wichmann-Verlag*, ISBN 3-87907-384-8

Dellaert, F.; Burgard, W.; Fox, D. & Thrun, S. (1999), Using the Condensation Algorithm for Robust, Vision-based Mobile Robot Localization, *IEEE Computer Society Conference on Computer Vision and Pattern Recognition (CVPR'99)*, p. 2588

El-Melegy, M.T. & Farag, A.A.; Statistically Robust Approach to Lens Distortion Calibration with Model Selection, *International Conf. on Computer Vision and Pattern Recognition*, CVPR-03, Workshop on Intelligent Learning, Madison, Wisconsin, June 16-22, 2003, pp. 150-156.

Fang, C.Y.; Chen, S.W. & Fuh, C.S. (2003), Road-sign detection and tracking, *IEEE Transactions on Vehicular Technology*, vol. 52, nr. 5, pp. 1329-1341

Franke, U.; Görzig, S.; Lindner, F.; Mehren, D. & Paetzold, F. (1997), Steps towards An Intelligent Vision System For Driver Assistance In Urban Traffic, *Intelligent Transportations Systems*, pp. 601–606

Franke, U.; Gavrila, D.M.; Görzig, S.; Lindner, F.; Paetzhold, F. & Wöhler, C. (1998), "Autonomous Driving Approaches Downtown", *IEEE Intelligent Systems*, vol.13, no.6, pp. 40-48

Fuerstenberg, K.C.; Dietmayer, J. & Lages, U. (2003), Laserscanner Innovations for Detection of Obstacles and Road, *AMAA 7th International Conference on Advanced Microsystems for Automotive Applications*

Gavrila, D.M. (2004), Pedestrian Detection from a Moving Vehicle, *Lecture Notes in Computer Science, Springer* , pp. 37-49, ISBN: 978-3-540-67686-7

Gupta & Rajesh (1995), Co-Synthesis of Hardware and Software for Digital Embedded Systems, *Kluwer Academic Publishers*, ISBN 0-7923-9613-8

Kaszubiak, J.; Tornow, M.; Kuhn, R.W.; Michaelis, B. & Knoeppel, C. (2005), Real-time vehicle and lane detection with embedded hardware, *IEEE Intelligent Vehicle Symposium*, pp. 618–623

Kluge, K. & Lakshmanan, S. (1995), A Deformable Template Approach to Lane Detection, *IEEE Intelligent Vehicle Symposium*, pp. 54–59

Knoeppel, C.; Regensburger, U. & Michaelis, B (2000), Robust Vehicle detection at Large Distance Using Low Resolution Cameras, *IEEE Intelligent Vehicle Symposium*, pp. 267-272

Lange, R. & Seitz, P. (2001), Solid-State Time-of-Flight Range Camera, *IEEE Journal of Quantum Electronics*, vol. 37, no. 3, pp. 390-397

Lee, S. & Kay, Y. (1990), A kalman filter approach for accurate 3d motion estimation from a sequence of stereo images, *10th International Conference on Pattern Recognition*, pp. 104–108

Noelle, M. (1996), Konzepte zur Entwicklung paralleler Algrithmen der digitalen Bildverarbeitung, *VDI-Verlag*, ISBN 3-18-341010-9

Saneyoshi, K. (1996), Drive assist using stereo image recognition, *IEEE Intelligent Vehicle Symposium*, pp. 230-235

Schenk, T. (1999), Digital Photogrammetry - Background, Fundamentals, Automatic Orientation Procedures, *Terra Science*, ISBN 0-203-30595-7

Stiller, C.; Pöschmüller, W. & Hürtgen, B. (1997), Stereo Vision in Driver Assistence Systems, *Intelligent Transportation Systems*

Tornow, M.; Michaelis, B.; Kuhn, R.W.; Calow, R. & Mecke, R. (2003), Hierarchical Method for Stereophotogrammetric Multi-objekt-Postion Measurement. *Pattern Recognition, DAGM Symposium*, pp. 164–171

Tornow, M.; Kaszubiak, J.; Schindler, T.; Kuhn, R.W. & Michaelis, B. (2006), Hardware Approach for Real Time Machine Stereo Vision, *Journal of Systemics, Cybernetics and Informatics*, vol. 4, no. 1, ISSN: 1690-4524

Tyrrel, J. (2004), Low-cost sensor puts 3D-cameras in the picture, *Opto and Laser Europe The European magazine for photonics professionals*, no. 123, pp. 20–21

Uhler, W.; Mathony, H.J. & Knoll, P.M. (2003), Driver Assistance Systems for Safety and Comfort / Robert Bosch GmbH, Driver Assistance Systems, *EU-Projekt EDEL im 5. Rahmenprogramm*, edel-eu.org

Venhovens, P. & Naab, K. (2000), Adiprasito, B.: Stop and Go Cruise Control. In: *Int. Journal of Automotive Technology* 1, S. 61–69

Yoshika, T.; Nakaue, H. & Uemura, H. (1999), Development of Detection Algorithm for Vehicles Using Multi-Line CCD Sensor, *Intelligent Transportation Symposium*

13

Projective Rectification with Minimal Geometric Distortion

Hsien-Huang P. Wu and Chih-Cheng Chen
National Yunlin University of Science and Technology
Taiwan

1. Introduction

There has been an increasing interest in the 3D imaging in the fields of entertainment, simulation, medicine, 3D visual communication, 3D tele-robotics, and 3D TV to augment the reality of presence or to provide vivid and accurate structure information. In order to provide vivid information in these and other 3D applications, efficient techniques to generate, store, and view the stereoscopic video are essential. While many methods are available for acquiring stereoscopic video, the images pairs obtained might not be in rectified form. Therefore, rectification is usually needed to support comfortable viewing and effective compression for storage and transmission. Projective geometry has been proved to be a useful tool for solving the rectification problem without camera calibration. However, if the matrices used for projective rectification (homographies) are not constrained properly, the rectification process can cause great geometric distortion. For visual applications, rectification with minimum geometry distortion should be pursued. In this chapter, we propose an improved algorithm to minimize the distortion by combining a newly developed projective transform with a properly chosen shearing transform. This new method is equipped with flexibility and can be adapted to various imaging models. Experimental data show that the proposed method works quite well for all the image pairs taken different imaging conditions. Comparison with other available method based on visual inspection and numerical data demonstrates the superiority of the new approach.

2. Background

Stereo vision is a technique for estimating 3D structure based on two or more images taken from different viewpoints, and are most often used in robotics and vehicle navigation. Stereoscopic videos are vastly used in entertainment, gaming, simulation, tele-conferencing, and tele-operation to augment the reality of presence. One of the major issues in the application of stereo imagery is correspondence problem. The correspondence problem is defined as locating a pair of image pixels from two different images, where these two pixels are projections of the same scene element. Given a point in one image, its *correspondent point* (or point correspondence) must lie on an epipolar line in the other image. This relationship is well known as epipolar constraint (Faugeras, 1993). It is obvious that knowledge of this epipolar geometry, or codified as *fundamental matrix*, simplifies the stereo matching from a 2-D area search to a 1-D search along the epipolar line. If the images are acquired from a pair of identical cameras placed side-by-side and pointed in the same direction, known as a *rectilinear stereo rig*, the epipolar lines will coincide with scan lines (x-axis) of the images. Given this ideal epipolar geometry, the correspondent points will lie on the same scan line in the two images. However, for an arbitrary placement of cameras, the epipolar lines are skew and the 1-D search will still be time consuming. Whether the imagery is used for stereo vision or stereoscopic video, we would like the image pair to be taken from an ideal epipolar-geometry.

When the epipolar geometry is not in ideal form, the image pairs can be warped to make correspondent points lie on the same scan lines. This process is known as image rectification, and can be accomplished by applying a 2D projective transforms, or *homographies*, to each image. The homography is a linear one to one transformation of the projective plane, which is represented by a 3×3 non-singular matrix. The rectified images can then be treated as obtained by a rectilinear stereo rig and the correspondence problem is greatly simplified. Since most stereo algorithms assume input images having ideal epipolar geometry, image rectification is usually a pre-requisite operation for stereoscopic related applications.

The idea of rectification has long been used in photogrammetry (Slama, 1980). The techniques originally used were optical-based, but now are replaced by software methods that model the geometry of optical projection. The software-based photogrammetric approaches, similar to most of the computer vision ones, assume the knowledge of projection matrices or cameras parameters (Ayache & Hanse, 1988)(Ayache & Lustman, 1991)(Fusiello, et al., 2000)These methods require camera parameters to compute a pair of homographies for transformations. The necessity of camera calibration is one of their disadvantages.

In contrast to these traditional approaches, several researchers have developed techniques called *projective rectification* to rectify images directly without using camera parameters. They utilized the epipolar geometry of the acquired images and various criteria to compute the homographies. Robert *et al.* (Robert, 1997) attempted to find the transform that best preserves orthogonality around image centers. Hartley (Hartley, 1999) proposed using minimization of the differences between matching points for the solution of homographies. He also gave a detailed theoretical presentation of the projective rectification. Loop and Zhang (Loop & Zhang, 1999) suggested decomposing each homography into projective and affine components. They then found the projective component that minimizes a defined projective distortion criterion. Gluckman and Nayar (Gluckman & Nayar, 2001) recently presented a stereo rectification method, which takes geometric distortion into account and tries to minimize the effects of resampling. Pollefeys (Pollefeys et al., 1999) proposed a simple and efficient algorithm for general two view stereo image. The other available approaches include (Papadimitriou and Dennis, 1996) which considers only the special case of partially aligned cameras, and (Al-Shalfan et al., 2000) which requires the estimation of the epipolar geometry. Although these proposed methods provided many possibilities for projective rectification, they all solve the problem indirectly. That is, they must explicitly estimate the fundamental matrix before rectification. Since the solution of fundamental matrix has its own uncertainty (Zhang, 1998) this indirect approach might obtain unpredictable rectifying results.

Isgrò and Trucco (Isgrò & Trucco, 1999) adopted a different procedure and obtained homographies directly without first computing the fundamental matrix. However, in order to solve the problem of uniqueness in rectification, their method requires disparity minimization along the *x-axis* to generate a unique solution. In certain applications, this modification of *x-axis* disparity in rectification might be harmless; however, in applications where original *x-axis* disparity must be maintained (e.g. for stereoscopic viewing purpose), this constraint will make the algorithm useless. Moreover, the enforcement of minimizing *x-axis* disparity to obtain a single solution sometimes greatly distorts the image.

In this chapter, we propose a different approach for rectifying two uncalibrated images with reduced geometric distortion. Its novelty is to formulate a new set of parameters for homographies, and solves the rectification problem using least square distance as a criterion. This new approach possesses similar advantage to that of the IT method (Isgrò & Trucco, 1999), that is, performing uncalibrated rectification without explicit computation of the epipolar geometry (fundamental matrix). However, the new method contains a shearing transform which greatly reduces geometric distortion caused by rectification.

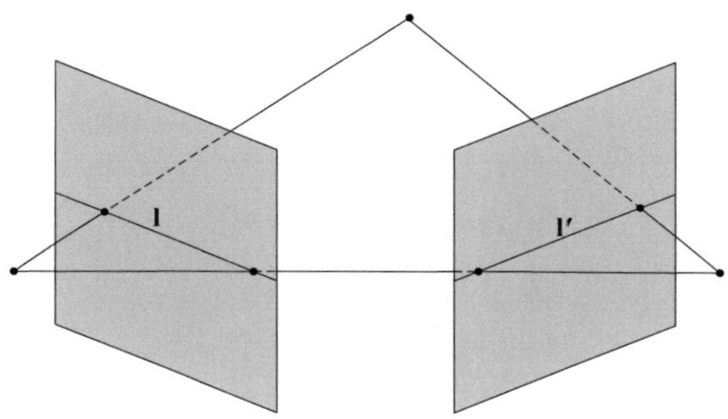

Figure 1. Epipolar geometry of a pair of stereo images

3. Epipolar geometry

The derivation of our algorithm is presented from the viewpoint of projective geometry (Faugeras, 1993). The image point is expressed in homogeneous coordinate and represented by a 3-dimensional column vector. Column vectors are denoted by bold lower-case letters, such as $\mathbf{m}$ and $\mathbf{l}$. Matrices are represented by bold upper-case letter, such as $\mathbf{F}$ and $\mathbf{H}$. Transposed vectors and matrices are expressed by adding a letter T as superscript, e.g., $\mathbf{m}^T$ and $\mathbf{F}^T$.

3.1 Epipolar constraint

Consider two images I and I' of a common scene. Let C and C' represent the optical centers of the left and right cameras in the 3D coordinate, respectively. Points $\mathbf{m}$ and $\mathbf{m}'$ are the projections of a certain 3D point M on the left (I) and right (I') images, as shown in Fig. 1. There are two points called the epipoles of the left and right images; one epipole $\mathbf{e}'$ is the point where the center of projection C of the left camera would be visible in the right image, and the other epipole $\mathbf{e}$ is the point where the center of projection C' of the right camera is seen in the left image. In the 3D coordinate, $\mathbf{e}$ and $\mathbf{e}'$ are the intersection points of the baseline, $\overline{CC'}$, with the left and right image planes. Any plane that contains the baseline and a 3D scene point (e.g. M above) is called *epipolar plane.*

The *epipolar lines* ($\mathbf{l}$ and $\mathbf{l}'$ in Fig. 1) are defined as the intersection of the epipolar plane and the left and right image planes. The ray goes through the optical center of one camera (C), which creates an image point ($\mathbf{m}$) on the image plane, will generate an image of epipolar line on the other camera ($\mathbf{l}'$). One specific matrix called *fundamental matrix* describes this mapping between points in one image and the corresponding epipolar line in the other image. Given the scene point *M*, and its two projections ($\mathbf{m}$ and $\mathbf{m}'$) on the left and right image planes, the *epipolar constraint* (Faugeras, 1993) asserts that point $\mathbf{m}'$ must lie on the epipolar line $\mathbf{Fm}$ and can be expressed as

$$\mathbf{m}'^T\mathbf{F}\mathbf{m} = \mathbf{0} \text{ or } \mathbf{m}^T\mathbf{F}^T\mathbf{m}' = \mathbf{0} \tag{1}$$

Where $\mathbf{F}$ is called fundamental matrix, or *F matrix,* and $\mathbf{0} = \begin{bmatrix} 0 & 0 & 0 \end{bmatrix}^T$ is a zero column vector. The matrix $\mathbf{F}$ is a 3×3 matrix with rank 2, and the epipoles for the left ($\mathbf{e} \in I$) and the right image ($\mathbf{e}' \in I'$) satisfy

$$\mathbf{Fe} = \mathbf{F}^T\mathbf{e}' = \mathbf{0} \tag{2}$$

That is, the epipoles $\mathbf{e}$ and $\mathbf{e}'$ are the null space of $\mathbf{F}$ and $\mathbf{F}^T$, respectively. Furthermore, all the epipolar lines ($\mathbf{l}$ and $\mathbf{l}'$) will pass the epipoles, or

$$\mathbf{l}^T\mathbf{e} = \mathbf{l}'^T\mathbf{e}' = 0 \tag{3}$$

3.2 Epipolar geometry after stereo image rectification

Image rectification can be treated as a process of converting the epipolar geometry of an image pair into a canonical form. This can be done by applying a homography, which maps the epipole to a point at infinity, to each image. We designate these two epipoles after rectification as $\mathbf{e}_\infty$ and $\mathbf{e}'_\infty$, where $\mathbf{e}_\infty = \mathbf{e}'_\infty = \begin{bmatrix} 1 & 0 & 0 \end{bmatrix}^T$, and fundamental matrix of a pair of rectified images has the form of

$$\mathbf{F}_\infty = \begin{bmatrix} 0 & 0 & 0 \\ 0 & 0 & -1 \\ 0 & 1 & 0 \end{bmatrix} \tag{4}$$

Let $(\bar{\mathbf{m}}, \bar{\mathbf{m}}')$ be an image pair in the rectified images corresponding to the original $(\mathbf{m}, \mathbf{m}')$ pair. From equation (1), the epipolar constraint after rectification can be rewritten as

$$\bar{\mathbf{m}}'^T\mathbf{F}_\infty\bar{\mathbf{m}} = 0 \tag{5}$$

Meanwhile, the rectification can be accomplished by the following operations:

$$\bar{\mathbf{m}} = \mathbf{Hm}\,,\ \bar{\mathbf{m}}' = \mathbf{H}'\mathbf{m}' \tag{6}$$

where $\mathbf{H}$ and $\mathbf{H}'$ are the rectifying *homographies* (or *H matrices*) for the left and right images, respectively. Combining (5) and (6) we obtain the following equation:

$$\mathbf{m}'^T\mathbf{H}'^T\mathbf{F}_\infty\mathbf{H}\mathbf{m} = 0 \qquad (7)$$

Given several point correspondences, or $(\mathbf{m},\mathbf{m}')$ pairs, equation (7) can be solved to obtain homographies ($\mathbf{H}$ and $\mathbf{H}'$). However, solution for the pair of *H matrices* $(\mathbf{H},\mathbf{H}')$ is not unique. Some of the solutions are even far from ideal and can cause huge geometric distortion. Various approaches have been proposed to find a unique pair of homographies $(\mathbf{H},\mathbf{H}')$ that minimize image distortion. This and other rectification related backgrounds are the topics of the next section.

4. Image Rectification

Several projective rectification methods have been proposed recently, and the backgrounds on these methods that are most related to our algorithm will be described below. On the basis of these methods, we propose our new approach to solving the projective rectification problem.

4.1 Review of projective rectification

Rectification based on epipolar geometry was originally developed by Hartley (Hartley, 1999). In order to constrain the geometric distortion caused by rectification, Hartley proposed that one of the two homographies, say $\mathbf{H}'$, should be close to a rigid transformation in the neighborhood of a selected point $\mathbf{p}_0$. That is, the homography for one of the image (I') can be represented by

$$\mathbf{H}' = \mathbf{KRT} \qquad (8)$$

where $\mathbf{T}$ is a translational vector taking $\mathbf{p}_0$ to the origin, $\mathbf{R}$ is a rotation matrix mapping the epipole to a point $\begin{bmatrix}1 & 0 & f\end{bmatrix}^T$ on the *x-axis*, and $\mathbf{K}$ is a transformation matrix mapping $\begin{bmatrix}1 & 0 & f\end{bmatrix}^T$ to a point $\begin{bmatrix}1 & 0 & 0\end{bmatrix}^T$ at infinity along the *x-axis*. Moreover, matrix $\mathbf{K}$ can be expressed as

$$\mathbf{K} = \begin{bmatrix} 1 & 0 & 0 \\ 0 & 1 & 0 \\ -f & 0 & 1 \end{bmatrix} \qquad (9)$$

In this way, $\mathbf{H}'$ depends only on two parameters: f and rotation angle θ. If the translational vector $\mathbf{T}$ is neglected, then $\mathbf{H}'$ becomes

$$\mathbf{H}' = \begin{bmatrix} \cos\theta & \sin\theta & 0 \\ -\sin\theta & \cos\theta & 0 \\ -f\cos\theta & -f\sin\theta & 1 \end{bmatrix} \qquad (10)$$

Given the **F** matrix, positions of the epipoles can be found by Equation (2). By following the above process, we can then obtain $\mathbf{H}'$ to rectify the image I' by mapping the epipole $\mathbf{e}'$ to the infinite point $\begin{bmatrix}1 & 0 & 0\end{bmatrix}^T$ and transforming the epipolar lines to lines parallel with the x-axis. The next step is to find the matrix $\mathbf{H}$ which can be applied to the other image to match up these new epipolar lines.

The strategy that Hartley took to find $\mathbf{H}$ (a matching transformation) is to minimize the sum-of-squared distances (Hartley, 1999):

$$\sum_i d(\mathbf{Hm}_i, \mathbf{H}'\mathbf{m}_i')^2 \tag{11}$$

The searching of $\mathbf{H}$ by minimizing $\sum_i d(\mathbf{Hm}_i, \mathbf{H}'\mathbf{m}_i')^2$ is not as straightforward as it seems. That is, the matrix $\mathbf{H}$ is first decomposed into a form of $\mathbf{H} = \mathbf{H}_A\mathbf{H}_0$ where

$$\mathbf{H}_A = \begin{bmatrix} a & b & c \\ 0 & 1 & 0 \\ 0 & 0 & 1 \end{bmatrix}, \text{ and } \mathbf{H}_0 = \mathbf{H}'\mathbf{M} \tag{12}$$

and $\mathbf{H}_A$ matrix represents an affine transformation. It was proven (Hartley, 1999) that *F matrix* can be factorized as $\mathbf{F} = [\mathbf{e}]_\times \mathbf{M}$ where $\mathbf{M}$ is a three-parameter family of non-singular matrices, and $[\mathbf{e}]_\times$ is an antisymetric matrix generated from vector $\mathbf{e}$ as follows:

$$[\mathbf{e}]_\times = \begin{bmatrix} 0 & -e_3 & e_2 \\ e_3 & 0 & -e_1 \\ -e_2 & e_1 & 0 \end{bmatrix} \tag{13}$$

Note that $\mathbf{e} = [e_1 \quad e_2 \quad e_3]^T$ is the epipole of the image I. Therefore, instead of minimizing $\sum_i d(\mathbf{Hm}_i, \mathbf{H}'\mathbf{m}_i')^2$ directly, the following steps are taken:

1. Matrix $\mathbf{H}'$ is found first.
2. The feature points on both images are transformed by

$$\begin{aligned} \hat{\mathbf{m}}_i &= \mathbf{H}_0\mathbf{m}_i = \mathbf{H}'\mathbf{M}\mathbf{m}_i \\ \hat{\mathbf{m}}_i' &= \mathbf{H}'\mathbf{m}_i' \end{aligned} \tag{14}$$

3. $\sum_i d(\mathbf{H}_A\hat{\mathbf{m}}_i, \hat{\mathbf{m}}_i')^2$ is minimized to find the matrix $\mathbf{H}_A$ by least square. (Note that this step would remove the x-disparity)
4. Matrix $\mathbf{H}$ is obtained by $\mathbf{H} = \mathbf{H}_A\mathbf{H}_0$

To further evaluate performance of the proposed algorithm, Hartley's method will be implemented and applied to the same sets of image pairs for comparisons in the later section of experiments. Algorithm of Hartley's approach has been briefly described above and is summarized below.

Outline of Hartley's Algorithm

1. Identify a set of point correspondences $\{ \mathbf{m}_i \leftrightarrow \mathbf{m}'_i, i = 1 \ldots N \}$ between the two input images. Seven points at least are needed, though more are preferable.
2. Compute the fundamental matrix **F** and find the epipoles $\mathbf{e}$ and $\mathbf{e}'$ in the two images.
3. Select a projective transformation $\mathbf{H}'$ that maps the epipole $\mathbf{e}'$ to the point at infinity on the x-axis, $\begin{bmatrix} 1 & 0 & 0 \end{bmatrix}^T$.
4. Find the matching transformation H that minimizes the least-squares distance $\sum_i d(\mathbf{H}\mathbf{m}_i, \mathbf{H}'\mathbf{m}'_i)^2$.
5. Resample the first image according to the transformation $\mathbf{H}$ and the second image according to the projective transformation $\mathbf{H}'$.

The number of parameter needs to be estimated is ten in the above process which includes the computation of matrix **F** that requires estimation of seven parameters. The Matlab codes for implementation of the Hartley's method are available from (Hartley, 2004).

4.2 Proposed method and *F matrix* parameterization

In this section, taking a distinct approach in representing the matrix $\mathbf{H}$, we propose a new method to solving the two homographies. Unlike the way **H** is parameterized in as $\mathbf{H} = \mathbf{H}_A \mathbf{H}_0$ in Hartley's approach, the proposed method adopts a more direct form of parameterization for $\mathbf{H}$, that is

$$\mathbf{H} = \begin{bmatrix} h_1 & h_2 & h_3 \\ h_4 & h_5 & h_6 \\ h_7 & h_8 & 1 \end{bmatrix} \tag{15}$$

Since the homography pair, **H** and $\mathbf{H}'$, are determined up to a scale factor, we can set $\mathbf{H}(3,3) = \mathbf{H}'(3,3) = 1$. Combining equations (5), (6) and (7) gives us

$$\bar{\mathbf{m}}'^T \mathbf{F}_\infty \bar{\mathbf{m}} = \mathbf{m}'^T \mathbf{H}'^T \mathbf{F}_\infty \mathbf{H}\mathbf{m} = \mathbf{m}'^T \mathbf{F}\mathbf{m} = 0 \text{, where } \mathbf{F} = \mathbf{H}'^T \mathbf{F}_\infty \mathbf{H} \tag{16}$$

By following Hartley's proposition that $\mathbf{H}'$ is very close to a rigid transformation, as shown in (10), and substituting $\mathbf{F}_\infty$, $\mathbf{H}'$, and $\mathbf{H}$ in equations (4), (10) and (15) into $\mathbf{F}$, we can parameterize and estimate *F matrix* as follows:

$$\hat{\mathbf{F}} = \begin{bmatrix} \cos\theta & \sin\theta & 0 \\ -\sin\theta & \cos\theta & 0 \\ -f\cos\theta & -f\sin\theta & 1 \end{bmatrix}^T \begin{bmatrix} 0 & 0 & 0 \\ 0 & 0 & -1 \\ 0 & 1 & 0 \end{bmatrix} \begin{bmatrix} h_1 & h_2 & h_3 \\ h_4 & h_5 & h_6 \\ h_7 & h_8 & 1 \end{bmatrix}$$
$$= \begin{bmatrix} -h_4 f\cos\theta + h_7\sin\theta & -h_5 f\cos\theta + h_8\sin\theta & -h_6 f\cos\theta + \sin\theta \\ -h_4 f\sin\theta - h_7\cos\theta & -h_5 f\sin\theta - h_8\cos\theta & -h_6 f\sin\theta - \cos\theta \\ h_4 & h_5 & h_6 \end{bmatrix} \tag{17}$$

Obviously, the *F matrix* is determined by only seven parameters, as shown in vector form

$$\mathbf{\Phi} = \begin{bmatrix} f & \theta & h_4 & h_5 & h_6 & h_7 & h_8 \end{bmatrix}^T \tag{18}$$

However, due to the characteristics of $\mathbf{F}_\infty$, only five out of eight parameters in matrix **H** are obtained, which leaves the solution for **H** not unique. To solve this uniqueness problem, Hartley's method suggests minimizing the discrepancy after rectification, as is described in Equation (11). In contrast, we propose using shearing transform formulated in section 3.4 to obtain a unique solution. Our approach results in lower geometric distortion as will be seen in the result section. Note that we have combined the problems of rectification and estimation of *F matrix*. In the next subsection, we will show how to derive a least-square solution for the rectification problem from the viewpoint of *F matrix* estimation. This novel parameterization scheme combining with a shearing transform, leads to a unique solution.

4.3 Projection rectification based on least square distance

The quantity used in Hartley's method for minimization, as shown in equation (11), is a linear criterion without physical meaning. In rectification, we would like the criterion to be something geometrically meaningful and to be measurable in the image plane. One such quantity is the distance from a point $\mathbf{m}'_i$ to its corresponding epipolar line $\mathbf{l}'_i = \mathbf{F}\mathbf{m}_i = \begin{bmatrix} l'_1 & l'_2 & l'_3 \end{bmatrix}^T$, as shown in Fig. 2. This distance is given by the following equation:

$$d(\mathbf{m}'_i, \mathbf{l}'_i) = d(\mathbf{m}'_i, \mathbf{F}\mathbf{m}_i) = \frac{\mathbf{m}'^T_i \mathbf{l}'_i}{\sqrt{l'^2_1 + l'^2_2}} = \frac{\mathbf{m}'^T_i \mathbf{F}\mathbf{m}_i}{\sqrt{l'^2_1 + l'^2_2}} \tag{19}$$

Conversely, distance for a point $\mathbf{m}_i$ to its corresponding epipolar line $\mathbf{l}_i = \mathbf{F}^T\mathbf{m}'_i = \begin{bmatrix} l_1 & l_2 & l_3 \end{bmatrix}^T$ is

$$d(\mathbf{m}_i, \mathbf{l}_i) = d(\mathbf{m}_i, \mathbf{F}^T\mathbf{m}'_i) = \frac{\mathbf{m}^T_i \mathbf{l}_i}{\sqrt{l^2_1 + l^2_2}} = \frac{\mathbf{m}^T_i \mathbf{F}^T\mathbf{m}'_i}{\sqrt{l^2_1 + l^2_2}} \tag{20}$$

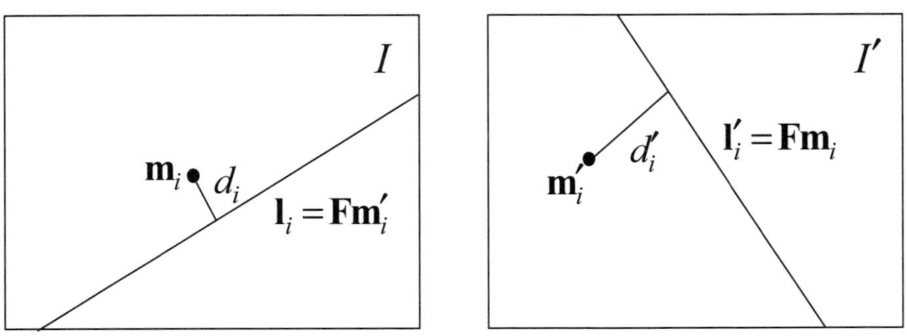

Figure 2. Distance from a point to the epipolar line of its correspondent point

Minimization of this distance is originally used to estimate *F matrix* (Zhang, 1998), which generates 36 possible modes of solution. Surprisingly, it turns out to be a very good *H matrix* estimator with a unique solution under our new formulation. We now demonstrate how to find the solution by minimizing the distance defined above.
To prevent inconsistency of the epipolar geometry between the left and right images, we choose to operate simultaneously on both images and minimize the mean-square distance. Hence, the problem becomes

$$\min_{\mathbf{F}} \sum_i \frac{1}{2}\left(d^2(\mathbf{m}'_i, \mathbf{F}\mathbf{m}_i) + d^2(\mathbf{m}_i, \mathbf{F}^T\mathbf{m}')\right) \tag{21}$$

Using equations (19), (20) and the fact that $\mathbf{m}_i'^T \mathbf{F}\mathbf{m}_i = \mathbf{m}_i^T \mathbf{F}^T \mathbf{m}'_i$, we reformulate the minimization problem in (21) as:

$$\min_{\mathbf{F}} \sum_i \frac{1}{2}\left[\frac{(\mathbf{m}_i'^T\mathbf{F}\mathbf{m}_i)^2}{l_1'^2 + l_2'^2} + \frac{(\mathbf{m}_i^T\mathbf{F}^T\mathbf{m}'_i)^2}{l_1^2 + l_2^2}\right] = \min_{\mathbf{F}} \sum_i w_i \frac{(\mathbf{m}_i'^T\mathbf{F}\mathbf{m}_i)^2}{2} \tag{22}$$

where $w_i = \frac{1}{l_1^2 + l_2^2} + \frac{1}{l_1'^2 + l_2'^2}$.

Given N point correspondences from the image pair ($\mathbf{m}_i \leftrightarrow \mathbf{m}'_i, i = 1 \ldots N$), the search for parameter vector $\mathbf{\Phi}$, which is to be used in $\mathbf{F} = \mathbf{F}(\mathbf{\Phi})$, $\mathbf{H} = \mathbf{H}(\mathbf{\Phi})$, and $\mathbf{H}' = \mathbf{H}'(\mathbf{\Phi})$, becomes a nonlinear optimization problem, that is

$$\min_{\mathbf{F}} \frac{1}{N}\sum_{i=1}^{N} w_i \frac{(\mathbf{m}_i'^T\mathbf{F}\mathbf{m}_i)^2}{2} \tag{23}$$

To simplify the derivation, we can restructure the matrix equation by turning a matrix into a vector. Assume that the 3×3 fundamental matrix in vector form is $\mathbf{F} = [\mathbf{F}_1 \quad \mathbf{F}_2 \quad \mathbf{F}_3]$; then we can use **vec** operator to convert the matrix $\mathbf{F}$ into a column vector $\mathbf{f}$ by stacking the columns of $\mathbf{F}$, or

$$\mathbf{f} = \mathbf{vec}(\mathbf{F}) = \begin{bmatrix} \mathbf{F}_1 \\ \mathbf{F}_2 \\ \mathbf{F}_3 \end{bmatrix} \tag{24}$$

Let symbol $\otimes$ denote Kronecker product; then

$$\mathbf{m}_i'^T\mathbf{F}\mathbf{m}_i = (\mathbf{m}'_i \otimes \mathbf{m}_i)^T \mathbf{f} \tag{25}$$

Substituting (25) into (23) yields the objective function in vector form. That is

$$\frac{1}{N}\sum_{i=1}^{N} w_i \frac{(\mathbf{m}_i'^T\mathbf{F}\mathbf{m}_i)^2}{2} = \frac{1}{2N}\sum_{i=1}^{N}(w_i^{1/2}\mathbf{m}_i'^T\mathbf{F}\mathbf{m}_i)^2 = \frac{1}{2N}\left\|\mathbf{W}^{1/2}\mathbf{U}_N\mathbf{f}\right\|^2 \tag{26}$$

where $\mathbf{W}$ is an $N\times N$ diagonal matrix and $\mathbf{U}_N$ is an $N\times9$ matrix :

$$\mathbf{W} = \text{diag}\begin{bmatrix} w_1 & w_2 & \cdots & w_N \end{bmatrix} = \begin{bmatrix} w_1 & 0 & \cdots & 0 \\ 0 & w_2 & 0 & \vdots \\ \vdots & 0 & \ddots & 0 \\ 0 & \cdots & 0 & w_N \end{bmatrix}, \mathbf{U}_N = \begin{bmatrix} (\mathbf{m}'_1 \otimes \mathbf{m}_1)^T \\ (\mathbf{m}'_2 \otimes \mathbf{m}_2)^T \\ \vdots \\ (\mathbf{m}'_N \otimes \mathbf{m}_N)^T \end{bmatrix}.$$

Given these new notation, minimization of the mean-square distance in (23) can now be rewritten as

$$\min_{\mathbf{f}} \frac{1}{2N} \left\| \mathbf{W}^{1/2} \mathbf{U}_N \mathbf{f} \right\|^2 \tag{27}$$

The solution for **f** in (27) can be found by any standard nonlinear minimization method. We chose the Levenberg-Marquardt algorithm because of it effectiveness and popularity. Before applying this minimization process, we need to derive the Jacobian matrix of (26), or $\frac{\partial}{\partial \mathbf{\Phi}}(\mathbf{W}^{1/2}\mathbf{U}_N\mathbf{f})$. In order to simplify the computation of this Jacobian matrix, we modify our iteration of the minimization process by using the old **W** value from the previous iteration to compute the new Jocobian matrix. That is,

$$\frac{\partial}{\partial \mathbf{\Phi}_k}\left\{\mathbf{W}^{1/2}(\mathbf{\Phi}_{k-1})\mathbf{U}_N\mathbf{f}(\mathbf{\Phi}_k)\right\} = \mathbf{W}^{1/2}(\mathbf{\Phi}_{k-1})\mathbf{U}_N \frac{\partial}{\partial \mathbf{\Phi}_k}\mathbf{f}(\mathbf{\Phi}_k)$$

Therefore, even though **W** is a function of $\mathbf{\Phi}$, we can treat it as a constant to $\mathbf{\Phi}$ in current iteration. Since factor $\mathbf{W}^{1/2}\mathbf{U}_N$ inside the partial derivative can be treated as constant for $\mathbf{\Phi}$, the Jacobian matrix can then be reduced to a simpler form

$$\frac{\partial}{\partial \mathbf{\Phi}}(\mathbf{W}^{1/2}\mathbf{U}_N\mathbf{f}) = (\mathbf{W}^{1/2}\mathbf{U}_N)\frac{\partial}{\partial \mathbf{\Phi}}\mathbf{f} \tag{28}$$

Therefore, we only need to compute $\frac{\partial}{\partial \mathbf{\Phi}}\mathbf{f}$ for the Jocobian matrix of (26) as follows

$$\frac{\partial}{\partial \mathbf{\Phi}}\mathbf{f} = \frac{\partial}{\partial \mathbf{\Phi}} \begin{bmatrix} -h_4 f\cos\theta + h_7 \sin\theta \\ -h_4 f\sin\theta - h_7 \cos\theta \\ h_4 \\ -h_5 f\cos\theta + h_8 \sin\theta \\ -h_5 f\sin\theta - h_8 \cos\theta \\ h_5 \\ -h_6 f\cos\theta + \sin\theta \\ -h_6 f\sin\theta - \cos\theta \\ h_6 \end{bmatrix}$$

$$= \begin{bmatrix} -h_4\cos\theta & h_4 f\sin\theta + h_7\cos\theta & -f\cos\theta & 0 & 0 & \sin\theta & 0 \\ -h_4\sin\theta & -h_4 f\cos\theta + h_7\sin\theta & -f\sin\theta & 0 & 0 & -\cos\theta & 0 \\ 0 & 0 & 1 & 0 & 0 & 0 & 0 \\ -h_5\cos\theta & h_5 f\sin\theta + h_8\cos\theta & 0 & -f\cos\theta & 0 & 0 & \sin\theta \\ -h_5\sin\theta & -h_5 f\cos\theta + h_8\sin\theta & 0 & -f\sin\theta & 0 & 0 & -\cos\theta \\ 0 & 0 & 0 & 1 & 0 & 0 & 0 \\ -h_6\cos\theta & h_6 f\sin\theta + \cos\theta & 0 & 0 & -f\cos\theta & 0 & 0 \\ -h_6\sin\theta & -h_6 f\cos\theta + \sin\theta & 0 & 0 & -f\sin\theta & 0 & 0 \\ 0 & 0 & 0 & 0 & 1 & 0 & 0 \end{bmatrix} \tag{29}$$

The Jacobian matrix can be obtained by substituting (29) into (28), which is then used in an iterative process of Levenberg-Marquardt algorithm to find the parameter vector $\mathbf{\Phi}$. This minimization algorithm contains an iterative process, which must start with an initial estimate of the *F matrix*, and the ideal *F matrix* of a pair of rectified images can be used, that is,

$$\hat{\mathbf{F}}_0 = \begin{bmatrix} 0 & 0 & 0 \\ 0 & 0 & -1 \\ 0 & 1 & 0 \end{bmatrix} = \mathbf{F}_\infty$$

A comparison of $\hat{\mathbf{F}}_0$ with the parameterization of $\hat{\mathbf{F}}$ in (17) shows that $\hat{\mathbf{F}}_0$ corresponds to an initial parameter vector of $\mathbf{\Phi}_0 = \begin{bmatrix} f & \theta & h_4 & h_5 & h_6 & h_7 & h_8 \end{bmatrix}^T = \begin{bmatrix} 1 & 0 & 0 & 1 & 0 & 0 & 0 \end{bmatrix}^T$. An iterative process can now be applied to find the solution of $\mathbf{\Phi}$ after proper stop conditions have been set.

4.4 Homography with minimal geometric distortion

After the parameter vector $\mathbf{\Phi} = \begin{bmatrix} f & \theta & h_4 & h_5 & h_6 & h_7 & h_8 \end{bmatrix}^T$ has been found, the values of the vector can be used to calculate the pair of rectifying homographies shown as below

$$\mathbf{H} = \begin{bmatrix} h_1 & h_2 & h_3 \\ h_4 & h_5 & h_6 \\ h_7 & h_8 & 1 \end{bmatrix}, \ \mathbf{H}' = \begin{bmatrix} \cos\theta & \sin\theta & 0 \\ -\sin\theta & \cos\theta & 0 \\ -f\cos\theta & -f\sin\theta & 1 \end{bmatrix} \tag{30}$$

Obviously, the only parameters left to be estimated are $[h_1 \ \ h_2 \ \ h_3]$. Since this vector does not affect the coordinate of y-axis, we can simply set it to $[1 \ 0 \ 0]$ and obtain satisfactory rectifying results. However, to achieve a certain purpose, we can apply specific constraint on the transformed coordinate of x-axis and obtain different values for $[h_1 \ \ h_2 \ \ h_3]$. For example, minimization of equation (11) has been used as an extra constraint to reduce the disparity of x-axis between two rectified images. This approach can reduce the range of search for stereo matching and increase the speed on solving the correspondence problem. However, in applications where the *x-axis* disparity should not be modified too much, other constraint can be used for acquiring the values of $[h_1 \ \ h_2 \ \ h_3]$. One suitable constraint is to keep the aspect ratio of the original image invariant after rectification. We will adopt the idea of shearing transform described in (Loop & Zhang, 1999) to achieve this purpose, and the procedure will be stated below. As will be shown in the experimental section, this approach not only maintains the aspect ratio of the original image but also reduces the overall geometric distortion.

Assume that the parameter vector $\mathbf{\Phi} = \begin{bmatrix} f & \theta & h_4 & h_5 & h_6 & h_7 & h_8 \end{bmatrix}^T$ has been found by following the procedure described in the previous section. Let $[h_1 \ \ h_2 \ \ h_3] = [1 \ \ 0 \ \ 0]$; then we have a preliminary solution of homographies

$$\mathbf{H}_0 = \begin{bmatrix} 1 & 0 & 0 \\ h_4 & h_5 & h_6 \\ h_7 & h_8 & 1 \end{bmatrix}, \; \mathbf{H}'_0 = \begin{bmatrix} \cos\theta & \sin\theta & 0 \\ -\sin\theta & \cos\theta & 0 \\ -f\cos\theta & -f\sin\theta & 1 \end{bmatrix}$$

To keep the aspect ratio invariant after rectification, these two homographies can further be combined with the shearing transform defined below

$$\mathbf{H}_s = \begin{bmatrix} a & b & 0 \\ 0 & 1 & 0 \\ 0 & 0 & 1 \end{bmatrix}, \; \mathbf{H}'_s = \begin{bmatrix} a' & b' & 0 \\ 0 & 1 & 0 \\ 0 & 0 & 1 \end{bmatrix} \tag{31}$$

The final homographies for the rectification can then be written as

$$\mathbf{H} = \mathbf{H}_s\mathbf{H}_0 = \begin{bmatrix} a & b & 0 \\ 0 & 1 & 0 \\ 0 & 0 & 1 \end{bmatrix}\mathbf{H}_0 \;, \; \mathbf{H}' = \mathbf{H}'_s\mathbf{H}'_0 = \begin{bmatrix} a' & b' & 0 \\ 0 & 1 & 0 \\ 0 & 0 & 1 \end{bmatrix}\mathbf{H}'_0 \tag{32}$$

Using $\mathbf{H}_0$ and $\mathbf{H}'_0$ alone can rectify the image pair such that the coplanar condition is satisfied; however, combined with $\mathbf{H}_s$ and $\mathbf{H}'_s$ respectively, we can further improve the appearance of the final rectification results. A detailed description of the shearing transform can be found in (Loop & Zhang, 1999), but its adaptation to our usage will be briefly described below.

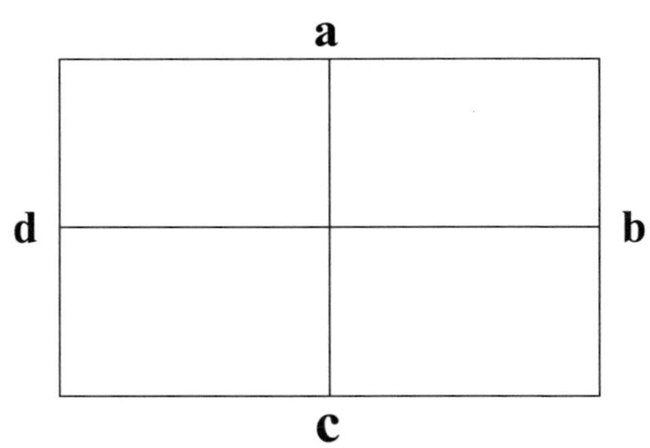

Figure 3. Center points used for computing shearing transform matrices

For a given image with width w and height h, coordinates of the midpoints on its four boundaries are shown in Fig. 3 and can be represented as

$$\mathbf{a} = \begin{bmatrix} \frac{w-1}{2} & 0 & 1 \end{bmatrix}^T, \mathbf{b} = \begin{bmatrix} w-1 & \frac{h-1}{2} & 1 \end{bmatrix}^T, \mathbf{c} = \begin{bmatrix} \frac{w-1}{2} & h-1 & 1 \end{bmatrix}^T, \mathbf{d} = \begin{bmatrix} 0 & \frac{h-1}{2} & 1 \end{bmatrix}^T$$

The two central lines are expressed as

$$\mathbf{x} = \mathbf{b} - \mathbf{d} \;, \; \mathbf{y} = \mathbf{c} - \mathbf{a}$$

Let $\hat{\mathbf{a}}, \hat{\mathbf{b}}, \hat{\mathbf{c}}, \hat{\mathbf{d}}$ be the coordinates of these four midpoints after transformation by $\mathbf{H}_0$, or

$$\hat{\mathbf{a}} = \begin{bmatrix} \hat{a}_u \\ \hat{a}_v \\ \hat{a}_w \end{bmatrix} = \mathbf{H}_0\mathbf{a} \xrightarrow{normalize} \begin{bmatrix} \hat{a}'_u \\ \hat{a}'_v \\ 1 \end{bmatrix}, \ \hat{a}'_u = \frac{\hat{a}_u}{\hat{a}_w}, \ \hat{a}'_v = \frac{\hat{a}_v}{\hat{a}_w} \tag{33}$$

The other three points ($\hat{\mathbf{b}}, \hat{\mathbf{c}}, \hat{\mathbf{d}}$) can be found by the same way, and the two central lines after rectification become
$\hat{\mathbf{x}} = \hat{\mathbf{b}} - \hat{\mathbf{d}} = \begin{bmatrix} x_u & x_v & 0 \end{bmatrix}^T$, $\hat{\mathbf{y}} = \hat{\mathbf{c}} - \hat{\mathbf{a}} = \begin{bmatrix} y_u & y_v & 0 \end{bmatrix}^T$

The perspective component of $\mathbf{H}_0$ causes the projective rectification to generate distortion, and the shearing transform $\mathbf{H}_s$, which is used to reduce the distortion, can be found by satisfying the following two constraints:

1. Orthogonal:: $$\mathbf{x}^T\mathbf{y} = (\mathbf{H}_s\hat{\mathbf{x}})^T(\mathbf{H}_s\hat{\mathbf{y}}) = 0 \tag{34}$$

2. Invariant aspect ratio: $$\frac{\mathbf{x}^T\mathbf{x}}{\mathbf{y}^T\mathbf{y}} = \frac{(\mathbf{H}_s\hat{\mathbf{x}})^T(\mathbf{H}_s\hat{\mathbf{x}})}{(\mathbf{H}_s\hat{\mathbf{y}})^T(\mathbf{H}_s\hat{\mathbf{y}})} = \frac{\mathrm{w}^2}{\mathrm{h}^2} \tag{35}$$

where $\mathbf{H}_s = \begin{bmatrix} a & b & 0 \\ 0 & 1 & 0 \\ 0 & 0 & 1 \end{bmatrix}$. Expanding equations (34), (35) and solving the quadratic polynomials of a and b based on the techniques similar to that were described in (Loop & Zhang, 1999), we obtain

$$a = \frac{\mathrm{h}^2 x_v^2 + \mathrm{w}^2 y_v^2}{\mathrm{hw}(x_v y_u - x_u y_v)}, \ b = \frac{\mathrm{h}^2 x_u x_v + \mathrm{w}^2 y_u y_v}{\mathrm{hw}(x_u y_v - x_v y_u)} \tag{36}$$

Substituting a,b into equation (31) yields shearing transform matrix $\mathbf{H}_s$. In order to make all the rectified pixels appear within the visible range, a must be positive. If a is a negative value, then both a and b are multiplied by -1. Elements a' and b' of matrix $\mathbf{H}'_s$ can be found by the same way. After $\mathbf{H}_s$ and $\mathbf{H}'_s$ were obtained, the final homographies used for rectification with minimal distortion become $\mathbf{H} = \mathbf{H}_s\mathbf{H}_0$, $\mathbf{H}' = \mathbf{H}'_s\mathbf{H}'_0$. They then can be used for resampling to complete the process of projective rectification.

5. Results and discussion

To evaluate performance of the proposed method, several indoor image pairs acquired from the INRIA web site and CMU (please see Acknowledge section) were tested. For each image pair, a set of ten point correspondences were selected from each image and used to compute the *H matrices* for rectification. Selection of these point correspondences takes a semi-automatic approach to avoid inaccuracy. That is, each point is chosen approximately by hand, and then a precise (subpixel accuracy) feature point close-by is then detected by Harris corner finder (Harris, 1998) inside a local search window. This approach not only makes the selection very easy, it also greatly improves the accuracy. To achieve the best results, these points are chosen to be evenly distributed over the entire image area.

5.1 Visual evaluation of rectifying results

The original and rectified image pairs are shown in Figures 4~8 for visual comparison, where the top is the original image pair, the middle and the bottom are the rectified results of the method proposed and the Hartley's method, respectively. To achieve a more robust estimation of **F** matrix in Hartley's method, RANSAC (Torr & Murry, 1997) is used. RANSAC calculates for each **F** the number of inliers, in which the chosen **F** is the one that maximizes it. Once the outliers are removed, **F** is recalculated with the aim of obtaining a better estimation. The solution for the pair of homogphies in the proposed method can be found in less than 100 iterations by Levenberg-Marquardt algorithm, and the re-sampling can be done in real time by look up table. As shown in these figures, all the re-sampled image pairs are properly rectified by the proposed method with minimal geometric distortions. In order to make visual evaluation of the rectified results more convenient, four horizontal lines are added to identify the difference of y-disparity before and after rectification.

In all the figures, it's obvious that our proposed method has less geometric distortion than that of Hartley's method. In Fig. 4, the Hartley's method greatly distorts the right image in the process of minimizing x disparity. Our method shows its capability in maintaining the angle and aspect ratio of the objects in the scene. However, the Hartley's method is not able to keep these properties invariant. The main reason for the distortion after rectification is because the image content contains a variety of depth values and therefore many different amounts of y-disparity. When the rectification algorithm tries to minimize the disparity all over the image region, distortion occurs. Overall, the proposed method keeps the objects in better shape than that of the Hartley's method. The greater geometric distortion of the Hartley's method is due to its minimization of the x-disparity.

5.2 Quantitative evaluation of rectifying results

In addition to the above visual comparisons, quantitative evaluation based on the changes in y disparity is also conducted as follows. The (x,y) coordinates for the ten chosen point correspondences in one image pair (Balmouss) before and after rectification by the proposed method are shown in Tables 1 for numerical evaluation. Obviously, the x disparities for the selected points have not changed too much after rectification. To estimate the accuracy of the rectification process numerically, we define the mean of the absolute difference (MAD) of y coordinate, $\overline{|\Delta y|}$, for the original and rectified image pair as

$$\overline{|\Delta y|} = \begin{cases} \varepsilon_{org} = \dfrac{1}{N}\sum_{i=1}^{N} |(\mathbf{m}_i)_y - (\mathbf{m}'_i)_y|: & \text{original} \\ \varepsilon_{rec} = \dfrac{1}{N}\sum_{i=1}^{N} |(\mathbf{H}\mathbf{m}_i)_y - (\mathbf{H}'\mathbf{m}'_i)_y|: & \text{rectified} \end{cases} \tag{37}$$

where $(\cdot)_y$ indicates the y coordinates and $(\mathbf{m}_i, \mathbf{m}'_i)$ represents the coordinates of the ith pair of the point correspondences.

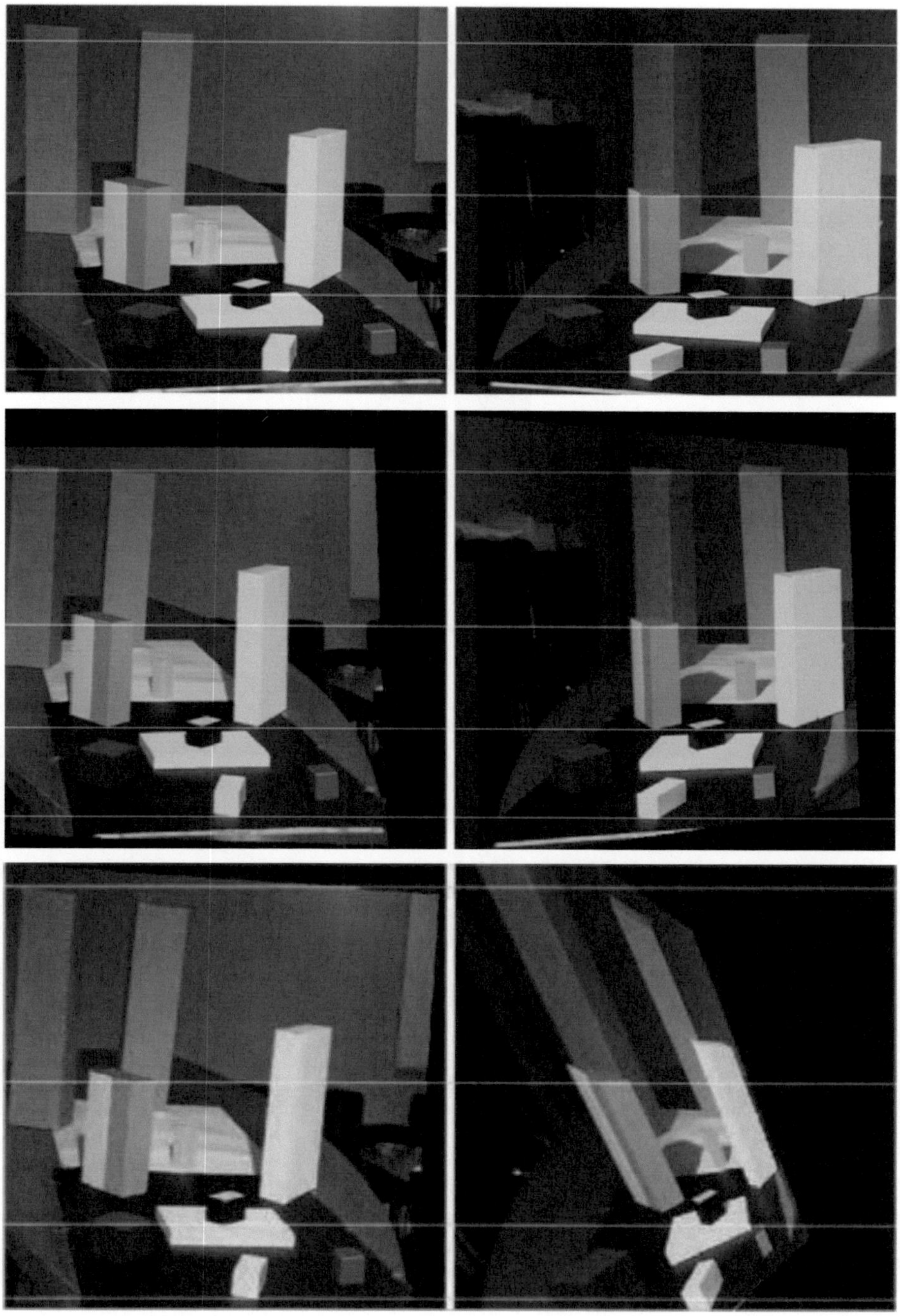

Figure 4. **Aɔut** image pair of INRIA. (a)Top row: original images. (b)Middle row: rectified images using the proposed method. (c)Bottom row: rectified images using Hartley's method. The proposed method has much lower visual distortion.

Figure 5. Rectifying results of the **castle** image from CMU/CIL (vary large y-disparity)

(a) Top row: original images.

(b) Middle row: rectified images using the proposed method.

(c) Bottom row: rectified images using Hartley's method.

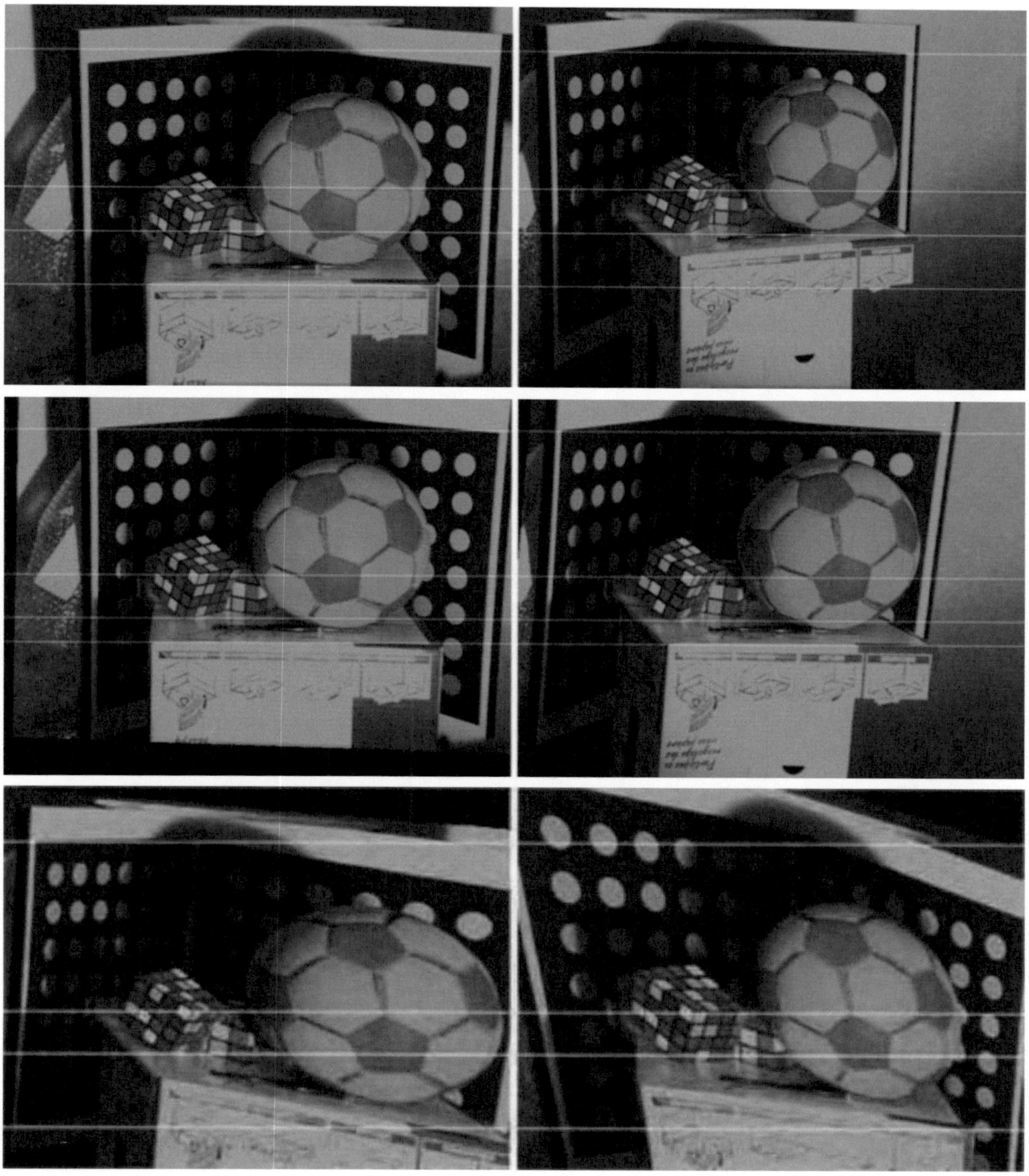

Figure 6. Rectifying results of the **BalMouss** image pair

(a) Top row: original pair of images.

(b) Middle row: rectified images using the proposed method.

(c) Bottom row: rectified images using Hartley's method

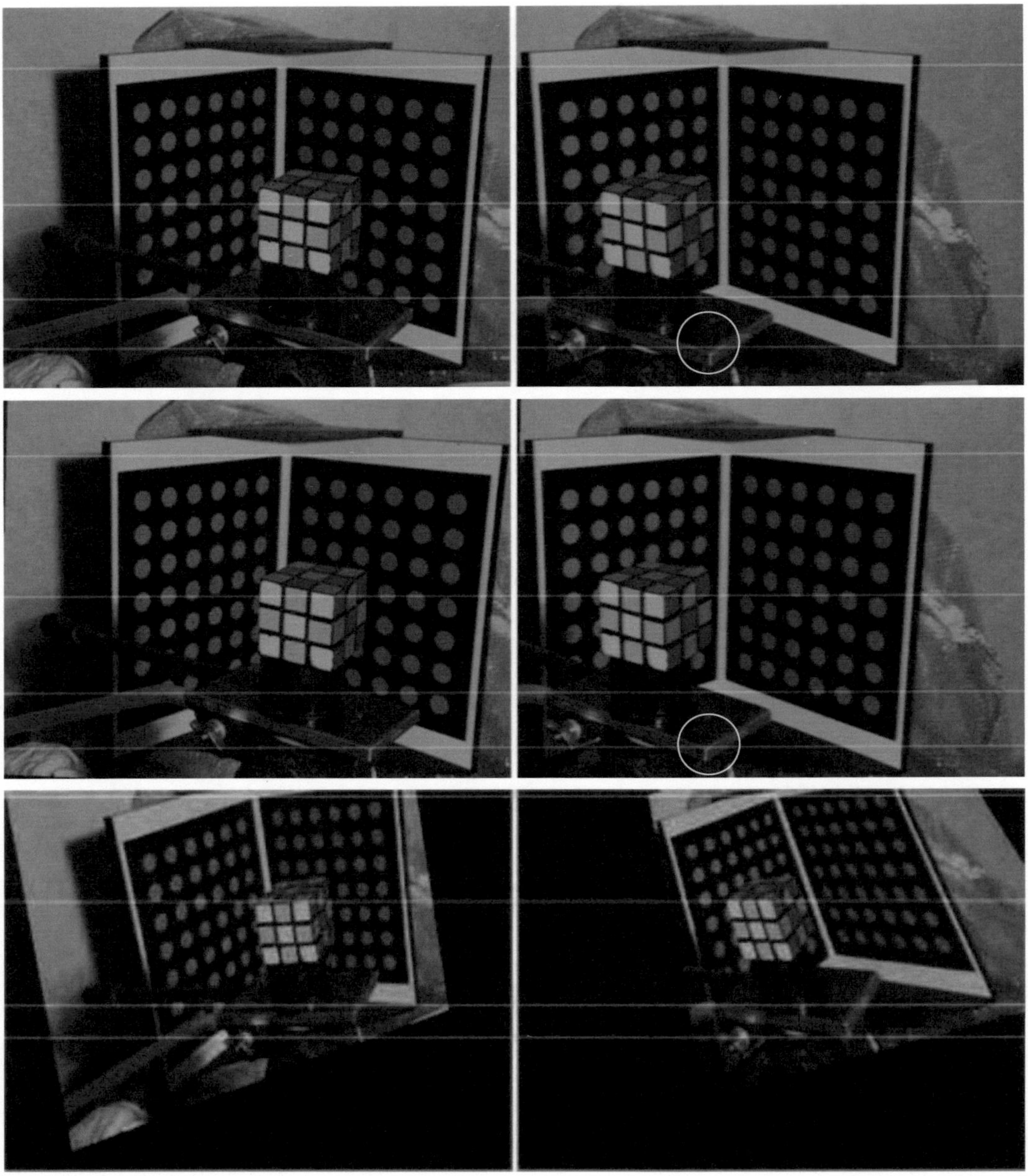

Figure 7. Rectifying results of **Rubik** image pair from INRIA

(a) Top row: original images.

(b) Middle row: rectified images using the proposed method.

(c) Bottom row: rectified images using Hartley's method

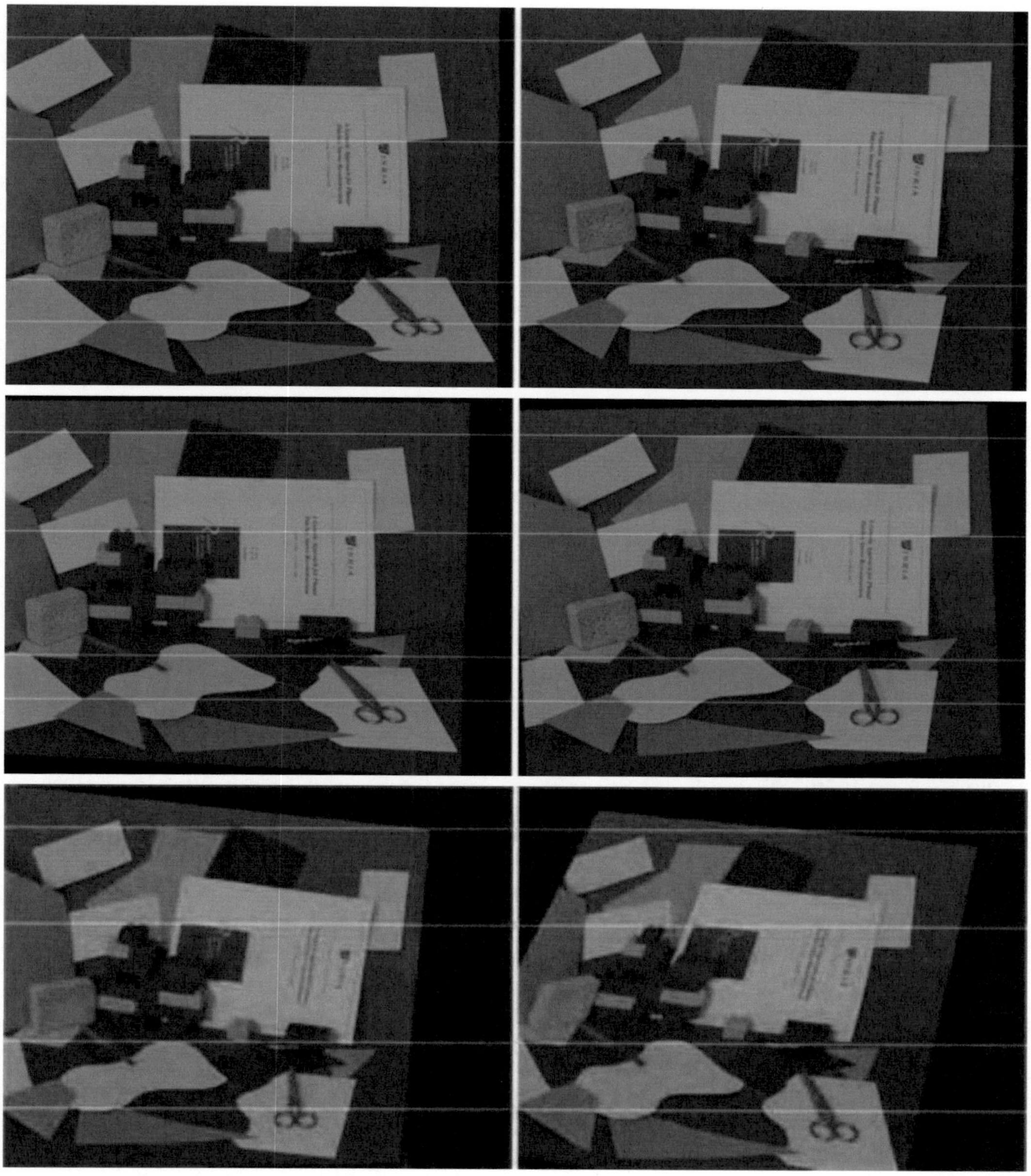

Figure 8. Rectifying results of **Tot** image pair from INRIA

(a) Top row: original images.

(b) Middle row: rectified images using the proposed method.

(c) Bottom row: rectified images using Hartley's method

A desirable property of the method is to *minimize* the $\overline{|\Delta y|}$, but keep the value of $\overline{|\Delta x|}$ *invariant* after rectification. When these ten chosen point correspondences were used for $\overline{|\Delta y|}$ computation, the results before and after rectification for the above six image pairs are listed in Table 2. If an image pair is ideally rectified, $\overline{|\Delta y|}$ of the point correspondences after rectification should be zero. As can be seen from the table, for all the image pairs, values of $\overline{|\Delta y|}$ after rectification of our proposed method (ε_{rec}) are all less than 1 pixel. They are greatly reduced compared with the values before rectification (ε_{org}), indicating the effectiveness of the proposed method. However, some image pairs can not be satisfactorily rectified by the Hartley's method.

Before rectification

Left image	x-axis	127	136	231	253	411	271	275	361	528	736
	y-axis	91	533	336	312	65	321	481	349	499	93
Right image	x-axis	55	64	208	235	255	255	297	320	508	587
	y-axis	77	501	302	277	49	286	428	307	426	69

After rectification

Left image	x-axis	127.37	136.81	233.38	256.66	419.84	274.49	278.59	368.33	543.28	766.42
	y-axis	77.376	509.38	318.49	295.32	53.493	304.77	462.15	333.97	487.31	82.733
Right image	x-axis	54.952	63.16	217.2	248.1	271.86	270.85	317.76	345.53	576.92	682.91
	y-axis	77.7	509.42	318.34	294.79	53.058	305.45	462.12	333.87	487.32	82.917

Table 1. Coordinates of point correspondences before and after rectification for **Balmouss** image pair based on the proposed method.

Image name / MAD_y	Aout Image pair	Castle image pair	Balmouss Image pair	Rubik image pair	Tot image pair
ε_{org} (pixel)	13.6	26.7084	35.8598	12.8	13.9577
ε_{rec} (pixel)	0.6322	0.5084	0.2477	0.6389	0.2779
ε_{rec_H} (pixel)	14.9539	0.4731	21.8769	14.2357	4.8668

Table 2. MAD of y-coordinate before (ε_{org}) and after rectification with the proposed (ε_{rec}) or Hartley's method (ε_{rec_H}). Evaluation based on 10 selected point correspondences.

6. Comparisons and discussion

Compared with the results presented in Hartley (Hartley, 1999), our new method has the following advantages:

1. Our method has much less geometric distortion visually, even when the image pair has large difference of viewpoints (Fig. 4). Further comparisons with the Hartley's method on geometric distortion are presented in Figs. 5-8 using four other image pairs.
2. The new method avoids using the similar constraint shown in (11) in order to obtain a unique solution. This extra x-axis disparity minimization step, which is used in deriving the Hartley's method, will be unreasonable if the rectified result is used for stereoscopic viewing. Instead of minimizing x-axis disparity, shearing transform is used in our algorithm to preserve aspect ratio and reduce geometric distortion.
3. Solving the rectification problem directly without first computing the **F** matrix makes the proposed method avoid the problem of selecting proper method for **F** matrix estimation.
4. Initial value of the nonlinear solution by iteration is much easier to set. The initial parameter vector $\mathbf{\Phi}_0$ is simply set to $\begin{bmatrix}1 & 0 & 0 & 1 & 0 & 0 & 0\end{bmatrix}^T$.

We use the same initial guess of the optimization process for all the images tested and the solutions always converge. The iteration stops after the error is smaller than a preset threshold. Although we are not sure if the true minimum is obtained, the rectified results show its robustness, even for image pair with very different view like Fig. 4. Since we are not looking for the true minimum to obtain an optimal solution, the convergence towards the true minimum is not guaranteed. If further improvement is needed, some approaches which can avoid local minimum might be taken.
Most of the projective rectification methods proposed all base their algorithms on an estimation of the *F* matrix. However, as has been stated in (Zhang, 1998), the *F* matrix estimator has its own uncertainty. Our approach, similar to the IT method (Isgrò & Trucco, 1999), avoids *F* matrix estimation procedure and obtains homographies directly. Furthermore, it improves on the Hartley's method and obtains rectifying results with reduced geometric distortion.

7. Conclusion

This chapter presented a new way of parameterizing the homography, which leads to a new approach of projective rectification for stereo images. Compared with the previous works, the novelty of this new algorithm is that it uses mean-square distance as minimization criterion which has more well-defined geometric meaning. Furthermore, instead of putting constraint on x-axis disparity, we use shearing transform to achieve a single solution for the projective rectification problem, and greatly reduce the geometric distortion. Visual inspection and quantitative evaluation of the rectification results show the accuracies of the proposed method and its low geometric distortion. Experiments on different types of image pairs with various *y*-disparity values have been conducted, and the results show that the proposed method can effectively reduce the geometric distortion.

8. Acknowledgement

The authors gratefully acknowledge the sources of some of the stereo image pairs used in this paper, which are kindly available from INRIA and CMU/CIL under Copyright.
INRIA: http://www-rocq.inria.fr/mirages/SYNTIM_OLD/analyse/paires-eng.html
CMU/CIL: http://www-2.cs.cmu.edu/afs/cs.cmu.edu/project/cil/www/cil.html

The Matlab codes of rectification implementation offered by (Hartley, 2004) for comparison is greatly appreciated.

9. References

Al-Shalfan, KA.; Haigh, JGB. & Ipson, SS. (2000). Direct algorithm for rectifying pairs of uncalibrated images, *Electronics Letters*, **36**(5), pp. 419-420.

Ayache, N. & Hansen, C. (1988). Rectification of images for binocular and trinocular stereovision, *IEEE ICPR*, pp. 11-16, Nov , Rome, Italy.

Ayache, N. & Lustman, F.(1991). Trinocular stereo vision for robotics. *IEEE Trans. on PAMI*, 13, Jan, pp. 73-85, ISSN: 0162-8828.

Faugeras, O. (1993). *Three-Dimensional Computer Vision*, MIT Press, Cambridge, MA, ISBN: 0387151192.

Fusiello, A.; Trucco, E. & Verri, A. (2000). A compact algorithm for rectification of stereo pairs. *Machine Vision and Applications*, **12**, July, pp. 16–22, ISSN: 0932-8092.

Gluckman, J. & Nayar, S. (2001). Rectifying Transformations That Minimize Resampling Effects, *IEEE CVPR'01*, pp. 111-117, Dec, Kauai, HI, USA.

Harris, C. & Stephens, M. (1998). A Combined Corner and Edge Detector, *Alvey Vision Conf*, pp. 147-151.

Hartley, R. (1997). In Defense of the Eight-Point Algorithm, *IEEE Transactions on PAMI*, **19**, pp. 580-593

Hartley, R. (1999). Theory and Practice of Projective Rectification. *International Journal of Computer Vision*, **35** , pp. 115-127.

Hartley, R (2004). http://www.robots.ox.ac.uk/~vgg/hzbook/code

Isgrò, F. & Trucco, E. (1999). On Robust Rectification for Uncalibrated Images, *IEEE International Conference on Image Analysis and Processing*, pp. 297-302, Sep.

Loop, C. & Zhang, Z. (1999). Computing Rectifying Homographies for Stereo Vision, *IEEE CVPR'99*, pp. 125-131, June, Fort Collins, CO, USA.

Papadimitriou, DV. & Dennis, TJ. (1996). Epipolar line estimation and rectification for stereo image pairs, *IEEE Transactions on Image Processing*, **5**(4), pp. 672-676.

Pollefeys, M.; Kock, R. & Gool, LV. (1999). A Simple and Efficient Rectification Method for General Motion, *Proc. ICCV*, pp. 496-501, Corfu, Greece.

Robert, L.; Zeller, C. & Faugeras, O. et al., (1997). Applications of non-metric vision to some visually-guided robotics tasks, In : *Visual Navigation: From Biological Systems to Unmanned Ground Vehicles (Vol. II of Advances in Computer Vision, Lawrence Erlbaum Associates)*, Aloimonos Y, ed.

Slama, C. (1980). *Manual of Photogrammetry*, American Society of Photogrammetry, ISBN: 0937294012.

Torr, P.H.S. & Murry D.W. (1997). The development and comparison of robust methods for estimating the fundamental matrix, *International Journal of Computer Vision* 24 (3) , pp.271–300.

Zhang, Z. (1998). Determining the Epipolar Geometry and its Uncertainty : A Review, *International Journal of Computer Vision*, **27**, pp. 161-195.

14

Non-rigid Stereo-motion

Alessio Del Bue[1] and Lourdes Agapito[2]
[1] *Instituto Superior Técnico*
Portugal
[2]*Queen Mary University of London*
United Kingdom

1. Stereo, motion and structure

Using a calibrated stereo pair is a common and practical solution to obtain reliable 3-D reconstructions. In its simpler formulation, once the stereo rig is calibrated, the depth of points in the image is estimated by applying triangulation (Trucco & Verri, 1998). In order to obtain accurate depth estimates, the cameras are usually separated from each other by a significant baseline thus creating widely spaced observations of the same object. The disadvantage of this configuration though, is that having a wide baseline makes the matching of features between pairs of views a more challenging problem.

On the other hand, the task of computing temporal tracks from single camera sequences is relatively easier since the images are closely spaced in time. As a drawback, disparities may be insufficient to obtain a reliable depth estimation and, as a result, longer sequences are needed to infer the 3-D structure. Particularly, in the case of non-rigid structure, a sufficient overall rigid motion is necessary to allow the algorithms to estimate the reconstruction parameters correctly.

Hence, a question of relevant interest is the feasibility of an approach that efficiently fuses the positive aspects of both methods. The problem of recovering 3-D structure using a stereo-rig moving in time or a stereo rig looking at a moving object has been defined for the rigid case as the stereo-motion problem (Waxman & Duncan, 1998; Dornaika & Chung, 1999; Stein & Shashua 1998; Mandelbaum et al., 1999). Ho and Chung (Ho & Chung, 2000) were the first to formulate this problem within the factorization scenario. Following a similar direction, we introduce a multi-camera motion model that is able to deal with a time-varying shape and we present a linear solution based on the factorization framework that is subsequently optimized with a non-linear procedure.

Schematically, the chapter is structured as follows. The inference of 3-D structure from an image sequence (single camera case) is introduced in Section 2, focusing particularly on the case of a deforming body. The next section will show how the presented framework, based on a factorization solution of the problem, can be consistently extended to the case of multiple cameras viewing a deforming body and a linear solution to the problem will be as well provided. Section 3 introduces a non-linear optimization strategy to refine the linear solution obtained with the previous method and Section 4 will validate the presented approaches with experimental tests on synthetic and real deforming bodies. Finally we present further considerations over the presented framework and its future extensions.

2. Background: the monocular case

2.1 Rigid factorization

Tomasi and Kanade's factorization algorithm (Tomasi & Kanade, 1992) for rigid structure provides a maximum likelihood estimate for affine structure and motion under the assumption of isotropic Gaussian noise. The key idea is to gather the 2-D image coordinates of a set of P points tracked throughout F frames into a measurement matrix $W_{2F \times P}$. Assuming affine viewing conditions, the measurement matrix can be expressed analytically as a product of two matrices: $W = M\,S$ where M is a $2F \times 3$ motion matrix which expresses the pose of the camera and S is the $3 \times P$ shape matrix which contains 3-D locations of the reconstructed scene points. Therefore the rank of the measurement matrix is constrained to be $r \leq 3$. This constraint can be easily imposed by taking the Singular Value Decomposition of the measurement matrix and truncating it to rank 3: $\mathrm{SVD}(W) = U_{2F \times 3}\, D_{3x3}\, V_{3xP} = M_{2F \times 3}\, S_{3xP}$. In this way the image measurement matrix can be factorized into its motion and shape components.

2.2 Non-Rigid motion: the single camera case

Tomasi and Kanade's factorization algorithm has recently been extended to the case of non-rigid deformable 3-D structure (Bregler et al., 2000). Here, a model is needed to express the deformations of the 3-D shape in a compact way. The chosen model is a simple linear model where the 3-D shape of any specific configuration of a non-rigid object is approximated by a linear combination of a set of D basis-shapes which represent the D principal modes of deformation of the object for P points. A perfectly rigid object would correspond to the situation where D=1. Each basis-shape ($S_1\ S_2 \ldots S_D$) is a $3 \times P$ matrix which contains the 3-D locations of P object points for that particular mode of deformation. The 3-D shape of any configuration can then be expressed as a linear combination of the basis-shapes S_i:

$$S = \sum_{d=1}^{D} l_d S_d \qquad S, S_d \in \Re^{3\times P} \qquad l_d \in \Re \tag{1}$$

where l_i are the deformation weights. If we assume a scaled orthographic projection model for the camera, the coordinates of the 2-D image points observed at each frame i are related to the coordinates of the 3-D points according to the following equation:

$$W_i = \begin{bmatrix} u_{i1} & \cdots & u_{iP} \\ v_{i1} & \cdots & v_{iP} \end{bmatrix} = R_i \left(\sum_{d=1}^{D} l_{id} S_d \right) + T_i \tag{2}$$

where

$$R_i = \begin{bmatrix} r_{i1} & r_{i2} & r_{i3} \\ r_{i4} & r_{i5} & r_{i6} \end{bmatrix} \tag{3}$$

is a 2×3 matrix which contains the first and second rows of the camera rotation matrix and T_i contains the first two components of the camera translation vector. Weak perspective is a good approximation when the depth variation within the object is small compared to its distance to the camera. The weak perspective scaling (f/Z_{avg}) is implicitly encoded in the l_i coefficients. We may eliminate the translation vector T_i by registering image points to the centroid in each frame. In this way, the 3-D coordinate system will be centred at the centroid of the shape S. If the same P points can be tracked throughout an image sequence we may stack them into a $2F \times P$ measurement matrix W and we may write:

$$W = \begin{bmatrix} W_1 \\ \vdots \\ W_F \end{bmatrix} = \begin{bmatrix} l_{11}R_1 & \dots & l_{1D}R_1 \\ \vdots & & \vdots \\ l_{F1}R_F & \dots & l_{FD}R_F \end{bmatrix} \begin{bmatrix} S_1 \\ \vdots \\ S_D \end{bmatrix} = MS \tag{4}$$

Since M is a $2F \times 3D$ matrix and S is a $3D \times P$ matrix, the rank of W when no noise is present must be at most 3D. Note that, in relation to rigid factorization, in the non-rigid case the rank is incremented by three with every new mode of deformation. The goal of factorization algorithms is to exploit this rank constraint to recover the 3-D pose, and shape (basis-shapes and deformation coefficients) of the object from the correspondence points stored in W.

2.3 Non-rigid factorization

The rank constraint on the measurement matrix W can be easily imposed by truncating the SVD of W to rank $3D$. This will factor W into a motion matrix $\tilde{M}$ and a shape matrix $\tilde{S}$. However, the result of the factorization of W is not unique since any invertible $3D \times 3D$ matrix Q can be inserted in the decomposition leading to the alternative factorization $W = (\tilde{M}Q)(Q^{-1}\tilde{S})$. The focal problem is to find a transformation matrix Q that imposes the replicated block structure on the motion matrix $\tilde{M}$ shown in (4) and that removes the affine ambiguity upgrading the reconstruction to a metric one. Whereas in the rigid case the problem of computing the transformation matrix Q to upgrade the reconstruction to a metric one can be solved linearly (Tomasi & Kanade, 1992), in the non-rigid case imposing the appropriate repetitive structure to the motion matrix $\tilde{M}$ results in a non-linear problem. It is important to note that while the block structure is not required if we only wish to determine image point motion, it is crucial for the recovery of 3-D shape and motion.

Most of the model-free approaches to non-rigid factorization are based either on closed-form solutions (Xiao et al., 2004), assuming prior knowledge over the structure of the basis shapes, or iterative non-linear optimisation techniques (Brand, 2005; Del Bue et al., 2007; Torresani et al., 2001), which require an appropriate initialisation in order to converge.

3. The stereo camera case

The main contribution we present here is to extend the non-rigid factorization methods to the case of a stereo rig, where the two cameras remain fixed relative to each other throughout the sequence. However, the same framework could be used in the case of 3 or more cameras. Torresani et al. (Torresani et al., 2001) first introduced the factorization problem for the multiple camera case but they did not provide an algorithm or any experimental results.

3.1 The stereo motion model

When two cameras are viewing the same scene, the measurement matrix W will contain the image measurements from the left and right cameras resulting in a $4F \times P$ matrix where F is the number of frames and P the number of points. Assuming that not only the single-frame tracks but also the stereo correspondences are known we may write the measurement matrix W as:

$$W = \begin{bmatrix} W^L \\ W^R \end{bmatrix} \tag{5}$$

where for each frame i the stereo correspondences are:

$$W_i^L = \begin{bmatrix} w_{i1}^L & \dots & w_{iP}^L \end{bmatrix} \quad W_i^R = \begin{bmatrix} w_{i1}^R & \dots & w_{iP}^R \end{bmatrix} \tag{6}$$

Note that, since we assume that the cameras are synchronized, at each time step i the left and right cameras are observing the same 3-D structure and this results in the additional constraint that the structure matrix S and the deformation coefficients l_{id} are shared by left and right camera. The measurement matrix W can be factored into a motion matrix M and a structure matrix S which take the following form:

$$W = \begin{bmatrix} l_{11}R_1^L & \dots & l_{1D}R_1^L \\ \vdots & & \vdots \\ l_{F1}R_F^L & \dots & l_{FD}R_F^L \\ l_{11}R_1^R & \dots & l_{1D}R_1^R \\ \vdots & & \vdots \\ l_{F1}R_F^R & \dots & l_{FD}R_F^R \end{bmatrix} \begin{bmatrix} S_1 \\ \vdots \\ S_D \end{bmatrix} \tag{7}$$

where R^L and R^R are the rotation components for the left and right cameras. Once more, we have eliminated the translation for both cameras by registering image points to the centroid in each frame. Note that the assumption that the deformation coefficients are the same for the left and right sequences relies on the fact that the weak perspective scaling f/Z_{avg} must be the same for both cameras. This assumption is generally true in a symmetric stereo setup where f and Z_{avg} are usually the same for both cameras.

It is also possible to express the stereo motion matrix M by including explicitly the assumption that a fixed stereo rig is being used. In this case the rotation pair for the left and right cameras can be expressed in terms of the matrix that encodes their relative orientation matrix R_{rel} such that: $R^R = R_{rel}\, R^L$. The motion matrix M in equation (6) can be consequently expressed as:

$$M = \begin{bmatrix} l_{11}R_1^L & \dots & l_{1D}R_1^L \\ \vdots & & \vdots \\ l_{F1}R_F^L & \dots & l_{FD}R_F^L \\ l_{11}R_{rel}R_1^L & \dots & l_{1D}R_{rel}R_F^L \\ \vdots & & \vdots \\ l_{F1}R_{rel}R_F^L & \dots & l_{FD}R_{rel}R_F^L \end{bmatrix} \tag{8}$$

3.2 Non-rigid stereo factorization

Once more the rank of the measurement matrix W is at most 3D since M is a 4F x 3D matrix and S is a 3D x P matrix, where P is the number of points. Assuming that the single frame tracks and the stereo correspondences are all known, the measurement matrix W may be factorized into the product of a motion matrix M and a shape matrix S by truncating the SVD of W to rank $3D$ (see section 2.3):

$$SVD(W) = \tilde{W} = \begin{bmatrix} \tilde{M}^L \\ \tilde{M}^R \end{bmatrix} \tilde{S} \tag{9}$$

3.3 Computing the transformation matrix *Q*

The result of the factorization is not unique since $\tilde{W} = (\tilde{M}Q)(Q^{-1}\tilde{S})$ would give an equivalent factorization. We proceed to apply the metric constraint by correcting each $4F$ x 3 vertical block in $\tilde{M}$ independently. Note that in this case we have used five constraints per frame: 2 orthogonality constraints (one from each camera) and 3 equal norm constraints (computed from rows $2i$-1, $2i$, $2i$+$2F$-1, $2i$+$2F$ of the motion matrix $\tilde{M}$ where i is a generic frame). Each vertical block will then be corrected as: $\hat{M}_d \leftarrow \tilde{M}_d Q_d$. The overall transformation Q is a block diagonal matrix such that:

$$Q = \begin{bmatrix} Q_1 & 0 & \dots & 0 \\ 0 & Q_2 & \dots & 0 \\ \vdots & \vdots & \ddots & \vdots \\ 0 & 0 & \dots & Q_D \end{bmatrix} \tag{10}$$

The shape matrix will be corrected with the inverse of the block-diagonal transformation: $\hat{S} \leftarrow Q^{-1}\tilde{S}$.

3.4 Factorization of the motion matrix *M*

In the stereo case we factorize each 4 x $3D$ sub-block of the motion matrix (which contains left and right measurements for each frame i) into its truncated 2 x 3 rotation matrices R_i^L and R_i^R and the deformation weights l_{id} using an orthonormal decomposition. The structure of the sub-blocks can be expressed as:

$$\mathbf{M}_i = \begin{bmatrix} \mathbf{M}_{il}^{L} & \dots & \mathbf{M}_{iD}^{L} \\ \mathbf{M}_{il}^{R} & \dots & \mathbf{M}_{iD}^{R} \end{bmatrix} = \begin{bmatrix} \mathbf{l}_{il} \begin{bmatrix} \mathbf{R}_i^L \\ \mathbf{R}_i^R \end{bmatrix} & \dots & \mathbf{l}_{iD} \begin{bmatrix} \mathbf{R}_i^L \\ \mathbf{R}_i^R \end{bmatrix} \end{bmatrix} \tag{11}$$

The approach used to estimate the rotation components for the left and right cameras use the orthogonality constraints on each block of the motion matrix. Since now we have 4 rows per frame, we arrange the motion sub-blocks such that:

$$\tilde{\mathbf{M}}_i \rightarrow \overline{\mathbf{M}}_i = \begin{bmatrix} \mathbf{l}_{il} \begin{bmatrix} \overline{\mathbf{r}}_i^L \\ \overline{\mathbf{r}}_i^R \end{bmatrix} & \mathbf{l}_{i2} \begin{bmatrix} \overline{\mathbf{r}}_i^L \\ \overline{\mathbf{r}}_i^R \end{bmatrix} & \dots & \mathbf{l}_{iD} \begin{bmatrix} \overline{\mathbf{r}}_i^L \\ \overline{\mathbf{r}}_i^R \end{bmatrix} \end{bmatrix} \tag{12}$$

where $\bar{r}_i^L = [r_{i1}^L \ldots r_{i6}^L]^T$ is a column vector which contains the coefficients of the left rotation matrix R_i^L and similarly for $\bar{r}_i^R$. Post-multiplying the rearranged matrix M_i by the 2D unity vector $c = [1 \ldots 1]^T$ gives a column vector a_i:

$$a_i = \overline{M}_i c \tag{13}$$

which may be rearranged into a 4 x 3 matrix A_i with analytic form:

$$A_i = \begin{bmatrix} kr_{i1}^L & kr_{i2}^L & kr_{i3}^L \\ kr_{i4}^L & kr_{i5}^L & kr_{i6}^L \\ kr_{i1}^R & kr_{i2}^R & kr_{i3}^R \\ kr_{i4}^R & kr_{i5}^R & kr_{i6}^R \end{bmatrix} = \begin{bmatrix} A_i^L \\ A_i^R \end{bmatrix} \tag{14}$$

where $k = l_{i1} + \ldots + l_{iD}$. Since R^L and R^R are orthonormal matrices, the following equation is satisfied:

$$\begin{bmatrix} R_i^L & 0 \\ 0 & R_i^R \end{bmatrix}_{4\times 6} \begin{bmatrix} \left(A_i^L\right)^T & 0 \\ 0 & \left(A_i^R\right)^T \end{bmatrix}_{6\times 4} = \sqrt{\begin{bmatrix} A_i^L\left(A_i^L\right)^T & 0 \\ 0 & A_i^R\left(A_i^R\right)^T \end{bmatrix}_{4\times 4}} \tag{15}$$

Therefore, a linear least-squares fit can be obtained for the rotation matrices R^L and R^R and the weights l_{id} can be subsequently estimated by rearranging the sub-block matrix M_i in a different way from equation (11):

$$\widetilde{M}_f \rightarrow M_i' = \begin{bmatrix} l_{i1}\bar{r}_i^T \\ \ldots \\ l_{iD}\bar{r}_i^T \end{bmatrix} \tag{16}$$

where $\bar{\mathbf{r}}_i = \left[\left(\bar{\mathbf{r}}_i^{\,\mathrm{L}}\right)^{\mathrm{T}} \ \left(\bar{\mathbf{r}}_i^{\,\mathrm{R}}\right)^{\mathrm{T}}\right]^{\mathrm{T}}$. The configuration weights for each frame i are then derived exploiting the orthonormality of R_i since:

$$M_i'\bar{r}_i^T = \begin{bmatrix} l_{i1}\bar{r}_i^T\bar{r}_i \\ \ldots \\ l_{iD}\bar{r}_i^T\bar{r}_i \end{bmatrix} = 4\begin{bmatrix} l_{i1} \\ \ldots \\ l_{iD} \end{bmatrix} \tag{17}$$

The linear estimation can be furthermore refined by using a regularization scheme similar to the one used by Brand in his flexible factorization algorithm (Brand, 2001) which enforces the deformations in $\widetilde{S}$ being as small as possible relative to the mean shape. The idea here is that most of the image point motion should be explained by the rigid component. This is similar to the shape regularization used by other authors (Torresani et al. 2001; Aanæs & Kahl, 2002).

So far we have presented an extension of non-rigid factorization methods to the case of a stereo camera pair. In particular our algorithm follows the approach by Brand (Brand, 2001). While this new method improves the quality of the 3-D reconstructions with respect to those using a monocular sequence, it still performs a partial upgrade of the motion and 3-D structure matrices since Q is computed initially as a block diagonal matrix and then corrected with Brand's flexible factorization. In order to obtain a solution which completely respects the structure of equation (7), we will now describe a non-linear optimization scheme which renders the appropriate structure to the motion matrix, allowing to disambiguate between the motion and shape parameters.

4. Stereo non-linear optimization

4.1 The non-rigid cost function

The goal is to estimate the motion parameters R_i, the relative orientation between cameras R_{rel}, the 3-D basis shapes S_d and the deformation weights l_{id} such that the distance between the measured image points w_{ij} and the reprojection of the estimated 3-D points is minimised. However, the coordinates in W are extracted by a measurement process and, therefore, they are affected by noise or by a certain degree of uncertainty n_{ij}. The measured coordinates w_{ij} for the left and right camera at frame i can be expressed in terms of the exact measurements x_{ij} such that:

$$w_{ij} = \begin{bmatrix} w_{ij}^L \\ w_{ij}^R \end{bmatrix} = x_{ij} + n_{ij} \tag{18}$$

The projection equation for a 3-D point j in image frame i is given by:

$$x_{ij} = \begin{bmatrix} R_i^L \sum_d l_{id} S_{dj} \\ R_{rel} R_i^L \sum_d l_{id} S_{dj} \end{bmatrix} \tag{19}$$

where x_{ij} are the image coordinates of the point for the left and right cameras and S_i is the $3D$ x 1 parameterisation of the shape basis for a deformable point j such that:

$$S_j = \begin{bmatrix} S_{1j} \\ S_{2j} \\ \vdots \\ S_{Dj} \end{bmatrix} \tag{20}$$

with the 3-vector S_{dj} defining the d basis component for point j.

Following equation (18), the uncertainty over the measurements is obtained from the residual given by $n_{ij} = w_{ij} - x_{ij}$. This residual is generally referred to as the reprojection error of the image coordinates in the literature and it expresses the difference between the image coordinates given the estimated model parameters and the measured data. Hence, it is possible to recast the problem of estimating the non-rigid structure and motion parameters by minimizing the norm of the reprojection error of all the points in all the frames such that:

$$\min_{R_i^L R_{rel} l_{id} S_{dj}} \sum_{i,j}^{F,P} \left\| n_{ij} \right\|^2 = \min_{R_i^L R_{rel} l_{id} S_{dj}} \sum_{i,j}^{F,P} \left\| w_{ij} - x_{ij} \right\|^2 \tag{21}$$

Note that the error is a sum of *FP* quadratic cost functions. Assuming the noise can be modelled with a Gaussian distribution, the minimization of equation (21) provides a true Maximum Likelihood (ML) estimate of the parameters.

The definition of this non-rigid cost function could rise two major criticisms. First, the number of parameters can increase dramatically with the number of frames composing the scene and the complexity of the modelled object. This may render the minimization of equation (21) computationally unfeasible given the size of the parameter space. Second, the high non-linearity of the cost function is likely to produce multiple minima which would result in a difficult convergence to the global minimum of the function. The solution proposed is a reformulation of bundle-adjustment techniques for deformable structure from motion which we describe in the following sections.

4.2 A bundle-adjustment approach to deformable modelling

The non-linear optimization of the cost function in (21) is achieved using a Levenberg-Marquardt (Levenberg, 1944; Marquardt 1963; Moré, 1977) iterative minimization scheme modified to take advantage of the sparse block structure of the matrices involved. This method is generically termed bundle-adjustment in the computer vision (Triggs et al. 2000) and photogrammetry (Atkinson, 1996) communities and it is a standard procedure successfully applied to numerous 3-D reconstruction tasks (Hartley & Zisserman, 2000). Our main contribution here is an analysis of its applicability to the non-rigid modelling framework.

In the next section, we will review the concepts involved in bundle-adjustment (Levenberg-Marquardt minimization and sparse computation) and reformulate the factorization framework as a non-linear, large-scale minimization problem.

4.3 Levenberg-Marquardt minimization

Levenberg-Marquardt methods use a mixture of Gauss-Newton and gradient descent minimization schemes switching from the first to the second when the estimated Hessian of the cost function is close to being singular. An algorithm with mixed behaviors usually obtains a higher rate of success in finding the correct minimum than other approaches. Other similar second-order or quasi-Newton algorithms may be used to minimize the cost function. However, Levenberg-Marquardt techniques have been studied and tested thoroughly in many Computer Vision applications (Hartley & Zisserman, 2000) and they have been found to deliver satisfactory results. Examples are mostly given for classical inference problems in Computer Vision such as fundamental matrix computation (Bartoli & Sturm, 2004), camera calibration (Pollefeys, 1999), and 3-D sparse reconstruction (Guilbert et al., 2004). However second-order methods have been successfully applied to less conventional geometric problems such as model-based face reconstruction (Fua, 2000), mosaicing (McLauchlan & Jaenicke, 2002) and reconstruction of curves (Berthilsson, 2001).

Most of the computational burden of iterative second-order methods is represented by the Gauss-Newton descent step, each iteration of which requires the calculation of the inverse of the Hessian of the cost function *C*. Specifically to the deformable factorization case, *C* can be expressed in terms of the N-vector Θ containing the model parameters such that $\Theta = (\Theta_{l1},\ldots,\Theta_{lF},\ \Theta_{R1},\ldots,\Theta_{RF},\Theta_{S1},\ldots,\Theta_{SP})^T$, where Θ_{li}, Θ_{Ri} and Θ_{Sj} represent respectively the parameters for the configuration weights, orthographic cameras and 3-D basis shapes for each view and each point. Hence, the cost function C can be written as a sum of squared residuals:

$$C(\Theta) = \sum_{i,j}^{F,P} \left\| n_{ij} \right\|^2 \tag{22}$$

where the residual for each frame and each point can be expressed as a $2FP$ x 1 vector n such that $n = [n_{11}^T \ldots n_{FP}^T]^T$. At each iteration t of the algorithm, an update Δ^t is computed in order to descend to the minimum of the cost function such that the new set of parameters is given by $\Theta^{t+1} = \Theta^t + \Delta^t$. By dropping the iteration index t for notation clarity, it is necessary to express the generic increment Δ in the model parameters as a second order Taylor expansion assuming local linearities in the cost function such that:

$$C(\Theta + \Delta) \approx C(\Theta) + g^T \Delta + \frac{1}{2} \Delta^T H \Delta \tag{23}$$

where $g = J^T n$ is the N x 1 gradient vector and H is the N x N Hessian matrix that can be approximated as $H = J^T J$ (Gauss-Newton approximation of the Hessian matrix; see (Triggs et al. 2000) for details) with $J = \frac{\partial n}{\partial \Theta}$ representing the $2FP$ x N Jacobian matrix in the model parameters. In order to find the increment Δ, the minimum of the quadratic function $e = g^T \Delta + \frac{1}{2} \Delta^T H \Delta$ is computed by imposing $\frac{\partial e}{\partial \Delta} = 0$. Thus, the expression of the Gauss-Newton descent step can be finally expressed as:

$$H\Delta = -g \tag{24}$$

Levenberg-Marquardt algorithms differ from a pure Gauss-Newton method since they apply a damping term to equation (24) obtaining:

$$(H + \lambda I)\Delta = -g \tag{25}$$

The added term λI has a twofold effect in the minimization. Firstly, by modifying the parameter λ, it is possible to control the behavior of the algorithm that can switch between first order (for high values of λ) and second order (low λ) iterations. Secondly, λI makes the solution of (17) numerically stable by forcing that $H + \lambda I$ is a full-rank matrix and thus properly invertible.

4.4 Sparse structure of the Jacobian

Solving for the normal equations in equation (22) is a problem of complexity $O(N^3)$ and this step has to be repeated at each iteration. In order to render the computation feasible as the number of parameters increases, it is possible to exploit the sparse structure of the Jacobian J. Motion components (configuration weights and camera parameters) are unrelated

between different views and, similarly, structure components are unrelated between different point trajectories. As a result, the Jacobian matrix contains a large number of entries for which the partial derivatives are zero.
It is possible to solve for the increment Δ in (25) efficiently by calculating the inverse of H using the sparse structure of J. Standard approaches for sparse computation are described in (Hartley & Zisserman, 2000) and (Triggs et al. 2000). Notice that, again, this property is valid for any rigid and non-rigid factorization model, since the sparseness relation is given by the independency between motion parameters (for each frame) and 3-D structure (for each point) in the multi-view cost function and thus independent of the chosen model.

4.5 Proposed implementation

The cost function of a deformable object presents more degrees of freedom than in the rigid case, which could lead to the existence of multiple local minima for the motion, deformation and structure components. It is possible to reduce the chance of falling into local minima by carefully designing the algorithm with respect to the following two aspects: initialisation and model parameterisation.
The camera matrices R_i are parameterised using unit quaternions (Horn 1987) giving a total of 4 x F rotation parameters, where F is the total number of frames. Quaternions ensure that there are no strong singularities and that the orthonormality of the rotation matrices is preserved by merely enforcing the normality of the 4-vector. This would not be the case with the Euler angle or the rotation matrix parameterisations, where orthonormality of the rotations is more complex to preserve. The quaternion normalization is directly enforced in the cost function by dividing the quaternion with its norm. Indeed, in an initial implementation the 3-D pose was parameterised using the 6 entries of the rotation matrices R_i and R_{rel}, however the use of quaternions led to improved convergence and to much better results for the rotation parameters and the 3-D pose.
The method proposed by Bar-Itzhack (Bar-Itzhack, 2000) in an attitude control context is used to obtain the quaternions from the set of rotation matrices R_i. The algorithm has the main advantage of yieldieng the closest quaternion representation if the constraints of matrix orthonormality are not exactly satisfied. This eventuality usually appears during the initialisation of the non-linear optimization scheme after the first computation of the corrective transform Q. Schematically, the method first defines the matrix B given the singular elements $\{r_{mn}\}$ belonging to a generic 3 x 3 rotation matrix R_i:

$$B = \frac{1}{3}\begin{bmatrix} r_{11}-r_{22}-r_{33} & r_{21}+r_{12} & r_{31}+r_{13} & r_{23}+r_{32} \\ r_{21}+r_{12} & r_{22}-r_{11}-r_{33} & r_{32}+r_{23} & r_{31}-r_{13} \\ r_{31}+r_{13} & r_{32}+r_{23} & r_{33}-r_{22}-r_{11} & r_{12}-r_{21} \\ r_{23}-r_{32} & r_{31}-r_{13} & r_{12}-r_{21} & r_{11}+r_{22}+r_{33} \end{bmatrix} \quad (26)$$

The algorithm then follows with the following three steps:

- Compute the eigenvalues of B.
- Find the largest eigenvalue λ_{max}.
- Extract the eigenvector of B which corresponds to λ_{max}.

The given eigenvector is the closest quaternion to the matrix R. In the case of an exact orthonormal matrix we would obtain $\lambda_{max} = 1$. Finally, the structure is parameterised with the $(3 \times D) \times P$ coordinates of the S_d shape bases and the $D \times F$ deformation weights l_{id}.
The linear method proposed in the previous section is used to obtain an initial estimation of the model parameters. The initial estimate for the constant relative orientation R_{rel} between the left and right cameras is estimated from the camera matrices R^L and R^R using a least squares estimation. If the internal and external calibration of the stereo rig were known in advance after a process of calibration or self-calibration, an alternative initialisation could be computed by recovering the 3-D structure and performing Principal Component Analysis (PCA) on the data to obtain an initial estimate for the basis shapes and the coefficients. However, our choice was to use an initialisation that does not require a pre-calibration of the cameras.

5. Experimental results

This section shows the performance of the proposed stereo-motion algorithms. Firstly, synthetic stereo sequences are generated under different Gaussian noise and deformation conditions to assess the validity of the method. A further synthetic test using a computer graphic (CG) generated face model will show the behaviour of the configuration weights and motion components when the object in the stereo sequence is static (only deforming). We then carry out some real experiments where the object underwent only a small amount of rigid motion (apart from the deformations) and we will show the improvement of the method by comparing the output of the monocular factorization and the stereo algorithms. Non-linear optimization will follow the computed linear solutions.

5.1 Experiments with a synthetic non-rigid cube

A set of deformable points is randomly sampled inside a cube of 50 x 50 x 50 units. A minimal overall rigid motion is introduced to avoid possible ambiguities arising from a completely static object. The 3-D structure computed at each frame is then projected with 2 orthographic cameras displaced by a baseline of 20 units and relatively rotated by 30 degrees about the y-axis. Finally, different levels of Gaussian noise ($\sigma = 0.5, 1, 1.5, 2$) are added to the measurements obtained by the stereo pair. Notice that the setup is constructed in such way that the overall rigid motion is not enough to reconstruct the sequences using monocular factorization followed by bundle adjustment. We performed a test and we obtained a relative 3-D reconstruction error of 50% resulting in a meaningless reconstruction.
The results show the plots for the relative 3-D error, rotation error and reprojection error tested over 25 trials with a 3-D shape deforming with different numbers of basis shapes (see Fig. 1) and different degrees of non-rigidity (see Fig. 2) defined as $ratio = \|S_{rigid}\| / \|S_{nonrigid}\|$.
Notice in this case a higher reconstruction error of the relative 3-D structure compared to the monocular case with higher degrees of deformation.

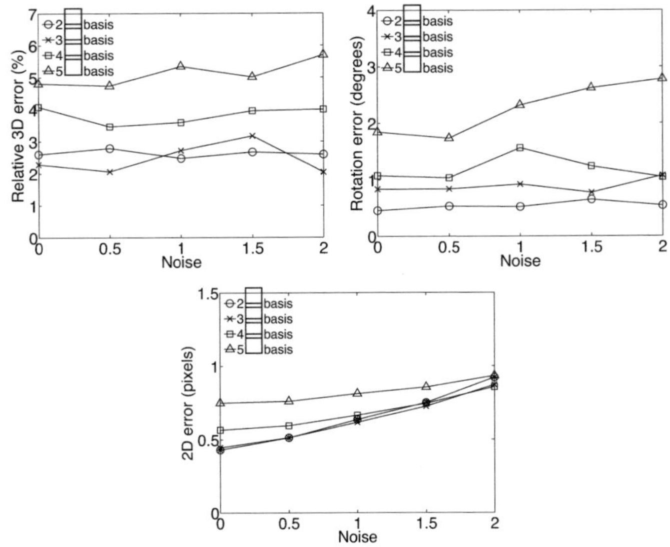

Figure 1. Relative 3-D error (%), r.m.s. rotation error (degrees) and 2-D reprojection error for the synthetic experiments with a stereo pair for different basis shapes $D = 2 \ldots 5$ and increasing levels of Gaussian noise. The ratio of non rigidity is fixed to 40% for all the trials.

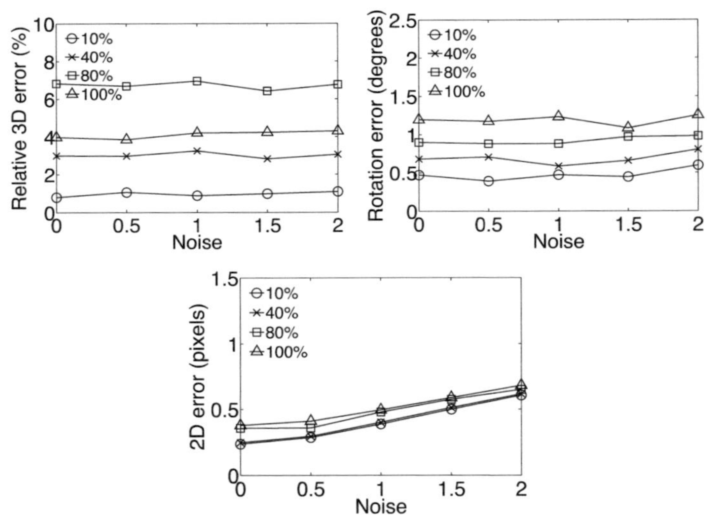

Figure 2. Relative 3-D error (%), r.m.s. rotation error (in degrees) and 2-D reprojection error for the synthetic experiments for different ratios of deformation (10%, 40%, 80%, 100%) and increasing levels of Gaussian noise.

5.2 Synthetic experiments with a CG generated face

In this section we have generated a sequence using a synthetic face model originally developed by (Parke & Waters, 1996). This is a 3-D model which encodes 18 different muscles of the face. Animating the face model to generate facial expressions is achieved by actuating on the different facial muscles. In particular we have used a sequence where the head did not perform any rigid motion, only deformations a situation where, clearly, monocular algorithms would fail to compute the correct 3-D shape and motion. The sequence was 125 frames long. The model deforms between frames 1 and 50, remains static and rigid until frame 100 and deforms once again between frames 100 and 125.

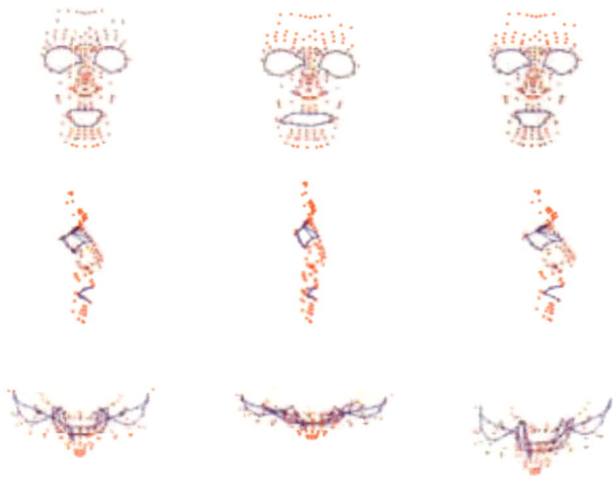

Figure 3. Front, side and top views of the 3-D synthetic face for frame 20. The first column shows the shape ground truth while the following two columns present the 3-D reconstructions for the linear and bundle adjustment algorithms. Deformations are present mainly in the mouth region. Notice that the face does not perform rigid motion for the whole sequence.

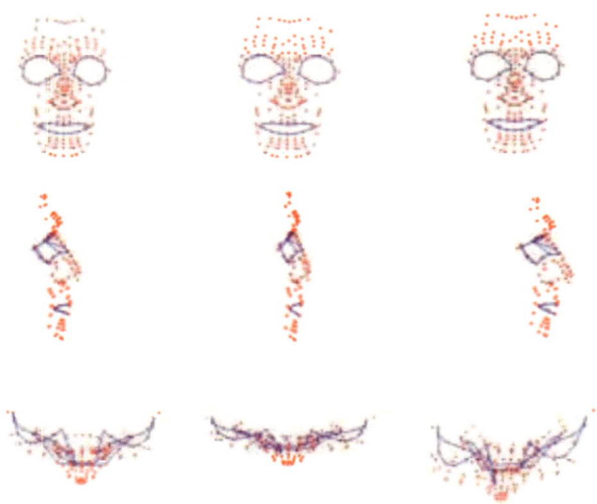

Figure 4. Front, side and top views of the 3-D synthetic face for frame 70. The first column shows the shape ground truth while the following two columns present the 3-D reconstructions for the linear and bundle adjustment algorithms. The shape is completely static in this frame.

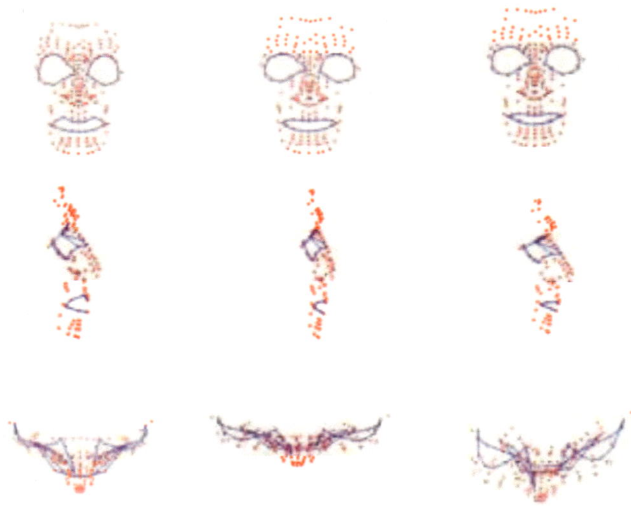

Figure 5. Front, side and top views of the 3-D synthetic face for frame 125. The first column shows the shape ground truth while the following two columns present the 3-D reconstructions for the linear and bundle adjustment algorithms. Deformations are localized in the mouth and cheek regions.

Once the model was generated we projected synthetically 160 points evenly distributed on the face, onto a pair of stereo cameras. The geometry of the cameras was such that both optical axes were lying on the XZ plane and each pointing inwards by 15 degrees. Therefore the relative orientation of the cameras about the Y axis was 30 degrees and 0 about the X and Z axes. The camera model used to project the points was a projective model however, the viewing conditions were such that the relief of the scene was small compared to the overall depth

We show in the following figures the comparisons between three key frames of the synthetic sequence providing the 3-D ground truth and the 3-D reconstructions for the linear and bundle adjustment algorithms. Fig. 3 presents a deformation localised in the mouth region at frame 20. A first visual inspection shows that the result obtained by the bundle adjustment has a qualitative advantage over the stereo linear algorithm. While the general mean shape is close to the ground truth, only the optimised solution with bundle adjustment can model properly the deformations. Frame 70 (see Fig. 4) shows the synthetic face (ground truth) with no deformations appearing. The static pose of the shape permits to compare the 3-D depth reconstructed by the algorithms. Compared to the ground truth, the shape obtained by the stereo algorithm shows a good frontal reconstruction but the estimation of the relief is not satisfactory (see side and top views). The non-linear solution obtains a depth estimate qualitatively closer to the ground truth. Finally Fig. 5 presents the reconstruction obtained for frame 125 where the synthetic face shows consistent deformations in the cheeks and mouth area. The stereo algorithm obtains a reasonable mean 3-D shape but it fails in capturing the deformations appearing in the ground truth.

Fig. 6 shows the results for the estimated rotation angles and configuration weights before and after the non-linear optimization step. The results after bundle adjustment describe fairly accurately the geometry of the cameras and the deformation of the face. In particular, the stereo setup was such that there was no rigid motion of the face (only deformation), the optical axes of the left and right cameras lay on the XZ plane and the relative rotation of the cameras about the Y axis was constant and equal to 30 degrees. In this case we have ground truth values for the relative orientation of the cameras since the sequence was generated synthetically. Notice how the values obtained for the rotation angles before bundle adjustment -- left -- exhibit some problems around frames 10 and 115, when the deformations are occurring. After the bundle adjustment step the relative rotation about the Y axis is estimated with a final result of 27 degrees resulting in a 3 degrees error given the ground truth. The relative orientations about the X and Z axes are correctly estimated to 0 degrees -- notice that the graphs for the left and right angles are superimposed.

Once more, the estimated values for the deformation weights after bundle adjustment have larger values than before the optimization. This explains the fact that the model succeeds to explain the non-rigid deformations accurately. Interestingly, the coefficients remain constant between frames 50 and 110, when no deformations were occurring.

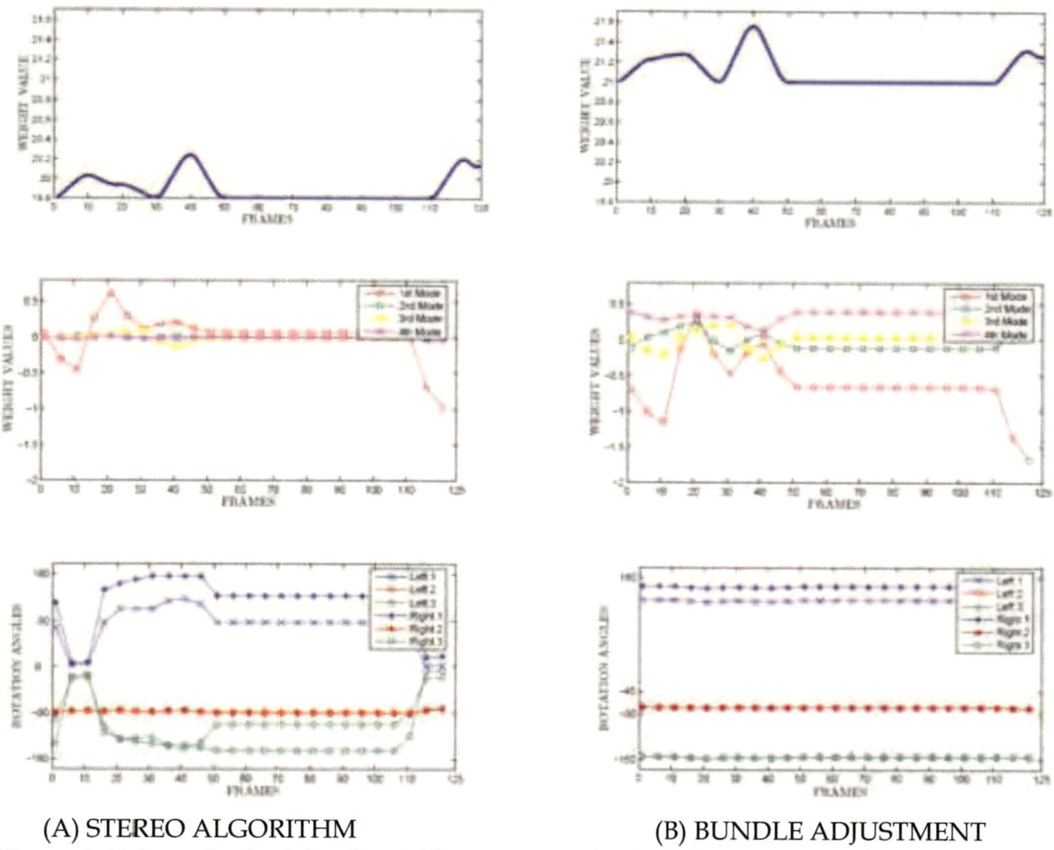

(A) STEREO ALGORITHM (B) BUNDLE ADJUSTMENT

Figure 6. Values obtained for the rigid component (top), deformation weights (middle) and rotation angles (bottom) before (A) and after bundle adjustment (B) for the synthetic sequence

5.3 Experiments with real data: comparison with the monocular solution

In this section we compare the performance of our stereo factorization algorithm -- before the non-linear optimization -- with Brand's single camera non-rigid factorization method. We present some experimental results obtained with real image sequences taken with a pair of synchronized Fire-i digital cameras with 4,65mm built in lenses. The stereo setup was such that the baseline was 20cm and the relative orientation of the cameras was around 30 degrees. Two sequences of a human face undergoing rigid motion and flexible deformations were used: the SMILE sequence (82 frames), where the deformation was due to the subject smiling and the EYEBROW (115 frames) sequence where the subject was raising and lowering the eyebrows. Fig. 7 shows 3 frames chosen from the sequences taken with the left and right cameras.

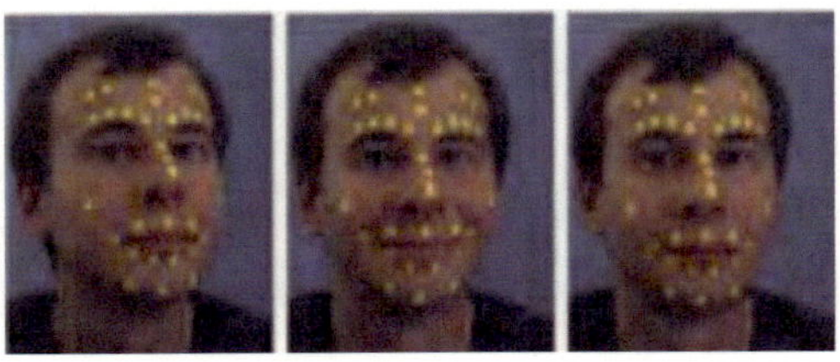

a) SMILE sequence: left view

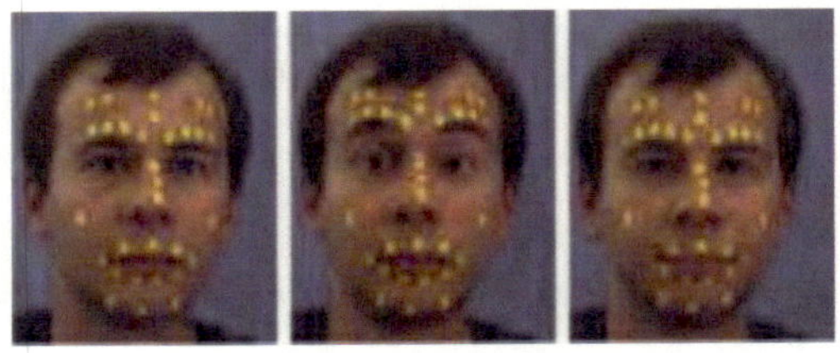

b) EYEBROW sequence: left view

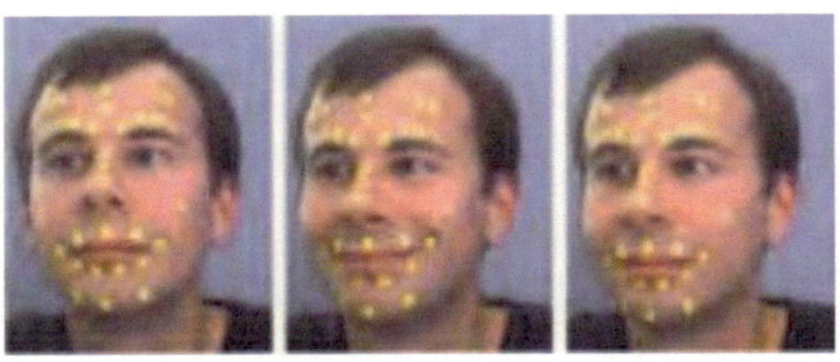

c) SMILE sequence: right view

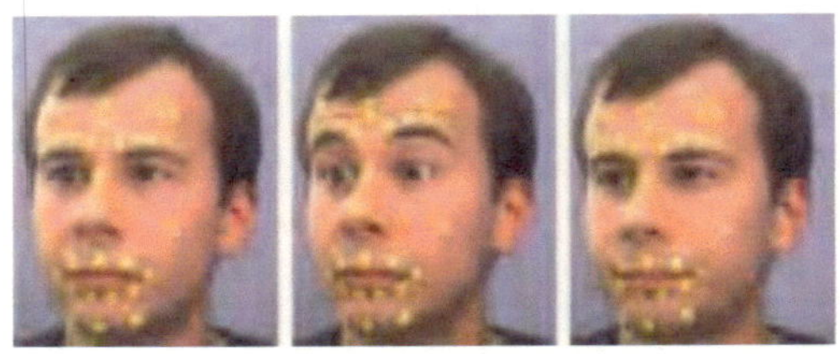

d) EYEBROW sequence: right view

Figure 7. Three images from the left (a) and right (c) views of the SMILE sequence and left (b) and right (d) views of the EYEBROW sequence

In order to simplify the temporal and stereo matching the subject had some markers placed on relevant points of the face such as along the eyebrows, the chin and the lips. A simple colour model of the markers using HSV components provided the representation used to track each marker throughout the left and right sequences respectively. The stereo matching was initialized by hand in the first image pair and then the temporal tracks were used to update the stereo matches.

Fig. 8 shows front, side and top views of the 3-D reconstructions obtained for the SMILE sequence. First we applied the single camera factorization algorithm developed by Brand to the left and right monocular sequences. We then applied the proposed stereo algorithm to the stereo sequence. In all cases the number of tracked points was P=31 and the chosen number of basis shapes was heuristically fixed to D=5.

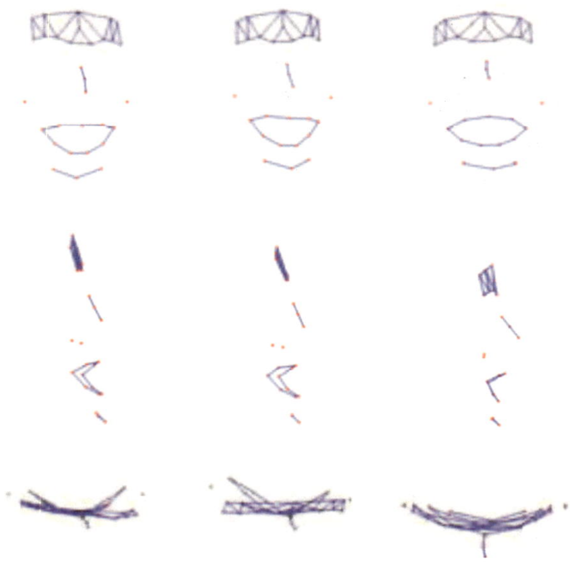

a) Left camera b) Right camera c) Stereo

Figure 8. SMILE sequence: Front, side and top views (above, middle, bottom) of the 3-D model for the a) left camera, b) right camera and c) stereo setup for D=5

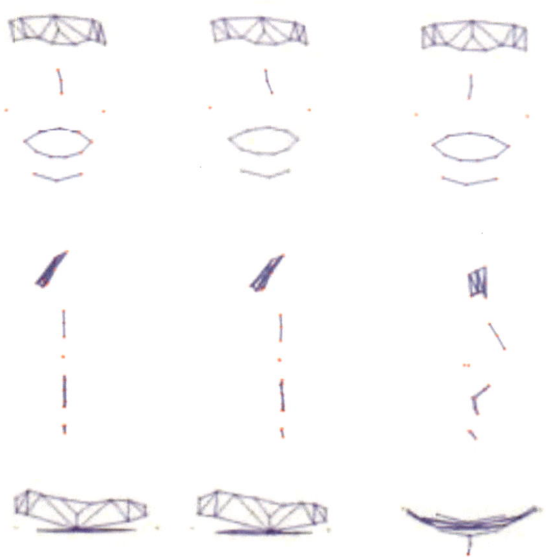

a) Left camera b) Right camera c) Stereo

Figure 9. EYEBROW sequence: Front, side and top views (above, middle, bottom) of the 3-D model for the a) left camera, b) right camera and c) stereo setup sequences for D=5

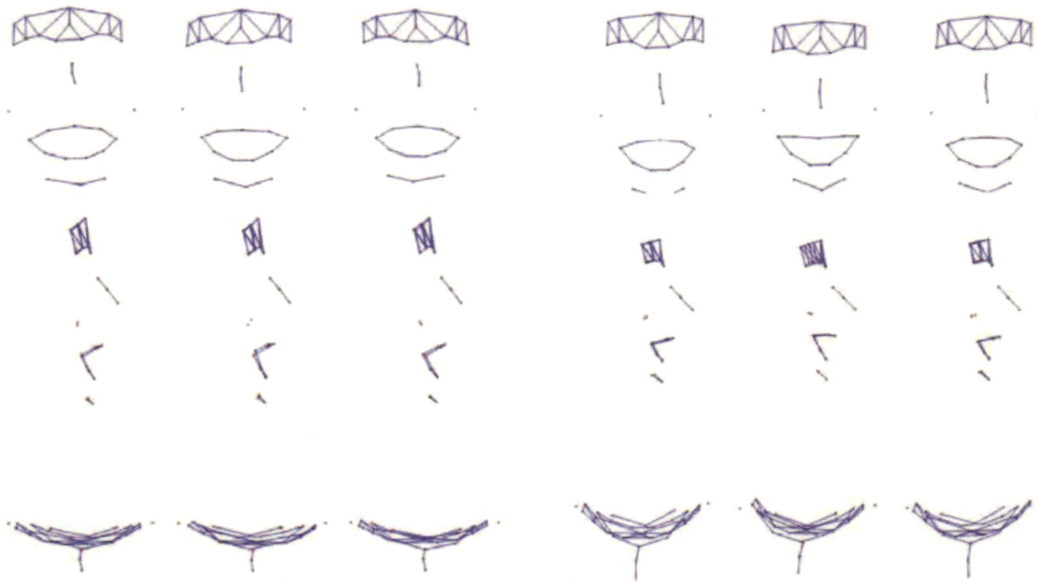

Frame 16 Frame 58 Frame 81 Frame 16 Frame 58 Frame 81

(A) STEREO ALGORITHM (B) BUNDLE ADJUSTMENT

Figure 10. Front, side and top views of the reconstructed face for the SMILE sequence using the stereo algorithm (left) and after bundle adjustment (right). Reconstructions are shown for frames 16, 56 and 81 of the sequence

Fig. 8c shows how the stereo reconstruction provides improved results. The reconstructions obtained using singularly the information from the left and right sequences have worse depth estimates that can be noticed especially in the side and top views. The reconstructed face is strongly asymmetric especially in the mouth region and the points on the forehead are almost belonging to a plane. Differently, after merging the data from both sequences in the stereo algorithm, we obtained a symmetric shape and a satisfactory curvature of the forehead.

Fig. 10(A) shows the front, side and top views of the 3-D reconstructions obtained for frames 16, 58 and 81 of the SMILE sequence. While the 3-D shape appears to be well reconstructed, the deformations are not entirely well modelled. Note how the smile on frame 58 is not well captured. This was caused by the final *flexible factorization* step proposed by Brand. We found that while this regularization step is essential to obtain good estimates for the rotation parameters it fails to capture the full deformations in the model. This is due to the fact that the assumption is that the deformations should be small relative to the mean shape so that most of the image motion is explained by the rigid component which results in a poor description of the deformations. However, we will see in the following paragraphs that the bundle adjustment step resolves the ambiguity between motion and shape parameters and succeeds in modelling the non-rigid deformations.

Fig. 9 shows the 3-D reconstructions obtained for the EYEBROW sequence. Once more, the single camera factorization algorithm was applied to the left and right sequences and the stereo algorithm was then applied to the stereo sequence. In this sequence the 3-D model obtained using stereo factorization is significantly better than the ones obtained with the left and right sequences. In fact, the left and right reconstructions have very poor quality, particularly the depth estimates. The points belonging to the nose, mouth and chin are almost planar (see side view) while the ones on the forehead have a particularly wrong depth estimate (see top view). Note that there was less rigid motion in this sequence and therefore the single camera factorization algorithm is not capable of recovering correct 3-D information whereas the stereo algorithm provides a good deformable model.

5.4 Experiments with real data: results after non-linear optimization

In this section we show the results obtained after the final non-linear optimization step. Fig. 10(B) shows the front, side and top views of the 3-D reconstructions before and after the bundle adjustment step for three frames of the SMILE sequence. The initial estimate is shown on the left and the results after bundle adjustment are shown on the right. While the initial estimate recovers the correct 3-D shape, the deformations on the face are not well modelled. However, bundle adjustment succeeds to capture the flexible structure -- notice how the upper lip is curved first and then straightened.

Fig. 11 shows the results obtained for the estimated motion parameters and configuration weights using the initial stereo factorization method and the improved results after bundle adjustment. The bottom graphs show the rotation angles about the X, Y and Z axes recovered for each frame of the sequence for the left and right cameras (up to an overall rotation). The recovered angles for the left and right camera after bundle adjustment reflect very well the geometry of the stereo camera setup. This was such that both optical axes lay approximately on the XZ plane -- therefore there was no relative rotation between the cameras about the X and Z axes -- and the relative rotation about the Y axis was about 15 degrees. Note that these values are not ground truth and only approximate as they were not measured accurately. Also note that the rotation matrices for the right camera are calculated as $R^R = R_{rel}\, R^L$ where R_{rel} is the estimated relative orientation. Fig. 11(B) shows how the estimates of the rotations about the X and Z axes (in blue and green) for the left and right views are close to being zero. The relative rotation between left and right cameras about the Y axis (in red) is closer to 15 degrees after bundle adjustment than before.

Fig. 11 also shows the evolution throughout the sequence of the values of the configuration weights associated with the mean component (top) and the 4 modes of deformation (middle). The values appear to be larger after bundle adjustment confirming that the non-linear optimization step has achieved to model the deformations of the face. It is also interesting to note how the first mode of deformation experiences a big change starting around frame 40 until frame 75. This coincides with the moment where the subject started and finished the smile expression.

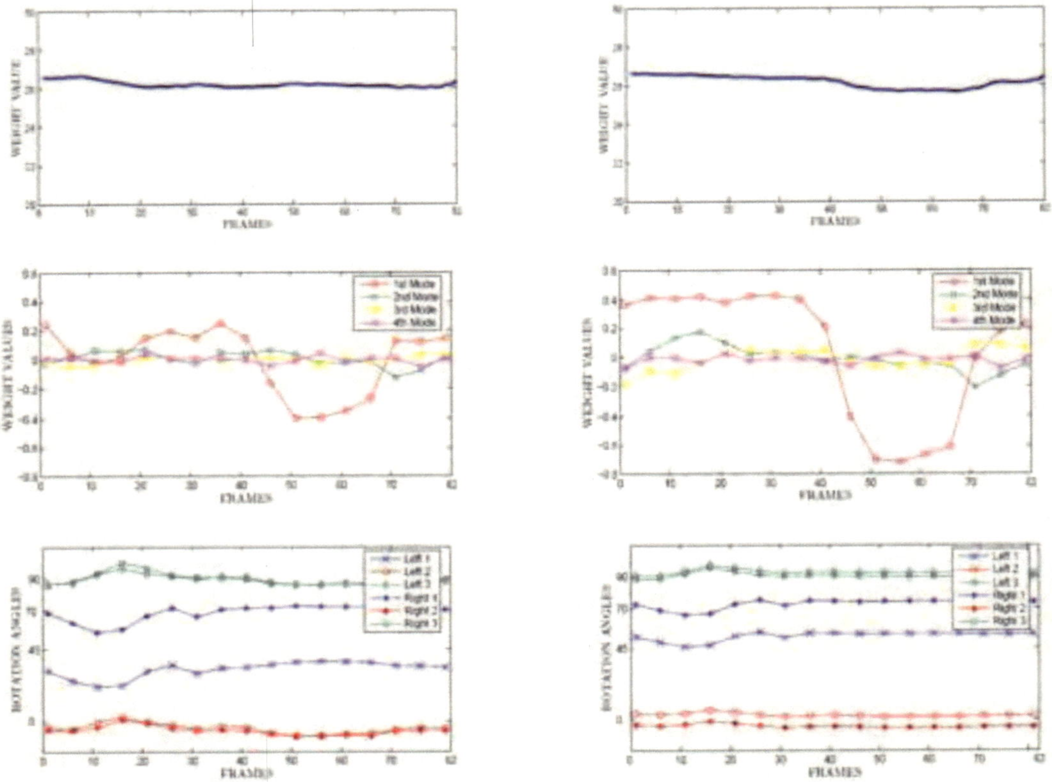

(A) STEREO ALGORITHM (B) BUNDLE ADJUSTMENT

Figure 11. Values obtained for the rigid component (top), deformation weights (middle) and rotation angles (bottom) before (A) and after bundle adjustment (B) for the SMILE sequence

6. Summary

A stereo-motion approach has been presented with the aim to reconstruct the 3-D shape of a deformable object using image sequences extracted from a stereo-pair. As a result, the non-rigid factorization framework has been accordingly updated to accommodate the constraint that trajectories in the left and right camera refer to the same 3-D object.

By construction, the method fuses naturally the advantages of motion and stereo approaches. A global solution for the time varying motion and 3-D structure is obtained from the image tracks without any prior calibration of the stereo pairs. Widely separated stereo views allow a more reliable estimation of motion and deformation parameters even in the absence of rigid motion of the object.

Additionally, non-linear optimization, as presented in the previous chapter, is performed to obtain the correct replicated structure in M. Results show a relevant improvement in the motion and structure estimates and thus the optimization stage is strongly recommended to obtain a correct solution.

The main assumption of our method is that the cameras must be synchronized and stereo matches be available. Synchronization can be enforced using the method presented in (Tresadern & Reid, 2003) but nowadays it is common to obtain synchronized video from

stereo cameras. Stereo matching could be tackled by extending current techniques (Ho & Chung, 2000; Oliveira et al., 2005} to deal with the non-rigid case.
Finally, notice that the solution for a stereo pair is trivially extendable to the case of multiple cameras both for the linear and non-linear approach. Moreover, the constraint over the fix baseline can be loosened to permit freely moving cameras; in this case the stereo-motion model needs to include parameters for the weak perspective scaling for each camera. This will allow to solve for a general multi camera system modelling non-rigid shapes from uncalibrated data.

7. Acknowledgements

The authors would like to thank the Royal Society European Science Exchange Programme, EPSRC Grant GR/S61539/01 and the Spanish Ministry of Science project TIC2002-00591 for financial support. Enrique Muñoz, Jose Miguel Buenaposada and Luis Baumela provided the code for the synthetic 3D face model. Thanks to Andrew Fitzgibbon for matlab functions for bundle adjustment. Alessio Del Bue is supported by Fundação para a Ciência e a Tecnologia (ISR/IST plurianual funding) through the POS_Conhecimento Program that includes FEDER funds.

8. References

Aanæs, H. & Kahl, F. (2002). Estimation of deformable structure and motion. *Workshop on Vision and Modelling of Dynamic Scenes*, Copenhagen, Denmark.

Atkinson, K. B. (1996). *Close Range Photogrammetry and Machine Vision. Engineering and Science*. Whittles Publishing.

Bar-Itzhack, I. Y. (2000). New method for extracting the quaternion from a rotation matrix. *Journal of Guidance, Control and Dynamics*, Vol. 23, No. 3, pp. 1085–1087.

Bartoli, A. & Sturm, P. (2004). Nonlinear estimation of the fundamental matrix with minimal parameters. *IEEE Transactions on Pattern Analysis and Machine Intelligence*, Vol. 26, No. 4, pp. 426– 432, 2004.

Berthilsson, R.; Astrom, K. & Heyden A. (2001). Reconstruction of general curves, using factorization and bundle adjustment. *International Journal of Computer Vision*, Vol . 41, No. 3, pp. 171–182.

Brand, M. (2001) . Morphable models from video. *Proc. IEEE Conference on Computer Vision and Pattern Recognition*, pp 456–463, Vol. 2, Kauai, Hawaii , December 2001.

Brand, M. (2005). A direct method for 3d factorization of nonrigid motion observed in 2d. *Proc. IEEE Conference on Computer Vision and Pattern Recognition*, San Diego, California, pp. 122–128, 2005.

Bregler, C.; Hertzmann, A. & Biermann, H. (2000). Recovering non-rigid 3d shape from image streams. *Proc. IEEE Conference on Computer Vision and Pattern Recognition*, Hilton Head, South Carolina, pages 690–696, June 2000.

Del Bue, A.; Smeraldi, F. & Agapito, L. (2007). Non-rigid structure from motion using ranklet–based tracking and non-linear optimization. *Image and Vision Computing*, Vol. 25, No. 3, pp. 297-310, March 2007.

Dornaika, F. & Chung, R. (1999). Stereo correspondence from motion correspondence. *Proceedings IEEE Conference on Computer Vision and Pattern Recognition*, pp. 70–75, Fort Collins, Colorado, June 1999.

Fua, P. (2000). Regularized bundle-adjustment to model heads from image sequences without calibration data. *International Journal of Computer Vision*, Vol. 38, No. 2, pp. 153–171, 2000.

Guilbert, N.; Kahl, F.; Astrom, K.; Oskarsson, M.; Johansson, M. & A. Heyden (2004). Constraint enforcement in structure and motion applied to closing an open sequence. *Asian Conference of Computer Vision*, Vol. 1, Jeju, South Korea.

Hartley, R. I. & Zisserman, A. (2000). *Multiple View Geometry in Computer Vision*. Cambridge University Press.

Ho, P. & Chung, R. (2000). Stereo-motion with stereo and motion in complement. *IEEE Transactions on Pattern Analysis and Machine Intelligence*, Vol. 22, No. 2, pp. 215–220, February 2000.

Horn, B. K. P. (1987). Closed-form solution of absolute orientation using unit quaternions. *Jounal of the Optical Society America*, pp. 629–642, Vol. 4, No. 4, 1987.

Levenberg, K. (1944). A method for the solution of certain problems in least squares. *The Quarterly of Applied Mathematics*, Vol. 2, pp. 164–168, 1944.

Mandelbaum, R. ; Salgian G. & H. Sawhney (1999). Correlation-based estimation of ego-motion and structure from motion and stereo. *Proceedings 7th International Conference on Computer Vision*, pp. 544–550. Kerkyra, Greece, 1999.

Marquardt, D. (1963). An algorithm for least-squares estimation of nonlinear parameters. *Journal of the Society for Industrial and Applied Mathematics*, Vol. 11, No. 2, June 1963, pp. 431-441.

McLauchlan, P. F. & Jaenicke, A. (2002). Image mosaicing using sequential bundle adjustment. *Image and Vision Computing*, Vol. 20, No. 9, pp. 751–759, 2002.

Moré, J. (1977). The Levenberg–Marquardt algorithm: Implementation and theory. *Numerical Analysis, Lecture Notes in Mathematics*, Vol. 630, pp. 105–116, 1977.

Pollefeys, M. (1999). *Self-Calibration and Metric 3D Reconstruction from Uncalibrated Image Sequences*. PhD thesis, Katholieke Universiteit Leuven, Belgium.

Stein, G. & Shashua (1998). Direct estimation of motion and extended scene structure from a moving stereo rig. *Proceedings IEEE Conference on Computer Vision and Pattern Recognition*, pp. 211–218, Santa Barbara, California, 1998.

Tomasi, C. & Kanade, T. (1992). Shape and motion from image streams under orthography: A factorization approach. *International Journal of Computer Vision*, Vol. 9, No. 2, pp. 137–154, 1992.

Torresani, L.; Yang, D.; Alexander, E. & Bregler, C. (2001). Tracking and modeling non-rigid objects with rank constraints. *Proceedings IEEE Conference on Computer Vision and Pattern Recognition*, Kauai, Hawaii, 2001.

Triggs, B.; McLauchlan, P.; Hartley, R. I. & Fitzgibbon, A. (2000). Bundle adjustment – A modern synthesis. In: *Vision Algorithms: Theory and Practice*, pp. 298–375. Springer Verlag, 2000.

Trucco, E. & Verri, A. (1998). *Introductory Techniques for 3-D Computer Vision*. Prentice-Hall.

Waxman, A. & Duncan, J. (1986). Binocular image flows: steps toward stereo-motion fusion. *IEEE Transactions on Pattern Analysis and Machine Intelligence*, Vol. 8, No. 6, 1986, pp. 715–729.

Xiao, J.; Chai, J. & Kanade, T. (2004). A closed-form solution to non-rigid shape and motion recovery. *Proc. 8th European Conference on Computer Vision*, Copenhagen, Denmark, pp. 573–587, May 2004.

15

Continuous Machine Learning in Computer Vision – Tracking with Adaptive Class Models

Rustam Stolkin
Stevens Institute of Technology
USA

1. Introduction

A fundamental (and popular) task in computer and robot vision is the tracking of an object which moves relative to the camera, essentially segmenting the object region of each successive frame. There are a great many published approaches, which are often variations, combinations or advances on well known techniques such as background subtraction, image differencing, predictive filtering and Bayesian estimation. Generally, these techniques rely on simple models of the tracked object and/or models of the background.

Many techniques in computer vision derive from ideas previously established in the pattern recognition community, where it is usual to learn models offline from historical training data sets. Hence these models, once learned, typically remain static during the online tracking process.

Such static models are ultimately of limited robustness in real world computer vision tracking scenarios where the appearance of both the background and the tracked object may change significantly and frequently due to camera motion (resulting in background change), object motion or deformation, introduction and removal of additional objects and clutter (e.g. passing traffic on a road) and changes in lighting and visibility conditions (either changes in ambient conditions or, for example, spotlights mounted on and moving with an underwater robot).

In contrast, this chapter will discuss a variety of tracking algorithms and techniques which are highly adaptable. These techniques have in common that they incorporate models which are continuously relearned from new input image frames while simultaneously performing tracking on those frames.

These techniques are powerful, in that they offer a way of successfully adapting to a changing environment. However, the price paid for adaptability can be a tendency towards certain kinds of instability. In simple terms, any system that continuously relearns (e.g. models of the tracked object and the background), has a risk of relearning incorrectly (e.g. relearning that background looks like object). Therefore, this chapter will also discuss various techniques for automatically detecting and correcting such errors as they occur, and survey techniques by which algorithms might continuously monitor their own performance.

It is also useful to consider continuous machine learning techniques in vision in terms of the rate of relearning. Firstly we will consider well established algorithms which incrementally re-learn models, very gradually, over many frames. Later we will look at very recent work, in which models are entirely relearned at every frame or even several times during an iterative analysis of each frame. We will see that this re-learning rate often has implications for the trade off between the capacity of an algorithm to adapt and its inherent stability.

2. Adaptive background subtraction with a stationary camera

2.1 Relearning simple uni-modal background models

If the camera is fixed (e.g. in visual surveillance applications), and the tracked object is also moving, the simple but powerful technique of background subtraction can be employed in order to segment the image region representing the tracked object of interest. Typically, this involves thresholding the difference between the current image and a historical model of what the image looked like before any objects of interest were present. In its simplest form, this relies on the assumption that background pixel values remain constant. While this assumption can be effective for short term tracking in indoor environments with fixed lighting, it fails in longer term use in changing environments, especially for outdoor scenes which involve lighting and shadow changes, repetitive motion of clutter or slowly acting long-term changes to the scene. Thus it becomes desirable to enable the background model to gradually be re-learned.

A simple approach (Kanade et al., 1998, Collins et al., 1999) involves, essentially, modelling each background pixel intensity as a weighted moving average of recent pixel values. At the tth video frame, the grey-scale intensity, I_{ij}, of each pixel, (i, j), is examined. If it is determined that this pixel represents background then the background model intensity, B_{ij}, for that pixel is updated as:

$$B_{ij}^{t+1} = \alpha B_{ij}^{t} + (1-\alpha) I_{ij}^{t} \tag{1}$$

otherwise the background model for that pixel is left unchanged. Classification of each pixel is determined by thresholding the difference between its intensity and that of the current background model, i.e. the pixel is classified as foreground if:

$$\left| I_{ij} - B_{ij}^{t} \right| > T_{ij}^{t} \tag{2}$$

Each pixel is assigned its own individual threshold, T_{ij}^{t}, which can itself be updated to take account of increases or decreases in the amount of temporal variation of background intensity. If a pixel is classified as background, then its threshold is updated as:

$$T_{ij}^{t+1} = \alpha T_{ij}^{t} + (1-\alpha)\left(\beta \times \left| I_{ij}^{t} - B_{ij}^{t} \right|\right) \tag{3}$$

i.e., the threshold for classifying foreground pixels is increased if the variation of background intensity from frame to frame increases and is decreased as this temporal variation decreases. Thus the threshold, T_{ij}^{t}, is analagous to β times the local temporal standard deviation of intensity. This process effectively moderates the fundamental tradeoff between false positives (erroneously classifying background pixels as foreground due to the threshold being too low) and false negatives (erroneously classifying foreground pixels as background because the threshold is set too high).

2.2 Relearning multi-modal background models

The above method is useful in that it continuously adapts to a (slowly) varying background scene. However, the simple uni-modal model cannot adequately account for the multi-modality that typically occurs in background pixels of real scenes, even when the camera is stationary. As an example, consider a fixed surveillance camera where a small part of the image views the branch of a tree. As the tree (or even the camera mounting) sways in the wind, a particular pixel colour might vary between blue (sky) and brown (tree branch). In such a situation we might wish for a bi-modal background model which can represent both of these common pixel values. A tri-modal model might further enable us to handle scenes in which background pixels typically represented tree branch, blue sky, or grey cloudy sky. Such multi-modal background variation occurs for myriad reasons, e.g. reflections from a rippling water surface in an outdoor scene or computer monitor flicker in an indoor office environment.

A continuosly relearnable model, which both addresses the multi-modality in background pixels and also adapts itself to temporal background changes, was first developed by Grimson and Stauffer (Grimson et al., 1998, Stauffer and Grimson, 1999, Grimson et al., 2000). Grimson models the recent history of each pixel colour (e.g. rgb value) over the previous t frames, $\{\overline{\mathbf{C}}_0,\ldots,\overline{\mathbf{C}}_{t-1}\}$, as a mixture of K Gaussian distributions. The probability of observing the current pixel colour is:

$$P(\overline{\mathbf{C}}_t)=\sum_{k=1}^{K}\omega_{k,t-1}N(\overline{\mathbf{C}}_t,\overline{\boldsymbol{\mu}}_{k,t-1},\boldsymbol{\Sigma}_{k,t-1}) \tag{4}$$

where $\omega_{k,t}$ is a weight (that portion of the data which is represented by this Gaussian) of the kth of K Gaussians at time t, $\overline{\boldsymbol{\mu}}_{k,t}$ and $\boldsymbol{\Sigma}_{k,t}$ are the means and covariance matrices respectively and N denotes the Gaussian probability density function. At each frame, every new pixel value is checked against the K Gaussians and assigned to the best match. If none of them match (e.g. the pixel does not lie within 2 standard deviations of any Gaussian) then the least probable Gaussian is removed and replaced with a new Gaussian having the current value as its mean, a high initial variance and a small weight.

Now the weights of all K Gaussians are updated as:

$$\omega_{k,t}=\begin{cases}(1-\alpha)\omega_{k,t-1}+\alpha & \text{if the new pixel belongs to the } k\text{th Gaussian}\\ (1-\alpha)\omega_{k,t-1} & \text{otherwise}\end{cases} \tag{5}$$

After this update the weights are all re-normalized. α determines the rate at which the background model is relearned and has important consequences which we will discuss in more detail later. The weights, $\omega_{k,t}$, could be thought of as prior probabilities of each kind of background mode (e.g. the tree branch or the sky). Analagous with recursive Bayesian filtering, this prior has, in effect, been approximated as a weighted average of the previous posterior probabilities, with exponentially decaying emphasis on past values.

Grimson also seeks to adaptively relearn the means and variances of each Gaussian in the mixture. A simplifying (though usually untrue) approximation is to assume that red, blue and green components of each pixel are independent and share similar variances, i.e.:

$$\mathbf{\Sigma}_{ki,t} = \sigma_{k,t}^2 \mathbf{I} \tag{6}$$

Values of $\overline{\boldsymbol{\mu}}_{k,t}$ and $\sigma_{k,t}^2$ for those Gaussians which do not match the current pixel value remain unadjusted. Values of $\overline{\boldsymbol{\mu}}_{k,t}$ and $\sigma_{k,t}^2$ for the Gaussian to which the new pixel value does belong are updated as follows:

$$\overline{\boldsymbol{\mu}}_t = (1-\beta)\overline{\boldsymbol{\mu}}_{t-1} + \beta\overline{\mathbf{C}}_t \tag{7}$$

$$\sigma_t^2 = (1-\beta)\sigma_{t-1}^2 + \beta\left(\overline{\mathbf{C}}_t - \overline{\boldsymbol{\mu}}_t\right)^T\left(\overline{\mathbf{C}}_t - \overline{\boldsymbol{\mu}}_t\right) \tag{8}$$

The second learning rate, β, is simply the overall learning rate, α, weighted by the probability that the observed pixel value truly belongs to the Gaussian being modified, i.e.:

$$\beta = \alpha N\left(\overline{\mathbf{C}}_t, \overline{\boldsymbol{\mu}}_k, \mathbf{\Sigma}_k\right) \tag{9}$$

To determine the background model for each pixel individually, all K Gaussians for that pixel are ordered on the basis of ω_k / σ_k^2 . This is a heuristic that assigns importance to modes which are both frequent and consistent (have a small variance). Once the Gaussians have been ordered in importance, the first B distributions are selected that account for a predefiend fraction, F, of observations, i.e.:

$$B = \arg\min_b \left(\sum_{k=1}^{b} \omega_k > F \right) \tag{10}$$

Now, any new pixel which is more than 2 standard deviations from the means of all of the B background distributions is classified as part of a foreground moving object.

Grimson and Stauffer's method provides a relatively sophisticated description of the background, which can be continuously relearned to enable powerful adaption capabilities for slowly changing scenes. A significant advantage of the method is that new characteristics of the background can be acquired without destroying the existing model. Statistically important colours will remain in the model until they become the Kth most probable mode and a new colour is observed. This enables for example, the background model to cope robustly with objects that move into the scene, temporarily stop, and then move on. Even if the stationary vehicle has temporarily been incorporated into the background model, it will quickly be removed again once it recomences motion.

2.3 Relearning non-parametric background models

Elgammal et al., 1999, suggest an alternative model for relearning backgrounds with a stationary camera. Grimson and Stauffer's mixture model approach builds a background model very slowly over a large number of image frames. This is unable to respond sufficiently sensitively to higher frequency background variations. To address this difficulty,

Elgammal et al. use a different kind of model that can be completely relearned over a much smaller, recent set of frames (good results are reported with 100 frames).
Given the colours of a pixel over the previous t frames, $\{\overline{\mathbf{C}}_0,\ldots,\overline{\mathbf{C}}_{t-1}\}$, the probability density that this pixel will have rgb colour $\overline{\mathbf{C}}_t = \left(C_1^t, C_2^t, C_3^t\right)^T$ in the current frame can be non-parametrically estimated using a kernel estimator, K, as:

$$p\left(\overline{\mathbf{C}}_t\right) = \frac{1}{t}\sum_{i=1}^{t} K\left(\overline{\mathbf{C}}_t - \overline{\mathbf{C}}_i\right) \tag{11}$$

The kernel estimator function, K, is typically chosen to be a Normal function, $N(0,\mathbf{\Sigma})$, giving the density in terms of the multivariate Normal distribution:

$$p\left(\overline{\mathbf{C}}_t\right) = \frac{1}{t}\sum_{i=1}^{t} \frac{1}{(2\pi)^{\frac{3}{2}}\left|\mathbf{\Sigma}\right|^{\frac{1}{2}}} e^{-\frac{1}{2}\left(\overline{\mathbf{C}}_t - \overline{\mathbf{C}}_i\right)^T \mathbf{\Sigma}^{-1}\left(\overline{\mathbf{C}}_t - \overline{\mathbf{C}}_i\right)} \tag{12}$$

As with grimson's work, a simplifying approximation is to assume independence between the r,g and b colour values of the pixel so that:

$$\mathbf{\Sigma} = \begin{pmatrix} \sigma_1^2 & 0 & 0 \\ 0 & \sigma_2^2 & 0 \\ 0 & 0 & \sigma_3^2 \end{pmatrix} \tag{13}$$

conveniently reducing the density estimation to:

$$p\left(\overline{\mathbf{C}}_t\right) = \frac{1}{t}\sum_{i=1}^{t}\prod_{j=1}^{3} \frac{1}{\sqrt{2\pi\sigma_j^2}} \exp\left\{-\frac{1}{2}\frac{\left(C_j^t - C_j^i\right)^2}{\sigma_j^2}\right\} \tag{14}$$

This pixel is now labelled as foreground if $p\left(\overline{\mathbf{C}}_t\right) < T$, where T is a global threshold for the whole image. To estimate the variances for each colour, σ_j^2, the median, m_j, is computed of the deviations between each successive pair of values in the sample, e.g. the median, m_j, of $\left|C_j^n - C_j^{n-1}\right|$ for each consecutive pair of the previours 100 frames. Now each standard deviation is estimated as:

$$\sigma_j = \frac{m}{0.68\sqrt{2}} \tag{15}$$

2.4 Relearning rate

The background subtraction methods described so far are unable to detect objects which move slower than a critical "re-learning speed" since the object itself would simply become re-learned as background. Therefore there is a fundamental trade off in the choice of learning rate. It must be rapid enough to cope with the fastest anticipated background change but slow enough to enable the most slowly moving objects to be detected. Thus two kinds of error must be considered when choosing an appropriate learning rate. Failing to relearn rapidly enough causes rapidly changing background pixels to be falsely detected as object (false positive). Failure to relearn slowly enough causes slow moving objects to pass undetected (false negative). In the extreme case, without the use of additional techniques, tracking based simply on background subtraction will eventually lose the tracked object if it stops moving since it will become incorporated into the relearned background model.

As an example of the complexity of these tradeoffs, Elgammal's model is able to adapt rapidly to background changes which would cause false positive detections with Grimson and Stauffer's method. However, Grimson and Stauffer's method is able to learn new background features without destroying its existing model. In contrast Elgammal's model is unable to remember background data from longer ago than 100 frames (or whatever length of frame history is chosen). Elgammal goes a certain way to overcoming this trade off by incorporating a procedure for combining both a short-term and long-term background model which are each updated over different timescales.

Since all of the methods so far described, including the faster responding non-parametric method, involve relatively slow relearning over many frames, they are all unable to cope with the rapidly changing backgrounds that result from a moving camera. The following sections describe recent work, in which rapid changes due to camera motion can be handled by a very different approach which enables the background to be completely relearned with every new frame.

3. The ABCshift algorithm – adapting backgrounds with a moving camera

3.1 Bayesian mean shift tracking with static colour models

The CAMSHIFT tracker (Bradski, 1998a, 1998b) is a colour based tracking algorithm which is popular for its elegant simplicity and speed. The qualities of speed and simplicity would suggest useful applications to mobile robot vision or wide area surveillance tasks which necessitate moving cameras. Unfortunately, CAMSHIFT was originally designed by Bradski for face tracking at close range from a stationary camera in relatively simple indoor environments. It often fails if the camera moves, because it relies on static models of both the background and the tracked object.

For each frame of an image sequence, the CAMSHIFT algorithm looks at pixels which lie within a subset of the image defined by a search window (green box in figures 1-5). Each pixel in this window is assigned a probability that it belongs to the tracked object, creating a 2D distribution of object location over a local area of the image. The centroid of this distribution can be regarded as the probabilistic expectation of the true object position, and thus provides an improved object position estimate. The search window is now repositioned at this centroid and the process is iterated until convergence. Since this iterative shift towards the mean (expectation) position is an example of the mean shift procedure (Comaniciu, 2002, 2003), Bradski's algorithm is known as the "Continuously Adaptive Mean Shift" or CAMSHIFT tracker. However, Bradski's use of the term "adaptive" is not the same as that of this chapter and does not imply any continuous machine learning. CAMSHIFT is only "adaptive" in the sense that the tracked object size is re-estimated at each frame to indicate whether the object is moving towards or away from the camera.

The size of the tracked object region (in pixels) is estimated by summing the probabilities of all the pixels within the search window. The object region can now be indicated by marking out a simple area of this size around the object centroid (the red box in figures 1-5). The search window is now resized so that its area is always in a fixed ratio to this estimated object area.

The tracked object is modeled as a class conditional colour distribution, $\mathrm{P}(\overline{\mathbf{C}} \mid O)$. Depending on the application, 1D Hue, 3D normalised RGB, 2D normalised RG, UV or ab histograms may all be appropriate choices of colour model, the important point being that these are all distributions which return a probability for any pixel colour, given that the pixel represents the tracked object. These object distributions can be learned offline from training images, or during initialisation, e.g. from an area which has been user designated as object in the first image of the sequence.

The object location probabilities can now be computed for each pixel using Bayes' law as:

$$\mathrm{P}(O \mid \overline{\mathbf{C}}) = \frac{\mathrm{P}(\overline{\mathbf{C}} \mid O)\mathrm{P}(O)}{\mathrm{P}(\overline{\mathbf{C}})} \tag{16}$$

where $\mathrm{P}(O \mid \overline{\mathbf{C}})$ denotes the probability that the pixel represents the tracked object given its colour, $\mathrm{P}(\overline{\mathbf{C}} \mid O)$ is the colour model learned for the tracked object and $\mathrm{P}(O)$ and $\mathrm{P}(\overline{\mathbf{C}})$ are the prior probabilities that the pixel represents object and posesses the colour, $\overline{\mathbf{C}}$, respectively.

The denominator of equation (16) can be expanded as:

$$\mathrm{P}(\overline{\mathbf{C}}) = \mathrm{P}(\overline{\mathbf{C}} \mid O)\mathrm{P}(O) + \mathrm{P}(\overline{\mathbf{C}} \mid B)\mathrm{P}(B) \tag{17}$$

where $\mathrm{P}(B)$ denotes the prior probability that the pixel represents background.

Bradski recommends values of 0.5 for both $\mathrm{P}(O)$ and $\mathrm{P}(B)$. However, this choice is difficult to justify if one takes these terms to denote the expected fractions of the total search window area containing object and background pixels respectively. It seems preferable to assign values to object priors in proportion to their expected image areas. If the search window area is always resized to be r times bigger than the estimated tracked object area, then $\mathrm{P}(O)$ is assigned the value $1/r$ and $\mathrm{P}(B)$ is assigned the value $(r-1)/r$.

The colour histograms, $\mathrm{P}(\overline{\mathbf{C}} \mid O)$ and $\mathrm{P}(\overline{\mathbf{C}} \mid B)$, are the class conditional object and background models respectively. As for the object model, Bradski also suggests learning the background model offline, presumably building a static $\mathrm{P}(\overline{\mathbf{C}} \mid B)$ histogram from an initial image. While it is often reasonable to maintain a static distribution for the tracked object (since objects are not expected to change colour), a static background model is unrealistic when the camera moves. The CAMSHIFT algorithm can rapidly fail when the background scenery changes since colours may exist in the new scene which did not exist in the original distribution, such that the expressions in Bayes law will no longer hold true and calculated probabilities no longer add up to unity.

Particular problems arise with CAMSHIFT if the tracked object moves across a region of background with which it shares a significant colour. Now a large region of background may easily become mistaken for the object, figure 1.

3.2 Incorporating an adaptive background model

Recent work (Stolkin et al. 2006) addresses these problems by using a background model which can be continuously relearned. An interesting aspect of the work is that, in contrast to Grimson and Stauffer's mixture model representation (section 2.2), this model can be relearned without the need to decisively classify pixels as being object or background. Due to the continuously relearnable background model, Stolkin et al. have named this tracker the ABCshift (Adaptive Background CAMSHIFT) algorithm.

Rather than using an explicit $P(\overline{\mathbf{C}} \mid B)$ histogram, Stolkin et al. build a $P(\overline{\mathbf{C}})$ histogram which is recomputed every time the search window is moved, based on all of the pixels which lie within the current search window. $P(\overline{\mathbf{C}})$ values, looked up in this continuously relearned histogram, can now be substituted as the denominator for the Bayes' law expression of equation 16. Since the object distribution, $P(\overline{\mathbf{C}} \mid O)$, remains static throughout the tracking, this process becomes equivalent to implicitly relearning the background distribution, $P(\overline{\mathbf{C}} \mid B)$, because $P(\overline{\mathbf{C}})$ is composed of a weighted combination of both these distributions (see equation 17). Relearning the whole of $P(\overline{\mathbf{C}})$, rather than explicitly relearning $P(\overline{\mathbf{C}} \mid B)$, avoids the need to make hard decisions about the class of any particular pixel and helps ensure that probabilities add up to unity,e.g. if there are small errors in the static object model, $P(\overline{\mathbf{C}} \mid O)$.

Adaptively relearning the background distribution helps prevent tracking failure when the background scene changes, particularly useful when tracking from a moving camera (figures 1-4). Additionally, it enables objects to be tracked, even when they move across regions of background which are the same colour as a significant portion of the object, (figure 1-4). This is because, once $P(\overline{\mathbf{C}})$ has been relearned, the denominator of Bayes' law (equation 16) ensures that the importance of this colour will be diminished. In other words, the tracker will adaptively learn to ignore object colours which are similar to the background and instead tend to focus on those colours of the object which are most dissimilar to whatever background is currently in view.

It is interesting to note that the continual relearning of the $P(\overline{\mathbf{C}})$ histogram need not substantially increase computational expense. Once the histogram has been learned for the first image it is only necessary to remove from the histogram those pixels which have left the search window area, and add in those pixels which have newly been encompassed by the search window as it shifts with each iteration. Provided the object motion is reasonably slow relative to the camera frame rate, the search window motion will be small, so that at each iteration only a few lines of pixels need be removed from and added to the $P(\overline{\mathbf{C}})$ histogram.

If the $P(\overline{\mathbf{C}})$ histogram is relearned only once every frame, the speed should be similar to that of CAMSHIFT. However, if the histogram is relearned at every iteration, some additional computational expense is incurred, since to properly exploit the new information it is necessary to recompute the $P(O \mid \overline{\mathbf{C}})$ values for every pixel, including those already analysed in previous iterations. In contrast, with the CAMSHIFT algorithm, $P(O \mid \overline{\mathbf{C}})$ values only ever need to be computed once for any pixel. Theoretically, updating at each iteration should produce more reliable tracking, although good tracking results are observed with both options.

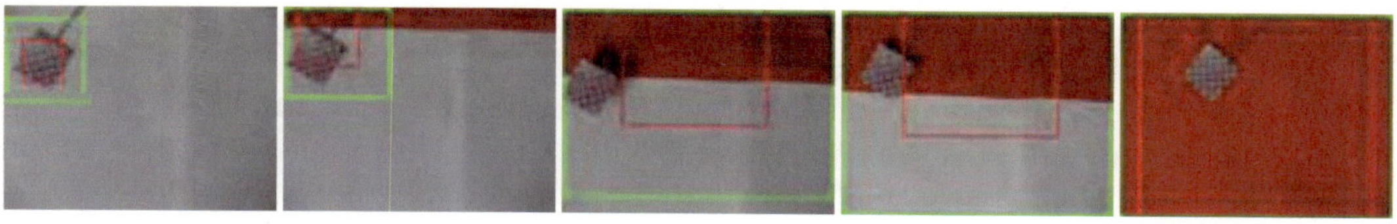

Figure 1. A simple blue and red chequered object, moving from a region of white background into a region of red background. CAMSHIFT fails as soon as the object moves against a background with which it shares a common colour. Frames 350, 360, 380, 400, and 450 shown. Green and red squares indicate the search window and estimated object size respectively. This movie, RedWhite1CAMSHIFT.avi, can be viewed at the project website (see references).

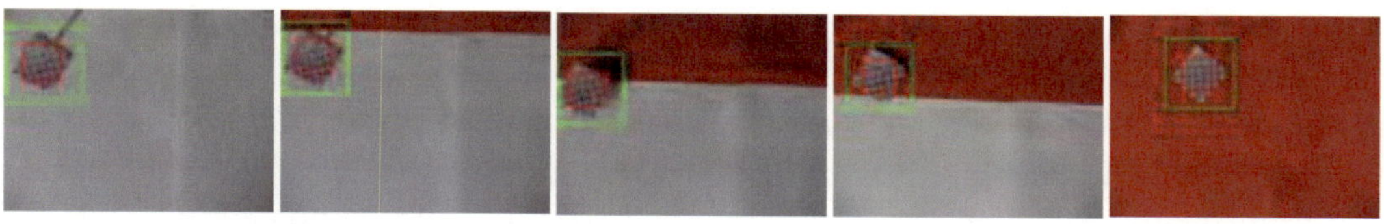

Figure 2. ABCshift tracks successfully. Frames 350, 360, 380, 400, and 450 shown. Green and red squares indicate the search window and estimated object size respectively. This movie, RedWhite1ABCshift.avi, can be viewed at the project website (see references).

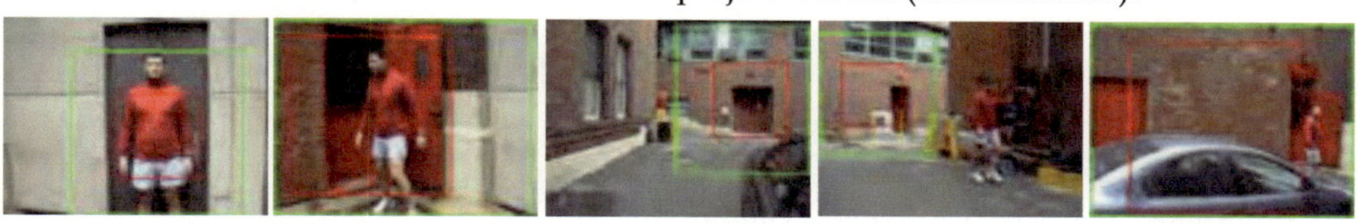

Figure 3. Person tracking with CAMSHIFT from a moving camera in a cluttered, outdoors environment. Frames 1, 176, 735, 1631 and 1862 shown. Since the tracked person wears a red shirt, CAMSHIFT tends to fixate on red regions of background, including brick walls and doors, and repeatedly loses the tracked person. Green and red squares indicate the search window and estimated object size respectively. This movie, PeopleTracking1CAMSHIFT.avi can be viewed at the project website (see references).

Figure 4. ABCshift successfully tracks throughout the sequence and is not distracted by red regions of background, despite being initialised in image 1 which contains no red background. Frames 1, 176, 735, 1631, and 1862 shown. Green and red squares indicate the search window and estimated object size respectively. This movie, PeopleTracking1ABCshift.avi, can be viewed at the project website (see references).

In practice, ABCshift may often run significantly faster than CAMSHIFT. Firstly, the poor background model can cause CAMSHIFT to need more iterations to converge. Secondly, the less accurate tracking of CAMSHIFT causes it to automatically grow a larger search window area, so that far greater numbers of pixels must be handled in each calculation.

3.3 Summary of the ABCshift tracker

The key difference between ABCshift and the conventional CAMSHIFT tracker is that CAMSHIFT uses a simple, static background model that is typically initialized from the first frame and then remains constant throughout the duration of the tracking. In contrast, ABCshift is able to completely relearn the background at every frame or even many times per frame, with little additional computational cost.

The ABCshift algorithm is summarized as:

1. Identify an object region in the first image and train the object model, $P(\overline{\mathbf{C}} \mid O)$.
2. Center the search window on the estimated object centroid and resize it to have an area r times greater than the estimated object size
3. Learn the colour distribution, $P(\overline{\mathbf{C}})$, by building a histogram of the colours of all pixels within the search window.
4. Use Bayes' law (equation 16) to assign object probabilities, $P(O \mid \overline{\mathbf{C}})$, to every pixel in the search window, creating a 2D distribution of object location.
5. Estimate the new object position as the centroid of this distribution and estimate the new object size (in pixels) as the sum of all pixel probabilities within the search window.
6. Repeat steps 2-5 until the object position estimate converges.
7. Return to step 2 for the next image frame.

4. Algorithms that detect and correct their own errors

4.1 Automatic online performance evaluation

Förstner, 1996, suggests that:

1. Vision systems should contain tools for self diagnosis and be able to estimate their own performance.
2. Vision systems should know their own limitations, detect their own cases of failure and be able to report failures and possible causes.
3. To enable such self diagnosis, quality measures need to be determined and specified for both algorithm inputs and outputs.

There seem to be two fundamental mechanisms by which a vision algorithm might determine when it is (or is likely to be) failing or performing sub-optimally. These can broadly be divided into techniques that examine the algorithm's inputs and those that examine its outputs. Firstly, it might be possible to test the kinds of tracking conditions under which a particular algorithm tends to fail. By comparing these with the current input data to the algorithm during tracking, it might be possible to infer when imminent failure or poor performance is likely. Secondly, it may be possible to apply quality measures to output features of the algorithm such as characteristics of an estimated trajectory or a learned representation of the tracked object. The first strategy is difficult since it would require an extensive survey of the performance of an algorithm on a large number of image sequences, under many conditions, as well as some way of characterizing and comparing the conditions, i.e. some metrics which summarise the nature of any input video sequence. This approach is theoretical and, to the best of the author's knowledge has not so far been attempted. Therefore, this section briefly examines some simple techniques that attempt to implement the second of these strategies.

There are two reasons for including this material in the chapter. The concept of algorithms which continuously monitor their own performance and recognise and correct their own errors, seems intuitively to be closely related to the principals of continuous machine learning and autonomous adaptability which are the subject of this discussion. Additionally, these techniques are particularly useful to help correct certain kinds of instability, which occasionally result from continuous model relearning. Simplistically, if an algorithm is allowed to continuously relearn without supervision, there is always a danger that it will learn incorrectly (e.g. learning that background looks like object). Once this process begins and is left uncorrected, it can sometimes escallate, creating an unstable feedback situation which results in failure. This is a previously underexplored area of research. The intention of this section is to highlight some examples and suggest a few possible research directions in the hopes of stimulating further interest within the vision community.

4.2 Bhattacharyya resizing

The ABCshift algorithm is powerful, in that it can cope with rapidly changing backgrounds due to camera motion, by completely relearning a background model at every frame. However, this continual relearning itself can introduce a special mode of instability which occasionally causes problems. If the search window should shrink (due to the object region being temporarily underestimated in size) to such an extent that the boundaries of the search window approach the boundaries of the true object region, then the background model will be retrained predominantly using object pixels. This in turn will lead to many object pixels being assigned a high probability of belonging to the background and even more object pixels beome incoporated into the background model. Thus the estimated object region shrinks in size with a corresponding shrinking of the search window. This results in an unstable feedback cycle with the estimated object region and search window gradually (and unrecoverably) collapsing.

Stolkin et al., 2007, solve this problem by noting that, as the search window shrinks and approaches the size of the object region, the learned search window distribution, $P(\overline{\mathbf{C}})$, must become increasingly similar to the static distribution known for the tracked object, $P(\overline{\mathbf{C}} \mid O)$. If this increasing similarity can be detected, then both the object region and search window can be easily resized, see figure 5, the correct enlargement factor being r, the desired ratio of search window size to object region size.

Several statistical measures exist for comparing the similarity of two histograms. Stolkin et al. utilise a Bhattacharyya metric (Bhattacharyya, 1943) sometimes referred to as Jeffreys-Matsusita distance (Jeffreys, 1946) which for two histograms, $p = \{p_i\}_{i \in \{1,2,\ldots K\}}$ and $q = \{q_i\}_{i \in \{1,2,\ldots K\}}$ is defined as:

$$d(p,q) = \sqrt{\sum_{i=1}^{K} \left(\sqrt{p_i} - \sqrt{q_i}\right)^2} \tag{18}$$

$0 \leq d \leq \sqrt{2}$. Note that this metric can easily be shown to be the same, modulo a factor of $\sqrt{2}$ as that referred to elsewhere in the literature (Comaniciu, 2002, 2003, Perez, 2002, Numiaro, 2002).

At each iteration of the ABCshift algorithm, Stolkin et al., 2007, evaluate the Bhattacharyya metric between the static object distribution, $P(\overline{\mathbf{C}} \mid O)$, and the continuously relearned search window distribution, $P(\overline{\mathbf{C}})$ (which implicitly encodes the background distirbution, $P(\overline{\mathbf{C}} \mid B)$. If the Bhattacharyya metric approaches zero, it is inferred that the search window is approaching the true object region size while the estimated object region is collapsing. Both windows are therefore resized by the factor r . In practice it seems useful to resize when the Bhattacharyya metric drops below a preset threshold. Useful threshold values typically lie between 0.2 and 0.7.

Note that, because of the special way that ABCshift implicitly relearns the background by relearning the $P(\overline{\mathbf{C}})$ histogram, the Bhattacharyya metric is used to compare this histogram with the object model, $P(\overline{\mathbf{C}} \mid O)$. In other kinds of algorithm, where the literal background distribution itself is available, it would be equally advantageous to measure the Bhattacharyya metric betwen $P(\overline{\mathbf{C}} \mid O)$ and $P(\overline{\mathbf{C}} \mid B)$.

This is an unusual application of the Bhattacharyya metric. It has previously become common in the vision literature (Comaniciu, 2002, 2003, Perez, 2002, Numiaro, 2002) to use this metric to evaluate the similarity between a candidate image region and an object distribution for tracking (i.e. comparing potential object with known object). In contrast, Stolkin et al., 2007, use the metric to compare an object distribution with a background distribution, inferring an error if the two begin to converge.

Figure 5. Bhattacharyya resizing. A simple red and blue checkered object is tracked across red, white and blue background regions by the ABCshift tracker, augmented with Bhattacharyya resizing. Frames 180, 200, 205, 206 shown. Due to rapid, jerky motion from frames 180 to 205, the search window has shrunk until it falls within the object region, risking relearning that background looks like object. ABCshift has detected this instability using the Bhattacharyya metric, and automatically corrects the estimated object region and search window size in frame 206. Green and red squares indicate the search window and estimated object size respectively. This movie, PeopleTracking1ABCshift.avi, can be viewed at the project website (see references).

4.3 Other kinds of online auto-performance evaluation

Other related work includes Correia and Pereira, 2002, 2003, and Erdem et al., 2004. This work is not explicitly concerned with the concept of algorithms that constantly monitor their own performance during tracking. However the techniques are applicable, since the authors are broadly interested in performance evaluation without the need for ground truth data (which can be very difficult to generate, see Stolkin, 2006). Erdem divides these performance metrics, which could be used to auto-evaluate tracking performance online (without any external ground-truth data), into two classes as intra-object homogeneity and inter-object disparity, i.e. the tracked object should be consistent with itself but different from the background or other objects.

Intra-object homogeneity metrics might examine shape regularity, spatial uniformity, temporal stability and motion uniformity. The Bhattacharyya resizing technique described above is similar to inter-object disparity metrics, which evaluate colour or motion contrast between pixels, labelled as lying inside and outside the tracked object.

For tracking schemes which output a detailed segmentation of the tracked object, Erdem et al. suggest evaluating spatial colour contrast along object boundaries. Pairs of pixels are selected which lie slightly inside and outside the boundary of the estimated segmented object region. Then colour differences are evaluated along the object boundary. If the tracking algorithm enables a colour histogram of the tracked object to be re-calculated at each frame (e.g. by defining a segmented object region or by relearning a colour model), then this histogram can be compared with a smoothed or average histogram from several previous frames, to measure temporal consistency. It is also possible to evaluate the differences in motion vectors of points estimated to lie inside and outside the tracked object.

In the author's opinion, the use of such techniques, even in very simple ways, to enable tracking algorithms to detect their own errors or modify their parameters in response to deteriorating performance has so far received very little attention, and this would seem to be a useful and open area of ongoing research.

5. Continuously adaptive models of the tracked object

So far, this chapter has provided an overview of various examples of continuous machine learning in the context of background models which adapt with time. Adaptive tracking research predominantly focuses on dynamic relearning of background models, rather than foreground models, because it is often reasonable to assume that the appearance (e.g. colour distribution or texture) of a tracked object remains relatively constant during the tracking process. This section will examine the possibilities for creating algorithms with the additional capabilities of adapting to changes in the tracked object.

Might it be possible to create a simple colour based blob tracker which can track a chameleon? Or how about tracking a person who, while strolling down the street, pulls off a red jacket to reveal a yellow shirt underneath (or Clark Kent as he changes into Superman on the fly)? At present, these kinds of problems (or the similar problem of tracking "camouflaged" objects) tend to be approached with contour tracking, e.g. the ConDensation algorithm (Isard and Blake, 1996), but might fast and simple algorithms such as Mean Shift Tracking (Comaniciu et al., 2003) or ABCshift (Stolkin et al., 2007) be modified to handle these tasks by continuously relearning the appearance of the tracked object?

Let us consider the case of region based object tracking with representations of objects in the form of distributions of intensity, colour or other simple features. In order to update such distributions based on the intensities of pixels in each new frame, some decision must be made about whether or not each new pixel belongs to the tracked object. Note that ABCshift successfully adapts to a changing background without any explicit classification of background pixels, but this is enabled by the assumption of a static object model, combined with some cunning manipulation of Bayes' law. It is relatively easy to update a background model given a static object model and presumably vice versa, but it is much less obvious how to mutually refine both models at the same time. A method is needed by which entirely new colours, which previously did not exist in the object at all, could still be acquired by the object model as they appear. It does not seem logically feasible to manage this without fitting some kind of boundary or contour around the tracked object region at each frame.

Figure 6. Possible mechanism for object model relearning. Firstly the old object model (e.g. colour distribution) is used to classify new image pixels as object. Next a boundary is fitted around these pixels, defining the object region. Finally all pixels within the object region are relearned as the new object model.

A simple theoretical example of such a scheme is illustrated in figure 6. If the object model is a class conditional intensity or colour distribution, then pixels in the current image, with high probabilities according to the existing model, can be identified as belonging to the object. Some object pixels are missed, since the object appearance has changed somewhat since the previous image and the current model is out of date. Hence it may be possible to estimate the object region by fitting a boundary around the detected object pixels. This boundary will include regions of colours which are missing from the current object model. The new colours can be incorporated by relearning the object model according to all pixels which lie in side the bounding contour. Depending on the application, this boundary might be a simple shape (e.g. an ellipse or a square), a flexible contour or snake or the projection of a known 3D model of a tracked rigid body.

An example of an algorithm which continuously relearns both object and background models, is the EM/E-MRF algorithm (Stolkin et al., 2000, 2007b, 2007c), which combines simple, Gaussian models of the object and background pixel intensities with a 3D CAD model of the rigid tracked object. The EM/E-MRF algorithm was an attempt to tackle images under conditions of extremely poor visibility, by combining observed image data with prior knowledge in various forms.

Given the recent trajectory of the camera relative to the observed object, a new relative camera pose is predicted for the current observed image. This pose is used to project a known 3D model of the object, yielding a prediction of the object region in the observed image. The projected/predicted object region can be used to roughly define those image pixels which represent the object. This then enables the creation of object and background distributions (1D Gaussians) from the observed image pixel intensities which lie in these regions.

The object and background distributions can now be used to segment the observed image (the EM/E-MRF algorithm probabilistically combines these distributions with predicted image data during segmentation, using the Extended-Markov Random Field procedure).

The 3D object model can now be best fitted to the segmented image to yield an improved camera pose estimate as well as a cleaner image segmentation. Now the camera pose can be recycled as a new input and the process is iterated. Camera pose, intensity distributions and image interpretation are mutually improved via an Expectation Maximisation-like iterative process. This iterative cycle is illustrated in figure 7.

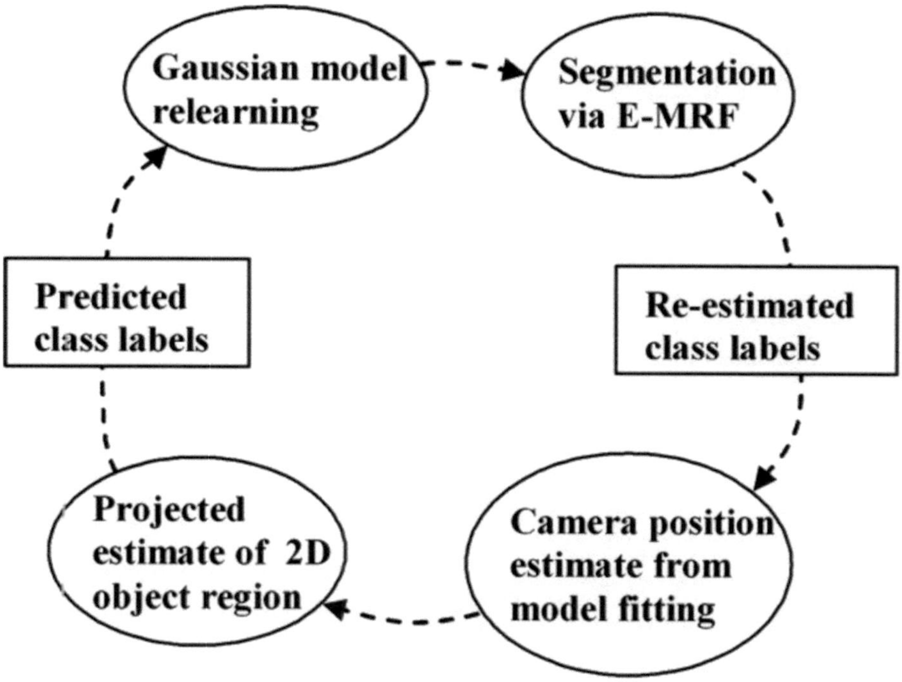

Figure 7. Iterative model relearning with the EM/E-MRF algorithm. Best fitting a projection of the tracked object provides a hard boundary to the estimated object region of the image. This enables object and background intensity distributions to be relearned accordingly.

The EM/E-MRF algorithm achieves some success at interpreting extraordinarily poor visibility images, due to the large amount of predicted information that it incorporates into the segmentation process. It is an interesting exercise in probabilistically fusing two images of the same scene, in this case an observed image and a predicted image. However, this algorithm uses object and background distributions which are overly simplistic for many scenes. At the same time, the Extended-Markov Random Field (E-MRF) optimisation, used in the segmentation process, is excessively computationally expensive.

Despite these drawbacks, the approach is included here as an interesting example of an algorithm which is able to simultaneously relearn both object and background distributions at every frame, see figure 8.

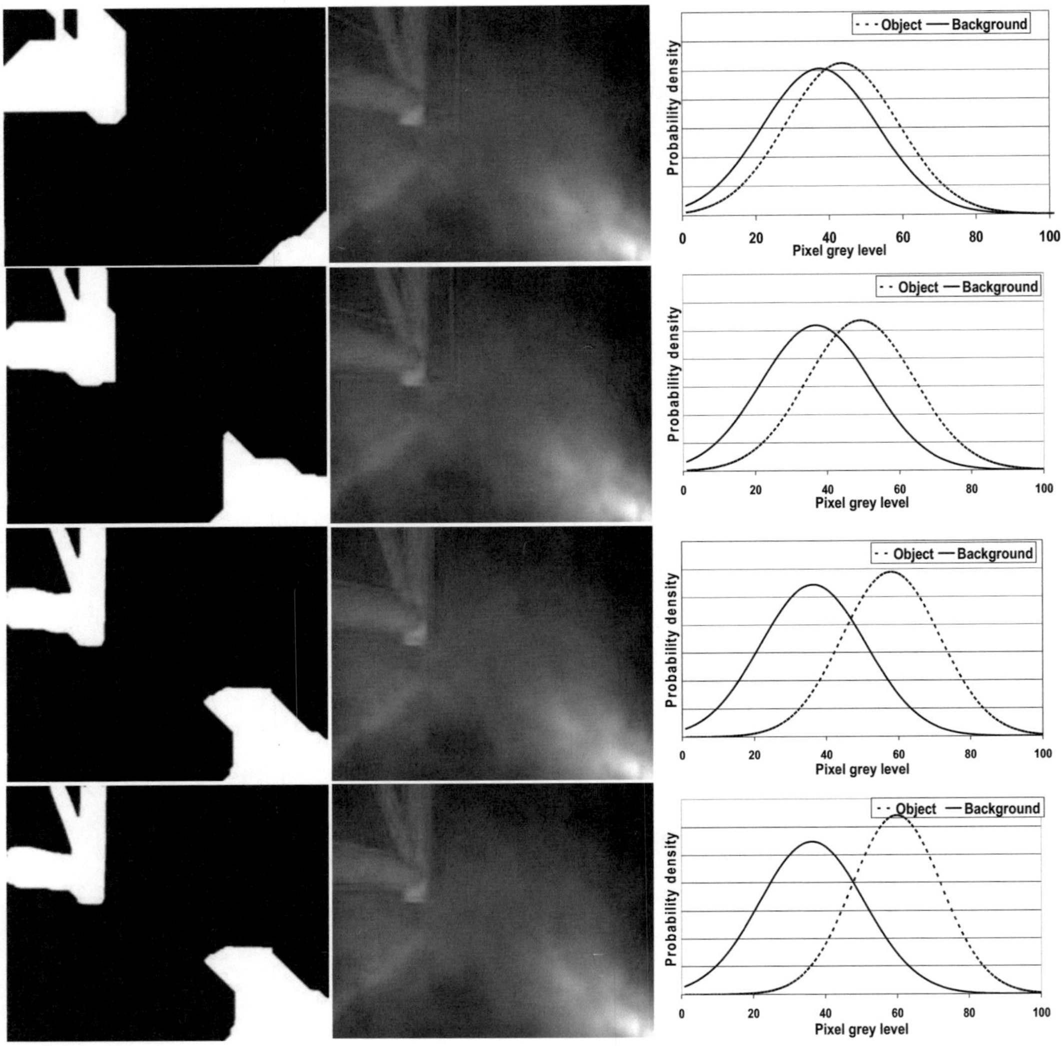

Figure 8. Example of EM/E-MRF tracking on a poor visibility image. Difficult, turbid conditions, encountered with underwater robotics, have been simulated in the lab with dry ice fog and focussed beam spot lights, mounted on and moving with the camera, leading to severe backscattering. Over four iterations, the EM/E-MRF algorithm homes in on an oil-rig like structure. Note how the algorithm mutually refines image interpretation, camera/object pose and the Gaussian object and background models. The two Gaussians separate as the algorithm progressively learns that object is relatively bright whereas background is relatively dark.

7. Conclusion

This chapter has explored a number of techniques in vision based tracking, with the common theme of continuous relearning of models of the background and the tracked object. The majority of well known work in this area has focussed on relearnable background models for stationary cameras. These tend to be robust and stable, but adapt relatively slowly. More recent work has proposed models which can be completely relearned at every frame, enabling tracking with rapid camera motion and also robust tracking of objects which move across regions of background with which they share significant colours.

It is important to note that, although the ABCshift algorithm can relearn the background at every frame, it is only able to do so because it is initialised with a known, static model of the tracked object. In contrast, the adaptive models for stationary camera background subtraction adapt much more slowly, but are able to detect and track new objects without any prior information about the objects' appearance. This might suggest a hybrid scheme, whereby background subtraction techniques with stationary cameras are used to detect new objects and acquire their characteristics, and these characteristics are then passed to object model based techniques which can, for example, continue to follow objects of interest by servoing a pan, tilt, zoom camera.

In order to enable continuous relearning of object models in addition to background models, it seems necessary to define the object region in each frame by a contour or boundary. Thus region based tracking, effectively requires the fusion of contour tracking techniques in order to achieve full adaptability. It is interesting to note that these ideas naturally correspond with calls from elsewhere in the vision community (e.g. Blake, 2005) for hybrid trackers, incorporating both contours and regions, as a way forwards in robust tracking research.

8. References

ABCshift movies at http://www.math.stevens.edu/~ifloresc/ABCshift.htm, 2006.

A. Blake. (2005). Visual tracking: a short research roadmap. *Mathematical Models of Computer Vision: The Handbook,* Eds. O. Faugeras, Y. Chen and N. Paragios, Springer, in press.

Bhattacharayya, A. (1943) On a measure of divergence between two statistical populations defined by their probability distributions. *Bulletin of the Calcutta Mathematical Society*, Vol. 35, 1943, pages 99-110.

Bradski, G. (1998a). Computer video face tracking for use in a perceptual user interface, *Intel Technology Journal,* Q2, 1998.

Bradski, G. (1998b). Real time face and object tracking as a component of a perceptual user interface, *Proceedings of the 4th IEEE Workshop on Applications of Computer Vision,* pages 214-219, 1998.

Collins, R.; Lipton, A., Kanade, T., Fujiyoshi, H., Duggins, D., Tsin, Y., Tolliver, D., Enomotos, N., Hausegawa, O., Burt, P. & Wixson, L. (1999). A System for Video Surveillance and Monitoring, *Proceedings of the American Nuclear Society (ANS) Eighth International Topical Meeting on Robotic and Remote Systems,* April, 1999.

Comaniciu, D.; Meer, P. (2002) Mean shift: A robust approach toward feature space analysis, *IEEE Transactions on Pattern Analysis and Machine Intelligence,* Vol. 24, No. 5, May 2002, pages 603-619.

Comaniciu, D.; Ramesh, V., Meer, P. (2003) Kernel-based object tracking, *IEEE Transactions on Pattern Analysis and Machine Intelligence,* Vol. 25, 2003, pages 564-577.

Correia, P.; Pereira, P. (2002) Stand-alone objective segmentation quality evaluation. *EURASIP Journal of Applied Signal Processing,* No. 4, pages 390-402, 2002.

Correia, P.; Pereira, P. (2003) Objective evaluation of video segmentation quality. *IEEE Transactions on Image Processing*, Vol. 12, February, 2003, pages 186-200.

Elgammal, A.; Harwood, D., Davis, L. (1999) Non-Parametric Model for Background Subtraction. *Proceedings of the IEEE Frame Rate Workshop*, 1999.

Erdem, C.; Sankur, B., Tekalp, A. (2004) Performance Measures for Video Object Segmentation and Tracking. *IEEE Transactions on Image Processing*, Vo. 13, No. 7, July, 2004.

Förstner, W. (1996). Pros and cons against performance characterization of vision algorithms. *Proceedings of the European Conference on Computer Vision, Workshop on Performance Characteristics of Vision Algorithms*, 1996, pages 13-29.

Grimson, W.; Stauffer, C., Romano, R., Lee, L. (1998). Using adaptive tracking to classify and monitor activities in a site, *Computer Vision and Pattern Recognition*, June 1998.

Jeffreys, H. (1946). An invariant form for the prior probability in estimation problems. *Proceedings of the Royal Society (A)*, Vol. 186, pages 453-461.

Kanade, T.; Collins, R., Lipton, A., Burt, P. & Wixson, L. (1998). Advances in cooperative multi-sensor video surveillance, *Proceedings of the 1998 DARPA Image Understanding Workshop*, volume 1, 1998, pages 3-24.

Nummiaro, K.; Van Gool, L., Koller-Meier, E. (2002). Object tracking with an adaptive color-based particle filter. *Pattern Recognition : 24th DAGM Symposium, Proceedings*, Vol. 2449 of Lecture Notes in Computer Science, pages 353-360, 2002, Zurich, Switzerland.

Perez, P; Hue, C., Vermaak, J., Gangnet, M. (2002). Color-based probabilistic tracking. *Proceedings of the 7th European Conference on Computer Vision*, Vol. 2350, Part 1, Lecture Notes In Computer Science, 2002, pages 661-675.

Stauffer, C; Grimson, W. (1999). Adaptive background mixture models for real-time tracking. *Proceedings of Computer Vision and Pattern Recognition*, June 1999.

Stolkin, R.; Hodgetts, M., Greig, A. (2000). An EM/E-MRF strategy for underwater navigation, *Proceedings of the British Machine Vision Conference*, 2000.

Stolkin, R.; Greig, A., Gilby, J. (2006). A calibration system for measuring 3D ground truth for validation and error analysis of robot vision algorithms. *Journal of Measurement Science and Technology*. Institute of Physics, 2006.

Stolkin, R.; Florescu, I., Kamberov, G. (2007a). An adaptive background model for CAMSHIFT tracking with a moving camera. *Proceedings of the 6th International Conference on Advances in Pattern Recognition*, Kolkatta, January, 2007.

Stolkin, R.; Hodgetts, M., Greig, A., Gilby, J. (2007b). Extended Markov Random Fields for predictive image segmentation, *Proceedings of the 6th International Conference on Advances in Pattern Recognition*, Kolkatta, January 2007.

Stolkin, R., Greig, A., Hodgetts, M., Gilby, J. An EM / E-MRF algorithm for adaptive model based tracking in extremely poor visibility. *Journal of Image and Vision Computing*, Elsevier, 2007c.

16

A Sensors System for Indoor Localisation of a Moving Target Based on Infrared Pattern Recognition

Nikos Petrellis, Nikos Konofaos and George Alexiou
Computer Engineering and Informatics Dept., University of Patras
Greece

1. Introduction

Estimating the position of a robot, a vehicle or a person in an indoor area is a significant issue for a number of applications in Robotics, Automation and Ubiquitous/Pervasive Computing. Several approaches have already been proposed in order to locate indoors the position of a moving target. These approaches rely on a wide range of media including RF signals, lasers, ultrasound, magnetic fields, visible light, infrared beams, speedometers etc. A combination of heterogeneous approaches is often adopted (Borenstein et al., 1996) in order to increase the accuracy of the position estimation.

Cameras are widely used in a number of robotics applications (Jin et al, 2004); (Porta & Krose, 2006); (Clerentin et al, 2005); (Kzecka et al, 2005); (Gramegna et al, 2004); (Arras et al, 2001). The views captured by these cameras are processed in order to locate scale invariant landmarks that indicate the position of the robot in a familiar area (Tovar et al, 2006). Moreover, the function of the human eyes can be imitated by a pair of cameras focusing at the same direction (Se et al, 2002). The shape, the depth and the distance of the surrounding objects may be estimated by comparing the images retrieved by these cameras. It is obvious that both the computational and the architectural cost of such a solution is high.

Laser scanning is often used in conjunction with the image processing techniques mentioned above (Miura et al, 2006); (Clerentin et al, 2005); (Victorino et al, 2003); (Arras et al, 2001); (Thrun, 2001). A rotating beacon is transmitting a laser beam which is reflected by the surrounding objects. The round trip time of the signal can be used for the estimation of the distance between the target and an object (e.g., a wall). An ultra high speed controller connected to sensors with fast response is required in this case, since the laser travels with the speed of light and the slightest deviation in the measured time intervals would fail to estimate the distance with adequate accuracy. The strength of the reflected beam may also provide an indication of the distance between the target and an object.

In a similar way, sonar or ultrasonic waves can be used instead of lasers (Jin et al, 2004); (Bicho, 2000); (Minami et al, 2004); (Holmberg, 1994); (Ullate, 1993) . In this case, it is easier to measure the round trip time of the reflected wave since it travels with a significantly lower speed than the laser but the sound can not be treated as a directional beam. Moreover, it is difficult to isolate the sonar transmitter from the receiver. In other words, the receiver cannot be sure if it "listens" to a reflected sound wave or to a sound coming from the sound source itself. The distance that can be measured using sonar data is of the order of several centimetres.

Another popular indoor and outdoor localisation method relies on the signal strength of multiple transmitters (Ladd et al, 2005); (Flora et al, 2005). For example, the Received Signal Strength Indication (RSSI) of the Wireless Local Access Network (WLAN) or Bluetooth networks can be used to estimate the distance of a mobile computer from an Access Point. Another example of this approach concerns the position estimation of a user in a cellular phone network. The signal of the three RF base stations: *B1, B2* and *B3* of Fig. 1 is received at the target with different strength. The strength of each signal indicates the distance of the target from the corresponding base station (*d1, d2* and *d3* from *B1, B2* and *B3* respectively). The point where the three circles centred at *B1, B2* and *B3* (with radius *d1, d2* and *d3* respectively), intersect is the real position of the target. The estimation accuracy depends on the precision that the signal strength can be measured. Although the existing infrastructure of the base stations can be exploited, expensive high precision analogue sensors are required at the side of the target.

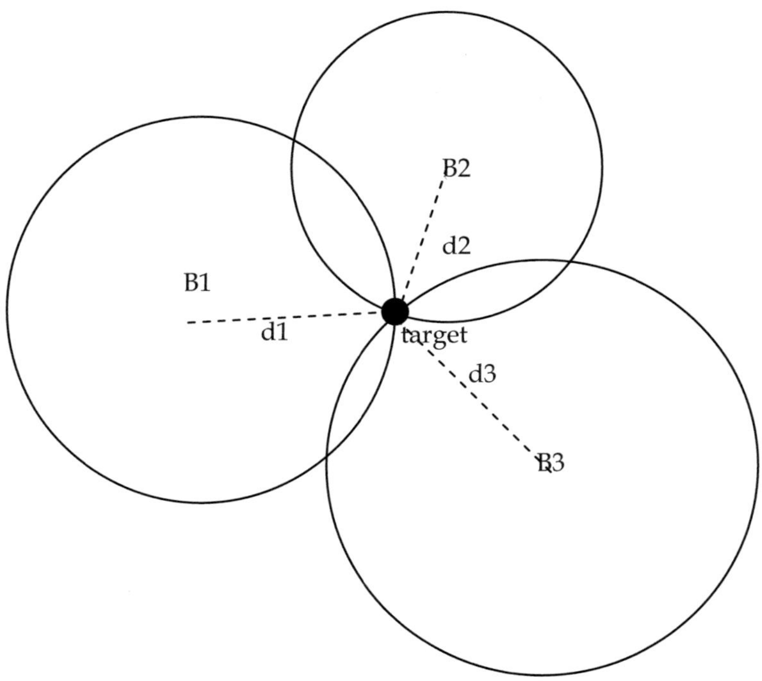

Fig. 1. Position estimation using the triangulation method

Magnetic fields have also been employed in order to accurately control in a non-contact way some machinery tools or medical instrumentation (Schlageter et al, 2001); (Kosel et al, 2005); (Arana et al, 2005). The distances covered in these cases range from a few millimetres to several tenths of centimetres. Nevertheless, distance estimation of up to 10m has also been reported in (Prigge & How, 2004).

Passive and active Infrared sensors have been employed in order to estimate distances of less than one meter (Jin et al, 2004); (Bicho, 2000). Infrared scanning is performed in the

same way as laser scanning. Additional properties of the object that is scanned can also be identified including surface shape and texture (Aytac & Barshan, 2004); (Benet et al, 2002); (Novotny & Ferrier, 1999).
An **absolute** position estimation method locates the current position of the target regardless of his previous movements. All the aforementioned methods can be considered as absolute. A **relative** position estimation approach is based on measuring how much distance has been walked since the last observation and in which direction. This kind of information can be retrieved by monitoring the speed and the steering of a vehicle (Jin et al, 2004); (Victorino et al, 2003); (Thrun, 2001). Stochastic processing can also be applied in order to evaluate how possible an estimated position is.
The position localisation method presented in this chapter is based on the statistical processing of digital infrared patterns that are received at the target (Petrellis et al, 2005); (Petrellis et al, 2006). These patterns are transmitted by at least two infrared emitting devices positioned at the borders of the covered area at a proper topology. The various supported pattern types are recognised with a different "success rate" at the target according to its current position. The term "success rate" refers to the number of patterns received compared to the expected ones for a specific type. The success rates of all the supported pattern types form a multidimensional identity of a specific position. The digital processing of the infrared patterns is carried out by an ultra low cost system since neither high precision sensors nor high speed controllers are required.
The target familiarises with the environment by visiting specific positions during a calibration stage. The reflections caused on the surrounding objects and walls are static and dynamic. The static reflections are encountered during the calibration stage and are exploited as an additional dimension to the position identity. The dynamic reflections caused by obstacles or persons that instantly appear in the covered area during real time operation can be considered as unpredictable dynamic noise. In order to overcome the effect of this noise a number of rules that confine the acceptable future positions can be applied.
The interference of other infrared sources like sunlight are avoided by sending the infrared patterns over a carrier. The frequency of the carrier determines how fast a position estimation can be carried out. If a standard 38KHz carrier is selected, the time needed for a position estimation exceeds 1sec. This time can be reduced to less than 100ms if a 1MHz carrier is used instead. The area covered by two infrared transmitters is more than $15m^2$ and can be further expanded if additional transmitters are used in a proper topology. The absolute position estimation error is less than 10cm in most of the covered area (Petrellis et al 2006b).

2. System Architecture and Setup

The architecture of the infrared pattern transmitter (IRTX) used in our system is presented in Fig. 2. A control unit generates the digital pattern signal. This signal is mixed with the carrier and the amplified output drives the infrared emitting diode. The carrier can be generated either by the control unit or by an external square wave generator. The power dissipation and the beam angle of the emitting diode is a significant issue since it is desirable to cover a wide enough area. In order to achieve this goal, more than one diodes can be connected in parallel (Fig. 2), positioned in a circular arrangement. If more than one IRTX devices are used they may share the same control unit if wiring is not an issue.

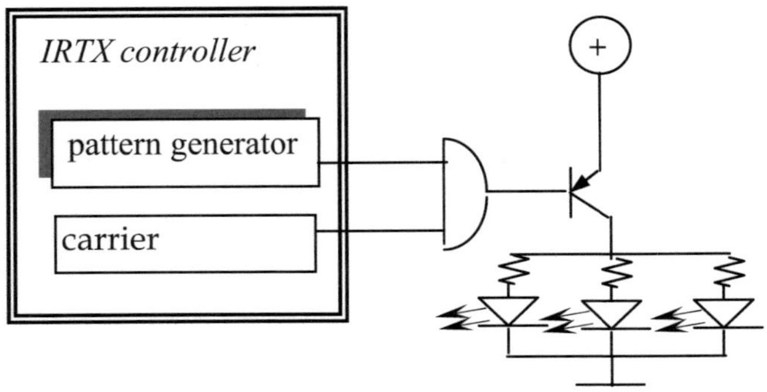

Fig. 2. The architecture of the IRTX device

The structure of an infrared pattern is presented in Fig. 3. Each pattern consists of a series of n identical pulses with period equal to $H+L$. The specific pattern type is named MODn. If $i \neq j$, the pattern types MODi and MODj should be recognised with different degree of difficulty at the receiver. The parameters H and L are chosen longer for MODi than MODj if $i<j$. In this way, the MODi patterns are received without errors in longer distance than MODj since it has longer and smaller number of pulses. The transmission starts with a preamble that can be a special code or a long enough pause interval. Then, a set of M identical patterns of each supported type is transmitted. The successive patterns are separated by a pause interval P longer than H or L. This procedure is repeated by sending a new preamble. The success rate of a pattern type is defined as the number of patterns received compared to the number of the expected ones (M).

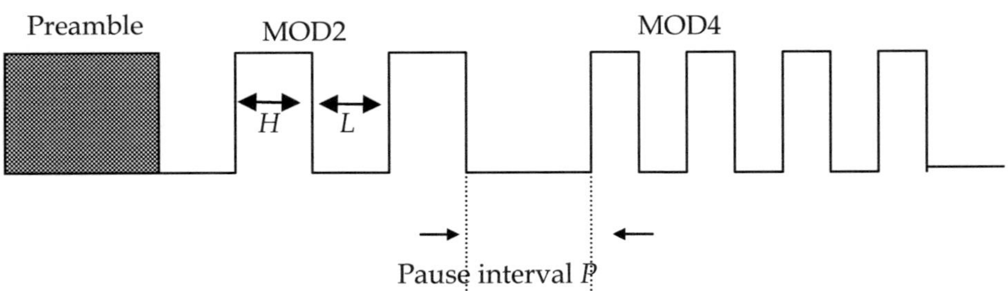

Fig. 3. The structure of the digital infrared patterns

The architecture of an infrared receiver (IRRX) is presented in Fig. 4. The modulated signal received by the infrared sensor is driven to a bandpass filter that allows only the pulses that are modulated at the specific carrier frequency. Then, an integrator rejects the carrier and the resulting digital pulses are sampled directly by a controller that recognises the pattern types from the pulses and the pause intervals. The number of patterns of a specific type that were recognised between two successive preambles is the success rate of this type and can be directly used to estimate the current position. The estimation can be carried out by the control unit itself or by a host computer that communicates with the controller and uses the

estimation results at the target application. At our experimental setup, the controller is connected to a laptop through a serial port. A custom application running at the laptop is performing the position estimation algorithm and presents the position estimation results.
Two IRRX devices are connected to the controller at the side of the target facing opposite directions. The orientation of these IRRX devices should be kept stable, because a slight rotation may drastically affect the success rates measured and the consequent position estimation results. At the present setup, it is assumed that the target can move on a plane but can not rotate i.e., it has two degrees of freedom. Nevertheless, the target may be allowed to rotate around itself if this can be done independently of the IRRX devices.

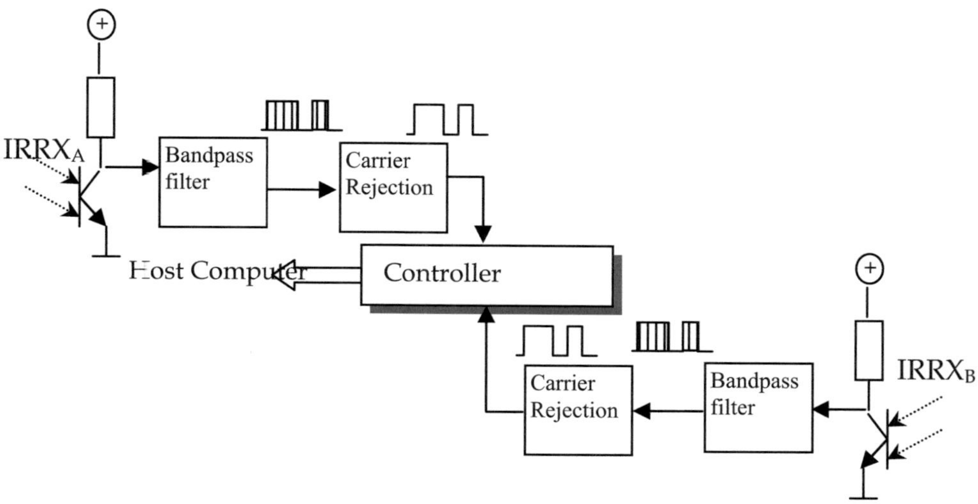

Fig. 4. The architecture of the IRRX devices.

3. Position Estimation Method

The success rate r_i of the MOD*i* type, is the number of MOD*i* patterns retrieved between two successive preambles. A calibration stage is necessary before the real time operation in order to familiarise with the environment. During this stage, the target visits specific positions in the covered area and records the retrieved success rate. If the topology of Fig. 5 is assumed, the target visits positions in regular distance and angular steps around an IRTX device. The success rates measured for a specific angular displacement can be drawn as a function of the distance as shown in Fig. 6.
The discrete values measured during the calibration can be approximated by a continuous non linear model like Richards' (Bates & Watts, 1988), before the real time operation of the system:

$$r_i = p_1 /(1 + e^{-p_2(d-p_3)})^{1/p_4} \tag{1}$$

The success rate r_i is approximated as a function of the distance d for a specific angle, while the parameters p_1, p_2, p_3 and p_4 are estimated by an external off the shelf optimisation tool. If the IRTX device supports k types of patterns, the calibration is performed in l directions and m positions are visited in each direction, then a set of $k \cdot l \cdot m$ equations like (1) have to be estimated. In fact, only the parameters p_i have to be stored requiring a memory of $4{\cdot}k{\cdot}l{\cdot}m$ floating point values.

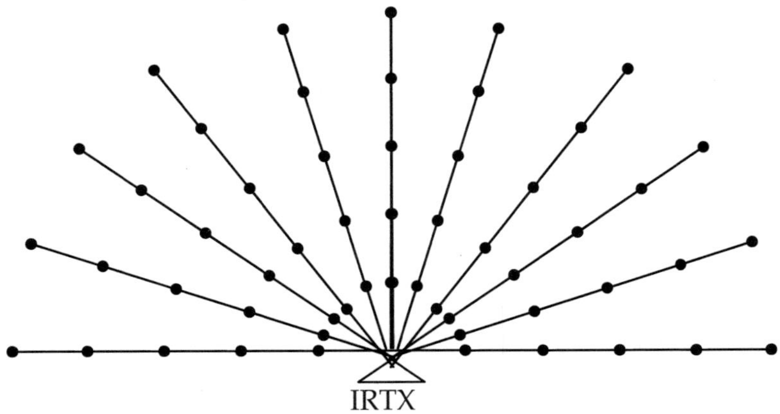

Fig. 5. Calibration at regular angle and distance steps.

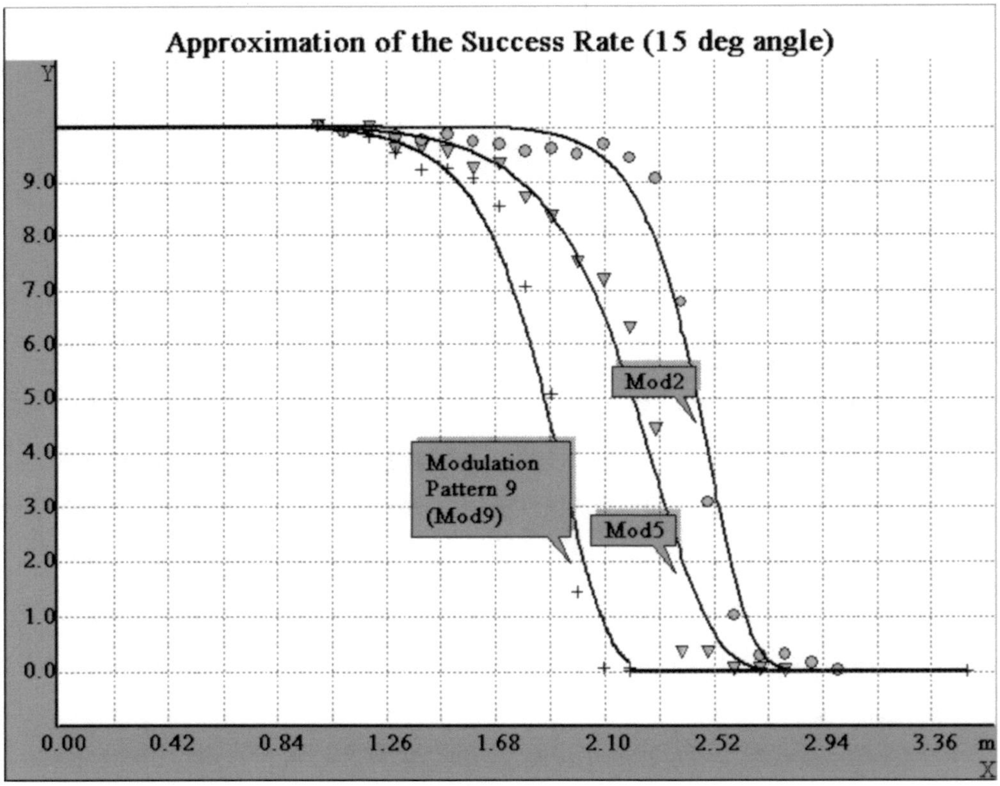

Fig. 6. Approximation of the calibration values with a nonlinear model (Petrellis et al 2006a).

Alternatively, the success rates for a specific distance can be drawn as a function of the angular displacement as shown in Fig. 7.

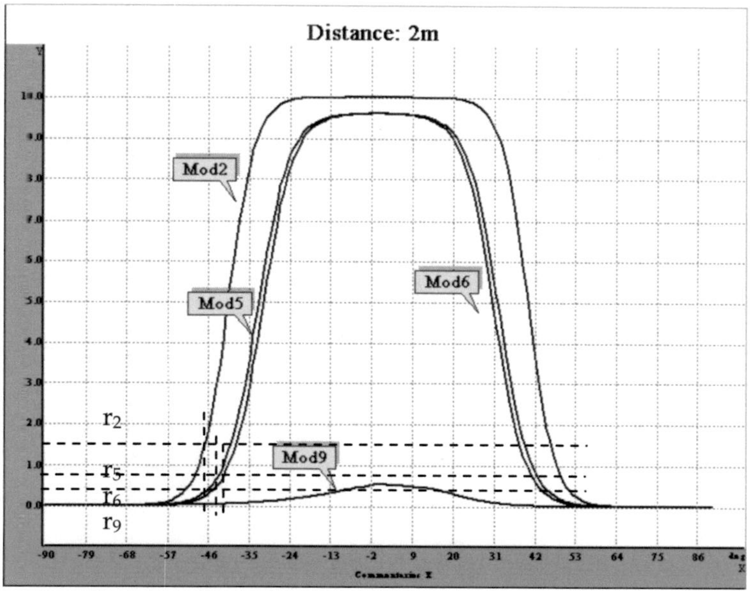

(a)

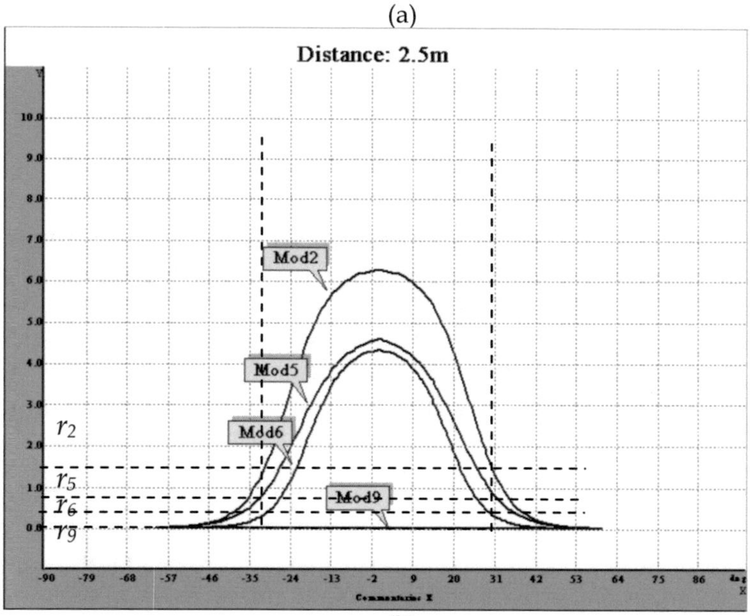

(b)

Fig. 7. The success rates as a function of the angular displacement for a specific distance (Petrellis et al 2006a).

The polar coordinates of the target related to the IRTX device can be estimated as follows (Petrellis et al, 2006a): if the pattern types MOD2, MOD5, MOD6 and MOD9 are supported by the IRTX device of Fig. 5 and the success rates r_2, r_5 , r_6 and r_9 are retrieved by the target at a specific position during real time operation then the curve sets of all the specific distances have to be checked out. For example, if the set of curves at a distance of 2m are used, the success rate values do not converge to the same angular displacement (Fig. 7a). On the contrary, if the curves retrieved at a distance of 2.5m are used, the measured r_i values converge to a ±30° angular displacement (Fig. 7b). The ambiguity of whether the target is located at the right or at the left side of the IRTX device can be clarified if a second IRTX device is positioned in a topology like the one presented in Fig. 8. Hence, the IRTX2 device is used in order to break the symmetry and extend the covered area.

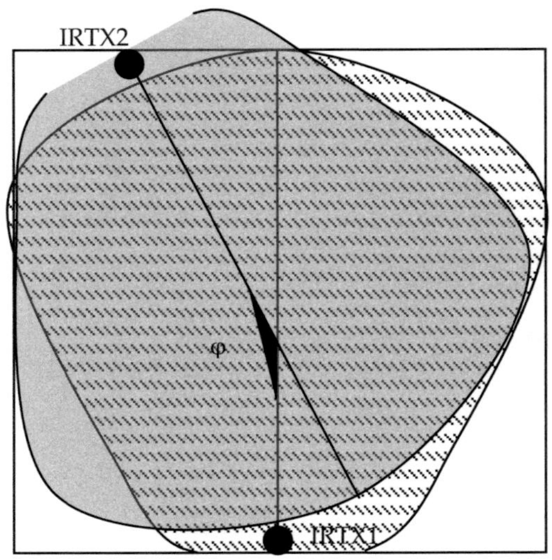

Fig. 8. Placing a second IRTX device in the covered area.

The approach described above suffers from two important drawbacks. First of all, the reflections from the surrounding area have to be negligible. Otherwise, the behaviour of the success rate is not similar to the one presented in Fig. 6 and 7 and a unique model like Richards' is not applicable. For the same reason, the two IRTX devices should not transmit their patterns concurrently in order to avoid scrambling.

These limitations can be overcome if the calibration and position estimation method is based on a grid (Petrellis et al, 2006b). The grid plane extends to all the covered area. During the calibration stage, the target visits the grid nodes and registers the retrieved success rates in the vectors *A*, *B*, *A′* and *B′*. The patterns retrieved "in order" by the $IRRX_A$ device are stored in *A* while patterns that are recognised "out of order" by the same device are stored in *A′*. In a similar way, the vectors *B* and *B′* refer to patterns that are received by the terminal $IRRX_B$. For example, if the $IRRX_A$ device points towards the IRTX1 that supports the pattern types MOD3, MOD4, MOD7 and MOD8, then the vector positions *A[3]*, *A[4]*, *A[7]* and *A[8]* store the corresponding number of patterns received "in order" between two preambles. If the IRTX2 device supports MOD2, MOD5, MOD6 and MOD9 types, the corresponding vector positions for the patterns received "in order" are *B[2]*, *B[5]*, *B[6]* and *B[9]* since $IRRX_B$ is facing towards IRTX2. Nevertheless, $IRRX_A$ may also receive patterns transmitted by IRTX2 through reflections. The corresponding number of patterns are stored in *A[2]*, *A[5]*, *A[6]* and *A[9]* and are viewed as "unexpected".

The success rate vectors *A, A′, B* and *B′* form the identity of a position. The reflections and the scrambling are encountered as different dimensions in these vectors ("expected", "unexpected" and "out of order" patterns). Thus, instead of viewing them as a drawback we exploit their effect in order to increase the estimation accuracy and eliminate the limitations posed by the polar coordinates approach. Consequently, static reflections are allowed in this approach and the IRTX devices may transmit their patterns concurrently.
During real time operation, the current success rates retrieved by the target are compared with the grid node rates that were retrieved during the calibration stage. The comparison is based on the relative differences estimated by the equations (2) and (3):

$$d_{ij} = \begin{cases} \frac{v_j - r_{ij}}{v_j}, if (v_j > r_{ij}) \\ \frac{r_{ij} - v_j}{r_{ij}}, if (v_j \le r_{ij}) and (r_{ij} \neq 0) \\ 1, if (v_j = 0) or (r_{ij} = 0) \end{cases} \quad (2)$$

$$D_i = \sum_j d_{ij} \quad (3)$$

The parameter v_j is the j-th position of the composite vector *C=[A A′ B B′]* while r_{ij} is the corresponding value of the success rate vectors retrieved during calibration for node *i*. The individual success rate differences for all the *C* vector positions are summed up and the grid node *i* with the smaller D_i value is selected as the closer to the target position.
Although no model has been used to describe how the success rate of a pattern varies in neighbouring positions, it may be assumed that if the grid nodes are close enough it changes linearly between two successive nodes. Thus, if the success rate of a pattern at the nodes *i* and *j*, are r_i and r_j, the success rate *r* at the middle of these nodes is

$$r = (r_i + r_j)/2 \quad (4)$$

The selection of the grid node distance is critical and a trade off has to be made between the calibration speed and the estimation accuracy. If the node distance is very short, the high number of grid nodes will increase the duration of the calibration stage and the memory requirements. Moreover, if there are too many grid nodes then there will be an increased possibility that nodes with almost identical success rate identities will exist. These nodes may be confused in real time operation leading to erroneous position estimations. On the other hand, if a long distance is selected, then the assumption that the success rate of a pattern changes linearly between two neighbouring nodes is not valid.
In Fig. 9, the success rate of an expected (a) and an unexpected (b) pattern is drawn in an area of 1mX1m. A study of several 2D graphs like the ones presented in Fig. 9 leads to the conclusion that a grid with a 20cm node distance is appropriate for our system since the concept of the linear success rate variation between neighbouring nodes is preserved in most of the cases without significantly increasing the number of the grid nodes.

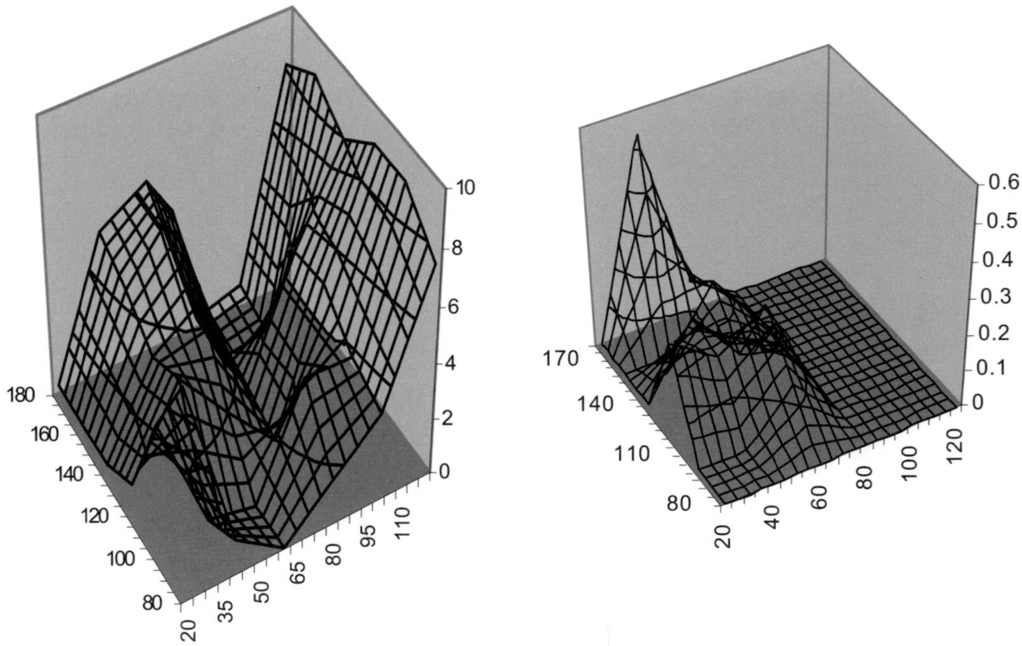

(a) (b)

Fig. 9. Success rate variation in 2D of an expected (*a*) and unexpected (*b*) MOD7 pattern.

A refinement step follows the selection of the initial grid node in order to estimate more accurately the real position of the target. This step is basically an extension of the interpolation search algorithm in two dimensions. A new grid with the half node distance is defined by estimating the success rate identities of the new nodes using the equation (4). Consider for example Fig. 10 where the node *E0* of the initial grid is selected by the first comparison between the current and the calibration success rates. The success rates of the virtual nodes at the middle of *E0* and its neighbouring nodes *Ex* are estimated using equation (4) and their differences from the current rates are extracted using equations (2) and (3). The virtual node with the smallest D_i value is selected as the centre of the new grid (node E0′ in Fig. 10). The aforementioned procedure is repeated for the nodes of the new grid and a new position between *E0′* and the rest of the *Ex′* nodes is selected (*E0″*). If the definition of a new grid does not lead to a lower D_i value, then the recursive refinement procedure terminates.

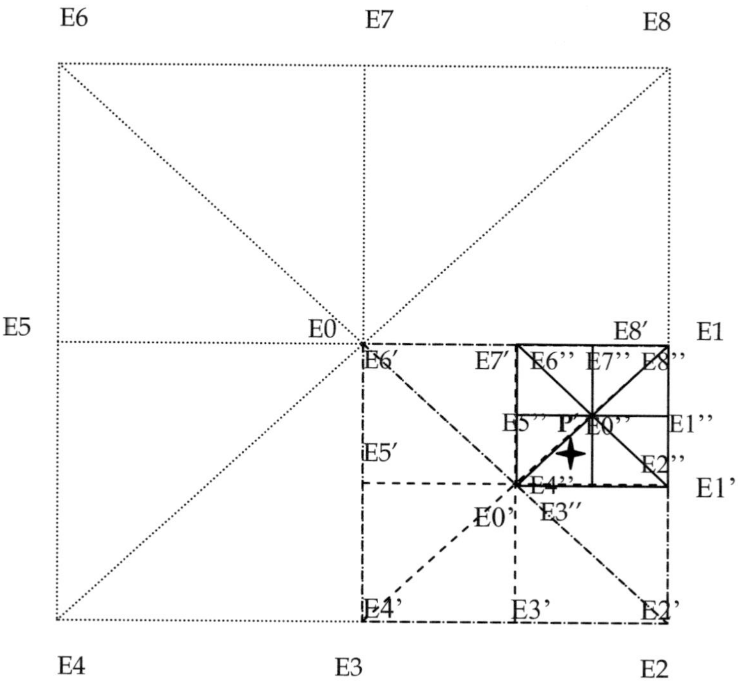

Fig. 10. The refinement step in the position estimation

4. Carrier Signal Options

As already mentioned in section 2, the patterns are transmitted over a carrier (F_c) in order to make it feasible for the receiver to abort the interfering infrared noise. A high pulse of an infrared pattern MOD*i* should last for multiple carrier periods in order to reassure the effectiveness of the receiver bandpass filter:

$$H_i = k / F_c \tag{5}$$

If $H=L$ the time needed to transmit the set of the identical MOD*i* patterns is

$$T_i = M(P + 2ik / F_c) \tag{6}$$

If T_{pream} is the duration of the preamble, the total time T that is needed to transmit all of the supported patterns is

$$T = T_{pream} + \sum_i M(P + 2ik / F_c) \tag{7}$$

It is obvious from equation (7) that the position estimation procedure is slow if a low frequency carrier is chosen. For example, using the standard 38KHz carrier, the location of a position requires more than one second but low cost sensors with embedded carrier rejection circuitry can be employed at the side of the receiver. A significant reduction in this time can be achieved if a higher carrier frequency is used. In this case, higher processor speed, fast infrared emitters/sensors and a custom carrier filter are required.

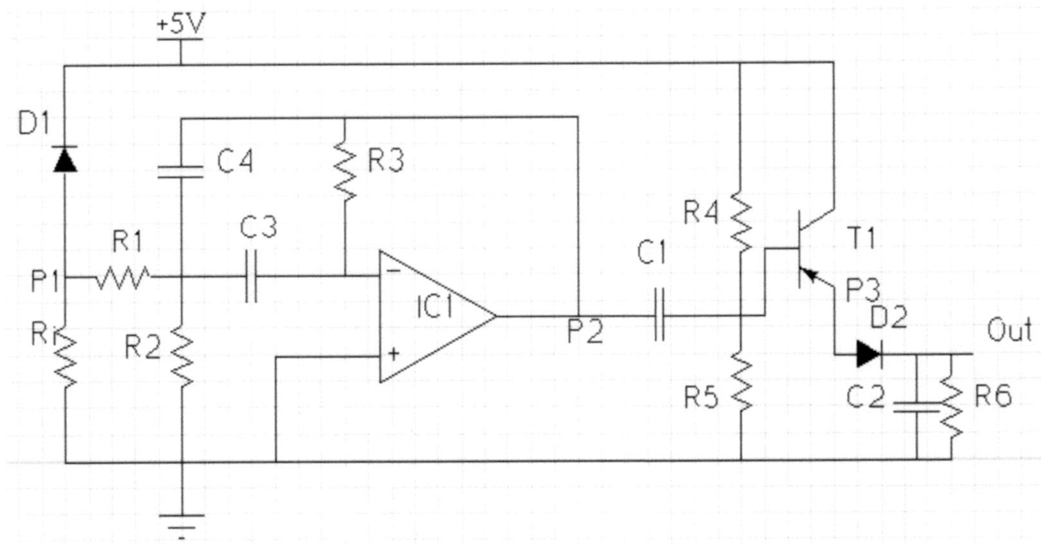

Fig. 11. A custom filter for high frequency carrier.

For example, the filter of Fig. 11 is used in this case. The infrared diode *D1* is connected inversely allowing a low current in the absence of infrared light (e.g., less than 50uA if the device model SFH203 is used). This current is increased to 80uA if infrared light falls on *D1*. The resistance *Ri* converts the current levels of *D1* to voltage input at the Multiple Feed Back Filter (MFBF) that consists of *R1, R2, C3, C4, R3* and *IC1*. If *B* is the desired bandwidth i.e., the frequency range where the signal is attenuated less than -3dB compared to the centre frequency f_c, the quality factor *Q* is defined as

$$Q = f_c / B \tag{8}$$

If *G* is the desired filter gain (*Q* and *G* should not be much greater than 1) and the capacitors *C1* and *C2* are equal to a selected value *Cp*, the resistors *R1, R2* and *R3* can be estimated using the following equations (Lancaster, 1995):

$$R1 = Q / 2\pi f_c CpG \tag{9}$$

$$R2 = Q / (2Q^2 - G)\pi f_c Cp \tag{10}$$

$$R3 = Q / \pi f_c Cp \tag{11}$$

The operational amplifier *IC1* is a high speed device capable of providing unity gain at much higher frequencies than f_c. For example, if the carrier frequency is 1MHz, the gain flatness of *IC1* should be kept less than 0.1dB for frequencies up to 60MHz. This requirement is harder to achieve if single power supply is used. The output of the *IC1* is amplified by *T1* through *C1* that isolates the MFBF filter from the amplification stage. The values of *C1* and *R5* are chosen in order to further attenuate the frequencies that are lower than f_c. The simple circuitry consisting of the components *D2, C2* and *R6* acts as an AM demodulator rejecting the current as can be seen in Fig. 12.

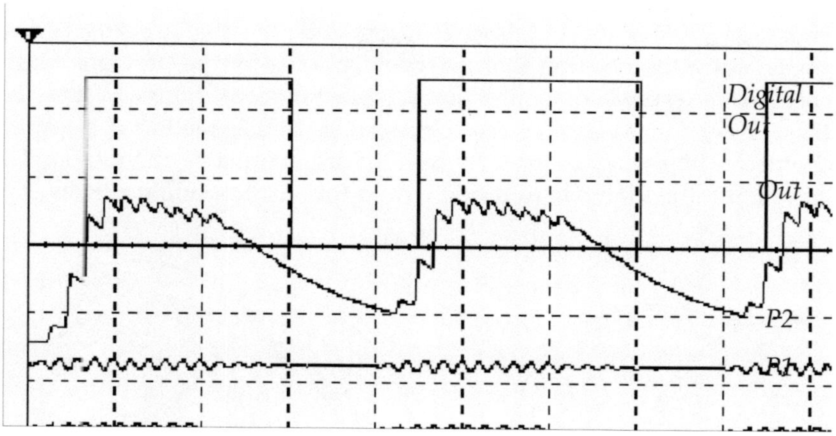

Fig. 12. The form of the received 1MHz signal at various stages of the MFBF filter.

Fig. 12 presents the behaviour in time of a 1MHz filter that attenuates by -30dB the signals with frequencies lower than 800KHz and greater than 1.2MHz. An input signal modulated at 1MHz appears at the junction *P1,* while *P2* is the output of the MFBF filter. Although the output of the demodulator (*Out*) is slightly rippling the signal can be safely sampled by a digital input

Although several alternative passive or active filters could have been employed, the study of these options is out of the scope of this chapter. Using a 1MHz filter like the one presented above, the duration of the position estimation procedure can be reduced to less than 100ms.

5. Real Time Position Validation Rules

The results of successive position estimations may differ significantly even if the target stands still. This is due to the fact that dynamic noise and reflections have not been considered during the calibration stage. The rules described in this section can help the system reject the estimation results that differ significantly from the original target position (Petrellis et al, 2006c). Some of these rules can be used as estimation correction techniques or they may simply force the system to repeat the estimation process. As the target moves within the covered area, it performs position localisation processes at regular intervals T_s. Each process includes S successive position estimations. Thus, the duration of a localisation process is $S{\cdot}T$ where the time T was estimated by equation (7).

5.1 Limited Speed Rule (LSR)

The speed of the vehicle or the person that is considered as a target is always limited and slow. Thus, the distance R_s that may be walked between the successive localisation processes is also limited by the following relations:

$$V_{mn}(T_s + s \cdot T) \leq R_s \leq V_{mx}(T_s + s \cdot T) \tag{12}$$

The parameters V_{mn} and V_{mx} are the minimum and the maximum speed of the target respectively, while s is the sequence of the specific estimation within a localisation process

($1 \le s \le S$). There is always an upper limit for the speed of the target but not a lower one since the target may not move for a while. In this case, $V_{mn} = 0$ and the value of s defines disks that have as a common centre the position that has been selected by the previous localisation process. The coordinates estimated by the current position localisation process have to reside within these disks, otherwise they are rejected (Fig. 13a). If the target always moves ($V_{mn} > 0$), then homocentric rings that possibly overlap are defined by the relation (12) and the result of a position estimation has to reside within the corresponding ring as shown in Fig. 13b.

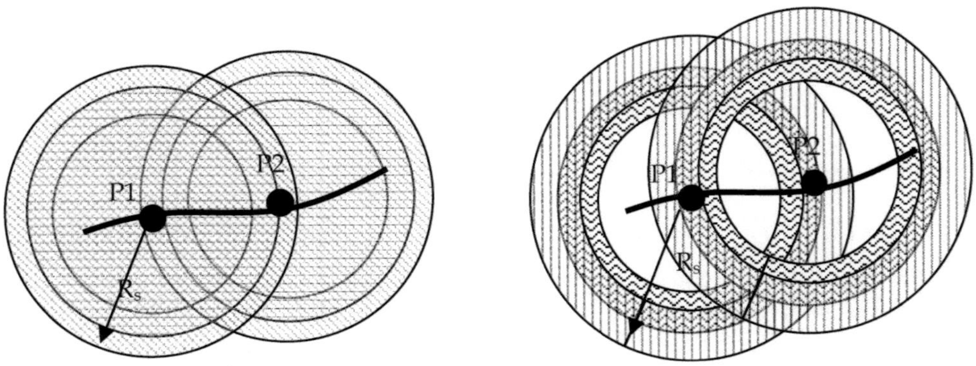

(a) (b)

Fig. 13. The limitations in the speed of the target define disks (a) or rings (b) where the acceptable positions reside.

The LSR rule can be used as a correction method if all the estimated positions are outside the limits of the disks or the rings. If P is the centre of the disk and P' is the closer estimated position outside the disk, then the point P'' selected. This is the point where the border of the disk intersects with the line that connects P with P' as shown in Fig. 14.

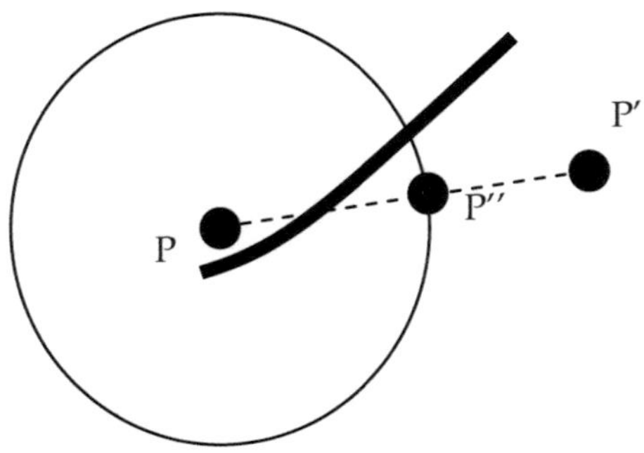

Fig. 14. Correction of the estimated results using LSR.

5.2 Neighbouring Regions Rule (NRR)

The way that the success rate of the patterns varies within the covered area may be used to divide this area in neighbouring regions. The concept of the NRR rule is that the target may cross neighbouring regions but cannot be found suddenly in a distant region. The NRR is actually a relaxed LSR rule and its basic purpose is the extension of the covered area by using more than 2 IRTX devices.

If the success rates presented in Fig. 9a and 9b are used, the regions *A, B, C* and *D* of Fig. 15 can be defined. The success rate class of *A7* in the range [0,10] is considered high (*H*) if it is more than 7, medium (*M*) if it is between 4 and 7, low (*L*) if it is between 1 and 4 and zero (*Z*) if it is less than 1. In a similar way, the success rate class of *B7* is defined as *H, M, L, Z* in the range [0,0.6]. Thus, the symbol *C(M,Z)* for example defines the region *C* where the success rates class of *A7* is *M* and *B7* is *Z*. A more accurate definition of the regions can be achieved if more than two success rate types are considered.

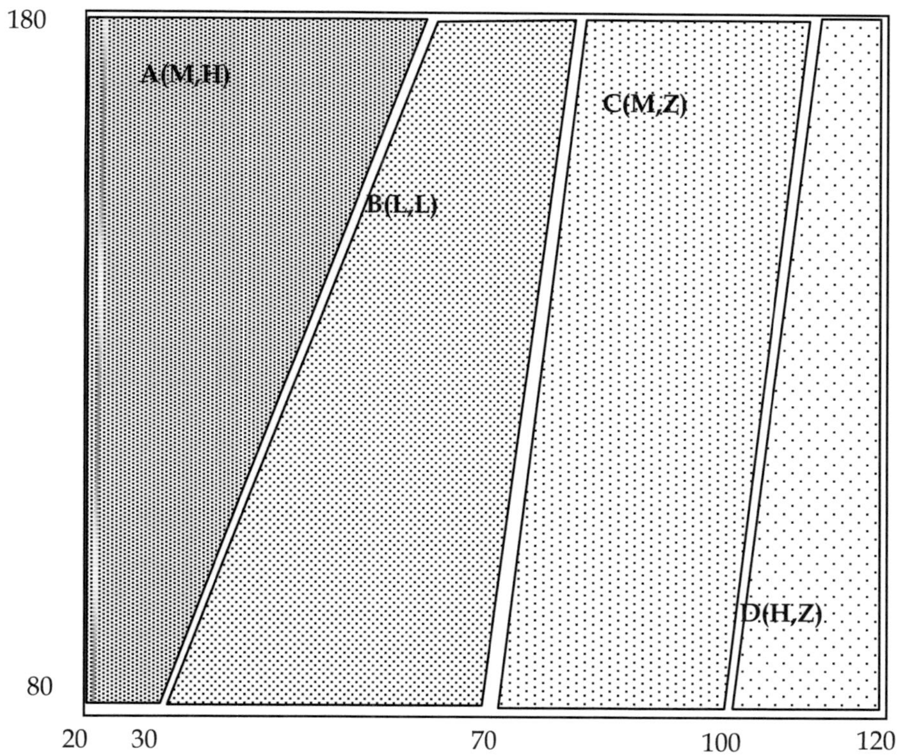

Fig. 15. Regions defined by the success rates of Fig. 9

If the speed of the target is low enough, it is assumed that it can only be found in the same or neighbouring regions in successive localisation processes. For example, if it is initially found in region *B*, the next acceptable position is allowed to be in regions *A*, *B* or *C* but not in *D*.

The area that is covered may be extended if the concept of the NRR rule is used with three or more IRTX devices. If the IRTX devices that are presented in Fig. 16 are used, the draft regions drawn in the same figure are defined. Each one of the IRTX1, IRTX2 and IRTX3 transmitters supports a different set of patterns. In this way, the target distinguishes the source of the patterns it receives. For example, if the reflections and the scrambling are negligible in the area of Fig. 16, the target receives high success rates from IRTX1 on $IRRX_A$ and lower success rates from IRTX2 on $IRRX_B$ when it is in region A. Similarly, in region B it receives high success rates from IRTX2 on $IRRX_B$ and lower from IRTX1 and IRTX3 on $IRRX_A$.

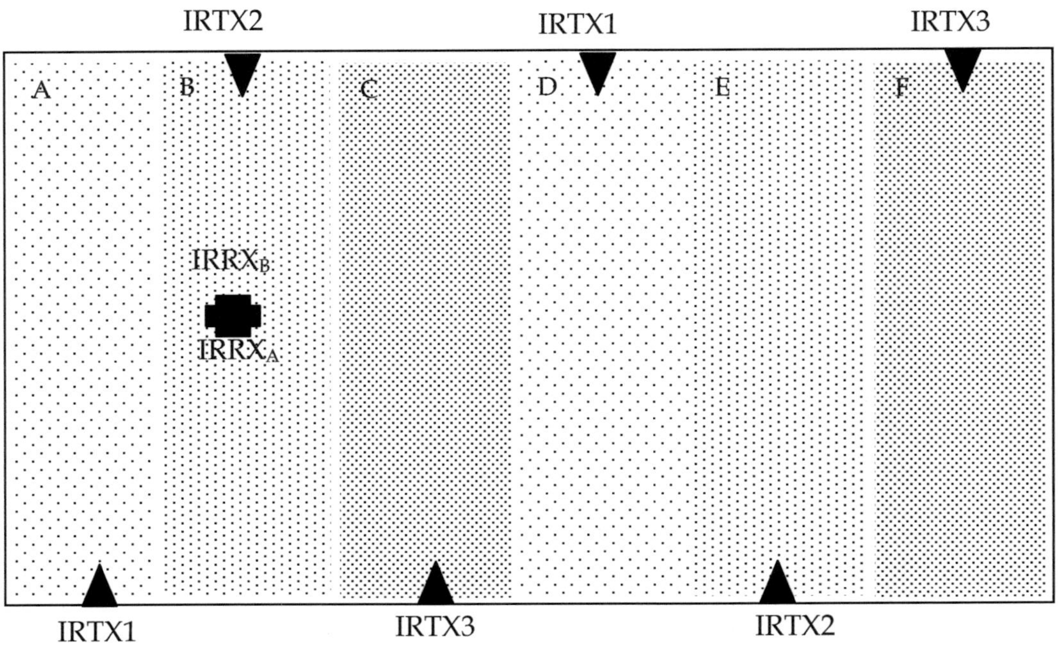

Fig. 16. Extending the area covered by using three or more IRTX devices.

In a real environment the regions neither have the regular shape presented in Fig. 16, nor the same size. They are defined using the information of 3D graphs like the ones presented in Fig. 9 and some distant regions have the same features if three types of IRTX devices are used repeatedly. The target should keep track of the regions that it has crossed in order to distinguish the exact region of its current position. For example, in regions *B* and *E* the target receives patterns with high success rate from IRTX2 on one IRRX device and lower success rates from IRTX1 and IRTX3 on the other IRRX device. This may cause a confusion of whether being in region *B* or *E*. Nevertheless, if it knows that the previous regions crossed were *C* and *D* in this specific turn, then the region *E* will be selected.

5.3 Direction Preserving Rule (DPR)

The third rule is based on the fact that the target is moving on the same rough direction most of the time. Although this is not true if for example the target follows a circular track, this rule can be very helpful in the general case. If *k* successive positions of the target are considered then *k-1* lines starting from the first position are defined as shown in Fig. 17. Two of these lines determine the wider angle that is considered as the rough direction where the next position is assumed to reside. The lower value that *k* can get is 3. In this case the two lines determine a single angle. For example, the positions *P0, P1* and *P2* determine the initial rough direction in Fig. 17. The next position (*P3*) should reside within the angle defined by *P0, P1* and *P2*. Then, the direction is updated using *P1, P2* and *P3* and the next position (*P4*) should reside within the angle defined by these three points.

The angle of *P0, P1* and *P2* is defined by:

$$\cos(P_1\hat{P}_0P_2) = \frac{(w_1 - w_0)(w_2 - w_0) + (l_1 - l_0)(l_2 - l_0)}{\sqrt{(w_1 - w_0)^2 + (l_1 - l_0)^2}\sqrt{(w_2 - w_0)^2 + (l_2 - l_0)^2}} \quad (13)$$

In the general case k points define $(k-1)(k-2)/2$ angles. The wider angle is chosen as the one with the lowest cosine value. The next position should reside within the wider angle. If $P0$, $P1$ and $P2$ define the wider angle then the next position Pn should comply with the following relations:

$$\cos(P1\hat{P}0Pn) \geq \cos(P1\hat{P}0P2) \quad (14)$$

$$\cos(Pn\hat{P}0P2) \geq \cos(P1\hat{P}0P2) \quad (15)$$

The applicable values used for k are 4 to 6. Using k=3 is too restrictive since the angle defined is narrow and may often be 0°. On the other hand, using a high value for k leads to extremely wide angles that do not reject any of the estimated positions in a localisation process .

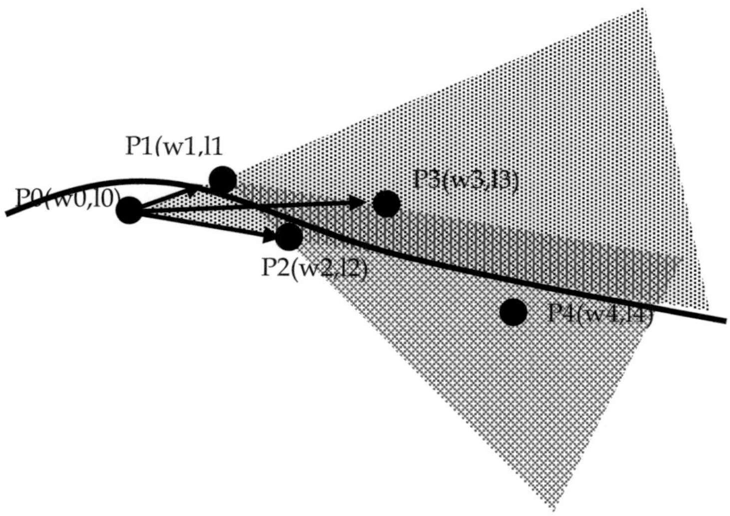

Fig. 17. Direction Preserving Rule

5.4 Steering Control Rule (SCR)

The SCR rule can be applied if the target is allowed to change his direction in specific angles. If Φ is the set of the allowed angles φ, then three successive positions $P1(w_1,l_1)$, $P2(w_2,l_2)$ and $P3(w_3,l_3)$ should satisfy the following relation:

$$\cos(\varphi) = \frac{(w_1 - w_2)(w_3 - w_2) + (l_1 - l_2)(l_3 - l_2)}{\sqrt{(w_1 - w_2)^2 + (l_1 - l_2)^2}\sqrt{(w_3 - w_2)^2 + (l_3 - l_2)^2}} \quad (16)$$

The SCR rule can also be used as an error correction rule if the closer position to an acceptable direction is rotated as shown in Fig. 18. In the general case presented in this figure, four angles are allowed (0°, φ_1, φ_2 and φ_3). If *P3* is the estimated position that is closer to an allowed direction (φ_2), the position *P3* is rotated by equations (17)-(19) and the resulting position *P3′* has the same distance *d* from *P2* but in an acceptable direction.

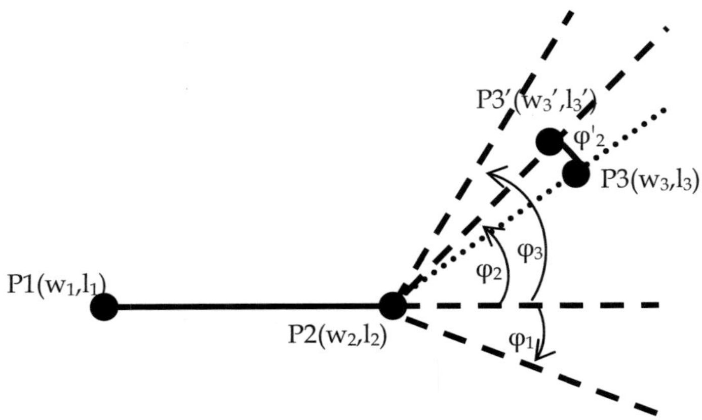

Fig. 18. Error correction using the SCR rule

$$w_3' = w_2 + d \cdot \cos\varphi_2 \tag{17}$$

$$l_3' = l_2 + d \cdot \sin\varphi_2 \tag{18}$$

$$d = \sqrt{(w_3' - w_2)^2 + (l_3' - l_2)^2} = \sqrt{(w_3 - w_2)^2 + (l_3 - l_2)^2} \tag{19}$$

6. Case Study

The experimental topology presented in Fig. 19 is used as a case study. Two IRTX devices are positioned in 1.8m horizontal and 3m vertical distance. Each IRTX device has two infrared emitting diodes of different type connected in parallel, placed in 45° angle. The external continuous line defines the range of at least one IRTX device signal. The area covered exceeds 15m² but the quality of the estimation results is not the same everywhere.

If a grid covering the whole area with long node distance (40cm) is considered then an estimation with an absolute error that is less than the half of the node distance (20cm) is acceptable. Each position localisation process carries out 5 successive estimations (*S*=5) and is considered successful if at least one of them has an absolute error of less 20cm. In this case, a 65% of the positions visited experimentally were localised successfully. If the four rules described in Section 5 are applied, then more than 90% of the positions visited are estimated successfully.

The absolute error can be reduced if a shorter node distance is used. In this case, it is difficult to cover the whole area since the number of grid nodes is significantly increased leading to a longer calibration time and possibly to poor results as already described in

Section 3. If we focus on the 1m² area in the dotted square of Fig. 19 and use a 20cmX20cm grid, then all the positions visited are localised with an error of less than 10cm.

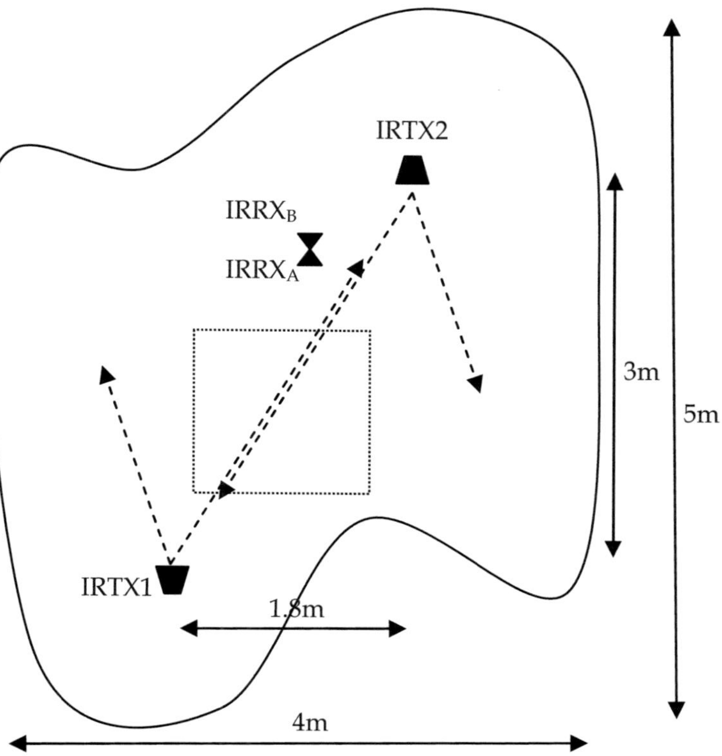

Fig. 19. The area covered by two IRTX devices

The dotted area of Fig. 19 and the corresponding success rate variation of Fig. 9 and Fig. 15 are used in order to describe how the LSR, NRR and DPR rules of Section 5 are used. The SCR is not applied since the target is free to turn in any direction. The real track of the target is the one depicted with the bold continuous line in Fig. 20. The dashed circles indicate the maximum LSR distance that the target was allowed to walk between two localisation processes. For simplicity reasons we only refer here to multiple estimation results of a localisation process when they are used by the position restriction rules.

The LSR and NRR rules are applied first while the DPR rule is used in a supplementary way. If we assume that the positions *P1, P2* and *P3* have already been estimated, the position *P4* is selected as a next step instead *P4′* since the last one deviates the LSR rule. Note that both of *P4* and *P4′* are compliant with the NRR rule but this is not a problem since the NRR is a relaxed LSR rule targeted for the potential extension of the covered area. In the next localisation process none of the estimated positions complies to any of the three rules. If *P5′* is one of the unaccepted positions that is closer to *P4* then the position *P5* is the result of the error correction performed by LSR. In the following localisation process both *P6* and *P6′* are acceptable by LSR and NRR. In this case, the DPR rule can be used to abort *P6′*. The previous positions *P2, P3, P4* and *P5* (i.e., *k=4)* are used by the DPR rule in order to define the rough direction depicted by the dotted lines starting from *P2* in Fig. 20. Finally, the two alternative positions: *P7′* and *P7′′* deviate both the LSR and the DPR rules in the next localisation process but *P7′* is compliant with NRR. Thus, *P7′* is selected in the LSR error correction method that leads to *P7* as the last position of the target in this example. The bold-dashed line of Fig. 20 is the estimated target track.

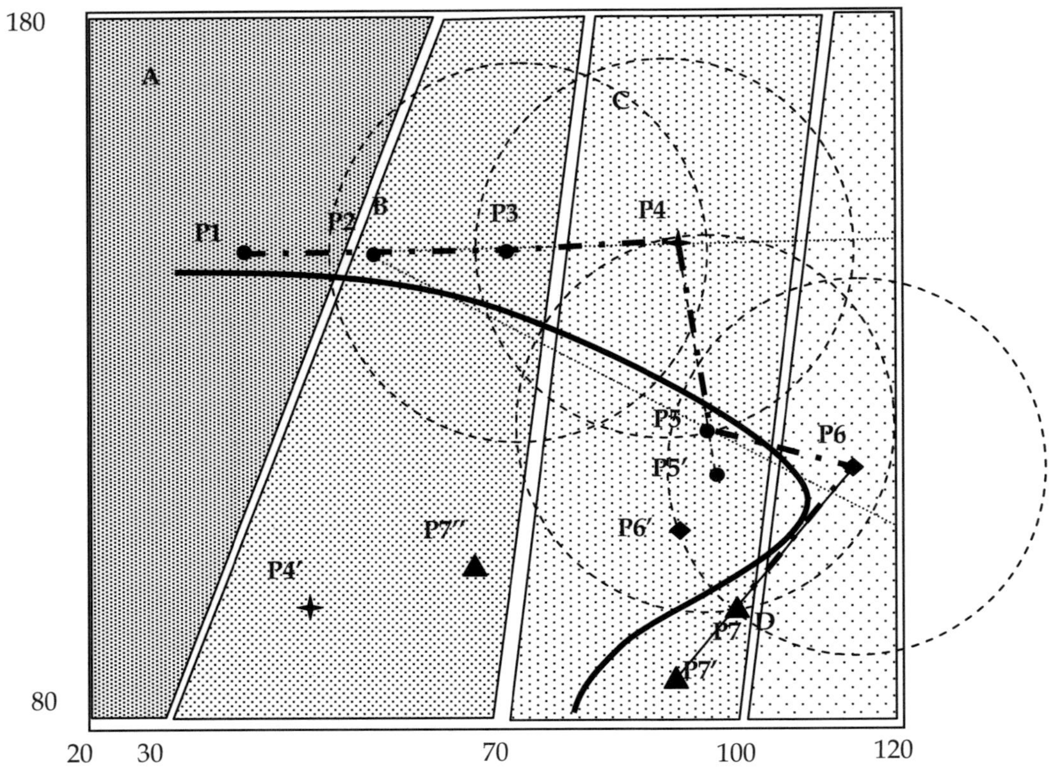

Fig. 20. The use of the LSR, NRR and DPR rules.

7. Conclusions

A novel method for the indoor localisation of a target was presented in this chapter. This method is based on measuring the number of the digital infrared patterns received by the target in a specific time interval (success rate). At least two transmitting devices are placed around the covered area that exceeds 15m², while a pair of infrared receivers are mounted on the target. This area is supposed to be covered by a virtual grid and can be further extended if more transmitters are employed. The grid nodes are visited by the target during a calibration stage when it familiarises with the retrieved success rates. At real time operation the closer grid node is selected and a refinement step based on a 2D interpolation search follows leading to a more accurate position estimation.

The absolute error that can be achieved is less than 10cm but may vary significantly if successive estimations are carried out at the same position. Four deterministic rules are described in order to abort the false estimations caused by dynamic noise and stabilise the estimation procedure. The speed of the localisation procedure depends on the frequency of the carrier that is used in order to shield the patterns from the interference of other infrared sources. The rather long estimation time that is needed for a standard 38KHz carrier frequency can be reduced to less than 100ms if a higher frequency is selected. The design of a custom 1MHz carrier filter was presented as an example.

Future work will focus on experimenting with various infrared pattern structures and system topologies in order to increase the estimation speed and accuracy and expand the area covered. Finally we will attempt to utilise the concept of our system in the case of targets with more degrees of freedom (moving in three dimensions, rotating etc).

8. References

Arana, S. Arana, N., Gracia, J. & Castano, E., High Sensitivity Linear Position Sensor Developed Using Granular Ag-Co, Giant Magnetoresistances. *Sensors And Actuators,* A 123-124, 2005, pp. 116-121.

Arras, K., Tomatis, N., Jensen, B. & Siegward, R., Multisensor On-the-Fly Localisation : Precision and Reliability for Applications. *Elsevier Robotics and Autonomous Systems,* 43(2001), pp. 131-143.

Aytac, T. & Barshan, B., Simultaneous Extraction of Geometry and Surface Properties of Targets Using Simple Infrared Sensors. *Optical Engineering,* 43(10), Oct. 2004, pp. 2437-2447

Bates, D. & Watts, D. (1988). *Nonlinear Regression Analysis and Its Applications,* Wiley Series in Probability and Statistics, Hoboken, NJ

Benet, G, Blanes, F., Simo, J. & Perez, P. Using Infrared Sensors for Distance Measurement in Mobile Robots. *Robot Autonomy Systems,* Vol. 30, 2002, pp. 255-266

Bicho, E., Mallet, P. & Schoner, G. Target Representation on an Autonomous Vehicle with Low Level Sensors, *Int. Journal of Robotics Research,* Vol. 19, No. 5, May 2000, pp. 424-447

Borenstein, J. Everett, B. & Feng, L. (1996). *Navigating Mobile Robots: Systems and Techniques,* A.K. Peters Ltd Wellesley, MA

Clerentin A., Delahoche, A., Brassart, E. & Drocourt, C. Self Localisation: A New Uncertainty Propagation Architecture. *Elsevier Robotics and Autonomous Systems,* 51(2001), pp. 151-166

Flora, C., Ficco, M., Russo, S. & Vecchio, V. Indoor and Outdoor Location Based Services for Portable Wireless Devices. *Proceedings of 1st IEEE Int. Workshop on Services and Infrastructure for Ubiquitous and Mobile Internet,* pp. 244-250, June 2005, Columbus OH

Gramegna, T., Venturino, L., Cicirelli, G., Attolico, G. & Distante, A. Optimisation of the POSIT Algorithm for Indoor Autonomous Navigation. *Elsevier Robotics and Autonomous Systems,* 48(2004), pp. 145-162

Holmberg, P. Ultrasonic Sensor Array for Positioning and Rotation Estimates of Planar Surfaces. *Sensors and Actuators A,* 44(1994), pp. 37-43

Jin, T., Lee, J. & Tso, S. A New Space and Time Sensor Fusion Method for Mobile Robot Navigation. *Wiley Journal of Robotics Systems,* 21(7), 2004, pp. 389-400

Kosel, J. Pfutzner, H., Mehnen, L., Kaniusas, E., Meydan, T., Vazquez, N., Rohn, M., Merlo, A. & Marquardt, B. Non Contact Detection of Magnetoelastic Position Sensors. *Elsevier Sensors and Actuators A,* 123-124 (2005), pp. 349-353

Kzecka, J. Li, F. & Yang, X. Global Localisation and Relative Positioning Based on Scale Invariant Keypoints. *Elsevier Robotics and Autonomous Systems,* 52(2005), pp. 27-38

Ladd, A., Bekiris, K., Rudys, A., Kavraki, L. & Wallach, D. Robotics Based Location Sensing Using Wireless Ethernet. *Wireless Networks,* Vol. 11, No. 1-2, Jan 2005, pp. 189-204

Lancaster, D. (1995). *Active Filter Cookbook.* 2nd Edition Newnes-Elsevier Science, MA

Minami, M., Fukuju, Y., Hirasawa, K., Yokoyama, S., Mizumachi, M., Morikawa, H. & Aoyama, T. Dolphin: A Practical Approach for Implementing a Fully Distributed Indoor Ultrasonic Positioning System. *Lect Not Comp Sci,* 3205, 2004, pp. 347-365

Miura, J., Negishi, Y. & Shirai, Y. Adaptive Robot Speed Control by Considering Map and Motion Uncertainty. *Elsevier Robotics and Autonomous Systems,* 54(2006), pp. 110-117

Novotny, P. & Ferrier, N. Using Infrared Sensors and the Phong Illumination Model to Measure Distances. *Proceedings of the IEEE Int. Conf. On Robotics and Automation,* pp. 1644-1649, 1999, Detroit MI

Petrellis, N. Konofaos, N. & Alexiou, G. Testing IR photon sensors for target localisation applications. *Proceedings of the 1st Int. Workshop on Advances in Sensors and Interfaces.* Aula Magna "Attilo Alto", pp. 153-158, Apr 2005, Bari, Italy

Petrellis, N. Konofaos, N. & Alexiou, G. Target Localisation Utilising the Success Rate in Infrared Pattern Recognition. *IEEE Sensors Journal,* 6(5), 2006, pp. 1355-1364

Petrellis, N. Konofaos, N. & Alexiou, G. Position Estimation on a Grid Based on Infrared Pattern Reception Features. *Int. Workshop on Ubiquitous Computing (IWUC),* pp. 21-28, May 2006, Paphos, Cyprus

Petrellis, N. Konofaos, N. & Alexiou, G. Utilising Infrared Pattern Recognition Features for Indoor Localisation Validated by Future Position Restrictions. 2nd IET Int. Conf. On Intelligent Environments (IE '06), pp. 307-311, July 2006, Athens, Greece

Porta, J. & Krose B. Appearance-based Concurrent Map Building and Localisation. *Elsevier Robotics and Autonomous Systems,* 54(2006), pp. 159-164

Prigge, E. & How, J. Signal Architecture for Distributed Magnetic Local Positioning System. *IEEE Sensors Journal.* Vol. 4, No. 6, 2004, pp. 864-873

Schlageter, V., Besse, P., Popovic, R. & Kucera, P. Tracking System with 5deg of Freedom Using a 2D Array of Hall Sensors and a Permanent Magnet. *Elsevier Sensors and Actuators A,* 92, 2001, pp. 37-42

Se, S., Lowe, D. & Little, J. Mobile Robot Localisation and Mapping With Uncertainty Using Scale Invariant Visual Landmarks. *Int. Journal of Robotics Research.* Vol. 21, No. 8, 2002, pp. 735-758

Thrun, S. A Probabilistic On Line Mapping Algorithm for Team of Robots. *Int Journal of Robotics Research.* Vol. 20, No. 5, May 2001, pp. 335-363

Tovar, B., Gomez, L., Cid, R., Miranda, M., Monroy, R. & Hutchinson, S. Planning Exploration Strategies for Simultaneous Localisation and Mapping. *Elsevier Robotics and Autonomous Systems.* 54(2006), pp. 314-331

Ullate, L., Sanchez, M., Villanueva, E., Parilla, M. & Anaya, J. A Three-Transducer Ultrasonic System for Object Location in the Air. *Elsevier Sensors and Actuators A,* 37-38(1993), pp. 391-396

Victorino A., Rives, P. & Borelly, J. Safe Navigation for Indoor Mobile Robots Part II: Exploration, Self Localisation and Map Building. *Int. Journal of Robotics Research.* Vol. 22, No. 12, Dec 2003, pp. 1019-1039

17

Pseudo Stereovision System (PSVS): A Monocular Mirror-based Stereovision System

Theodore P. Pachidis
Kavala Institute of Technology and Education
Greece

1. Introduction

For the autonomous movement of a robotic system, in real time, it has to perceive its environment, to calculate the position of a target or of a block and to move properly. For this reason, many types of sensors and apparatus have been proposed. The target state is required to be accurately calculated and a desired task or procedure to be safely and successfully integrated. In cases of limited intelligence of the system, mainly in industrial environments, the adaptation of the system to new data is necessary. The advantages of the proper use of sensors mounted on the end effector of a manipulator or on a mobile robot are multiple.

Using cameras as sensors it is possible to have mainly vision systems with one or more cameras. A stereovision system is composed of two cameras. For the recovery of a 3-D scene from a pair of stereo images of the scene, it is required to establish correspondences. Correspondence between points in images is a major step in stereo depth perception. This step is known as the correspondence process, and many algorithms for it have been developed. Another major step is the computation of depth values from the point correspondences.

The stereo process can be summarized by the following steps: 1) detection of features in each image 2) matching of features between images under certain geometric and other constraints and 3) calculation of depth using the disparity values and the geometric parameters of the imaging configuration. While each of these steps is important in the stereo process, the matching of features (correspondence between points) is generally thought to be the most difficult step and can easily become the most time consuming.

Depth perception via stereo disparity is a passive method that does not require any special lighting or scanner to acquire the images. This method may be used to determine depths of points in indoor as well as outdoor scenes, and depths of points that are centimeters or kilometers away from the viewer.

A correspondence algorithm can produce more reliable matches if the underlying images have smaller intensity and geometric difference. If the scene has Lambertian surfaces, there would be no difference in the intensities of corresponding points in images. For stereo images acquired by the two cameras, the focal lengths and zoom levels of the cameras are often slightly different. Differences in the optical properties of the two cameras cause intensity differences between corresponding points in stereo images. The optical axes of the cameras may not lie in the same plane also. These unwanted geometric and intensity differences should be reduced as much as possible to increase the ability to find correspondences reliably.

In cases of monocular (single camera) stereovision systems the above problems are reduced. In these systems, a single camera and some mirrors or a biprism, properly placed, are used, so that the reception of a stereo pair of images to be possible. The correspondence points are usually found on a single line (epipolar line), the intensity differences of these points are reduced and the two virtual cameras, which constitute the stereovision system, have the same geometric properties and parameters.

In this chapter, the design and the construction of a new apparatus for stereovision with a single CCD camera, is presented. It is called Pseudo Stereo Vision System (PSVS) and it is composed of a camera, three mirrors and a beam-splitter. PSVS, compared with other monocular or binocular stereovision systems (Section 2), has the following advantages:

1. It is a relatively low cost and robust apparatus, it has no moving parts and it can be used in place of any vision system.
2. It uses only one common CCD camera and thus the two created virtual cameras of the stereo system have the same geometric properties and parameters.
3. It receives a complex image (the superposition of a stereo pair of images), which is directly processed (pseudo stereo), in a single shot.
4. It has the double resolution of other monocular systems and the same resolution with an ordinary stereo system.
5. It can be constructed to any dimensions covering every type of camera, length of baseline, accurate measurement of depth.
6. Using the correspondence algorithm (Pachidis & Lygouras, 2002a), (Pachidis et al., 2002) and (Pachidis & Lygouras, 2006), it is easy to find points disparities.

Drawbacks of PSVS could be the following:

1. Known correspondence algorithms cannot be implemented to complex images. For this reason, a new correspondence algorithm capable to find correspondences in edges has been developed.
2. Correspondences cannot be found when the two different views of an object are overlapped. In these cases the proposed correspondence algorithm can find correspondences in edges of overlapped objects or parts of them. Moreover, in this chapter, two methods to separate complex images into pairs of stereo images (where any correspondence algorithm can be implemented) are described.

The chapter is organized as follows. In Section 2, single camera stereovision systems, described by other researchers, are examined. In Section 3, construction details of PSVS and refraction phenomena due to the beam-splitter are presented. In Section 4, recalculation of the final equations, taking into consideration refraction phenomena and camera calibration parameters, of the coordinates of a point by using PSVS, are introduced. In Section 5, basic concepts of the correspondence algorithm used are presented. In Section 6, two methods for the separation of a complex image into a pair of stereo images and the reconstruction of them are given. In Section 7, some experimental results are depicted. Finally, in Section 8, conclusions of this work and future plans are presented.

2. Existing Single Camera Stereovision Systems

Many single camera stereovision systems have been proposed in the literature. Teoh and Zhang (Teoh & Zhang, 1984) described a single-lens stereo camera system. Two mirrors, fixed to the body of the camera, make a 45° angle with the optical axis of the camera. A third mirror that can rotate is placed directly in front of the lens. The rotating mirror is made parallel to one of the fixed mirrors and an image is obtained. Then, it is made parallel to the other fixed mirror and another image is obtained. Here, although a single camera is used, the result is the same as using two cameras with parallel optical axes.

Nishimoto and Shirai (Nishimoto & Shirai, 1987) proposed a single-lens camera system that can obtain stereo images. In this system, a glass plate is placed in front of the camera, and images are obtained with the plate at two different rotational positions. When the glass plate is rotated, the optical axes of the camera shifts slightly, simulating two cameras with parallel optical axes. The obtained stereo images have very small disparities making the point correspondence easy. However, only coarse depth values can be obtained from the disparities. This camera system requires two shots from a scene and therefore should be used only in static environments. Otherwise, the scene will change during the time the images are obtained, and the positions of the corresponding points will no longer relate to the depths of points in 3D.

Both of these cameras considerably reduce unwanted geometric and intensity difference between stereo images. But the cameras have parts that should be rotated when obtaining a pair of images. Exact rotation of the parts is a major design issue in these systems, and two shots of a scene are required.

Several researchers demonstrated the use of both curved and planar mirrors to acquire stereo data with a single camera. Curved mirrors have been primarily used to capture a wide field of view. Nayar (Nayar, 1988) suggested a wide field of view stereo system consisting of a conventional camera pointed at two specular spheres. Later, Southwell et al. (Southwell et al., 1996) proposed a similar system using two convex mirrors, one placed on top of the other.

Gosthasby and Gruver (Gosthasby & Gruver, 1993) proposed a single camera system that can obtain images in a single shot using a single lens. The obtained images are reflected about the image of the mirrors axis. This camera system can obtain images in a single shot and through a single camera. But, the reversed image should be transformed to appear as if obtained by cameras with parallel optical axes, before carrying out the correspondence and measuring the depth values from the correspondence. The inter-reflection between the mirrors causes intensity difference between corresponding points in stereo images.

Stereo systems using four planar mirrors were proposed by both Inaba et al (Inaba et al., 1993) and Mathieu and Devernay (Mathieu & Devernay, 1995). In their recent work, Nene and Nayar (Nene & Nayar, 1998) proposed four stereo systems that use a single camera pointed toward planar, hyperboloidal, ellipsoidal, and paraboloidal mirrors. By using of non-planar reflecting surfaces such as hyperboloids and paraboloids, a wide field of view (FOV) images are easily obtained. However, their stereo system needs a complex mirror mechanism. Gluckman and Nayar (Gluckman & Nayar, 1998a) and Gluckman and Nayar (Gluckman & Nayar, 1999) demonstrated how two mirrors in an arbitrary configuration could be self-calibrated and used for single camera stereo. Gluckman and Nayar (Gluckman & Nayar, 1998b) presented the design of a compact panoramic stereo camera, which uses parabolic mirrors and is capable of producing 360° panoramic depth maps. Gluckman and

Nayar (Gluckman & Nayar, 2000) also presented a novel catadioptric sensor, which uses mirrors to produce rectified stereo images.
Lee, Kweon and Cipolla (Lee et al., 1999) and Lee and Kweon (Lee & Kweon, 2000) proposed a practical stereo camera system that uses only one camera and a biprism placed in front of the camera. The equivalent of a stereo pair of images is formed as the left and right halves of a single charge coupled device (CCD) image using a biprism. This system is more accurate for nearby objects than for far ones. Their system is simple but a biprism cannot be found easily. Peleg et al. (Peleg et al., 2001) presented two stereovision systems with one camera by using a spiral-like mirror or lens. These systems, right now, cannot be used in real time applications. By imaging an object and its mirror reflection, a stereo image can also be obtained using only a single mirror, Wuerz et al (Wuerz et al., 2001).
Song et al (Song et al., 2002) presented an apparatus with a rotated mirror. For the measurement of depth, they observed that from the sequence of the captured images, the velocity of pixels is increased when the distance of objects in a scene is increased. Finally, Kawasue and Oya (Kawasue & Oya, 2002) presented an apparatus based on a single camera and a rotated mirror. The apparatus can be only used in a small number of applications.

3. System Description and Analysis

3.1 System Description

The main idea is based on using three mirrors with a 100% reflection of their incident light and a 50% beam-splitter. Refraction phenomena do not appear to first three mirrors because the first surface of them is used (first surface mirrors).
To determine the relative location of mirrors in PSVS, a right-hand orthogonal coordinate system is defined. *Z*-axis of this system coicides with the optical axis of the real camera and the origin of it is the optical center *O* of the camera. *X*-axis, vertical to *Z*-axis, is parallel with the direction of columns increment in the image plane and *Y*-axis is vertical to the plane *XZ*. Mirrors of PSVS are vertically located to *XZ* plane and form 45° angle with *Z*-axis (Fig. 1(a)).
It is considered that initially no refraction phenomena exist due to mirror (1) (i.e. by using a Pellicle beam-splitter). Then two virtual cameras are created with their optical axes parallel to the optical axis of the real camera. These cameras are symmetrically located to *Z*-axis. They have the same geometric properties and parameters (the same of the real camera). Consequently, these virtual cameras constitute an ideal stereovision system with two cameras. This vision system, as it presented here, receives in a single shot one complex image. This image consists of two superimposed images captured from the left and right views of the apparatus.
If the intensity of each pixel of an image captured from the left and from the right view are $I_L(i,j)$ and $I_R(i,j)$ respectively, the intensity of each pixel of the complex image is given as:

$$I_C(i,j) = k \cdot I_L(i,j) + (1-k) \cdot I_R(i,j) \tag{1}$$

Where *i*, *j*, are indices of the current row and column of a pixel in the image. *k* is a parameter (*k*=0.5 with the beam-splitter used) declaring the reduction of the intensity of pixels of each view because of the beam-splitter. It is obvious that the intensity in a complex image never exceeds its maximum value, (for gray-scale images $\mathrm{I_C(i,j)} \leq 255$). The baseline of this stereo system is *b* and it is the distance between the two virtual parallel optical axes (Fig. 1(a)).

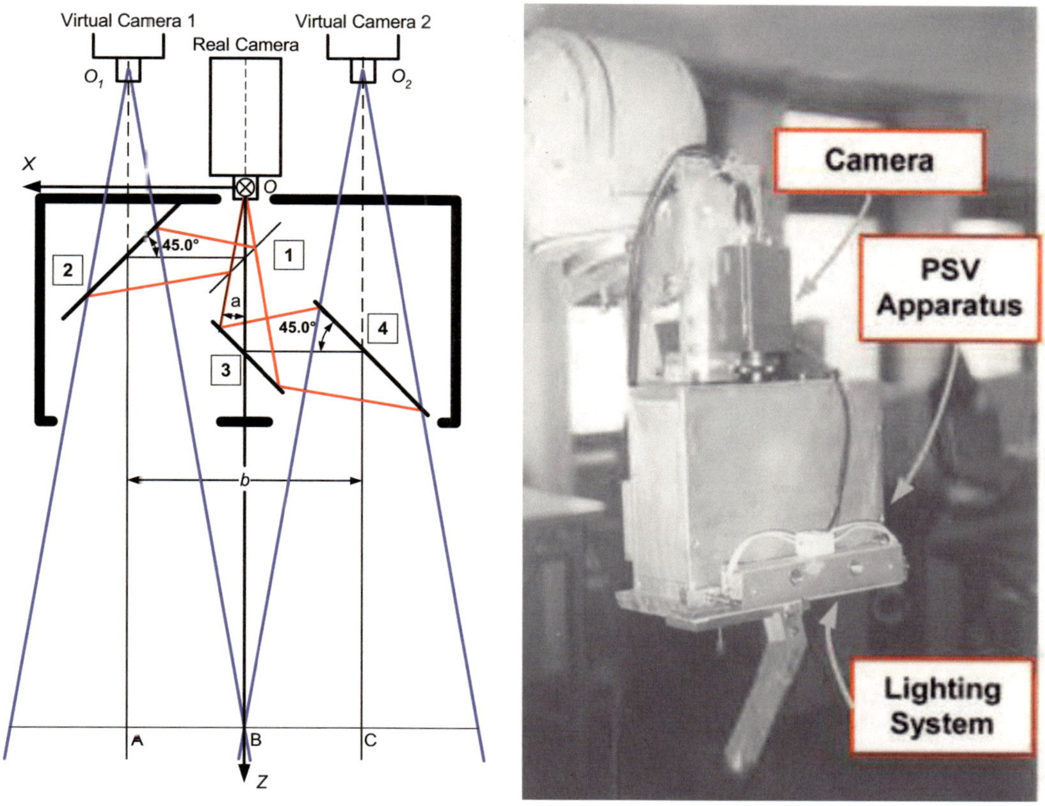

(a) (b)

Figure 1. PSVS: (a) Mirrors position (b) PSV apparatus mounted on the end effector of a PUMA 761 robotic manipulator

Problems with correct luminosity are reduced from the system by using a regulated lighting system on the apparatus (Fig. 1(b)). A small laser module is incorporated to the apparatus. The red spot laser beam is used to periodically check the alignment of mirrors. The front view of the PSVS is properly formulated to accept "spatial" or color filters.

3.2 PSVS Geometry Equations

In PSVS, to avoid probable shades of parts of complex images because of the improper size or of the location of mirrors and the appearance of ghost images, the calculation of mirrors dimensions is required. The equation providing these dimensions is the following:

$$AC = AB + BC \Rightarrow AC = \left(\frac{OB \cdot \tan a \cdot \cos \omega_1}{\tan(\omega_1 - a)} + OB \cdot \tan a \cdot \sin \omega_1 \right) + \left(\frac{OB \cdot \tan a}{\sin \omega_1 + \cos \omega_1 \cdot \tan a} \right) \quad (2)$$

Angle $2a$ represents the angular field of view of the lens while ω_1 is the angle the optical axis forms with a mirror plane (Fig. 2). OB is the path a light beam follows along the optical axis from the optical center of the real camera to a mirror. From equation (2) partial cases for ω_1=45° and ω_1=90° are derived.

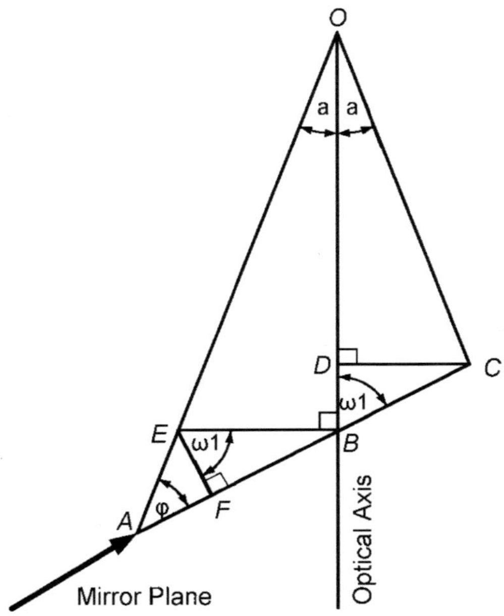

Figure 2. Calculation of mirror dimensions

Case studies:

1. $\omega_1 = 45°$. Then:

$$AC = AB + BC = \frac{\sqrt{2} \cdot OB \cdot \tan a}{1 - \tan a} + \frac{\sqrt{2} \cdot OB \cdot \tan a}{1 + \tan a} = \sqrt{2} \cdot OB \cdot \tan 2a \tag{3}$$

Equation (3), permits the calculation of the dimension of each mirror which forms an angle of $\omega_1 = 45°$ with the optical axis. More details can be found in (Pachidis & Lygouras, 2005). The other dimension of each mirror is vertical to the optical axis, namely $\omega_1 = 90°$.

2. $\omega_1 = 90°$. Then:

$$AC = AB + BC = OB \cdot \tan a + OB \cdot \tan a = 2 \cdot OB \cdot \tan a \tag{4}$$

Sections *AB* and *BC* are equal, when $\omega_1 = 90°$. From the previous relations and taking into consideration that the optical axes are vertical to the sub-frames (left and right views), it results that each virtual optical axis will pass from the geometric center of the corresponding sub-frame (view) captured by PSVS.

In PSVS, the four mirrors are grouped in two pairs. The first pair consists of mirrors (1) and (2) and it is responsible for the creation of the virtual camera 1, while the second pair consists of the mirrors (3) and (4) and it is responsible for the creation of the virtual camera 2.

By definition the distance of the two pairs of mirrors is the distance *AB* (Fig. 3). The estimation of distance *OB* used in the previous equations (Fig. 2), giving the dimensions of mirrors, presuppose the knowledge of the length of baseline *b* or and the distance *AB* of the two mirror pairs. The minimum length of the baseline b_{min} depends on the angular field of view 2*a* of the lens, the distance of the beam-splitter from the optical center *O* and the distance *AB* of the mirror pairs.

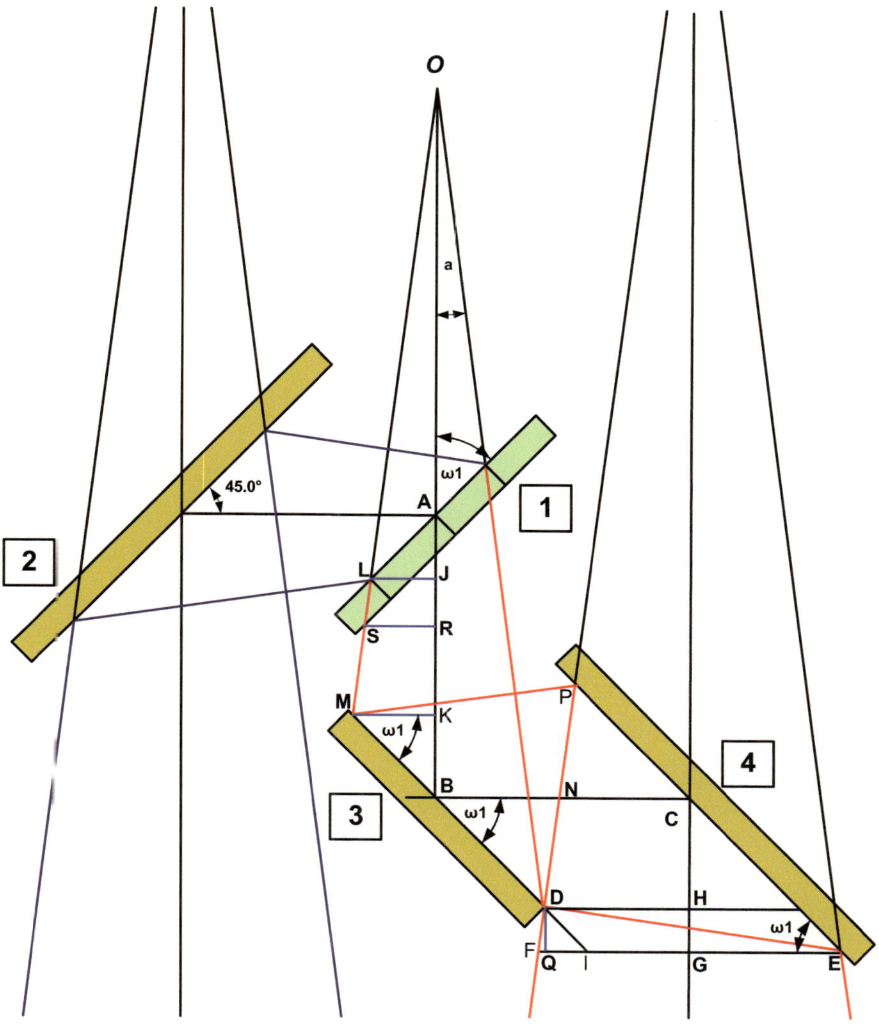

Figure 3. Calculation of b_{min} and AB_{min}

The design of PSVS permits to freely select the distance OA of the real camera optical center from the beam-splitter. Only a maximum value of it, OA_{max}, is necessary to be determined. Equation (5) provides the minimum length of the baseline, b_{min} in its general form and equation (6) b_{min} when the angle of mirrors with the optical axis is 45°:

$$b_{min} = \frac{4 \cdot \tan a \cdot (\tan \omega_1 - \tan a)}{\tan \omega_1 \cdot (1 + \tan^2 a) \cdot (1 - \tan \omega_1 \cdot \tan a_1) - 2 \cdot \tan a \cdot (\tan \omega_1 - \tan a)} \cdot (OA + AB_{min}) \quad (5)$$

$$b_{min} = \frac{4 \cdot \tan a}{(1 - \tan a)^2} \cdot (OA + AB_{min}) \quad (6)$$

It is considered that the distance OA has its maximum value.

The minimum distance of the two pairs of mirrors, $AB_{\min}$, in its general form, is given by the relation (7):

$$AB_{\min} = \frac{\sin\omega_1 + \cos\omega_1 \cdot \tan a}{\sin\omega_1 + \cos\omega_1 \cdot \tan a - \tan a \cdot \sin\omega_1} \cdot \left[\frac{OA \cdot \tan a \cdot \cos^2\omega_1}{\tan(\omega_1 - a)} + OA \cdot \tan a \cdot \sin\omega_1 \cdot \cos\omega_1 + \frac{OA \cdot \tan a \cdot \sin\omega_1}{\sin\omega_1 + \cos\omega_1 \cdot \tan a} + \frac{d}{\cos\omega_1} \cdot \cos a \right] \tag{7}$$

For angle $\omega_1 = 45^o$, (7) is simplified to:

$$AB_{\min} = OA \cdot \frac{2 \cdot \tan a}{(1 - \tan a)} + \sqrt{2} \cdot d \cdot \cos a \cdot (1 + \tan a) \tag{8}$$

To calculate the *Minimum Distance of Common View*, Fig. 1(a) is used. The distance of interest is *OB*. The point *B* represents the first common point, which is created from the two virtual cameras, where no refraction phenomena are taken into consideration. From the right triangle (O_1AB), it results:

$$\tan a = \frac{AB}{O_1A} \Rightarrow O_1A = \frac{AB}{\tan a} \Rightarrow OB + \frac{b}{2} = \frac{\frac{b}{2}}{\tan a} \Rightarrow OB = \frac{b}{2\tan a} - \frac{b}{2} \tag{9}$$

3.3 Refraction Phenomena

In this part, the influence of refraction phenomena due to mirror (1) of PSVS is examined. It is desirable, the left and right view of a scene captured by means of PSVS to coincide and to have exactly the same magnification. The second virtual camera, due to refraction phenomena to beam-splitter, undergoes a parallel displacement to the optical axis of the real camera. Simultaneously the optical center O_2 shifts on the virtual optical axis (Fig. 4).

To accurately calculate paths of a light beam in two different directions, created by these two virtual cameras, the displacement of the virtual axis and the shifting of the virtual optical center O_2 must be calculated. Using Snell law, (Pedrotti & Pedrotti, 1998), the refraction angle of a light ray from the optical center *O*, along the optical axis, is the following:

$$\theta_r = \sin^{-1}\left(\frac{n_{air}}{n_{glass}} \cdot \sin\theta_i \right) \tag{10}$$

Where θ_i is the incidence angle. If ω_1 is the angle formed by the optical axis with mirror (Fig. 4), then $\theta_i = 90^o - \omega_1$. If *d* is the mirror (1) thickness the displacement *m* of the second virtual camera, after some simple trigonometric calculations, can be calculated as:

$$m = \frac{d \cdot \cos(\omega_1 + \theta_r)}{\cos\theta_r} = \frac{d \cdot \sin(\theta_i - \sin^{-1}(\frac{n_{air}}{n_{glass}} \cdot \sin\theta_i))}{\sqrt{1 - \frac{n^2_{air}}{n^2_{glass}} \cdot \sin^2\theta_i}} \tag{11}$$

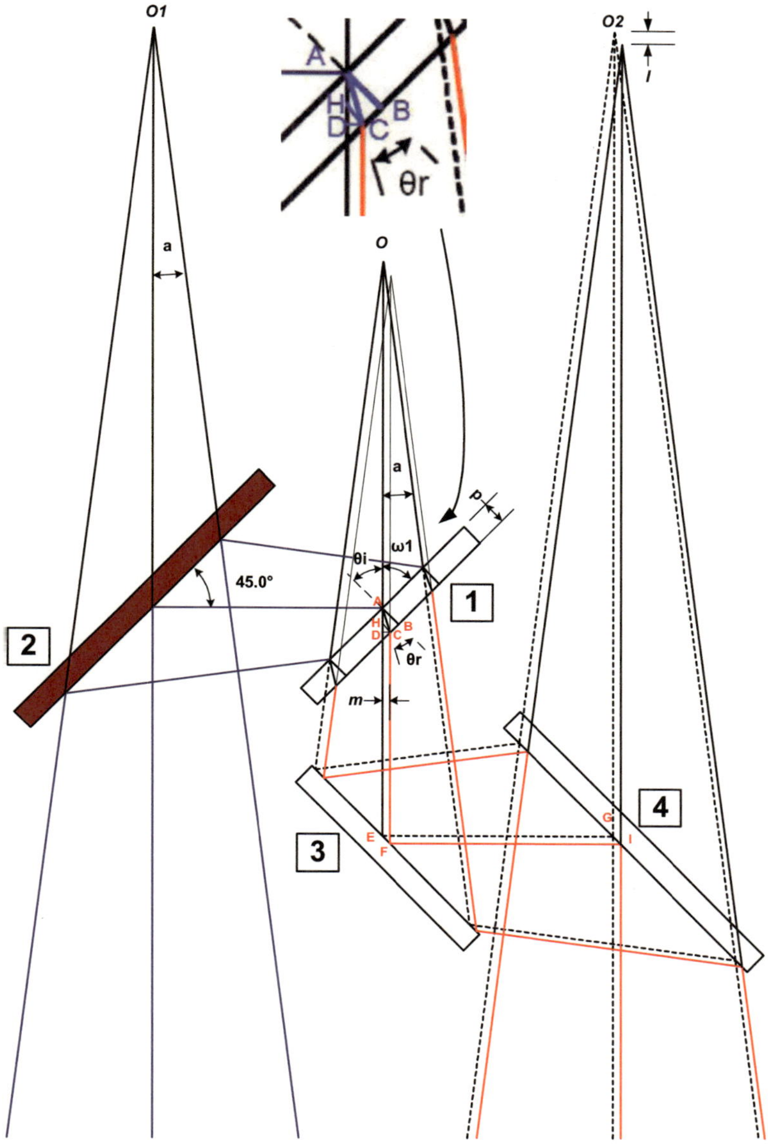

Figure 4. Refraction phenomena due to beam-splitter

The shifting of the optical center O_2, l, is calculated as the difference in distance of a ray from the optical center O_2 until mirror (4), when this ray is radiated through mirror (1) with refraction and without refraction. The result is the following relation:

$$l = \frac{d}{\cos\theta_r}\left(1 - \sin(\omega_1 + \theta_r) + \cos(\omega_1 + \theta_r)\cdot\tan\omega_1\right) = \frac{d}{\sqrt{1 - \frac{n^2_{air}}{n^2_{glass}}\cdot\sin^2\theta_i}}\left(1 - \frac{n_{air}}{n_{glass}}\right) \qquad (12)$$

We can see that parameters m and l are depending on the refraction indices and the beam-splitter thickness. For incidence angle $\theta_i = 45^o$, m and l have the values of Table 1.

m (mm)	0.329142
l (mm)	0.377964

Table 1. Values of parameters m and l in mm

By means of the above results for the displacement m and the shifting l the construction of the apparatus could be separated in two partial cases. In first case the simplicity in construction and in mirrors alignment is desirable. The distance between mirrors (1) and (2) or (3) and (4) is selected to be exactly the same and equal to $b/2$. Then, the second virtual camera optical axis, due to refraction phenomena to mirror (1), is displaced along X-axis by m and the optical center O_2 is shifted along Z-axis by l. Shifting by l means that the left view of the apparatus, in relation with the right view, is a bit magnified. This means that not all the corresponding points are found in exactly the same scan line (epipolar line) and a correspondence algorithm should be able to manipulate this kind of points.

In second case, during construction and calibration the distance between mirrors (3) and (4) is regulated to be $b/2+l$. Then the result is a ray radiated from the optical center O to follow slightly different in length paths in two different directions. The magnification of the two virtual cameras is exactly the same and the displacement of the second virtual axis with respect to the optical axis of the real camera is $b/2+m+l$. In this case the construction and the calibration procedure requires the careful placement of mirrors (3) and (4). The corresponding points are always found in the same scan line (epipolar line).

4. Coordinates of a Random Point in 3D Space - Recalculation

To calculate the modified equations, giving the coordinates of a random point in 3D space, we solve the stereo problem using as cameras the two virtual cameras created by PSVS. Each of the above virtual cameras can be separately calibrated and the matrix $\boldsymbol{A}$ with the intrinsic parameters can be found. A right hand ortho-normal coordinate system with origin the optical center O of the real camera and Z-axis to coincide with the optical axis of the real camera is established (Fig. 5). The coordinates of a point P in space, with respect to this coordinate system, are expressed by the vector $\boldsymbol{X}=[x,y,z,1]^T$ while the coordinates of optical centers O_1 and O_2 are provided from vectors $\boldsymbol{X_{oL}}=[x_{oL},y_{oL},z_{oL}]^T$ and $\boldsymbol{X_{oR}}=[x_{oR},y_{oR},z_{oR}]^T$ respectively. Then, using matrix relations, the calculation of vectors $\boldsymbol{m_L}=[u_L,v_L,1]^T$, $\boldsymbol{m_R}=[u_R,v_R,1]^T$ in the image plane for each virtual camera of a point P is possible. Here, the assumption made, is that the two virtual cameras are parallel to the real camera as a result of PSVS mirrors alignment and checking procedure (Pachidis & Lygouras, 2002b). Thus, rotation matrices $\boldsymbol{R_{oL}}$, $\boldsymbol{R_{oR}}$ describing the orientation of the virtual cameras with respect to the real camera are equal to the identified matrix $\boldsymbol{I_{3x3}}$. The calculation methodology provides equations giving the coordinates of a point in space, in a more general form. Then, special case studies concerning PSVS are examined.

$$\boldsymbol{m}_L = \lambda \cdot \boldsymbol{A}_L \cdot [\boldsymbol{R}_{oL} \quad -\boldsymbol{X}_{oL}] \cdot \boldsymbol{X} \tag{13}$$

$$\boldsymbol{m}_R = \lambda \cdot \boldsymbol{A}_R \cdot [\boldsymbol{R}_{oR} \quad -\boldsymbol{X}_{oR}] \cdot \boldsymbol{X} \tag{14}$$

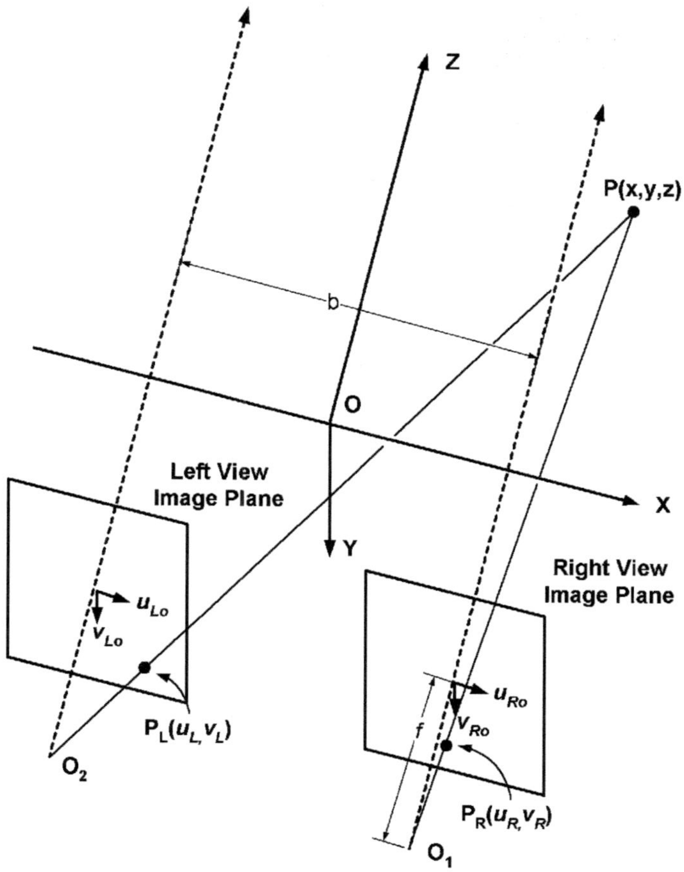

Figure 5. In this figure the established ortho-normal coordinate system is illustrated

Matrices A_L, A_R, (providing intrinsic parameters of cameras) as they are calculated, using the calibration method proposed by Z. Zhang (Zhang, 2000) , are of the form:

$$A_L = \begin{bmatrix} a_{u_L} & c_L & u_{Lo} \\ 0 & a_{v_L} & v_{Lo} \\ 0 & 0 & 1 \end{bmatrix}, \quad A_R = \begin{bmatrix} a_{u_R} & c_R & u_{Ro} \\ 0 & a_{v_R} & v_{Ro} \\ 0 & 0 & 1 \end{bmatrix} \tag{15}$$

In the previous matrices, (u_{Lo}, v_{Lo}) and (u_{Ro}, v_{Ro}) are the coordinates of the principal points in each image view, a_{u_L} , a_{u_R} are the horizontal scale factors and a_{v_L} , a_{v_R} are the vertical scale factors. The parameters c_L and c_R describe the skew of the corresponding image axes. The mean value of parameters c_L, c_R is near zero, thus c_L=c_R=0. Making some multiplications from relations (13) and (14) the following systems of equations are derived:

$$\begin{bmatrix} u_L \\ v_L \\ 1 \end{bmatrix} = \lambda \cdot \begin{bmatrix} a_{u_L} \cdot (x - x_{oL}) + u_{Lo} \cdot (z - z_{oL}) \\ a_{v_L} \cdot (y - y_{oL}) + v_{Lo} \cdot (z - z_{oL}) \\ (z - z_{oL}) \end{bmatrix} \tag{16}$$

and

$$\begin{bmatrix} u_R \\ v_R \\ 1 \end{bmatrix} = \lambda \cdot \begin{bmatrix} a_{u_R} \cdot (x - x_{oR}) + u_{Ro} \cdot (z - z_{oR}) \\ a_{v_R} \cdot (y - y_{oR}) + v_{Ro} \cdot (z - z_{oR}) \\ (z - z_{oR}) \end{bmatrix} \tag{17}$$

Where λ is a parameter. By the solution of the previous systems the following equations, providing coordinates of a point in a 3D space are calculated:

$$x = \frac{(u_R - u_{Ro})}{a_{u_R}} \cdot (z - z_{oR}) + x_{oR} \text{ or } x = \frac{(u_L - u_{Lo})}{a_{u_L}} \cdot (z - z_{oL}) + x_{oL} \tag{18}$$

$$y = \frac{(v_R - v_{Ro})}{a_{v_R}} \cdot (z - z_{oR}) + y_{oR} \text{ or } y = \frac{(v_L - v_{Lo})}{a_{v_L}} \cdot (z - z_{oL}) + y_{oL} \tag{19}$$

$$z = \frac{a_{u_L} \cdot (u_R - u_{Ro}) \cdot z_{oR} - a_{u_R} \cdot (u_L - u_{Lo}) \cdot z_{oL} + a_{u_L} \cdot a_{u_R} \cdot (x_{oL} - x_{oR})}{a_{u_L} \cdot (u_R - u_{Ro}) - a_{u_R} \cdot (u_L - u_{Lo})} \tag{20}$$

To find the form of final equations, adapted to PSVS, some simplifications were made. These simplifications are:

$$x_{oL} = -\frac{b}{2} - m,\ y_{oL} = 0,\ z_{oL} = -\frac{b}{2} + l, \quad x_{oR} = \frac{b}{2},\ y_{oR} = 0,\ z_{oR} = -\frac{b}{2} \tag{21}$$

Where the parallel displacement m and the shifting l (Fig. 4) due to refraction phenomena in mirror (1) are given from equations (11) and (12).
Substituting the equal values from (21), equations (18-20), are simplified to:

$$x = \frac{1}{a_{uR}} \cdot \left(z + \frac{b}{2}\right) \cdot (u_R - u_{Ro}) + \frac{b}{2} \text{ or } x = \frac{1}{a_{uL}} \cdot \left(z + \frac{b}{2} - l\right) \cdot (u_L - u_{Lo}) - \frac{b}{2} - m \tag{22}$$

$$y = \frac{1}{a_{vR}} \cdot \left(z + \frac{b}{2}\right) \cdot (v_R - v_{Ro}) \text{ or } y = \frac{1}{a_{vL}} \cdot \left(z + \frac{b}{2} - l\right) \cdot (v_L - v_{Lo}) \tag{23}$$

$$z = \frac{a_{uR} \cdot a_{uL} \cdot (b + m) + a_{uR} \cdot l \cdot (u_L - u_{Lo})}{a_{uR} \cdot (u_L - u_{Lo}) - a_{uL} \cdot (u_R - u_{Ro})} - \frac{b}{2} \tag{24}$$

Equations (22-24) are more simplified, if the origins of images from the two different views coincide and the scale factors horizontally and vertically are equal. Then the relations in (25), as result of mirrors alignment in PSVS and careful calibration of virtual cameras, are valid.

$$u_{Lo} = u_{Ro} = u_o,\ v_{Lo} = v_{Ro} = v_o,\ a_{uR} = a_{uL} = a_u,\ a_{vR} = a_{vL} = a_u \tag{25}$$

The simplified equations are:

$$x = \frac{1}{a_u} \cdot \left(z + \frac{b}{2}\right) \cdot (u_R - u_o) + \frac{b}{2} \text{ or } x = \frac{1}{a_u} \cdot \left(z + \frac{b}{2} - l\right) \cdot (u_L - u_o) - \frac{b}{2} - m \tag{26}$$

$$y = \frac{1}{a_v} \cdot \left(z + \frac{b}{2} \right) \cdot (v_R - v_o) \text{ or } y = \frac{1}{a_v} \cdot \left(z + \frac{b}{2} - l \right) \cdot (v_L - v_o) \tag{27}$$

$$z = \frac{a_u \cdot (b+m) + l \cdot (u_L - u_o)}{u_L - u_R} - \frac{b}{2} \tag{28}$$

Equations (25-28) correspond to the first case of mirrors location and alignment as it is described in a previous section. According to the second case of mirrors location and alignment, equations (30-32) are derived. Coordinates of the optical centers O_1 and O_2 are given from the relations in (29):

$$x_{oL} = -\frac{b}{2} - m - l,\ y_{oL} = 0,\ z_{oL} = -\frac{b}{2},\ \ x_{oR} = \frac{b}{2},\ y_{oR} = 0,\ z_{oR} = -\frac{b}{2} \tag{29}$$

$$x = \frac{1}{a_u} \cdot \left(z + \frac{b}{2} \right) \cdot (u_R - u_o) + \frac{b}{2} \text{ or } x = \frac{1}{a_u} \cdot \left(z + \frac{b}{2} \right) \cdot (u_L - u_o) - \frac{b}{2} - m - l \tag{30}$$

$$y = \frac{1}{a_v} \cdot \left(z + \frac{b}{2} \right) \cdot (v_R - v_o) \text{ or } y = \frac{1}{a_v} \cdot \left(z + \frac{b}{2} \right) \cdot (v_L - v_o) \tag{31}$$

$$z = \frac{a_u \cdot (b + m + l)}{u_L - u_R} - \frac{b}{2} \tag{32}$$

According to the previous analysis, coordinates of the tracks of a point in 3D space, in a complex image, have different values along *X*-axis but the same values along *Y*-axis. Solving equations (27) or (31) in relation to v_R and v_L, the difference $v_L - v_R$ represents the difference in coordinates of the tracks of a point *P* along *Y*-axis (*Y* disparity) respectively:

$$v_L - v_R = y \cdot a_v \cdot \frac{1}{\left(z + \frac{b}{2} - l \right) \cdot \left(z + \frac{b}{2} \right)} \ \text{(a)} \quad \text{and } v_L - v_R = 0 \ \text{(b)} \tag{33}$$

It is concluded that when the first set of equations is used (26-28) the two tracks of point P in the complex image are not found in the same line (33(a)). However, this deviation creates a measurement error less than one pixel, which it is decreased as the depth z is increased. Consequently, it is considered that $v_L - v_R \cong 0$. When the second set of equations (30-32) is used (with the proper location and alignment of mirrors), the tracks of a point P are found in exactly the same scan line as the equation (33(b)) shows.

5. Correspondence Algorithm - Basic Concepts

The proposed correspondence algorithm belongs in high-level feature-based algorithms and particularly in algorithms that can find correspondences in curves (Dhond & Aggarwal, 1989) (Goulermas & Liatsis, 2001). It is based on the concept of seeds and it is executed in two stages. To implement the proposed correspondence algorithm, a complex image or a stereo pair of images are initially processed. In the application developed in Visual C++ (Pachidis et al., 2002), (Pachidis & Lygouras, 2006), (Pachidis et al., 2006), a variety of filters and edge detection methods may be used. In the final edge images, the desired edges are selected as left view edges, in a semi-automatic procedure; i.e., by coloring a pixel manually and then by propagating the pixel to the whole edge. When all the desired edges are colored, with different color values, the corresponding edges are detected. In an automatic procedure, each left view edge is automatically selected first, the corresponding edge is detected and the whole procedure is repeated until all the pairs of corresponding edges are detected. Three criteria are used to select the corresponding edge:

1. The horizontal upper and lower limits of the initial edge plus a small permissible deviation measured in pixels.
2. The number of pixels in each initial edge extended by a predefined percentage of the initial number of pixels.
3. The criterion of the most probable edge. According to this criterion, the most probable candidate edge corresponds to the maximum population of pixels at the same distance from the initial image. At this distance, at least one pixel of the candidate edge is detected.

Using this algorithm the selection and processing of 11 independent edges or lines with different colors, of an image of the same scene, is possible. The results, namely, the color of points, their image plane coordinates and the disparities are stored in a matrix and at the same time in a file for future use.

An example is illustrated in Fig. 6(a). The color of the initial desired edge is on gray-scale. The other edges are excluded when the first two criteria are applied. Only one of them has the same upper and lower limits and a smaller number of pixels than the predefined one. For the application of the third criterion, seven points are automatically selected from the initial edge. After the criterion is applied, only one seed is found. This seed is propagated and the corresponding edge is created. Then, having implemented the second stage of the algorithm, the corresponding pairs of points are found. This mapping is illustrated with the parallel lines in Fig. 6(b).

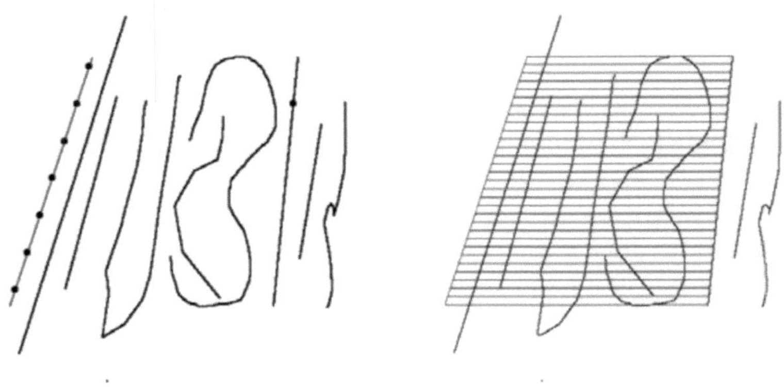

(a) (b)

Figure 6. The correspondence procedure is illustrated. a) In the first stage, seven points are selected for correspondence from the desired edge. Only one corresponding point was found. b) In the second stage, thirty corresponding pairs of points were found. Parallel lines show this mapping

6. Complex Image Separation and Stereo Images Reconstruction

PSVS, as it was presented right here, could be successfully used to calculate coordinates of random points in space, as well as to find edge or point correspondences of objects in any depth. This system, contrary to other monocular systems, captures two different stereo views in a single shot and with accuracy in measurements better of previous systems because of the angular field of view. The disparity values, detected by the system for an object, are the same with an ordinary stereo system with two cameras. But PSVS is faster and cheaper than an ordinary stereo system (one camera, one frame grabber card, one shot, one image processing). Using a high frame rate camera could be used to any application needs a fast vision system. In systems, where accurate measurements are required, in small distances, it can be used with success. Our system was initially developed for an arc welding system where the camera and the torch are mounted on the end-effector of a PUMA robotic manipulator. In this application, the PSVS is near the torch and consequently scene views are simple. A plethora of robotic tasks and procedures can be successfully manipulated by using PSVS (Pachidis et al., 2005).

When calculation of point locations in separated views of a scene is desirable, the separation of the complex image into a pair of stereo images is required. After their initial separation, the left and right images are reconstructed and can be processed as images of an ordinary stereo system. The complex image separation is examined in two cases. In the first case, a monochrome CCD camera is used. If $I_R(x,y)$, $I_L(x,y)$ and $I_C(x,y)$ are functions of the right, left, and complex images respectively, then the intensity of each pixel of the complex image is given by:

$$I_C(x,y) = k\, I_R(x,y) + (1-k)\, I_L(x,y) \qquad (34)$$

where k ($0<k<1$) is the portion of the reflecting and the transmitting radiation from the beam-splitter. Here, k=0.5 (50% beam-splitter). In this case the intensities of the corresponding pixels of the right and left images are added and the separation of the complex image is not possible. Generally the intensities of the corresponding pixels of these sub-images, in each location, have different intensities.

Figure 7. Complementary spatial filters

For the separation of a complex image into a pair of stereo images, the concept of "spatial filters" is introduced. With the term "spatial filters" we consider filters made from plastic film with specific form of transparent and black areas, i.e. chessboard like with squares, or rectangles, or parallel lines. The filter of one view must act complementary to the filter of the other view (Fig. 7). The size of still elements is determined to be equal or multiple of the apparent size of a pixel in the distance where the filters are mounted on the PSVS. The filters are mounted on the front view of PSVS creating this way shading areas to left and right sub-images. As these images are superimposed, illuminated areas of the initial images create the complex image. For the separation of the complex image is required:

1. Alignment of the spatial filters by means of the regulators adapted on the PSVS and the related software developed for this reason.
2. Storage of the initial images (mask-images) captured by each view separately, in white background (white scene). In normal operation, these images are used for extraction of the pair of images from the complex image.

Then, separation of a complex image into a pair of stereo images is possible by selecting from the complex image only pixels that their corresponding pixels to each mask-image pixels have intensities greater than zero. The intensity of each pixel of mask-images is defined as $I_{RM}(x,y)$, $I_{LM}(x,y)$, for the right and left image respectively. Then, the intensities of pixels of the right and left images are of the form:

$$I_R(x,y) = \begin{cases} I_C(x,y) & if\ I_{RM}(x,y) > 0 \\ 0 & if\ I_{RM}(x,y) = 0 \end{cases} \tag{35}$$

$$I_L(x,y) = \begin{cases} I_C(x,y) & if\ I_{LM}(x,y) > 0 \\ 0 & if\ I_{LM}(x,y) = 0 \end{cases} \tag{36}$$

These images have black areas and areas with pixel intensities from only one view. For the reconstruction of these images, we borrow a concept and the related theory used in error recovery approaches for MPEG encoded video over Asynchronous transfer Mode (ATM) networks. From the proposed approaches, spatial error concealment has been adopted (Salama et al.,1995), (Salama, 1999), (Asbun & Delp, 1999). The method is used to reconstruct video images after their reception through the net. Because of the important percentage of black areas in the separated images, the above method, that is the estimation of missing blocks by using spatial interpolation, was modified and adapted to the requirements of this specific application.

According to our method two new concepts were used. The first one is the estimation of each block's start point (up and left pixel) as well as of the size of the block. Then the size of the block continuously changes as block pixels are reconstructed. The second concept is referred to the sequence each pixel in a block is examined. We propose a method, called "the Meander Method (MM)", where pixels in a block are scanned from the start point to a block center pixel, following a circular path, so that a meander to be created (Fig. 8).

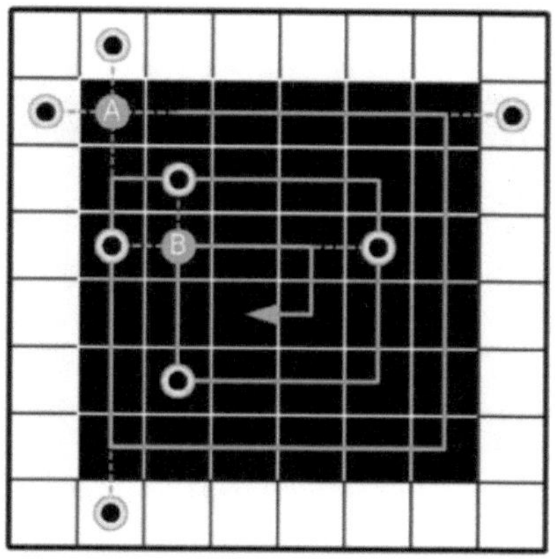

Figure 8. A typical block (black pixels) and a meander are depicted. With A and B, the reconstruction of two pixels from the adjacent non-black pixels is presented.

MM is more efficient than simple spatial error concealment, permitting the reconstruction of variable size blocks with the block densities appeared to the separated images. If the block is restricted to one black pixel the new value of it is the mean value of the 4-neighbor pixels surrounding the pixel. If the coordinates of a start point in a block are (k, l) and the size of the block is nxo, the intensity of each black pixel is calculated by using the following equation:

$$I(k+i,l+j)=\frac{o-\left(j+\frac{1}{2}\right)}{\lambda\cdot o}\cdot I(k+i,l-1)+\frac{j+\frac{1}{2}}{\lambda\cdot o}I(k+i,l+o+1)+ \\ +\frac{n-\left(i+\frac{1}{2}\right)}{\lambda\cdot n}\cdot I(k-1,l+j)+\frac{i+\frac{1}{2}}{\lambda\cdot n}\cdot I(k+n+1,l+j) \tag{37}$$

Where i, j are the variable indices in the block and λ is a parameter that determines the number of terms. Factors, multiplying pixel intensities, determine the contribution of each term to the final intensity.

When the whole image has been reconstructed, a proper smoothing filter is implemented to each image. The basic steps of the proposed algorithm are:

1. Scan each image from the upper left corner and find the start point and size of each black area in the image according to a pre-specified threshold.
2. Store the parameters in a matrix (start point location, n, o, dimension).
3. For each shape, beginning from the start point, move right and down and replace the intensity of a black pixel with a new value, calculated from adjacent non black pixels.
4. Repeat the procedure until all black pixels of the shape to be replaced by non-black pixels.
5. Repeat steps 3 and 4 for all black pixels of shapes until the whole image to be reconstructed.
6. Apply a smoothing filter to each image of the pair of the reconstructed images.

A number of problems are encountered by trying to use this method. If the shape's size is too small, diffusion of images and Moiré effects are observed and the complex image cannot be separated. From the other side if the shape's size is large the separation of the complex image is possible but the reconstruction has as result low quality images. An important portion of the information is lost.

In the second case for our study a simple color camera was used. For a color image, $I_{Color}(x,y)$, let be $I_{Red}(x,y)$, $I_{Green}(x,y)$ and $I_{Blue}(x,y)$ the gray scale images derived from the color image by using the RGB model. The idea here is to filter the initial views by using dichroic red and blue filters in each input view of PSVS. These filters are mounted again on the front view of PSVS but no alignment is necessary. Then the color image will be:

$$I_C(x,y) = I_{Color}(x,y) = k\, I_{Red}(x,y) + (1-k)\, I_{Blue}(x,y) \tag{38}$$

The red filter is placed in front of the left virtual camera and the blue filter in front of the right camera. The red filter operates as high pass filter with frequency f>600nm where the blue filter behaves as a low pass filter with frequency f<500nm. Then by splitting the color complex image captured by PSVS the left as red and the right as blue image of a stereo pair of images are created. Because of the frequencies cut of the previous filters a small portion of the green image might be appeared. Using this method, problems can be created if there are reflections on filters. Problems could also be created if the filters used have a common area in spectra. In such a case the complex image is not completely separated. The gray scale images, generated by the above method can be directly used for processing. However, if it is necessary to have gray scale images with normal distribution of pixel intensities, as it happens when a single camera captures a gray scale image, pixel intensities of the generated image could be replaced by new pixel intensities by means of an intensity map. This map might be created taking into consideration pixel intensity changes after their filtering through a color filter (here red and blue).

If a monochrome camera and the previous color filters are used then the separation is possible for simple scenes using histogram functions. The separation could be made because the effect of these filters to gray scale images is to emphasize some colors more than others.

7. Experimental Results

In experimental results presented in this section, PSVS is mounted on the end-effector of a PUMA 761 robotic manipulator or on an aluminum tube. Depending on the experiment, two Pulnix monochrome cameras, models TM-520 and TM-6705, two parallel IEEE-1394 (firewire) cameras composing a stereovision system, as well as a typical color camera for the reception of color images are used. The first case of mirrors alignment is examined. The whole procedure is supported by two personal computers, running Windows. In the first computer, at 350 MHz, the developed robotic software application, called *HumanPT*, is installed. An important number of operations and applications can be executed by means of *HumanPT* (i.e. high level robot control, visual servo control, image processing, communication, calibration, e.t.c.). In the second computer, at 700 MHz, a small part of *HumanPT* is installed (Pachidis et al., 2006). This part is responsible for the reliable and stable communication of the computer (server) with the robot controller through ALTER communication port at 38400 bps and with the first computer (client) through Ethernet.

7.1 Examples of Complex Images

Images of Fig. 9 are captured by means of PSVS from the environment of a PUMA 761 robotic manipulator. Images are referred to simple scenes, where the two views are separately appeared and to more complicated scenes where the different views of objects are superimposed.

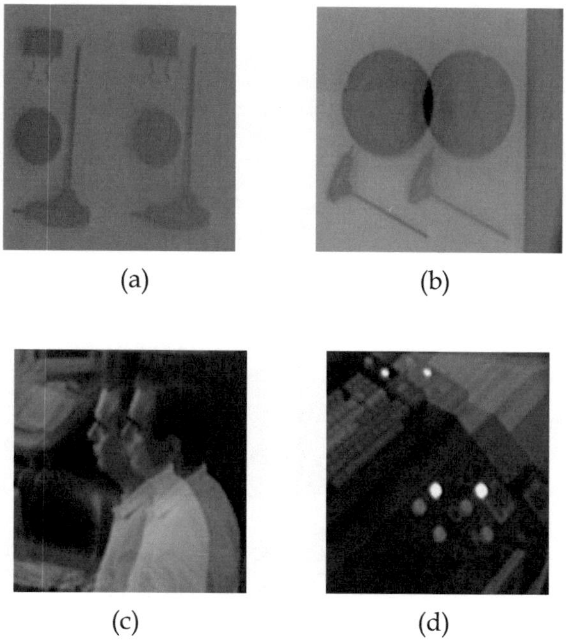

Figure 9. (a) Simple complex image captured by means of PSVS (b) One image where the overlapping of the ashtrays is shown. (c) (d) Images of complex scenes are presented

7.2 Measurements Accuracy

To test the accuracy in measurement for different distances, a pattern with circular areas is used. Distances between the centers of the circular areas are 20 mm and their diameters are 10 mm. The manipulator is moving, along the world coordinate system Z-axis (axis of the world coordinate system, established on the robot), 50 mm each time.

Totally, sixteen complex images are captured by means of PSVS (Fig. 10). After the initial processing of these images (filtering, conversion to binary, Roberts edge detection), geometric centers of two circular areas per image are found. The measured and the calculated distance in mm and the distance error in mm with respect to the calculated depth z are illustrated in Fig. 11(a) and (b) respectively.

As a second experiment the complex image of a pair of pliers is processed (Fig. 12(a)). After the initial processing (mean filtering, conversion to binary image, median filtering, Roberts edge detection) and the implementation of the correspondence algorithm, image coordinates of 500 points for this pair of pliers, are calculated. The disparity map is illustrated in Fig. 12(b).

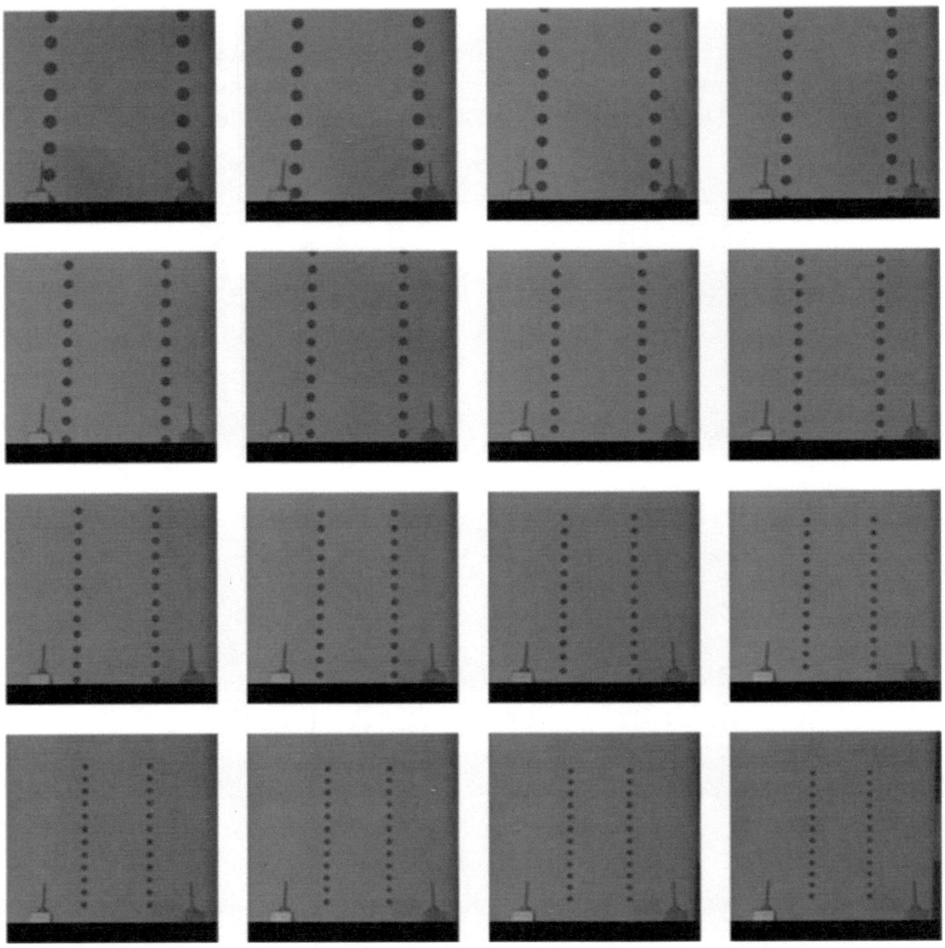

Figure 10. Complex images captured by means of PSVS, from different distances

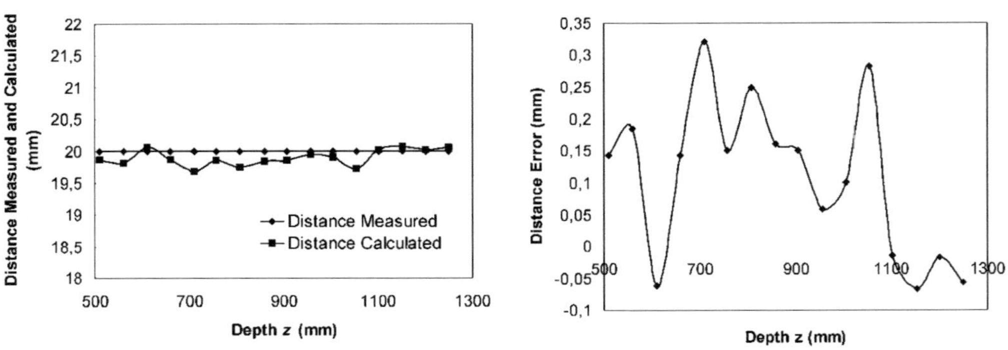

(a) (b)

Figure 11. a) Distance Measured and Calculated vs. Depth z. b) Distance Error vs. Depth z

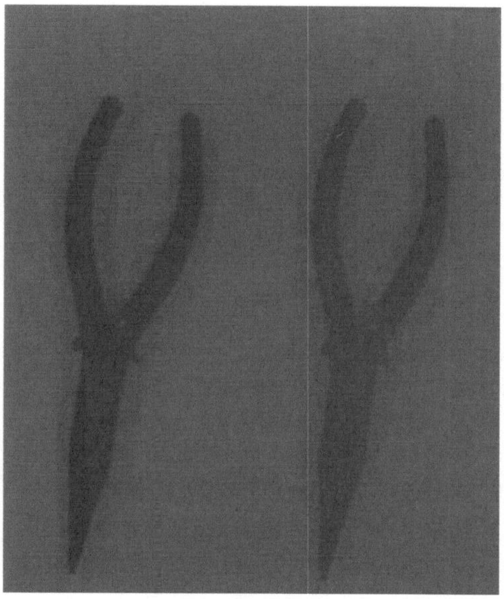

(a)

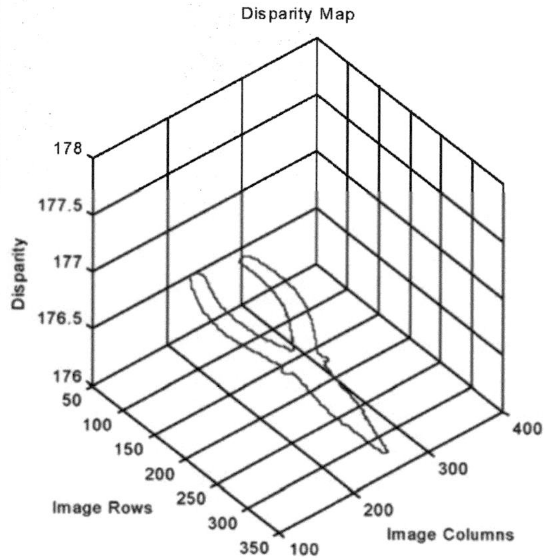

(b)

Figure 12. a) The complex image of pair of pliers. b) The disparity map

7.3 Comparison With Other Systems

To compare the performance of PSVS with respect to a standard stereovision system and to have the same measure, two parallel IEEE-1394 (firewire) cameras are used composing a stereovision system. The baseline length *b* of this vision system is again 10 cm (as PSVS). This stereovision system is calibrated (Zhang, 2000) and (Zhuang et al., 1994). The stereo system is mounted on a square profile 8x8 cm aluminum tube two meters long. Along this tube a target similar with this of Fig. 13(a), mounted on a specially constructed thick aluminum base, can be accurately moved. Stereo pair of images are acquired every 100 mm from 500 to 1900 mm. The experiment is repeated using one camera in the same location with respect to Z-axis and PSV apparatus instead of the stereovision system. Complex images are captured again every 100 mm. Images acquired by means of the two vision system are processed using the proposed correspondence algorithm. In each case, the depth z is calculated and the results of errors are illustrated in Fig. 14.

(a)

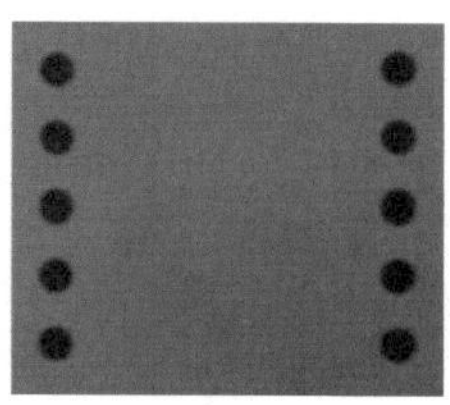

(b)

Figure 13. (a) The original pattern (b) A sample of complex images

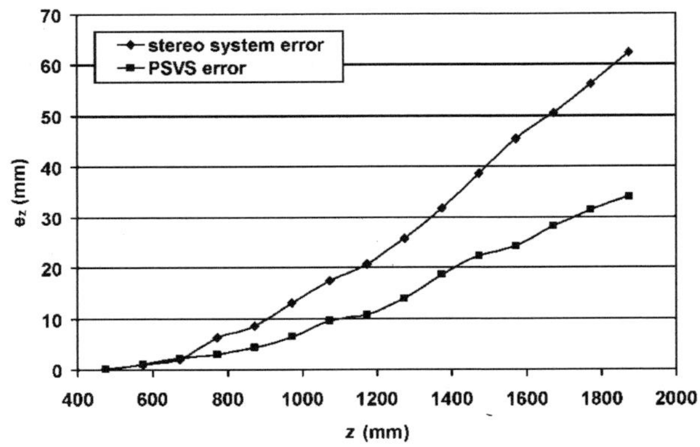

Figure 14. Errors measured with respect to the real distance of each vision system from the target

Comparing the results in Fig. 14 it is realized that a) the accuracy of PSVS is much better than the accuracy of the standard stereo vision system along Z- axis, b) PSVS can measure in smaller distances (smaller blind zone). Moreover cameras parallelism was a difficult procedure (that is why rectification in a stereo pair of images is usually implemented increasing the computational cost) and a computer is always necessary for the alignment of cameras while alignment of PSVS mirrors is possible (when it is necessary) by means of a simple laser beam. Comparing with the results presented in papers (Teoh & Zhang, 1984), (Lee et al., 1999) and (Lee & Kweon, 2000), results in Fig. 14 are more accurate also.

7.4 Complex Images Separation

7.4.1 Monochrome Camera and Spatial Filters

In this part of experimental results the procedure of the separation of a complex image by using a monochrome camera and spatial filters is presented. The filters used are of the form of Fig. 7. The dimension of each square in the spatial filters is 2X2 mm. These filters, first, are carefully aligned. The alignment is made by means of a part of the software application *HumanPT* (http://users.otenet.gr/~pated). During the alignment, the scene (the background) is white. Thus, images captured from PSVS, by means of spatial filters, contain only spatial information. When the alignment is completed the captured image must be an almost white image of the area of interest. Then, the right side of the apparatus is closed and an image is captured. This image contains information only for the left filter. The same procedure is repeated for the left side and an image containing information for the right filter is captured. These two initial images are stored. Following the above steps the system is ready to separate a complex image.

An example of this procedure in case of PSVS is illustrated in Fig. 15. In this example, mirrors are not completely regulated but for the separation, the two spatial filters are carefully aligned. The pair of images can be reconstructed by using the theory of section 6. The results are illustrated in Fig. 16. As smoothing filter a median filter is used.

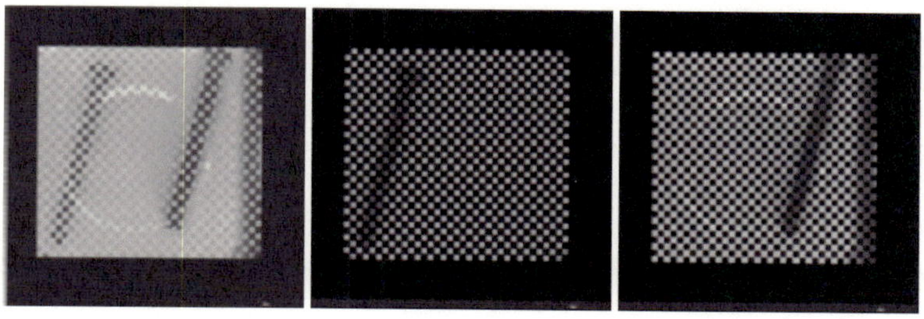

(a) (b) (c)

Figure 15. Complex image separation a) The complex image b) The left view (right image) c) The right view (left image)

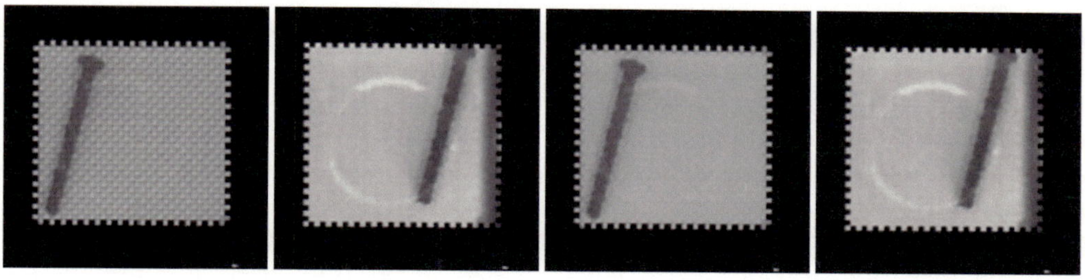

(a) (b) (c) (d)

Figure 16. Complex image reconstruction and smoothing a), b) images reconstruction, c), d) Filtering with a median filter

Figure 17. Complex color images separation

7.4.2 Color Camera and Color Filters

To separate an image by using a color camera, as it mentioned previously, blue and red dichroic filters are mounted on the apparatus closing this way the front area of PSVS. No alignment is necessary and the apparatus is ready to capture images.
The complex image is the superposition of a "red" and a "blue" image. The separation of two complex images captured by means of PSVS and using a color camera is illustrated in Fig. 17. Some areas in the new images, as result of color filtering, are emphasized. However, these images can be used as they are for processing.

8. Conclusions and Future Plans

A system for stereovision based on mirrors and a beam-splitter, was presented. PSVS, as it is called, is a low cost system with well-located features (accuracy, stability, compact constru-ction). Equations and relations, concerning its construction and calculation of points coordinates in 3D space, taking into consideration refraction phenomena due to beam-splitter, were derived. Keeping always in mind the low construction cost and the possibility to easy constructed and used by anyone, new methods were introduced. These methods concern the correspondence algorithm used complex images separation and stereoscopic images reconstruction. Some problems during separation and reconstruction of images were explained. However, more research for this issue is required (i.e. integration of a spatial filter on a beam-splitter). The PSVS, as it is obvious from the experimental results can be successfully used for robotic applications. It was successfully used in different tasks, methods for robot path generation and stereo visual servo control. Moreover, it can be used to measure in space (to measure big distances) or in underwater applications.
Our future plans include implementation of PSVS in more robotic applications, the development of a new PSVS calibration method, the improvement of complex images separation method. They also include the construction of different in size PSVS devices that could accurately measure ultra small distances in the micro world or distances in space.

9. References

Asbun, E. & Delp, E. J. (1999). Real-Time Error Concealment in Compressed Digital Video Streams, *Proceedings of the Picture Coding Symposium*, pp. 345-348, April 1999 Portland, Oregon

Dhond, U.R. & Aggarwal, J.K. (1989). Structure from Stereo—A Review, *IEEE Transactions on Systems, Man, and Cybernetics*, Vol. 19, No. 6, November/December 1989, 1489-1510, ISSN 0018-9472

Gluckmam, J. M. & Nayar, S. K. (1998a). A Real-Time Catadioptric Stereo System Using Planar Mirrors, *Proceedings of DARPA Image Understanding Workshop, IUW98*, pp.309-313, November 1998, Morgan Kaufmann Publishers, Monterey, CA

Gluckman, J. & Nayar, S. (1999). Planar catadioptric stereo: geometry and calibration, *Proceedings of the 1999 Conf. on Computer Vision and Pattern Recognition*, pp. 22-28, ISBN 0-7695-0149-4, June 1999, IEEE Computer Society, Ft. Collins, CO, USA.

Gluckman, J. M. & Nayar, S. K. (1998b). Real-time Omnidirectional and Panoramic Stereo, *Proceedings of DARPA Image Understanding Workshop, IUW98*, pp.299-303, November 1998, Morgan Kaufmann Publishers, Monterey, CA

Gluckman, J. M. & Nayar, S. K. (2000). Rectified Catadioptric Stereo Sensors, *Proceedings of the IEEE Conference on Computer Vision and Pattern Recognition*, pp.224-236, ISBN 0-7695-0662-3, June 2000, IEEE Computer Society, Hilton Head, SC, USA

Goshtasby, A. & Gruver, W. A. (1993) Design of a single-lens stereo camera system, *Pattern Recognition* Vol. 26, No. 6, 1993, 923–936, ISSN 0031-3203

Goulermas, J.Y. & Liatsis, P. (2001). Hybrid Symbiotic Genetic Optimization for Robust Edge-based Stereo Correspondence, *Pattern Recognition,* Vol. 34, No. 12, December 2001, 2477-2496, ISSN 0031-3203

Inaba, M.; Hara, T. & Inoue, H. (1993) A stereo viewer based on a single camera with view-control mechanism, *Proceedings of the International Conference on Intelligent Robots and Systems*, pp.1857-1864, ISBN 0-7803-0823-9, July 1993, IEEE / RSJ, Yokohama, Japan

Kawasue, K. & Oya, Y. (2002). Circular Dynamic Stereo and its Image Processing, *Proceedings 2nd WSEAS Int. Conf. on Robotics, Distance Learning and Intelligent Communication Systems (ICRODIC 2002)*, pp.1311-1315, ISBN 960-8052-68-8, September 2002, WSEAS Press, Skiathos, Greece

Lee, D. H. & Kweon, I. S. (2000). A novel stereo camera system by a biprism, *IEEE Trans. On Robotics and Automation*, Vol. 16, No. 5, October 2000, 528-541, ISSS 1042-296X

Lee, D. H. & Kweon, I. S., & Cipolla, R. (1999). A biprism stereo camera system, *Proceedings of IEEE Comput. Soc. Conf. Computer Vision and Pattern Recognition (CVPR'99)*, pp.82–87, ISBN 0-7695-0149-4, June 1999, IEEE Computer Society, Ft. Collins, CO, USA

Mathieu, H. & Devernay., F. (1995). Systéme de miroirs pour la stereoscopie, *Technical Report 0172*, 1995, INRIA Sophia-Antipolis, FRANCE.

Nayar. S. (1988). Robotic vision system, *United States Patent 4,893,183*, 1988.

Nene S. & Nayar, S. (1998). Stereo with mirrors, *Proceedings of Int. Conf. on Computer Vision (ICCV'98)*, pp.1087–1094, ISBN 81-7319-221-9, January 1998, Bombay, India.

Nishimoto, Y. & Shirai, Y. (1987). A feature-based stereo model using small disparities, *Proceedings of the IEEE International Workshop on Industrial Applications of Machine Vision and Machine Intelligence*, pp. 192-196, February 1987, Seiken Symposium, Tokyo, Japan

Pachidis T. & Lygouras J. (2005). Pseudo Stereo Vision System: A Detailed Study, *Journal of Intelligent and Robotic Systems*, Vol. 42, No. 2, February 2005, 135-167, ISSN 0921-0296

Pachidis T. & Lygouras J. (2006). Vision-based Path Generation Method for a Robot-based Arc-Welding System, *Journal of Intelligent and Robotic Systems,* 2006, ISSN 0921-0296 (Accepted)

Pachidis T.; Lygouras J.; Tarchanidis K. & Kodogiannis V. (2006), HumanPT: Architecture for Low Cost Robotic Applications,. *Proceedings of IEEE International Conference on Virtual Environments, Human - Computer Interfaces and Measurement Systems (VECIMS)*, pp. 154 - 159, ISBN 1-4244-0243-3, July 2006, La Coruna, Spain.

Pachidis T.; Tarchanidis K.; Lygouras J. & Tsalides P. (2005). Robot Path Generation Method for a Welding System Based on Pseudo Stereo Visual Servo Control, *EURASIP Journal on Applied Signal Processing Advances in intelligent vision systems: methods and applications. Part II*, Vol. 2005, No. 14, 2005, 2268-2280, ISSN 1110-8657

Pachidis, T. & Lygouras, J. (2002a). A Pseudo Stereo Vision System as a Sensor for Real Time Path Control of a Robot, *Proceedings of IEEE Instrumentation and Measurement Technology Conference*, pp.1589-1594, ISBN 0-7803-7218-2, Mai 2002, IEEE/IMS, Anchorage, Alaska, USA

Pachidis, T. & Lygouras, J. (2002b). Pseudo Stereo Vision System: Modifications for Accurate Measurements in 3D Space by Using Camera Calibration, *Proceedings of IEEE/ISA Sensors for Industry Conference (Sicon'02)*, pp.66-70, ISBN: 1-55617-834-4, November 2002, IEEE/ISA, Houston, Texas, USA

Pachidis, T.; Lygouras, J. & Tsalidis, P. (2002). A Graphical User Interface for the Initial Path Generation of a Robotic Manipulator for an Arc Welding System, *Proceedings of 2nd WSEAS Int. Conf. on Robotics, Distance Learning and Intelligent Communication Systems (ICRODIC 2002)*, pp.1601-1607, ISBN 960-8052-68-8, September 2002, WSEAS Press. Skiathos, Greece.

Pedrotti, L. S. & Pedrotti, F. L. (1998). *Optics and Vision*, Prentice-Hall, Inc., ISBN 0-13-242223-9, New Jersey

Peleg, S.; Ben-Ezra, M. & Pritch, Y. (2001). Omnistereo: Panoramic Stereo Imaging, *IEEE Trans. On Pattern Analysis and Machine Intelligence*, Vol. 23, No. 3, (March 2001), 279-290, ISSN 0162-8828

Salama, P. (1999). *Error concealment in encoded images and video*, PhD Thesis, Purdue University, School of Electrical Engineering

Salama, P.; Shroff, N.; Coyle, E. & Delp, E. (1995) Error Concealment Techniques for Encoded Video Streams, *Proceedings of the International Conference on Image Processing*, pp. 9-12, ISBN 0-8186-3122-2, October 1995, IEEE Computer Society, Washington, DC, USA

Song, J.; Na, S.; Kim, H.; Kim, H. & Lin, C. (2002). A Depth Measurement System Associated with a Mono-camera and a Rotating Mirror, *Proceedings of the Third IEEE Pacific Rim Conference on Multimedia: Advances in Multimedia Information Processing*, pp. 1145-1152, ISBN 3-540-00262-6, 2002, Springer-Verlag, London, UK

Southwell, D.; Basu, A.; Fiala, M. & Reyda, J. (1996). Panoramic Stereo, *Proceedings of the Int' l Conference on Pattern Recognition*, pp.378-382, ISBN 0-8186-7282-X August 1996, Vienna, Austria

Teoh W. & Zhang, X. D. (1984). An inexpensive Stereoscopic vision system for robots *Proceedings of Int. Conf. on Robotics and Automation*, pp. 186–189, March 1984

Wuerz, A.; Gehrig, S. K. & Stein, F. J. (2001). Enhanced Stereo Vision Using Free-Form Surface Mirrors, *Proceedings of Robot Vision: International Workshop RobVis 2001*, pp.91–98, **ISBN** 3-540-41694-3, February 2001, Auckland, New Zealand

Zhang, Z. (2000). A Flexible New Technique for Camera Calibration, *IEEE Transactions on Pattern Analysis and Machine Intelligence*, Vol. 22, No. 11 (November 2000), 1330-1334, ISSN 0162-8828

Zhuang, H.; Roth, Z. & Sudhakar, R. (1994). Simultaneous robot/world and tool/flange calibration by solving homogeneous transformation of the form AX=YB, *IEEE Transactions on Robotics and Automation*, Vol. 10, No. 4, (August 1994), 549-554, ISSN 1042-296X

18

Tracking of Facial Regions Using Active Shape Models and Adaptive Skin Color Modeling

Bogdan Kwolek
Rzeszow University of Technology
Poland

1. Introduction

It is widely accepted that skin-color is an effective and robust cue for face detection, localization and visual tracking. Well-known methods of color modeling, such as histograms and Gaussian mixture models enable creation of appropriately exact and fast detectors of skin. In particular, skin color-based methods are robust to changes in scale, resolution and partial occlusion. In real scenarios an object undergoing tracking may be shadowed by other objects or even by the object itself. However, many color-based tracking approaches assume controlled lighting. These methods construct or learn models in advance and then use them in tracking, without adaptation to suit new conditions. Consequently, these techniques usually fail or have significant drifts after some period of time, mainly due to variation of lighting in the surrounding. Thus, such techniques are not as good as can be for use in real environments because skin-color perceived by a camera usually changes when the lighting conditions vary. Therefore, for reliable detection of skin pixels a dynamic color model that can cope with nonstationary skin-color distribution over time should be applied in vision systems. Two types of information are typically used to perform segmentation during face tracking. The first is color information (Bradski, 1998; Comaniciu et al., 2000; Fieguth & Terzopoulos, 1997; Perez et al., 2002; Sobottka & Pitas, 1996). The second is the geometric configuration of the face shape (Chen et al., 2002). It is often not easy to separate skin colored objects from non-skin objects like wood, which can appear to be skin colored. Therefore, both skin-color modeling and contours are used to separate the facial region undergoing tracking (Birchfield, 1998). The oval shape of the head is often approximated by an ellipse (Birchfield, 1998; Srisuk et al., 2001). To cope with varying illumination conditions the color model is accommodated over time using the past color distribution and newly extracted distribution from the ellipse's interior. However, such tracker pays little attention to what lies inside the ellipse and what is utilized to accommodate the color model. The kernel density-based tracking has recently emerged as robust and accurate method due to its robustness to appearance variations and its low computational complexity (Bradski, 1998; Comaniciu et al., 2000; Perez et al., 2002). Due to the use of a simple pixel-based representation as well as reduced adaptation capabilities of Mean-Shift methods the algorithm performs poorly under large illumination change.

Updating the color model is one of the crucial issues in color-based tracking. A technique for color model adaptation was addressed in (Raja et al. 1998). A Gaussian mixture model was

used to represent the color distribution and the linear extrapolation was utilized to adapt the model parameters via a set of labeled training data from a subimage within the bounding box. A non-parametric method that in histogram adaptation employs only pixels which fall in the skin locus was proposed in work (Soriano et al., 2003a). In work (Sigal et al., 2000) the modeling of the color distribution over time is realized through predictive histogram adaptation. Histograms are dynamically updated using affine transformations, warping and resampling. The pixel-wise skin color segmentation is often not sufficient to select the pixels for adaptation of a color model because pixels in the image background may also have colors similar with skin colors and this can then lead to over-segmentation. Another issue which should be taken into account is that nearby pixel from skin-colored background may blend with the true skin regions and this can have an adverse effect on subsequent processing of skin regions. The adaptive skin-color filter (Cho et al., 2001) performs initial skin candidate detection at the beginning and then more accurate tuning of a skin model takes place. The adaptation takes into account the skin-like background colors. The method uses the HSV color space in which the H coordinates are additionally shifted by 0.5. A comparative study of four state-of-the-art techniques of skin detection under changing illumination conditions can be found in (Soriano et al., 2003b).
A few attempts have been proposed to track objects under large change in illumination (Hager & Belhumeur, 1996; La Cascia et al., 2000). These algorithms follow the same idea consisting in the usage of a low dimensional linear subspace to approximate the space of all feasible views of the object under different lighting conditions. To perform the tracking one needs to construct the basis images from a set of images collected at fixed pose under different lighting conditions.
The *key* idea of the proposed approach is an improved selection of pixels to determine the parameters of models expressing the evolution of skin color over time. Even when a background region situated close to a face region has skin colored pixels, there always exists a boundary between the true skin region and the background. Our aim is to delineate such a boundary under varying illumination conditions by means of Active Shape Models. In context of dealing with skin-color segmentation under time varying illumination the Gabor filters are particularly useful as they are robust to variability in images arising due to variation in lighting and contrast. Active Shape Models (ASM) were originally proposed by Cootes (Cootes, 2000). They allow for considerable variability of instances of models represented in a subspace spanned by eigenvectors.
The algorithm for segmenting and tracking a face in a sequence of color images enables reliable segmentation of facial region during face tracking despite variation of skin-color perceived by a camera. A second order Markov model is utilized to forecast the skin distribution of facial regions in the next frame. The histograms that are constructed from the predicted distribution are backprojected to generate candidates of facial regions. The detected skin-colored regions are then refined with regard to spatio-temporal coherence. The algorithm reviews the image focusing the action around the location of the face in the previous frame. In particular, the connected component analysis is applied in the binary image to label separate regions. Spatial morphological operations for hole and object size filtering are used afterwards. Using prior knowledge about the target shape the Active Shape Model seeks to match a set of model points to the image. While interpreting the image contents we employ statistical shape models built on intensity gradients, distance between color of pixels in subsequent frames and the phase of Gabor filter responses. In the

first iteration we always utilize the distance to the edge of extracted in advance facial mask to find a plausible starting configuration. The coherence score between corresponding characteristic points, which is determined using phase of the Gabor filter responses, improves considerably the tracking capabilities of the method. The outcome is a shape fitted to the tracked face.

The user only needs to initialize the tracker in the first frame. After a fixed number of frames the tracker automatically switches from tracking with the learning phase to the model-based tracking. A second order Markov model is applied to predict the evolution of colors of skin pixels, gathered within shape interiors in certain number of the last frames. During the tracking, the matching are not performed between only image pairs, but also between the current frame and the shape model. The accommodation of the skin histogram over time takes place on the basis of feedback from shape, newly classified skin pixels and predictions of the skin color evolution.

The following section briefly outlines some topics related to statistical shape models. The details of the shape alignment are given in Section 3. Section 4 describes how the Active Shape Model is used in our system to conduct tracking and to support the skin segmentation. It presents in detail all ingredients of our ASM-based tracker and reports results, which were obtained in experiments with various cues. The model of skin colors and their evolution is described in Section 5. Experiments conducted in varying illumination are described as well.

2. Point Distribution Model

The method for segmentation and tracking of facial regions, which is presented in this chapter utilizes the statistical shape models. A shape model is utilized to constrain the configuration of a set of candidate skin pixels. An efficient algorithm allows the detection of facial pixels to be tested and verified. Thus, it deals with failures of a skin detector. The non-skin pixels that are placed outside of the shape are not considered in the skin-color model.

During shape guided verification of the facial region a set of candidate skin pixels is inspected using shape constraints in two ways. Firstly, a shape model is fitted to the candidate facial region. Secondly, limits are prescribed on the position, orientation and scale of a set of candidate skin pixels relative to the position, orientation and scale according to their values from the last frame. The aim is to extract pixels belonging only to the tracked face, using the candidate facial mask, intensity gradient, coherence of the phase of Gabor filter responses, and the shape constraints. The facial mask is generated from a skin probability image. The skin probability image is extracted on the basis of a skin histogram that is accommodated over time. There are two broad approaches for representing a two-dimensional shape: region-based and contour-based. The region-based methods encode the place occupied by the object through a mask. The methods belonging to this group are sensitive to noise and they cannot cope with partly obscured objects. In contour-based approach the boundary of the object is modeled as an outline. Therefore, such methods can better deal with partially obscured objects and partial occlusions. A contour-based model can be built by placing landmark markers on distinctive features and at some pixels in between. The contour-based instances are usually normalized to canonical scale, translation and rotation in order to make possible comparison among distinct shapes. A distance between corresponding points from the two normalized shapes can be utilized to express the similarity between them.

Active Shape Models (ASMs or smart snakes) were originally designed as a method for locating given shapes or outlines within images (Cootes, 2003). An ASM-based procedure starts with the base shape, approximately aligned to the object, iteratively distorts it and refines its pose to obtain a better fit. It seeks to minimize the distance between model points and the corresponding pixels found in the image. A shape consisting of n points can be considered as one data point in 2n -dimensional space. A classical statistical method for dealing with redundancy in multivariate data is the principal component analysis (PCA). PCA determines the principal axes of a cloud of npoints at locations $\mathbf{x}_i$. The principal axes, explaining the principal variation of the shapes, compose an orthonormal basis $\mathbf{\Phi}=\{\mathbf{p}_1, \mathbf{p}_2,..., \mathbf{p}_n\}$ of the covariance matrix $\mathbf{\Sigma}=\frac{1}{n-1}\sum_{i=1}^{n}(\mathbf{x}_i-\overline{\mathbf{x}})(\mathbf{x}_i-\overline{\mathbf{x}})^T$. It can be shown that the variance across the axis corresponding to the *i*-th eigenvalue λ_i equals the eigenvalue itself. By deforming the mean shape $\overline{\mathbf{x}}$, using a linear combination of eigenvectors $\mathbf{\Phi}$, weighted by so-called modal deformation parameters **b**, we can generate an instance of the shape. Therefore, the new shape can be expressed in the following manner: $\mathbf{x}=\overline{\mathbf{x}}+\mathbf{\Phi b}$. By varying the elements of b we can modify the shape. By applying constraints we ensure that the generated shape is similar to the mean shape from the original training data. Through applying limits of $\pm 3\sqrt{\lambda_i}$ to each element b_i of **b**, where λ_i is the variance of the i - th parameter b_i, we can operate on plausible values of **b**. The deformation of the shape is constrained to a subspace spanned by a few eigenvectors corresponding to the largest eigenvalues. We can achieve a trade-off between the constraints on the shape and the model representation by varying the number of eigenvectors. If all principal components are employed, ASM can represent any shape and no prior knowledge about the shape is utilized.

3. Shape Alignment

Given two 2D shapes, $\mathbf{x}_1$ and $\mathbf{x}_2$ our aim is to determine the parameters of a transformation *T*, which, when applied to $\mathbf{x}_2$ can best align it with $\mathbf{x}_1$ with one-to-one point correspondence. During alignment we utilize an alignment metric that is defined as the weighted sum of the squares of the distances between corresponding points on the considered shapes. Thus we seek to choose the parameters *t* of the transformation *T* to minimize:

$$E=\sum_{i=1}^{n}(\mathbf{x}_{1i}-T_t(\mathbf{x}_{2i}))^T\mathbf{W}(\mathbf{x}_{1i}-T_t(\mathbf{x}_{2i})), \tag{1}$$

where **W** is a diagonal matrix of weights $\{w_1, w_2,..., w_n\}$. Expressing T_t in the following form:

$$T_t \equiv \begin{bmatrix} s\cos(\theta) & -s\sin(\theta) & t_x \\ s\sin(\theta) & s\cos(\theta) & t_y \\ 0 & 0 & 1 \end{bmatrix}\begin{bmatrix} x_{2i} \\ y_{2i} \\ 1 \end{bmatrix} \tag{2}$$

and denoting a_x=s cos(θ), a_y=s sin(θ) we can rewrite (1) in the following form: $E=\sum_{i=1}^{n}w_i\left((a_x x_{2i}-a_y y_{2i}+t_x-x_{1i})^2+(a_y x_{2i}+a_x y_{2i}-t_y-y_{2i})^2\right)$. The error E assumes a minimal value when all the partial derivatives are zero. Differentiating the last equation with regard to a_x we obtain: $\sum_{i=1}^{n} w_i \left(a_x(x_{2i}^2 + y_{2i}^2) + t_x x_{2i} + t_y y_{2i}(x_{1i}x_{2i} + y_{1i}y_{2i})\right) = 0$. Diferentiating *w.r.t.* remaining parameters and equating to zero gives:

$$\begin{bmatrix} C_1 \\ C_2 \\ X_1 \\ Y_1 \end{bmatrix} = \begin{bmatrix} D & 0 & X_2 & Y_2 \\ 0 & D & -Y_2 & X_2 \\ X_2 & -Y_2 & W & 0 \\ Y_2 & X_2 & 0 & W \end{bmatrix} \begin{bmatrix} t_x \\ t_y \\ a_x \\ a_y \end{bmatrix}, \quad (3)$$

where $X_k = \sum_{i=1}^{n} w_i x_{ki}$, $Y_k = \sum_{i=1}^{n} w_i y_{ki}$, $C_1 = \sum_{i=1}^{n} w_i (x_{1i}x_{2i} + y_{1i}y_{2i})$, $C_2 = \sum_{i=1}^{n} w_i (y_{1i}x_{2i} + x_{1i}y_{2i})$, $D = \sum_{i=1}^{n} w_i (x_{2i}^2 + y_{2i}^2)$, $W = \sum_{i=1}^{n} w_i$. The parameters t_x, t_y, a_x and a_y constitute a solution which best aligns the shapes. An iterative approach to find the minimum of square distances between corresponding model and image points is as follows (Cootes, 2003):

1. Initialize shape parameter $\mathbf{b}$ to zero.
2. Generate the model instance $\mathbf{x} = \bar{\mathbf{x}} + \mathbf{\Phi b}$.
3. Find the pose parameters using (3), which best map $\mathbf{x}$ to $\mathbf{Y}$.
4. Invert the pose parameters and then use to project image pixels $\mathbf{Y}$ into the model co-ordinate frame: $\mathbf{y} = T_t^{-1}(\mathbf{Y})$.
5. Project $\mathbf{y}$ into the tangent plane to $\bar{\mathbf{x}}$ through scaling it by $1/(\mathbf{y}.\bar{\mathbf{x}})$: $\mathbf{y}' = \mathbf{y}/(\mathbf{y}.\bar{\mathbf{x}})$.
6. Update $\mathbf{b}$ to match $\mathbf{y}'$ as follows: $\mathbf{b} = \mathbf{\Phi}^{\mathrm{T}}(\mathbf{y}' - \bar{\mathbf{x}})$.
7. If not converged, repeat starting from 2.

4. Active Shape Model-Based Tracking

Tracking can be perceived as a problem of assigning consistent labels to objects being tracked. This is done through maintaining the observations of objects in order to label these so that all observations of a given object in a sequence of images are given the identical label. During shape aligning our algorithm reviews the binary image focusing the action around the pose that has been determined in the previous frame. The algorithm requires that there is an overlap between the image region occupied by the object in the previous iteration and the new object region. Such an assumption is utilized in Mean-Shift trackers (Bradski, 1998; Comaniciu et al. 2000), which require significant overlap on the target kernels in consequent frames. In our system limits are prescribed on the position, orientation and scale of the target according to their values in the last frame. The binary image is generated prior to shape fitting on the basis of the skin histogram that is accommodated over time.

The standard ASM aligns the shape model to outlines in an image using only contours. It works well on images with consistent shape and appearance. It requires good initialization and is inadequate when the shape variations are highly non-linear. To cope with such constraints we initialize the locating of the face in each frame by the use of the binary mask. Its boundary indicates a rough location as well as shape of the face. In work (Koschan et al., 2003) an incorporation of color cues into the ASM framework has been proposed. However, the mentioned approach does not apply color segmentation. It is based on the minimization of energy functions in the color components. Therefore it admits of only a small change in illumination between two successive frames.

Fig. 1. demonstrates the performance of the ASM attempting to match the head model to a given binary mask that has been extracted on the basis of color model. To demonstrate the usefulness of statistical shape models in tracking two artifacts at the left and the right side of face border have been manually added. Despite large deformation of the shape outline we can observe how precisely the algorithm can align the shape to such a face mask. The shape on the left is the base shape in the initial pose that has been utilized in depicted shape alignment. This figure exemplifies also how the statistical shape models can support the selection of pixels for color model adaptation and thus the prediction of skin evolution over time.

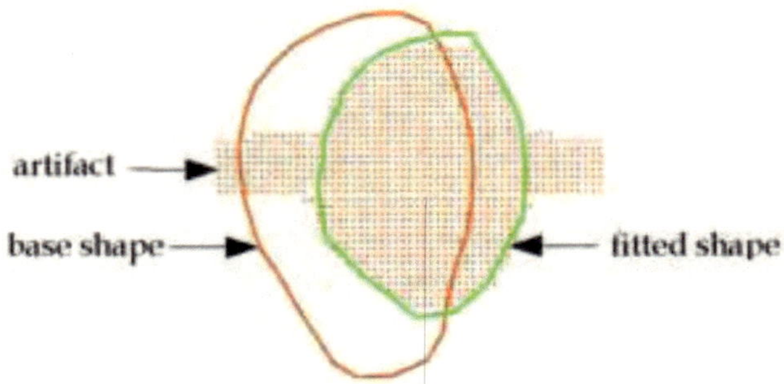

Fig. 1. Shape alignment in presence of manually added artifacts to extracted facial mask.

The shape model has been prepared on the basis of 10 manually segmented images with frontal faces, each represented by 30 characteristic points. The faces have been normalized with regard to orientation and size in order to obtain a set of points with similar physical correspondence across the training collection. All training faces were manually aligned by eye position.
The oval shape of the head can be reasonably well approximated by an ellipse. During preparing the statistical model of the head shape the model shapes are normalized by aligning the average shape to a fixed circle of landmark points. Such an approach has the advantage that the model can be scaled to a needed size via setting only the size of the circle. The pose of the shape during the tracking is determined on the basis of the distance to the edge of face mask, intensity gradient near the edge of the outline, matching score of colors from the candidate outline and from the outline determined in the previous iteration, and phase of the Gabor filter responses. In the following subsections we present how each of the mentioned above cues contributes to the cost function that is calculated during searching for the best fit to the tracked face.

4.1. Distance to the Edge of the Facial Mask

In work (Isard & Blake, 1996) a search for the edges in direction perpendicular to the shape border has been shown as optimal. Therefore, a search for the points along profiles normal to the shape border is employed in our system. Fig. 2. demonstrates sample shape and location of the normals corresponding to characteristic points of our face representation.

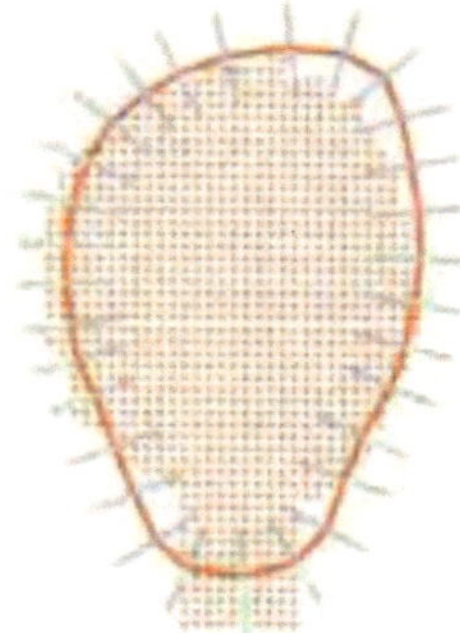

Fig. 2. The location of the normals to base shape.

Fig. 3. shows some shapes that were determined using the distance to the edge of the binary mask undergoing fitting. The binary images indicating skin color like areas were extracted on the basis of histograms accommodated over time. The experiments were conducted in home/office environment in front of wooden doors and a piece of furniture.

Fig. 3. ASM-based face tracking using distance to the edge of the face mask. Frames #1, #2, #20, #40, #60, #80, #100 and #120 (from left to right and from top to bottom). Left images in the pairs are binary ones, whereas right images depict the outlines fitted to the face.

The candidates of facial region are extracted on the basis of histograms modeling the distribution of skin color. Histograms are accommodated over time from newly classified skin pixels and predictions of the skin-color evolution. The backprojected histograms are employed to generate binary images. Such images are then used in determining the connected components. Spatial morphological operations, such as size and hole filtering are employed next. Using the location of the face in the previous frame, a single binary component is extracted finally. The Active Shape Model seeks to match a set of model points to such a facial mask. In the images shown above we can perceive that only the usage of distance to the edge of the mask can lead to shapes that are well fitted to the face. The results demonstrate that the mask can be very useful in the initialization of the shape fitting.

4.2. Intensity Gradient

Figure 4 demonstrates some results that were achieved using intensity gradient while shape fitting to the tracked face. We apply the binary mask in the first iteration that initializes the matching of the set of model points to the edges. The gradient magnitude is calculated on the basis of the Sobel mask. The filtering with Gaussian mask precedes the extraction of the intensity gradient. The search is done along lines perpendicular to the shape.

Fig. 4. ASM-based face tracking, using gradient. Frames #1, #2, #20, #60, #80, #100, #120.

Comparing the extracted shapes at Fig. 3. and Fig. 4. we can observe that the shapes generated on the basis of intensity gradient tend to fit the upper part of the person's head. Such an effect occurs because the strongest edge is not always the object edge. The number of pixels indicating skin like areas in the background is slightly larger in images shown in Fig. 4.

4.3. Intensity Gradient and Color

As demonstrated in (Birchfield, 1998), the contour cues combined with color can be very useful to distinguish the tracked head when both a model of the color distribution and the elliptical model are accommodated over time. When the contour information is poor or is temporary unavailable, color information can be very useful alternative to extract the tracked object. Some tracking results that were obtained using color and intensity gradient cues are depicted in Fig. 5. As in previous experiments, the searching starts from the final location in the previous frame and proceeds iteratively to find the best fit of the shape to the face. In the first iteration the distance to the edge of the face mask is employed. The incorporation of information about the temporal coherence of color results in tracking with small shape's jumps, even in the presence of skin like colors in the background.

Fig. 5. ASM-based face tracking using intensity gradient and color. Frames #1, #2, #20, #40, #60, #80, #100 and #120.

4.4. Phase of Gabor Filter Responses

In order to improve further the quality of shape fitting we exploit Gabor filter responses. This choice is biologically motivated since it has been shown that they model the response the human cortical cells, which are both orientation and frequency selective. In context of dealing with skin-color segmentation under time varying illumination, the Gabor filters can be particularly useful as they are robust to variability in images arising due to variation in lighting and contrast.

A 2-D Gabor filter is created by modulating a 2-D sine wave with a Gaussian envelope. The 2-D kernel of the Gabor filter is given by:

$$g(x,y,\theta_k,\lambda) = \exp\left[-\frac{(x\cos\theta_k + y\cos\theta_k)^2}{2\sigma_x^2} - \frac{(-x\sin\theta_k + y\cos\theta_k)^2}{2\sigma_y^2}\right]\exp\left\{\frac{2\pi(x\cos\theta_k + y\sin\theta_k)}{\lambda}\right\} \quad (4)$$

where σ_x and σ_y denote the standard deviations of the Gaussian envelope along the x and y, respectively, whereas λ and θ are the wavelength and orientation of the 2-D sine wave, respectively. The spread of the envelope is determined via the sine wavelength λ . θ_k is defined as follows: $\theta_k = \frac{\pi}{n}(k-1)$, where k =1, 2,..., n and n represents the number of the considered orientations.The Gabor filter response is calculated by convolving the filter kernel specified by θ_k and λ with the gray-level image I :

$$O(x,y,\theta_k,\lambda) = I(x,y) * g(x,y,\theta_k,\lambda) \ . \quad (5)$$

Fig. 6. shows the real part of Gabor filtered images. The images show the advantages of multiscale image representation-based on Gabor functions in feature matching. In results shown here, we have used four scales and four orientations in representing the landmark points. In our system we employ the efficient Gabor filter implementation of Nestares (Nestares et al., 1998). This pyramidal multiscale Gabor transform that allows very efficient implementation in the spatial domain is faster than conventional FFT implementations.

Given a characteristic point of our shape model we are interested in a correspondence score between the considered pixel at the normal and the corresponding pixel that has been acquired at the initial outline. Such a correspondence score can be estimated using the phase of the Gabor filter responses. Suppose that for a Gabor filter with orientation θ and wavelength λ the phase at a point x_t is $\phi_{\lambda,\theta}$. Given a response of a single filter the similarity between points x_t and x_1 is proportional to $\exp(-(\phi_{\lambda,\theta}(\mathbf{x}_t) - \phi_{\lambda,\theta}(\mathbf{x}_1))^2)$. The matching score between points x_t and x_1 can be computed in the following manner:

$$G(\mathbf{x}_1,\mathbf{x}_t) = C_h \prod_{\lambda,\theta}\left(\exp(-(\phi_{\lambda,\theta}(\mathbf{x}_t) - \phi_{\lambda,\theta}(\mathbf{x}_1))^2) + 1\right), \quad (6)$$

where C_h is a normalization constant ensuring that G varies between 0 and 1. By adding 1 to each factor during multiplication we limit the predominance of a single filter in the filter outcome.

Fig. 7. illustrates the coherence score between the landmark points that were acquired from the shape in the first frame and pixels from the frame #10. For visualization purposes a face subimage is included in the probability image. The brighter the pixel representing probability is, the higher is the coherence probability. The images demonstrate the

usefulness of phase in precise alignment the shape to the facial landmarks. The location of the landmark points for which the coherence probability has been computed can be found at Fig. 8c.
To achieve a better fit of the model shape to image data the method elaborated by (Cootes, 2000) uses searching profiles. Within such profiles this method looks for a sub-profile with statistics that best match the training profile. A representation of the training profile of each landmark is constructed off-line using a collection of the gray level values along the search profiles. The best match is determined by searching for a sub-profile for which a square error function takes the minimal value. The searching starts at the top level of the multi-resolution pyramid and continues at the lover level using the search outcome of the previous level. However, this method is sensitive to changes in illumination. One of the main advantages of our method is its robustness to variations in illumination and contrast. Our method does not require an off-line training stage and takes also the advantages of multiresolution analysis.

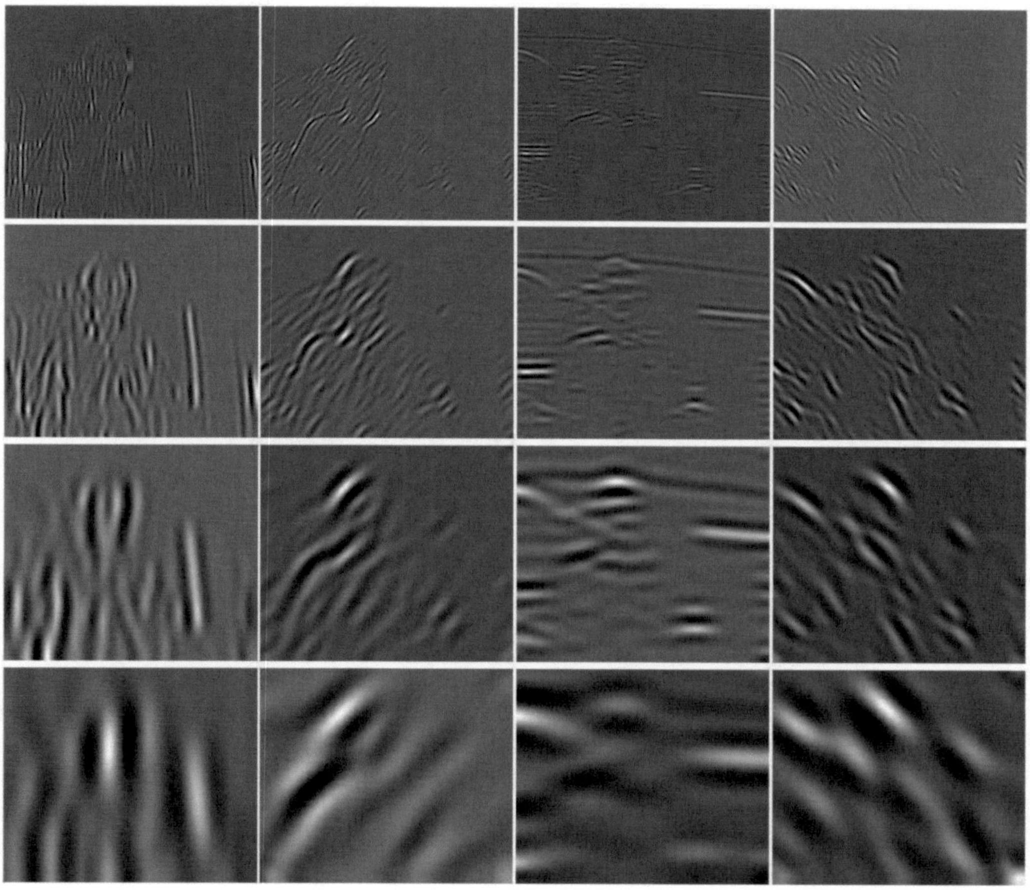

Fig. 6. Gabor decomposition of the test image.

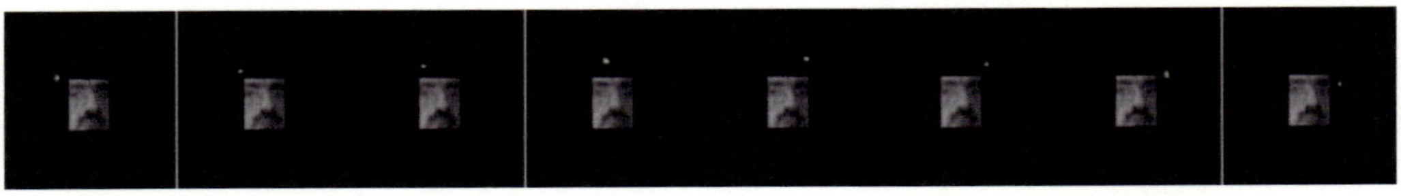

Fig. 7. Gabor filter-based coherence score between the pixels located at landmark points of the shape fitted to face in frame #1 and image pixels from frame #10.

The initialization of the tracker begins with a separation of skin and non-skin colors, see Fig. 8a, using a database of skin and non-skin pixels. The face mask obtained in such a way is utilized to determine the initial pose of the base shape, see Fig. 8b. Experiments demonstrated that such a rough initialization is sufficient to conduct successful tracking in typical scenarios. Good choices for reference pixels to compute the phase score are points at corners or borderlines. Pixels located at the borderline between the shirt and the face are examples of such pixels too. Therefore, after the automatic determination of the shape pose we manually correct the pose of the shape in order to place some of the landmark points of the shape at mentioned above points. Fig. 8c illustrates a typical fit of the base shape to the face after manual correction of the pose. It has been obtained through clock-wise rotation of the shape depicted in Fig. 8b. Although our algorithm does not require very precise initialization, a far more precise initial fit of the shape to the face can be obtained. In case of such a need our graphical interface provides sufficient support and flexibility. For example, we can choose a mode of variation and its weight and then visualize the generated shape. In particular, thanks to such functionality we can determine the number of eigenvalues that are needed to approximate any tracking example within a given accuracy. After specifying the max weight and step we can animate the deformations of the shape in front of the face. This helps in selecting a set of parameters preventing the algorithm from convergence to an unrealistic shape. In another option of the program, through a specification of the weight for each mode we can observe deformation of the shape and its fit to the face. The mentioned above functionality acknowledged also its usefulness at the training stage.

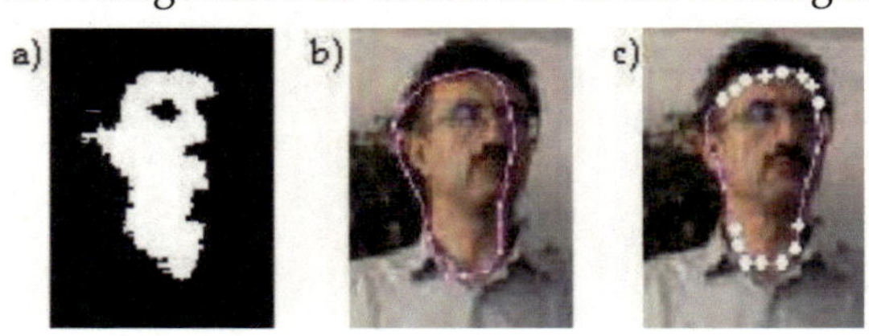

Fig. 8. Initialisation of the tracker.

Fig. 9. illustrates some tracking results that were obtained using the distance to the edge of mask, the intensity gradient and the phase coherence. Through this sequence we want to highlight an improved fit of the shape to the face while the tracking. Comparing images from this figure with corresponding images from Fig. 3.-5. we can notice that thanks to Gabor filter responses, the upper part of the shape is located almost in all frames at the border between the face and hairs of the person's head. A similar effect consisting in a close location of the bottom part of the outline to the face-shirt boundary can also be observed. The accuracy of locating the boundary of the face is constrained by the assumed shape model.

Fig. 9. ASM-based face tracking using the distance to the edge of face mask, intensity gradient and coherence of the phase. Frames #1, #2, #20, #40, #60, #80, #100 and #120.

In the experiments described above we used two modes to approximate the oval shape of the human head. We constructed also shape models with increasing number of modes in order to test their ability to approximate the outline of the face as well as their ability to generalize. The shapes we can obtain arise via linear combinations of the shapes seen in a training set. Thus, the examples of the training repository have also an influence on the approximation as well as generalization capabilities. Some results from the tracking experiments using four modes are presented in Fig. 10. An improved fit to the face can be observed. Our experimental findings show that the 2-3 nodes provide sufficient approximation having on regard comparable face sizes in the image. The model employed in this work has been utilized in our former work (Kwolek, 2006). It has been prepared on the basis of images not containing the faces from the presented here test sequences. A very simple model built on landmark points constituting a shape like an egg can be sufficient to approximate the oval shape of the head in many tracking scenarios. The number of landmark points can be smaller as well. The model parameterized by the number of landmarks, which we decided to use in our experiments provides sufficient approximation for faces occupying larger areas of image.

Fig. 10. ASM-based face tracking using distance to the edge of the face mask, intensity gradient and coherence of the phase. The number of modes is set to four. Each 10-th frame of 120 frames long sequence is presented.

The presented above experimental results were achieved using 10 iterations and they were conducted in front of wooden doors and a piece of furniture. Large shape deformations are made in the first few iterations, which give the scale and shape roughly correct, see Fig. 11b-d. While the searching progresses the deformations are smaller. Fig. 11c demonstrates the shape in first iteration, whereas Fig. 11d shows shapes in 9-th and 10-th iteration, respectively. The images depict also how the statistical shape models can support the selection of pixels for adaptation of the skin model. The skin-color based image segmentation under time-varying illumination is described in next section.

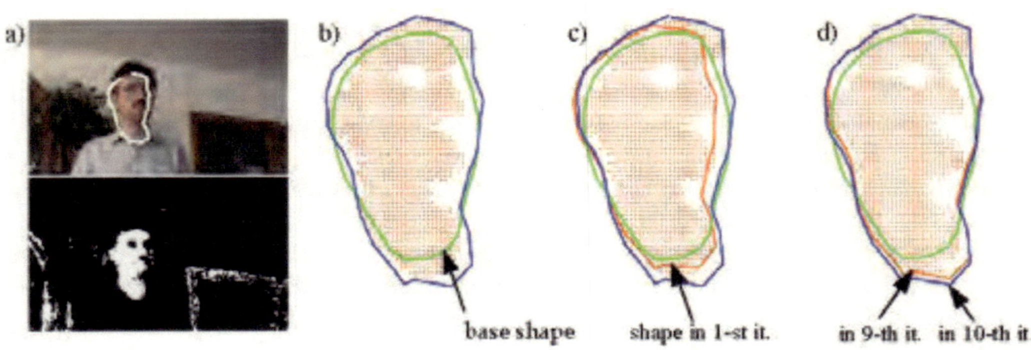

Fig. 11. Examples of search. Input and binary images (a). Process of searching (b-d).

5. Skin Color Segmentation under Time-Varying Illumination

The face detection scheme within tracking framework must operate flexibly and reliably regardless of lighting conditions, background clutter in the image, as well as variations in face position, scale, pose and expression. Some tracking applications, for example using a moving camera, do require good detection rates even in case of abrupt changes of illumination. Fast and reliable face segmentation techniques in image sequences are highly desirable capability for many vision systems. Skin color-based detection methods are independent to scale, resolution and to some degree of face orientation in the image. A problem with robust detection of skin pixels arises under varying lighting conditions. The same skin patch can look like two different patches under two different conditions. An important issue for any skin-color based tracking system is to provide an accommodation mechanism which could cope with varying illumination conditions that may occur during tracking. In our approach, color distributions are estimated over time and then are predicted under the assumption that lighting conditions vary smoothly over time. The prediction is used to reflect the changing tendency in appearance of the object being tracked. A ground-truth is an evident need during adapting a color model over time to changing illumination conditions (Raja et al., 1998). In this approach the evolution of distribution is constrained via statistical shape model and skin locus mechanism. In work (Sigal et al., 2000) the current segmentation and predictions of Markov model were applied to provide a feedback for accommodation. In other work (Raja et al., 1998) the accommodation process is controlled via mechanism for detecting errors accompanying tracking.

One significant element that should be considered while constructing a statistical model of skin color is the choice of color space. One of the advantages of the HSV color space is that it yields minimum overlap between skin and non-skin distributions. Hue is invariant to certain types of highlights, shadows and shading. A shadow cast does not change significantly the hue color component. It decreases mainly the illumination component and changes the saturation. This color space was utilized in several face detection systems (Raja et al., 1998; Sigal et al., 2000; Sobottka & Pitas, 1996). The only disadvantage of the HSI color space is the costly conversion from the RGB color space. We handled this problem by using lookup tables. The histogram is the oldest and most broadly employed non-parametric density estimator. In the standard form it is computed by counting the number of pixels that have given color in region of interest. This operation allows alike colors to be clustered into the separate bin. The quantization into bins reduces the memory and computational requirements. Due to their statistical nature the color histograms can only reflect the content of images in a limited way (Swain & Ballard, 1991). Therefore, such representation of color densities is tolerant to noise. Histogram-based techniques are effective only when the number of bins can be kept relatively low and when sufficient data are in disposal (Raja et al., 1998). One of the drawbacks of the histogram-based density estimation is the lack of convergence to the true density if the data set is small. In certain applications, the color histograms are invariant to object translations and rotations. They vary slowly under change of angle of view and with change in scale.

The target is represented by the set $S=\{\mathbf{u}_i\}_{i=1}^{N}$, where N is the number of pixels and $\mathbf{u}_i$ denotes vector with HSV components of the i -th pixel. Given a set of samples S we can obtain estimate of $p(\mathbf{u})$ using multivariate kernel density estimation (Comaniciu et al., 2000; Elgammal et al., 2003):

$$p(\mathbf{u}) = p\left(u^{(1)} = H, u^{(2)} = S, u^{(3)} = V\right) = \frac{1}{N}\sum_{i=1}^{N}\prod_{l=1}^{3} K_h\left(u^{(l)} - u_i^{(l)}\right), \tag{7}$$

where $K_h(\mathbf{u}) = \frac{1}{(\sqrt{2\pi}h)^d}\exp\left(-\frac{\|\mathbf{u}\|^2}{2h^2}\right)$ is a Gaussian kernel of bandwidth h, whereas d denotes the dimension. The quantization with 32x32x32 bins has been used to represent both the target as well as the background.

An initial skin histogram, along with the model for non-skin background pixels, has been used to compute the probability of every pixel in the first input color image and thus to give the skin likelihood. A model for human skin color distribution was built using a repository of labeled skin pixels that has been prepared in advance. Given the histograms ϕ_{fg} and ϕ_{bg}, the log-likelihood ratio for a pixel with color $\mathbf{u}$ is given by (Han & Davis, 2005):

$$L(\mathbf{u}) = \max\left(-1, \min\left(1, \log\frac{\max(\phi_{fg}(\mathbf{u}), \delta)}{\max(\phi_{bg}(\mathbf{u}), \delta)}\right)\right), \tag{8}$$

where δ is a very small number, whereas $\phi_{fg}(\mathbf{u})$ and $\phi_{bg}(\mathbf{u})$ denote the frequency of pixels with color $\mathbf{u}$ in the foreground and background, respectively. Given the probability image the thresholding takes place. After that, the binary image is analyzed via a labeling procedure, which isolates connected components in order to detect the presence of face candidates in the image. Next, the candidate regions are subjected to morphological operations, such as size and hole filtering, to clean up the mask and to generate the mask indicating which pixels belong to the face. After alignment of the model shape with the current mask, the refined face mask is utilized to select from the newly classified pixels the representation of the skin distribution. Using such samples gathered over an initial sequence of frames the sequence-specific motion patterns are learned. A second-order Markov process has been chosen to model the evolution of the color distribution over time (Blake & Isard, 1998; Sigal et al., 2000).

Many studies have indicated that the skin tones differ mainly in their intensity value while they form compact cluster in chrominance coordinates (Yang et al., 1998). Hence, the evolution of skin cluster can be parameterized at each time instant t by translation, rotation and scaling. The translation parameters $\mathbf{t}_p$ can be extracted on the basis of means from samples constituting a learning distribution, whereas the scaling parameters $\mathbf{s}_p$ can be estimated from their standard deviations. The eigenvectors of the covariance matrices of samples from two consecutive frames define two coordinate frames, which can be then used to estimate the rotations $\mathbf{r}_p$.

The work (Blake & Isard, 1998) demonstrated that affine motion can be described via a second-order auto-regressive Markov process:

$$\mathbf{X}(t+1) - \overline{\mathbf{X}} = A_2\left(\mathbf{X}(t_{k-1}) - \overline{\mathbf{X}}\right) + A_1\left(\mathbf{X}(t_k) - \overline{\mathbf{X}}\right) + B_0\mathbf{w}_k, \tag{9}$$

where $\mathbf{X} = \{\mathbf{t}_p^{\mathrm{T}}, \mathbf{s}_p^{\mathrm{T}}, t_p^{\mathrm{T}}\}$ is the vector parameterizing the skin evolution. The parameters which should be learned are $\mathbf{A}_0$, $\mathbf{A}_1$ and $C = BB^{\mathrm{T}}$ because B cannot be observed directly. It was shown in (Blake et al., 1995) that the matrices $\mathbf{A}_0$ and $\mathbf{A}_1$ can be estimated on the basis of the following equations:

$$S_{20} - \hat{A}_0 S_{00} - \hat{A}_1 S_{10} = 0 \tag{10a}$$

$$S_{21} - \hat{A}_0 S_{01} - \hat{A}_1 S_{11} = 0\,, \tag{10b}$$

where $S_{ij} = \sum_{k=1}^{m-2} \left(\mathbf{X}(t_{(k-1)+i}) \mathbf{X}^T (t_{(k-1)+j}) \right)$, i, j =0,1, 2, and m denotes number of learning frames. Given $\mathbf{A}_0$ and $\mathbf{A}_1$ we can estimate C from the following equation: $\hat{C} = \frac{1}{m-2} Z(\mathbf{A}_0, \mathbf{A}_1)$, where $Z(\mathbf{A}_0, \mathbf{A}_1) = S_{22} + A_1 S_{11} A_1^T + A_0 S_{00} A_0^T - S_{21} A_1 - S_{20} A_0^T + A_1 S_{10} A_0^T - A_1 S_{02} + A_0 S_{01} A_1^T$.

On the basis of predicted distribution the histogram $\phi_{fg^{(p)}}$ of skin colors is extracted. After normalization of the histogram we perform an adaptation which combines the histogram that had been obtained from the predicted distribution and the histogram from the last frame. Adaptation is made according to the following equation:

$$\phi_{fg^{(u)}}(t) = (1 - \alpha_1)\phi_{fg}(t-1) + \alpha_1 \phi_{fg^{(p)}}(t) \tag{11}$$

where the adaptation coefficient α has been determined empirically. The histogram $\phi_{fg^{(u)}}(t)$ has been subjected to segmentation procedure to produce the face mask. The refined face mask by statistical shape model, as discussed in Section 4, has been then used to collect the newly classified skin pixels in a list.

The refined face mask by statistical shape model can contain non-skin pixels. Experiments demonstrated that the part of face below the hair was a source of such inadequate pixels. To deal with this undesirable effect, the pixels collected in the mentioned above list were additionally inspected if they fall within the prepared in advance skin locus. A prepared off-line two-dimensional table defining possible skin chromaticities has been used at this stage. It has shown to be useful especially in eliminating non-skin pixels from the representation of the skin distribution in a sudden change of illumination.

The list prepared in such a way has been utilized to generate the histogram $\phi_{fg^{(n)}}$. Finally, this histogram has been updated in the following manner:

$$\phi_{fg}(t) = (1 - \alpha_2)\phi_{fg}(t-1) + \alpha_2 \phi_{fg^{(n)}}(t)\,. \tag{12}$$

This histogram has been utilized to generate the skin image probability during tracking.

5.1 Experiments in Time-Varying Illumination

To test the elaborated method of skin color segmentation under time-varying illumination we performed various experiments on real images. Some images from one of our test sequences are shown at Fig. 12. Through this sequence we want to highlight the behavior of the tracking algorithm in varying illumination as well as in case of errors in color-based target segmentation. We can notice in frame #56 that even if the segmentation does not separate the object of interest from the background, the contour generated from the active shape model supports greatly the extraction of the target. In case of such an abrupt change of illumination and without the ASM-based shape refinement the color model would be influenced by the background colors. Thanks to precise delineation of face from the background and the adaptation mechanism the skin model contains only face colors, see frame #60, #70. The accommodation of the skin histograms over time takes place on the basis of feedback from shape, newly classified skin pixels and predictions of the skin color evolution. Once a face is being tracked, the color model adapts according to changes in illumination and improves tracking performance. In this sequence we can also observe how the size of the shape is scaled in response to varying distance between the moving camera and moving person. The number of learning images has been set to 10.

Fig. 12. ASM-based face tracking in varying illumination using intensity gradient and phase of Gabor filter responses. Frames #1, #50, #55, #56, #60, #70, #100 and #200.

To study the adaptation performance in time-varying illumination conditions we conducted experiments with two configurations of the tracking algorithm. In the first configuration only the newly classified pixels were used to accommodate the histogram, whereas in the second one we utilized the predictions of the skin evolution. The predictions lead to better segmenta-tion of the tracked face in varying illumination, see Fig. 13. and Fig. 14. Until significant change of illumination in frame #56, both algorithms produce almost the same results, compare frame #55 at Fig. 13. and Fig. 14. Something better segmentation can be observed as early as in frame #57. Significantly better segmentation can be perceived in frame #70 and all frames behind it. A tracker built on an ellipse can not track the face in frames acquired after the change of the illumination. The presented system runs at 320x240 image resolution at frame rates of 9-11 Hz on a 2.4 GHz PC.

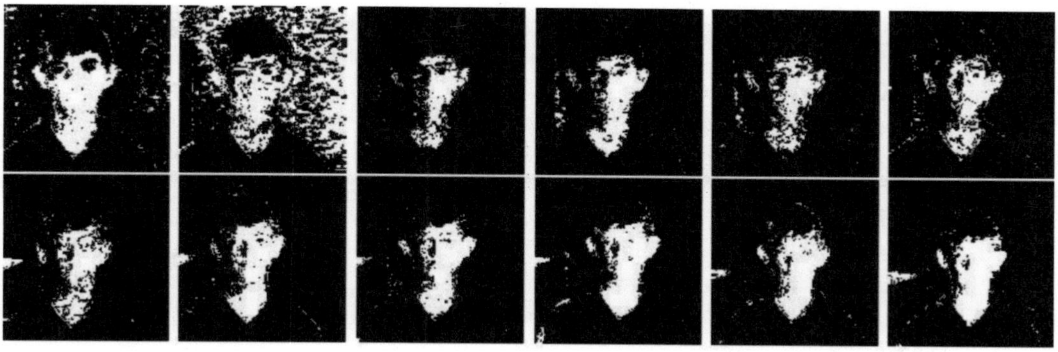

Fig 13. Skin-like regions during adaptation-based on newly classified skin pixels. Frames #55, #56, #57, #58, #59, #60, (top row), #70, #80, #90, #100, #150, #200 (bottom row).

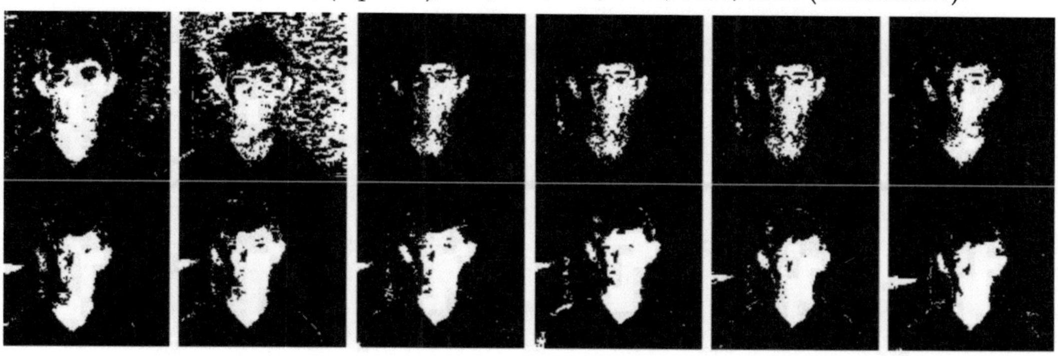

Fig 13. Skin-like regions in learning-based adaptation. Frames #55, #56, #57, #58, #59, #60, (top row), #70, #80, #90, #100, #150, #200 (bottom row).

6. Acknowledgment

This work has been supported by Polish Ministry of Education and Science (MNSzW) within the projects 3 T11C 057 30 and N206 019 31/2664.

7. References

Birchfield, S. (1998). Elliptical Head Tracking Using Intensity Gradients and Color Histograms, In *Proc. IEEE Conf. on Comp. Vision and Patt. Rec.*, Santa Barbara, 232-237

Blake, A., Isard, M., Reynard, D. (1995). Learning to Track the Visual Motion of Contours, *Artificial Intelligence*, Vol. 78, 101-133

Blake, A., Isard, M. (1998). Active Contours, Springer Bradski, G. R. (1998). Computer Vision Face Tracking as a Component of a Perceptual User Interface, In *Proc. IEEE Workshop on Appl. of Comp. Vision*, 214-219

Chen, Y., Rui, Y., Huang, T. (2002). Mode-based Multi-Hypothesis Head Tracking Using Parametric Contours, In *Proc. IEEE Int. Conf. on Aut. Face and Gesture Rec.*, 112-117

Cho, K. M., Jang, J. H., Hong, K. S. (2001). Adaptive Skin Color Filter, *Pattern Recognition*, Vol. 34, No. 5, 1067-1073

Comaniciu, D., Ramesh, V., Meer, P. (2000). Real-Time Tracking of Non-Rigid Objects Using Mean Shift, In *Proc. IEEE Conf. on Comp. Vision and Patt. Rec.*, 142-149

Cootes, T. (2000). An Introduction to Active Shape Models, *Model-Based Methods in Analysis of Biomedical Images,* [in:] *Image Processing and Analysis,* Eds., R. Baldock and J. Graham, Oxford University Press

Elgammal, A., Duraiswami, R., Davis L. S. (2003). Probabilistic Tracing in Joint Feature-Spatial Spaces, In *Proc. IEEE Conf. on Comp. Vision and Patt. Rec.*, 16-22

Fieguth, P., Terzopoulos, D. (1997). Color-Based Tracking of Heads and Other Mobile Objects at Video Frame Rates, In *Proc. IEEE Conf. on Comp. Vision Patt. Rec.*, 21-27

Han, B., Davis, L. (2005). Robust Observations for Object Tracking, In *Proc. Int. Conf. on Image Processing,* 442-445

Hager, G., Belhumeur, P. (1996). Real-Time Tracking of Image Regions with Changes in Geometry and Illumination, In *Proc. IEEE Conf. on Comp. Vis. and Patt. Rec.*, 403-410

Isard, M., Blake, A. (1996). Contour Tracking by Stochastic Propagation of Conditional Density, *European Conf. on Computer Vision,* Cambridge, 343-356

Koschan, A., Kang, A., Paik, J., Abidi, B., Abidi, M. (2003). Color Active Shape Models for Tracking Non-Rigid Objects, *Pattern Recognition Letters,* Vol. 24, 1751-1765

Kwolek, B. (2006). Active Shape Model-Based Segmentation and Tracking of Facial Regions in Color Images, Int. *Conf. on Image Analysis and Recognition,* Povoa de Varzim, Portugal, Lecture Notes in Computer Science, Vol. 4141, Springer-Verlag, 295-306

La Cascia, M., Sclaroff, S., Athitsos V. (2000). Fast, Reliable Head Tracking under Varying Illumination: An Approach Based on Registration of Texture-Mapped 3D Models, *IEEE Trans. on Pattern Analysis and Machine Intelligence,* Vol. 22, 322-336

Nestares, O., Navarro, R., Portilla, J., and Tabernero, A. (1998). Efficient Spatial-Domain Implementation of a Multiscale Image Representation Based on Gabor Functions, *J. of Electronic Imaging,* Vol. 7, 166-173.

Perez, P., Hue, C., Vermaak, J., Gangnet, M. (2002). Color-Based Probabilistic Tracking, *European Conf. on Computer Vision,* 661-675

Raja, Y., McKenna, S. J., Gong, S. (1998). Color Model Selection and Adaptation in Dynamic Scenes, In *Proc. European Conf. on Computer Vision,* 460-474

Soriano, M., Martinkauppi, B., Huovinen, S., Laaksonen, M. (2003). Adaptive Skin Color Modelling Using the Skin Locus for Selecting Training Pixels, *Pattern Recognition,* Vol. 36, 681-690

Soriano, M., Martinkauppi, B., Pietikainen M. (2003). Detection of Skin under Changing Illumination: A Comparative Study, *Int. Conf. on Image Analysis and Proc.*, 652-657

Sigal, L., Sclaroff, S., Athitsos, V. (2000). Estimation and Prediction of Evolving Color Distributions for Skin Segmentation under Varying Illumination, In *Proc. IEEE Conf. on Comp. Vision and Patt. Rec.*, 2152-2159

Sobottka, K., Pitas, I. (1996). Segmentation and Tracking of Faces in Color Images, In *Proc. 2-nd Int. Conf. on Automatic Face and Gesture Rec.*, 236-241

Srisuk, S., Kurutach, W., Limpitikeat, K. (2001). A Novel Approach for Robust Fast and Accurate Face Detection, *Int. J. of Uncertainty, Fuzziness and Knowledge-Based Systems,* Vol. 9, No. 6, 769-779

Swain, M. J., Ballard, D. H. (1991). Color Indexing, Int. J. of Comp. Vision, Vol. 7, No. 1, 11-32 Yang, J., Weier, L., Waibel, A. (1998). Skin-Color Modelling in Color Images, In Proc. *Asian Conf. on Computer Vision,* II:687-694

19

Bimanual Hand Tracking based on AR-KLT

Hye-Jin Kim, Keun-Chang Kwak and Jae Jeon Lee
Intelligent Robot Research Division
Eelectronics and Telecommunications Resarsh Institute,
Korea

1. Introduction

Robot and human interaction has received a significant amount of attention in the robot vision research community in the past decades. This has been motivated by the desire of understanding human gesture/motion tracking and recognition. If you solve tracking problems under the circumstance of fast movement, occlusion, and illumination, then you need to complicate calculation, and hence the computational complex prevents to work in real time. For example, particle filter is an useful algorithm to track objects, even under occlusion and non-rigid motion difference. However, particle filter needs to enough samples to support reliability of the potential candidates of the target. There have done many works in hand tracking. To track hands in real time, Shan(Shan, 2004) made particle filter faster by reducing sample size according to mean shift. On the other hand, Kolsch (Kolsch&Turk, 2004) designed a fast tracking algorithm that combined Kanade-Lucas-Tomasi(KLT) flocks and k-nearest neighborhood.
Some papers concentrated on the particular properties of hands and their features. Non-rigidity of the hand causes difficulties to track because of non-linear dynamics of the articulation. Fei and Reid(Fei&Reid, 2003) dealt with deformation of the hand by constructing two models according to non-rigid motion from rigid motion. HLAC (Higher-Order Local Auto-Correlation) features of Ishihara (Ishihara&Otsu, 2004) achieved efficient information over time domain by Auto-Regressive model.
The size of interesting objects is another critical factor for tracking because if its size is too small or changes too fast, object tracking becomes very challenging problem. Francçis(Francçis,2004) dealt with blobs varying their resolution, hence made it possible to track the object with various size in the image sequence. Both hands tracking is simultaneously different from one hand tracking since features such as shape, color etc. between both hands is almost the same each other. Shamaie (Shamaie&Sutherland, 2003) built the model of the movements of bimanual limbs. However, the model needs large enough time to compute distance transform in the image. McAllister(McKenna et al., 2002) solved the both hands tracking by employing contour distance transform and 2D geometric model.
In this paper, we propose a new 2D both hands tracking algorithm based on the articulated structure of human body in real time. This method is efficient enough to perform in real time due to the limb model tracking. The model enables to deal with the deformation of hands and nonrigid motion because of the articulate structure of the arm for both hands.

The model can be tracked by a linear line obtained from the regression of KLT features in order to represent the target information. Unlike Shamaie and McAllister, the proposed algorithm outperforms previous method in occlusion handling of both hands. For instance, some methods require restricting occlusion cases because similar features prevent a hand to differentiate from another. However, this method tracks superimposed hands correctly by virtue of its prediction of the moving direction.

In the next section, we will elaborate our proposed algorithm step by step. In the section 2 A-B, we will illustrate key algorithms to build our model. In Section 2.3, we give brief explanation about how to segment and extract hands from the background. The section 2.4 is dedicated to the dynamic model and the algorithms for occlusion detection and tracking. Some experimental results are presented in the section 3. Our contribution in hand tracking and conclusion are presented at the end of paper.

2. Articulate Hand Motion Tracking Method

2.1 Building the auto-regression model

Auto-regression model is one of dynamical mode that is a statistical framework for motion tracking. Through accumulated motion sequences, dynamical model obtains the information to predict motion in the next frame. Second-order auto-regression model is a special Markov process model with gaussian priors $\mathbf{X} \sim N(\overline{X}, \mathbf{V})$, the dynamical model

$$p(X(t_k) \mid X(t_{k-1})) \propto \exp\{-\frac{1}{2}\left\|B^{-1}(X(t_k) - AX(t_{k-1}))\right\|^2\} \tag{1}$$

Also the Markov process can be expressed in a generative form:

$$X(t_k) - \overline{X} = A_2(X(t_{k-2}) - \overline{X}) + A_1(X(t_{k-1}) - \overline{X}) + B_0 w_k \tag{2}$$

where A_2, $A_1$and B_0 are all $N_X \times N_X$ AR coefficients. We set the order of auto-regression model as 2 because it can handle motions with different velocity and noisy direction [8].

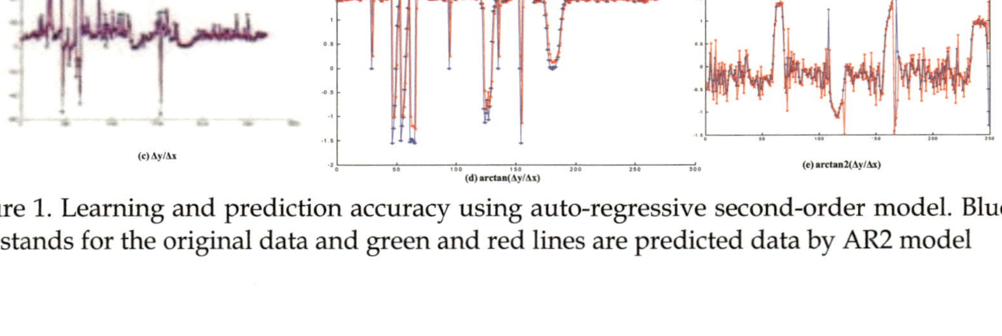

Figure 1. Learning and prediction accuracy using auto-regressive second-order model. Blue line stands for the original data and green and red lines are predicted data by AR2 model

AR2 coefficients were learned from the manually marked ground truth data. Training data consist of 100 samples and test data 53 samples with 7 dimensions with respect to x and y point of 2D hand, elbow and shoulder points, and a slope between an elbow and an hand. The AR2 model predicts most points well except for the gradients. Fig.1 (a) is the image of test samples (above row). Fig.1 (b) shows how to estimate the slope. We attempt to extract the slope in several ways: (1) $\Delta y/\Delta x$ (2) $\theta_1 = tan^{-1}(\Delta y/\Delta x)$ (3) $\theta_2 = tan_2^{-1} (\Delta y/\Delta x)$. The period of θ_1 ranges from $-\pi/2$ to $\pi/2$ and that of θ_2 ranges $-\pi$ to π. We emphasize on the gradient factor because it gives useful clues that a predicted hand belongs to which side when both predicted hands are crossed each other.

2.2 KLT features and linear regression

KLT features, named after Kanade, Lucas and Tomasi, provide steepest density gradients along the x and y directions (see [9]). The features are corner points with the largest eigenvalues. The size of each feature represents the amount of context knowledge and depends on two factors: quality level of a corner' intensity and minimum distance between corner points. To match the image I and J, the current and the next image, we minimize the error function ε by the following equation:

$$\varepsilon = \iint_W [J(x) - I(x)]dx \tag{3}$$

where W is the given feature window and w(**x**) is a weighting function. Minimizing Eq.(3), you find the A and d corresponding to the affine motion field and the translation of the feature window's center, respectively. The largest eigenvalue of A estimates feature quality. In the presented system, KLT features calculate their density gradient on the skin and motion image when the object has motion or on the skin image if there is no object to move.

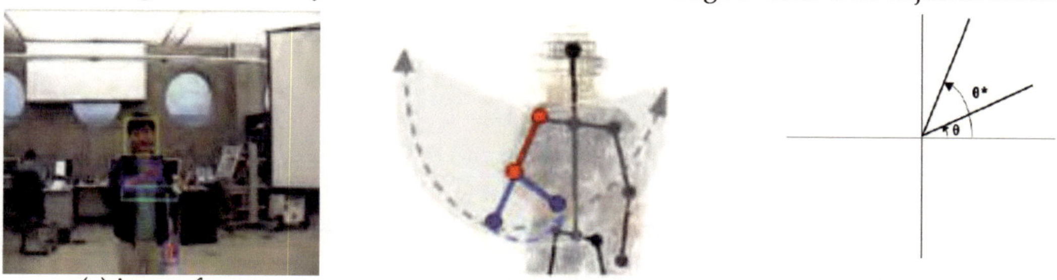

(a) image frame (b) body structure (c) slope estimation

Figure 2. We define a body structure consists of hands, shoulders and elbows. The elbow points, green cross marks in (a), represent the base point of the arm's slope. In the first frame, the elbow points are assumed by the ratio of the length between a shoulder and an elbow and the length between the elbow and a hand. For the slope estimation, the difference between slope($\theta^*-\theta$)is considered to predict the next change of the slope.

By adjusting the feature size in the skin image or in the skin-motion image, KLT features can be spread out over the whole image plane. Therefore, we filtered KLT features using mean and variance constraint. That is, we removed all KLT features of which variances are more than 2.5 times the overall variance. Linear regression is applied to the filtered KLT features in order to get the slope and find the end point of each hand. Here, we note that the end point extraction needs a reference point because the slope and y-axis intercept need to fit the exact tracking position by removing noisy data and abstract the structural information of the arm by linear regression. This bias will be adjusted and removed by the reference point. As you can see in Fig.2, we construct the arm model for reflecting articulate motion of hands in tracking issue. There are three points for each arm: the shoulder, elbow and hand points. We take each elbow point into the reference point instead of the shoulder point because if you set the shoulder point up as the reference point, then you may lose the elbow point and cannot figure out the status of arms : stretched out , curved and so on. Fig. 2(c) shows the elbow and hand points and the line between them and the slope of the line illustrating in Fig. 2(c) gives the directional information when the occlusions within hands and arms are detected.

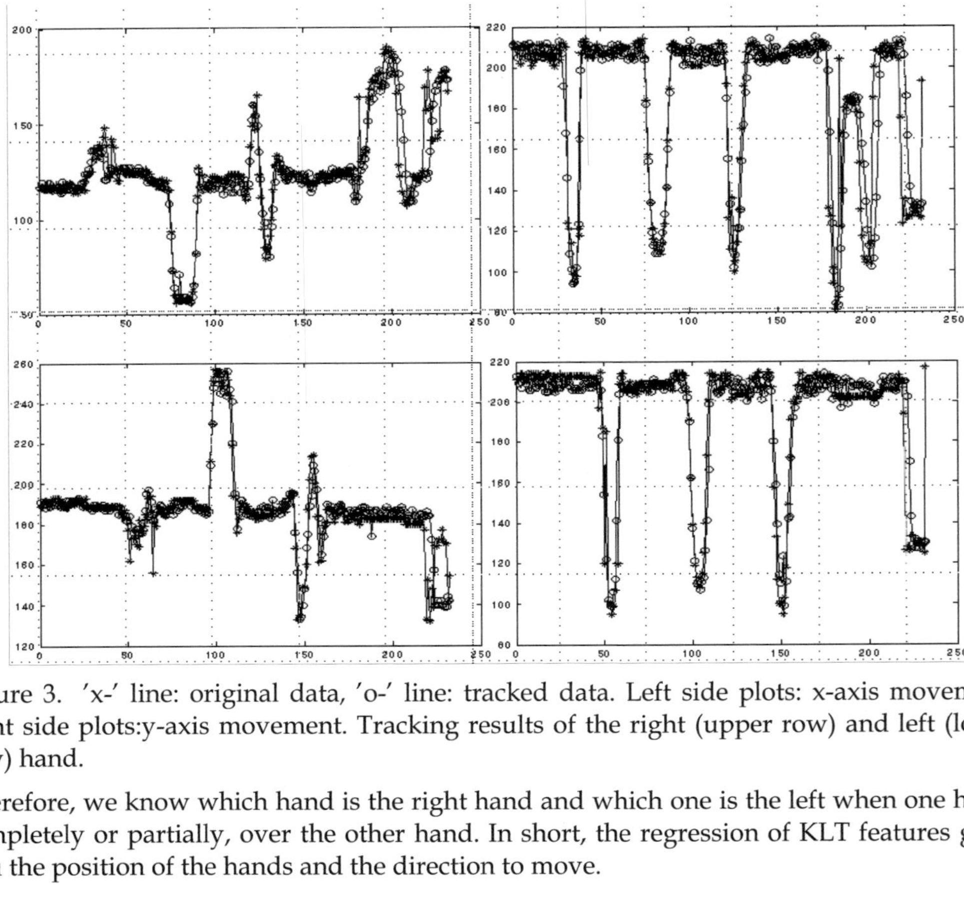

Figure 3. 'x-' line: original data, 'o-' line: tracked data. Left side plots: x-axis movement, right side plots:y-axis movement. Tracking results of the right (upper row) and left (lower row) hand.

Therefore, we know which hand is the right hand and which one is the left when one hand, completely or partially, over the other hand. In short, the regression of KLT features gives you the position of the hands and the direction to move.

2.3 Hand detection and pre-processing

Skin-color and motion cues are adopted for pre-processing the image. Motion cues are obtained from differentiating the current frame with the previous frame. Skin-color segmentation requires the following four steps.

1. Construct skin-color database with about one million size samples on RGB plan.
2. Generate non-skin color database.
3. Train the skin-color pixel and non-skin color pixel after transforming RGB spaces into YUV spaces.

4. Obtain the U-V image sequence along the Y plan.
5. Create the representative U-V lookup table of skin-color at the mean point of Y.
6. Find skin-color pixels in an input image using the U-V lookup table.

The fourth and fifth steps are essential steps to achieve real-time skin color segmentation. In the third step, skin-color detection scheme needs 256×256× 256 comparison per a pixel on the YUV space. However, it is revealed that the trained U-V ranges did not have much difference on Y-spaces. Therefore, U-V values are chosen at the average point of Y as the skin-color lookup table.

Finally, the interesting target the motion of skin-colored regions, the input image is processed by the logical AND operator between the color probability image and the difference image.

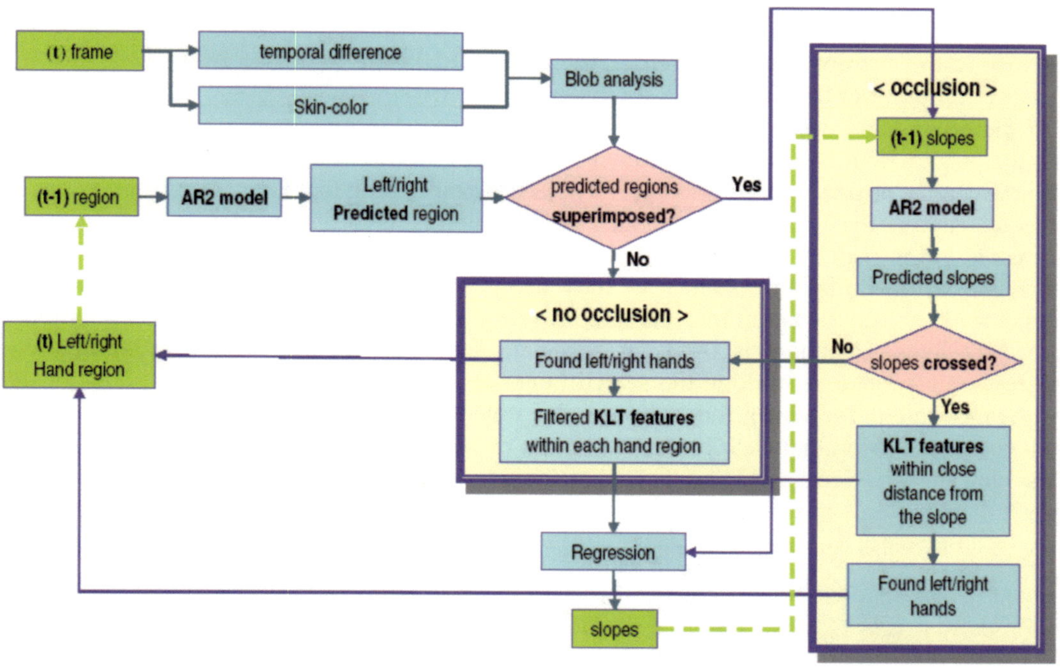

Figure 4. Overview of fast 2D both hands tracking with articulate motion prediction

2.4 A dynamic model for occlusion detection and tracking

In this section, detecting occlusion and tracking is dealt with for both hands at once as shown in Fig.4.

For tracking hands in an image, the limb model is useful to predict future movements of each hand and catch occlusion. Tracking is divided by two parts: crossed motion and uncrossed motion. Hand occlusion in the next frame can be detected by the following factors: (1)the size of superimposed region between predicted areas of both hands should be large enough; (2) the product of two slopes from left and right hands should be non-positive; (3) the amount of slope changes from one frame to a consecutive frame should be beyond threshold. If these three conditions are all satisfied, it is the alarm that two hands are crossed each other.

Detection and tracking issues highly depend on characteristic of targets. Therefore, it is hard to find targets such as both hands with similar color and similar shape. This fact invokes the need of special features that can decide whether a hand belongs to left or right one. The proposed method uses directivity of hands because the limb structure of human body enables to restrict discriminative movement for each hand. Directivity can be obtained by KLT features and its regression result as already shown in 2.2. When predictive both hands are occluded each other, KLT features are collected when they are close enough to the predicted linear line from the previous frame. Closeness is calculated by the following eq. (4). Where a line equation $ax + b - y = 0$ and a point $(x0, y0)$ are given, the distance d is obtained by

$$d = \frac{|ax_0 + b - y_0|}{\sqrt{a^2 + b^2}} \tag{4}$$

The close KLT feature to the predicted line is highly possible a candidate of the target feature in the current frame. Therefore, the filtered KLTs are regressed in order to find the proper end point of the hand.

On the other hand, this method analyzes blobs on the skin and motion image since blobs segments generic features without domain-dependent information. Difficulties that use blobs are the change of size and the velocity of a object corresponding to a blob. Such changes can be serious under the Ubiquitous Robotic Companion (URC) circumstance where image transmission is usually much slower than other mediums such as USB camera because of server-robot transmission system. Fast movement and sudden magnification/reduction of a target leads to lose the target information, preventing from tracking. In the proposed method, the AR2 dynamic model is used for eliminate such risk because second-order of auto-regression can enlarge/abridge the search range of the target according to the status of the target movement. Moreover, the 2nd-order dynamic model gives the alarm of the occlusion. It is a cue of occlusion that each predictive region of both hands coincides with the same place. Tracking system selects occlusion process as shown in Fig.4 based on that cue.

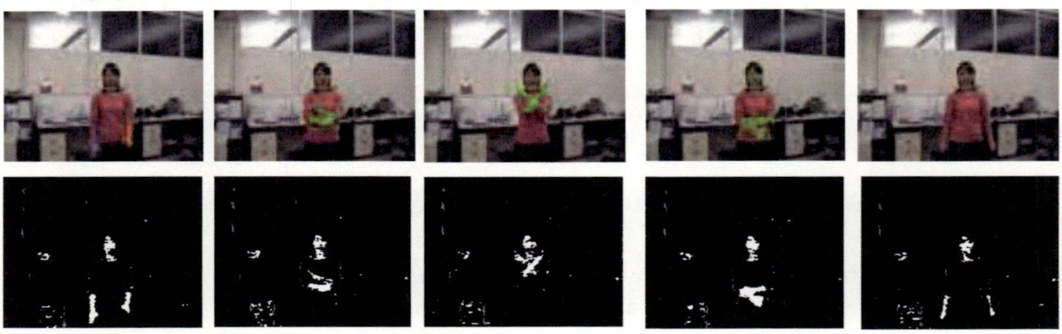

Figure 5. Both hands are crossed each other

3. Experimental results

Fig.1 (a) and (b) are the image of test samples (above row). We attempt to extract the slope in several ways: (1) $\Delta y/\Delta x$ (2) $\theta_1 = tan^{-1}(\Delta y/\Delta x)$ (3) $\theta_2 = tan_2{}^{-1} (\Delta y/\Delta x)$. The period of θ_1 ranges from $-\pi/2$ to$\pi/2$ and that of θ_2 ranges $-\pi$ to π. We emphasize on the gradient factor because it gives useful clues that a predicted hand belongs to which side when both predicted hands are crossed each other. Fig.1 (a) and (b) represented how well the learned AR2 parameters predicted $\Delta x/\Delta y$ coordinates of both hands. Especially in Fig.1 (b), predicted points were well tracked even if fast movement - the rapid change at x or y coordinate axes of the hand occur. On the other hand, Fig.1(c)-(e) showed that the gradient was hard to make a pre-estimation. Although various approaches such as tangent and arc tangent were taken to calculate gradients, it is revealed that the gradient was very sensitive to the difference of the x coordination, Δx between (t-1) frame and (t) frame. For example, negligible Δx much less than 1 could cause remarkable change of its gradient but such difference in an image can be considered as roughly no change. In other words, although the hand stayed little motion along the x-axis in an image changes, robot considered it big hand movement while human-beings can ignore such changes. Therefore, the effort to reduce the effect of Δx was made by transforming the gradient $\Delta y/\Delta x$ into θ_1 = arctan($\Delta y/\Delta x$), or θ_2 = arctan2($\Delta y/\Delta x$). However, some parts still failed to get correct prediction because tangent and arc tangent is a trigonometrical function having own period. That is, prediction could not but be failed at the extreme point of its period, θ_1: $-\pi/2$ and $\pi/2$ and θ_2 : $-\pi$ and π, as shown in Fig.1(c)-(e). Despite of such restrictions of the slope prediction, the gradient information can provide the key clue that a hand belongs to left or right one. To adopt benefits of slope, tracking process was decomposed into two processes (see Fig.4). One is for the uncrossed hand tracking. Here, the slope information is kept in until the next frame. This process used x- and y-coordinates of both hands and confirmed the tracking result. Another handles the hand occlusion. That is, if the occlusion is detected by the AR2 model, then the previous slope for each hand is prepared for finding the correct hand position.

For the bimanual tracking, it is hard to figure out whether both hands are crossed each other as well as which hand is a left or right one because both hands' properties are almost the same. Our method proposes a good feature to discriminate two hands: directivity. The well-known law of inertia can tell that a hand belongs to a right or left hand because moving objects suddenly do not change its direction. The directivity can be obtained from the slope. Fig.4 shows that the slope gives a cue whether both hands are superimposed. According to this information, we can track both hands simultaneously as shown in Fig.5.

In order to measure the performance of the algorithm, 900 experiments were performed on many different hand shapes. The result of the experiments is listed in Table 1. Fig.3 shows a part of our experimental results. We performed the experiment using multimodal hand gesture database such as drawing 'O' and 'X', pointing left and right and so on. In Fig.3, the movement velocity along y-axis is higher than x-axis direction. Despite the velocity difference, our proposed algorithm adaptively found correct hand position whether its velocity is fast or slow.

Another important issue in tracking is that an algorithm can be simulated under the real time system. Wever, a robot for cheap practical use, has limited computing power, can transport an image through the internet only in 6.5 frames per a second on average without additional image processing. Furthermore, the target, hand, was often found out of detectable range because of slow image transportation. Under this circumstance we achieved real-time tracking in 4.5 frames per a second.

Side	Left	Right
Hand(x –axis)	94.39±0.62	94.84±0.56
Hand(y –axis)	93.01± 1.96	91.32± 1.75
Elbow(x-axis)	99.09±0.68	99.78±0.30
Elbow(y-axis)	99.77±0.33	99.57±0.61

Table 1. Tracking accuracy

4. Conclusion

Our ARKLT method is very useful for tracking and gesture recognition. As mentioned before, the ARKLT method consists of three points for each hand: the shoulder, elbow and hand. Since the model reflects the articulated motion of the human body which is restrained by the each limb's degree of freedom. That is, the possible region for hand movement is restricted in the elongated region of the shoulder and elbow movement. Therefore, the proposed method can devise effective prediction method, which enables to pre-detect crossing hands based on the body structure. In addition, the proposed method applies the KLT features and their regression line so that the body structure can effectively be fitted into the target. Also, the well-fitted KLT line can provide the exact point of a hand; meanwhile most tracking methods provide the broad region of the target. When it comes to practical uses such as gesture recognition, the find location of the target improves to draw accurate outcome, for example, gesture recognition.

5. Acknowledgement

This work was supported in part by IT R&D program of MIC & IITA [2005-S-033-03, Embedded Component Technology and Standardization for URC].

6. References

Blake, A. & Isard K. (2000) *Active Contours* Springer ISBN3-540-76217-5 Springer-Verlag Berlin Heidelberg New York

Francçis, A. (2004) Real-time multi-resolution blob tracking *IRIS Technical Report*

Shamaie, A & Sutherland A. (2003) A dynamic model for real-time tracking of hands in bimanual movements *Gesture Worshop*

Shan, C. et al., Real time hand tracking by combining particle filtering and mean shift *IEEE International Conference on Automatic Faces and Gesture Recognition*

Fei, H. & Reid, I (2003) Probablistic tracking and recgonition of non-rigid hand motion *IEEE International Workshop on Analysis and Modeling of Faces and Gestures*

Shi, J. and Tomasi, T. (1994) Good feature to track *Proc. IEEE Conference on Computer Vision and Pattern Recognition*

Kolsch, M. & Turk, M. Fast (2004) Fast 2D Hand Tracking with Flocks of Features and Multi-Cue Integration Proceeding of the 2004 IEEE Computer Society Conference on Computer Vision and Pattern Recognition Workshop (CVPR'04)

McKenna, S. J. and McAllister, G. and Ricketts, I. W. (2002) Hand Tracking for Behavior Understanding *Image and Vision Computing* Vol. 20 pp 827-840

Ishihara, T. & Otsu, N. Gesture Recognition Using Auto-Regressive Coefficients of Higher-order Local Auto-Correlation Features *Proceedings of IEEE International Conference on Automatic Face and Gesture Recognition* 2004

20

An Introduction to Model-Based Pose Estimation and 3-D Tracking Techniques

Christophe Doignon
LSIIT - University of Strasbourg
France

1. Chapter overview

The aim of this chapter is to present a general overview of the feature-based 3-D pose estimation and tracking techniques. Principles, classical techniques and recent advances are presented and discussed in the context of a monocular camera. The objective is to focus on techniques employed within both the visual servoing and registration fields for the wideclass of rigid objects. The main assumption to this problem rely on the availability of a 3-D model of the object to track.

2. Introduction: Model-based tracking and pose estimation

The recovery of the 3-D geometric information from 2-D images is a fundamental problem in computer vision. When only one view is available, the appearance or the relative arrangement of the object features of interest should be modelled in a symbolic description so as to be compared with the image descriptors thanks to a similarity criterion. Geometric-based approaches restrict the search for correspondence to a sparse set of geometrical features. They use numerical and symbolic properties of entities available. To automatically compute a rigid-body transformation (the pose), it is necessary to match a 3-D model features with part of the visible 2-D image features, a process referred to as the correspondence problem, and for the past four decades, the model-based pose estimation of objects with a simple geometry has been intensively studied.
The major goal is tracking at camera frame rate the pose parameters in the world space. Therefore, features such as points, lines, ellipses are not only extracted from 2-D images, but the 3-D model and the pose of the object has to be also exploited.

2.1 Related work on model-based 3-D tracking

The modelbased 3-D tracking is closely related to the pose estimation problem. It can cope with abrupt motions and it is generally more efficient to deal with partial occlusions of the object of interest than 2-D tracking. However, it needs the correspondence problem to be solve at least once. The definition of object tracking algorithms in image sequences is an important issue for research and applications related to robot vision. A robust extraction and realtime spatiotemporal tracking of measurements is one of the keys to a successful visual servoingbased tracking, in particular for positionbased visual servoing approaches

(PBVS) (Hutchinson, 1996), where the tracking error is computed in the task space and thereafter used by the robot control system.
The reference work on visionbased navigation is the dynamic tracking approach introduced by Dickmanns and Graefe (Dickmanns, 1988). In this work, the steering of cars, vehicle docking and aircraft landing are performed by dynamic modelling and edge feature extraction and processing.
Feature extraction and matching play an important role, and restriction of matching is commonly done by windowing technique. Harris and Stennet (Harris, 1990), Papanikolopoulos et al. (Papanikolopoulos, 1993) and Hager and Toyama (Hager, 1998) with the XVision system restrict the search space of matching to a neighbourhood of the searched features. This reduces computational costs because only small parts of the image are processed. More recently, Thompson et al. (Thompson, 2001) use robust methods for line fitting and pose estimation by applying iterative median filters in order to detect outliers. In (Marchand, 2004), Marchand & Chaumette described both feature tracking issues and modelbased tracking for visual servoing techniques. Compared to Thompson's work, robust methods are used for tracking visual 2-D features which are related in turn to the 3-D motion (the motion field applied to imagebased visual servoing purposes). In this work, the pose estimation problem is seen as the dual problem of 2-D visual servoing: for a given pose, a set of virtual 2-D measurements are computed (the virtual camera). The approach consists of estimating the real pose by minimizing visual measurements errors (thus, by moving the virtual pose to the real one) with a robust control law. This approach can be thought as a minimization technique driven by the the 2-D/3-D mapping (perspective law herein) at each iteration, and which restricts the path from a guess solution to the desired one.

2.2 The pose determination versus camera calibration

Generally, the identification of some of the camera parameters - the intrinsic parameters - is needed to achieve the pose. This process named as the camera calibration can be done as a preliminary step or it can be achieved in some situations simultaneously with the estimation of the pose (Sturm, 1997). The extrinsic parameters of the pose relate the world coordinates to the camera orientation and position and there is a lot of related works in the computer vision and photogrammetry literatures both on the pose estimation and camera calibration (Horn, 1986; Tsaï, 1987; Haralick, 1992; Hartley, 2000) as the two problems are strongly connected. With a single view, the accuracy of the intrinsic and extrinsic parameters estimates relies on the ability to extract the perspective effect in a reliable fashion from the imaged 3-D objects or from a couple of sets of planar patterns (Doignon, 1999; Zhang, 1999). Non linear effects and electronic synchronizations has been modelled by (Tsaï, 1987) twenty years ago and are significant disturbing factors in the captured perspective image. The radial alignment constraint (RAS) described by Tsaï alleviates some of the above mentioned problems for parts of extrinsic parameters, mainly the orientation and the direction of the position vector.
The practical use of a camera calibration procedure is strongly limited by the socalled correspondence problem since many methods used points (Faugeras, 1987 ; Tsaï, 1987) or lines features (Liu, 1990) for that purpose. Recently, Meng and Hu have proposed a calibration based on circular points which does not need any correspondences (Meng, 2003) and nor computation of extrinsic parameters. A complete review of most of calibration techniques is reported in (Salvi, 2002).

2.3 The importance of feature grouping

The pose determination from a single perspective view requires a local geometric description of objects and image features of interest. The space search for the onetoone correspondence may be very large when no constraint is used to associate them. Various recognition schemes have been proposed in the past to solve the search of the correspondence problem like the interpretation tree (Grimson, 1990), geometric hashing (Lamdan, 1988), aspect graphs (Ikeuchi, 1987; Hansen, 1989), focal features (Bolles, 1982 and 1986), pose clustering (Olson, 2001), the soft assignment (Gold, 1998; David, 2002) and alignment techniques (Huttenlocher, 1990; Torr, 1999; Bartoli, 2001).

Many authors have presented solutions to this problem in the context of the registration with alignment techniques. The goal is then to match two subsets (a subset of image features with a subset of features of the 3-D model) corresponding to a geometric transformation consistent with the data 2 (Haralick, 1984; Lowe, 1987; Ikeuchi, 1987; Thompson, 1987; Sugihara, 1988; Grimson, 1991; Jurie, 1999; David, 2002). For linear primitives such as points (vertices of a polyhedra, corners, zerocurvature points, intersections of lines,...) or straight lines (edges, tangent lines at zerocurvature points, polar lines,...), the search space of a consistent viewpoint[1] is large as several features are needed to constrain it (typically 3 to 5 matched linear features are required).

Quadratic primitives constrain more the viewpoint. In many situations, only one quadratic feature is needed to find a small set of consistent pose parameters. In counterpart, quadratic primitives are more tricky to detect with a sufficient level of reliability (see (Weiss, 1993; Werghi, 1995; Pilu, 1996)).

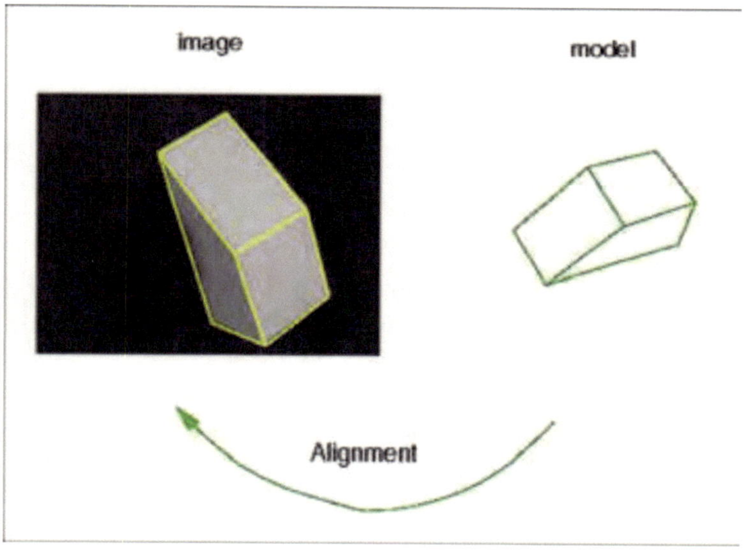

Figure 1. The 2D/3D rigid registration as an alignment technique from a subset of model features (in green) to a subset of visible image features

[1]The parameters of the viewpoint are corresponding to the determination of the pose or attitude of the viewed object. It is a imagetoworld (2-D/ 3-D) rigid registration. For a camerabased vision sensor, it is equivalent to the recovery of extrinsic parameters of a calibrated camera.

The size of these subsets are depending both on the geometric transformation and the number of dof which are constrained by the features used. Features grouping and classification are then important stages, to speed up the correspondence problem by rejecting *a priori* several very probable inconsistent subsets. For instance, the determination of a onedimensional homography between two sets of points requires the grouping of 3 collinear points in both sets, since a onedimensional projective basis is defined with three points on the same line[2].

2.4 An introduction to the correspondence problem

We introduce the correspondence problem as it is an essential vision component for automate the pose and to detect outliers. A set of n_m 3-D model features and a set of n_I 2-D image features are used through a matching process to determine the "best" Euclidean transformation. Usually n_m and n_I are different for many reasons. A model feature may be occluded or outofthe camera field of view or some irrelevant feature may be detected in the image, because of the acquisition and segmentation processes. These artefacts act as outliers and they must be discarded. Anyway, even if $n_I = n_m$, a featurebased pose determination algorithm needs the onetoone correspondence between subsets of all available features. A naive approach could be done by computing the large set of geometric transformations with all combinations of n_m ordered model features and n_m unordered image points, and to select the transformation with the lowest target registration error (the "best" transformation). However, this is unpractical since the number of combinations is increasing very quickly with the number of features and lead to a cumbersome computing time.

The matching process must be fast and as few timesensitive as possible to a small variation of the number of features involved. That's why, it is of prime importance to design pose algorithms with few features even if the final registration computation takes advantage of all available inliers.

For instance, when one solves the solutions for the pose by means of the wellknown *perspective 3-points problem* (Horaud, 1987; Haralick 1989; DeMenthon 1992; Alter 1994), n_m model points should be matched with n_I image points, considering every arrangement of triples of feature points. Hence, for n_m 3-D model points and n_I image points, there are $A_{n_m}^3 C_{n_I}^3$ candidates (couples of triples) (Huttenlocher, 1990). To register the polyhedra with respect to the camera frame in Figure 1, there are typically $n_m = 8$ vertices and at most $n_I = 7$ visible points in the image. This lead to a large search space since 11760 putative couples of triples should be scanned so as to find the right alignment[3]. One more image point issuing from artefacts extends the number of candidates up to 18 816, two more image points up to 28 224.

To provide a practical solution, some authors proposed to turn towards the estimation theory. There are many existing robust estimation algorithms and we relate one the most popular family of techniques referred to as the *hypothesizeandtest* approach (Grimson, 1990) where a small set of correspondences are first hypothesized, and the corresponding

---

[2] If a fourth point (collinear to the three others) is included in the subset, a wellknown projective invariant can be computed, the crossratio, which is equivalent (but not equal) to the projective coordinate of this extra point in the projective basis

[3] Considering a calibrated camera, every alignment provides 4 solutions for the pose following the perspective 3points approach, only two with the paraperspective approximation.

transformation is computed. The best known example of this approach is the RANdom SAmple Consensus (RANSAC) algorithm of Fischler and Bolles (Fischler, 1981) which is able to cope with a large amount of outliers and to automatically compute the a geometrical transformation. Another close algorithm is that of Rousseeuw & Leroy (Rousseeuw, 1987) applied by Rosin (Rosin, 1999) for the pose determination.

3. Some pose estimation problems

We begin this section with a short review of wellknown techniques for the pose with feature points and lines in general configuration, so as to orient the discussion toward less wellknown techniques like collinear points, spheres, cylinders and multiple heterogeneous features.

3.1 Pose recovery from points

This problem has been addressed for many years and we suggest the interested reader to look for the following related work. The literature is vaste and the proposed solutions differ from the relative configurations of points (collinear points (Haralick, 1992), planar points (Tsaï 1987) or scattered 3-D data (Triggs, 1999)), the number of feature points used (Haralick, 1991; Triggs 99, Nister, 2003), the computational approach (closedform (Dhome, 1989; Haralick, 1989; Horaud, 1989) or numerical iterative approaches (Horaud, 1987; Lowe, 1987; Yuan, 1989; DeMenthon, 1995; Rosin, 1999; David, 2002), concurrent processing (Linnainmaa, 1988), solutions which take advantages of data redundancy (Quan, 1999), the imaging model used (perspective model (Triggs, 1999; Hartley, 2000), weak perspective (Huttenlocher, 1990), paraperspective (Aloimonos, 1990) or orthoperspective (Alter, 1994)).

3.2 Pose recovery from lines

Usually, the extension of the previous related methods to the case of lines is straightforward for some specific arrangements as lines and points are dual entities in a projective plane. For instance, with a non parametric planar curve, it is possible to extract zerocurvature points (which are invariants by perspective projection in most cases), but since this kind of points are very unlocalized, one may preferably used tangent lines instead of zerocurvature points to match the 2D image features with the object model (Mokhtarian, 1986; Richetin, 1991).
In the case of a polyhedra (see Figure 1 and Figure 3), a 3-D model can be built with a set of 3-D straight lines which are generally not in the same plane. The linepoint duality does not hold any more and a specific method with 3-D lines (4 dof) should be investigated. It's a more difficult problem than that of the pose from points, since the equations which relate the 3-D line representation (see Figure 2) and its perspective projection in the image are quadratic functions of the pose parameters (Hartley, 2000). Dhome et al. (Dhome89), Chen (Chen, 1991b), Liu et al. (Liu, 1990}, Navab & Faugeras. (Navab, 1993), Andreff et al. (Andreff, 2000), Bartoli & Sturm (Bartoli, 2001) and Ansar & Daniilidis (Ansar, 2003) have proposed some pose and displacement algorithms from lines. In (Dhome, 1989), the solution is given by solving a polynomial equation of degree 8 with at least three lines. Chen (Chen, 1991) points out some particular and important arrangements of 3 lines (concurrent lines, three lines with two parallel lines, coplanar lines, perpendicular lines,...) in order to reduce the degree of the polynomial equation, and consequently to reduce the number of solutions. The various approaches are differing from the geometric constraint used (Liu, 1990 and

Chen, 1991), and by the type of representation used like the Plückerian representation for the pose and motion analysis (Navab, 1993; Mitiche, 1995), for large displacements (Bartoli, 2001), with the normalized version of the Plückerian representation (Andreff, 2000) or to get a linear algorithm with large data redundancy (Ansar, 2003).

The perspective projection of a 3-D line Δ represented with the Plücker matrix **L** (whose components are described with $\mathcal{L} = (\boldsymbol{r}, \boldsymbol{w})$ with $\boldsymbol{r}^T \boldsymbol{w} = 0$ in the object frame) is the line $\boldsymbol{l}^c$ such that

$$[\boldsymbol{l}^c]_\times = P^c \, L \, (P^c)^T \qquad (1)$$

with

$$L = \begin{bmatrix} [\boldsymbol{w}]_\times & -\boldsymbol{r} \\ -\boldsymbol{r}^T & 0 \end{bmatrix} \qquad (2)$$

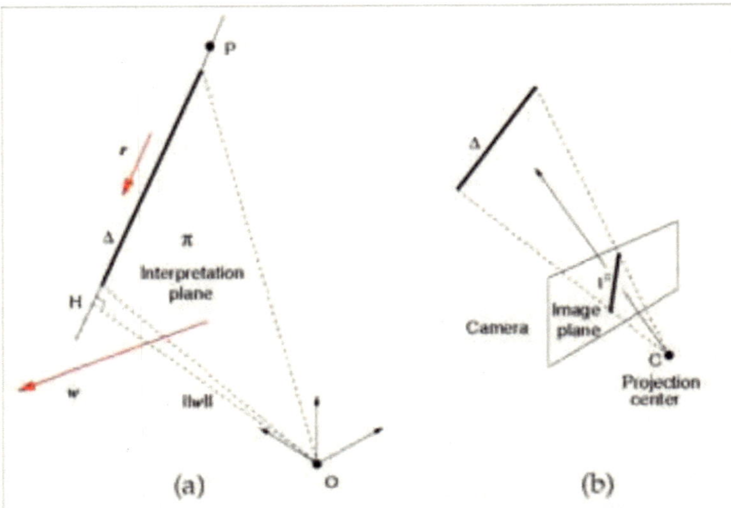

Figure 2. (a) The geometric representation of a 3-D line with the Plücker coordinates $\mathcal{L} = (\boldsymbol{r}, \boldsymbol{w})$. (b) A backprojection of an image line does not completely defines the 3-D line from which it came from

$\boldsymbol{w}$ is a vector with a direction perpendicular to the interpretation plane (also called pullback plane) which contains the straight line and the origin of the frame (the projection centre **C** in Figure 2b). It is a suitable representation since one may easily deal with geometrical transformations (Bartoli, 2001) including the perspective projection. The dual of the Plücker matrix, L^*, may also represent the 3-D straight line, with the intersection of two planes. L and L^* are related with a simple rule ($L\,L^* = 0$) and both representations are commonly used. These two (4 x 4) matrices are defined up to a scale, skewsymmetric and singular. The rank value (2) is expressing the orthogonality constraint between the two vectors $\boldsymbol{r}$ and $\boldsymbol{w}$. Moreover, with the derivation of the characteristic polynomial of the Plücker matrix, one can easily show that eigenvalues are complex conjugates scalars ($i\,\mu$, $-i\,\mu$, 0, 0) with the expression $\mu^2 = \|\boldsymbol{r}\|^2 + \|\boldsymbol{w}\|^2$. μ can be arbitrarily set to any nonzero value in order to normalize **L**.

$\boldsymbol{P}^c$ is the perspectivity, a (3 x 4) real matrix, composed of the camera parameters matrix $\boldsymbol{K}^c$, the 3-D rotation R and the position vector $\boldsymbol{t}$ of the object frame w.r.t. the camera frame:

$$P^c = K^c \begin{bmatrix} R & t \end{bmatrix} = K^c \begin{bmatrix} (r_1, r_2, r_3), t \end{bmatrix} = \begin{bmatrix} p_1^T \\ p_2^T \\ p_3^T \end{bmatrix} \tag{3}$$

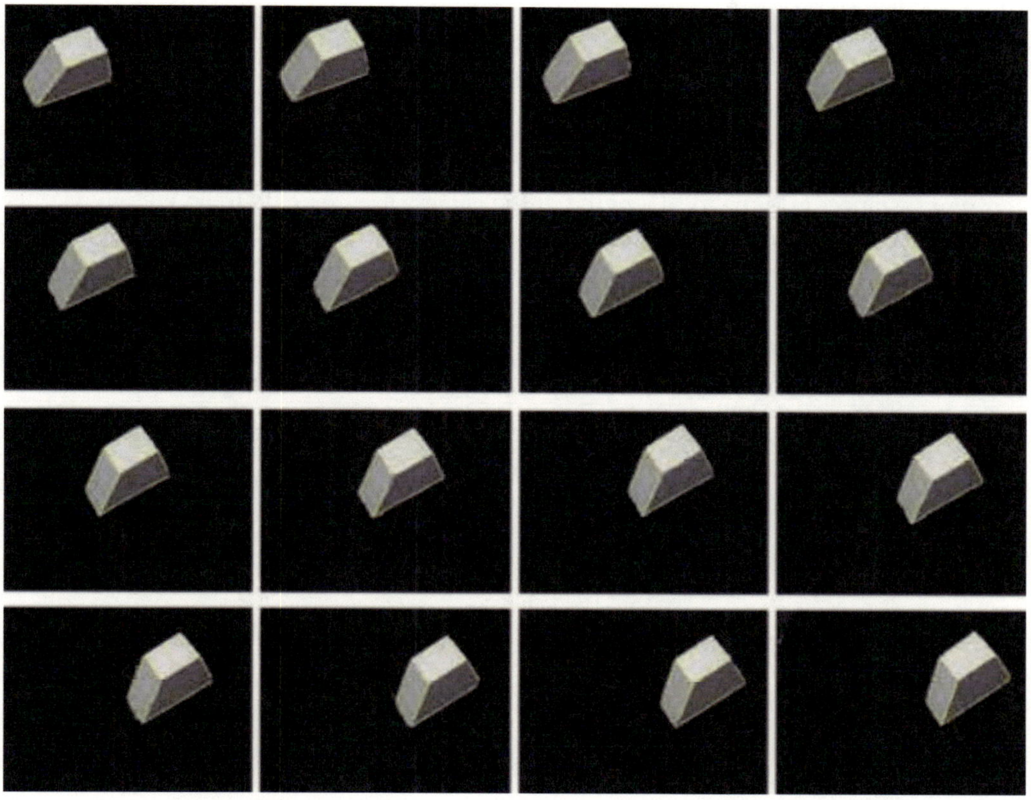

Figure 3. Tracking simple shape in a structured environment. The modelbased polyedral object pose estimation is used to compute the camera displacements during the image sequence

It is now clear that (1) is non linear with respect to the pose parameters r_1, r_2, r_3 and t. The pose computation needs to solve these parameters given a set of n 3-D lines Δ_i and the corresponding imaged lines l_i^c. It may be shown from equation (1) applied to the ith line, that we have

$$\left(\left[l_i^c \right]_\times \otimes \left(r_i^T , w_i^T \right) \right) \begin{pmatrix} r_3 \times t \\ -r_2 \times t \\ r_1 \\ r_1 \times t \\ r_2 \\ -r_3 \end{pmatrix} = 0 \tag{4}$$

where $\otimes$ is the matrix Kronecker product. This is a linear system with respect to the (18 x 1) vector of algebraically dependent unknowns, and it can be solved with at least $n = 3$ straight lines.

3.3 Pose recovery from collinear points

In this part, we discuss on a very particular case of pose from points, especially when points are all lying on a common line as it is with fiducial markers or for patterns with structured lighting.

Recovering the relative orientation (2 dof - a unit vector $\boldsymbol{r}$) and the position (a 3-vector $\boldsymbol{t}$) of a set of n collinear points such as the markers in Figure 4, with respect to the camera frame has been previously investigated by Haralick fifteen years ago (Haralick, 1992). The interpoint distances and the focal length f of the camera are assumed to be known. Haralick solved this problem with a linear algorithm.

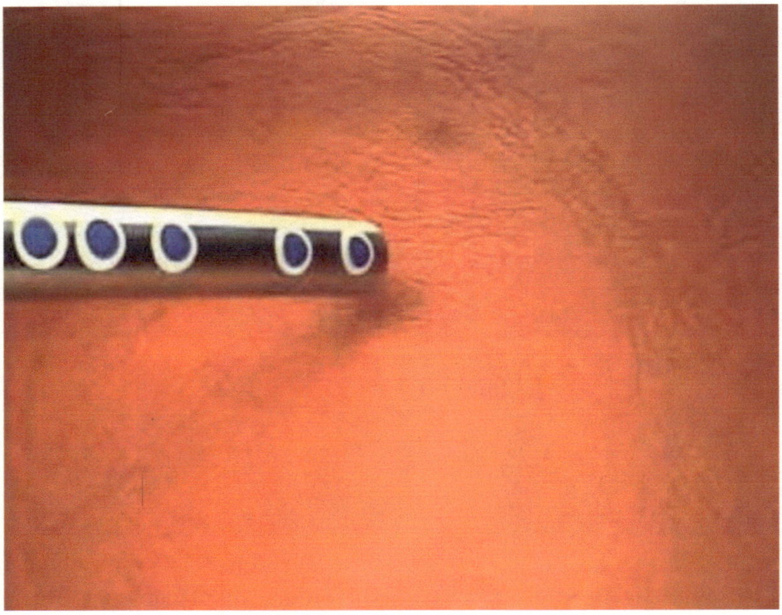

Figure 4. Collinear points (centroids of blue markers) stuck on a metallic and cylindrical surface

Let $\boldsymbol{P}_0 = \boldsymbol{t}$, $\boldsymbol{P}_1 = \boldsymbol{t} + \lambda_1 \boldsymbol{r}$, $\boldsymbol{P}_2 = \boldsymbol{t} + \lambda_2 \boldsymbol{r}$, ..., $\boldsymbol{P}_{n-1} = \boldsymbol{t} + \lambda_{n-1} \boldsymbol{r}$ be n distinct points where λ_i represents the distance between the $i+1^{th}$ and i^{th} points. The first point $\boldsymbol{P}_0$ is arbitrarily chosen as the origin ($\lambda_0=0$), hence the perspective projection $\boldsymbol{Q}_i$ of the ith point with homogeneous coordinates $(u_i, v_i, 1)$ is given by

$$\begin{bmatrix} 0 & 0 & 1 \end{bmatrix} (\boldsymbol{t}+\lambda_i \boldsymbol{r}) \begin{bmatrix} u_i \\ v_i \\ 1 \end{bmatrix} = \boldsymbol{K}^c (\boldsymbol{t}+ \lambda_i \boldsymbol{r}) \tag{5}$$

where $\boldsymbol{K}^c$ is a (3 x 3) upper diagonal matrix containing the parameters of the camera. From the above equation, Haralick built an homogeneous linear system with a univariate matrix $\boldsymbol{K}^c = \mathrm{diag}(f, f, 1)$ and vectors $\boldsymbol{t}$ and $\boldsymbol{r}$ as unknowns

$$\begin{bmatrix} A_r & A_t \end{bmatrix} \begin{bmatrix} r \\ t \end{bmatrix} = 0 \qquad (6)$$

A_r and by A_t are two ($2n$ x 3) real matrices whose components are functions of the camera parameters and the λ's. A closedform solution can be found with $n > 2$ distinct points. This system may be reformulated as a classical optimization problem with an equality constraint $\|r\|=1$. The solution for r is given by the eigenvector associated with the smallest eigenvalue of the following symmetric matrix $E = A_r^T (I - A_t (A_t^T A_t)^{-1} A_t^T) A_r$ and the position vector t is straightforwardly given by the expression $t = -A_t (A_t^T A_t)^{-1} A_t^T A_r r$. We end up with two estimates for r (a twofold ambiguity in the sign). However, for real objects placed in front of the camera, the third component of vector t must be strictly positive assuming that the camera zaxis (usually, the optical axis) is pointed towards the scene. This leads to the uniqueness of the solution for the pose.
It worth pointing out that in presence of both noisy data and close points in the object pattern, matrices Ar and At are illconditioned, which may introduce a significant bias in the results. The use of the least mean squares for $n > 3$ and the lack of data normalization in the original algorithm tend the solution to be sensitive to the matrix condition number. One has to pay attention to data normalization (Hartley, 1997) since the pose estimation may be computed with points not always well scattered. This may also lead to numerical problems. To lower the condition number, it seems advisable to normalize data coordinates with an affine transformation (Trucco, 1998).

3.4 Pose recovery from spheres

To deal with quadratic primitives, we begin with the pose from spheres in this paragraph. The projection of a sphere surface through the central projection is a cone with the vertex at the projection centre (see Figure 5a). The intersection of that cone with the sphere surface is called the contour generator (Γ) whereas intersections with the image plane provide the apparent contour (γ), both are elliptic planar curves in general.
To our knowledge, the mathematical formulation and a solution to the 3-D pose of spherical objects has been firstly proposed by Shin and Ahmad (Shin, 1989). The solution was based on 3-D analytical geometry and a closedform solution is given. SafaeeRad et al. (SafaeeRad, 1992) have also studied spherical objects pose in the context of mobile robotics and they have pointed out some major practical limitations in the pose accuracy, like the location of edges used in the ellipse parameters fitting, the uncertainty of intrinsic scale factors (due to timing mismatches that occur between camera scanning hardware and image acquisition hardware) and also the radial distortion of the lens. Ferri et al. (Ferri, 1993) present some algorithms for linear and quadratic primitives which include the computation of the 3-D pose and in particular a quadric of revolution. They provide a simple pose recovery procedure from the eigendecomposition of the matrix representation and they mentioned that in the case of a sphere, it must have two equal eigenvalues. Pose determination and camera calibration by means of images of spherical objects has also been studied, in particular by Teramoto and Xu (Teramoto, 2002), by Agrawal and Davis (Agrawal, 2003), by Dhome et al. (Dhome, 1990) and by Daucher et al. (Daucher, 1994).

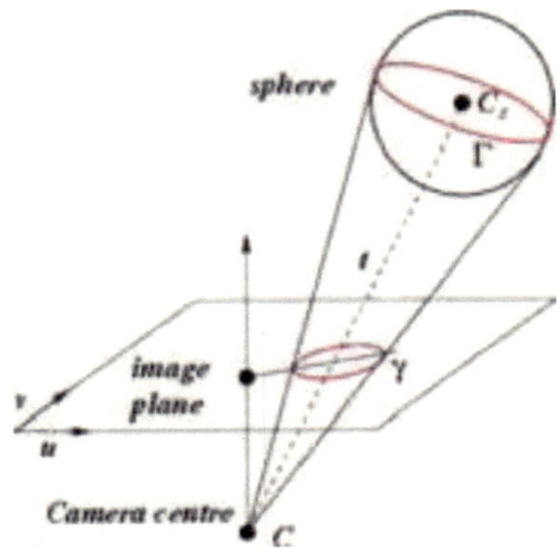

(a)

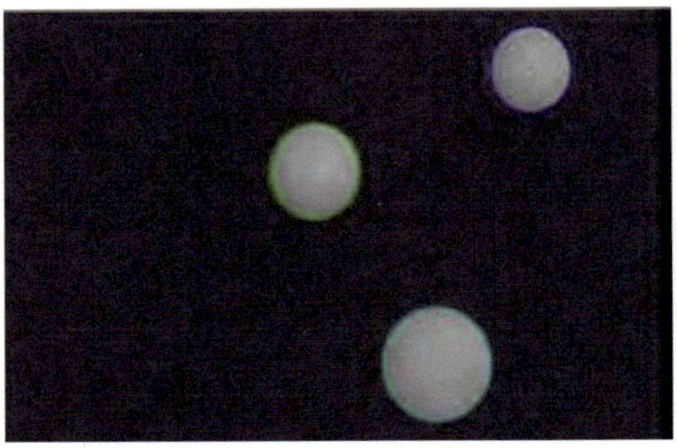

(b)

Figure 5. (a) A sphere, its contour generator (**Γ**) and its apparent contour (γ) in image plane is a conic. (b) Each detected ellipse is represented by a matrix E^* related to the 3-D position of the sphere centre

A sphere S is a quadric, and with the homogeneous coordinates of any point $\boldsymbol{M}$ on the sphere surface, it can be represented by a (4 x 4) symmetrical matrix S as $\boldsymbol{M}^T S \boldsymbol{M} = 0$. The matrix S depends on the radius r_s and the sphere position vector $\boldsymbol{t} = (t_x, t_y, t_z)^T$ from its centre to the world reference frame. When the camera reference frame coincides with the world reference frame, t_z is chosen in the direction perpendicular to the image plane, and pointing towards the scene. When expressed in that frame, it is provided by

$$S(r_s, \boldsymbol{t}) = \begin{bmatrix} I & -\boldsymbol{t} \\ -\boldsymbol{t}^T & \|\boldsymbol{t}\|^2 - r_s^2 \end{bmatrix} \tag{7}$$

where $\boldsymbol{I}$ is the identity matrix. Since $\|t\|$ is the distance between the sphere centre and the projection centre, $\boldsymbol{C}$, the scalar $\|t\|^2 - r_s^2$ must be positive as it is for a sphere placed in front of the camera, taken into account its own size. The dual of the sphere S is a sphere represented by the adjoint S^* of S since it is a symmetric matrix. It is given by $S^* = S^{-1}$. Both matrices S and S^* will be used hereinafter since a sphere and its image are easily related by dual matrices.

With the pinhole camera model and homogeneous coordinates, a 3-D point $\boldsymbol{M}$ is projected onto the image plane in a 2-D point $\boldsymbol{m}$ such that

$$m = P^c M \tag{8}$$

with

$$P^c = K^c \begin{bmatrix} 1 & 0 & 0 & 0 \\ 0 & 1 & 0 & 0 \\ 0 & 0 & 1 & 0 \end{bmatrix} \tag{9}$$

where the (3 x 4) camera matrix P^c is a perspectivity (or camera matrix) and λ is a non null scalar. When expressed in the camera frame with the projection centre C as the origin, the camera matrix is of the form given by (8). Under the camera matrix P^c, the outline of the sphere S is an ellipse E in the image which can be represented with a (3 x 3) symmetric matrix E. The dual of E is the adjoint E^* which can be related to the adjoint of S as follow

$$E^* = P^c\, S^*\, (P^c)^T \tag{10}$$

By substituting equations (7) and (9) in (10), it has been shown by Agrawal (Agrawal, 2003) that

$$(K^c)^{-1}\, E^*\, (K^c)^{-T} = I - \frac{1}{r_s^2}\, t\, t^T \ , \quad \mu \in \mathbb{R}^* \tag{11}$$

The work of Teramoto et al. (Teramoto, 2002) is a pose determination method in which the position direction and the size of a ball is derived in the case of known intrinsic parameters. It is extended here to the recovery of the full 3-D position with a slightly modification of the original work which will serve to analyze the eigendecomposition in presence of noisy data. Given the dual matrix E^*, let us denote with $t_u = t/s$, a unit vector with a nonnull scalar ($s=\pm\|t\|$). Starting from equation (7), we have:

$$Q^* = I - \frac{s^2}{r_s^2}\, t_u t_u^T \tag{12}$$

with $Q^*=(K^c)^{-1}\, E^*\, (K^c)^{-T}$. Since s/r_s is always greater 1, the righthandside of the above equation is a rank-3 matrix, it can be written as:

$$[t_1, t_2, t_u]\, diag\left(1, 1, 1-\frac{s^2}{r_s^2}\right) [t_1, t_2, t_u]^T \tag{13}$$

and the lefthandside can be decomposed as $U\, diag\, (\lambda_1, \lambda_2, \lambda_3)\, U^T$ with $U=[U_1, U_2, U_3]$ is an orthonormal matrix. It's clear that we have

$$1-\frac{s^2}{r_s^2} = \lambda_3 / \lambda_2 \tag{14}$$

and

$$t = s\, U_3 \tag{15}$$

The solution is unique since the sign for t_z ($t_z > 0$) reveals the sign for the scalar s. It is worth pointing out that in one hand the symmetrical matrix E^* has 5 independent components as it represents an ellipse in the image. In the other hand, the symmetrical matrix $I - t\, t^T/r_s^{\,2}$ has two eigenvalues equal to one (clearly $t\, t^T$ is a rank-1 matrix), hence representing a "calibrated ellipse". So, it's clear that the geometric information issued from equation (11) has not been fully exploited. This means that either the position vector t can be solved with an overdetermined system (with data redundancy) or other parameters (like intrinsic parameters) may be determined from a unique sphere and its corresponding ellipse in a single image. Let us now considering the former case. Following this remark, a simple improvement of the Teramoto's method consists of a slightly modification of equation (14) since the two singular values λ_1 and λ_2 must be equal with uncorrupted data. Thus, we propose to replace equation (14) to by

$$1-\frac{s^2}{r_s^2} = 2\lambda_3 / (\lambda_1+\lambda_2) \tag{16}$$

that is λ_1 is replaced by the midvalue of the first two singular values in presence of noise. The resulting matrix Q_m* is then the closest symmetrical matrix to Q* with the Frobenius norm and is given by $Q_m^* = U\, diag\left((\lambda_1+\lambda_2)/2, (\lambda_1+\lambda_2)/2, \lambda_3\right) U^T$. Once the matrix Q_m* has been derived, the (4 x 4) matrix $\hat{S}$ may be computed with the estimated position vector $\hat{t}$ thanks to the Teramoto's method, that is with $Q_m^* = I - \frac{1}{r_s^2}\hat{t}\,\hat{t}^T$.

Simulation results reported in Figure 6 show a better behaviour with respect to noise for the modified version we propose compared to the original algorithm. It is simple to implement and it does not require more computations. It has been used as an efficient tool while tracking the 3-D position of a moving camera mounted on a wheeled robot for robotic competition (see Figure 7).

Windowing techniques are used to define the search space of the area of interest (the closest red ball). The diagonal of the inner blue square that area is corresponding to the estimated depth, whereas the the blue cross are corresponding to the position of the centre. (add at the end of figure caption)of the centre.

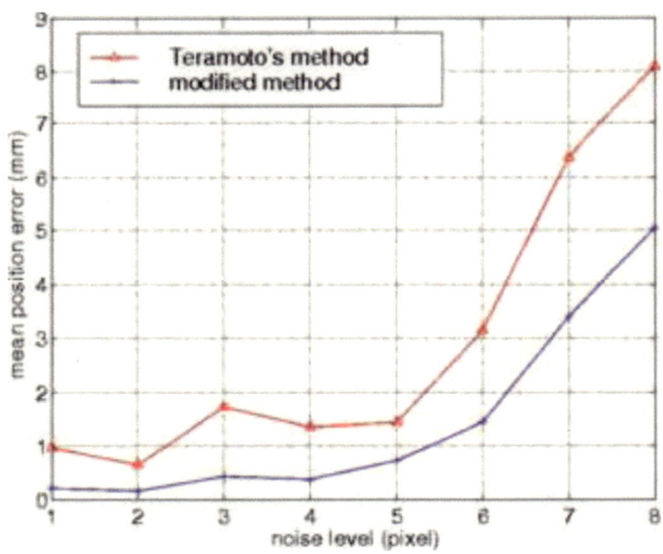

Figure 6. Mean position errors with the Teramoto's method (red) and with the modified version (blue) with respect to varying noise level

Figure 7. 3-D tracking of red balls. A camera is mounted on a wheeled robot which is moving in the ground plane (basketball robot players). Given the radius, red balls should be tracked and picked up

3.5 Pose estimation from cylinders

To go ahead with quadratic primitives, we now discuss on the pose from cylinders, especially with straight homogeneous circular cylinders (SHCC), that is the class of cylinders with a straight axis and a circular section with constant radius (see Figure 8).

In the late 80s and early 90s, shape from contour approaches have been developed in an attempt to determine constraints on a threedimensional scene structure based on different assumptions about the shape. The understanding of the relations between image contours geometry and the shape of the observed object and the viewing parameters is still a challenging problem and it is essential that special shapes are not represented by freeform surfaces without regard to their special properties, but treated in a way more appropriate to their simple nature. Explicit relations from occluding contours to the model of a curved threedimensional object have been presented for objects with geometrical properties such as generalized cylinders or surfaces of revolution (Dhome, 1992; Ferri, 1993; Kriegman, 1990 ; Ponce, 1989).

More recent works are based on the image contour of a cylinder crosssection when it is visible. Puech et al. (Puech, 1997) used the image of two crosssections to locate a straight uniform generalized cylinder in 3-D space and Shiu and Huang (Shiu, 1991) solve the problem for a finite and known cylinder height, that is a 3-D pose determination for 5 degrees of freedom. SafaeeRad et al. (SafaeeRad, 1992) estimate the 3-D circle centre and orientation from the projection of one of the two circles on the cylinder ends. However, ellipse fitting generally becomes inaccurate when the cylinder radius is small with respect to the cylinder height and also since both circles on the cylinder are not completely visible. Huang et al. (Huang, 1996) solve the pose determination of a cylinder through a reprojection transformation which may be thought as a rectification transformation. The computed transformation is applied to the image of the cylinder and brings the camera optical axis to perpendicularly intersect the cylinder axis, which is then parallel to one of the two image axes. The new image (called "canonical" image) is a symmetrical pattern which simplify the computation of the pose. It is an interesting method which provides an analytical solution of the problem, including the recovery of the height of the cylinder. However, it's requiring an image transformation and errors for estimating the reprojection transformation may lead to significant bias in the contours location of the resulting canonical image and consequently to the pose parameters. In a similar way, Wong et al. (Wong, 2004) take advantage of the invariance of surface of revolution (SOR) to harmonic homology and have proposed to recover the depth and the focal length (by assuming that the principal point is located at the image center and that the camera has unit aspect ratio) from the resulting silhouette which exhibits a bilateral symmetry. It is also a rectification which brings the revolution axis to coincide with the *y*axis of the image. If the image of a latitude circle in the SOR can be located, the orientation of the revolution axis can also be estimated.

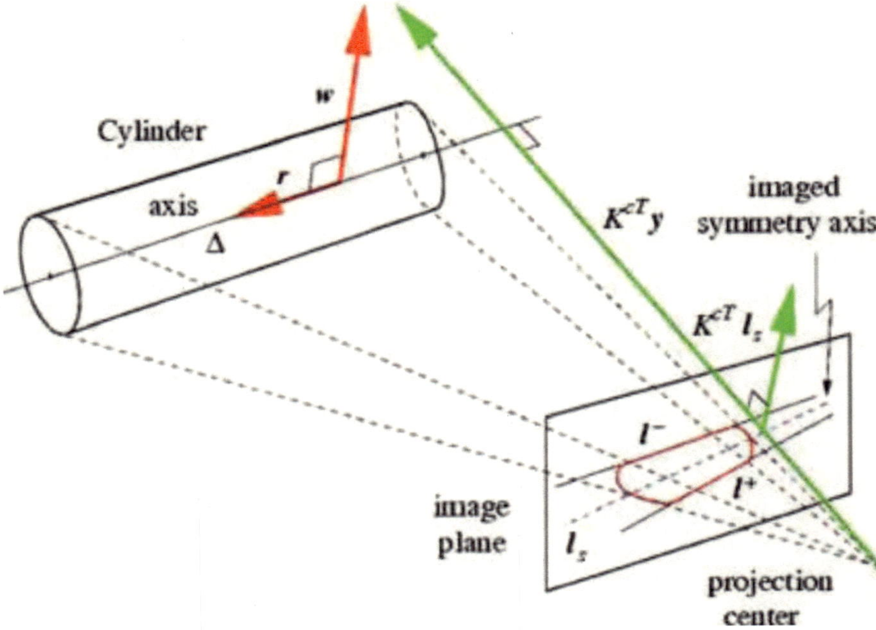

Figure 8. A straight homogeneous circular cylinder and its perspective projection. The backprojection of apparent lines (l^-, l^+) is a couple of planes $(P^c)^T l^-$ and $(P^c)^T l^+$ passing through the centre. The image of the cylinder axis Δ is the axis l_s of the harmonic homology H relating the two apparent lines

Some other approaches based on contours and shading have also been proposed. Asada et al. (Asada, 1992) provide a technique to recognize the shape of a cylinder crosssection and to determine the orientation axis under the weak Lambertian assumption for the reflectance of the object surface when the surface does not include specular component. Caglioti and Castelli (Caglioti, 1999) focus their work rather on metallic surfaces (cylinders and cones) and they recover the pose parameters by means of the axial symmetric reflection model. However, although methods which do not solely involve geometric features should be more investigated to achieve an accurate pose estimation, these two latter methods assume an orthographic projection for the camera model, a too strong approximation when cylinder orientation is partly embedded in the perspective effect. It has been shown in (Doignon, 2007) that the estimation of the Plücker coordinates $(\boldsymbol{r},\boldsymbol{w})$ of the cylinder axis can be directly recovered from the degenerate conic $C = l^- (l^+)^T + l^+ (l^-)^T$ built with the two apparent lines (l^-, l^+) and the cylinder's radius r_c with a calibrated camera. In one hand, we have

$$(K^c)^T \, C \, K^c = U \, D \, U^T = U \, diag(\lambda_1 \;\; \lambda_2 \;\; 0) \, U^T \qquad (17)$$

and in the other hand (after some computations , see (Doignon, 2007) for details).

$$(K^c)^T \, C \, K^c \equiv (I - r\,r^T - z\,z^T) = [a \; z_u \; r] \begin{bmatrix} 1 & 0 & 0 \\ 0 & 1-\sigma^2 & 0 \\ 0 & 0 & 0 \end{bmatrix} \begin{bmatrix} a^T \\ z_u^T \\ r^T \end{bmatrix} \quad (18)$$

with $z = (\sqrt{1-\alpha^2}/\|w\|)\, r \times w$, $\alpha = r_c/\sqrt{\|w\|^2 - r_c^2}$ and the unit vector $z_u = z/\sigma$. It is easy to see that $U = [a \; z_u \; r]$, $w \equiv z_u \times r = a$ and finally $\|w\| = r_c \sqrt{1 + \lambda_1/\lambda_2}$.

Some results illustrated in Figure 9 and Figure 10, show the efficacy of the proposed fitting and pose determination. Firstly, the pose determination is performed in a simple and controlled environment (Figure 9). Second, in a complex environment with a moving background (the abdomen of a pig), a cylindricalshaped laparoscopic instrument is detected (thanks to a joint huesaturation colour attribute). Plücker coordinates are computed with the method described above. It is shown in (Doignon, 2007) that the direction of vector **w** is directly related to the image of the cylinder's axis.

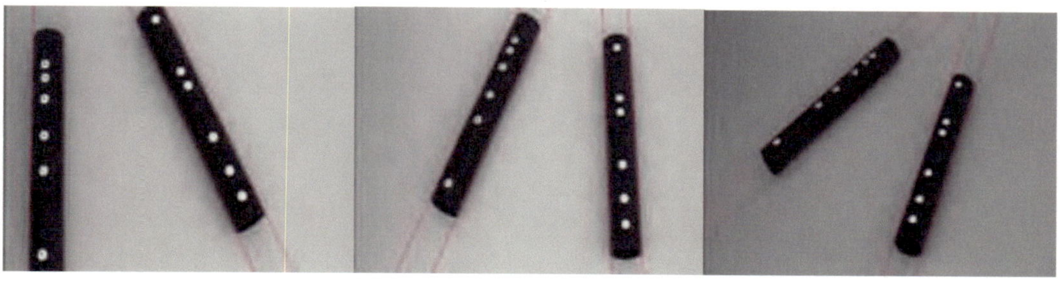

Figure 9. The 3-D tracking of the cylinder's axis through the detection of the conjugate apparent lines in a uniform background

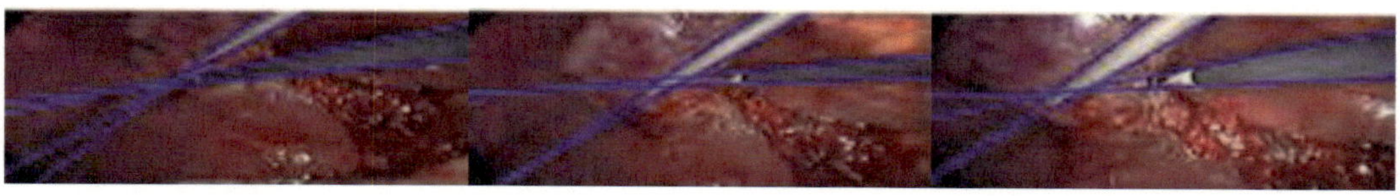

Figure 10. The 3-D of the cylinder's axis of cylindricalshaped laparoscopic instruments through the detection of the conjugate apparent lines in a complex environment (abdomen of a pig)

3.6 Pose estimation with multiple types of geometrical features

We now turn to a little bit towards more complex environments. As some features may be occluded during the tracking, it is necessary to estimate the pose with multiple features. We introduce this approach with an example in Figure 11. The virtual visual servoingbased pose estimation (see the end of paragraph 2.1) is carried out with three geometrical features : a cylinder, a circular needle and marker points. Only four degrees of freedom are necessary to estimate the attitude of the instrument axis. The 4 dof of the pose can be determined using the contour generator and its image (the apparent contour) of the cylinder (see paragraph 3.5). However, the positions of the marking spots not only define the proper rotations and translations, but also give information on the orientation and position of the axis of the

shaft. We then chose to estimate the 6 dofs of the instrument with all the available features. This can be done with analytical methods using both the apparent contours and one known point at the cylinder's surface (Nageotte, 2006).
The full pose estimation is interesting for robustness considerations only if all the available information given by the apparent lines and all the spots is used. To this purpose, the Virtual Visual Servoing (VVS) due to Sundareswaran (Sundareswaran, 1998) and also by Marchand (Marchand, 2002) and may handle the information redundancy. VVS is a numerical iterative method for minimizing the error between the extracted features and the forward projection of the object in the images and based on the imagebased visual servoing (IBVS) schemes. This process needs the computation of an interaction matrix which relates the variations of each image feature and the camera velocity screw $\boldsymbol{\tau}$. With these image features, the full interaction matrix L_s has the following generic form:

$$\begin{vmatrix} \dot{l}^+ \\ \dot{l}^- \\ \dot{p}_1 \\ \dot{p}_2 \\ \vdots \\ \dot{p}_n \\ x_e \\ y_e \\ r_{min} \\ r_{max} \\ \alpha_e \end{vmatrix} = \begin{vmatrix} L_{line}(l+) \\ L_{line}(l-) \\ L_{pt}(p_1) \\ L_{pt}(p_2) \\ \vdots \\ L_{pt}(p_n) \\ L_{ellipse} \end{vmatrix} \boldsymbol{\tau} = L_s \boldsymbol{\tau} \tag{19}$$

The interaction matrices associated to a point $\boldsymbol{p}$, $\boldsymbol{L}_{pt}$, to a line $\boldsymbol{l}$, $\boldsymbol{L}_{line}$, and associated to an ellipse $\boldsymbol{E}=(x_e, y_e, r_{min}, r_{max}, \alpha_e)$, $\boldsymbol{L}_{ellipse}$, can be found in Espiau et al. (Espiau, 1992) or in Chaumette et al. (Chaumette, 1993). In order to guarantee a fast convergence and a good stability of the VVS, it is useful to initialize the algorithm close enough to the real pose. For this purpose, we use the modifed version of the Haralick's method and the DeMenthon iterative method (DeMenthon, 1995) for points, that of Dhome (Dhome, 1992) to get the 4 solutions for the pose of a circle and the pose determination of the axis of a circular cylinder described at the paragraph 3.5. With this initial pose parameters estimates for the attitude of the camera with respect to the object of interest (a laparoscopic surgical instrument, see Figure 11), the following control law is applied to the virtual camera

$$\boldsymbol{\tau} = -G\, \widehat{L_s^+}\, (s - s^*) \tag{20}$$

until the control vector becomes smaller than a specified value. The process converges quickly towards the real pose of the camera (see Figure 11).

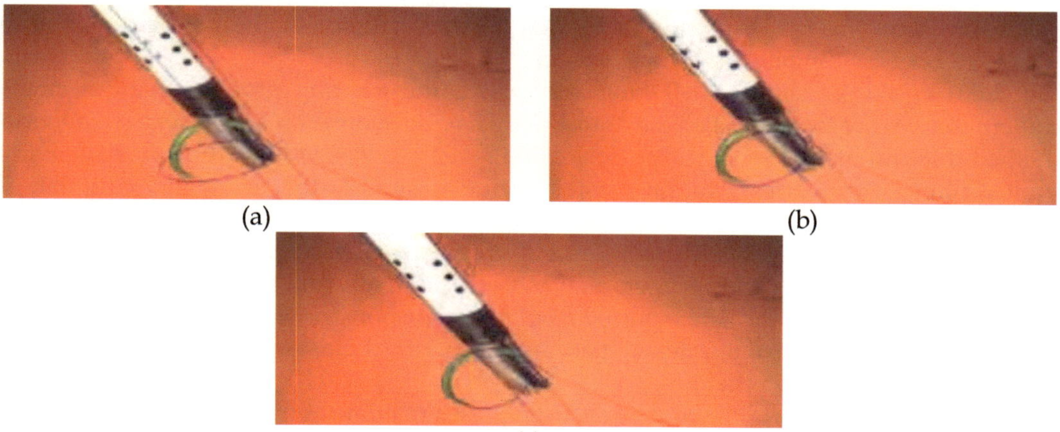

Figure 11. The pose estimation as a Virtual Visual Servoing process with multiple geometric features (apparent lines, markers and a circular needle). (a) The blue lines are the projections with the initial virtual camera position. (bc). The projections when the error vector (s - s^*) tends to 0

4. Further Readings : Pose estimation with multiple cues

We close the chapter by touching upon the difficult problem of the pose estimation and tracking in a complex and unknown environment. In many situations, like for assistance domestic environments, outdoor navigation or tracking inside the human body, the observed scene is unstructured and the background is not uniform nor constant. It is then not a trivial task to detect object of interests or patterns, since brightness and colour are changing and the background moves due to human displacements, the wind or the breathing or heart beating in the third case, leading to shadows, occlusions or specularities. Some rather recent works integrate multiple visual cues like colour (Vincze, 2005), texture (Pressigout, 2006) or global&local descriptions (Kragic, 2002) or a learning stage (Vacchetti, 2004) to improve the tracking process.

The Vision for Robotics (V4R) software package proposed by Vincze et al. (Vincze, 2005) integrates multiple cues like edge gradient, colour, intensity, topological interrelations among features and pose from preceding frames to provide an efficient visual modelbased tracking tool in realistic and unconstrained environments. These cues are derived not only from the images but also from object parameters (the model) and pose information stored within previous tracking cycles. A fourstage tracking scheme is designed, from the 2-D feature extraction to the pose computation and validation.

For domestic environment (living room), Kragic & Christensen propose to use both the appearance and geometrical models to estimate the position and orientation of the object relative to the camera/robot coordinate system. Following a threestage strategy (initialization, pose estimation, tracking), this system may be seen as a coarsetofine tracking. The initialization step provides an approximation to the current object pose by means of the Principle Components Analysis. Once the model is found, a local fitting is used to extract linear primitives from which the pose is computed. Finally, if the object or the eyeinhand robot start to move, the Drummond's method (Drummond & Cipolla, 2000) is adopted to provide a realtime estimate of the object pose.

Vacchetti et al. (Vacchetti, 2004) have formulated the tracking problem using a single camera in terms of local bundle adjustment and have developed an image correspondences method that can handle short and widebaseline matching. The video information of a very limited number of reference images created during a training stage is merged with that of preceding frames during the tracking. The tracking process needs a 3-D model of any object that can be represented by a 3-D mesh. Thus, keyframes serve to register an incoming image by means of a set of extracted corners thanks to the minimization of the reprojection error with the Tukey Mestimator. The reported results have demonstrated a very good robustness with respect to aspect changes, model inaccuracies, partial occlusions, focal length and scale changes, and illumination changes.

Pressigout and Marchand (Pressigout, 2006) propose a realtime hybrid 3-D tracking with the integration of the texture information in a nonlinear edgebased pose estimation algorithm. Pose and camera displacements are formulated in terms of a full scale nonlinear optimization instead of a point of interestbased pose estimation. In particular, the camera displacement estimation is based on a two images intensity matching. A non linear criterion based on intensity mapping error is defined to that purpose from which an interaction matrix is derived.

5. Conclusion

With this article, we have addressed some issues in pose estimation with geometrical features and a modelbased approach in the context of monocular vision. While the 3-D tracking/estimation may be performed with optimal estimators (with the Kalman filter and its extended/nonlinear versions or with the particle filter also referred to as the sequential Monte Carlo method), system models and state vectors need the pose parameters recovery or the 3-D motion recovery from the motion field. The pose determination is needed for applications with high accurate 3-D positioning requirements, when occlusions, shadows or abrupt motions have to be handle. To this purpose, several geometrical featurebased approaches have been reviewed for solving the pose with various constrained degrees of freedom.

Cue integration leads to robustness and automatic measurement of scene complexity. This is of prime importance to exploit the video information captured in a complex environment with dynamical changes. Composite features, colour, edges, texture integration are some additional data which have brought significant improvements of the tracker's behaviour thanks to robust and Mestimators. This is a key factor of success for a visionbased module with some autonomous capabilities, hence for the achievement of some visionbased (semi) autonomous tasks.

6. References

Agrawal, M. & Davis, L.S. (2003). Camera calibration using spheres: A semidefinite programming approach, *Proceedings of the IEEE Int'l Conf. on Computer Vision*, Vol. 2, p. 782789, Nice, France

Aloimonos, Y. (1990). Perspective approximations, *Image and Vision Computing*, Vol. 8, No 3, p. 177192, Elsevier Science

Alter, T.D. (1994). 3-D Pose from 3 Points Using WeakPerspective, *IEEE Transactions on Pattern Analysis and Machine Intelligence*, Vol. 16, No 8, p. 802808, IEEE Computer Society Press

Andreff, N.; Espiau, B. & Horaud, R. P. (2000). Visual Servoing from Lines, *Proceedings of the IEEE Int'l Conf. on Robotics and Automation*, p. 20702075

Ansar, A. & Daniilidis, K. (2003). Linear Pose Estimation from Points or Lines. *IEEE Transactions on Pattern Analysis and Machine Intelligence*, Vol. 25, No 5, p. 578589, IEEE Computer Society Press

Asada, M.; Nakamura, T. & Shirai, Y. (1992). Weak Lambertian Assumption for Determining Cylindrical Shape and Pose from Shading and Contour, *Proceedings of the IEEE Int'l Conf. on Computer Vision and Pattern Recognition*, p. 726729, IEEE Computer Society

Bartoli, A. & Sturm, P. (2001). The 3-D line motion matrix and alignment of line reconstructions, *Proceedings of the IEEE International Conference on Computer Vision and Pattern Recognition*, Hawaii, USA. p. 287292, IEEE Computer Society Press NY

Bolles, R.C. & Cain, R.A. (1982). Recognizing and locating partially visible objects, the localfeaturefocus method, *Int'l Journal of Robotics Research*, Vol. 1, No 3, p. 5782, SAGE Publications, Thousand Oaks

Bolles, R.C. & Horaud, R.P. (1986). 3-DPO: A threedimensional part orientation system, *Int'l Journal of Robotics Research*, Vol. 5, No 3, p. 326, SAGE Publications, Thousand Oaks

Caglioti, V. & Castelli, E. (1999). Recovering cylindric and conic surfaces from contours and reflections, *Pattern Recognition Letters*, Vol. 20, p. 367382, Elsevier Science

Chaumette, F.; Rives, P. & Espiau, B. (1993). Classification and realization of the different visionbased tasks. *In Visual Servoing, K. Hashimoto (ed.)*, Vol. 7, p. 199228, World Scientific Series in Robotics and Automated Systems, Singapore

Chen, H. (1991). Pose Determination from linetoplane correspondences: Existence of solutions and closedform solutions, *IEEE Transactions on Pattern Analysis and Machine Intelligence*, Vol. 13, No 6, p. 530541, IEEE Computer Society Press

Daucher, N.; Dhome, M. & Lapresté, J.-T. (1994). Camera Calibration From Spheres Images, *Proceedings of the third European Conference on Computer Vision*, Vol. 1, p. 449454, Stockholm, Sweden

David, P.; DeMenthon, D. & Duraiswami, R. & Samet, H. (2002). SoftPOSIT: Simultaneous Pose and Correspondence Determination, *Proceedings of the European Conference on Computer Vision*, Copenhagen, Denmark, SpringerVerlag

DeMenthon, D. & L.S. Davis, L.S. (1992). Exact and Approximate Solutions of the PerspectiveThreePoint Problem, *IEEE Transactions on Pattern Analysis and Machine Intelligence*, Vol. 14, No 11, p. 11001105, IEEE Computer Society Press

Dementhon, D. & Davis, L.-S. (1995). ModelBased Object Pose in 25 lines of Code, *Int'l. Journal of Computer Vision*, Vol. 15, No 1, p. 123141, Kluwer Academic Publishers

Dhome, M.; Richetin, M. & Lapresté, J.-T. & Rives, G. (1989). Determination of the attitude of 3-D objects from a single perspective view, *IEEE Transactions. on Pattern Analysis and Machine Intelligence*, Vol. 11, No 12, p. 12651278, IEEE Computer Society Press

Dhome, M; Lapresté, J.-T. & Rives, G. & Richetin, M. (1992). Spatial localization of modelled objects of revolution in monocular perspective vision, *Proceedings of the European Conference on Computer Vision*, Antibes, France

Dickmanns, E. D. & Graefe, V. (1988). Dynamic monocular machine vision, *Machine Vision Applications*, Vol. 1, p. 223240

Doignon C. & Abba G. (1999). A practical multiplane method for a lowcost camera calibration technique, *Proceedings of the fifth European Control Conference*, Karlsruhe, Germany, SpringerVerlag

Doignon, C. & De Mathelin, M. (2007). A Degenerate ConicBased Method for a Direct Fitting and 3-D Pose of Cylinders with a Single Perspective View, T*o appear in the proceedings of the IEEE Int'l. Conf. on Robotics and Automation*, Roma, Italy

Drummond, T. & Cipolla, R. (2000). RealTime Tracking of Multiple Articulated Structures in Multiple Views. *In proceedings of the European Conference on Computer Vision*, Vol. 2, p. 2036, SpringerVerlag, Dublin, Ireland

Espiau, B.; Chaumette, F. & Rives, P. (1992). A new approach to visual servoing in robotics. *IEEE Transactions on Robotics and Automation*, Vol. 8, No 3, p. 313326

Faugeras, O.D. & Toscani, G. (1987). Camera Calibration for 3-D Computer Vision, *Proceedings of the Int'l Workshop on Machine Vision and Machine Intelligence*, Tokyo, Japan

Ferri, M.; Mangili, F. & Viano, G. (1993). Projective Pose Estimation of Linear and Quadratic Primitives in Monocular Computer Vision, *Computer Vision, Graphics and Image Processing: Image understanding*, Vol. 58, No 1, p. 6684, Elsevier Science

Fischler, M.A. & Bolles, R.C. (1981). Random sample consensus: A paradigm for model fitting with application to image analysis and automated cartography, *Communications of the ACM*, Vol. 24, No 6, p. 381395

Gold, S.; Rangarajan, A. & Lu, C.P. & Pappu, S. & Mjolsness, E. (1998). New Algorithms for 2-D and 3-D Point Matching: Pose Estimation and Correspondence, *Pattern Recognition*, Vol. 31, p. 10191031, Elsevier Science

Grimson, W. E. L. (1990). *Object Recognition by Computer: The Role of Geometric Constraint*, MIT Press, Cambridge, MA. ISBN 0262071304

Grimson, W.E.L. & Huttenlocher, D.P. (1991). On the Verification of Hypothesized Matches in ModelBased Recognition, *IEEE Transactions on Pattern Analysis and Machine Intelligence*, Vol. 13, No 12, p. 12011213, IEEE Computer Society Press

Hager, G. D. & Toyama, K. (1998). The Xvision system: A portable substrate for realtime vision applications, *Computer Vision and Image Understanding*, Vol. 69, No 1, p. 2337, Elsevier Science

Hansen, C. & Henderson, T.C. (1989). CAGDbased computer vision, *IEEE Transactions on Pattern Analysis and Machine Intelligence*, Vol. 11, No 11, p. 11811193.

Haralick, R. M. & Chu, Y.H. & Watson, L.T. & Shapiro, L.G. (1984). Matching wire frame objects from their 2-D perspective projection, *Pattern Recognition*, Vol. 17, No 6, p. 607619, Elsevier Science

Haralick, R. M. (1989). Monocular vision using inverse perspective projection geometry: Analytic relations, *Proceedings of the IEEE Conference on Computer Vision and Pattern Recognition*, p. 370378, IEEE Press

Haralick, R. M.; Lee, C. & Ottenberg, K. & Nölle, M. (1991). Analysis and Solutions of the ThreePoint Perspective Pose Estimation Problem, *IEEE Conf. Computer Vision and Pattern Recognition*, p. 592598, Maui, Hawaï, USA, IEEE Computer Society Press

Haralick, R. M. & Shapiro, L.G. (1992). *Computer and Robot Vision*, vol. 1, AddisonWesley Publishing. ISBN 0201108771

Harris, C. G. & Stennet, C. (1990). RAPID A video rate object tracker, *Proceedings of the British Machine Vision Conf.*, p. 233236

Hartley, R. (1997). In defense of the eightpoint algorithm, *IEEE Transactions on Pattern Analysis and Machine Intelligence*, Vol. 19, No 6, p. 580593, IEEE Computer Society Press

Hartley, R. & Zisserman, A. (2000). *Multiple view geometry in computer vision*, Cambridge University Press, UK. ISBN 0521623049

Horaud, R.P. (1987). New Methods for Matching 3-D Objects with Single Perspective Views, *IEEE Transactions on Pattern Analysis and Machine Intelligence*, Vol. 9, No 3, p. 401412, IEEE Computer Society Press

Horaud, R.P.; Conio, B. & Leboulleux, O. & Lacolle, B. (1989). An Analytic Solution for the Perspective 4Point Problem, *Computer Vision, Graphics, and Image Processing*, vol. 47, p. 3344, Elsevier Science

Horn, B.K.P. (1986). *Robot Vision*, MIT Press, McGrawHill, Cambridge. ISBN 0262081598

Huang,J.-B.; Chen, Z. & Chia, T.-L. (1996). Pose determination of a cylinder using reprojection transformation, Vol. 17, p. 10891099, *Pattern Recognition Letters*, Elsevier Science

Hutchinson, S.; Hager, G. D. & Corke, P. I. (1996). A tutorial on visual servo control, *IEEE Transactions on Robotics and Automation*, Vol. 12, No 5, p. 651670

Huttenlocher, D. P. & Ullman, S. (1990). Recognizing Solid Objects by Alignment with an Image, *Int'l. Journal of Computer Vision*, Vol. 5, No 2, p. 195212, Kluwer Academic Publishers

Ikeuchi, K. (1987). Generating an interpretation tree from a CAD model for 3-D object recognition in binpicking tasks, *Int'l Journal of Computer Vision*, Vol. 1, No 2, p. 145165, Kluwer Academic Publishers

Jurie, F. (1999). Solution of the Simultaneous Pose and Correspondence Problem Using Gaussian Error Model, *Computer Vision and Image Understanding*, Vol. 73, No 3, p. 357373, Elsevier Science

Kragic, D & Christensen, H.I. (2002). Modelbased Techniques for Robotic Servoing and Grasping, *Proceedings of the IEEE/RSJ Int'l Conf. on Intelligent Robots and Systems*, p. 299304, ISBN 0780373987, Lausanne, Switzerland.

Kriegman, D.-J. & Ponce, J. (1990). On Recognizing and Positioning Curved 3-D Objects from Image Contours, *IEEE Transactions on Pattern Analysis and Machine Intelligence*, Vol. 12, No 12, p. 11271137, IEEE Computer Society Press

Lamdan, Y. & Wolfson, H.J. (1988). Geometric hashing: A general and efficient modelbased recognition scheme, *Proceedings of the IEEE Int'l Conf. on Computer Vision*, p. 238249, Tampa, FL, USA

Linnainmaa, S. ;Harwood, D. & Davis, L. S. (1988). Pose Determination of a ThreeDimensional Object Using Triangle Pairs, *IEEE Transactions on Pattern Analysis and Machine Intelligence*, Vol. 10, No 5, p. 634647, IEEE Computer Society Press

Liu, Y.; Huang, T.S. & Faugeras, O.D. (1990). Determination of camera location from 2-D to 3-D line and point, *IEEE Transactions on Pattern analysis and Machine Intelligence*, Vol. 12, No 1, p. 2837, IEEE Computer Society Press

Lowe, D.G. (1987). Threedimensional object recognition from single twodimensional images, *Artificial Intelligence*, Vol. 31, No 3, p. 355395, Elsevier Science

Marchand, E. & Chaumette, F. (2002). Virtual visual servoing: a framework for realtime augmented reality, *Proceedings of the EUROGRAPHICS Conference*, Vol. 21 (3 of Computer Graphics Forum), p. 289298, Saarbrücken, Germany

Marchand, E & Chaumette, F. (2004). Feature tracking for visual servoing purpose. *Proceedings of the Int'l. Workshop on Advances in Robot Vision: From Domestic Environments to Medical Applications, in conjunction with the IEEE:RSJ Int'l. Conf. on Inteeligent Robots and Systems*, p. 1020, Sendaï, Japan.

Marchand, E.; Spindler, F. & Chaumette, F. (2005). ViSP for visual servoing: a generic software platform with a wide class of robot control skills. *IEEE Robotics and Automation Magazine*, Vol. 12, No 4, p. 4052, ISSN 10709932

Meng, X & Hu, Z. (2003). A new easy camera calibration technique based on circular points, *Pattern Recognition*, Vol. 36, p. 11551164, Elsevier Science

Mitiche, A. (1995). *Computational Analysis of Visual Motion*, Advances in Computer Vision and Machine Intelligence Series, ISBN 9780306447860, SpringerVerlag

Mokhtarian, F. & Mackworth, A. (1986). Scalebased Description and Recognition of Planar Curves and TwoDimensional Shapes, *IEEE Transactions on Pattern Analysis and Machine Intelligence*, Vol. 8, No 1, p. 3443, IEEE Computer Society Press

Nageotte, F; Zanne, P. & Doignon, C. & de Mathelin, M. (2006). Visual ServoingBased Endoscopic Path Following for RobotAssisted Laparoscopic Surgery, *Proceedings of the IEEE/RSJ Int'l Conf. on Intelligent Robots and Systems*, Beijin, China

Navab, N. & Faugeras, O. D. (1993). Monocular Pose Determination from Lines : Critical sets and Maximum Number of Solutions, *IEEE Int'l Conf. on Computer Vision and Pattern Recognition*, p. 254260, IEEE Computer Society Press

Navab, N; Vieville, T. & Faugeras, O. D. (1993). The Critical Sets of Lines for Camera Displacement Estimation: A Mixed EuclideanProjective and Constructive Approach, *Proceedings of the IEEE Int'l Conf. on Computer Vision*, p. 713723, IEEE Computer Society Press

Nister, D. (2003). An efficient solution to the fivepoint relative pose problem, *Proceedings of the IEEE Int'l Conf. on Computer Vision and Pattern Recognition*, Vol. 2, p. 195202, IEEE Computer Society Press, Madison, WI, USA

Olson, C.F. (2001). A General Method for Geometric Feature Matching and Model Extraction, *Int'l Journal of Computer Vision*, Vol. 45, No 1, p. 3954, Kluwer Academic Publishers

Papanikolopoulos, N. P.; Khosla, P. K. & Kanade, T. (1993). Visual Tracking of a Moving Target by a Camera Mounted on a Robot: A Combination of Control and Vision, *IEEE Transactions on Robotics and Automation*, Vol. 9, No 1, p. 1435

Pilu, M.; Fitzgibbon, A.W. & Fisher R.B. (1996). Ellipsespecific Direct leastsquare Fitting, *Proceedings of the IEEE Int'l Conf. on Image Processing*, Vol. 3, p. 599602, Lausanne, Switzerland, IEEE Press, Dublin

Ponce, J.; Chelberg, D. & Mann, W. (1989). Invariant properties of straight homogeneous generalized cylinders and their contours", *IEEE Trans. on Pattern Analysis and Machine Intelligence*, Vol. 9, No 11, p. 951966, IEEE Computer Society Press

Pressigout, M & Marchand, E. (2006). Realtime 3-D ModelBased Tracking: Combining Edge and Texture Information. *In proceedings of the IEEE Int. Conf. on Robotics and Automation*, p. 27262731, Orlando, Florida, USA

Puech, W.; Chassery, J.-M. & Pitas, I. (1997). Cylindrical surface localization in monocular vision, *Pattern Recognition Letters*, Vol. 18, p. 711722, Elsevier Science,

Quan, L. & Lan, Z. (1999). Linear NPoint Camera Pose Determination, *IEEE Transactions on Pattern Analysis and Machine Intelligence*, Vol. 21, No 8, p. 774780, IEEE Computer Society Press

Richetin, M.; Dhome, M. & Lapresté, J.-T. & Rives, G., Inverse Perspective Transform Using ZeroCurvature Contour Points: Application to the Localization of Some Generalized Cylinders from a Single View, *IEEE Transactions on Pattern Analysis and Machine Intelligence*, Vol. 13, No 2, p. 185192, IEEE Computer Society Press

Rosin, P.L. (1999). Robust Pose Estimation, IEEE Transactions on Systems, Man, and Cybernetics (Part B), Vol. 29, No 2, IEEE Press

Rousseeuw, P. &Leroy, A. (1987). *Robust Regression and Outlier Detection*, ISBN 9780471488552 (new edition), Wiley, NY SafaeeRad,

R; Tchoukanov, I. & Smith, K. -C. & Benhabib, B. (1992). ThreeDimensional Location Estimation of Circular Features for Machine Vision, *IEEE Transactions on Robotics and Automation*, Vol. 8, No 5, p. 624640

Salvi, J.; Armangué, X. & Batalle, J. (2002). A Comparative Review of Camera Calibrating Methods with Accuracy Evaluation, *Pattern Recognition*, Vol. 35, No 7, p. 16171635, Elsevier Science

Shin, Y. C. & Ahmad, S. (1989). 3-D location of circular and spherical features by monocular modelbased vision, *Proceedings of the IEEE International Conference on System, Man and Cybernetic*, p. 576581, Boston, USA

Shiu, Y.-C. & Huang, C. (1991). Pose Determination of Circular Cylinders Using Elliptical and Side Projections, *Proceedings of the Int'l Conf. on Systems Engineering*, p. 265268, Dayton, OH, USA

Sturm, P. (1997). Critical motion sequences for monocular selfcalibration and uncalibrated Euclidean reconstruction, *Proceedings of the IEEE Int'l. Conference on Computer Vision and Pattern Recognition*, Puerto Rico, p. 11001105

Sugihara, K. (1988). Some location problems for robot navigation using a single camera, *journal of Computer Vision, Graphics and Image Processing*, Vol. 42, No 1, p. 112129, Elsevier Science

Sundareswaran, V & Behringer, R. (1998). VisualServoingbased Augmented Reality, *Proceedings of the first IEEE Int'l. Workshop on Augmented Reality*, San Francisco, USA

Teramoto, H. & Xu, G. (2002). Camera calibration by a Single Image of Balls: From Conics to the Absolute Conic, *Proceedings of the Asian Conf. on Computer Vision*, Vol. 2, p. 499506, Melbourne, Australia

Thompson, D.W. & Mundy, J.L. (1987). Threedimensional model matching from an unconstrained viewpoint, *Proceedings of the IEEE Int'l Conf. on Robotics and Automation*, Raleigh, NC, USA, p. 208220, IEEE Press

Thompson, R. L.; Reid, I. D. & Munoz, L. A. & Murray, D. W. (2001). Providing synthetic views for teleoperation using visual pose tracking in multiple cameras, *IEEE Transactions System, Man and Cybernetics*, Vol. 31, No 1, p. 4354, IEEE Press

Torr, P. H. S. & Zisserman, A. (1999). Feature based methods for structure and motion estimation, In: *Vision Algorithms Workshop.: Theory and Practice*, p. 278294, ISBN 3540679731, Springer Verlag, London, UK

Triggs, W. (1999). Camera Pose and Calibration from 4 or 5 Known 3-D Points, *Proceedings of the IEEE Int'l Conf. on Computer Vision*, Vol. 1, p. 278284

Trucco, E. & Verri, A. (1998). *Introductory Techniques for 3-D Computer Vision*, ISBN 0132611082, Prentice Hall Upper Saddle River, NJ 07458

Tsaï, R.Y. (1987). A versatile camera calibration technique for highaccuracy 3-D machine vision metrology using offthe shelf TV cameras and lenses, *IEEE Journal of Robotics and Automation*, Vol. 3, No 4, p. 323344, IEEE Press NY

Vacchetti, L; Lepetit, V. & Fua, P. (2004) Stable RealTime 3-D Tracking Using Online and Offline information, *IEEE Transactions on Pattern Analysis and Machine Intelligence*, Vol. 26, No 10, p. 13851391, IEEE Computer Society

Vincze, M.; Schlemmer, M. & Gemeiner, P. & Ayromlou, M. (2005). Vision for Robotics: A tool for ModelBased Object Tracking, *IEEE Robotics and Autonomous Magazine*, Vol. 12, No 4, p. 5364.

Weiss, I. (1993). NoiseResistant Invariants of Curves, *IEEE Transactions on Pattern Analysis and Machine Intelligence*, Vol. 15, No 9, p. 943948, IEEE Computer Society Press

Wong, K.-Y.; Mendonça, P.-R. -S. & Cipolla, R. (2004). Reconstruction of surfaces of revolution from single uncalibrated views, *Image and Vision Computing*, Vol. 22, p. 829836, Elsevier Science

Werghi, N. & Doignon, C. (1995). Contour decomposition with wavelet transform and parametrisation of elliptic curves with an unbiased extended Kalman filter, *Proceedings of the Second Asian Conference on Computer Vision*, Vol. 3, p. 186190, Singapore

Yuan, J.-C. (1989). A general photogrammetric method for determining object position and orientation, *IEEE Transactions on Robotics and Automation*, Vol. 5, No 2, p. 129142

Zhang, Z. (1999). A flexible new technique for camera calibration, *Proceedings of the International Conference on Computer Vision*, p. 666673, Corfu, Greece, IEEE Computer Society Press

21

Global Techniques for Edge based Stereo Matching

Yassine Ruichek, Mohamed Hariti, Hazem Issa
University of Technology of Belfort-Montbéliard
France

1. Introduction

Depth perception is one of the most active research areas in computer vision. Passive stereo vision is a well known technique for obtaining 3-D depth information of objects seen by two or more video cameras from different viewpoints (Hartley & Zisserman, 2000 | Brown et al., 2003). The difference of the viewpoint positions causes a relative displacement of the corresponding features in the stereo images. Such relative displacement, called disparity, encodes the depth information, which is lost when the three dimensional scene is projected on an image The key problem, which is difficult to solve and computationally expensive (Barnard & Fisher, 1982), is hence to compare each feature extracted from one image with a number, generally large, of features extracted from the other image in order to find the corresponding one, if any. Once the matching process is established and the stereo vision system parameters are known, the depth computation is reduced to a simple triangulation (Jane & Haubecker, 2000 | Dooze, 2001).
This chapter presents some recent research works proposed to solve the stereo matching problem. The presented methods are based on a global approach, which can be viewed as a constraint satisfaction problem where the objective is to highlight a solution for which the matches are as compatible as possible with respect to specific constraints. These methods are tested and evaluated for real-time obstacle detection in front of a vehicle using linear stereo vision.

2. Related Works

Many approaches have been proposed to solve the stereo matching problem. According to the considered application, the existing techniques are roughly grouped into two categories: area-based and feature-based (Haralick & Shapiro, 1992). Area-based methods use correlation between brightness patterns in the local neighbourhood of a pixel in one image with brightness patterns in the local neighbourhood of the other image (Scharstein & Szeliski, 2002 | Saito & Mori, 1995 | Han et al., 2001 | Tang et al., 2002). These methods, which lead to a dense depth map, are generally used for 3D scene reconstruction applications. Feature-based methods use zero-crossing points, edges, line segments, etc. and compare their attributes to find the corresponding features (Lee & Leou, 1994 | Lee & Lee, 2004 | Nasrabadi, 1992 | Tien, 2004 | Pajares & de la Cruz, 2004 | Candocia & Adjouadi, 1997 | Starink & Backer, 1995). These methods, which lead to a sparse depth map, are generally used to ensure environment perception, as for obstacle detection. Feature-based methods can be used also for 3D scene reconstruction by interpolating the sparse depth map. To resolve matching ambiguities, feature-based and area-based methods use some constraints like epipolar, uniqueness, smoothness and ordering (Wang & Hsiao, 1999 | Zhang et al., 2004).

In the robot vision domain, the stereo matching problem is generally simplified by making hypotheses about the type of objects being observed and their visual environment so that structural features, such as corners or vertical straight lines, can be more or less easily extracted (Kriegman et al., 1989). Indoor scenes, including a few rigid objects scattered without occlusions against a featureless background, are much easier to analyze than natural outdoor scenes of the real world (Nitzan, 1988). With such restrictive assumptions, the number of candidate features for matching is substantially reduced so that computing times become acceptable for real-time processing without an important loss of useful information. Unfortunately, none of these hypotheses can be used in outdoor scenes, such as road environments, for detecting and localizing obstacles in front of a moving vehicle, because the features are too numerous to allow a reliable matching within an acceptable computer time (Bruyelle & Postaire, 1993).

Considering these difficulties, some authors have proposed to use linear cameras instead of matrix ones (Bruyelle & Postaire, 1993 | Inigo & Tkacik, 1987 | Colle, 1990). With these cameras, the information to be processed is drastically reduced since their sensor contains only one video line, typically 2 500 pixels, instead of, at least, 250 000 pixels with standard raster-scan cameras. Furthermore, they have a better horizontal resolution than video cameras. This characteristic is very important for an accurate perception of the scene in front of a vehicle.

To solve the problem of matching edges extracted from stereo linear images, a classical approach is to use correlation techniques (Bruyelle & Postaire, 1993). In order to improve this basic approach, it has been proposed to explore the edges of the two linear images sequentially, from one end to the other. A majority of candidate edges can be matched without ambiguities by means of this scheme, performed forward and backward (Burie et al., 1995). However, this sequential procedure can leave some unmatched edges, and may lead to false matches, which are difficult to identify.

This chapter is concerned with the stereo matching problem for obstacle detection using linear cameras. The proposed approach is based on a global formulation of the stereo matching problem. Considering only possible matches that respect local constraints, the principle of this approach consists in searching a solution for which the matches are as compatible as possible with respect to global constraints. Thus, the stereo matching problem can be viewed as a constraint satisfaction problem. This approach is turned in different methods, which are evaluated and compared for obstacle detection using linear stereo vision.

3. Linear Stereo Vision

3.1 How to Build a Linear Stereo Vision Set-up

A linear stereo set-up is built with two line-scan cameras, so that their optical axes are parallel and separated by a distance E (see Figure 1). Their lenses have identical focal lengths f. The fields of view of the two cameras are merged in one single plane, called the optical plane, so that the cameras shoot the same line in the scene. A specific calibration method has been developed to adjust the parallelism of the two optical axes in the common plane of view attached to the two cameras (Bruyelle, 1994). This calibration technique necessitates a specific planar calibration chart (see Figure 2), which bears two horizontal and two vertical calibration marks. The stereo set-up is calibrated when the vertical calibration marks are seen by the two cameras and when the horizontal calibration marks are at the centre of the two linear images. A set of oblique lines is provided so that the user knows if he is adjusting the positions of the cameras in the right direction.

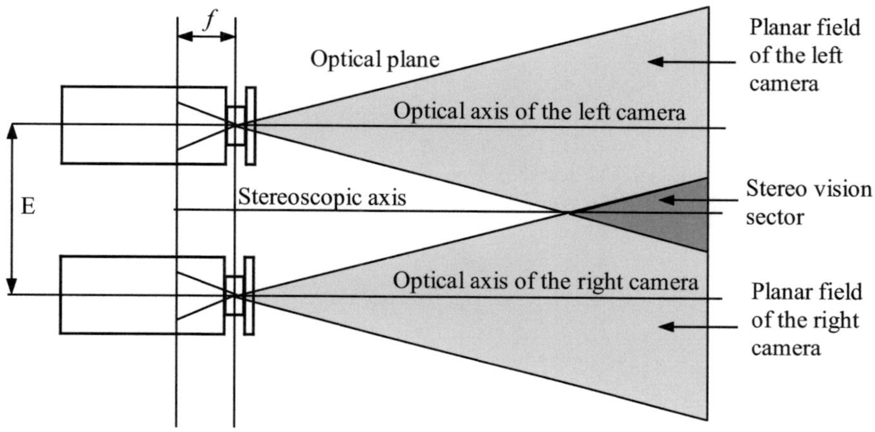

Figure 1. Geometry of the cameras

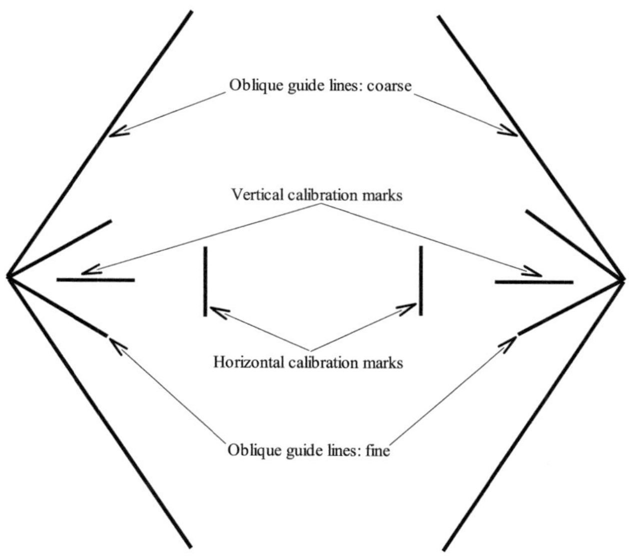

Figure 2. Calibration chart of the linear stereo set-up

If any object intersects the stereo vision sector, which is the common part of the two fields of view in the optical plane, it produces a disparity between the two linear images and, as a consequence, can be localized by means of triangulation.

Let the base-line joining the perspective centers O_l and O_r be the X-axis, and let the Z-axis lie in the optical plane, parallel to the optical axes of the cameras, so that the origin of the *{X,Z}* coordinate system stands midway between the lens centers (see Figure 3). Let us consider a point $P(X_p,Z_p)$ of coordinates X_p and Z_p in the optical plane. The image coordinates x_l and x_r represent the projections of the point *P* in the left and right imaging sensors, respectively. This pair of points is referred to as a corresponding pair. Using the pin-hole lens model, the coordinates of the point *P* in the optical plane can be found as follows:

$$z_P = \frac{E \cdot f}{d} \tag{1}$$

$$X_P = \frac{x_l \cdot z_P}{f} - \frac{E}{2} = \frac{x_r \cdot z_P}{f} + \frac{E}{2} \tag{2}$$

where *f* is the focal length of the lenses, *E* is the base-line width and $d = |x_l - x_r|$ is the disparity between the left and right projections of the point *P* on the two sensors.

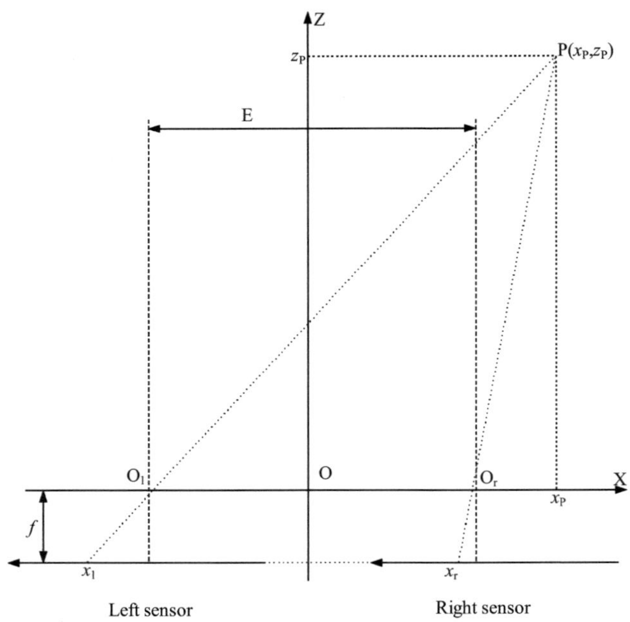

Figure 3. Pin-hole lens model

3.2 Feature Extraction

The low-level processing of a couple of two stereo linear images yields the features required in the correspondence phase. Edges appearing in these simple images, which are one-dimensional signals, are valuable candidates for matching because large local variations in the gray-level function correspond to the boundaries of objects being observed in a scene.

Edge detection is performed by means of the Deriche's operator (Deriche, 1990). After derivation, the pertinent local extrema are selected by splitting the gradient magnitude signal into adjacent intervals where the sign of the response remains constant (Burie et al., 1995) (see Figure 4). In each interval of constant sign, the maximum amplitude indicates the position of a unique edge associated to this interval when, and only when, this amplitude is greater than a low threshold value t. The application of this thresholding procedure allows to remove non significant responses of the differential operator lying in the range $[-t,+t]$. The adjustment of t is not crucial. Good results have been obtained with t adjusted at *10%* of the greatest amplitude of the response of the differential operator.

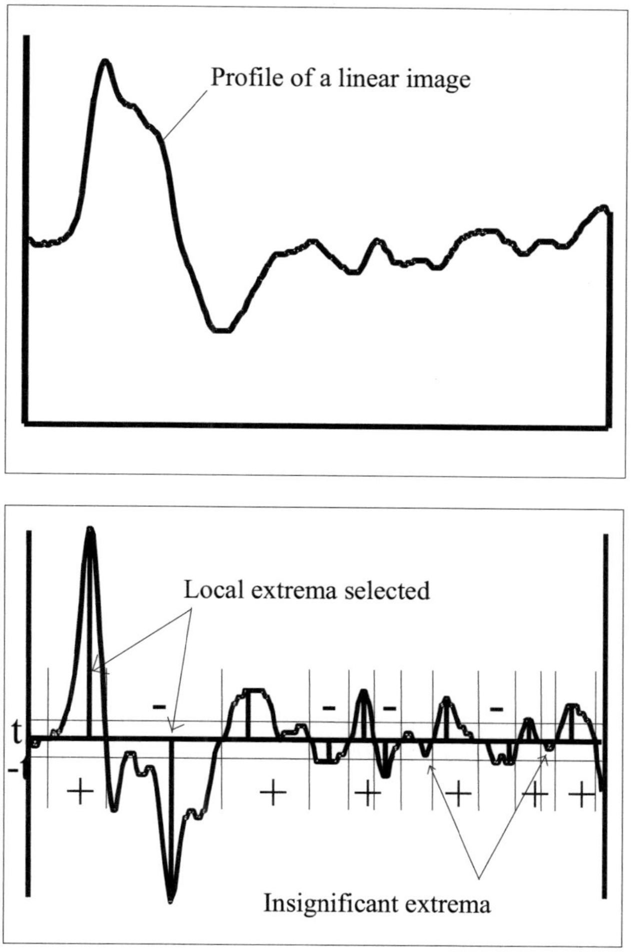

Figure 4. Edge extraction

Applied to the left and right linear images, this edge extraction procedure yields two lists of edges. Each edge is characterized by its position in the image, the amplitude and the sign of the response of the Deriche's operator.

4. Hopfield Neural Network Based Stereo Matching

4.1 Problem formulation

Let L and R be the left and right lists of the edges, respectively. The matching between L and R is first formulated as an optimization problem where an objective function, which represents the constraints on the solution, is to be minimized. The objective function,

defined such that the best matches correspond to its minimum value, is then mapped onto a Hopfield neural network for minimization.
The objective function is defined from three global constraints. The first one is the uniqueness constraint, which assumes that one edge in L matches only one edge in R (and vice-versa). The second global constraint is the ordering constraint, which is used to preserve the order, in the images, between the matched edges. This means that if an edge l in L is matched with an edge r in R, then it is impossible for an edge l' in L, such that $x_{l'} < x_l$, to be matched with and edge r' in R for which $x_{r'} > x_r$, where x denotes the position of the edge in the image. The third constraint is the smoothness constraint, which assumes that neighboring edges have similar disparities.
Combining the three global constraints, the objective function, representing the stereo correspondence problem, is defined so that its minimum value corresponds to the best solution. It can be expressed as:

$$H = \frac{K_u}{2}\sum_{l\in L}\left(1-\sum_{r\in R/(l,r)\in\Omega}E_{lr}\right)^2 + \frac{K_u}{2}\sum_{r\in R}\left(1-\sum_{l\in L/(l,r)\in\Omega}E_{lr}\right)^2 + \frac{K_o}{2}\sum_{(l,r)\in\Omega}\sum_{(l',r')\in\Omega}O_{lrl'r'}E_{lr}E_{l'r'} - \frac{K_s}{2}\sum_{(l,r)\in\Omega}\sum_{(l',r')\in\Omega}S_{lrl'r'}E_{lr}E_{l'r'} \tag{3}$$

where K_u, K_o, and K_s are weighting positive constants, which are set experimentally to *5*, *1* and *1*, respectively. E_{lr} represents the matching state between the edge l in L and the edge r in R: if $E_{lr} = 1$, then the edges l and r are matched; otherwise they are not matched. Ω is the set of all possible matches between the edges in L and those in R, i.e. the set of all pairs of edges (l,r) that satisfy the two following local constraints. Resulting from the sensor geometry, the first one is the geometric constraint, which assumes that a couple of edges l and r appearing in L and R, respectively, represents a possible match only if the constraint $x_l > x_r$ is satisfied. The second local constraint is the slope constraint, which means that only edges with the same sign of the gradient are considered for a possible matching.

$$\Omega = \{(l,r)\in L\times R \,/\, (l,r) \text{ satisfy the local constraints}\} \tag{4}$$

The two first terms of the objective function correspond to the uniqueness constraint. It can be seen that these terms tend to increase when multiple matches occur (i.e. when an edge in L (respectively R) has more than one corresponding edge in R (respectively L)). The first term (respectively second term) tends to a minimum value when the sum of the matching states of all possible matches of an edge in L (respectively R) is equal to *1*.
The third term allows the ordering constraint to be respected. The coefficient $O_{lrl'r'}$ indicates whether the order between the two pairs (l,r) and (l',r') is respected:

$$O_{lrl'r'} = \left|s(x_l - x_{l'}) - s(x_r - x_{r'})\right| \tag{5}$$

with:

$$s(a) = \begin{cases} 1 & if \quad a>0 \\ 0 & otherwise \end{cases} \tag{6}$$

The fourth term of the objective function is used to enforce the smoothness constraint. The coefficient $S_{lrl'r'}$ indicates how compatible the two pairs (l,r) and (l',r') are:

$$S_{lrl'r'} = S(X_{lrl'r'}) = \frac{2}{1+e^{\alpha\cdot(X_{lrl'r'}-\omega)}} - 1 \tag{7}$$

where $X_{lrl'r'}$ is the absolute value of the difference of disparities of the pairs (l,r) and (l',r'). The nonlinear function $S(X)$ scales the compatibility measure smoothly between *-1* and *1*. The parameter ω is adjusted so as to allow some tolerance with respect to noise and distortion. It is chosen such that a high compatibility is reached for a good match when X is close to *0*, while a low compatibility corresponds to a bad match when X is very large. A satisfying value of this parameter is experimentally selected as $\omega = 20$. The parameter α controls the slope of the function $S(X)$ when $X = \omega$. This parameter is set experimentally to *0.1*.

4.2 Objective Function Mapping onto a Hopfield Neural Network

After the mathematic formulation of the stereo correspondence problem as an optimization task, the next step is to map the objective function onto a Hopfield neural network for minimization. The neural network consists of a set of neurons mutually interconnected: each neuron is connected to all the other ones, except itself (Hopfield & Tank, 1985). A neuron n_{lr} of the network represents a possible match between the edges l and r appearing in L and R, respectively (see Figure 5). Note that only the pairs satisfying the local constraints are represented in the Hopfield neural network. The output of the neuron n_{lr} corresponds to the matching state E_{lr}.

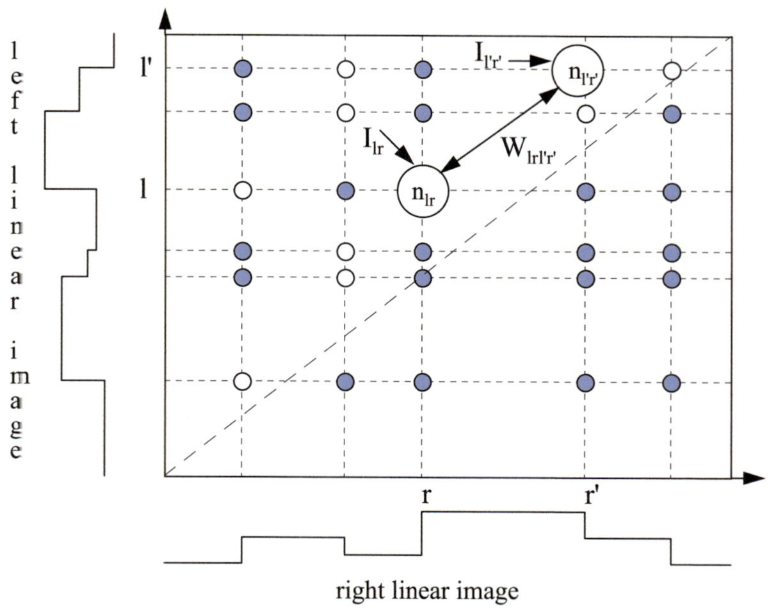

Figure 5. Hopfield neural network architecture. The white circles correspond to the neurons representing possible matches whereas the black ones correspond to the neurons representing impossible matches with respect to the local constraints

To determine the connection weights $\{W_{lrl'r'}\}$ between the neurons and the external inputs $\{I_{lr}\}$, the objective function is rearranged in the form of the energy function of the Hopfield neural network:

$$H = \sum_{(l,r)\in\Omega}\sum_{(l',r')\in\Omega} W_{lrl'r'}E_{lr}E_{l'r'} - \sum_{(l,r)\in\Omega} I_{lr}E_{lr} \tag{8}$$

with:

$$\begin{aligned} W_{lrl'r'} = & -K_u \cdot \left[\delta_{ll'}(1-\delta_{rr'}) - \delta_{rr'}(1-\delta_{ll'})\right] \\ & - K_o \cdot O_{lrl'r'}(1-\delta_{ll'})(1-\delta_{rr'}) \\ & + K_s \cdot S_{lrl'r'}(1-\delta_{ll'})(1-\delta_{rr'}) \\ & \text{and } \; I_{lr} = 2K_u \end{aligned} \tag{9}$$

where:

$$\delta_{ij} = \begin{cases} 1 & if \quad i > j \\ 0 & otherwise \end{cases} \tag{10}$$

Once the objective function has been mapped onto the Hopfield neural network, the minimization process is achieved by letting the so-defined network evolve so that it reaches a stable state (i.e. when no change occurs in the state of its neurons during the updating procedure). For the neural network relaxation, we have chosen a continuous dynamic evolution in which the output of the neurons is allowed to vary continuously between *0* and *1*. It has been shown that continuous Hopfield neural networks perform better than discrete ones in which the neuron outputs are restricted to the binary values *0* and *1*. With a continuous Hopfield network, the output of a neuron can be interpreted as a matching probability or quality, which is quantified continuously from *1* for a correct match to *0* for a wrong match. To start the network evolution, the neural states are set to *0.5*, i.e. all the possible matches are considered with the same probability. During the network evolution, the state of neurons representing good matches converges toward *1* and the state of neurons representing bad matches converges toward *0*.

The equation describing the time evolution of a neuron n_{lr} in a continuous Hopfield neural network is:

$$\frac{du_{lr}}{dt} = -\frac{u_{lr}}{\tau} + \sum_{(l',r')\in\Omega} W_{lrl'r'}E_{l'r'} + I_{lr} \tag{11}$$

where u_{lr} is the internal input of the neuron n_{lr} and τ is a time constant, which is set to *10*. The internal input u_{lr} and the output E_{lr} of the neuron n_{lr} are coupled as:

$$E_{lr} = \frac{1}{2}\left(1 + \tanh\left(\frac{u_{lr}}{\lambda}\right)\right) \tag{12}$$

where λ is a parameter, which determines how close the final state of the neurons is to the binary values *0* and *1*. This parameter is set experimentally to *0.01*.

To extract the pairs of corresponding edges from the final state of the network, a procedure is designed to select the neurons for which the output is maximum in each row and each column of the network. This is achieved by selecting, in each row of the network, the neuron with the largest response. However, this procedure can select more than one neuron in a same column. To discard this configuration, which corresponds to multiple matches, the same procedure is applied to each column of the network. The neurons selected by this two-step procedure indicate the correct matches.

4.3 Application to Obstacle Detection

A linear stereo set-up is installed on top of a car, 1.5 m above the level of the road, for periodically acquiring stereo pairs of linear images as the car travels (see Figure 6). The tilt angle is adjusted so that the optical plane intersects the pavement at a distance D_{max} = 50 m in front of the car. This configuration ensures that every object that lies on the road in front of the vehicle is seen by the two cameras, even if its height is very small.

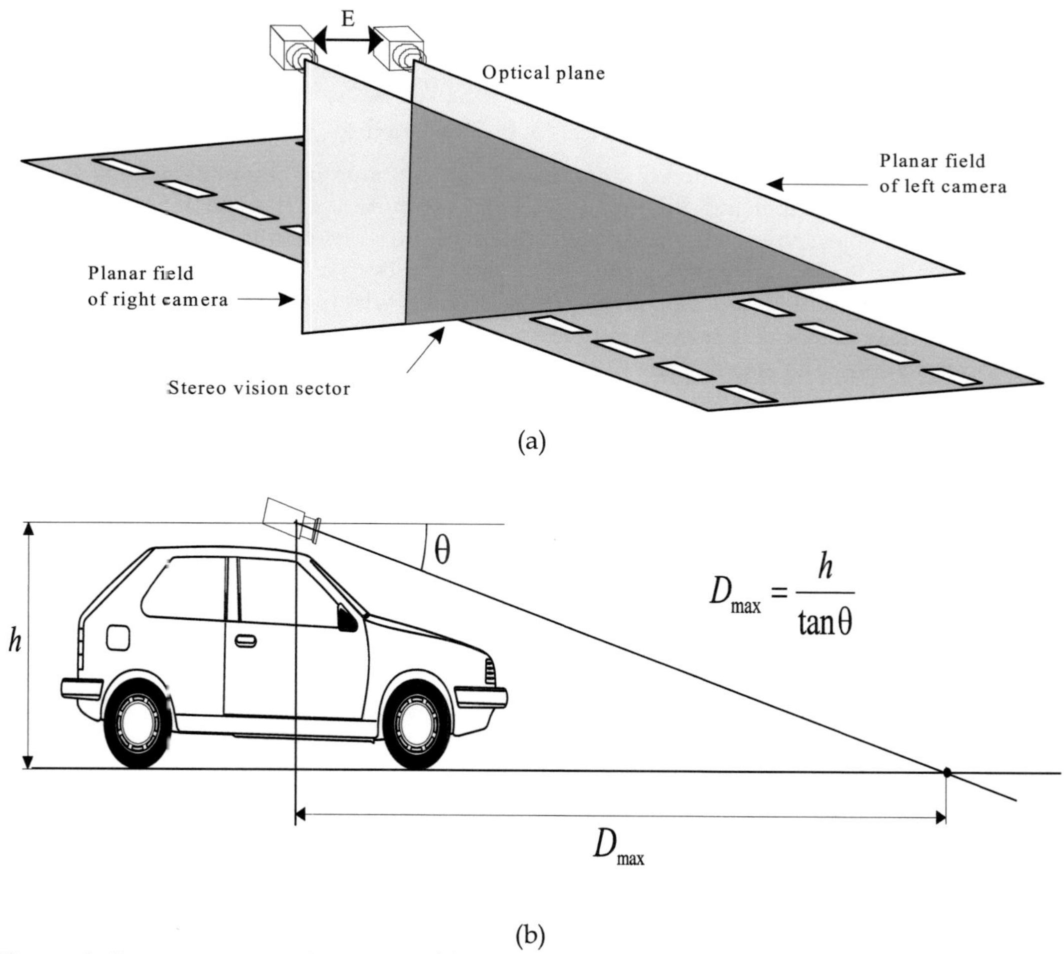

Figure 6. Stereo set-up configuration. (a) Top view. (b) Side view

One of the sequences shot in field conditions by this set-up is shown in Figure 7. In these pictures, the linear images are represented as horizontal lines, time running from top to bottom. In this example, the left and right sequences are composed by 200 linear images each. In this sequence, a pedestrian travels in front of the car according the trajectory shown in Figure 8. On the images of the sequence, we can clearly see the white lines of the pavement. The shadow of a car, located out of the vision plane of the stereoscope, is visible on the right of the images as a black area.

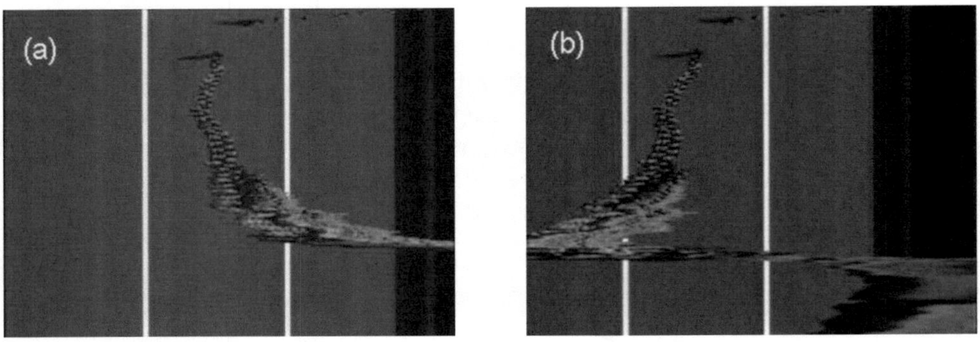

Figure 7. Stereo sequence. (a) Left sequence. (b) Right sequence

The neural processing of this stereo sequence allows determining the matched edge pairs. The disparities of all matched edges are used to compute the horizontal positions and distances of the object edges seen in the stereo vision sector. The results are shown in Figure 9 in which the horizontal positions are represented along the horizontal axis and the distances are represented by color levels, from the red, which corresponds to the farther distance, to the blue, which corresponds to the closer distance. As in Figure 7, time runs from top to bottom. The edges of the two white lines have been correctly matched and their detection is stable along the sequence. Indeed, the positions and distances remain constant from line to line. The pedestrian is well detected as he comes closer and closer to the car. The transition between the pavement and the area of shadow is also well detected. The presence of a few bad matches is noticed when occlusions occur (i.e. when the pedestrian hides one of the white lines to the left or right camera). These errors are caused by matching the edges of the white line, seen by one of the cameras, with those representing the pedestrian. Using an *AMD Athlon XP 2800+ PC* with *1.67 GHz* and *512 Mo RAM*, the processing rate is about *90* pairs of stereo linear images per second.

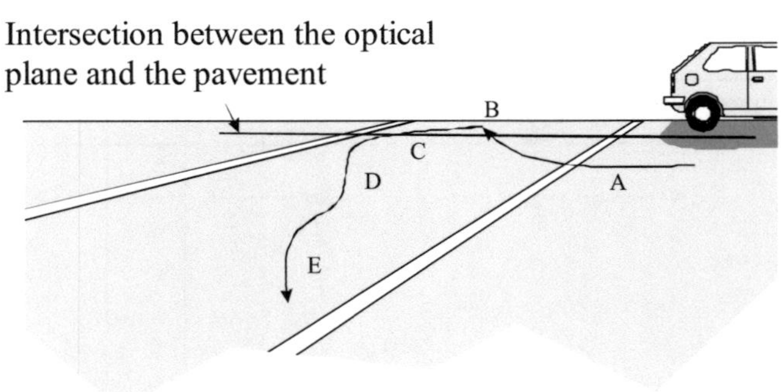

Figure 8. Trajectory of the pedestrian during the sequence

Figure 9. Neural stereo reconstruction

5. Genetic Algorithm Based Stereo Matching

It is known that Hopfield neural networks can perform only a local optimization process, and thus, they do not always guarantee to reach the global optimum, which corresponds to the best matching solution.
Genetic Algorithms (GAs) are randomized searching and optimization techniques guided by the principles of evolution and natural genetics (Goldberg, 1989). They are efficient, adaptive and robust search processes, and they are not affected by the presence of spurious local optimum in the solution space. Indeed, GAs span the solution space and can concentrate on a set of promising solutions that reach the global optimum or converge near the optimal solution. GAs have been applied successfully in many fields such as image processing, pattern recognition, machine learning, etc. (Goldberg, 1989).

5.1 Integer Encoding Scheme

To solve the stereo correspondence problem by means of a genetic algorithm, one must find a chromosome representation in order to code the solution of the problem. Let L and R be the lists of the edges extracted from the left and right linear images, respectively. Let N_L and N_R be the numbers of edges in L and R, respectively. A classical encoding scheme is to encode all the possible matches that meet the local constraints as a binary string B (see Figure 10). Each element B_k of this binary string contains two records. The first one, which is static, represents a possible match between an edge i in the left image and an edge j in the right one. The second record, which takes binary values, indicates if the hypothesis that the edge i is matched with the edge j is valid or not. If this record is set to 1, then the edges i and j are matched; otherwise they are not matched. This encoding scheme is referred hereafter to as a binary encoding scheme since it allows manipulating binary chromosomes. Note that a binary chromosome can be represented as a N_LxN_R array M in which each element M_{ij} validates or not the hypothesis that the edge i in the left image matches the edge j in the right image (see Figure 11). If $M_{ij} = 1$, then the edges are matched; otherwise, they are not matched. Note that only the possible matches, which respect the local constraints, are represented in this array. Figure 11 shows an example of a binary chromosome represented by an array. *NbPix* is the number of pixels in the linear images.

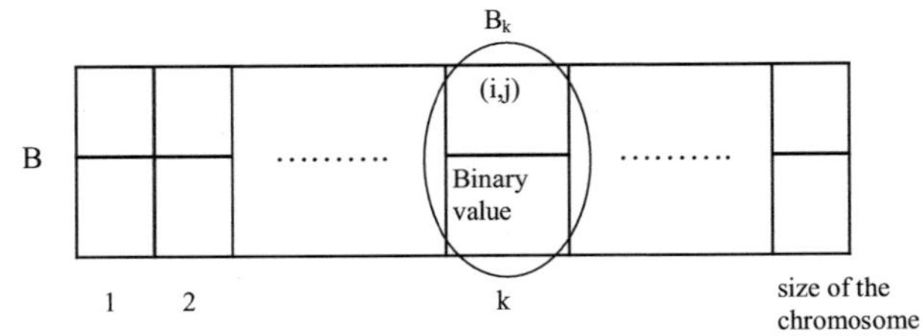

Figure 10. Binary chromosome

As we can see in Figure 11, the binary encoding scheme may produce chromosomes with many ambiguities when multiple possible matches appear simultaneously on the lines and columns of their corresponding arrays. Therefore, a genetic algorithm based on this encoding scheme will not explore efficiently the solution space and, as a consequence, it will be necessary to perform a great number of iterations to reach an acceptable solution. Furthermore, handling binary chromosomes, which are large-sized chromosomes, requires an important computing effort. To overcome the limitations that appear when handling classical binary chromosomes, we propose a new encoding scheme, which produces compact chromosomes with less matching ambiguities.

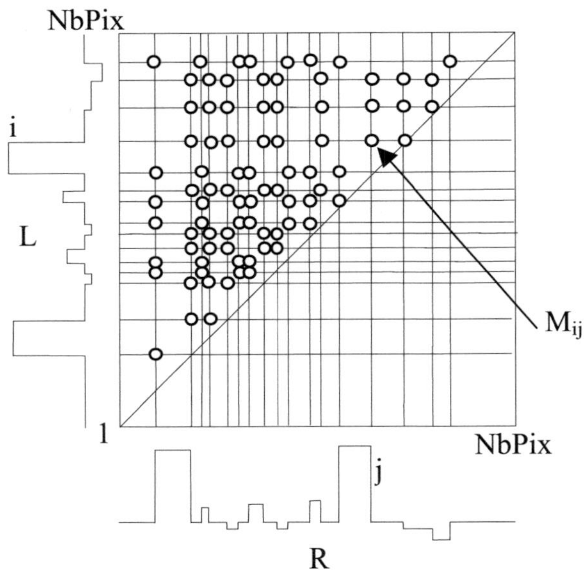

Figure 11. Array representation of a binary chromosome

Let $T_{max} = \{1,2,\ldots,N_{max}\}$ and $T_{min} = \{1,2,\ldots,N_{min}\}$ be the edge lists to be matched, where $N_{max} = max\ (N_L,N_R)$ and $N_{min} = min\ (N_L,N_R)$ are the sizes of T_{max} and T_{min}, respectively. This means that if $N_{max} = N_L$, then $T_{max} = L$ and $T_{min} = R$ (and vice-versa). The new encoding scheme, referred hereafter to as an integer encoding scheme, consists in representing a solution as a chain C indexed by the elements of the list T_{max} and which takes its values in the list $\{0\} \cup T_{min}$. The interpretation of the new encoding scheme is as follows. If $C_i = 0$, then the edge i in T_{max} has no corresponding edge; otherwise, the edges i in T_{max} and C_i in T_{min} are matched. As for binary chromosomes, the integer ones encode only possible matches, which respect the local constraints. Figure 12 gives an example of an integer chromosome, which represents a matching possibility between the edge lists L and R of Figure 11. In this example, $N_{max} = N_R = 17$ and $N_{min} = N_L = 15$, thus $T_{max} = R$ and $T_{min} = L$.

C_i =	1	2	4	3	3	5	5	13	13	12	12	13	12	12	12	0	15
i=	1	2	3	4	5	6	7	8	9	10	11	12	13	14	15	16	17

Figure 12. Chromosome based on the integer encoding scheme

Note that it is easy to represent an integer chromosome C as a $N_L x N_R$ array M'. For $i \in T_{max}$ and $j \in T_{min}$, $M'_{ij} = 1$ if $C_i = j$; otherwise $M'_{ij} = 0$. Figure 13 illustrates the array representation of the integer chromosome of Figure 12. We can see in this figure that there are no ambiguities in the columns of this array. In general, if $T_{max} = L$, then the integer encoding scheme produces chromosomes with no ambiguities in the lines of their corresponding arrays. In the opposite case, i.e., if $T_{max} = R$, as in Figure 13, the integer encoding scheme produces chromosomes with no ambiguities in the columns of their corresponding arrays.

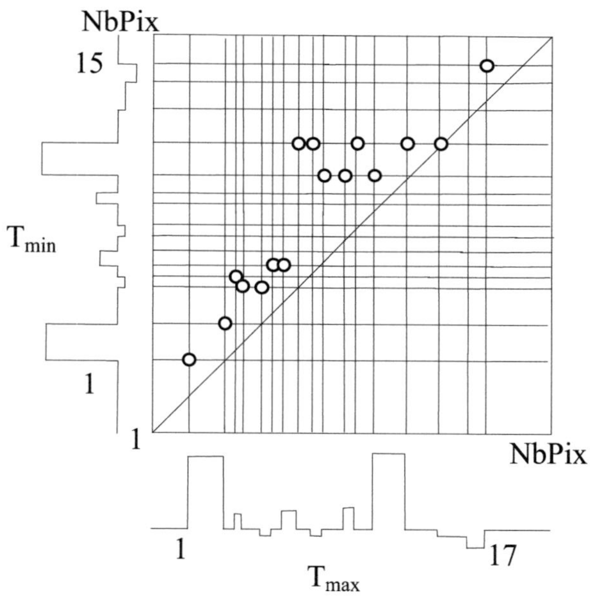

Figure 13. Array representation of the integer chromosome of Figure 12

The integer encoding scheme will therefore allow a genetic algorithm to explore more efficiently the solution space and, thus, to converge toward a better solution within a lower number of generations than when using the binary encoding scheme. Furthermore, the integer chromosomes, which are smaller than the binary ones, will require less computing time for their mutation and evaluation. In the examples given above, the integer chromosomes are 17-sized whereas the binary ones are 84-sized.

5.2 Integer Chromosome Evaluation

A genetic algorithm needs a fitness function for evaluating the chromosomes. The fitness function is defined from the global constraints so that the best matches correspond to its minimum:

$$\begin{aligned}F_{integer}(C) &= K_u \sum_{i=1}^{N_{max}-1} \sum_{k=i+1}^{N_{max}} U(C_i, C_k) \\ &+ K_m \left(N_{max} - N_{min} - \sum_{i=1}^{N_{max}} Z(C_i) \right)^2 \\ &+ K_o \sum_{i=1}^{N_{max}-1} \sum_{k=i+1}^{N_{max}} O(C_i, C_k) \\ &- K_s \sum_{i=1}^{N_{max}} \sum_{k=1 / k \neq i \, and \, C_i \neq C_k}^{N_{max}} S(C_i, C_k)\end{aligned} \quad (13)$$

where C is the integer chromosome to be evaluated. K_u, K_m, K_o and K_s are weighting positive constants, which are experimentally set to *5, 5, 5* and *1*, respectively.

The first term of the fitness function corresponds to the uniqueness constraint, where the quantity $U(C_i,C_k)$ represents a penalty when the constraint is not respected, i.e., when the two edges i and k have a same corresponding one. This penalty is computed as follows:

$$U(C_i, C_k) = \begin{cases} 1 \; if \; C_i = C_k \; and \, (C_i \neq 0 \, , C_k \neq 0) \\ 0 \; otherwise \end{cases} \quad (14)$$

The second term allows promoting chromosomes with an important number of matches. This term tends to a minimum when the number of matches is equal to N_{min}. The quantity $Z(C_i)$ is computed as follows:

$$Z(C_i) = \begin{cases} 1 \; if \; C_i = 0 \\ 0 \; otherwise \end{cases} \quad (15)$$

The third term is used to respect the ordering constraint. The quantity $O(C_i,C_k)$ represents a penalty when the order between the two pairs of edges (i,C_i) and (k,C_k) is not respected:

$$O(C_i, C_k) = \begin{cases} 1 \; if \; C_k < C_i \; and \, (C_i \neq 0, C_k \neq 0) \\ 0 \; otherwise \end{cases} \quad (16)$$

The fourth term supports the smoothness constraint. The quantity $S(C_i,C_k)$ indicates how compatible are the two pairs of edges (i,C_i) and (k,C_k) with respect to the smoothness constraint. This compatibility measure is computed as follows:

$$S(C_i, C_k) = Q(X_{C_iC_k}) = \frac{2}{1 + e^{\alpha \cdot (X_{C_iC_k} - \omega)}} - 1 \quad (17)$$

where $X_{C_iC_k}$ is the absolute value of the difference between the disparities of the pairs of edges (i,C_i) and (k,C_k), expressed in pixels. The non-linear function Q is identical to the one described in section 4.1 (see Equation 7). The parameters α and ω are experimentally set to *1* and *20*.

5.3 Genetic Stereo Matching Algorithm

The genetic algorithm for the edge stereo correspondence problem consists first in generating randomly an initial population of chromosomes representing possible matches that satisfy the local stereo constraints. The evolution process is then performed during some generations thanks to reproduction and selection operations in order to highlight the best chromosome, which minimizes the fitness function.

Starting from a current population in which each chromosome is evaluated, particular chromosomes are chosen with a selection probability proportional to the fitness value. These selected chromosomes are first reproduced using a single point crossover operation, i.e., two chromosomes are divided at a random position, and a portion of each chromosome is swapped with each other. The offspring chromosomes that are the result of the crossover operation are then submitted to a mutation procedure, which is randomly performed for each gene. The mutation of a gene number i of an integer chromosome C is performed by replacing its value by a new one chosen randomly in $\{0\} \cup T_{min} - \{C_i\}$ (see section 5.1).

After the crossover and mutation phases, a new population is obtained by means of two selection procedures: a deterministic selection and a stochastic one. These two selection procedures are applied to the set containing the chromosomes of the current population and those produced by the crossover and mutation operations. Based on an elitist strategy, the deterministic procedure is applied to select the best chromosomes, which represent 10% of the population. The remainder of the new population is obtained thanks to the stochastic selection, which is based on the same principle used to select chromosomes to be reproduced, i.e., with a selection probability proportional to the fitness value.

The algorithm is iterated until a pre-specified number of generations is reached. Once the evolution process is completed, the optimal chromosome, which corresponds to the minimum value of the fitness function, indicates the pairs of matched edges.

5.4 Genetic Parameter Setting

It is known that the convergence time of a genetic algorithm depends generally on the size of the population and the number of generations. To obtain good matching results, the values of these two parameters are chosen by taking into account the complexity of the problem, i.e., the sizes of the stereo edge lists to be matched. Thus, if the complexity of the problem is important, it is necessary to set these parameters to large values in order to reach a good solution. Furthermore, our experiment tests show that when there is a large difference between the sizes of the stereo edge lists, large values are required for these two parameters to converge toward a good solution. Considering these two observations, we propose the following empirical expressions for setting the size of the population *SizePop* and the number of generations N_{gen}:

$$SizePop = W_1 \cdot (N_L + N_R) + W_2 \cdot |N_L - N_R| \tag{18}$$

$$N_{gen} = W_3 \cdot SizePop \tag{19}$$

where N_L and N_R are the total numbers of edges in the left and right images, respectively. W_1, W_2 and W_3 are weighting positive constants, which are experimentally set to *5*, *2* and *1*, respectively. Concerning the other genetic parameters, the crossover probability is set to *0.6* and the mutation probability is equal to the inverse of the number of genes in a chromosome.

5.5 Performance Analysis of the Integer Encoding Scheme

To compare the performances of the integer and binary encoding schemes, two genetic algorithms are run separately. The first one, named integer genetic algorithm (IGA), uses integer chromosomes. The second one, named binary genetic algorithm (BGA), manipulates binary chromosomes. The chromosome evaluation is performed using a common fitness function, which is adapted to the array representation (see section 5.1). This fitness function allows evaluating both integer and binary chromosomes. It is constructed from the global constraints so that the best matches correspond to its minimum:

$$
\begin{aligned}
F_{array}(M) = {} & K_u \sum_{i \in L} \left(1 - \sum_{j \in R / (i,j) \in \Omega} M_{ij} \right)^2 \\
& + K_u \sum_{j \in R} \left(1 - \sum_{i \in L / (i,j) \in \Omega} M_{ij} \right)^2 \\
& + K_m \left(N_{\min} - \sum_{(i,j) \in \Omega} M_{ij} \right)^2 \\
& + K_o \sum_{(i,j) \in \Omega} \sum_{(k,l) \in \Omega} O_{ijkl} M_{ij} M_{kl} \\
& - K_s \sum_{(i,j) \in \Omega} \sum_{(k,l) \in \Omega} S_{ijkl} M_{ij} M_{kl}
\end{aligned}
\tag{20}
$$

where M is the array representation of the integer or binary chromosome to be evaluated. K_u, K_m, K_o and K_s are weighting positive constants. Ω is the set of all possible matches between the edges in the lists L and R, i.e., the set of all pairs of edges (i,j) that satisfy the local constraints (see Equation 4).

The two first terms of the fitness function correspond to the uniqueness constraint. These terms tend to a minimum when the sum of the elements lying in each line and each column of the array is equal to *1*. The third term is used to enforce an important number of matches in the array. This term tends to a minimum when the number of matches is equal to $N_{min} = min(N_L, N_R)$. The fourth term is introduced to respect the ordering constraint. The coefficient O_{ijkl} indicates if the order between the pairs of edges (i,j) and (k,l) is respected (see Equation 5). The last term is used to support the smoothness constraint. The quantity S_{ijkl} indicates how compatible are the two pairs of edges (i,j) and (k,l) with respect to the smoothness constraint (see Equation 7).

The two genetic algorithms, i.e., the binary chromosome-based algorithm (BGA) and the integer chromosome-based algorithm (IGA), are applied to a couple of stereo linear images. There are 27 and 21 edges in the left and right linear images, respectively. Let us recall that during their evolution, the two algorithms evaluate the chromosomes by using the fitness function F_{array}, associated with the array representation of the chromosomes (see Equation 20).

Figure 14 illustrates the evolution of the fitness function F_{array} using the integer genetic algorithm. Figure 15 and 16 show the evolution of the fitness function F_{array} using the binary genetic algorithm, with different values for the population size and the number of generations. Table 1 gives the fitness function values corresponding to the best chromosome obtained by the integer (IGA) and binary (BGA) genetic algorithms. With a population of *100* chromosomes, the fitness function reaches a minimum of *-128* after 300 generations using the integer genetic algorithm. Using the same values for the population size and the number of generations, the fitness function reaches a minimum of *112* when applying the binary genetic algorithm. By increasing the population size and the number of generations to *300* and *600*, respectively, the binary genetic algorithm leads the fitness function to a minimum value of *-99* .

As a conclusion to this discussion, the integer encoding scheme allows the genetic algorithm to explore more efficiently the solution space and, thus, to converge toward a better solution within a lower population size and a lower number of generations than when using the binary encoding scheme.

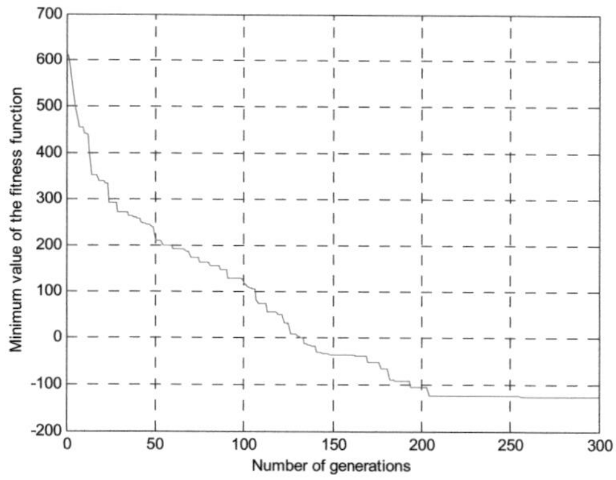

Figure 14. Evolution of the fitness function using the integer genetic algorithm

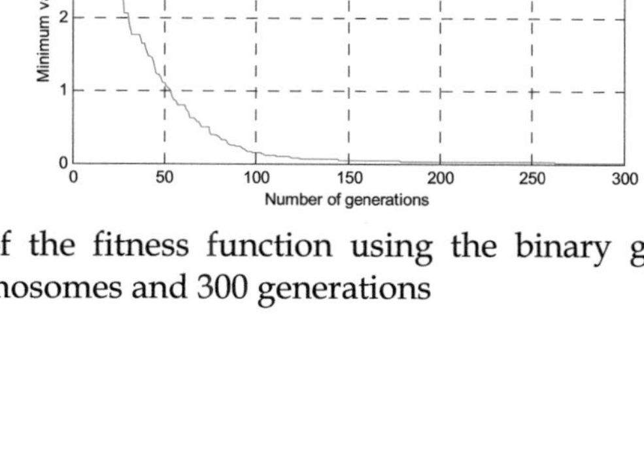

Figure 15. Evolution of the fitness function using the binary genetic algorithm, with a population of 100 chromosomes and 300 generations

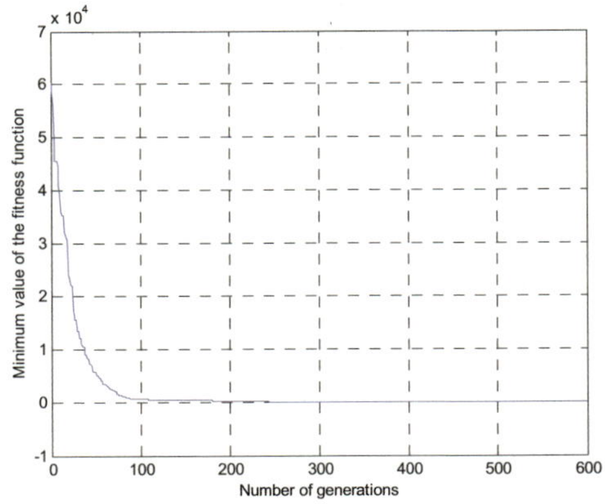

Figure 16. Evolution of the fitness function using the binary genetic algorithm, with a population of 300 chromosomes and 600 generations

Algorithm	Population size and number of generations	Fitness value
BGA	100 chromosomes and 300 generations	112
	300 chromosomes and 600 generations	-99
IGA	100 chromosomes and 300 generations	-128

Table 1. Performance comparison between the integer and binary encoding schemes

5.6 Genetic Stereo Matching Result

The integer genetic processing of the stereo sequence of Figure 7 provides the reconstructed scene represented in Figure 17. When compared to the binary genetic algorithm, the integer genetic algorithm allows reducing significantly the computing time. Indeed, the processing rate is about 2.7 stereo linear images per second instead of 0.1 stereo linear images per second (see Table 2).

The stereo matching results are comparable with those obtained by the neural stereo matching procedure (see Figures 9 and 17). However, the processing rate of the genetic stereo matching procedure is much lower when compared to the processing rate of the neural stereo matching algorithm (see Table 2).

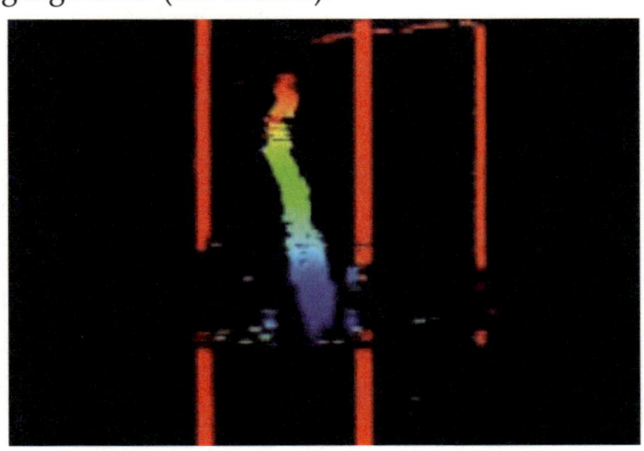

Figure 17. Integer genetic stereo reconstruction

Algorithm	Processing rate
BGA	0.1 pairs per second
IGA	2.7 pairs per second
Neural algorithm	90 pairs per second

Table 2. Processing rate comparison between the neural algorithm, integer genetic algorithm and binary genetic algorithm

6. Stereo Matching using a Multilevel Searching Strategy

Stereo matching is a combinatorial problem. To reduce the combinatory (resulting from the number of the edges considered in the stereo images) we propose a multilevel searching strategy, which decomposes hierarchically the problem into sub-problems with reduced complexities. The hierarchical decomposition performs edge stereo matching at different levels, from the most significant edges to the less significant ones. At each level, the process starts by selecting the edges with the larger gradient magnitudes. These edges are then matched and the obtained pairs are used as reference pairs for matching the most significant edges in the next level.

The multilevel searching strategy starts from level *1* in which all the left and right edges are considered. Let $L_1^0 = L$ and $R_1^0 = R$ be the lists of the edges extracted from the left and right images, respectively. We define from L_1^0 and R_1^0 a $NL_1^0 \times NR_1^0$ array MA_1^0 in which are represented all the possible matches that satisfy the local constraints (see Figure 18). NL_1^0 and NR_1^0 are the total numbers of edges in L_1^0 and R_1^0, respectively.

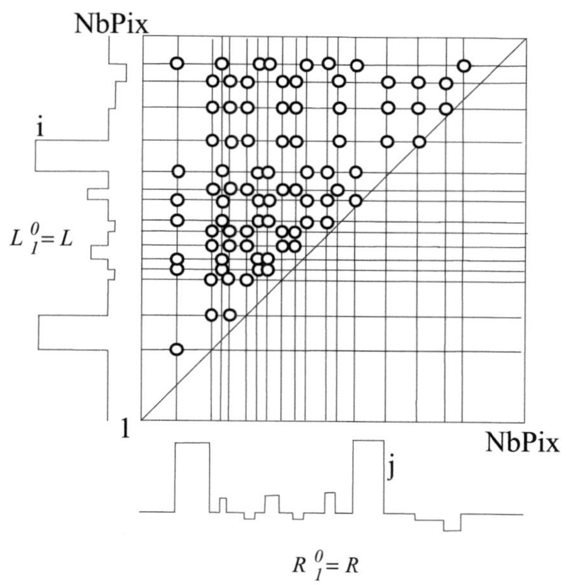

Figure 18. Array representation taking into account all the edges in the left and right images

The first step of the multilevel searching strategy consists of selecting, from L_1^0 and R_1^0, the edges with significant gradient magnitudes (see Figure 19). These selected edges are then matched and the obtained pairs, called reference pairs, define new sub-arrays, which are processed with the same searching strategy to match the most significant edges in level 2 (see Figure 20). In the example of Figure 20, four reference pairs are obtained from the first level. Thus, five sub-arrays, namely MA_2^0, MA_2^1, MA_2^2, MA_2^3 and MA_2^4, are considered in the second level.

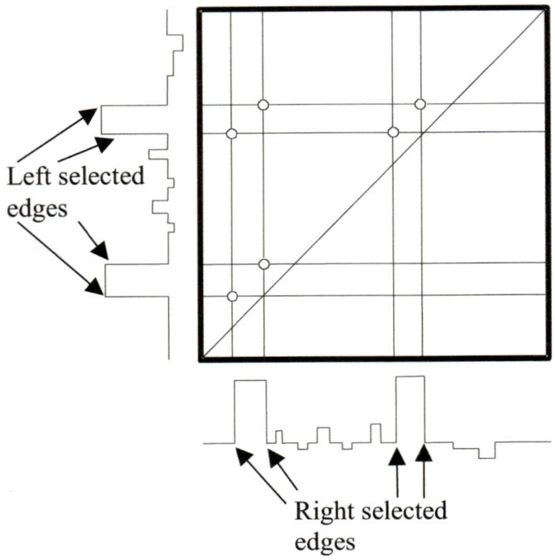

Figure 19. Level 1 of the multilevel searching strategy

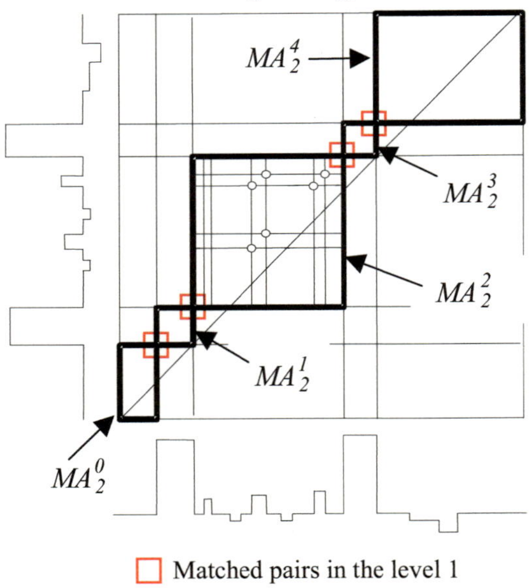

Figure 20. Level 2 of the multilevel searching strategy

Let MA_n^q be the sub-array number q in the level n. Let L_n^q and R_n^q be the left and right edge lists from which the sub-array MA_n^q is defined. The significant edges considered for the matching in the level n are selected in L_n^q and R_n^q such that their gradient magnitudes satisfy the following conditions:

$$\frac{\min_l}{2^{n-1}} \le mg_i \le \frac{\min_l}{2^n} \quad \text{or} \quad \frac{\max_l}{2^n} \le mg_i \le \frac{\max_l}{2^{n-1}} \qquad i \in L_n^q \tag{21}$$

$$\frac{\min_r}{2^{n-1}} \le mg_j \le \frac{\min_r}{2^n} \quad \text{or} \quad \frac{\max_r}{2^n} \le mg_j \le \frac{\max_r}{2^{n-1}} \qquad j \in R_n^q \tag{22}$$

where min_l and max_l (respectively min_r and max_r) are the smallest and largest gradient magnitudes of the edges extracted from the left (respectively right) image. mg_i and mg_j are the gradient magnitudes of the left edge i and right edge j, respectively.

Let K_n^q be the number of the matched pairs obtained from the matching of the selected edges in L_n^q and R_n^q. These pairs, called reference pairs, define new sub-arrays MA_{n+1}^0, $MA_{n+1}^1, \ldots, MA_{n+1}^{K_n^q}$, which are processed in the level $n+1$ using the same principle for matching the most significant edges in this level. In order to optimize its running, the multilevel searching strategy is implemented recursively.

The performance of the multilevel searching strategy is analyzed using the integer genetic algorithm, described in section 5. The using of the integer genetic algorithm with the multilevel searching strategy is referred hereafter to as a multilevel genetic algorithm (MiGA). On the other hand, the integer genetic algorithm performing stereo matching without the multilevel searching strategy, i.e., applied to all the edges extracted from the left and right linear images, is referred hereafter to as a basic genetic algorithm (BiGA).

Applied to the stereo sequence of Figure 7 (see section 4.3), the multilevel genetic algorithm provides the reconstructed scene shown in Figure 21. When we compare the reconstructed scenes obtained from BiGA (see Figure 17) and MiGA (see Figure 21), we can see that the matching results are globally similar. To evaluate quantitatively the performances of these two algorithms, we compare the matching solutions by means of an objective function constructed from the three terms corresponding to the uniqueness, ordering and smoothness constraints in the fitness function, which is defined by Equation 13 (see section 5.2). Figure 22 shows, for each genetic matching algorithm (BiGA and MiGA), the objective function values corresponding to the solutions obtained for each stereo pair of linear images of the sequence of Figure 7 (see section 4.3). We can see that the two algorithms behave almost identically except for the stereo pairs in the range [105,145] for which the multilevel scheme is less robust than the basic one. As we can see in Figure 7, some occlusions appear in these stereo pairs (i.e. when the pedestrian hides one of the white lines to the left or right camera). The partial fail of the multilevel scheme is due probably to the edge selection procedure, which is performed before stereo matching at each level. Indeed, the selection procedure can select an edge from the left image while the corresponding one is not selected from the right image (and vice-versa). This situation occurs frequently in presence of occlusions.

Figure 21. The reconstructed scene using the multilevel genetic algorithm

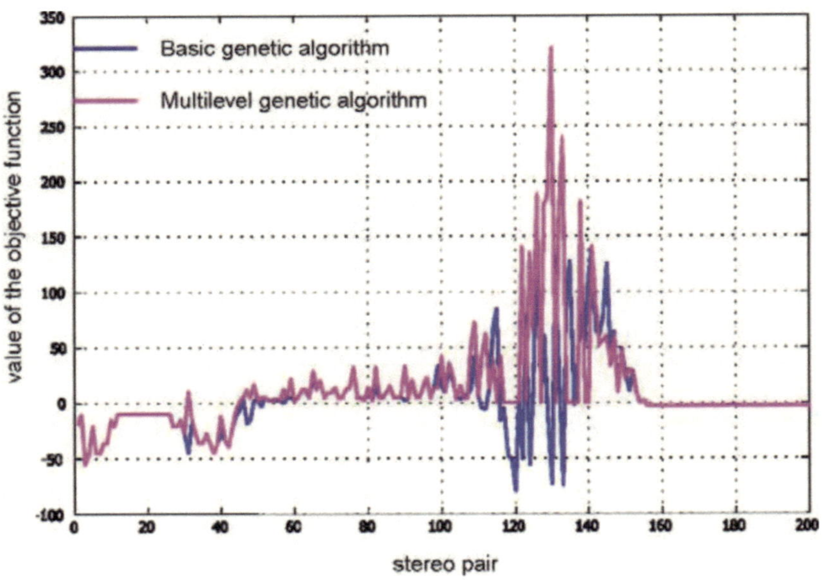

Figure 22. Quantitative analysis between the basic and multilevel genetic algorithms

This minor loss of robustness is the cost of the improvement in terms of processing time (see Table 3). With the multilevel searching strategy, the processing rate becomes 83 stereo pairs per second, while it was only equal to 2.7 stereo pairs per second with the basic scheme. The same observations are noted when the multilevel searching strategy is associated with the neural stereo processing (see Figure 23 and Table 3).

Method	Processing rate	
	Without the multilevel searching strategy	With the multilevel searching strategy
Genetic algorithm	2.7 stereo pairs per second	83 stereo pairs per second
Neural algorithm	90 stereo pairs per second	260 stereo pairs per second

Table 3. Processing rate comparison between the basic and multilevel schemes

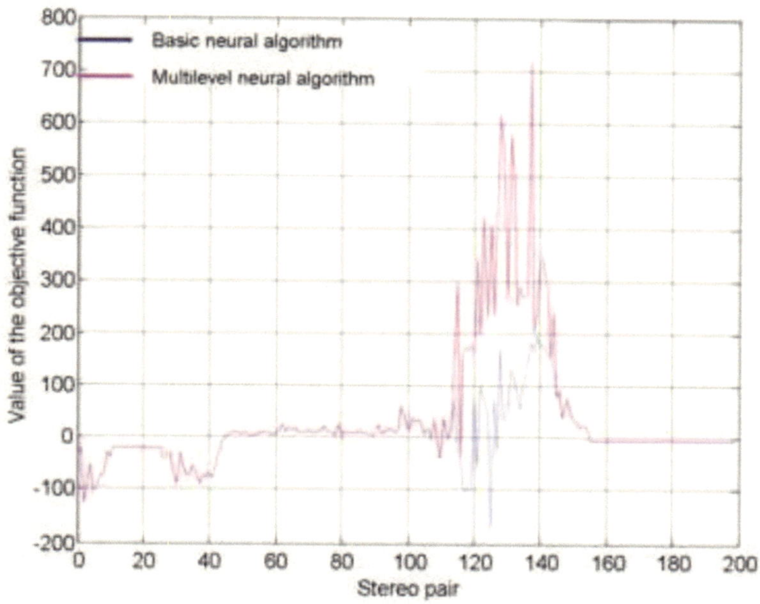

Figure 23. Quantitative analysis between the basic and multilevel neural algorithms

7. Voting Method Based Stereo Matching

The multilevel searching strategy allows improving significantly the stereo processing time. However, it may cause some difficulties because of the selection procedure applied at each level. Indeed, this procedure may select an edge from an image while the true corresponding one is not selected from the other image. Considering these difficulties, we propose an alternative stereo matching approach, which is based on a voting strategy.

7.1 Problem Mapping

Let L and R be the lists of the edges extracted from the left and right linear images, respectively. Let N_L and N_R be the numbers of edges in L and R, respectively. The edge stereo matching problem is mapped onto a $N_L x N_R$ array M, called matching array, in which an element M_{lr} explores the hypothesis that the edge l in the left image matches or not the edge r in the right image (see Figure 24). We consider only the elements representing the possible matches that met the position and slope constraints. For each element M_{lr} representing a possible match *(l,r)*, we associate a score SM_{lr}, which is set initially to zero.

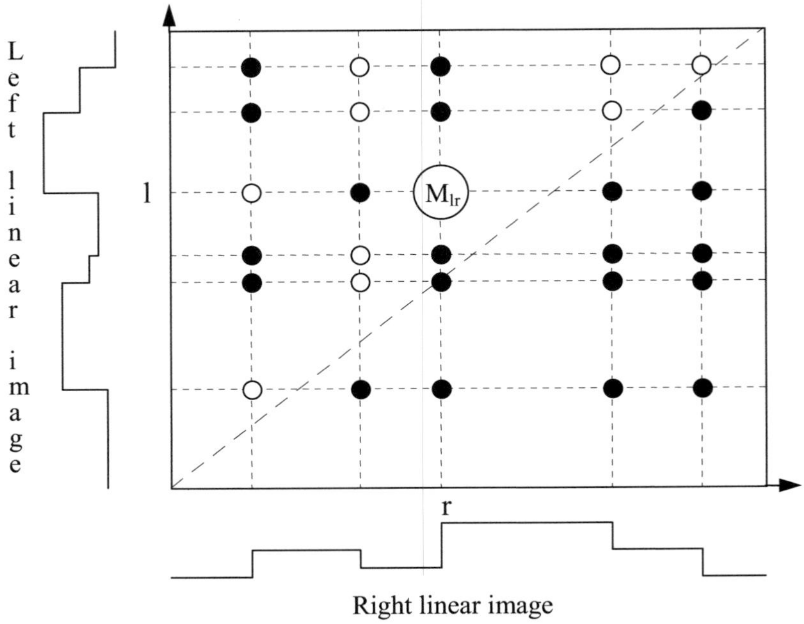

Figure 24. Matching array. The white circles represent the possible matches that met the position and slope constraints. The black circles represent the impossible matches that do not respect the position and slope constraints

7.2 Score Based Stereo Matching

The stereo matching process is performed thanks to a score-based procedure, which is based on the global constraints. The procedure is applied to all the possible matches that meet the local constraints, i.e., the position and slope constraints. This procedure consists in assigning for each possible match a score, which represents a quality measure of the matching regarding the global constraints. Let M_{lr} be an element of the matching array, representing a possible match between the edges l and r in the left and right images, respectively. The stereo matching procedure starts by determining among the other possible matches those that are authorized to contribute to the score SM_{lr} of the possible match M_{lr}. The contributor elements are obtained by using the uniqueness and ordering constraints: an element $M_{l'r'}$ is considered as a contributor to the score of the element M_{lr} if the possible matches *(l,r)* and *(l′,r′)* verify the uniqueness and ordering constraints (see Figure 25). The contribution of the contributors to the score of the element M_{lr} is then performed by means of the smoothness constraint. For each contributor $M_{l'r'}$, the score updating rule is defined as follows:

$$SM_{lr}(new) = SM_{lr}(previous) + G(X_{lrl'r'}) \tag{23}$$

where $X_{lrl'r'}$ is the absolute value of the difference between the disparities of the pairs *(l,r)* and *(l′,r′)*, expressed in pixels. G is a non linear function, which calculates the contribution of the contributors. This function is chosen such that a high contribution corresponds to a high compatibility between the pairs *(l,r)* and *(l′,r′)* with respect to the smoothness constraint, i.e. when $X_{lrl'r'}$ is close to 0, and a low contribution corresponds to a low smoothness compatibility, i.e. when $X_{lrl'r'}$ is very large. This function is chosen as:

$$G(X) = \frac{1}{1+X} \tag{24}$$

By considering the different steps of the score-based procedure, the final score FSM_{lr} of the possible match M_{lr} can be computed as follows:

$$FSM_{lr} = SM_{lr}(final) = \sum_{(l',r')\in\Omega_{lr}} G(X_{lrl'r'}) \tag{25}$$

where Ω_{lr} is the set of all the possible matches *(l′,r′)* such that the pairs *(l,r)* and *(l′,r′)* satisfy the uniqueness and ordering constraints.

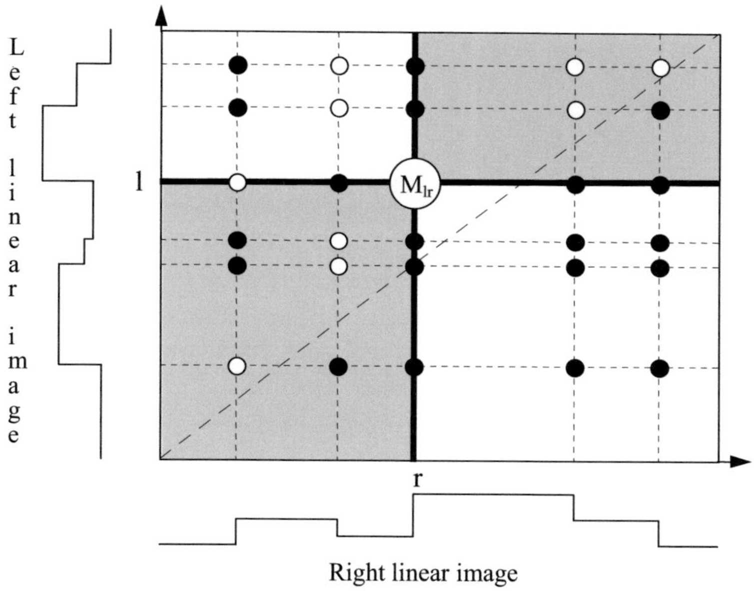

Figure 25. Determination of the contributors for calculating the score of a possible match: The contributors to the score of the possible match M_{lr} are the elements (white circles) situated in the gray area of the matching array

7.3 Extraction of the Correct Matches

To determine the correct matches, a procedure is designed to select the possible matches for which the final score is maximum. This is achieved by selecting in each row of the matching array the element with the largest score. However, this procedure can select more than one element in a same column of the matching array. To discard this configuration, which corresponds to multiple matches, the same procedure is applied to each column of the matching array. The elements selected by this two-steps procedure indicate the correct matches.

7.4 Voting Stereo Matching Result

The processing of the stereo sequence of Figure 7 (see section 4.3) using the voting procedure provides the reconstructed scene shown in Figure 26. We can see that the stereo matching results are very similar with those obtained by the neural and genetic algorithms (see Figures 9 and 17). The advantage of the voting technique is that it is fast, with a very high speed processing (see Table 4). Furthermore, the neural and genetic stereo techniques use many coefficients, which are usually difficult to adjust. The voting method is not confronted to this problem since it does not depend on any parameter.

Figure 26. Reconstructed scene using the voting stereo technique

Method	Processing rate
Neural network based method	90 stereo pairs per second
Genetic algorithm based method	2.7 stereo pairs per second
Voting method	220 stereo pairs per second

Table 4. Processing rate comparison between the neural, genetic and voting techniques

8. Conclusion

We proposed global techniques for edge stereo matching. The problem is formulated as a constraint satisfaction problem where the objective is to highlight a solution for which the matches are as compatible as possible with respect to specific constraints: local constraints and global ones. The local constraints are used to discard impossible matches so as to consider only potentially acceptable pairs of edges as candidates. The global constraints are used to evaluate the compatibility between the possible matches in order to determine the best ones.

In the first technique, the problem is turned into an optimization task where an objective function, representing the global constraints, is mapped and minimized thanks to a Hopfield neural network. This neural optimization method constitutes a local searching process, and thus, it does not always guarantee to reach a global minimum. As an alternative, we suggested to use genetic algorithms, which span the solution space and can concentrate on a set of promising solutions that reach the global optimum or converge near the optimal solution. A specific encoding scheme is presented and the analysis shows its efficiency to explore the solution space. However, the genetic technique necessitates a lot of time computation, and thus, it cannot be exploited for real-time applications such as obstacle detection in front of a moving vehicle. In order to improve the time computation, we proposed a multilevel searching strategy, which decomposes the stereo matching problem into sub-problems with reduced complexities. This searching strategy performs stereo matching from the most significant edges to the less significant ones. In each level, the procedure starts by selecting significant edges, using their gradient magnitude. The selected edges are then matched and the obtained pairs are used as reference pairs for matching the remaining edges according the same principle. The multilevel searching strategy allows improving significantly the stereo processing time. However, the limitation is that, in each level, the selection procedure may select an edge from an image while the true corresponding one is not selected from the other image. Considering this difficulty, we proposed a voting stereo matching technique, which consists to determine for each possible match a score based on the combination of the global constraints. This technique provides very similar stereo matching results with a high speed processing, compatible with real-time obstacle detection. Furthermore, unlike the neural and genetic stereo methods, the voting technique does not use any parameter, and hence, does not need any adjustment.

9. References

Hartley, R. & Zisserman, A. (2000). *Multiple View Geometry in Computer Vision,* Cambridge Univ. Press, Cambridge, U.K.

Brown, M.Z.; Burschka, D. & Hager, G.D. (2003). Advances in computational stereo. *IEEE Trans Pattern Anal Machine Intel.,* Vol. 25, (Aug. 2003) 993-1008)

Jane, B. & Haubecker, H. (2000). *Computer vision and applications,* Academic, New York

Dooze, D. (2001). *Conception et réalisation d'un stéréoscope bi-modal à portée variable: application à la détection d'obstacles à l'avant de véhicules guidés automatisés,* PhD Thesis, Université des Sciences et Technologies de Lille, France

Haralick, R.M & Shapiro, L.G. (1992). *Image matching, computer and robot vision, Part 2,* Addison-Wesley, New York

Scharstein, D. & Szeliski, R. (2002). A taxonomy and evaluation of dense two-frame stereo correspondence algorithms. *Int J Comput Vis,* Vol. 47, No. 1-3, (2002) 7-42

Saito, H. & Mori M. (1995). Application og genetic algorithms to stereo matching of images. *Pattern Recognit Lett,* No. 16, (1995) 815-821

Han, K.P.; Song, K.W.; Chung, E.Y.; Cho, S.J. & Ha, Y.H. (2001). Stereo matching using genetic algorithm with adaptive chromosomes. *Pattern Recognit,* No. 34, (2001) 1729-1740

Tang, L.; Wu, C. & Chen, Z. (2002). Image dense matching based on region growth with adaptive window. *Pattern Recognit Lett,* No. 23, (2002) 1169-1178

Lee, S.H. & Leou, J.J. (1994). A dynamic programming approach to line segment matching in stereo vision. *Pattern Recognit Lett,* Vol. 27, No. 8, (1994) 961-986

Lee, K. & Lee, J. (2004). Generic obstacle detection on roads by dynamic programming for remapped stereo images to an overhead view, *Proceedings of the IEEE International Conference on Networking, Sensing and Control,* pp. 897-902, 2004, Taipei

Nasrabadi, N.M. (1992). A stereo vision technique using curve-segments and relaxation matching. *IEEE Trans Pattern Anal Machine Intel,* Vol. 14, No 5., (1992) 566-572

Tien, F.C. (2004). Solving line-feature stereo matching with genetic algorithms in Hough space. *Journal of the Chinese Institute of Industrial Engineers,* Vol. 21, No. 5, (2004) 515-526

Pajares, G. & de la Cruz, J.M. (2004). On combining support vector machines and simulated annealing in stereovision matching. *IEEE Trans Man Cybern Part B,* Vol. 34, No. 4, (2004) 1646-1657

Candocia, F. & Adjouadi, A. (1997). A similarity measure for stereo feature matching. *IEEE Trans Image Processing,* No. 6, (1997) 1460-1464

Starink, J.P.P. & Backer, E. (1995). Finding point correspondences using simulated annealing. *Pattern Recognit,* Vol. 28, No. 2, (1995) 231-240

Wang, J.H. & Hsiao, C.P. (1999). On disparity matching in stereo vision via a neural network framework. *Proc Natl Sci Counc ROC(A),* Vol. 23, No. 5, (1999) 665-678

Zhang, P.; Lee, D.J. & Beard, R. (2004). Solving correspondence problems with 1-D signal matching, *Proceedings of the SPIE 5608,* pp. 207-217, 2004, Philadelphia

Kriegman, D.J.; Triendl, E. & Binford, T.O. (1989). Stereo vision and navigation in buildings for mobile robot. *IEEE Trans Robot Autom,* Vol. 5, No. 6, (1989) 792-803

Nitzan, D. (1988). Three-dimensional vision structure for robot application. *IEEE Trans Pattern Anal Machine Intel,* Vol. 10, No. 3, (1988) 291-309

Bruyelle, J.L. & Postaire, G.J. (1993). Direct range measurement by linear stereo vision for real-time obstacle detection in road traffic. *Robo Auton Syst,* No. 11, (1993) 261-268

Inigo, R.M. & Tkacik, T. (1987). Mobile robot operation in real-time with linear image array based vision, *Proceedings of the IEEE Intelligent Control Symposium,* pp. 228-233, 1987

Colle, O. (1990). *Vision stéréoscopique à l'aide de deux caméras linéaires: application à la robotique mobile,* PhD Thesis, Institut des Sciences Appliquées de Lyon, France

Burie, J.C.; Bruyelle, J.L. & Postaire, J.G. (1995). Detecting and localising obstacles in front of a moving vehicle using linear stereo vision. *Math Comput Model,* Vol. 22, No. 4-7, (1995) 235-246

Bruyelle, J.L. (1994). *Conception et réalisation d'un dispositif de prise de vue stéréoscopique linéaire: application à la détection d'obstacles à l'avant des véhicules routies,* PhD Thesis, Université des Sciences et Technologies de Lille, France

Deriche, R. (1990). Fast algorithms for low-level vision. *IEEE Trans Pattern Anal Machine Intel,* Vol. 12, No., 1 (1990) 78-87

Hopfield, J.J. & Tank, T.W. (1985). Neural computation of decisions in optimization problems. *Biol Cybern,* No. 52, (1985) 141-152

Lima, P.; Bonarini, A. & Mataric, M. (2004). *Name of Book in Italics,* Publisher, ISBN, Place of Publication

Li, B.; Xu, Y. & Choi, J. (1996). Title of conference paper, *Proceedings of xxx xxx,* pp. 14-17, ISBN, conference location, month and year, Publisher, City

Siegwart, R. (2001). Name of paper. *Name of Journal in Italics,* Vol., No., (month and year of the edition) page numbers (first-last), ISSN

Arai, T. & Kragic, D. (1999). Name of paper, In: *Name of Book in Italics,* Name(s) of Editor(s), (Ed.), page numbers (first-last), Publisher, ISBN, Place of publication

22

Local Feature Selection and Global Energy Optimization in Stereo

Hiroshi Ishikawa[1] and Davi Geiger[2]
[1]*Department of Information and Biological Sciences, Nagoya City University, Japan*
[2]*Courant Institute of Mathematical Sciences, New York University, U.S.A.*

1. Introduction

The human brain can fuse two slightly different views from left and right eyes and perceive depth. This process of stereopsis entails identifying matching locations in the two images and recovering the depth from their disparity. This can be done only approximately: ambiguity arising from such factors as noise, periodicity, and large regions of constant intensity makes it impossible to identify all locations in the two images with certainty. There has been much work on stereo (Ayache, 1991; Grimson, 1981; Marapane & Trivedi, 1994).

The issues in solving this problem include

i how the geometry and calibration of the stereo system are determined,

ii what primitives are matched between the two images,

iii what *a priori* assumptions are made about the scene to determine the disparity,

iv how the whole correspondence, i.e. the disparity map, is computed, and

v how the depth is calculated from the disparity.

In this chapter, we assume that (i) is solved, and that we know the stereo geometry exactly, including the correspondence between epipolar lines in the two images. Answering question (v) involves determining the camera parameters, triangulation between the cameras, and an error analysis, for which we refer the reader to (Faugeras, 1993).

In this chapter, we focus on the remaining issues (ii), (iii), and (iv). Main contributions of this chapter to these problems are summarized as follows:

ii In order to find corresponding points in the two images, an algorithm must have some notion of similarity, or likelihood that a pair of points in fact represents the same point in the scene. To estimate this likelihood, various features can be used, e.g., intensity, edges, junctions (Anderson, 1994; Malik, 1996), and window features (Okutomi & Kanade, 1993). Since none of these features is clearly superior to others in all circumstances, using multiple features is preferable to using a single feature, if one knows when to use which feature, or what combination of features. However, features are difficult to cross-normalize; how can we compare, for instance, the output from an edge matching with the one from correlation matching? We would like not to have to cross-normalize the output of the features, and still be able to use multiple features. We present a new approach that uses geometric constraints for matching surface to select, for each set of mutually-exclusive matching choices, optimal feature or combination of features from multiscale-edge and intensity features.

iii Various algorithms, as in the cooperative stereo (Marr & Poggio, 1976), have proposed *a priori* assumptions on the solution, including *smoothness* to bind nearby pixels and *uniqueness* to inhibit multiple matches. Occlusions and discontinuities must also be modelled to explain the geometry of the multiple-view image formation. There is now abundant psychophysical evidence (Anderson, 1994; Gillam & Borsting, 1988; Nakayama & Shimojo, 1990) that the human visual system does take advantage of the detection of occluded regions to obtain depth information. The earliest attempts to model occlusions and its relation to discontinuities (Belhumeur & Mumford, 1992; Geiger, Ladendorf, & Yuille, 1995) had a limitation that they restrict the optimization function to account only for interactions along the epipolar lines. Another aspect of the stereo geometry is the interdependence between epipolar lines. This topic was often neglected because of a lack of optimal algorithms until recently, when graph-based algorithms made it feasible to handle this in an energy-optimization scheme (Boykov, Veksler, & Zabih, 2001; Ishikawa & Geiger, 1998; Roy, 1999; Roy & Cox, 1998). We show that it is possible to account for all of these assumptions, including occlusions, discontinuities, and epipolar-line interactions, in computing the optimal solution.

iv To compute the most likely disparity map given the data, we define a Markov Random Field energy functional and obtain the MAP estimation globally and exactly. The energy minimization is done using a minimum-cut algorithm on a directed graph specifically designed to account for the constraints described above in (iii).

In the next section, we discuss the general probabilistic model of stereopsis, including the optimization space and various constraints, and introduce a general energy minimization formulation of the problem. In section 3, we introduce the more specific form of first-order Markov Random Field energy minimization problem that we actually solve. We devise a unique graph structure in section 4 to map the MRF problem to a minimum-cut problem on the graph, so that we can solve it exactly and globally. In section 5, we explain how various features can be used to compare points in the two images. Finally, we show experimental results in section 6.

2. Energy Formulation

In this section, we discus the probabilistic model of stereopsis and the Maximum A Posteriori (MAP) optimization of the model. First we define the space of parameters we wish to estimate, that is, the space of disparity maps. Then we formulate a model of the causal relationship between the parameters and the resulting images as a conditional probability distribution. In this way, the whole system is represented by the probability that different values of the parameters occur a priori and the probability that the image occurs under the assumption that the parameters have some given value. Then, for a given pair of images, we look for the disparity map that maximizes the probability that it occurs and gives rise to the images. We then define an energy minimization formulation that is equivalent to the MAP estimation.

2.1 Parameter Space

In binocular stereo, there are left and right images I_L and I_R; the parameter to be estimated is the matching between visible sites in the two images, which is directly related to the depth surface (3D scene) S in front of the cameras. We denote by $\hat{I}_L$ and $\hat{I}_R$ the domains of the image functions I_L and I_R; here we are assuming the two domains are identical rectangles. A match between the two images can naturally be represented as a surface in a 4D space $\hat{I}_L \times \hat{I}_R$, which is called the match space. A point in the match space is a pair of points in the left and right images, which is interpreted as a match between the points. Note that the parameter space in which we seek the best solution is not the match space, but the space of surfaces therein (with certain constraints.)

Two constraints in the geometry of stereo make the parameter space smaller.

Epipolar Constraint

Each point in the scene goes through a unique plane in the 3D space defined by it and the two focal points of the cameras; thus the points sharing such a plane form a line on each image. Hence each domain is stratified by such *epipolar lines* and there is a one-to-one correspondence between epipolar lines on the two images (see Fig. 1.)

Because of the epipolar constraint, we can assume that the surface in the match space is always included in the subspace

$$\{(x_L, x_R) \in \hat{I}_L \times \hat{I}_R \mid x_L \text{ and } x_R \text{ belong to the corresponding epipolar line}\}.$$

Thus, a match can be seen as a surface in a 3D space. In the rest of the chapter, the two images are always assumed to be rectified, i.e., points that belong to corresponding epipolar lines have the same y-coordinate in both images; a match occurs only between points with the same y-coordinate. Thus, a match is represented as a surface in the 3D space $\{(l,r,y)\}$, where $\{(l,y)\}$ and $\{(r,y)\}$ are the coordinates of the left and right image domains $\hat{I}_L$ and $\hat{I}_R$ respectively.

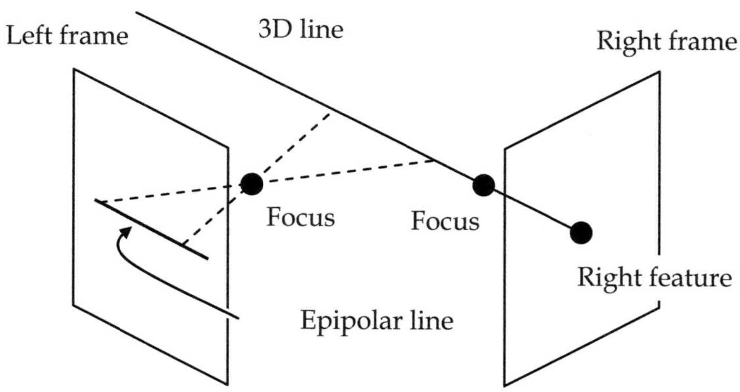

Figure 1. Each point in the scene goes through a unique plane in the 3D space defined by the two focal points of the cameras and itself; thus the points sharing such a plane form a line on each image. Hence each image is stratified by such *epipolar lines* and there is a one-to-one correspondence between epipolar lines on the two images.

Ordering Constraint

There is also another constraint known as the ordering constraint (Baker & Binford, 1981; Marr & Poggio, 1976). It states that if a point moves from left to right on the epipolar line in the left image, the corresponding point also moves from left to right in the right image. This can be characterized as a local condition (monotonicity constraint) on the tangent plane of the surface representing the match: the ratio of change in l by r must stay positive everywhere on the surface. This is not always strictly true for the real 3D scene in the sense that there can be a surface such that corresponding points move from left to right in the left image and from right to left in the right image. For instance, a plane that equally and perpendicularly divides the line segment between focal points would have this property. However, this is a rare situation and even the human visual system cannot handle this anyway. The ordering constraint further reduces the size of the search space. Note that the epipolar and ordering constraints together ensure the uniqueness constraint. This is because any point in one image is restrained to match only points on one epipolar line in the other image, and these potential points are strictly ordered so that it is impossible to match more than one point without violating the ordering constraint.

2.2 Prior Model

The prior model is an *a priori* statistical assumption about the 3D scenes that reveals which surfaces the system expects to find most often in a scene. It is described as a prior probability distribution $P(S)$ that gives a probability to each possible 3D scene output S of the process. In particular, the prior models how any ambiguity is resolved. Belhumeur (Belhumeur, 1996) analyzed stereo prior models in explicitly Bayesian terms. As in other low-level problems, commonly used prior models are local. They generally favour small disparity changes (fronto-parallel surfaces) and small disparity curvature (smooth surfaces). In our formulation, we enforce the ordering constraint as the prior model by giving a very low probability to any surface that violates this constraint.

2.3 Image Formation Model

The image formation model describes what images the cameras record when a 3D scene S is presented in front of them. It is basically a photometric model and can be expressed as a conditional probability distribution $P(I_L, I_R \mid S)$ of forming images I_L and I_R, given a 3D scene S.

Also modelled in the image formation model are occlusions, or appearances of scene locations in only one of the two images, which correspond to discontinuities in the match surface or a match surface that is perpendicular to the l or r axis, depending on how this situation is modelled (see Fig. 2.) It has been shown that the detection of occlusions is especially important in human stereopsis (Anderson, 1994; Nakayama & Shimojo, 1990). Occlusions have also been modelled in artificial vision systems (Belhumeur & Mumford, 1992; Geiger, Ladendorf, & Yuille, 1995).

Any effect on the images due to the shape and configuration of the 3D surface can be modelled in the image formation model. For instance, intensity edges and junctions can be seen as cues for the depth discontinuities. The significance of junctions in stereo vision has been pointed out (Anderson, 1994; Malik, 1996).

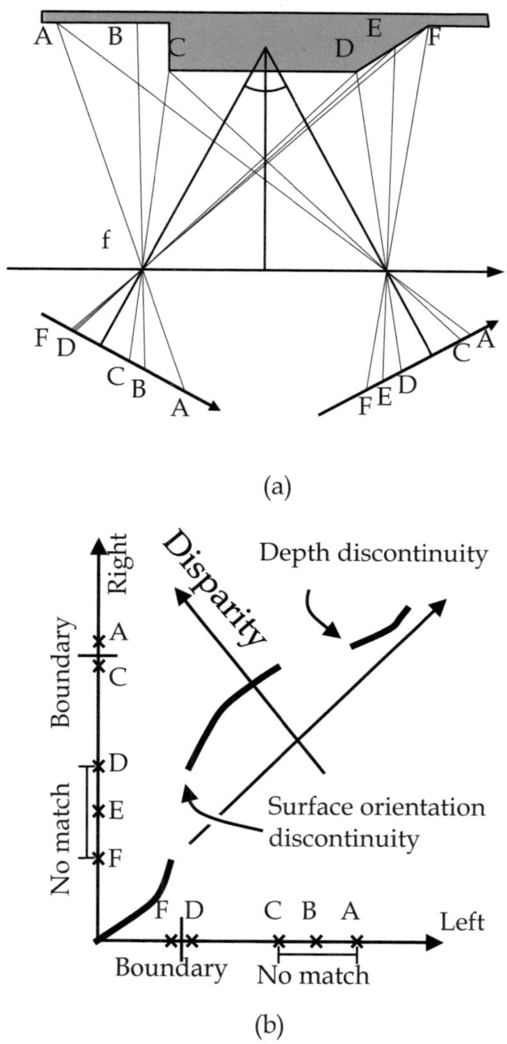

Figure 2. (a) A polyhedron (shaded area) with self-occluding regions and with a discontinuity in the surface-orientation at feature D and a depth discontinuity at feature C. (b) A diagram of left and right images (1D slice) for the image of the ramp. Notice that occlusions always correspond to discontinuities. Dark lines indicates where the match occurs.

2.4 MAP Formulation

Given the left and right images I_L and I_R, we want to find the surface S in the match space that maximizes the a posteriori probability $P(S \mid I_L, I_R)$. By Bayes' rule,

$$P(S \mid I_L, I_R) = \frac{P(I_L, I_R \mid S)P(S)}{P(I_L, I_R)}.$$

Since I_L and I_R are fixed, this value can be optimized by maximizing the $P(I_L, I_R \mid S)P(S)$ using the prior model $P(S)$ and the image formation model $P(I_L, I_R \mid S)$.

In the next section, we define the prior and image-formation energy functionals as the logarithms of the probability functionals so that

$$P(S) = \frac{1}{Z_1} e^{-E_1(S)}$$

$$P(I_L, I_R \mid S) = \frac{1}{Z_2(S)} e^{-E_2(I_L, I_R, S)}$$

Here, the normalization factor Z_1 and Z_2 are defined as

$$Z_1 = \sum_S e^{-E_1(S)}$$

$$Z_2(S) = \sum_{I_L, I_R} e^{-E_2(I_L, I_R, S)}$$

Then the maximization of the probability $P(I_L, I_R \mid S)P(S)$ is equivalent to the minimization of the energy

$$E(I_L, I_R, S) = E_1(S) + E_2(I_L, I_R, S) - \log Z_2(S). \tag{1}$$

The last term will be irrelevant since we define the energy $E_2(I_L, I_R, S)$ so that $Z_2(S)$ is constant.

3. Stereo Energy Functionals

In this section, we define the energy functionals that appeared in the preceding section.

3.1 Markov Random Field

First, we remind the reader of the Markov Random Field (MRF).

A graph $G = (V,E)$ consists of a finite set V of vertices and a set $E \subset V \times V$ of edges. An edge $(u,v) \in E$ is said to be from vertex u to vertex v. An undirected graph is a graph in which all edges go both ways:

$$(u,v) \in E \Leftrightarrow (v,u) \in E.$$

A clique is a set of vertices in an undirected graph in which every vertex has an edge to every other vertex.

An MRF consists of an undirected graph $G = (V,E)$ without loop edges (i.e., edges of the form (v,v)), a finite set L of labels, and a probability distribution P on the space $Z = L^V$ of label assignments. That is, an element X of Z, sometimes called a configuration of the MRF, is a map that assigns each vertex v a label X_v in L. Let N_v denote the set of neighbours $\{u \in V \mid (u,v) \in E\}$ of vertex v. Also, for an assignment $X \in Z$ and $S \subset V$, let X_S denote the event $\{Y \in Z \mid Y_v = X_v, \text{ for all } v \in S\}$, that is, the subset of Z defined by values at vertices in S. By definition, the probability distribution must satisfy the condition:

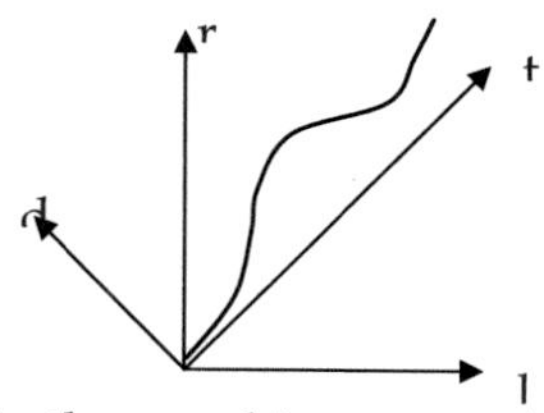

Figure 3. A cyclopean coordinate in the matching space. An epipolar slice is shown.

$$P(X) > 0 \text{ for all } X \in Z$$

$$P(X_{\{v\}} \mid X_{V \setminus \{v\}}) = P(X_{\{v\}} \mid X_{N_v}).$$

This condition states that the assignment at a vertex is conditionally dependent on other assignments only through its neighbours.

Note that the MRF is a conditional probability model. A theorem (Besag, 1974; Kinderman & Snell, 1980) connects it to a joint probability model: a probability distribution P on Z is an MRF exactly when it is a Gibbs distribution relative to G:

$$P(X) \sim e^{-E(X)},$$

$$E(X) = \sum_{C \in \Gamma} E_C(X),$$

where Γ denotes the set of cliques in G and E_C a function on Z with the property that $E_C(X)$ depends only on values of X on C.

The simplest interesting case is when only the edges and vertices, the two simplest kinds of cliques, influence the potential:

$$E(X) = \sum_{(u,v) \in E} g(u,v,X_u,X_v) + \sum_{v \in V} h(v,X_v).$$

This is called a first order MRF, and our stereo energy formulation is an example of it.

3.2 Stereo MRF

As explained in 2.1, the parameter space for stereo is the space of surfaces in the product space $\hat{I}_L \times \hat{I}_R$ restricted by the epipolar constraint (the match space). The match space has a natural coordinate system (l,r,y), where y parameterises epipolar lines, and l and r are the coordinates on the epipolar lines in the left and right images, respectively. We represent occlusions, or appearances of scene locations in only one of the two images, by a match surface that is perpendicular to the l or r axis.

We convert the (l,r,y) coordinate system into a "cyclopean" coordinate system (d,t,y), where $d = r - l$ and $t = r + l$ (see Fig. 3.) Because of the monotonicity constraint, the surface in this representation has a unique point for each (t,y) pair, i.e., it is the graph of some function on the (t,y) plane that gives a value d —the disparity —at each point.

At this point, we also move to the discrete notation so that we can formulate it as a first order MRF. We define the MRF by considering a graph embedded in the t-y plane that has nodes at integral lattice points and a label set consisting of integral disparity values d. The graph G for the MRF has a vertex for each pair of integral t and y in the range, and has the standard four-neighbor structure: the vertex for (t,y) is connected to the vertices for the coordinates $(t+1,y)$, $(t-1,y)$, $(t,y+1)$, and $(t,y-1)$, except at the boundary. The Label set L consists of integral disparity values; thus the configuration X is a function $d(t,y)$ that gives an integral disparity at each vertex of the graph. We denote the configuration by d rather than X. We define the first-order MRF energy functional as follows:

$$E(d) = E_1(d) + E_2(I_L, I_R, d)$$

$$= \sum_{(t,y),(t',y'):\ neighbours} g(t,y,t',y',d(t,y),d(t',y')) + \sum_{(t,y)} h(t,y,d(t,y)), \tag{2}$$

where d assigns a value in L to each vertex of the graph, i.e., a (t,y) pair.
The prior term is defined by

$$g(t,y,t',y',d(t,y),d(t',y')) = \begin{cases} 0 & \text{if } d_1 = d_2, \\ a\,|\,d_1 - d_2\,| & \text{if } y \neq y', \\ b & \text{if } y = y',\ |\,d_1 - d_2\,| = 1,\ \mathrm{t} + d_1 \text{ is even}, \\ c & \text{if } y = y',\ |\,d_1 - d_2\,| = 1,\ \mathrm{t} + d_1 \text{ is odd}, \\ K & \text{if } y = y',\ |\,d_1 - d_2\,| > 1, \end{cases} \tag{3}$$

where a, b, c, and K are positive constants. A change of disparity d across the epipolar line ($y \neq y'$) has a penalty proportional to the change. A disparity change that is larger than 1 along the epipolar line ($y = y'$) means a violation of the monotonicity constraint (e.g., if d changes from 0 to 3 as t changes from 2 to 3, l changes from 1 to 0 and r changes from 1 to 3, violating the monotonicity) and has a penalty K. We make K very large in order to enforce the monotonicity constraint by making it impossible for d to change by more than 1 as t changes its value by 1.

A change of d by 1 as t changes by 1 along the epipolar line has a penalty b or c according to the parity (even or odd) of $t+d$. This might seem odd, but it is because of the discretization: the parity of t and d must coincide for there to be corresponding integral l and r. Thus only those pairs (t,d) with $t+d$ even represent the actual matches of left and right pixels; let us call them the real matches and call the ones with odd $t+d$ the dummy matches. For a real match (t,d), if t and d both change by 1, the result is still a real match. In this case, either l or r stays the same while the other changes by 1 (for example, the change (t,d): $(0,2)\rightarrow(1,3)$ corresponds to (l,r): $(2,1)\rightarrow(2,2)$.) This represents the discrete case of tilted surface, i.e., one discretized interval in one image corresponding to two intervals in the other image. To this, we give a penalty of the positive constant b. If, on the other hand, (t,d) is a dummy match (i.e., $t+d$ is odd) and both t and d change by 1, it means there is a value of either l or r that does not have a match. For example, the change (t,d): $(1,2)\rightarrow(2,3)$, corresponding to (l,r): $(0.5,1.5)\rightarrow(0.5,2.5)$, implies that there is no real match that corresponds to $r = 2$. This models an occlusion, to which we give a penalty of the positive constant c.

The image formation model is given by the following term:

$$h(t,y,d) = \begin{cases} \text{dist}(f(I_L, \frac{t-d}{2}, y), f(I_R, \frac{t+d}{2}, y)), & \text{if } t+d \text{ is even,} \\ 0 & \text{otherwise,} \end{cases} \tag{4}$$

where $f(I,x,y)$ gives a feature at the point (x,y) in the image I and dist(f_1, f_2) gives a measure of the difference of two features f_1 and f_2. We will use a number of different functions $f(I,x,y)$ and dist(f_1, f_2), as explained in section 5.

Note that for this energy to be equivalent to the MAP energy (1), the normalization factor

$$Z_2(d) = \sum_{I_L,I_R} e^{-\sum_{(t,y)} h(t,y,d(t,y))} = \sum_{I_L,I_R} e^{-\sum_{(t,y)} \text{dist}(f(I_L, \frac{t-d}{2}, y), f(I_R, \frac{t+d}{2}, y))}$$

must be constant regardless of the disparity map d, so that it does not affect the outcome of the optimization. This essentially requires the total space of possible image pairs to be neutral with respect to the feature f, which usually is the case.

4. Global Energy Optimization via Graph Cut

In this section, we explain the stereo-matching architecture that utilizes the minimum-cut algorithm to obtain the globally optimal matching, with respect to the energy (2), between the left and right images.

4.1 The Directed Graph

We devise a directed graph and let a cut represent a matching so that the minimum cut corresponds to the optimal matching. It is a modification of the general MRF optimization algorithm introduced in (Ishikawa, 2003). The formulation explicitly handles the occlusion and is completely symmetric with respect to left and right, up to the reversal of all edges, under which the solution is invariant.

Let M be the set of all possible matching between pixels, i.e., $M = \{(l,r,y)\}$. We define a directed graph $G = (V,E)$ as follows:

$$V = \{ u^y_{lr} \mid (l,r,y) \in M \} \cup \{ v^y_{lr} \mid (l,r,y) \in M \} \cup \{s, t\}$$

$$E = E_M \cup E_C \cup E_P \cup E_E$$

In addition to the two special vertices s and t, the graph has two vertices u^y_{lr} and v^y_{lr} for each possible matching $(l,r,y) \in M$. The set E of edges is divided into subsets E_M, E_C, E_P, and E_E, each associated with a weight with a precise meaning in terms of the model (2), which we explain in the following subsections.

As before, we denote a directed edge from vertex u to vertex v as (u,v). Each edge (u,v) has a nonnegative weight $w(u,v) \geq 0$. A *cut* of G is a partition of V into subsets S and $T = V \setminus S$ such that $s \in S$ and $t \in T$ (see Fig. 4.) When two vertices of an edge (u,v) is separated by a cut with $u \in S$ and $v \in T$, we say that the edge is *in the cut*. This is the only case that the weight $w(u,v)$ of the edge contributes to the total cost, i.e., if the cut is through the edge (u,v) with $u \in T$ and $v \in S$, the cost is $w(v,u)$, which is in general different from $w(u,v)$. It is well known that by

solving a maximum-flow problem one can obtain a *minimum cut*, a cut that minimizes the total cost $\Sigma_{u\in S,\, v\in T}\, w(u,v)$ over all cuts.
Our method is to establish a one-to-one correspondence between the configurations of the stereo MRF and the cuts of the graph. By finding the minimum cut, we will find the exact solution for the MRF energy optimization problem.
Let us now explain each set of edges E_M, E_C, E_P, and E_E.

4.2 Matching Edges

Each pair of vertices are connected by a directed edge (u^y_{lr}, v^y_{lr}) with a weight

$$w(u^y_{lr}, v^y_{lr}) = h(r+l,y,r-l) = \mathrm{dist}(f(I_L, l, y), f(I_R, r, y)).$$

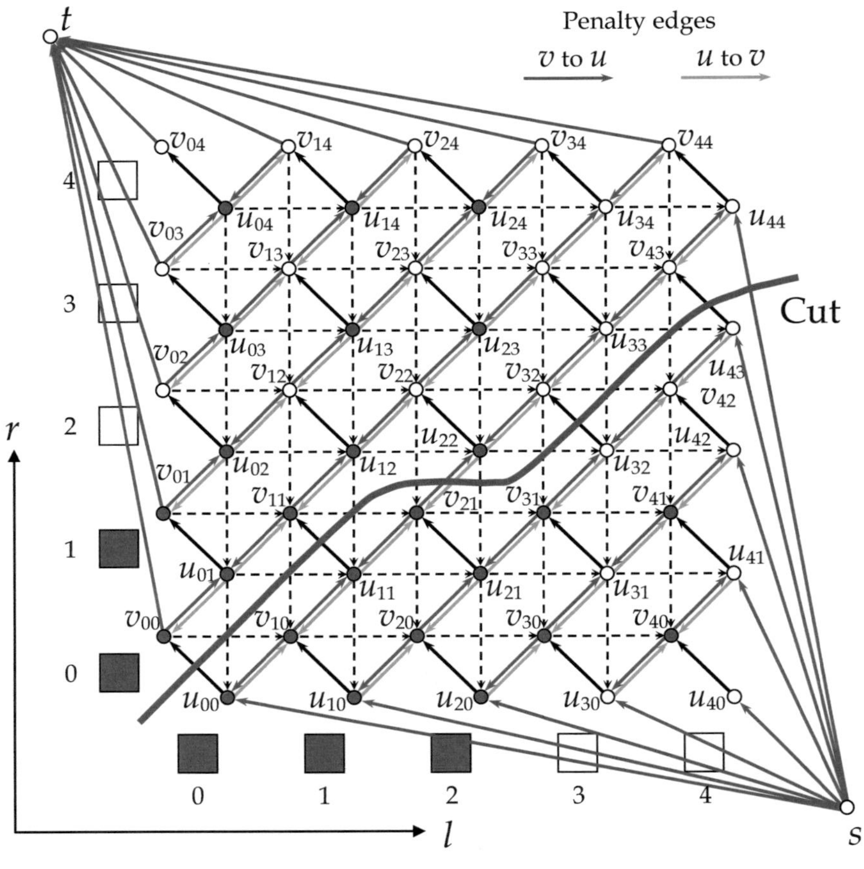

Figure 4. An epipolar slice of the graph representing the stereo model. The full graph is represented in 3D, with the third axis parameterising the epipolar lines. A cut of the graph can be thought of as a surface that separates the two parts; it restricts to a curve in an epipolar slice. The optimal cut is the one that minimizes the sum of the weights associated with the cut edges. In this example, the cut shown yields the matches $(l,r) = (0,0)$, $(1,1)$, $(3,2)$, and $(4,3)$; the cut also detects an occlusion at grey (white) pixel 2 (4) in the left (right) image.

This edge is called the *matching edge* and we denote the set of matching edges by E_M:

$$E_M = \{(u^y_{lr}, v^y_{lr}) \mid (l,r,y) \in M\}.$$

If a matching edge (u^y_{lr}, v^y_{lr}) is in the cut, we interpret this as a match between pixels (l,y) and (r,y). Thus, the sum of the weights associated with the matching edges in the cut is exactly E_2 in (2). This is the correspondence between the match surface and the graph cut:

> **Convention.** Given any cut of G, a matching edge (u^y_{lr}, v^y_{lr}) in the cut represents a match between pixels (l,y) and (r,y).

Fig. 4. shows the nodes and matching edges on an epipolar line. The cut shown represents a match $\{(l,r)\} = \{(0,0), (1,1), (3,2), (4,3)\}$. Note that pixel 2 in the left image has no matching pixel in the right image. Pixel 4 in the right image also has no match; these pixels are occluded. This is how the formulation represents occlusions and discontinuities, whose costs are accounted for by *penalty edges*.

4.3 Penalty Edges (Discontinuity, Occlusions, and Tilts)

Penalty edges are classified in four categories:

$$E_P = E_L \cup E'_L \cup E_R \cup E'_R,$$

$$E_L = \{(v^y_{lr}, u^y_{l(r+1)})\} \cup \{(s, u^y_{l0})\} \cup \{(v^y_{l(N-1)}, t)\},$$

$$E'_L = \{(u^y_{l(r+1)}, v^y_{lr})\},$$

$$E_R = \{(v^y_{lr}, u^y_{(l-1)r})\} \cup \{(s, u^y_{(N-1)r})\} \cup \{(v^y_{0r}, t)\},$$

$$E'_R = \{(u^y_{(l-1)r}, v^y_{lr})\},$$

where the indices run the whole range where indexed vertices exist and N is the width of the images. Edges in E_L are in the cut whenever a pixel in the left image has no matching pixel in the right image. If pixel (l,y) in the left image has no match, exactly one of the edges of the form $(v^y_{lr}, u^y_{l(r+1)})$, (s, u^y_{l0}), or $(v^y_{l(N-1)}, t)$ is in the cut (see Fig. 5(a).) By setting the weight for these edges to be the constant c in the definition of the prior term (3) of the energy functional, we control the penalty of occlusion/discontinuity according to the energy functional. Similarly, an edge in E_R corresponds to an occlusion in the right image.

Edges in E'_R are cut when a pixel in the right image matches two or more pixels in the left image. (Fig. 5(b).) This corresponds to a tilted surface. These edges have the constant weight of b in the definition of the prior term (3).

4.4 Epipolar edges

Epipolar edges are the only edges across epipolar lines. They simply connects vertices with the same (l,r) in both directions:

$$E_E = \{(u^y_{lr}, u^{y+1}_{lr})\} \cup \{(u^{y+1}_{lr}, u^y_{lr})\} \cup \{(v^y_{lr}, v^{y+1}_{lr})\} \cup \{(v^{y+1}_{lr}, v^y_{lr})\}.$$

where the indices run the whole range where indexed vertices exist. The weight a, from the definition of the prior term (3), of an epipolar edge controls the smoothness of the solution across epipolar lines.

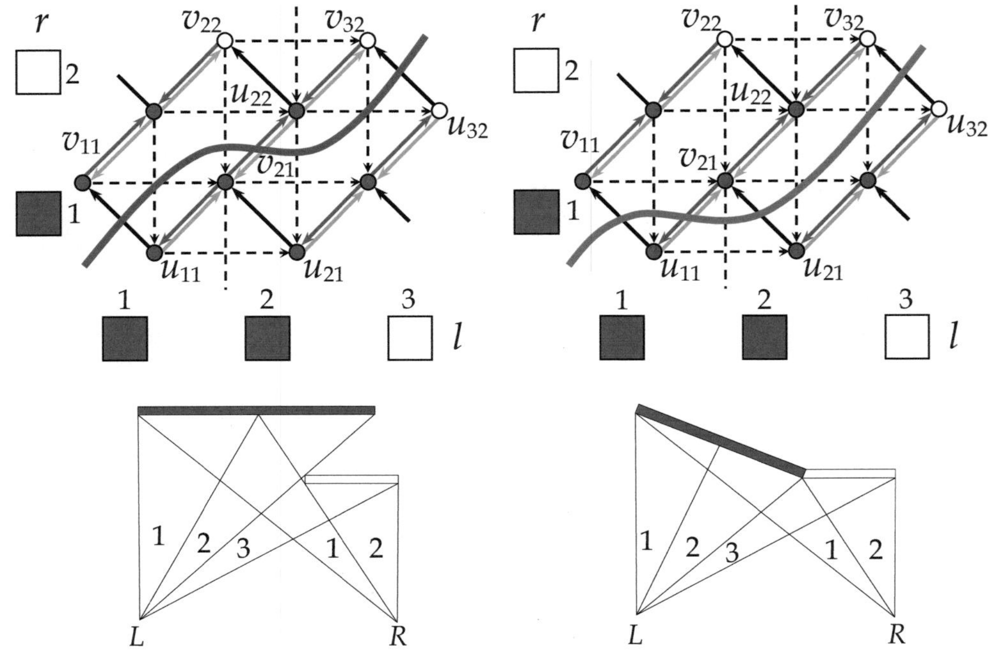

(a) (b)

Figure 5. (a) A close-up of the Fig. 4. The left-pixel 2 (the middle) does not have a matching right-pixel, i.e., it is occluded. (b) Another possibility, where the left-pixel 1 and 2 match the same right pixel; this happens when the surface is tilted. Note the different kinds of the penalty edges are cut in the two cases.

4.5 Constraint edges

Constraint edges are for enforcing the monotonicity constraint and defined as follows:

$$E_C = \{(u^y_{lr}, u^y_{(l+1)r})\} \cup \{(u^y_{lr}, u^y_{l(r-1)})\} \cup \{(v^y_{lr}, v^y_{(l+1)r})\} \cup \{(v^y_{lr}, v^y_{l(r-1)})\}.$$

where, as always, the indices run the whole range where indexed vertices exist. The weight of each constraint edge is set to K from the prior term (3) of the energy. This corresponds to a disparity change that is larger than 1 along the epipolar line, which violates the monotonicity constraint. We make K very large to enforce the monotonicity constraint. In Fig. 4, constraint edges are shown as dotted arrows. It can be seen that whenever the monotonicity constraint is broken, one of the constraint edges falls in the cut. Note that, because the edges have directions, a constraint edge prevents only one of two ways to cut them. This cannot be done with undirected graphs, where having an edge with a very large weight is akin to merging two vertices, and thus meaningless.

This concludes the explanation of the graph structure and the edge weights. We have defined the graph and the weights so that the value of a cut exactly corresponds to the stereo MRF energy functional (2) via the interpretation of the cut as a stereo matching and MRF configuration that we defined in 4.2.

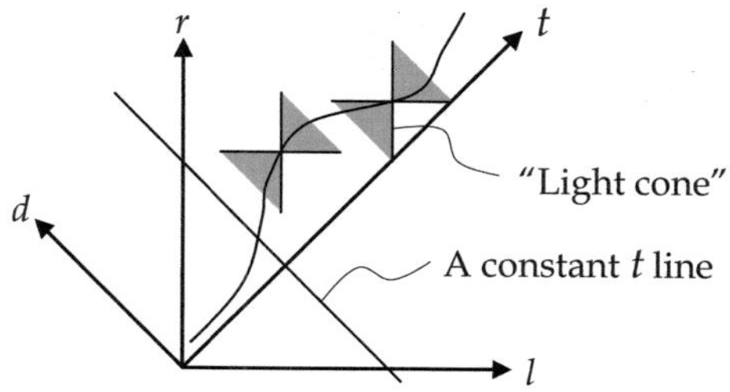

Figure 6. An epipolar slice of the match space. The matching surface appears as a curve here. The monotonicity constraint means that this curve crosses every constant t line once.

5. Feature Selection

In this section, we deal with the image formation local energy $h(t,y,d)$ in (4). In order to find corresponding points in the two images, an algorithm must have some notion of similarity, or likelihood that points in each image correspond to one another. To estimate this likelihood various features are used, e.g., intensity difference, edges, junctions, and correlation. Since none of these features is clearly superior to the others in all circumstances, using multiple features is preferable to using a single feature, if one knows which feature, or which combination of features, to use when. Unfortunately, features are difficult to cross-normalize. How can we compare the output from an edge matching with one from a correlation matching? We would like not to have to cross-normalize the outputs of the feature matchings, and still be able to use multiple features. Here, we use a consequence of the monotonicity constraint to select an optimal feature or combination of features for each set of mutually exclusive matching choices.

In the energy functional (2), the local feature energy function $h(t,y,d)$ gives a measure of difference between the points $((t-d)/2,\ y)$ in the left image and $((t+d)/2,\ y)$ in the right image. We assume that it gives a nonnegative value; a smaller value means a better match. In what follows in this section, the y coordinate will be omitted. Also, note that these functions of course depend on the images, although the notation does not show this explicitly.

Suppose we have a finite set Φ of local feature energy functions. On what basis should we choose from the set? Different features are good in different situations. For instance, edges and other sparse features are good for capturing abrupt changes of depth and other salient features, but can miss gradual depth change that can instead be captured by using dense features. What one cannot do is to choose functions at each point in the match space; the values of different local energy functions are in general not comparable. In general, the same local function must be used at least over the set from which a selection is made. In other words, across these sets of selections, different functions can be used. Then, what is the set of selections? Fig. 6. shows an epipolar slice of the match space. The surface that represents the matching appears as a curve here. In this figure, the monotonicity constraint means that the tangent vector of the curve must reside in the "light cone" at each point of the matching curve. This implies that the matching curve crosses each constant t line at exactly one point. This means that on each such line the matching problem selects one point (the match) from all the points on the line. Thus we can choose one particular local energy function on this line and safely choose a different one on another line. In the following, we will call these lines the "selection lines." The partition of the match space into selection lines is minimal in the sense that, for any sub-partition, the selection of the energy function cannot be local to each partition. There are, however, other minimal partitions with this local-selection property. For instance, the match can be partitioned into other "space-like" lines with an l to r tilt different from $-1:1$, as long as the ratio is negative.

5.1 Selection Rule

As we have said, on each selection line, we are free to choose any local energy function. Note that the information that we can easily utilize for the selection is limited. For instance, we cannot use any information concerning the matching surface that is eventually selected, as that would lead to a combinatorial explosion. Here, we employ a least "entropy" rule to select the energy function. It chooses the energy function that is most "confident" of the match on each selection line. After all, an energy function that does not discriminate between one match and another is of no use. Going to the other extreme, when we have ground truth, an energy function that gives the true match the value zero and every other match the value positive infinity is obviously the best; the energy function knows which match to choose with certainty. This intuition leads us to evaluate how ``sure'' each energy function is.

Let us define an ``entropy'' functional for a positive-valued function h on $\{d = D_0, D_0 + 1, \ldots, D_1\}\times\{t\}$ by:

$$E_t(h) = \sum_{d=D_0}^{D_1} h(d,t),$$

$$H_t(h) = -\sum_{d=D_0}^{D_1} \frac{h(d,t)}{E_t(h)} \log \frac{h(d,t)}{E_t(h)}.$$

This functional H_t gives a measure of the degree of concentration of the function h: it is smaller when h is more concentrated (see Fig. 7.) The more peaked the function, the lower the value of the functional. We use this functional to choose a preferred local energy function for each selection line. To use this functional for our purposes, where we need a dipped function rather than a peaked one, we invert the function and feed the result to the functional.

Thus, for each selection line, we choose the function h with the least value of $H_t(h^{\max_t}-h)$, where $h^{\max_t}$ is the maximum value of h on the selection line corresponding to the coordinate

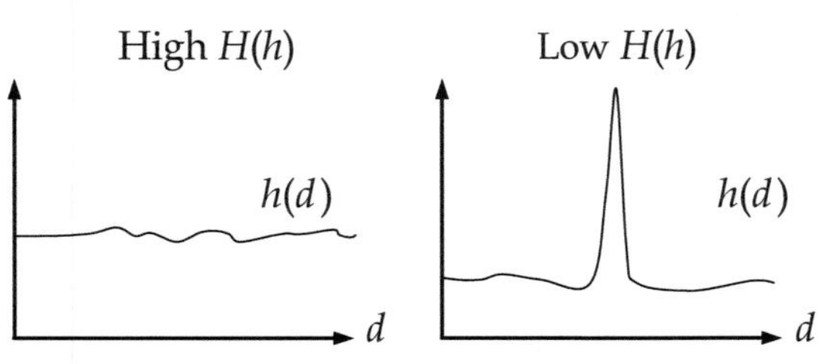

Figure 7. The functional H on function h. It measures the degree of concentration of the value of h.

value t:

$$h_t = \text{argmin}_{h \in H} H_t(h^{\max_t} - h).$$

This selection rule prefers a function that has a distinguished dip, which means, in our situation, one or few disparity values that have an advantage over other values. This method of selection allows us to avoid irrelevant measures locally and ensures the most confident selection of the disparity on each selection line.

6. Implementation and Results

We implemented the architecture explained in the preceding sections. For the minimum-cut algorithm, we used the standard push-relabel method with global relabeling (Cherkassky and Goldberg, 1997).

For the local energy functions, the following features are used:

1. **Intensity**. This is a simple squared difference between the points, i.e.,

$$h^2_{\mathrm{I}}(t,y,d) = \{I_{\mathrm{L}}(\frac{t-d}{2}, y) - I_{\mathrm{R}}(\frac{t+d}{2}, y)\}^2.$$

2. **Wavelet edge**. The derivative of Gaussian wavelet that detects an edge in the vertical direction at various scales:

$$h^s_{\mathrm{E}}(t,y,d) = \left| W_s\, I_{\mathrm{L}}(\frac{t-d}{2}, y) - W_s\, I_{\mathrm{R}}(\frac{t+d}{2}, y) \right|,$$

where

$$W_s I(x,y) = I * \psi_s(x,y),$$

$$\psi_s(x,y) = s^{-1}\psi(s^{-1}x, s^{-1}y),$$

$$\psi(x,y) = 2\pi^{-1} \exp(x^2 - y^2)x.$$

See (Mallat, 1999) Chapter 6 for the details of multi-scale edge detection.

3. **Multi-scale edges consistent across the scale**. This is a measure of the presence of an edge across scales.

$$h_{\mathrm{E}}(t,y,d) = \left| \sum_s W_s\, I_{\mathrm{L}}(\frac{t-d}{2}, y) - \sum_s W_s\, I_{\mathrm{R}}(\frac{t+d}{2}, y) \right|.$$

In Fig. 8, a comparison of the results for a sample image pair ((a), (b); 135×172 pixel 8-bit gray-scale images) using these energy functions is shown. The results (disparity maps) are shown using the intensity square difference h^2_{I} (c); the wavelet edge features h^s_{E} with scale s = 1 (d), s = 2 (e), and s = 4 (f); the multi-scale edge h_{E} (g) (the square difference of the sum of the wavelet coefficients for s = 1, 2, 4; and the minimum-entropy selection from the five energies (h). The Intensity feature h^2_{I} (c) gives the poorest result in this example. Wavelet edges for s = 1, 2, 4 (d), (e), and (f) are better, yet with a black artifact on the upper right, also present with the multi-scale edge (g). The gray-scale image (i) shows which of the five energy functions is used in (h) at each point of the left image. A black point represents an occluded point, where no match was found, resulting in no corresponding t defined for the l-coordinate. Other gray values are in the order (c) to (g), i.e., darkest: intensity h^2_{I}, lightest: multi-scale edge h_{E}.

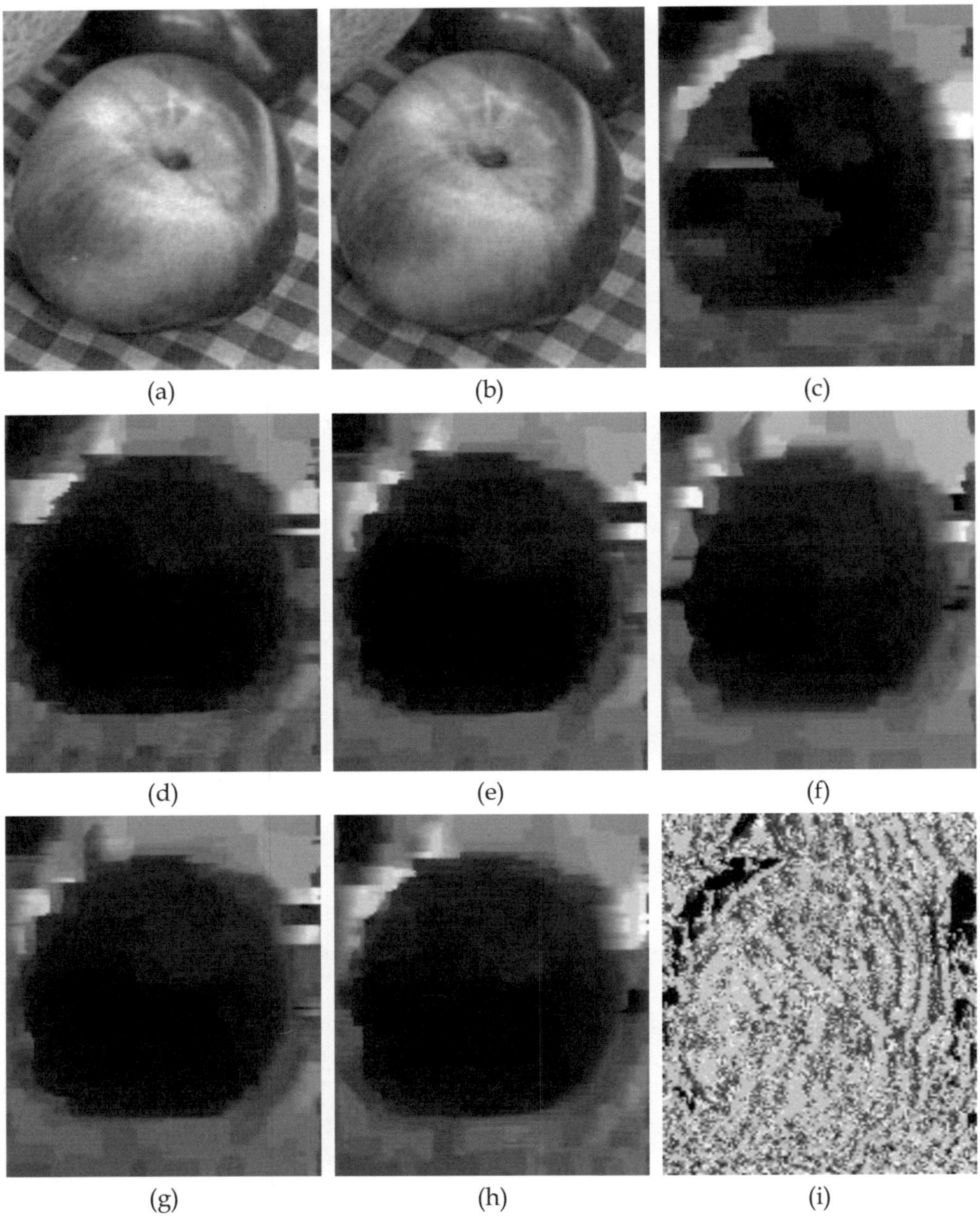

Figure 8. (a), (b): A sample image pair "Apple." Results (disparity maps) are shown using different local energy functions (c), (d), (e), (f), (g), and minimum-entropy selection from the five energies (h). The gray level in (i) shows which of five energy functions is used in (h) at each point of the left image.

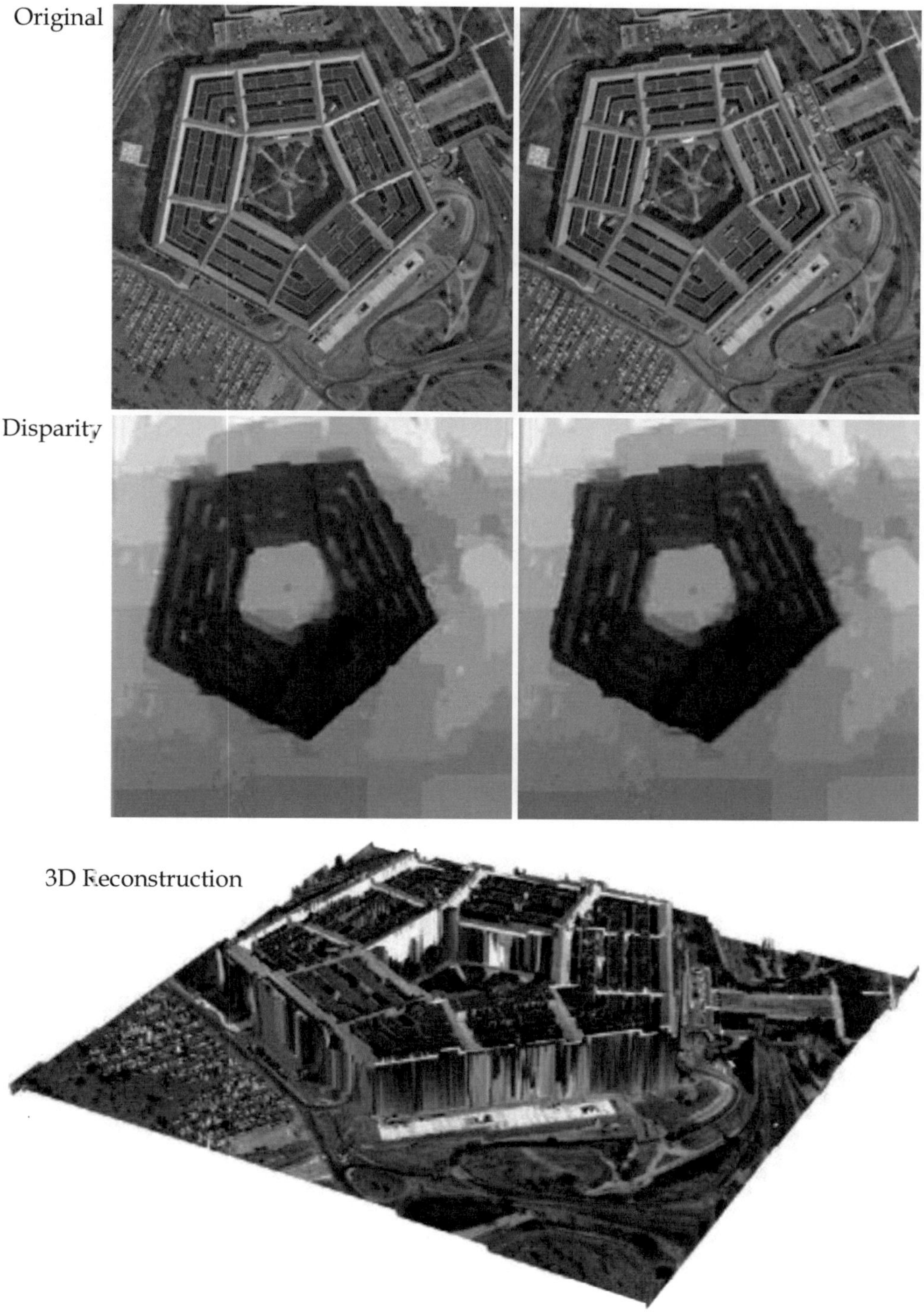

Figure 9. Stereo pair "Pentagon" (508×512 pixel 8-bit greyscale images,) disparity maps for both images, and a 3D reconstruction from the disparity

(a)

(b)

(c)

Figure 10. More results. Left and Middle columns show the left and right images. Right column shows the stereo disparity.

Fig. 9. shows a stereo pair "Pentagon" (508×512 pixel 8-bit greyscale images,) disparity maps for the left and right images, and a 3D reconstruction from the disparity map. To compute this example, it took about ten minutes on a 1GHz Pentium III PC with 1GB of RAM. A few more results are shown in Fig. 10.

7. Conclusion

We have presented a new approach to compute the disparity map, first by selecting optimal feature locally, so that the chosen local energy function gives the most confident selection of the disparity from each set of mutually exclusive choices, then by modelling occlusions, discontinuities, and epipolar-line interactions as a MAP optimization problem, which is equivalent to a first-order MRF optimization problem, and finally by exactly solving the problem in a polynomial time via a minimum-cut algorithm. In the model, geometric constraints require every disparity discontinuity along the epipolar line in one eye to *always* correspond to an occluded region in the other eye, while at the same time encouraging smoothness across epipolar lines. We have also shown the results of experiments that show the validity of the approach.

8. References

Anderson, B (1994). The role of partial occlusion in stereopsis. *Nature*, Vol. 367, 365-368.

Ayache, N. (1991) *Artificial Vision for Mobile Robots*, MIT Press. Cambridge, Mass.

Baker, H. H. & Binford, T. O. (1981). Depth from Edge and Intensity-based Stereo. *Proceedings of 7th International Joint Conferences on Artificial Intelligence*, Vancouver, Canada, August 1981, 631-636.

Belhumeur, P. N. (1996). A Bayesian Approach to Binocular Stereopsis. *International Journal of Computer Vision*, Vol. 19, No. 3, 237-262.

Belhumeur, P. N. & Mumford, D. (1992). A bayesian treatment of the stereo correspondence problem using half-occluded regions. *Proceedings of IEEE Computer Society Conference on Computer Vision and Pattern Recognition*, Champaign, IL, 506-512.

Besag, J. (1974). Spatial interaction and the statistical analysis of lattice systems (with discussion). *Journal of the Royal Statistical Society, Series B*, Vol. 36, 192-326.

Boykov, Y.; Veksler, O. & Zabih, R. (2001). Efficient Approximate Energy Minimization via Graph Cuts. *IEEE Transactions on Pattern Analysis and Machine Intelligence*, Vol. 20, No. 12, 1222-1239.

Cherkassky, B. V. & Goldberg, A. V. (1997). On Implementing Push-Relabel Method for the Maximum Flow Problem. *Algorithmica*, Vol. 19, No. 4, 390-410.

Faugeras, O. (1993) *Three-Dimensional Computer Vision*. MIT Press. Cambridge, Mass.

Geiger, D.; Ladendorf, B. & Yuille, A. (1995). Occlusions and binocular stereo. *International Journal of Computer Vision*, Vol. 14, 211-226.

Gillam B. & Borsting. E. (1988). The role of monocular regions in stereoscopic displays. *Perception*, Vol. 17, 603-608.

Grimson, W. E. L. (1981). *From Images to Surfaces*. MIT Press. Cambridge, Mass.

Ishikawa, H & Geiger, D. (1998). Occlusions, discontinuities, and epipolar lines in stereo. *Proceedings of Fifth European Conference on Computer Vision*, Freiburg, Germany. 232-248.

Ishikawa, H. (2003). Exact optimization for Markov random fields with convex priors. *IEEE Transactions on Pattern Analysis and Machine Intelligence*. Vol. 25, No. 10, 1333-1336.

Kinderman, R. & Snell, J. L. (1980). *Markov Random Fields and Their Applications*. American Mathematical Society. Providence, RI.

Malik, J. (1996) On Binocularly viewed occlusion Junctions. *Proceedings of Fourth European Conference on Computer Vision*, Cambridge, UK. , 167-174.

Mallat, S. (1999). *A Wavelet Tour of Signal Processing (Second Edition)*. Academic Press. 1999.

Marapane, S. B. & Trivedi, M. M. (1994). Multi-primitive hierarchical (MPH) stereo analysis. *IEEE Transactions on Pattern Analysis and Machine Intelligence*, Vol. 16, No. 3, 227-240.

Marr, D. & Poggio, T. (1976) Cooperative computation of stereo disparity. *Science*, Vol. 194, 283-287.

Nakayama, K. & Shimojo, S. (1990). Da Vinci stereopsis: depth and subjective occluding contours from unpaired image points. *Vision Research*, Vol. 30, 1811-1825.

Okutomi, M. & Kanade, T. (1993). A multiple-baseline stereo. *IEEE Transactions on Pattern Analysis and Machine Intelligence*, Vol. 15, No. 4, 353-363.

Roy, S. (1999). Stereo without epipolar lines : A maximum-flow formulation. *International Journal of Computer Vision*, Vol. 34, 147-162.

Roy, S. & Cox, I. (1998). A Maximum-Flow Formulation of the N-camera Stereo Correspondence Problem. *Proceedings of International Conference on Computer Vision*, Bombay, India. 492-499.

23

A Learning Approach for Adaptive Image Segmentation

Vincent Martin and Monique Thonnat
INRIA Sophia Antipolis, ORION group
France

1. Introduction

Image segmentation remains an issue in most computer vision systems. In general, image segmentation is a key step towards high level tasks such as image understanding, and serves in a variety of applications including object recognition, scene analysis or image/video indexing. This task consists in grouping pixels sharing some common characteristics. But segmentation is an ill-posed problem: defining a criterion for grouping pixels clearly depends on the goal of the segmentation. Consequently, a unique general method cannot perform adequately for all applications. When designing a vision system, segmentation algorithms are often heuristically selected and narrowly tuned by an image processing expert with respect to the application needs. Generally, such a methodology leads to *ad hoc* algorithms working under fixed hypotheses or contexts. Three major issues arise from this approach. First, for a given task, the selection of an appropriate segmentation algorithm is not obvious. As shown in Figure 1, state-of-the-art segmentation algorithms have different behaviours. Second, the tuning of the selected algorithm is also an awkward task. Although default values are provided by authors of the algorithm, these parameters need to be tuned to get meaningful results. But complex interactions between the parameters make the behaviour of the algorithm fairly impossible to predict (see Figure 2). Third, when the context changes, so does the global appearance of images. This can drastically affect the segmentation results. This is particularly true for video applications where lighting conditions are continuously varying. It can be due to local changes (e.g. shadows) and global illumination changes (due to meteorological conditions), as illustrated in Figure 3. The third issue emphasizes the need of automatic adaptation capabilities. As in (Martin et al., 2006), we propose to use learning techniques for adaptive image segmentation. No new algorithms are proposed, but rather a methodology that allows to easily set up a segmentation system in a vision application. More precisely, we propose a learning approach for context adaptation, algorithm selection and parameter tuning according to the image content and the application need.

In order to show the potential of our approach, we focus on two different segmentation tasks. The first one concerns figure-ground segmentation in a video surveillance application. The second segmentation task we focus on is static image adaptive segmentation.

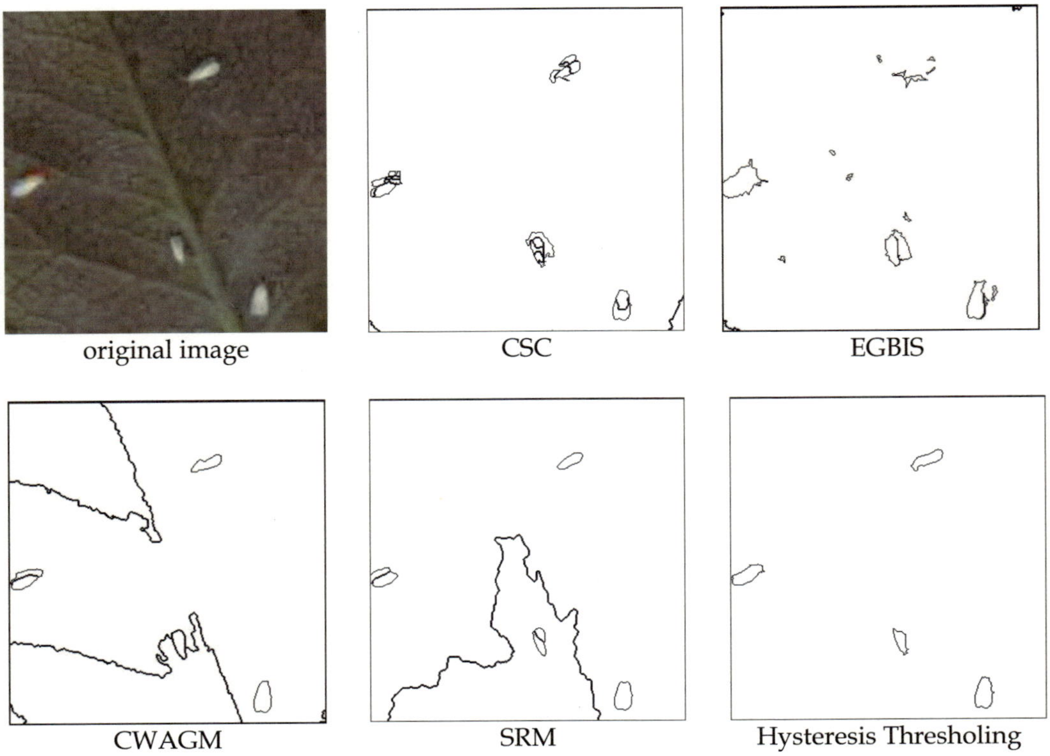

Figure 1. Illustration of the problem of segmentation algorithm selection. Five region-based segmentation algorithms (see Table 1 for details and references) are tuned with default parameters. For better visualization of very small regions, only region boundaries have been represented. Results show differences in terms of number of segmented regions and sensibility to small structures

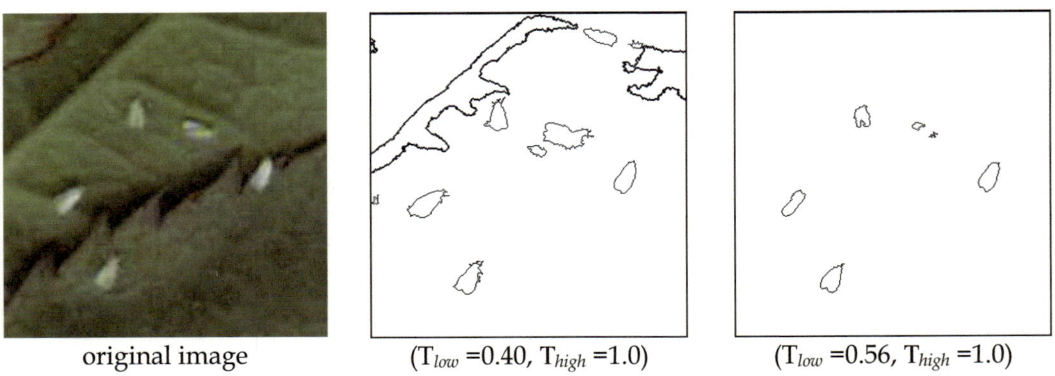

Figure 2. Illustration of the problem of segmentation algorithm parameter setting. The Hysteresis thresholding algorithm is tuned with two different sets of its two control parameters (T_{low} , T_{high}). A good parameter set might be between these two sets

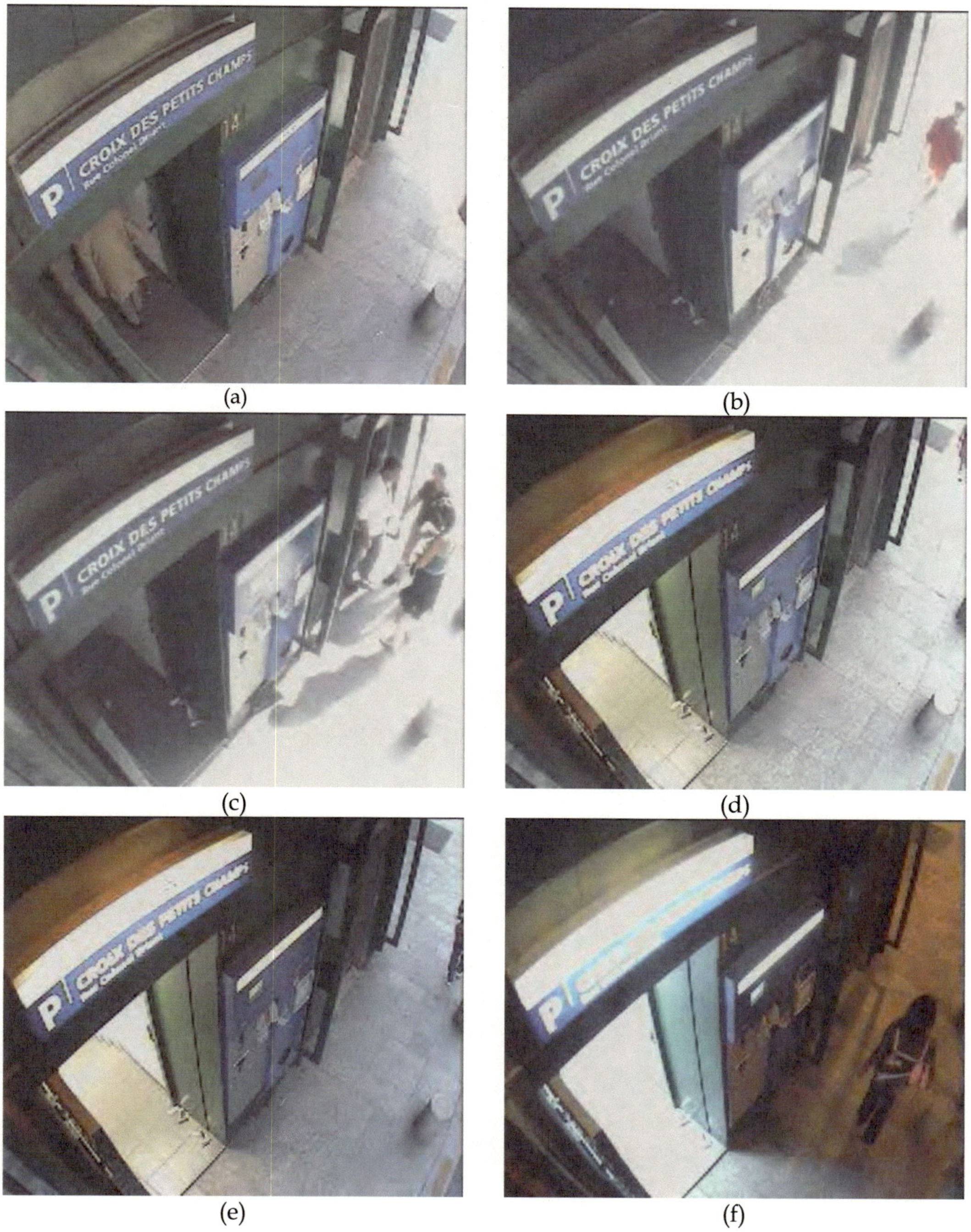

Figure 3. Illustration of the problem of context variation for a video application. Six frames (from a to f) from an outdoor fixed video surveillance camera have been captured along a day. As lighting conditions change, the perception of the scene evolves. This is visible at a local level as in the zone of pedestrian entrance of the car park (see frames c and d) and at a global level (see frames b and f)

Figure 4. Illustration of the problem of context variations for a static image application. Objects of interest are small, seen from different point of view and background is highly textured, with complex structures. This makes the segmentation task very difficult

In the first task, the goal is to detect moving objects (e.g. a person) in the field of view of a fixed video camera. Detection is usually carried by using background subtraction methods. A large number of techniques has been proposed in recent years mainly based on pixel intensity variation modeling techniques, e.g. using mixture of gaussians (Grimson & Stauffer, 1999), kernel density (Elgammal et al., 2000) or codebook model (Kim et al., 2005). Strong efforts have been done to cope with quick-illumination changes or long term changes, but coping with both problems altogether remains an open issue (see Figure 3 for example). In these situations, we believe that it should be more reliable to split the background modeling problem into more tractable sub-problems, each of them being associated with a specific context. For this segmentation task, the main contribution of our approach takes place at the context modeling level. By achieving dynamic background model selection based on context analysis, we allow to enlarge the scope of surveillance applications to high variable environments.
In the second task, the goal is to segment complex images where both background and objects of interest are highly variables in terms of color, shape and texture. This is well-illustrated in Figure 4. In other words, the segmentation setting of an image to an other one can be completely different. In this situation, the contribution of our approach arises from the need of adaptability of treatments (algorithm selection and parameter tuning) in order to segment the object of interest in an optimal manner for each image. Knowledge-based techniques have been widely used to control image processing (Thonnat et al., 1999; Clouard et al. 1999). One drawback is that a lot of knowledge has to be provided to achieve good parametrization. In our approach, we alleviate the task of knowledge acquisition for the segmentation algorithm parametrization by using an optimization procedure to automatically extract optimal parameters. In the following sections we describe a learning approach that achieves these objectives.
The organization of the chapter is as follows: Section 2 first presents an overview of the proposed approach then a detailed description is given for two segmentation tasks: figure-ground segmentation in video sequence and static image segmentation. In section 3, we present how we apply these techniques for a figure-ground segmentation task in a video surveillance application and a static image segmentation task for insect detection over rose leaves. Section 4 summarizes our conclusions and discusses the possibilities of further research in this area.

2. Proposed Approach

2.1 Overview

Our approach is based on a preliminary supervised learning stage in which the knowledge of the segmentation task is acquired in two steps.

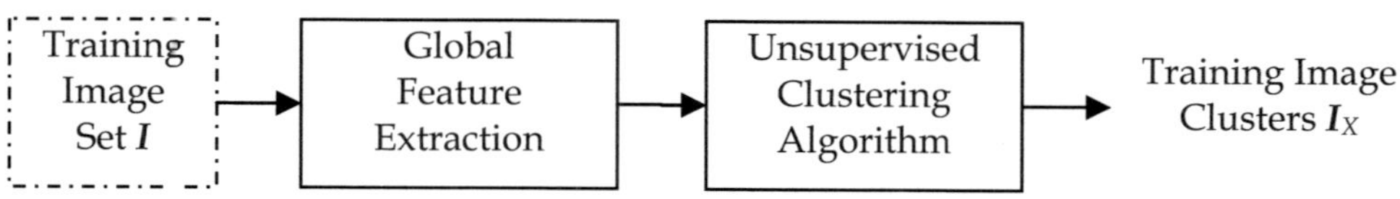

Figure 5. Context analysis schema. The input is a training image set selected by the user. The output is a set of clustered training image I_X

The first step of our approach is dedicated to handle context variations. It aims at modeling context variations based on global image characteristics (see Figure 5). The role of the user is to establish a training image set composed of samples that point out context variations. Low-level information is extracted from the training image set to capture image changes. Then, an unsupervised clustering algorithm is used to cluster this training data feature set. This makes further tasks such as high variable object-class modelization possible by restricting object-class model parameter space.
The second step consists in learning the mapping between the knowledge of the segmentation task and the image characteristics (see Figure 6). The user first defines a set of classes according to the segmentation goal (e.g. background, foreground, object of interest #1, object of interest #2, etc.). This set is used to annotate regions from initial training image segmentation (i.e. grid segmentation, manual segmentation). The goal is to train region classifiers. A region classifier allows to evaluate the membership of a region to a class. Then, a segmentation evaluation metric based on these trained classifiers is defined to assess the quality of segmentation results independently of the segmentation algorithm. This assessment will be further used both for parameter optimization and algorithm ranking.

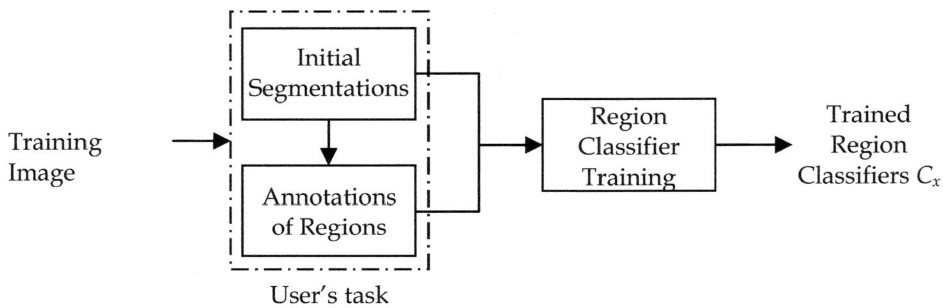

Figure 6. Region classifier training schema. For a cluster of training images I_x belonging to the same context x, the user is invited to annotate template regions from initial segmentations. The output is a set of trained region classifiers C_x, i.e. one classifier per class

After this learning stage our approach proposes an automatic stage for the adaptive segmentation of new images. This stage is devoted to segmentation algorithm parameter control using previously learned knowledge. For an input image, after the context analysis, a global optimization algorithm efficiently explores the parameter space driven by the segmentation quality assessment. The goal is to minimize the assessment value. The main advantage of this procedure is that the search process is independent of both the segmentation algorithm and the application domain. Therefore, it can be systematically applied to automatically extract optimal segmentation algorithm parameters. This scheme is applied to a set of algorithms. By ranking their assessment values, we can select the one which performs the best segmentation for the considered image.
The next sections describe in details each step of our approach for the two investigated segmentation tasks. Figure-ground segmentation task for video surveillance application requires real-time capabilities. In this case, the algorithm selection and parametrization steps are inappropriate because of the necessary computing-time. In static image segmentation task, the computing time is less important.

2.2 Figure-ground Segmentation in Video Sequences

We consider a figure-ground segmentation problem in outdoor with a single fixed video camera. The context variations are mainly due to scene illumination changes such as the nature of the light source (natural and/or artificial), the diffusion effects or the projected shadows. The goal is to segment efficiently foreground regions (i.e. mobile objects) from background regions.

2.2.1 Training Dataset Building by Context Analysis

Segmentation is sensitive to context changes. We study the variability of context in a quantitative manner by using an unsupervised clustering algorithm. The goal is to be able to identify context classes according to a predefined criterion. As context changes alter image both locally and globally, the criterion must be defined to take into account these characteristics. A straightforward approach is to use a global histogram based on pixel intensity distribution as in (Georis, 2006). However, such histograms lack spatial information, and images with different appearances can have similar histograms. To overcome this limitation, we use an histogram-based method that incorporates spatial information (Pass et al., 1997). This approach consists in building a coherent color histogram based on pixel membership to large similarly-colored regions. For instance, an image presenting red pixels forming a single coherent region will have a color coherence histogram with a peak at the level of red color. An image with the same quantity of red pixels but widely scattered, will not have this peak. This is particularly significant for outdoor scene with changing lighting conditions due to the sun rotation, as in Figure 3(a,b).

An unsupervised clustering algorithm is trained using the coherence color feature vectors extracted from the training image set $\boldsymbol{I}$. Let I be an image of the training dataset $\boldsymbol{I}$, for each $I \in \boldsymbol{I}$, the extracted global feature vector is noted g_I. The unsupervised clustering is applied on g_I. Its output is a set of clustered training images $\boldsymbol{I}_X$ composed of n clusters $\boldsymbol{I}_x$:

$$\boldsymbol{I}_X = \bigcup_{i=1}^{n} \boldsymbol{I}_{x_i} \tag{1}$$

The set of cluster identifiers (ID) is noted $X=[x_1,\ldots,x_n]$. In our experiments, we have used a density-based spatial clustering algorithm called DBScan proposed by Ester et al. (Ester et al., 1996). This is well-adapted for clustering noisy data as histograms. Starting from one point, the algorithm searches for similar points in its neighborhood based on a density criteria to manage noisy data.

The next section describes how each cluster of training images is used to train context-specific background classifiers.

2.2.2 Figure-ground Segmentation Knowledge Acquisition by Automatic Annotations of Buckets

Because the point of view of the video camera is fixed, we can easily capture spatial information on image. This is done by using an image bucket partioning where a bucket is a small region at a specific image location. For instance, a bucket can be a square of pixels (see Figure 7) or reduced to only one pixel. The size and the shape of a bucket must be fixed and are equals for all samples of the training image set $\boldsymbol{I}$.

b_1	b_2	b_3
b_4	b_5	b_6
b_7	b_8	b_9

Figure 7. Example of a bucket partioning using a grid segmentation. The image is segmented into nine regions of same size and shape. Each region is a bucket

Let us define the set of bucket partioning B as:

$$B = \bigcup_{i=1}^{m} \boldsymbol{b}_i \tag{2}$$

Where b_i is a bucket among m. Since training image sets are composed of background images, the task of bucket annotations is automatic for a figure-ground segmentation problem. In our approach, this is done by assigning the same background label l to each $b_i \in B$. The role of the user is limited to the selection of video sequences where no mobile objects are present. Then, for each bucket, a feature vector v_b is extracted and makes, with the label a pair sample noted (v_b, l_b). A pair sample represents the association between low-level information (v_b) and high-level knowledge (l_b). If the bucket is a pixel, v_b can be the (R,G,B) value of the pixel. If the bucket is a small region, v_b can be an histogram of the bucket pixel (R,G,B) values. Since all buckets have the same label, the set of all collected pair samples from $\boldsymbol{I}_x$ can be considered as the set of all feature vectors. This constitutes the training dataset T_x as:

$$T_x = \bigcup_{\substack{b \in \boldsymbol{B} \\ I_x \in \boldsymbol{I}_x}} v_b \tag{3}$$

and then,

$$T = \bigcup_{x \in \boldsymbol{X}} T_x \tag{4}$$

T represents the knowledge of the segmentation task. At the end of this automatic annotation process, we obtain $m*n$ training data sets (i.e. one training data set per bucket and per context cluster). The following task is to modelize this knowledge in order to train background classifiers.

2.2.3 Segmentation Knowledge Modelization

For each training image set $\boldsymbol{I}_x$, we have to train a set of specific background classifiers noted C_x with one background classifier c_x per bucket $b \in B$ as seen in Figure 8.

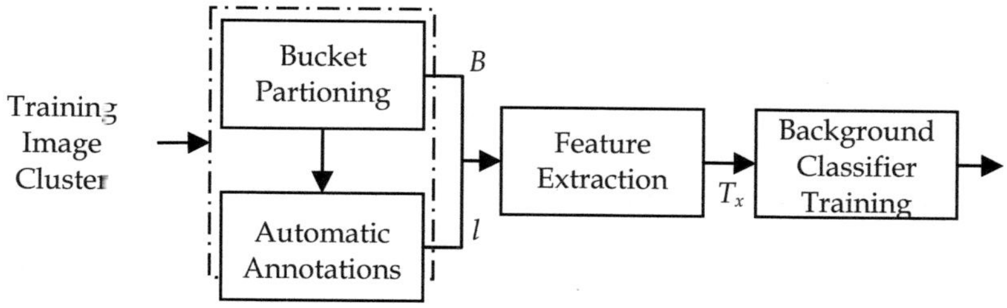

Figure 8. Background classifier training schema for figure-ground segmentation. Since training image sets are composed of only background images, the annotation task is fully automatic

In our approach, we use the background codebook model proposed by Kim et al. (Kim et al., 2005) as background classifier technique. This codebook algorithm adopts a quantization/clustering technique to construct a background model from long observation sequences. For each pixel, it builds a codebook consisting of one or more codewords. For each pixel the set of codewords is built based on a color distortion metric together with brightness bounds applied to the pixel values of the training images $\boldsymbol{I_x}$. The codewords do not necessarly correspond to single Gaussian or other parametric distributions.
According to this algorithm, a bucket is a pixel and the feature vector v_b is composed of four features: the three (R,G,B) values of the considered pixel and its intensity. At the end of the training, we obtain one background classifier (i.e. a codebook) for each bucket (i.e. a pixel) and for each background cluster $\boldsymbol{I_x}$.

2.2.3 Real-Time Adaptive Figure-ground Segmentation

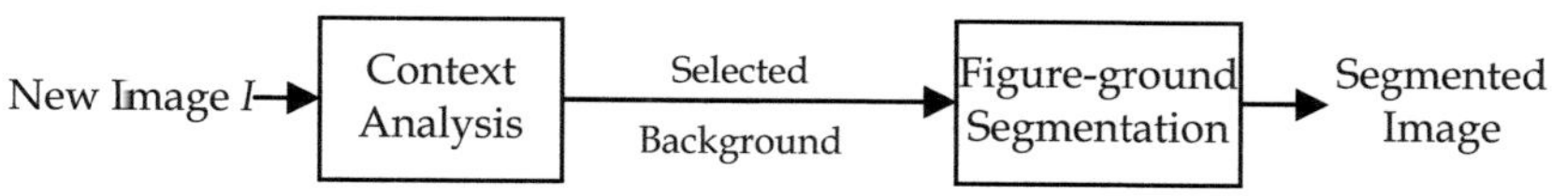

Fig 9. Adaptative segmentation schema for figure-ground segmentation

As illustrated in Figure 9, the first step is the dynamic selection of background classifiers. We also use a temporal filtering step to reduce unstability of the clustering algorithm. Indeed, in cluttered scenes, foreground objects can strongly interact with the environnement (e.g. light reflections, projection of shadows) and then add a bias to the context analysis. So, it is important to smooth the analysis by ponderating the current result with respect to previous ones. Our temporal filtering criterion is defined as follows. For an image I, let us define the probability vector of the context analysis ouput for an image I as:

$$p(X \mid g_I) = [p(x_1 \mid g_I), \ldots, p(x_n \mid g_I)] \tag{5}$$

The most probable cluster x_I with associated probability $p_{\max}(x_I)$ for the image I are then:

$$p_{\max}(x_I) = \max p(X \mid g_I)$$

$$x_I = \arg\max p(X \mid g_I) \tag{6}$$

Let us define x the context cluster identifier, x_I the cluster identifier for the incoming image I, μ_x the square mean of cluster probability computed On a temporal window. α is a ponderating coefficent related to the width w of the temporal filtering window. To decide if x_I is the adequate cluster for an incoming image I, we compare it with the square meanshift of cluster probability μ_x as in the algorithm described in Figure 13. In this algorithm, two cases are investigated. If x_I is the same as the previous one, μ_x is updated based on the context maximum probability $p_{max}(x_I)$ and α. Else if the current x_I is different from the previous one, the current $p_{max}(x_I)$ is tested against μ_x. The square value of $p_{max}(x_I)$ is used to raise the sensibility of temporal filtering to large variations of $p_{max}(x_I)$.
When the cluster identifier x is found, the corresponding background classifiers C_x are selected for the figure-ground segmentation of I as seen in Figure 9.

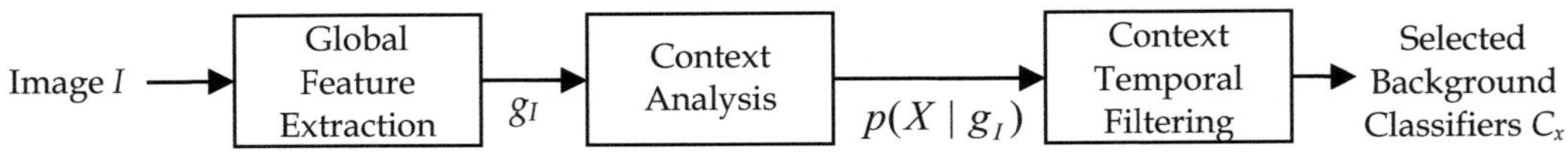

Figure 9. Context analysis in real-time segmentation. From an input image, a global feature vector g_I is first extracted. Then, context analysis computes the vector $p(X \mid g_I)$. Context temporal filtering uses this vector to compute the most probable cluster identifier x_I for the current image depending on previous probabilities

The figure-ground segmentation consists in a vote for each pixel. This vote is based on the results of the background classifiers for each pixel. If a pixel value satisfies both color and brightness distance conditions, it is classified as background ($l = bg$). Otherwise, it is classified as foreground ($l = fg$).
The major problem of this segmentation method is that no spatial coherency is taken into account. To overcome this limitation, we compute in parallel a region-based image segmentation. Our objective is to refine the segmentation obtained with background classifiers (see Figure 12) .

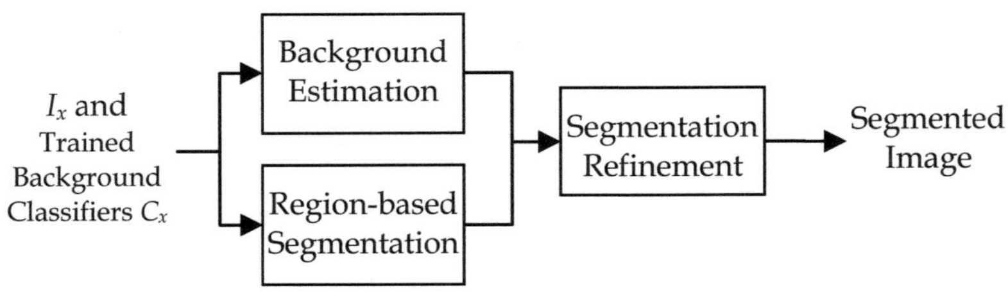

Fig 12. Figure-ground segmentation with region spatial refinement

For each region r of the region-based segmentation we compute its label l by testing the percentage of pixels of this region labelled as foreground by the background classifiers. The refinement criterion is defined as follows:

$$\textbf{if } \frac{1}{|r|}\sum_r l_{pix}^{fg} \geq \theta \quad \textbf{then } l = fg \quad \textbf{else } l = bg \tag{7}$$

where θ is a threshold and I_{pix}^{fg} is a pixel classified as being a foreground pixel by its corresponding background classifier.
So, if the foreground pixels inside the region r represent more or equal than θ percent of the region area $|r|$, the region r is considered as a foreground region. In our experiments, we have fixed the threshold θ to 90 percent.

Context Temporal Filtering Algortihm

Initialization step :

$x \leftarrow 0, \mu_x = 0, \alpha \leftarrow 0$

For each new image I

I. $[x_I, p_{\max}(x_I)] = ContextAnalysis(g_I)$ // extract $p(X|g_I)$ index of max and its corresp. value

II. If $(x = x_I \;||\; x = 0)$ // test the context identifier of I (0 = noise)

(i) $x \leftarrow x_I$

(ii) $\mu_x \leftarrow \dfrac{\alpha * \mu_c + p^2{}_{\max}(x_I)}{\alpha + 1}$ // update the value of μ_x

(iii) If $(\alpha < w)$ // test α within the width of the temporal window

$\alpha \leftarrow \alpha + 1$

Else If $(p^2{}_{\max}(x_I) \geq \mu_x)$

(i) $x \leftarrow x_I$

(ii) $\mu_x \leftarrow p^2{}_{\max}(x_I)$ // update the value of μ_x with square max prob of $p(X|g_I)$

(iii) $\alpha \leftarrow 1$ // reinitialize weight α

End If

III. return x

End For

Figure 13. Description of the context temporal filtering algorithm. In our experiment, we have fixed w to 40 to consider the last five seconds of the image sequence in the calculation of μ_x (i.e. 40 frames at eight frames per second correspond to five seconds)

Section 3.1 presents experiments of this proposed approach.

2.3 Static Image Adaptive Segmentation

We consider the segmentation task for a static image segmentation. The goal is to segment objects of interest from the background. The objects of interest are small, variable within the background and background is highly textured, with complex structures.

2.3.1 Training Image Set Building by Context Analysis

This step is conducted in the same way as in section 2.2.1. For this segmentation task, the user must provide training images containing both objects of interest and background.

2.3.2 Static Image Segmentation Knowledge Acquisition by Visual Annotations of Regions

In this section, we focus on the knowledge acquisition for static image segmentation. We use the example-based modeling approach as an implicit representation of the knowledge. This approach has been applied successfully in many applications such as detection and segmentation of objects from specific classes (e.g. Schnitman et al., 2006; Borenstein & Ullman, 2004). Starting from representative patch-based examples of objects (e.g. fragments), modeling techniques (e.g. mixture of gaussians, neural networks, naive bayes classifier) are implemented to obtain codebooks or class-specific detectors for the segmentation of images. Our strategy follows this implicit knowledge representation and associates it with machine learning techniques to train region classifiers. In our case, region annotations represents the high-level information. This approach assumes that the user is able to gather a representative set of manually segmented training images, i.e. a set that illustrates the variability of object characteristics which may be found. The result of a manual segmentation for a training image $I \in \boldsymbol{I}$ image is noted R_I where R is a set of regions.
First, let the user define a domain class dictionary composed of k classes as $L = \{l_1,\ldots,l_k\}$. This dictionary must be designed according to the problem objectives. Once L is defined, the user is invited, in a supervised stage, to label the regions of the segmented training image with respect to V. From a practical point of view, an annotation is done by clicking into a region r and by selecting the desired class label l. At the end of the annotation task, we obtain a list of labelled regions which belong to classes defined by the user. For each region, a feature vector v_r is also extracted and it makes, with the label a pair sample noted (v_r, l_r). The set of all collected pair samples from $\boldsymbol{I}$ constitutes the training dataset. This training dataset represents the knowledge of the segmentation task and is composed, at this time, of raw information.
In the following section, we address the problem of knowledge modeling by statistical analysis.

2.3.3 Segmentation Knowledge Modelization

The first step towards learning statistical models from an image partition is extracting a feature vector from each region. But which low-level features are the most representative for a specific partition ? This fundamental question, refering to the feature selection problem, is a key issue of most of the segmentation approaches. As said by Draper in (Draper, 2003), we need to avoid relying on heuristically selected domain features. A popular approach is to combine generic features, such as color, texture and geometric features. The final feature vector representing a region is a concatenation of the feature vectors extracted from each cue.

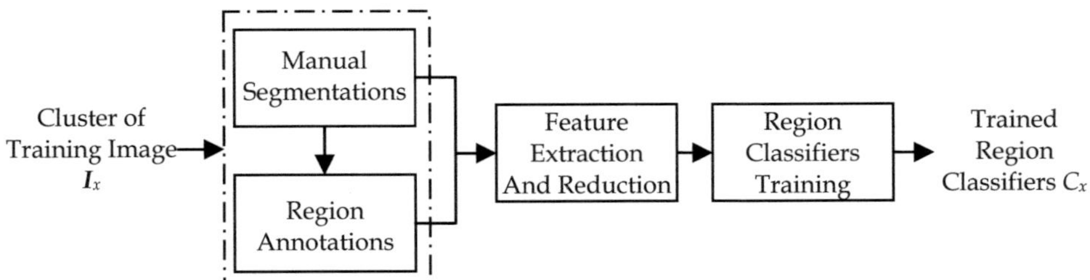

Figure 14. Region Classifier training schema for static image segmentation

Then, applying a feature reduction algorithm, discriminante information is extracted by using a linear component analysis method. In our approach, a generalization of linear principal component analysis, kernel PCA, is exploited to simplify the low-level feature representation of the training dataset T. Kernel PCA was introduced by Scholkopf (Mika et al., 1999) and has proven to be a powerful method to extract nonlinear structures from a data set (Dambreville et al., 2006). Comparing to linear PCA, which may allow linear combinations of features that are unfaithful to the true representation of object classes, kernel PCA combines the precision of kernel methods with the reduction of dimension in the training set. We denote v_r' as the vector of reduced features for the region r.
After reducing feature vector for each region of each training image, the next step is to modelize the knowledge in order to produce region classifiers (one classifier per class) as seen in Figure 14. For a feature vector v_r and a class c,

$$c_l(r) = p(l_r \mid v_r') \tag{9}$$

with $c_l(r) \in [0,1]$, is the probability estimate associated with the hypothesis: feature vector v_r' extracted from region r is a representative sample of l. The set of these trained region classifiers is noted $C = \{ c_1, \ldots, c_k \}$.
A variety of techniques have been successfully employed to tackle the problem of knowledge modeling. Here we have tested Support Vector Machine (SVM) (Burges, 1998) as a template-based approach. SVM are known to be an efficient discriminative strategy for large-scale classification problems such as in image categorization (Chen & Wang, 2004) or object categorization (Huan & LeCun, 2006). SVM training consists of finding an hyper-surface in the space of possible inputs (i.e. feature vectors labeled by +1 or -1). This hyper-surface will attempt to split the positive examples from the negative examples. This split will be chosen to have the largest distance from the hyper-surface to the nearest of the positive and negative examples. We adopt a one-vs-rest multiclass scheme with probability information (Wu et al., 2004) to train one region evaluator c per class l.
The goal of training region classifiers is not to directly treat the problem of the segmentation as a clustering problem but as an optimization one. Region classifiers express the problem knowledge. Used as performance assessment tools, they define a segmentation evaluation metric. Such functional can then be used in an optimization procedure to extract optimal algorithm parameters. Consequently, we can say that the segmentation optimization is guided by the segmentation task. Next section describes this approach.

2.3.4 Segmentation Knowledge Extraction via Parameter Optimization

While a lot of techniques (Sezgin et al., 2004) have been proposed for adaptive selection of key parameters (e.g. thresholds), these techniques do not accomplish any learning from experience nor adaptation independently of detailed knowledge pertinent to segmentation algorithm. The proposed optimization procedure overcomes such limitations by decomposing the problem into three fundamental and independent components: a segmentation algorithm with its free-parameters to tune, a segmentation evaluation metric and a global optimization algorithm (see Figure 15). To our knowledge, this scheme has already been applied for adaptive segmentation problems by Banu et al. (Bahnu et al., 1995) and by Abdul-Karim et al. (Abdul-Karim et al., 2005). Bahnu et al. used a genetic algorithm to minimize a multiobjective evaluation metric based on a weighted mix of global, local and symbolic information. Experiments are not very convincing since it has only been tested for one segmentation algorithm and one application (outdoor tv imagery). Abdul-Karim et al. used a recursive random search algorithm to optimize the parameter setting of a vessel-neurite segmentation algorithm. Their system uses the minimum description length principle to trade-off a probabilistic measure of image-content coverage against its conciseness. This trade-off is controlled by an external parameter. The principal limitation of the method is that the segmentation evaluation metric has been defined for the specific task of vessel-neurite segmentation and makes the system unsuitable for other applications. Our approach differs from these ones in the optimization method and above all, in the definition of the evaluation metric.

Let I be an image of the training dataset $\boldsymbol{I}$, A be a segmentation algorithm and $\mathbf{p}^A$ a vector of parameters for the algorithm A. The result R_I^A of the segmentation of I with algorithm A is defined as:

$$R_I^A = A(I, \mathbf{p}^A) \tag{10}$$

where R is a set of regions.

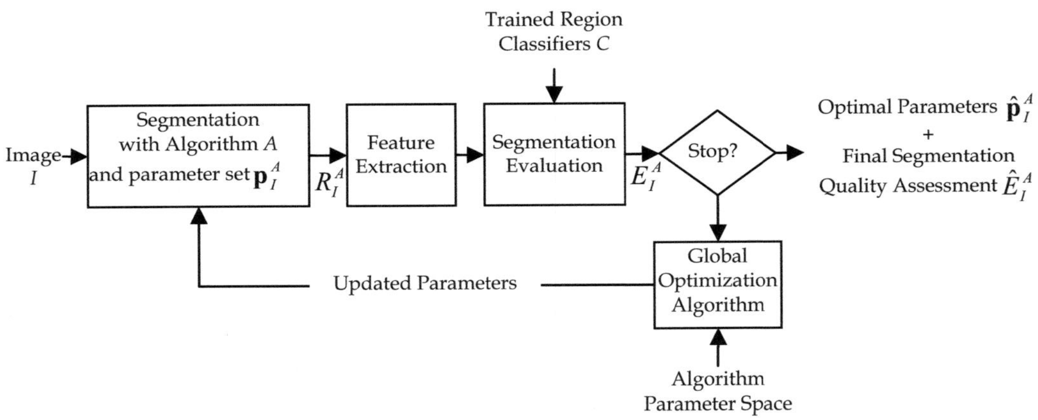

Fig 15. Algorithm parameter optimization schema. Given an input image and trained region classifiers, the ouput of the module is the set of optimal parameter for the segmentation algorithm associated with the final segmentation quality assessment value

Several considerations motivate the selection of a direct search method (the simplex algorithm in our implementation) as a preferred strategy compared to other available alternatives. First, exhaustive search is time prohibitive because of the size of the search space. Second, in our approach, the performance metric ρ has no explicit mathematical form and is non-differentiable with respect to $\mathbf{p}_I^A$, mainly because the mapping itself is not differentiable. Thus, standard powerful optimization techniques like Newton-based methods cannot be applied effectively. Simplex algorithm reachs these two conditions: it is able to work on non-smooth functions and the number of segmentation runs to obtain the optimal parameter settings is low (from experiments, under 50 runs in mean).

Let us define the performance evaluation of the segmentation as:

$$E_I^A = \rho(R_I^A, \mathrm{C}) \tag{11}$$

where E_I^A is a scalar, R_I^A the result of the segmentation of I with algorithm A and C the set trained region classifiers. The purpose of the optimization procedure is to determine a set of parameter values $\hat{\mathbf{p}}_I^A$ which minimizes E_I^A:

$$\begin{aligned}\hat{\mathbf{p}}_I^A &= \arg\min_{\mathbf{p}_I^A} \rho(R_I^A, \mathrm{C}) \\ &= \arg\min_{\mathbf{p}_I^A} \rho\left(A(I, \mathbf{p}^A), \mathrm{C}\right)\end{aligned} \tag{12}$$

In order to be goal-oriented, ρ must take into account the knowledge of the problem. In our approach, this knowledge is represented by the set of previously trained region classifiers C. Each region classifiers returns the class membership probability $c(r)$ depending on the feature vector v_r extracted from r. The analysis of the classifier output values allows to judge the quality of the segmentation of each segmented region. The performance metric ρ is then considered as a discrepency measure based of the responses of region classifiers as:

$$\rho\left(R_I^A, C\right) = \frac{1}{|I|} \sum_{r_i \in R} |r_i| \cdot \left(1.0 - \max_j c_j(r_i)\right) \tag{13}$$

where $|I|$ and $|r_i|$ are respectively the image area and the area of the ith region. ρ is borned between zero (i.e. optimal segmentation according to C) and one (i.e. all classifier responses to zero).Our metric takes also into account the region sizes by lowering the weight of small regions.

2.2.3 Adaptive Static Image Segmentation

From a new image and a set of algorithms, the clustering algorithm determines to which context cluster the image belongs to. Then, corresponding region classifiers are used for algorithm parameter optimizations. A set of segmentation assessment values is obtained (one per algorithm). This is used to rank algorithms. Finally, the algorithm with the best assessment value is selected and parametrized with the corresponding optimal parameter set for the segmentation of the image (see Figure 16).

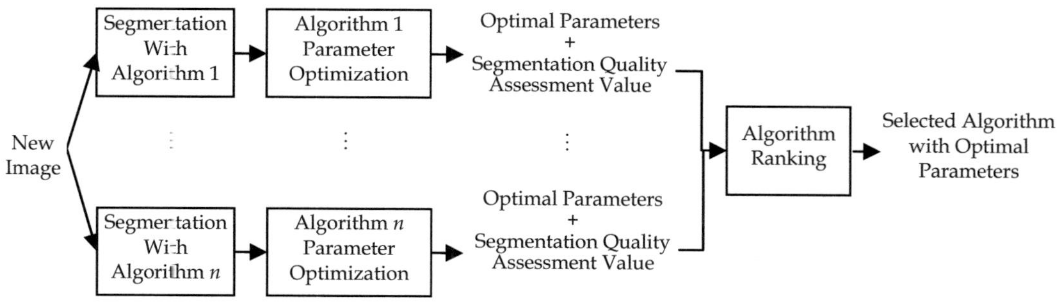

Figure 16. Adaptive static image segmentation schema

Section 3.2 presents experiments of this proposed approach.

3. Experiments

In this section, we present two experiments. The first experiment is a figure-ground segmentation task for video surveillance. It shows the interest of our approach for context adaptation issues. The second experiment is a segmentation task for object detection on static images. The application is in the scope of biological organism detection in greenhouse crops. It shows the interest of our approach for the three issues, i.e. context adaptation, algorithm selection and parameter tuning.

3.1 Figure-ground Segmentation in Video Sequences

The experimental conditions are the followings: the video data are taken during a period of 24 hours at eight frames per second, the field of view is fixed and the video camera parameters are set in automatic mode. In this application our goal is to be able to select the best appropriate background model according to the current context analysis. The size of the images is 352x288 pixels. Our approach is implemented in C++ and a 2,33 GHz Dual Core Xeon system with 4 Go of RAM is used for the experiments.

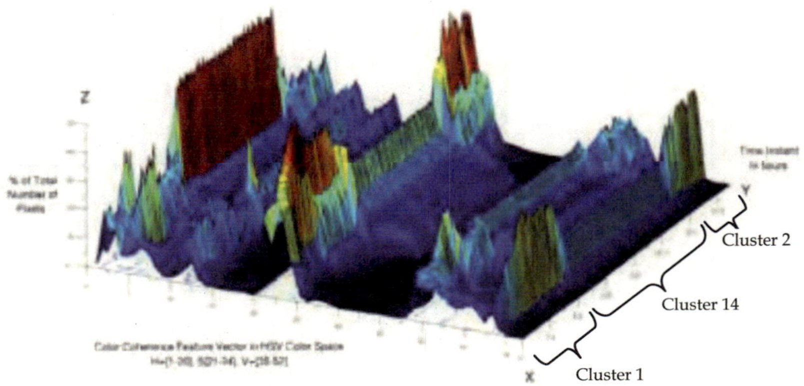

Figure 17. 3-D histogram of the image sequence used during the experiment (see Figure 3 for samples). Each X-Z slice is an histogram which represents the percentage of the number of pixels (Z axis) belonging to a given color coherent feature (X axis). The coherent color feature scale has been divided into 3 intervals for the three HSV channels. Histograms are ordered along the Y axis which represents the time in the course of a day. Several clusters of histograms can be easily visually disciminated as notified for cluster number 1, 14 and 2. Others clusters not represented here are intermediate ones and mainly correspond to transitions states between the three main clusters

In the learning stage, we have manually defined a training image set $\boldsymbol{I}$ composed of 5962 background frames (i.e. without foreground objects) along the sequence. This corresponds to pick one frame every 15 seconds in mean. First, the context clustering algorithm is trained using coherence color feature vectors g_I as inputs. Figure 17 gives a quick overview of the feature distribution along the sequence. Sixteen clusters $\boldsymbol{I}_x$ are found (see Figure 18 for context class distribution). For each cluster, the corresponding frames are put together and automatically annotated by assigning the same (background) label to each pixel. The resulting training data set T is used to train background classifiers C_x (i.e. codebooks).

In the automatic stage the figure-ground segmentation is performed in real-time. For each new frame I, context analysis with temporal filtering is used to select a background classifier C_x. Then, background segmentation is computed using the selected C_x. We compute in parallel a static region-based segmentation using the EGBIS algorithm with parameter σ set to 0.2 and parameter k set to 100. We use this segmentation to refine the one resulting from the background segmentation. Exemple of segmentation refinement is presented in Figure 19. The testing set is composed of 937 frames different from the training set $\boldsymbol{I}$. We present in Figure 20 four representative results of figure-ground segmentation illustrating different context situations. To show the potential of our approach, we have compared the results obtained with our approach with the results obtained without context adaptation, i.e. using background classifiers trained on the whole sequence. We can see that the detection of moving objects is improved with our approach.

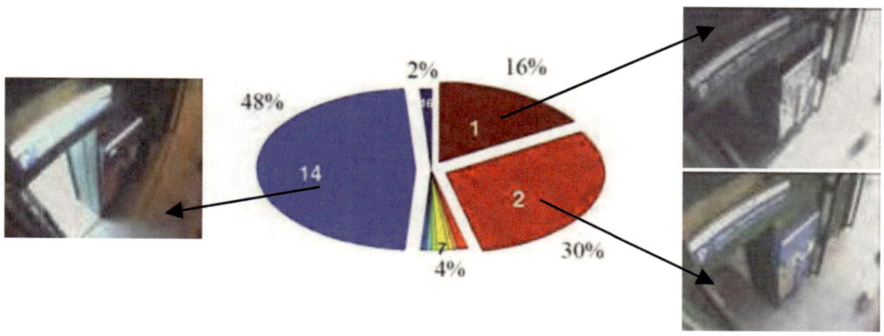

Figure 18. Pie chart of the context class distribution for the image sequence used for the experiments. Three major clusters can be identified (number 1, 2 and 14). The order of class representation does not necessary correspond to consecutive time instants. Cluster 1 corresponds to noon (sunny context), cluster 2 correspond to the morning (lower contrast) and cluster 14 to the night

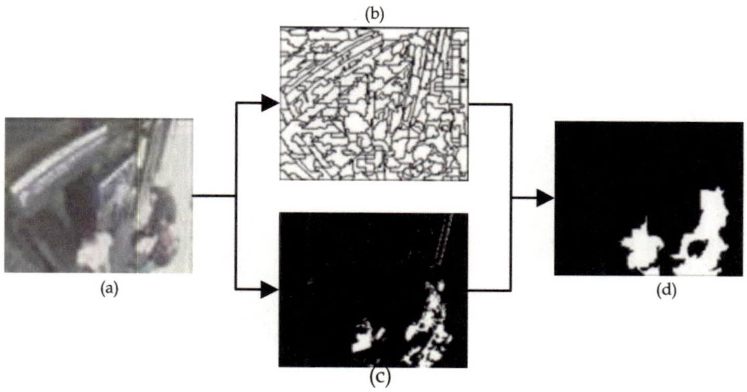

Figure 19. Illustration of the segmentation refinement. An input image (a) is segmented using a region-based segmentation algorithm. The result is presented in (b). In parallel, a figure-ground segmentation (c) is computed using the background classifiers. The final result (d) is a combination of the two segmentations with respect to the criteria defined in Equation 7

Concerning the computational-time, without any optimization of the implementation, the background segmentation takes less than 0,02 second and the region-based segmentation takes 0,4 second. The total processing time allows to segment two frames per second in mean. This validates our approach for real-time applications.

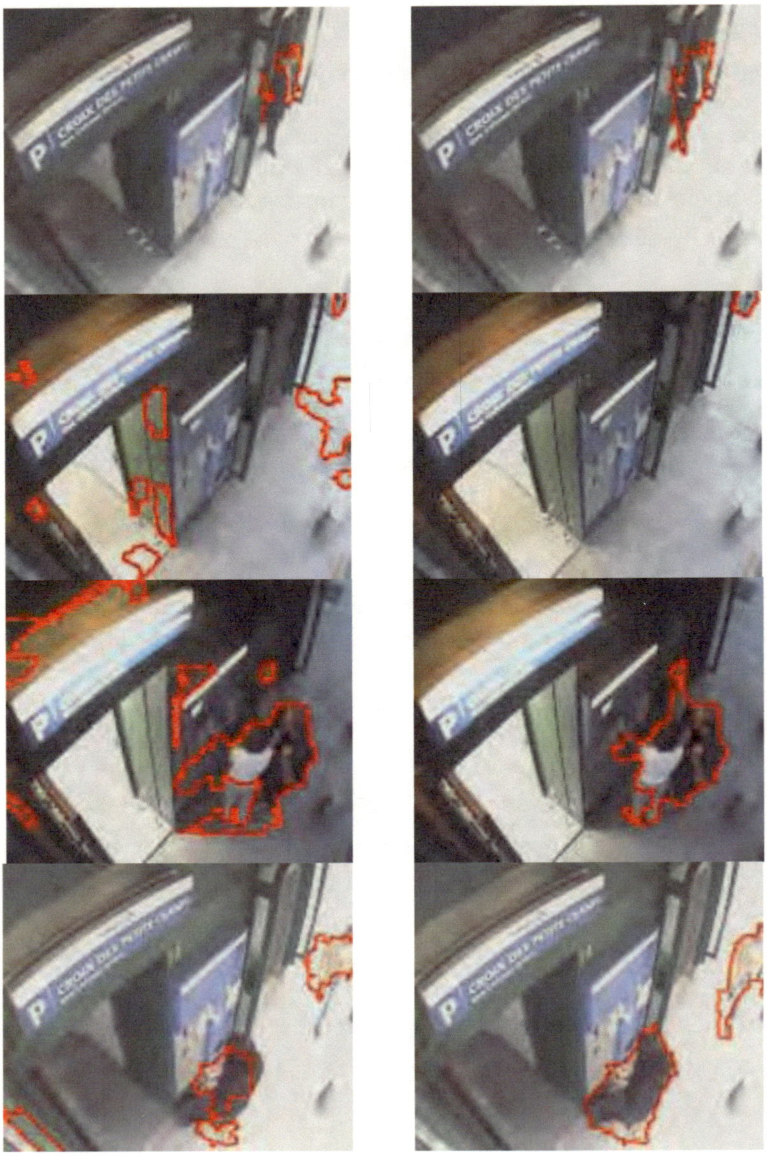

(a) Context 2

(b) Context 6

(c) Context 8

(d) Context 3

Figure 20. Segmentation results illustrating different context situations. Boundaries of the detected foreground regions (mobile objects) are shown in red. Images of the left column are those obtained without context adaptation. Images of the right column are segmentation results with context adaptation. The third column corresponds to the identified context cluster. We can see that the persons are better detected using our method (rows a, c and d). Moreover, false detection are reduced (rows b, c and d)

3.2 Static Image Adaptive Segmentation

This experiment is related to a major challenge in agronomy: the early pest detection in rose crops (Boissard et al., 2003). The experimental conditions are the followings: images are obtained from scanned rose leaves. The objects of interest are white flies (Trialeurode vaporariorum) at mature stage. The white fly wings are half-transparent and the insect has many appendices as antennas and paws. They are shown from different points of view. The image background (i.e. the rose leaf) is highly structured and textured and also varies in color in function of the specy and the age of the plant. Concerning the set of segmentation algorithms used for this experiment, we have selected from the literature (Freixenet et al, 2002), four algorithms which illustrate different state-of-the-art approaches of image segmentation: Efficient Graph-Based Image Segmentation (Felzenszwalb & Huttenlocher, 2004), Color Structure Code (Priese et al., 2002), Statistical Region Merging (Nock & Nielsen, 2004) and Color Watershed Adjency Graph Merge (Alvarado, 2001). They are summarized in Table 1, along with their free parameters and default values used in our experiment.

Algorithm	Free Parameter	Range	Default Value
EGBIS	σ: smooth control on input image	0.0-1.0	0.50
	k: color space threshold	0.0-2000.0	500.0
CSC	t: region merging threshold	5.0-255.0	20.0
SRM	Q: coarse-to-fine scale control	1.0-255.0	32.0
CWAGM	$\boldsymbol{M}$: Haris region merge threshold	0.0-2000.0	100.0
	k: Haris minimal region number	1.0-100.0	10.0
	t: Min prob for wathershed threshold	0.0-1.0	0.45

Table 1. Components of the segmentation algorithm bank, their names, parameters to tune with range and default values

In the learning stage, we have defined a training image set $\boldsymbol{I}$ composed of 100 sample images of white flies over rose leaves. The size of an image is 350x350 pixels. First, the context clustering algorithm is trained using coherence color feature vectors g_I as inputs. We have obtained four context clusters. Each training image cluster is manually segmented into regions by marking white fly boundaries out. This represent a total of 557 regions. Then, each region is annotated with a *white fly* or a *leaf* label and a feature vector v_r is extracted. We compute the (H,S,V) histogram of the region pixel values quantified into 48 bins (i.e. 16 bins per channel). Each cluster of feature vectors is reduced by using kernel PCA. The size of a reduced feature vector v_r' varies from 22 features to 28 depending on the context cluster. Then, the region classifiers C_x are trained using the linearly scaled feature vectors v_r'. We use SVM with radial basis function (RBF) as region classifiers. To fit the C and γ parameters of the RBF kernel to the problem data, we perform a five fold cross-validation on training data to prevent overfitting problems.

In the automatic stage, a new image I is initially segmented with an algorithm A tuned with default parameters $\mathbf{p}^A$ (i.e. with values given by the author of the algorithm). Then, parameter optimization is achieved and returns an optimal parameter set $\hat{\mathbf{p}}_I^A$ and a segmentation quality assessment quality value E_I^A as output. Once all segmentation algorithm parameter optimizations are processed, we can rank the segmentation algorithms in accordance to their E_I^A. This algorithm selection technique is illustrated in Figure 21. We can see that for the four presented algorithms, the assessment values are very closed. This is in accordance with the visual observation of the results. The small differences between the algorithms can be explained by the detection (or not) of small appendices of white flies (e.g. antenna, paw). We also see that the SRM algorithm gets the best result (i.e. the smallest assessment value) without performing the finest segmentation (appendices are not detected). This is mainly due to the fact that white fly classifiers have been trained with manually segmented regions for which, most of the time, small details like the appendices are missed. Consequently, segmentation is better evaluated when the appendices are not parts of white fly regions.

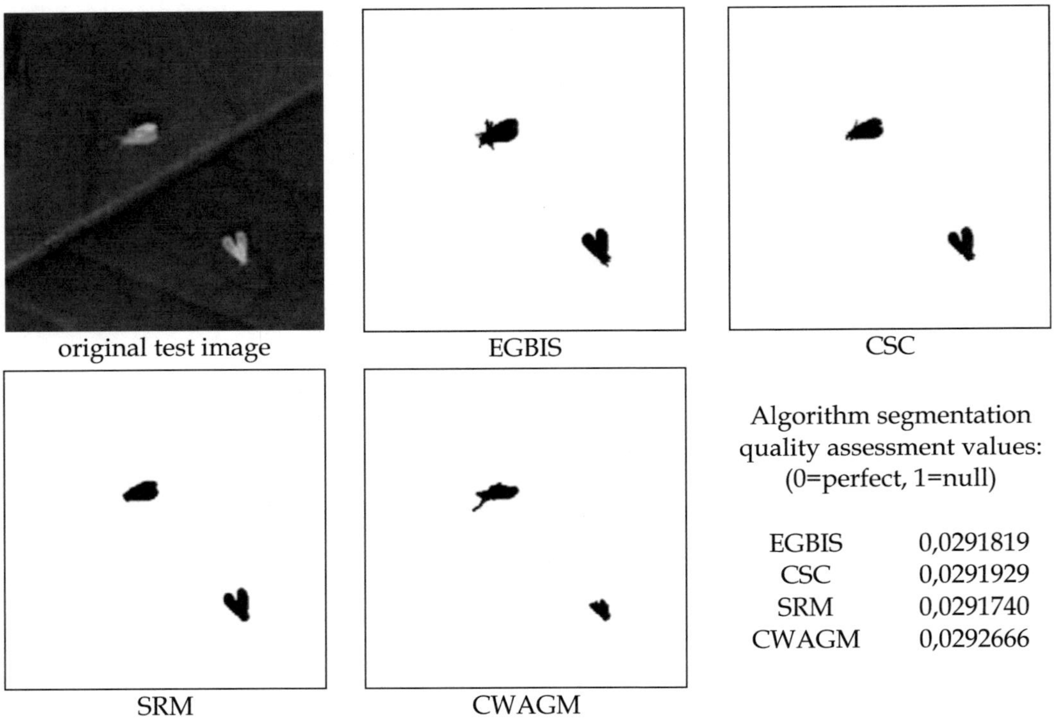

Figure 21. Segmentation results from test samples illustrating the algorithm selection issue. After parameter optimization, final algorithm segmentation quality assessment values can be compared to rank the algorithms

Figure 22 is shown to illustrate the parameter tuning issue. We clearly see that optimization of parameters is useful and tractable for different segmentation algorithms. However, we can see for the first image of Figure 22 that two white flies are miss-detected. This discrepancy has two explanations: first, it reveals that classifiers have not been trained enough and second, that our dictionary does not discriminate enough differences between classes. The first issue can be achieved by training classifiers on more training images and the second issue can be achieved by using more specific classes as one classe for each white fly body parts (e.g. head, wings and abdomen). Obviously, this also demands more efforts to the user.

Regarding the conputation-time, we have used the same hardware system than in section 3.2. Both context analysis and algorithm ranking are inconsiderable (less than 0,01 second).

An optimization closed-loop takes between 5 and 35 seconds for an image. The duration depends on the algorithm segmentation computation-time (between 0.08 second and 0.8 second), the number of iterations (between 8 and 50) and the segmentation evaluation time depending on the number of regions to process (between 1 and 300). So the total processing time of the automatic adaptive segmentation is between 5 and 35 seconds, using the same system as in section 3.1.

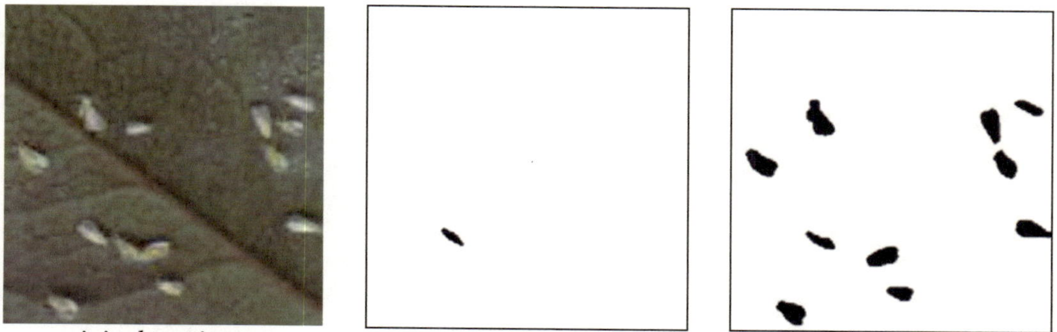

original test image | SRM with default parameters | SRM with optimal parameters

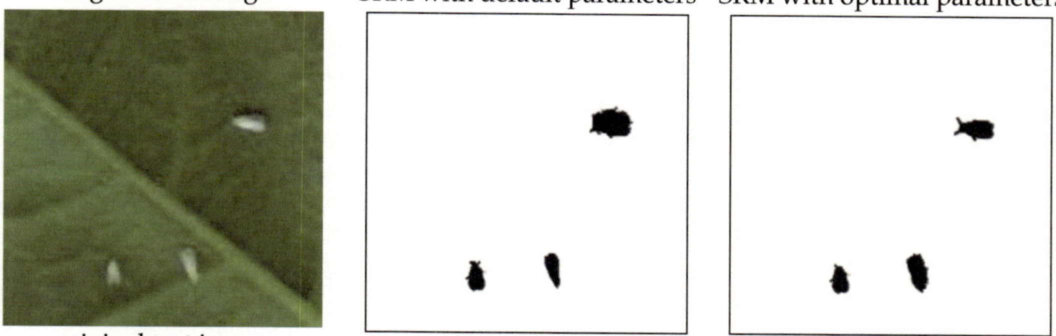

original test image | EGBIS with default parameters | EGBIS with optimal parameters

Figure 22. Segmentation results from test samples illustrating the algorithm parameter tuning issue. For two different images , two algorithms are first run with their default parameters (central column). Results after the parameter optimization step are presented in the last column. We can see that the detection of the object of interest is better with optimal parameters than with the default parameters

4. Conclusion and Discussion

In this chapter, we have proposed a learning approach for three major issues of image segmentation: context adaptation, algorithm selection and parameter tuning according to the image content and the application need. This supervised learning approach relies on hand-labelled samples. The learning process is guided by the goal of the segmentation and therefore makes the approach reliable for a broad range of applications. The user effort is restrained compared to other supervised methods since it does not require image processing skills: the user has just to click into regions to assign labels; he/she never interacts with algorithm parameters. For the figure-ground segmentation task in video application, this annotation task is even automatic. When all images of the training set are labelled, a context analysis using an unsupervised clustering algorithm is performed to divide the problem into context clusters. This allows the segmentation to be more tractable when context is highly variable. Then, for each context cluster, region classifiers are trained with discriminative information composed of a set of image features. These classifiers are then used to set up a performance evaluation metric reflecting the segmentation goal. The approach is independent of the segmentation algorithm. Then, a closed-loop optimization procedure is used to find algorithm parameters which yield optimal results.

The contribution of our approach is twofold: for the image segmentation community, it can be seen as an objective and goal-oriented performance evaluation method for algorithm ranking and parameter tuning. For computer vision applications with strong context variations (e.g. multimedia applications, video surveillance), it offers extended adaptability capabilities to existing image-sequence segmentation techniques.

The ultimate goal of this approach is to propose the best available segmentation for a given task. So, the reliability of the approach entirely depends on the inner performance of the segmentation algorithms used. One other limitation of the approach is that the adaptability ability is depending on the sampling of the training data. More the training dataset is representative of different contexts, more the system will be precise to select and tune the algorithms.

Future works consist in improving these issues. For instance, incremental learning could be used to learn on-the-fly new situations and then enrich the knowledge of the problem. In this chapter, we have proposed a method based on class models of visual objects. This method exploits features in a discriminative manner. For very difficult cases where intra-class information (i.e. object appearance) is very heterogeneous and/or inter-class information is poorly discriminative, selection of representative features is tricky and leads to poor performances. In this case, approaches based on shared visual features across the classes as boosted decision stumps should be more appropriated and effective. Finally, by addressing the problem of adaptive image segmentation, we have also addressed underlying problems such as feature extraction and selection, segmentation evaluation and mapping between low-level and high-level knowledge. Each of these well-known challenging problems are not easily tractable and still demands to be intensively considered. We have designed our approach to be modular and upgradeable so as to take advantage of new progresses in these topics.

5. Acknowledgments

We would like to thank colleagues P. Boissard, Guy Perez and P. Bearez for image contribution concerning the static image segmentation application. This work is partially financed by a grant of region PACA. This support is gratefully acknowledged.

6. References

Abdul-Karim, M.-A. and Roysam, B. and Dowell-Mesfin, N.M. and Jeromin, A. and Yuksel, M. and Kalyanaraman, S. (2005). Automatic Selection of Parameters for Vessel/Neurite Segmentation Algorithms, *IEEE Transactions on Image Processings*, Vol.14, No.9, September 2005, pp. 1338-1350, ISSN: 1057-7149

Alvarado, P. and Doerfler, P. and Wickel, J. (2001). Axon2 - A visual object recognition system for non-rigid objects, *Proceedings of the International Conference on Signal Processing, Pattern Recognition and Applications (SPPRA)*, pp.235-240, ISBN: 0-88986-293-1, July 2001, Rhodes, Greece

Bahnu, B. and Lee, S. and Das, S. (1995). Adaptive Image Segmentation Using Genetic and Hybrid Search Methods, *IEEE Transactions on Aerospace and Electronic Systems*, Vol.31, No.4, October 1995, pp.1268-1291, ISSN: 0018-9251

Boissard, P. and Hudelot, C. and Thonnat, M. and Perez, G. and Pyrrha, P. and Bertaux, F. (2003). An automated approach to monitor the sanitary status and to detect early biological attacks on plants in greenhouse – Examples on flower crops, *Proceedings of the International Symposium on Greenhouse Tomato*, Avignon, France, September, 2003

Borenstein, E. and Ullman, S. (2004). Learning to segment, *Proceedings of European Conference on Computer Vision*, pp. 315-328, ISBN 978-3-540-21982-8, Prague, Czech Republic, May 2004, Springer, Berlin / Heidelberg

Burges, Christopher J. C. (1998). A Tutorial on Support Vector Machines for Pattern Recognition, *Data Mining and Knowledge Discovery*, Vol.2 ,No.2 , pp.121-167, June 1998, Kluwer Academic Publishers, Hingham, MA, USA, ISSN:1384-5810

Chen, Y. and Wang, James Z. (2004). Image Categorization by Learning and Reasoning with Regions, *The Journal of Machine Learning Research* , Vol.5, pp.913-939, December, MIT Press, Cambridge, MA, USA, ISSN:1533-7928

Clouard, R. and Elmoataz, A. and Porquet, C. and Revenu, M. (1999). Borg: A knowledge-based system for automatic generation of image processing programs , *IEEE Transaction on Pattern Analysis and Machine Intelligence*, Vol. 21, No. 2, February, 1999, pp. 128-144, ISSN: 01 62-8828

Dambreville, S. and Rathi, Y. and Tannenbaum, A. (2006). Shape-Based Approach to robust Image Segmentation using Kernel PCA, *Proceedings of the IEEE Conference on Computer Vision and Pattern Recognition*, Vol.1, pp.977-984, ISBN: 0-7695-2597-0, ISSN: 1063-6919, June 2006, IEEE Computer Society, Washington, DC, USA

Draper, Bruce A. (2003). From Knowledge Bases to Markov Models to PCA, *Proceedings of Workshop on Computer Vision System Control Architectures*, Graz, Austria, March 2003

Elgammal A., Harwood D. and Davis L. (2000). Non-parametric Model for Background Subtraction, *Proceedings of the 6th European Conference on Computer Vision-Part II*, Vol.1843, pp. 751-767, ISBN:3-540-67686-4, Dublin, Ireland, June 2000, Springer-Verlag, London, UK

Ester M., Kriegel H-P., Sander J., Xu X. (1996). A Density-Based Algorithm for Discovering Clusters in Large Spatial Databases with Noise, *Proceedings of the Second International Conference on Knowledge Discovery and Data Mining*, pp. 226-231, Portland, Oregon, USA, 1996, AAAI Press, ISBN 1-57735-004-9

Felzenszwalb, Pedro F. and Huttenlocher, Daniel P. (2004). Efficient Graph-Based Image Segmentation, *International Journal of Computer Vision*, Vol.59, No.2, September 2004, pp. 167-181, Kluwer Academic Publishers, Hingham, MA, USA, ISSN: 0920-5691

Freixenet J., Muñoz X., Raba D., Martí J., Cufí X. (2002). Yet Another Survey on Image Segmentation: Region and Boundary Information Integration, *Proceedings of the 7th European Conference on Computer Vison Part III*, Vol. 2352/2002,pp.408-422, Copenhagen, Denmark, May 2002, Springer Berlin / Heidelberg, ISSN: 0302-9743

Georis, B. (2006). Program supervision techniques for easy configuration of video understanding ststems, Ph. D. Thesis. Louvain Catholic University, Belgium, January 2006

Grimson W.E.L and Stauffer C. (1999). Adaptive background mixture models for real-time tracking, *IEEE Computer Society Conference on Computer Vision and Pattern Recognition*, Vol.2, pp.252, ISBN: 0-7695-0149-4, Fort Collins, CO, USA, June 1999, IEEE Computer Society

Huang Fu Jie and LeCun Y. (2006). Large-scale Learning with SVM and Convolutional Nets for Generic Object Categorization, *Proceedings of the 2006 IEEE Computer Society Conference on Computer Vision and Pattern Recognition*, Vol.1, pp. 284 - 291, ISBN:1063-6919, New York, USA, June 2006, IEEE Computer Society, Washington, DC, USA

Kim, K. and Chalidabhongse, T.H. and Harwood, D. and Davis, L.S. (2005). Real-time foreground-background segmentation using codebook model, *Real-time imaging*, Vol.11,No.3,pp.172-185, June 2005, Elsevier, Oxford, United Kingdom, ISSN:1077-2014

Mika, S. and Scholkopf, B. and Smola, A. (1999). Kernel PCA and De-noising in Feature Spaces, *Proceedings of the 1998 conference on Advances in neural information processing systems II*, Vol.11, pp. 536-542, ISBN: 0-262-11245-0, Denver, Colorado, USA, December 1998, MIT Press, Cambridge, MA, USA

Martin, V. Thonnat, M. Maillot, N. (2006). A Learning Approach for Adaptive Image Segmentation, *IEEE International Conference on Computer Vision Systems,* pp.40, ISBN: 0-7695-2506-7, New York, NY, USA, January 2006, IEEE Computer Society

Nock, R. and Nielsen, F. (2004). Statistical Region Merging , *IEEE Transactions on Pattern Analysis and Machine Intelligence*, Vol.26, No.11, November 2004, pp.1452-1458, IEEE Computer Society , Washington, DC, USA, ISSN:0162-8828

Pass, G. and Zabih, R. and Miller, J. (1997). Comparing Images Using Color Coherence Vectors, *Proceedings of the fourth ACM international conference on Multimedia*, pp.65-73, ISBN: 0-89791-871-1, Boston, Massachusetts, United States, November 1996, ACM Press, New York, USA

Priese, Lutz Rehrmann, Volker and Sturm, P. (2002). Color Structure Code, url = http://www.uni-koblenz.de/

Sezgin M., Sankur B. (2004). Survey over image thresholding techniques and quantitative performance evaluation, Journal of Electronic Imaging, Vol.13, pp. 146-165, January 2004

Schnitman, Y. and Caspi, Y. and Cohen-Or, D. and Lischinski, D. (2006). Inducing Semantic Segmentation from an Example, *Proceedings of the 7th Asian Conference on Computer Vision - ACCV*, Vol.3852, No.22,pp. 384-393, Hyderabad, India, January 13-16, 2006, Springer-Verlag

Thonnat, M. and Moisan, S. and Crubezy M. (1999). Experience in integrating image processing programs, *Proceedings of the First International Conference on Computer Vision Systems*, pp.200-215, ISBN: 3-540-65459-3, Henrok Christensen, Las Palmas Gran Canaria, Spain, January 1999, Springer-Verlag

Wu T. and Lin C. and Weng R. (2004). Probability estimates for multi-class classification by pairwise coupling, *The Journal of Machine Learning Research*, Vol.5, December 2004, pp.975-1005, MIT Press, Cambridge, MA, USA, ISSN: 1533-7928

24

A Novel Omnidirectional Stereo Vision System with a Single Camera[1]

Sooyeong Yi, Narendra Ahuja
Dept. of Electrical Engineering, Seoul National University of Technology
Republic of Korea
Dept. of Electrical and Computer Engineering, Univ. of Illinois at Urbana-Champaign
USA

1. Introduction

The omnidirectional vision system has been given increasing attentions in recent years in many engineering research areas such as computer vision and mobile robot since it has wide field of view (FOV). A general method for 360° omnidirectional image acquisition is the catadioptric approach using a coaxially aligned convex mirror and a conventional camera. The catadioptric approach with the convex mirror is simple and fast compared to the mosaic approach using multiple cameras or a rotating camera. There are several types of commercially available convex mirrors such as conical, spherical, parabolic, or hyperbolic mirrors (Baker & Nayar, 1999)(Nayar, 1977)..

In order to extract 3D information from the camera vision, the stereo image with disparity should be taken. One obvious method for the stereo image acquisition is using two cameras with different view angles. However, two-camera stereo introduces difficulties in the image processing caused by the non-identical intrinsic camera parameters such as focal length, gain, and spectral responses etc (Gluckman & Nayar, 2001). Accordingly, there have been much work on single-camera stereo system to overcome the problems of the two-camera stereo. One straightforward method for the single camera stereo is sequential image acquisition with respect to camera movement. A typical application of the method is in the mobile robot area, where the camera system on a mobile robot takes a sequence of images, and extracts 3D information from the set of images. Due to the uncertainties in the sequential camera position, however, it is difficult to get the accurate 3D information in that method. Moreover, the information is basically not real-time due to the time-lag of the sequential images. In order to overcome the problems according to the sequential camera motion, additional optical devices are introduced to the single camera stereo system such as two planar mirrors which have different view angles (Gluckman & Nayar, 2001) or a biprim which gives two virtual images for an object (Lee & Kweon, 2000).

On the other hand, the stereo methods have also been developed in the omnidirectional vision area. An exemplar omnidirectional stereo vision is the direct application of two-camera stereo with two convex mirrors in (Gluckman et al., 1998)(Pajdlar et al., 2002). Since

---

[1] This work was published in part in Proc. of ICIAR 2006.

the omnidirectional stereo vision system obtains the distance information for all directions in one shot, it is especially useful for a mobile robot application. K. Koyasu *et al.* developed an omnidirectional stereo vision system with two pairs of cameras and convex mirrors for the map-making and the autonomous navigation of a mobile robot (Koyasu et al., 2002). For high resolution, the multiview panoramic cameras have been developed using a mirror pyramid (Nalwa, 1996). The single camera approach is also an important issue in the omnidirectional stereo vision area. A. Basu and D. Southwell proposed a double lobed mirror for the single camera stereo vision system (Southwell et al., 1996) and developed the required image processing algorithm (Fiala & Basu, 2005). E. Cabral *et al.* also designed the similar double lobed hyperbolic mirror for the single camera omnidirectional stereo vision (Cabral et al., 2004). Recently, another single camera approach using two pieces of hyperbolic mirrors is reported to improve the accuracy in 3D distance computation (Jang et al., 2005). The main advantages of the single camera omnidirectional stereo vision system are the reduced system complexity and the simple image processing due to the consistent intrinsic camera parameters.

A main aim of this paper is to present a new approach for the single camera omnidirectional stereo vision system. Eliminating the costly two pieces of mirrors or the double lobed mirrors, the proposed method uses a simple combination of the off-the-shelf convex mirror and concave lens. Thus, the resulting omnidirectional stereo vision system becomes compact and cost-effective. This paper is organized as follows: In Sec. 2, the principles of the proposed omnidirectional stereo system are briefly described. In Sec. 3, the closed-form depth estimate is addressed based on the simple optics for a convex mirror and a concave lens. A prototype of the proposed system and some preliminary experiments are described in Sec. 4. Sec. 5 presents some concluding remarks.

2. The Proposed Omnidirectional Stereo System

The optical part of the proposed omnidirectional stereo system consists of a convex mirror and a concave lens. A hyperbolic omnidirectional mirror is used as the convex mirror in this paper. However, a parabolic mirror could also be used instead.

Fig. 1 illustrates the principles of the proposed system, where $\mathbf{O}(r, z)$ denotes an object point. Light ray I from the object is reflected on the hyperbolic mirror, and the reflected ray passes through the pinhole. There is an image point on the sensor plane corresponding to the ray I as shown in Fig. 1 (a). The real object emits the light rays for all directions, not only the ray I of course. However, the other light rays having different directions from the ray I, e.g., the ray II in Fig. 1 (a) cannot reach the pinhole after the reflection, thereby, cannot have any image on the sensor plane.

On the contrary, the reflected ray from the ray II in Fig. 1 (b) can reach the pinhole owing to the refraction through the concave lens. The amount of refraction depends on the refraction index of the lens material, curvature, position, and thickness of the concave lens. It should be noted that the concave lens does not affect on the ray I. Since both the rays I and II come from the same object point, the image points, ρ_1 and ρ_2 on the sensor plane constitute the stereo pair with disparity. Therefore, it is possible to compute 3D distance to the object point based on the simple optics composed of the reflection on the hyperbolic mirror and the refraction through the concave lens.

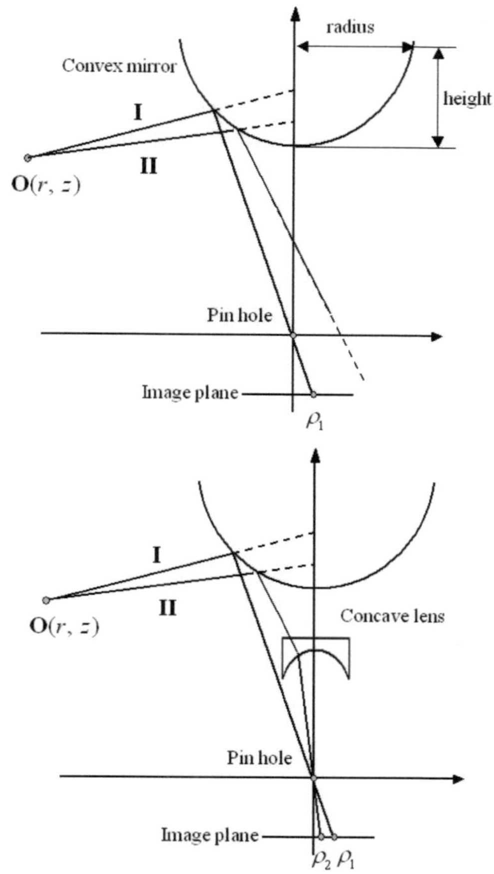

(a) (b)

Figure 1. The proposed single camera omnidirectional stereo vision system: (a) The omnidirectional imaging, (b) The omnidirectional stereo imaging with concave lens

3. Depth Computation

3.1 Refraction Through a Concave Lens

As passing through a concave lens, a light ray experiences the refraction as illustrated in Fig. 2, which is given by Snell's law (Jenkins & White, 1976). First order optics with Gaussian approximation gives the relationships between the incident ray and the refracted ray as follows:

$$p_2'' = p_2 - \frac{p_2 \cdot c}{p_2(n-1)+c} + d \cdot \frac{n-1}{n} \tag{1}$$

$$\theta_2'' = \frac{c+(n-1)\cdot p_2}{c}\cdot\theta_2 \tag{2}$$

where θ_2'' and p_2'' denote the incidence angle and the cross point with the vertical axis, and θ_2 and p_2 represent the angle of the refracted ray and the lens position as shown in Fig. 2. Derivation in detail is described in Appendix. It is assumed that the coordinate system is assigned at the pinhole position in this sequel. In (1) and (2), c, d, and n imply the curvature, thickness, and the refraction index of the lens material respectively. Here, a plano-concave lens with flat surface on one side is used without loss of generality. It is also possible to get the similar expressions for a biconcave lens.

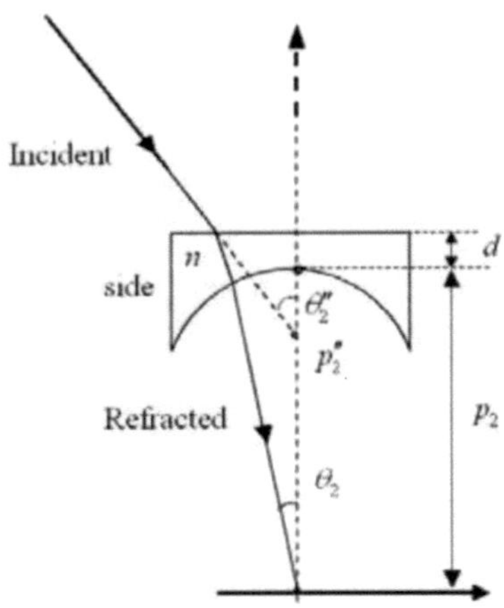

Figure 2. Refraction through a concave lens

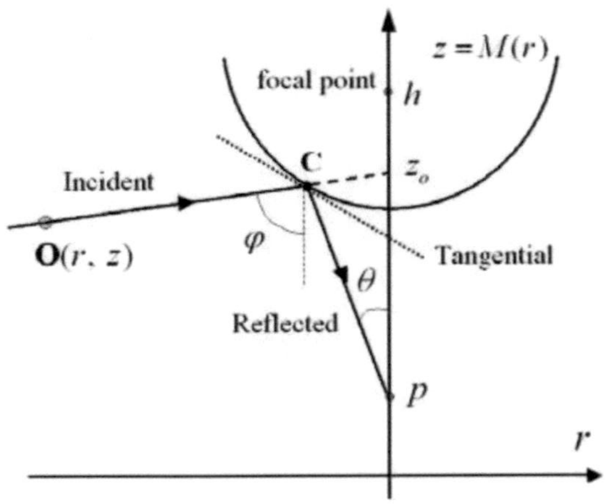

Figure 3. Reflection on a hyperbolic mirror

3.2 Reflection on the Hyperbolic Mirror Surface

The analysis in this paper is described on $r-z$ plane rather than in the whole 3D space. It is easy to extend this analysis to 3D space by rotating about the vertical $\mathbf{z}$ axis. Given the reflected ray with angle θ and cross point p as shown in Fig. 3, it is possible to obtain the equation for the incident ray from an object, $\mathbf{O}(r,z)$, based on the simple reflection law. At first, the hyperbolic curve, $M(r)$, with its focal point at h can be represented as (3) on $r-z$ plane.

$$\begin{aligned} &\frac{(z-h+f)^2}{a^2} - \frac{r^2}{b^2} = 1 \\ \equiv\quad & z = M(r) = h - f + \frac{a}{b}\sqrt{r^2+b^2} \end{aligned} \tag{3}$$

where a and b denote the parameters of the hyperbolic function, and f represents its focal point given by

$$f = \sqrt{a^2 + b^2} \tag{4}$$

The reflected ray is then described by the given angle θ and the cross point p as:

$$z = -\cot\theta \cdot r + p \tag{5}$$

The intersection point, $\mathbf{C}$ between the hyperbolic function (3) and the reflected ray (5) is denoted as $\mathbf{C}(r_c, z_c)$. Then, the incident ray from an object, $\mathbf{O}(r, z)$, can be parameterized as:

$$z = \cot\phi \cdot r + z_o \tag{6}$$

where ϕ and z_o represent vertical angle and cross point with $\mathbf{z}$ axis as shown in Fig. 3. By using the simple law of reflection on a specular surface and the geometry given in Fig. 3, it is possible to get the first parameter, ϕ for (6) as follows:

$$\phi = \theta + 2 \cdot \tan^{-1}\left(\left. \frac{dM(z)}{dr} \right|_{\mathbf{C}} \right) \tag{7}$$

$$\left. \frac{dM(z)}{dr} \right|_{\mathbf{C}} = \frac{a^2}{b^2} \cdot \frac{r_c}{z_c - h + f} \tag{8}$$

Since the incident ray (6) should pass through the intersection, $\mathbf{C}(r_c, z_c)$, the parameter, z_o, can be represented as:

$$z_o = z_c - \cot\phi \cdot r_c \tag{9}$$

In other words, given angle θ and cross point p of the reflected ray, the corresponding incident ray toward z_o is described in (6), where the parameters, ϕ and z_o can be obtained by (7) through (9).

It is assumed in this paper that the first focal point of the hyperbolic mirror is located at $h = 2f$, so that the pinhole position of a camera coincides with the second focal point of the hyperbolic mirror. According to the property of the hyperbolic function, all incident rays toward the first focal point, i.e., $z_o = 2f$, reach the pinhole at the origin after the reflection. Thus, the reflected ray always has $p = 0$ without regard to θ.

3.3 Depth Computation

As shown in Fig. 4, the position of the object point, $\mathbf{O}(r, z)$ is the solution of the simultaneous equations for the rays $\mathbf{I}$ and $\mathbf{II}$. Thus, it is necessary to get the expressions for the rays based on the measurement data in the system.

Given measured stereo pairs, ρ_1 and ρ_2 on the image plane in Fig. 4, the vertical angles of two rays toward the pinhole are described as follows:

$$\theta_1 = \tan^{-1}\left(\frac{\rho_1}{\lambda}\right), \quad \theta_2 = \tan^{-1}\left(\frac{\rho_2}{\lambda}\right) \tag{10}$$

where λ denotes the distance from the pinhole position to the image plane.

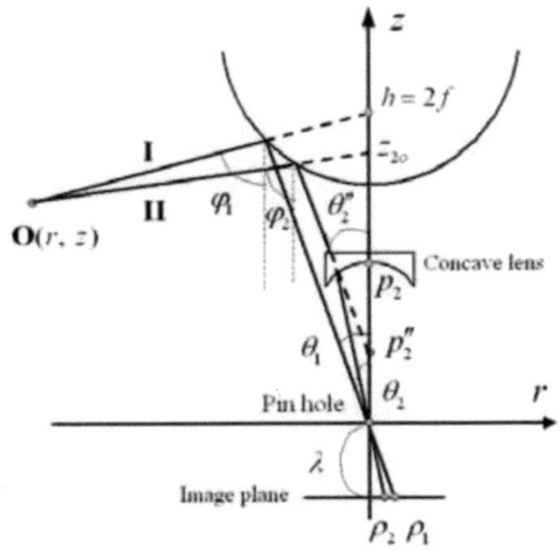

Figure 4. Depth computation given stereo pair

The equation for ray **I** in Fig. 4 can be obtained as follows. It should be recalled that only the incident ray toward the first focal point can reach the pinhole after the reflection on the hyperbolic mirror. Thus the other parameter, z_o for the ray (6) becomes $z_o = 2f$. The parameter, ϕ in (6) is obtained by inserting the measurement (10-1) into (7) together with (8). The equation of ray **I** is written as (11).

$$z = \cot\phi_1 \cdot r + 2f \tag{11}$$

In order to get the equation for the ray **II**, the refraction through the concave lens should be taken into consideration. As described in Sec. 3.1, it is possible to get θ_2'' and p_2'' by (1) and (2) with given θ_2 and p_2, where p_2 denotes the known position of the concave lens. Again, by inserting θ_2'' and p_2'' into (7) through (9), it is possible to get the parameters, ϕ_2 and z_{o2} for the ray equation (12).

$$z = \cot\phi_2 \cdot r + z_{o2} \tag{12}$$

Detailed expressions for the parameters are omitted here for brevity. The solution of the simultaneous equations consisting of (11) and (12) gives the object point, $\mathbf{O}(r, z)$ as follows:

$$\begin{bmatrix} r \\ z \end{bmatrix} = \begin{bmatrix} \cot\varphi_1 & -1 \\ \cot\varphi_2 & -1 \end{bmatrix}^{-1} \cdot \begin{bmatrix} -2f \\ -z_{o2} \end{bmatrix} \tag{13}$$

4. Experimental Results

A prototype of the system is implemented as shown in Fig. 5, and some preliminary experiments are carried out with the prototype. The parameters of the experimental system are tabulated in Table 1.

Fig. 6 (a) and Fig. 6 (b) show the omnidirectional images acquired by the proposed system without and with the concave lens respectively. As shown in Fig. 4, the side of the concave lens blocks the light rays incident from sufficiently horizontal directions, which causes the opaque ring at the boundary between the outer and the inner stereo image as shown in Fig. 6. By making the lens side inclined rather than vertical, it is possible to minimize the blocked angle, thereby the thickness of the opaque ring in the image. However, the vertical side of the lens is preferable for the case of a parabolic mirror and the orthographic imaging.

Parameter	a	b	f	Radius	Height
Value	28.095	23.4125	36.57	30.0	20

(a) Mirror (mm)

Parameter	n	d	c	p_2	Radius
Value	1.7	2 mm	58.8 mm	52 mm	15 mm

(b) Concave lens

Parameter	Focal length	Size, Resolution
Value	2.7 ~ 8 mm	1/3", 1024x768

(c) Camera

Table 1. Parameters of the experimental system

Figure 5. Prototype of the proposed system

Since the epipolar line is radial in the omnidirectional stereo image, it is relatively easy to match the stereo pair. Recently, many corresponding algorithms for the omnidirectional stereo image have been developed (Fiala & Basu, 2005)(Jang et al., 2005)(Zhu, 2001). The depth resolution in $r-z$ plane is depicted in Fig. 7, where each point represents the depth computed using the correspondences of all pixels along an epipolar line.

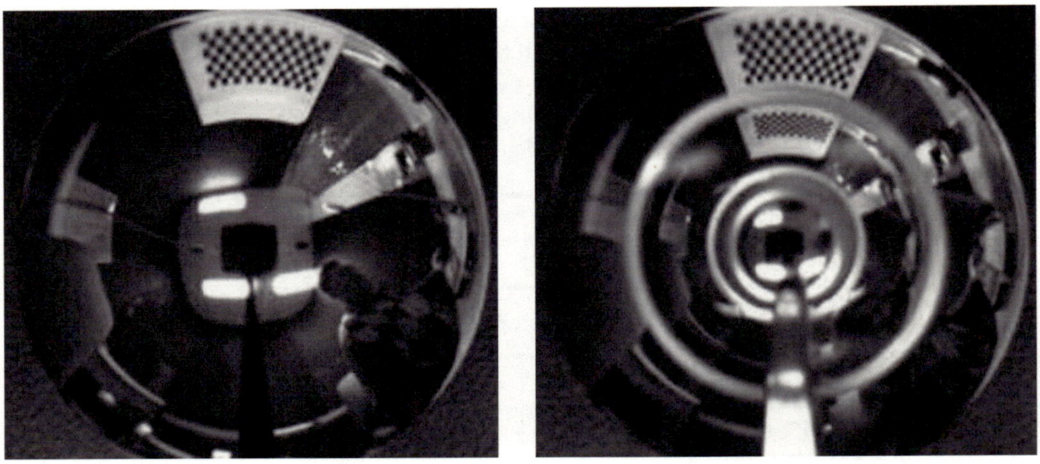

(a) Without concave lens (b) With concave lens

Figure 6. Experimental images

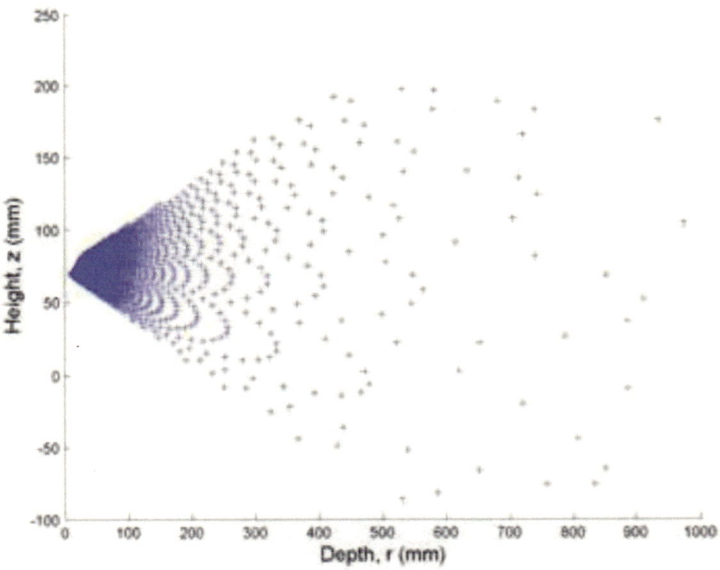

Figure 7. Depth resolution of the proposed system

Extension for longer range of sight:

It is possible to get longer range of sight by using a modified lens. The lens used in Fig. 8 (a) has the convex part in its outer side as well as the concave part in the inner side. As illustrated in Fig. 8 (a), the convex part and the concave part of the lens introduce the refractions in the opposite directions to a pair of light rays, II and III, thereby gives the large disparity in the image points. Fig. 8 (b) shows a simulation result for the depth resolution of the imaging system, which has the longer range of sight than Fig. 7.

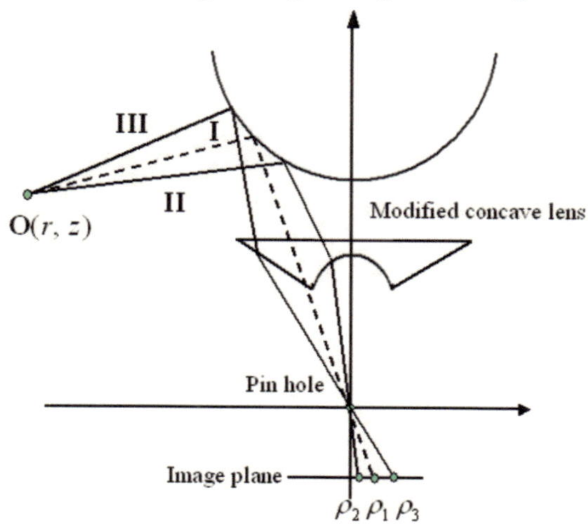

(a) The omnidirectional stereo imaging system

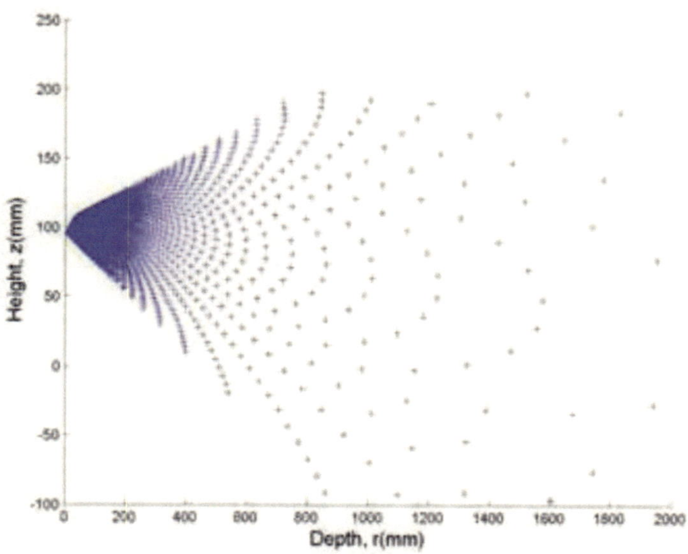

(b) Depth resolution

Figure 8. The omnidirectional stereo imaging system with the modified concave lens and the corresponding depth resolution

5. Conclusion

Wide field of view is the most attractive feature of the omnidirectional vision. There exist two approaches to omnidirectional stereo imaging with a single camera. They use: (1) a double lobed mirror (Fiala & Basu, 2005)(Cabral et al., 2004), or (2) two mirrors (Jang et al., 2005). In this paper, a third approach is described using a mirror and a concave lens. By adjusting the position of the concave lens, it is possible to control the disparity between two stereo images and the accuracy of the 3D distance computation. Since the optical components adopted in the proposed system are commercially available, the proposed omnidirectional stereo imaging system is compact and cost-effective.
Based on the simple optics composed of the reflection and the refraction on the convex mirror and the concave lens, an expression for the 3D distance is derived. The proposed method is versatile in the sense that it is also applicable to different types of convex mirrors, e.g., the parabolic mirror. The second approach (2) mentioned above involves a relatively lengthy baseline, and therefore a longer depth range than (1) and the approach proposed in this paper. Two simple ways of getting longer range of sight with (1) and the approach in this paper are to use a larger mirror or a camera with higher resolution.

6. References

Baker, S. & Nayar, S. (1999). A theory of Single-Viewpoint Catadioptric Image Formation, *International Journal of Computer Vision*, Vol. 35, No. 2, pp.175–196

Nayar, S. (1977). Catadioptric Omnidirectional Camera, *Proceedings of IEEE Conference on Computer Vision and Pattern Recognition*, pp.482-488

Gluckman, J. & Nayar, S. (2001). Catadioptric Stereo Using Planar Mirrors, *International Journal of Computer Vision*, pp.65-79

Lee, D. and Kweon, I. (2000). A novel stereo camera system by a bi-prism, *IEEE Transaction on Robotics and Automation*. Vol. 16, No. 5, pp.528-541

Gluckman, J., Nayar, S. & Thorek, K. (1998). Real-time omnidirectional and panoramic stereo. *Proceedings of DARPA Image Understanding Workshop*, Vol. 1, pp.299-303

Pajdlar, T., Svobda, T. & Hlavac, V. (2002). Epipolar geometry of central catadioptric camera, *International Journal of Computer Vision*, Vol. 49, No. ,. pp.23-37

Koyasu, H., Miura, J. & Shirai, Y. (2002). Recognizing moving obstacles for robot navigation using real-time omnidirectional stereo vision, *Journal of Robotics and Mechatronic,*. Vol. 14, No. 2, pp.147-156

Nalwa, V. (1996). A true omnidirectional viewer, *Bell lab. Tech. Report*

Tan, K., Hua, H. & Ahuja, N. (2004). Multiview Panoramic Cameras Using Mirror Pyramids, *IEEE Transaction on Pattern Analysis and Machine Intelligence,*. Vol. 26, No. 6

Southwell, D., Basu, A., Fiala, M. & Reyda, J. (1996). Panoramic Stereo, *Proceedings of International Conference on Pattern Recognition*, pp.378-382

Fiala, M. & Basu, A. (2005). Panoramic stereo reconstruction using non-SVP optics, *Computer Vision and Image Understanding*, Vol. 98, pp.363-397

Cabral, E., Souza, J. & Hunoid, C. (2004). Omnidirectional Stereo Vision with a Hyperbolic Double Lobed Mirror, *Proceedings of International Conference on Pattern Recognition*, pp.1-4

Jang, G., Kim, S. & Kweon, I. (2005). Single Camera Catadioptric Stereo System, *Proceedings of Workshop on Omnidirctional Vision, Camera Networks and Non-classical Cameras*

Zhu, Z. (2001). Omnidirectional Stereo Vision, *Proceedings of International Conference on Advanced Robotics*, pp.22-25

Jenkins, F. & White, H. (1976). Fundamentals of Optics, 4th ed. McGraw-Hill

7. Appendix: Refraction through Concave Lens

When passing through a concave lens, a light ray experiences the refraction according to the surface shape and the refraction index of the lens material. The refraction equations, (1) and (2) for θ'' and p'' are derived here in terms of θ and p of the light lay. The overall refraction through the lens consists of two stages: (1) Free space to lens material and (2) Lens material to free space.

The first stage: In Fig. 9 (a), the followings hold:

$$\frac{\sin\phi_0}{p-c}=\frac{\sin\theta}{c} \equiv \phi_0 = \sin^{-1}\left(\frac{p-c}{c}\cdot\sin\theta\right) \text{ at } \Delta\text{MTC} \tag{14}$$

$$\frac{\sin\theta'}{c}=\frac{\sin\phi_1}{p'-c} \equiv p'=c+c\cdot\frac{\sin\phi_1}{\sin\theta'} \text{ at } \Delta\text{M}'\text{TC} \tag{15}$$

$$\theta+\phi_0-\phi+\pi-\theta'=\pi \equiv \theta'=\theta+\phi_0-\phi \quad \text{ at } \Delta\text{MTM}', \tag{16}$$

From Snell's law, ϕ_1 is given by

$$\sin\phi_1=\frac{\sin\phi_0}{n} \equiv \phi_1=\sin^{-1}\left(\frac{\sin\phi_0}{n}\right) \tag{17}$$

Inserting (14) and (15) into (16) and (17) and applying the first-order optics give

The second stage: From Snell's law, the relation between ϕ_2 and ϕ_3 is given as $\sin\phi_3 = n\cdot\sin\phi_2$. It is noted here that $\phi_2=\theta'$ and $\theta''=\phi_3$ in Fig. 9 (b). Thus, θ'' is described in terms of θ' as

$$\sin\theta''=n\cdot\sin\theta' \equiv \theta''=\sin^{-1}\left(n\cdot\sin\theta'\right) \tag{19}$$

In Fig. 9 (b), the followings hold: $\tan\theta'=\dfrac{h}{p'+d}$ and $\tan\theta''=\dfrac{h}{p''_c+d}$. Combining these two equations gives

$$p''_c=(p'+d)\cdot\frac{\tan\theta'}{\tan\theta''}-d\,. \tag{20}$$

Inserting (18) into (19) and (20) and applying the first-order optics give

$$\theta'' = \frac{np - p + c}{c} \cdot \theta \cdot \tag{21}$$

$$p''_c = \frac{pc}{np - p + c} + d \cdot \frac{1-n}{n} \cdot \tag{22}$$

As a consequence, the distance from the origin of the coordinate system, M to M'' is given as follows:

$$\begin{aligned} p'' &= p - p''_c \\ &= p - \frac{pc}{np - p + c} - d \cdot \frac{1-n}{n} \cdot \end{aligned} \tag{23}$$

$$\theta' = \frac{np - p + c}{nc} \cdot \theta, \quad p' = \frac{npc}{np - p + c} \tag{18}$$

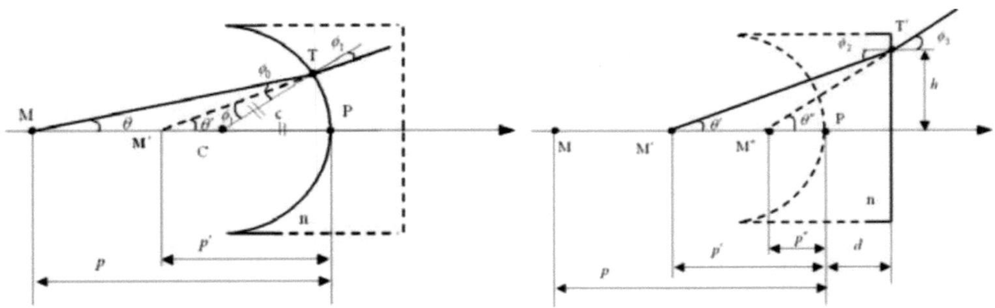

(a) The first stage (b) The second stage

Figure 9. Refraction through the concave lens

25

Image Processing Techniques for Unsupervised Pattern Classification

C. Botte-Lecocq, K. Hammouche, A. Moussa, J.-G. Postaire, A. Sbihi & A. Touzani
University of Science and Technology of Lille
France

1. Introduction

The aim of cluster analysis is to divide a set of multidimensional observations into subsets according to their similarities and dissimilarities. These observations are generally represented as data points scattered through an N-dimensional data space, each point corresponding to a vector of observed features measured on the objects to be classified. In the framework of the statistical approach, many clustering procedures have been proposed, based on the analysis of the underlying probability density function (pdf) (Devijver & Kittler, 1982).

Independently from cluster analysis, a large amount of research effort has been devoted to image segmentation. To humans, an image is not just an unstructured collection of pixels. We generally agree about the different regions constituting an image due to our visual grouping capabilities. Among the factors that lead to such perceptual grouping, the most important are similarity, proximity and connectedness. The segmentation process can be considered as a partitioning scheme such that:

-Every pixel of the image must belong to a region,

-The regions must be composed of contiguous pixels,

-The pixels constituting a region must share a given property of similarity.

These three conditions can be easily adapted to the clustering process. Indeed, each data point must be assigned to a cluster, and the clusters must be composed of neighbouring data points since the points assigned to the same cluster must share some properties of similarity. Considering this analogy between segmentation and clustering, some image segmentation procedures based on the gray-level function analysis can be adapted to multidimensional density function analysis for pattern classification, assuming there is a one-to-one correspondence between the modes of the underlying pdf and the clusters.

In this framework of unsupervised pattern classification, the underlying pdf is estimated on a regular discrete array of sampling points (Cf. section 2). The idea of using a pdf estimation for mode seeking is not new (Parzen, 1962) and, in very simple situations, the modes can be detected by thresholding the pdf at an appropriate level, using a procedure similar to image binarization. A solution for improving this thresholding scheme is to adapt a probalistic labelling scheme directly derived from image processing techniques (Cf. section 3).

In the clustering context, a mode boundary is similar to a region boundary in an image since it is an area where abrupt local changes occur in the pdf. The modes of a distribution of multidimensional observations can then be detected by means of generalized gradient operators (Cf. section 4). Although these spatial operators enhance substantially the discontinuities that delineate the modes, a relaxation labeling process, similar to the one used for thresholding, can be necessary for mode boundary extraction.
Beside procedures based on the concepts of similarity and discontinuity, mathematical morphology has proven to be a valuable approach for image segmentation. This theory is adapted to cluster analysis by considering the sets of multidimensional observations as mathematical discrete binary sets (Cf. section 5).
Another approach is to consider statistical texture measures to describe the spatial distribution of the data points. Similarly to texture segmentation, the approach consists first of selecting a set of features that characterize the local distribution of the data points in the multidimensional data space in terms of textures. The data points with similar local textures are aggregated to define compact connected components of homogeneous textures considered as the cores of the clusters (Cf. section 6).
Modeling spatial relationships between pixels by means of Markov random fields has proved to be relevant to the image segmentation problem. The Markovian approach can also be adapted to the mode detection problem in cluster analysis (Cf. section 7).
The algorithms presented in this chapter must be tuned carefully in order to detect the significant modes of the distributions (Cf. section 8). The observations falling in these detected cluster cores are considered as prototypes so that the remaining data points are finally assigned to their respective clusters by means of classical supervised procedures (Cf. section 9).

2. Discretization of the data set

In order to adapt image processing tools to clustering, it is necessary to introduce a discrete array of sampling points. Let us consider Q observations $Y_q = [y_{q,1}, y_{q,2}, \ldots, y_{q,n}, \ldots, y_{q,N}]^T$, $q=1,2,\ldots,Q$, where $y_{q,1}, y_{q,2}, \ldots, y_{q,n}, \ldots, y_{q,N}$ are the N coordinates of the observation Y_q in the data space. The range of variation of each component of the observations is normalized to the interval [0, K], where K is an integer, by means of the transformation:

$$y'_{q,n} = K \frac{y_{q,n} - \min\limits_{q=1}^{q=Q}\{y_{q,n}\}}{\max\limits_{q=1}^{q=Q}\{y_{q,n}\} - \min\limits_{q=1}^{q=Q}\{y_{q,n}\}}.$$

Let $Y'_q = [y'_{q,1}, y'_{q,2}, \ldots, y'_{q,n}, \ldots, y'_{q,N}]^T$, $q=1,2,\ldots,Q$, be the Q new observations in the normalized data space. Each axis of this space is partitioned into K exclusive and adjacent intervals of unit width. This discretization defines an array of K^N hypercubes of unit side length. The centers of these hypercubes constitute a regular lattice of sampling points denoted P_r, $r=1,2,\ldots,K^N$. The unit hypercubic cell centered at point P_r is denoted $H(P_r)$. It is defined by its coordinates $h_{r,1}, h_{r,2}, \ldots, h_{r,n}, \ldots, h_{r,N}$, which are the integer parts of the coordinates of its center P_r. The qth normalized observation Y'_q falls into the unit cell $H(P_r)$ of coordinates $h_{r,n} = \text{int}(y'_{q,n})$, $n=1,2,...,N$, where $\text{int}(y'_{q,n})$ denotes the integer part of the real number $y'_{q,n}$.

Taking the integer parts of the coordinates of all the available normalized observations yields the list of the non-empty cells whose coordinates are defined on the set Z^{+N}. If several observations fall into the same cell, this one appears many times in the list of non-empty cells. It is easy to determine the number $q[H(P_r)]$ of observations that fall into the hypercubic cell of center P_r by counting the number of times the cell $H(P_r)$ appears in that list (Postaire & Vasseur, 1982). Subsequently, the distribution of the data points can be approximated by the discrete multi-dimensional histogram $\hat{p}(P_r) = q[H(P_r)]$. Note that $\hat{p}(P_r)/Q$ can be considered as an approximate value of the underlying pdf at point P_r.

The result of this sampling procedure is a multidimensional regular array of discrete integers in the range $[0, p_{max}]$, where p_{max} is the maximum value of $\hat{p}(P_r)$, $r = 1,2,...,K^N$, that is well conditioned for a multidimensional analysis. Let $\underline{X}$ denote the set of the centers X of the non-empty hypercubic cells defined by this procedure.

3. Mode detection by relaxation

In very simple situations, the modes can be detected by thresholding the pdf at an appropriate level, using a procedure similar to image binarization. A «mode» label is associated with each point where the underlying pdf is above the threshold. Otherwise, the corresponding point is assigned a «valley» label.

However, in practical situations, it is often difficult, or even impossible, to select an appropriate threshold to detect the significant modes. A solution for improving this simple thresholding scheme is to consider the spatial relationships among the sampling points where the underlying pdf is estimated, rather than making a decision at each point independently of the decisions at other points. Probabilistic labelling, or relaxation, is a formalism through which object labels are iteratively updated according to a compatibility measure defined among the neighbouring labels (Hummel & Zucker, 1983). This approach, which has been mainly applied to image processing (Rosenfeld & Smith, 1981), has been adapted to cluster analysis to reduce local ambiguities in the mode/valley discrimination process (Touzani & Postaire, 1988).

To convey the general idea of the relaxation labelling procedure, which has been applied to a variety of image processing problems, we initially assign to each sampling point P_r a probability $p_r^{(0)}(M)$ that it belongs to a mode. The initial probability that P_r belongs to a valley is therefore $p_r^{(0)}(V)=1-p_r^{(0)}(M)$. These probabilities are then adjusted in parallel on the basis of the probability assignments at the neighbouring points of P_r. The process is iterated and finally each sampling point P_r is assigned the "mode" or the "valley" label according to the resulting probabilities $p_r(M)$ and $p_r(V)$. To be more specific, the initial probability $p_r^{(0)}(M)$ that P_r belongs to a mode is given by:

$$p_r^{(0)}(M)=\frac{\hat{p}(P_r)-p_{min}}{p_{max}-p_{min}},$$

where p_{min} is the minimum value of the estimated pdf over the whole data space, generally equal to 0.

For each pair of neighbouring sampling points $\{P_r\ P_{r'}\}$, we define a measure $C_{rr'}(\lambda,\lambda')$ of compatibility between label λ assigned to point P_r and label λ' assigned to point $P_{r'}$, where λ and λ' can be either the "mode" or the "valley" labels, such as :

$$C_{rr'}(\lambda,\lambda')=\frac{[p_r(\lambda)-\overline{p}(\lambda)]\,.\,[p_{r'}(\lambda')-\overline{p}(\lambda')]}{[p_{max}(\lambda)-\overline{p}(\lambda)]\,.\,[p_{max}(\lambda')-\overline{p}(\lambda')]}$$

and where :

$p_r(\lambda)$ is the probability associated with label λ at point P_r

$\overline{p}(\lambda)=(1/K^N)\sum_{r=1}^{K^N}p_r(\lambda)$

$p_{max}(\lambda)=\max_r\{p_r(\lambda)\}$, $r=1,2,\ldots,K^N$.

At the $(t+1)^{th}$ iteration, the new estimate of the probability of label λ at point P_r is updated as :

$$p_r^{(t+1)}(\lambda)=\frac{p_r^{(t)}(\lambda)\left[1+q_r^{(t)}(\lambda)\right]}{p_r^{(t)}(M)\left[1+q_r^{(t)}(M)\right]+p_r^{(t)}(V)\left[1+q_r^{(t)}(V)\right]}$$

where :

$$q_r^{(t)}(\lambda)=\frac{1}{(2\delta+1)^N}\sum_{\substack{P_{r'}\in V_\delta(P_r)\\ r'\neq r}}\left\{\rho(\lambda,M)C_{rr'}(\lambda,M)p_r^{(t)}(M)+\rho(\lambda,V)C_{rr'}(\lambda,V)p_r^{(t)}(V)\right\}.$$

$V_\delta(P_r)$ denotes the hypercubic neighbourhood of point P_r, of size $2\delta+1$ where δ is an integer, consisting of $(2\delta+1)^N$ neighbouring points, defined as :

$$V_\delta(P_r)=\left\{[x_1,\ldots,x_N]^T\ /\ h_{r,i}-\delta<x_i<h_{r,i}+\delta; i=1,2,\ldots,N\right\}$$

The weighting coefficients $\rho(\lambda,M)$ and $\rho(\lambda,V)$ must satisfy the condition:

$$\sum_{\lambda\in\{M,V\}}[\rho(\lambda,M)+\rho(\lambda,V)]=1\,.$$

When convergence of the sequence of probabilities $p_r^{(t)}(M)$ is completed, a value of 1 indicates an unambiguous "mode" label while a value of 0 indicates an unambiguous "valley" label. Experiments show that most label probabilities reach these extreme values after a few iterations. However, in some cases, the limiting values may be strictly between 0 and 1 but, due to the drastic reduction of ambiguities, thresholding these probabilities becomes trivial.

Figure 1 (b) shows a raw estimate of the pdf corresponding to 1000 bidimensional observations of figure 1 (a) distributed as three clusters of unequal weights. The probabilities at the last step of the relaxation process are displayed in figure 1 (c). This example demonstrates the considerable noise cleaning of the relaxation process.

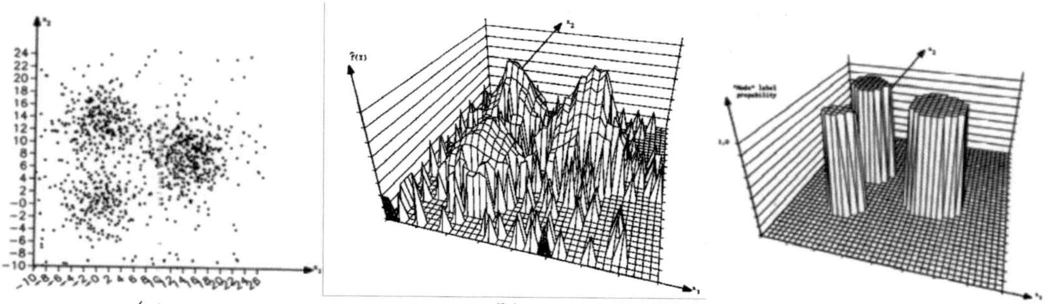

Figure 1. Mode detection by relaxation

(a) Scatter diagram of the data set
(b) Raw estimate of a bidimensional pdf
(c) Label probability diagram at the last iteration of the relaxation process

4. Mode boundary detection

4.1 Multidimensional differential operators

The segmentation of an image can be considered as a problem of edge detection. Similarly, in the clustering context, a mode boundary can be defined as an area of abrupt local changes in the pdf. It can be detected by means of generalized gradient operators designed to perform a discrete spatial differentiation of the estimated pdf (Touzani & Postaire, 1989).
In an N-dimensional space, the Robert's operator (Davis, 1975) is generalized by computing the $N(N-1)/2$ elementary gradients defined by :

$$\hat{G}_{\alpha,\beta}(P_r)=\left|\hat{p}(h_{r,1},\ldots,h_{r,\alpha},\ldots,h_{r,\beta},\ldots,h_{r,N})-\hat{p}(h_{r,1},\ldots,h_{r,\alpha}+1,\ldots,h_{r,\beta}+1,\ldots,h_{r,N})\right|$$
$$+\left|\hat{p}(h_{r,1},\ldots,h_{r,\alpha}+1,\ldots,h_{r,\beta},\ldots,h_{r,N})-\hat{p}(h_{r,1},\ldots,h_{r,\alpha},\ldots,h_{r,\beta}+1,\ldots,h_{r,N})\right|$$

where $\alpha=1,2,\ldots,N$, $\beta=1,2,\ldots,N$, $\alpha\neq\beta$.

Thanks to the algorithm used for pdf estimation, which yields the list of the nonempty hypercubes, the gradient operator is only applied to non empty regions of the data space, thus speeding up the procedure.
Another way to estimate the gradient of a multidimensional pdf is to generalize the Prewitt's operator by determining the hyperplane that best fits the estimated function $\hat{p}(P_r)$ at point P_r (Morgenthaler & Rosenfeld, 1981). This hyperplane, defined by:

$$\Pi(x_1,\ldots,x_N)\equiv a_0+\sum_{i=1}^{N} a_i\, x_i$$

is found by minimizing the squared error :

$$E_{rr} = \int_{V_\delta(P_r)} (\Pi(x_1,....,x_N) - \hat{p}(x_1,....,x_N))^2 \, dx_1....dx_N$$

Setting the origin at point P_r and then differentiating E_{rr} with respect to $a_0,....,a_N$ and setting the result to zero yields the coefficients of the hyperplane. In the discrete case, we obtain:

$$a_n = \frac{\sum_{P_r \in V_\delta(P_r)} h_{r',n} \hat{p}(h_{r',1},....,h_{r',N})}{\sum_{P_r \in V_\delta(P_r)} (h_{r',n})^2} \quad , n = 0,1,2,....,N \ .$$

Analogously to Robert's operator, Prewitt's operator is just applied in non empty regions of the data space.

The sampling points that have high gradient values are possible boundary elements. Since mode boundaries are closed hypersurfaces, the boundary extraction procedure must be an omnidirectional aggregation process. The candidate points lying in the neighbourhood of a current boundary point are evaluated on the basis of their satisfying a gradient magnitude criterion for acceptance. To be more specific, let $\hat{G}(P_0)$ be the estimated magnitude of the gradient at the starting point P_0 and let τ be a tolerance factor, so that the aggregation algorithm incorporates only points with gradient magnitude greater than the threshold value $\tau.\hat{G}(P_0)$. When the algorithm is successful in finding some boundary elements in the neighbourhood of the current point, these elements are added to the currently accepted piece of boundary and become available current points for the next stages of the growth process. If there are no acceptable candidates in the neighbourhoods of all available current points, the aggregation terminates. The aggregation algorithm is then reinitialised from a new starting point, which is the point with the highest gradient value among the points that do not belong to a reconstructed boundary.

The boundaries of the three clusters constituting the distribution of bidimensional observations of figure 2 (a) are displayed in figure 2 (b). They reflect the modal structure of the distribution and can be easily used to assign the data points to their respective clusters.

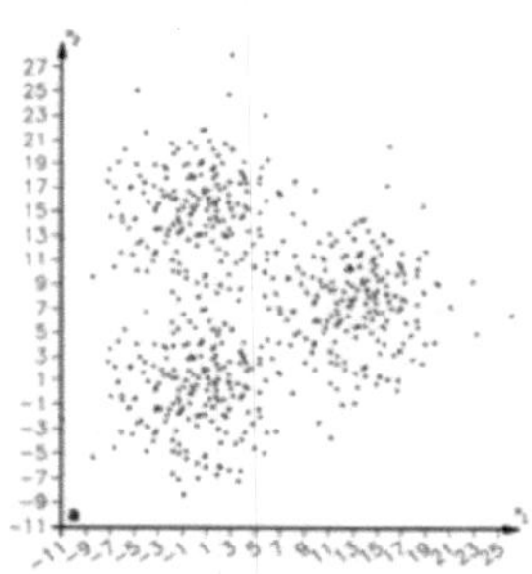

(a)

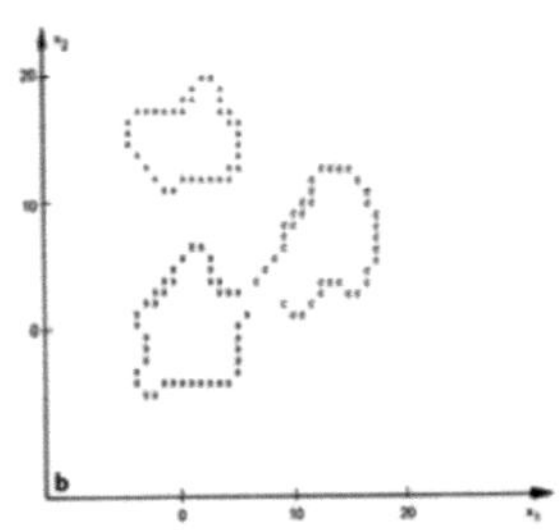

(b)

Figure 2. Mode boundary detection

(a) Scatter diagram of a two-dimensional data set

(b) Detected mode boundaries

These mode boundaries can be used for unsupervised identification of normal mixtures (Postaire & Touzani, 1990).

4.2. Relaxation for boundary detection

Although these spatial operators enhance substantially the discontinuities that delineate the modes, a relaxation labeling process, similar to the one used for thresholding, can be necessary for mode boundary extraction (Postaire & Touzani, 1989).

Figure 3 (b) shows the response of the generalized Prewitt's operator on the data set of figure 3 (a). The result of figure 3 (c) shows how an iterative relaxation scheme can be used to enhance the mode boundaries while weakening the effects of noise and irregularities in the distribution of the input data.

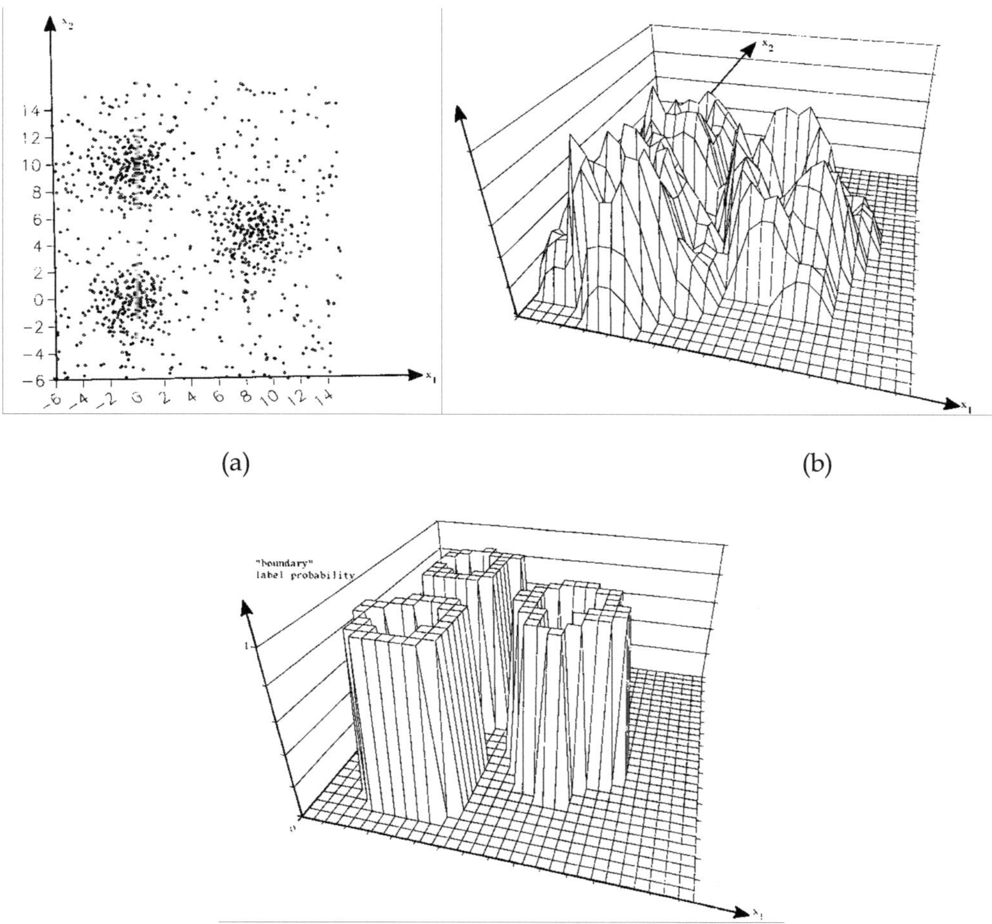

(a) (b)

(c)

Figure 3. Mode boundary detection by relaxation

(a) Scattered diagram of the data set
(b) Response of the generalized Prewitt's operator
(c) Result of 6 iterations of the relaxation process

5. Mode detection by morphology

5.1. Introduction

Mathematical morphology has been developed as an algebra of set-theoretic operations in Euclidean spaces for quantitative description of geometrical structures. As introduced by Matheron and Serra (Matheron, 1985) (Serra, 1987), this approach has been mainly concerned with binary and graylevel image analysis. Erosions, dilations, openings and closings are the simplest transformations derived from mathematical morphology but other transformations such as thinnings and thickenings are also widely used.

These operations can be adapted to cluster analysis by considering the set $\underline{X}$ of centers X of non empty hypercubes, determined from the data by means of the discretization procedure described in section 2, in terms of a mathematical set in a Z^{+N} space (Postaire et al., 1993). The underlying pdf is then viewed as a closed set in the Euclidean space $E = Z^{+N} \times R^{+*}$.

The structure of this discrete set $\underline{X}$ can then be analysed by means of binary morphological operations, in order to extract the significative connected components of $\underline{X}$, each connected component indicating the existence of a cluster in the original data set. Another approach consists of detecting the modes of the pdf by means of multivalued morphological transformations.

5.2. Binary morphology

The binary morphology is based on the comparison between the local structure of the discrete set $\underline{X}$, and the structure of a pre-specified subset $\underline{B}$, called structuring element, whose structure depends on the properties that have to be extracted from $\underline{X}$.

The dilation of $\underline{X}$ by a structuring element $\underline{B}$ is the Minkowski addition of $\underline{X}$ and $\underline{B}$, such as:

$$\underline{D} = \underline{X} \oplus \underline{B} = \bigcup_{B \in \underline{B}} (\underline{X})_B = [D \in Z^N | D = X + B, X \in \underline{X}, B \in \underline{B}].$$

The set $\underline{D}$ is found by translating $\underline{X}$ by all the elements of $\underline{B}$ and then taking the union. Dilation by a small compact structuring element can be used to expand the set $\underline{X}$. Dilation of $\underline{X}$ by $\underline{B}$ is the set $\underline{D}$ composed of all those elements D such as $\underline{B}$ translated to D intersects $\underline{X}$.

The erosion, which is the Minkowsky set subtraction of $\underline{B}$ from $\underline{X}$, is the operation dual to dilation with respect to complementation. It is defined by :

$$\underline{E} = \underline{X} \Theta \underline{B} = \bigcap_{B \in \underline{B}} (\underline{X})_B = [E \in Z^N | E + B = X, X \in \underline{X}, \text{for every } B \in \underline{B}]$$

The set $\underline{E}$ is found by translating $\underline{X}$ by all the elements of $\underline{B}$ and then taking the intersection. It consists of all the elements E for which $\underline{B}$ translated to E is contained in $\underline{X}$. Erosion by a compact structuring element $\underline{B}$ can be viewed as a shrinking transformation of the set $\underline{X}$.

In practice, erosion and dilation are seldom used alone. They are often combined in pairs, giving two other fundamental morphological operations called openings and closings.

The opening of $\underline{X}$ by $\underline{B}$, denoted $\underline{X}_{\underline{B}}$, is the set resulting from the erosion of $\underline{X}$ by $\underline{B}$, followed by the dilation of the eroded set by $\underline{B}$:

$$\underline{X}_{\underline{B}} = \underline{X} \Theta \underline{B} \oplus \underline{B}$$

At the completion of this sequence, the opening $\underline{X}_{\underline{B}}$ is generally different from $\underline{X}$. The opening suppresses irrelevant protuberant details of the set towards its boundary and yields a rather simplified version of $\underline{X}$.

By duality, the closing of $\underline{X}$ by $\underline{B}$, denoted $\underline{X}^{\underline{B}}$, is the result of first dilating $\underline{X}$ and then eroding the dilated set by $\underline{B}$:

$$\underline{X}^{\underline{B}} = \underline{X} \Theta \underline{B} \oplus \underline{B}$$

The closing tends to fill the holes and the gaps in the set $\underline{X}$.

The set $\underline{X}$ of figure 4 (a) is used to demonstrate the effects of these morphological transformations on bidimensional data. The opening and the closing of this discrete binary set by a (3x3) square structuring element are shown in figures 4 (b) and 4 (c), respectively.

The results show that these two transformations tend to produce new sets, with simpler shapes than the original ones. Opening and closing seem to be very effective to eliminate isolated groups of set points and holes, provided theses details do not exceed the size of the structuring element. All the irrelevant details are rubbed out, while the actual structure of the data remains unchanged.

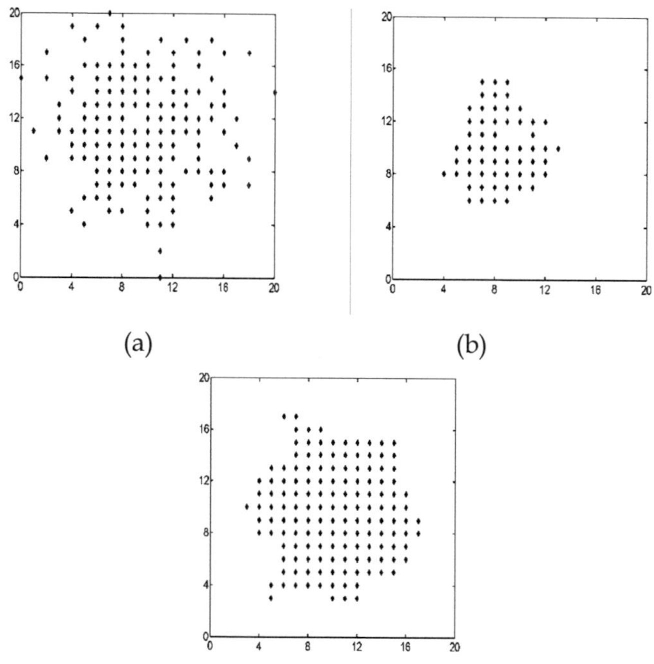

(a) (b)

(c)

Figure 4. Morphological transformations of a binary set

(a) Binary discrete set (* are the centers of the non-empty hypercubes)
(b) Opened set using a compact 3x3 structuring element
(c) Closed set using a compact 3x3 structuring element

In order to extract the connected components of $\underline{X}$, the cluster detection procedure consists of successively applying opening and closing operations, removing irrelevant details in the discrete set structure while preserving the global shapes of unsuppressed components. The procedure has been applied to the raw data of figure 5 (a). The three cluster cores of figure 5 (b) have been obtained by a single opening operation followed by a closing operation.

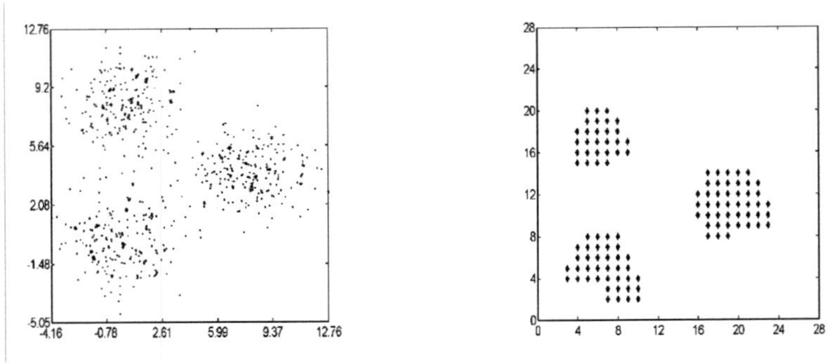

(a) (b)

Figure 5. Mode detection by binary morphology

(a) Raw bidimensional data set

(b) The three modes detected by an opening followed by a closing

The connected components of $\underline{X}$ can also be extracted by analysing the connectivity of $\underline{X}$ by means of a valley seeking technique using morphological thinnings (Botte-Lecocq & Postaire, 1994). Another solution is to extract the connected components of $\underline{X}$ by means of its ultimate eroded set (Benslimane et al. 1996).

5.3. Multivalue morphology

The binary morphological techniques, where only non-empty hypercubes are considered independently of the associated pdf value, are very simple to implement and very efficient unless the overlapping degree between the different clusters is small.

Modes can also be viewed as connected components in the space $E = Z^{+N} \times R^{+*}$ previously defined. If we consider the additive inverse of the pdf, each of its wells corresponds to a mode of the pdf, which can be detected by adapting watershed transforms (Meyer & Beucher, 1990), usually applied for two-dimensional image segmentation.

Let $f(X)$ be this additive inverse such as $f(X) = -\hat{p}(X)$. This function is shifted up so that its new version:

$$f^*(X) = -\hat{p}(X) + \left|\min_X\{-\hat{p}(X)\}\right| = -\hat{p}(X) + \max_X\{\hat{p}(X)\}$$

becomes positive with its absolute minimum at zero.

In image segmentation, the most commonly used algorithm for efficient divide determination consists of constructing a numerical skeleton by means of homotopic thinning transformations of the gray level function (Meyer, 1989). The idea behind this thinning process is to deepen the level of the function within the catchment basins so that

their bottoms become flat, while leaving unchanged the function along the divides separating these basins.
The thinning of a function consists in a morphological transformation using a composite structuring element $\underline{B}$ composed of two sets of configurations $\underline{B_0}$ and $\underline{B_1}$. $\underline{B_0}$ is the subset of points of $\underline{B}$ with a 0 value while $\underline{B_1}$ is the subset of the points with a 1 value in this composite structuring element. The application of the morphological transformation means that the structuring element $\underline{B}=(\underline{B_1},\underline{B_0})$ is moved systematically through the entire discretized data space so as to position it at every sampling point. The result of the thinning of the function $f^*(X)$ at the current position of the structuring element is given by:

$$\begin{cases} g(X)=\sup\limits_{X'\in \underline{B_0}}\{f^*(X')\} \text{ if and only if } \sup\limits_{X'\in \underline{B_0}}\{f^*(X')\}< f^*(X) \leq \inf\limits_{X'\in \underline{B_1}}\{f^*(X')\} \\ g(X)=f^*(X) \text{ else.} \end{cases},$$

The interpretation of this morphological operation is clear. Let $\underline{B_X}=(\underline{B_1},\underline{B_0})_X=(\underline{B_1}_X,\underline{B_0}_X)$ be the structuring element whose origin is shifted to the current position $X \in \underline{X}$. By this translation of $\underline{B}$, if for any point X' falling in the part $\underline{B_1}_X$ of the composite structuring element $f^*(X')\geq f^*(X)$, and if for any point X'' falling in the other part $\underline{B_0}_X$ $f^*(X'') < f^*(X)$, then $f^*(X)$ is replaced by the supremum of the function inside the part $\underline{B_0}_X$ of the shifted structuring element. Otherwise, $f^*(X)$ is not modified.
Thinning transformations are generally used sequentially. A sequential thinning can be obtained as a sequence of eight elementary thinnings using the structuring elements $\underline{L}^{(i)}$, $i=1,2,\ldots,8$ that are obtained by successive rotations by $\Pi/4$ of the composite structuring element $\underline{L}^{(1)}$ shown in figure 6 (a). A value of one indicates an element that belongs to part $\underline{L}_1^{(1)}$ of $\underline{L}^{(1)}$, while an element with a zero value belongs to part $\underline{L}_0^{(1)}$. The particular element denoted 1_0 is the center of the structuring element. An asterisk * in the matrix denotes an element belonging neither to $\underline{L}_0^{(1)}$ nor to $\underline{L}_1^{(1)}$. The transformations using this structuring family $L=\{\underline{L}^{(1)},\ldots,\underline{L}^{(8)}\}$ preserve the connectivity properties of the data sets since they are homotopic. Hence, the sequential thinning is iterated and converges to the so-called homotopic skeleton. Idempotence is reached when two consecutive iterations yield the same result, and the thinning process is stopped.
This homotopic sequential thinning is performed with the L family (cf. figure 6 (a)). Each structuring element of this family is used to process the $N.(N-1)/2$ bi-dimensional discrete data sets lying in the planes containing the current point X where the operation is carried out and parallel to the planes defined by the axis of the data space taken two by two. That means that the thinning at any point X is obtained as a combination of $N.(N-1)/2$ elementary planar thinnings operating in orthogonal directions. This procedure circumvents the difficulty of finding composite structuring elements in N dimensions that would lead to homotopic transformations. As these elementary operations are commutative and

associative, they are combined in a single N-dimensional hypercubic composite structuring element of size 3. The orthogonal planes, containing the center of this hypercube and parallel to the planes defined by the axis taken two by two, have the structure of the considered plane structuring element of the *L* family. All the other elements constituting this N-dimensional hypercubic structuring element will be assigned an asterisk, as they are not used in the thinning process.

0	0	0
*	1_0	*
1	1	1

(a)

0	0	0
0	1_0	*
0	0	*

(b)

Figure 6. 2-D composite structuring elements from the Golay alphabet (Golay, 1969).

(a) The $\underline{L}^{(1)}$ structuring element

(b) The $\underline{E}^{(1)}$ structuring element

Figure 7 (b) shows the effect of this sequential thinning on the pdf of figure 7 (a) when it is iterated until idempotence.

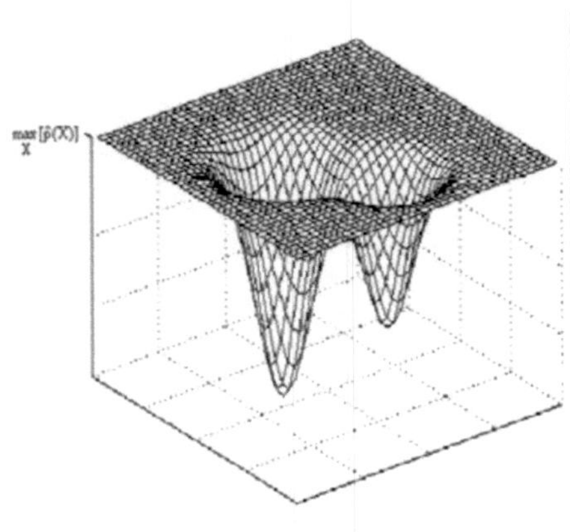

(a)

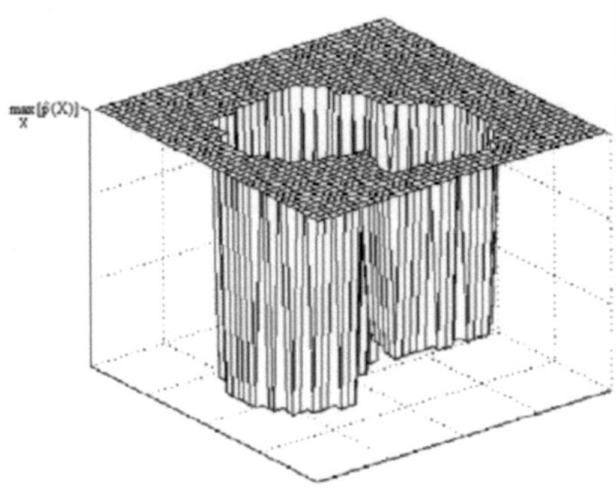

(b)

Figure 7. Sequential thinning of the shifted additive inverse of a pdf with the *L* family

(a) Shifted additive inverse of a bimodal pdf

(b) Result of the last iteration of the thinning process corresponding to idempotence

Note that the multidimensional skeletons resulting from the sequential thinning operations may present non-significant ramifications. They are removed by a pruning operation, performed by means of a sequential thinning with another family of structuring elements, i.e. the *E* structuring family, which is not homotopic (cf. figure 6 (b)). When sequentially thinning the function with the composite structuring family $E=\{\underline{E}^{(i)}\ ,\ i=1,2,...,8\}$, spurious divides are shortened from their free ends. If this pruning operation is iterated until stabilization of the result, only the true divides remain that are the true boundaries between the modes of the distribution.

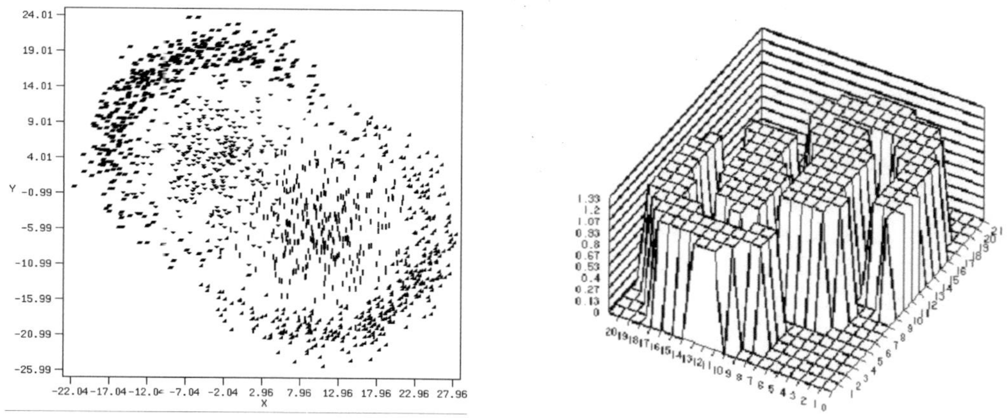

(a) (b)

Figure 8. Mode detection for a bidimensional data set
(a) Estimate of the multimodal underlying pdf
(b) Detected modal domains

The final thinned function consists of catchment basins separated by divides of unit width. Within a basin, the transformed function has a constant level equal to its local minimum value in the basin. The divides are easy to identify in the transformed function, since they are neighboured by catchment basins with lower levels. Figure 8 (b) shows the modes identified by means of this multidimensional watershed transform in the multidimensional pdf of figure 8 (a).

6. Clustering based on multidimensional texture analysis

Statistical texture measures can be used to describe the spatial distribution of the data points (Hammouche et al., 2006). Similarly to texture segmentation, the approach consists first of selecting a set of features that characterize the local distribution of the data points in the multidimensional data space in terms of textures. These textures, which reflect the spatial arrangement of data points, are then classified on the basis of these features. The data points with similar local textures are aggregated in the data space to define compact connected components of homogeneous textures. These multidimensional domains of uniform texture are finally considered as the modes of the distribution.

Textural properties are considered in terms of statistical models. The main difficulty is the selection of a set of relevant features to describe the properties of the spatial distribution of the observations. The concept of co-occurrence matrices, well-known in image processing, can be generalized to multidimensional data spaces. A large variety of features can then be derived from such matrices that combine spatial information with statistical properties (Haralick et al., 1973).

In the framework of image processing, an element $T(i,j)$ of a co-occurrence matrix is a count of the number of times a pixel $P_r = [x_{r,1}, x_{r,2}]^T$, with gray-level i, is positioned with respect to a pixel $P_{r'} = [x_{r',1}, x_{r',2}]^T$, with gray level j, such as :

$$P_{r'} = P_r + \begin{bmatrix} d\cos\theta \\ d\sin\theta \end{bmatrix}$$

where d is the distance in the direction θ between the two pixels.

A similar co-occurrence matrix can be determined to characterize the local distribution of the data points in a given neighbourhood of each non-empty hypercube. We use the classical hypercubic neighbourhood of side length $(2\delta+1)$ previously defined. As directionality and periodicity are obviously irrelevant characteristics of the data point distributions, it is not necessary to determine co-occurrence matrices for different sets of discrete values of the distance d and the orientation θ between the pairs of sampling points taken into account. Hence, only one co-occurrence matrix is determined for each sampling point. The co-occurrences $T(i,j)$ of any given pair (i, j) of discrete multidimensional histogram values such as $i=\hat{p}(P_r)$ and $j=\hat{p}(P_{r'})$, are simply counted for all the couples of adjacent sampling points encountered within this hypercubic neighbourhood. Two sampling points are considered as adjacent if they are the centers of two hypercubes that have at least one point in common. As the histogram $\hat{p}$ is quantized on a set of $p_{max}+1$ discrete values, the co-occurrence matrices have $p_{max}+1$ rows and $p_{max}+1$ columns.

Several local texture features can be computed from these specific co-occurrence matrices, which accumulate information on the data distribution in the neighborhood of each sampling point (Cf. Table 1). These features are expected to characterize such properties as roughness, smoothness, homogeneity, randomness or coarseness rather than textural properties such as directionality or periodicity, since each co-occurrence matrix summarizes the number of occurrences of pairs of histogram values for all possible pairs of adjacent sampling points lying within a given neighbourhood, without constraints on their orientations.

When the sampling points are characterized by a set of texture features, they can be represented as feature vectors in a multidimensional feature space. Texture classification consists of assigning the sampling points of the discrete data space to different texture classes defined in the feature space. This is an unsupervised classification problem since no a priori knowledge about the feature vectors associated with the textures to be identified is available. A simple solution is to use a well-established clustering procedure, such as the k-means algorithm.

Under the assumption that the cluster cores are multidimensional domains in the original data space, with homogeneous textures, it is expected that the hypercubes centered on sampling points assigned to the same class of texture give rise to connected components in the discrete data space. These components can be extracted by means of an aggregation procedure where two hypercubes whose centers belong to the same class of texture are assigned to the same component if they have at least one point in common. Small components resulting from this aggregation procedure may correspond to non-significant domains of the original data space containing only a small number of data points. Therefore, any domain containing less than 5% of the total number Q of observations is discarded.

Uniformity-1 (1st order)	$f_1 = \frac{1}{N_c} \sum_{i=0}^{P_{max}} T(i,i)$
Uniformity-2 (2nd order)	$f_2 = \frac{1}{N_c^2} \sum_{i=0}^{P_{max}} T(i,i)^2$
Homogeneity	$f_3 = \frac{1}{N_c} \sum_{i=0}^{P_{max}} \sum_{j=0}^{P_{max}} \frac{T(i,j)}{1+(i-j)^2}$
Correlation	$f_4 = \frac{1}{N_c} \sum_{i=0}^{P_{max}} \sum_{j=0}^{P_{max}} ijT(i,j)$
Energy	$f_5 = \frac{1}{N_c^2} \sum_{i=0}^{P_{max}} \sum_{j=0}^{P_{max}} T(i,j)^2$
Entropy	$f_6 = -\frac{1}{N_c} \sum_{i=0}^{P_{max}} \sum_{j=0}^{P_{max}} T(i,j) \log\left(T(i,j) / N_c \right)$
Inertia	$f_7 = \frac{1}{N_c} \sum_{i=0}^{P_{max}} \sum_{j=0}^{P_{max}} (i-j)^2 T(i,j)$
Means	$f_8 = \frac{1}{N_c} \sum_{i=0}^{P_{max}} \sum_{j=0}^{P_{max}} i * T(i,j)$ $f_9 = \frac{1}{N_c} \sum_{i=0}^{P_{max}} \sum_{j=0}^{P_{max}} j * T(i,j)$
Covariance	$f_{10} = \frac{1}{N_c} \sum_{i=0}^{P_{max}} \sum_{j=0}^{P_{max}} (i-f_8)(j-f_9)T(i,j)$
Cluster shade	$f_{11} = \frac{1}{N_c} \sum_{i=0}^{P_{max}} \sum_{j=0}^{P_{max}} ((i-f_8)+(j-f_9))^3 T(i,j)$
Cluster prominence	$f_{12} = \frac{1}{N_c} \sum_{i=0}^{P_{max}} \sum_{j=0}^{P_{max}} ((i-f_8)+(j-f_9))^4 T(i,j)$
Absolute value	$f_{13} = \frac{1}{N_c} \sum_{i=0}^{P_{max}} \sum_{j=0}^{P_{max}} \lvert i-j \rvert \, T(i,j)$

Table 1. Statistical texture features ($N_c = \sum_{i=0}^{P_{max}} \sum_{j=0}^{P_{max}} T(i,j)$ is a normalizing parameter)

Among the remaining domains, those corresponding to the actual modes of the distribution are expected to be more compact than those corresponding to their boundaries or to the valleys between them. Hence, they can be discriminated from other connected components by analyzing their compactness defined as:

$$C = [\text{total number of hypercubes}] / [\text{number of boundary hypercubes}]^N$$

which is as much as high as the component is compact. In these conditions, mode detection is straightforward by simple thresholding of the compactness.
Figure 9 (b) shows the modes identified as domains of homogeneous texture detected in the data set of figure 9 (a).

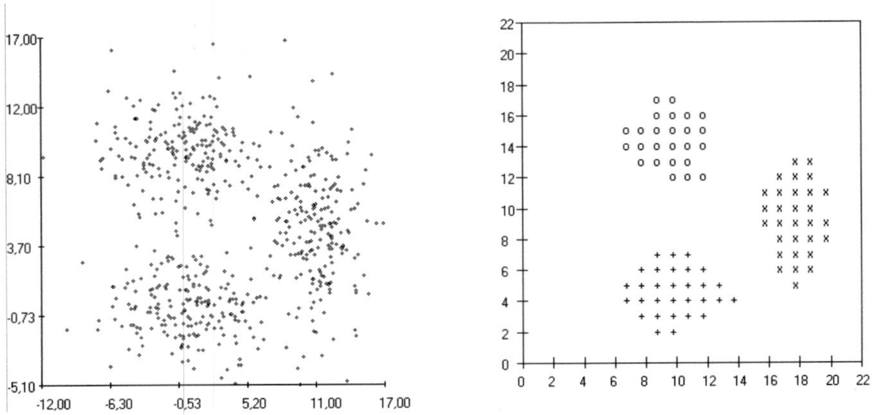

(a) (b)

Figure 9. Mode detection by texture analysis
(a) Data set
(b) Detected modes

7. Markov random field models for clustering

In the framework of the Markovian approach, each hypercube defined by the discretization process of section 2 corresponds to a site s whose coordinates are defined as the integer parts of the coordinates of its center. Let $\underline{S}$ denote the set of K^N sites defined in the data space. At each site s, $s=1,2,\dots,K^N$, a measure O_s is determined as :

$$O_s = \begin{cases} 1 & \text{if at least one observation falls into the site } s \\ 0 & \text{if the site } s \text{ is empty} \end{cases}$$

The resulting discrete binary set $O=\{O_s, s \in \underline{S}\}$ is the observable field which can be considered as a simplified binary representation of the distribution of the observations through the data space. This observable field O, which is composed of non-empty sites where $O_s = 1$ and empty sites where $O_s = 0$, is considered as an initial state of the hidden field Γ. In this initial hidden field, sites where $\Gamma_s = 1$ are considered as "mode sites"while, when $\Gamma_s = 0$, they are considered as "valley sites". As the field O is a simplified discrete binary version of the set of available observations, non-empty sites that belong to the modes tend to have a great number of non-empty sites among their nearest neighbours, due to the high concentration of observations within the modes. Similarly, empty sites tend to be more connected in the valleys than within the modes. In order to detect the modes of the distribution, the key problem is to assign the mode label to the sites that effectively define the modal domains and to assign the valley label to those that stand out of these modal domains (Sbihi et al., 2005).

A straightforward procedure for constructing connected subsets representing the modes in the data space is to use two sets of cliques (Moussa et al., 2001). For the sake of simplicity, let us consider an hypercubic neighbourhood $V_1(s)$ of side length 3 of each site s. The first set C_2^s is composed of the cliques c_2^s of size two that can be found in that neighbourhood and that contain the site s itself (Cf. figure 10 (a)). $\varphi_{c_2^s}$ is the potential corresponding to these cliques. The second set $\overline{C}_2^s$ is composed of all the cliques $\overline{c}_2^s$ of size two that can be found in $V_1(s)$ and that do not contain the site s itself (Cf. figure 10 (b)). $\overline{\varphi}_{\overline{c}_2^s}$ is the potential function associated to these cliques. The resulting potential function is:

$$\varphi_{(c_2^s,\overline{c}_2^s)} = \upsilon\varphi_{c_2^s} + (1-\upsilon)\overline{\varphi}_{\overline{c}_2^s}$$

The factor $\upsilon = \frac{\alpha}{\alpha+\beta}$, where α is the number of cliques in $\overline{C}_2^s$ and β their number in C_2^s, weights the relative influence of the two terms, so that the measure of compatibility does not depend on the number of considered sites.

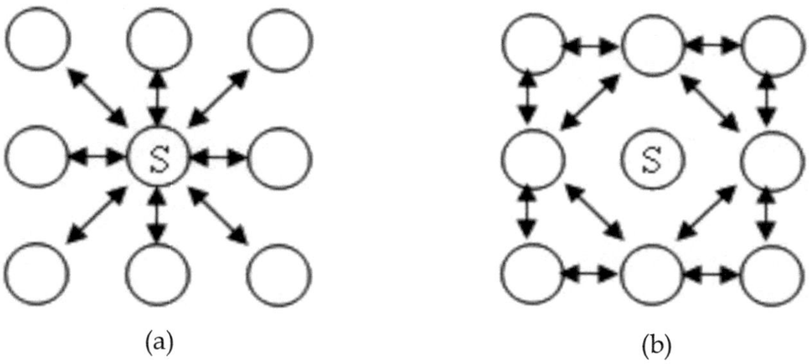

Figure 10. The set of cliques in the bidimensional case

(a) The set C_2^s of cliques c_2^s related to the potential function $\varphi_{c_2^s}(.)$

(b) The set $\overline{C}_2^s$ of cliques $\overline{c}_2^s$ related to the potential function $\varphi_{\overline{c}_2^s}(.)$

All the sites are visited sequentially. The conditional energy $U(\Gamma_s=\gamma_s/\Gamma_r=\gamma_r, r\in V_1(s))$ is computed at each site s, taking into account the label configuration existing at that time for all its neighbouring sites. The label corresponding to the lowest conditional energy, which maximizes the Gibbs conditional probability:

$$P(\Gamma_s=\gamma_s/\Gamma_r=\gamma_r, r\neq s, r\in V_1(s)) = \frac{\exp[-U(\Gamma_s=\gamma_s/\Gamma_r=\gamma_r, r\in V_1(s))]}{\sum_{\gamma_n\in\{0,1\}}\exp[-U(\Gamma_s=\gamma_n/\Gamma_r=\gamma_r, r\in V_1(s))]}$$

is selected. The process is iterated until no further change occurs in the global energy, defined as:

$$U(\Gamma=\gamma) = \sum_{s\in S}\ \sum_{c_2^s\in C_2^s,\overline{c}_2^s\in\overline{C}_2^s} \varphi_{(c_2^s,\overline{c}_2^s)}$$

The algorithm stops when $\Delta^t = U^t - U^{t-1} = 0$, where U_t is the value of the global energy $U(\Gamma=\gamma)$ at iteration number t.

Figure 11 shows the modes that can be detected by modelling a bidimensional distribution as a Markovian process.

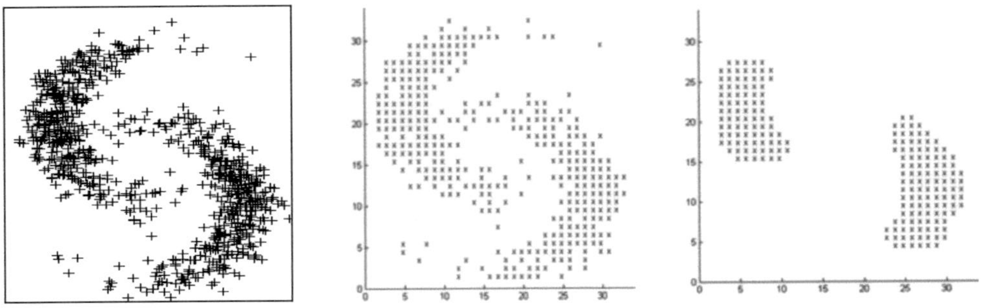

(a) (b) (c)

Figure 11. Mode detection by means of Markov Field Model

(a) Raw data set
(b) Sites where $O_s = 1$ in the observable field O
(c) Sites with the "mode" label in the hidden field Γ

8. Algorithms tunning

The performance of the above described algorithms depends mainly on the adjustment of the discretization parameter K and on the relevance of the chosen texture features.

Let us first consider the effect of the resolution of the discretization process. In fact, the adjustment of K depends on the sample size Q, on the dimensionality N of the data and on the structure of the distribution of the observations. It can be expected that, when true clusters exist, stable connected subsets of data points with similar properties appear for a wide range of values of K. Based on this assumption, the adjustment of K can be governed by the concept of cluster stability (Eigen et al., 1974). Choosing such a parameter in the middle of the largest range where the number of detected clusters remains constant, and different from one, has proved to be a good procedure to optimize a number of clustering algorithms when nothing is a priori known about the structure of the distribution of the observations (Postaire & Vasseur, 1981). Note that the larger the range is, the more reliable the tuning procedure is. Figure 12 shows the evolution of the number of detected modes with the discretization parameter K for the example of figure 9 (a). The largest range where this number remains constant appears for three modes. It is the reason why figure 9 (b) shows the detected modes in a discrete space with K=22, which is the middle of this range.

The concept of mode stability is very useful to improve the capabilities of clustering procedures. Indeed, in the specific framework of multidimensional texture analysis, the key problem is the selection of a set of suitable texture features. For choosing relevant features while reducing the dimensionality of the texture classification problem, a performance-dependent feature selection scheme, directly related to this concept, can be implemented. The effectiveness of a subset of features is evaluated by means of the width of the largest range of values of the discretization parameter K leading to the appropriate number of detected modes. As mentioned earlier, the larger this range, the more reliable the number of detected modes. This criterion is used to select a set of relevant features among the available ones by means of a sequential forward selection technique (Siedlecki & Sklansky, 1988).

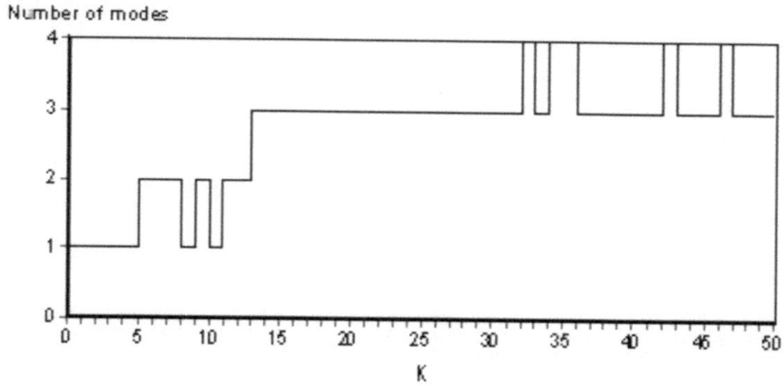

Figure 12. Effect of the parameter K on the number of detected modes

9. Final classification

Each detected mode reveals the presence of a cluster in the data space. Many grouping procedures can be used to assign the available observations to the so-detected clusters. One solution uses the input observations falling into the modal domains as prototypes. The remaining observations are finally assigned to the clusters attached to their nearest (Euclidean) neighbours among these prototypes (Cover & Hart, 1967).
When implementing this basic nearest neighbour classifier, experiments have shown that the results can be fairly improved if the remaining observations are assigned one by one to the clusters in a specific order depending on their distances to the prototypes (Gowda & Krishna, 1978). At each step of this procedure, we consider the distances between all the unassigned observations and all the prototypes. The smallest among these distances indicates the specific observation that must be considered. This observation is assigned to the cluster attached to its nearest neighbour and is integrated within the set of prototypes defining this cluster. This updating rule is iterated until all the observations are classified.

11. Conclusion and perspectives

All the clustering methods presented in this chapter tend to generalize bi-dimensional procedures initially developed for image processing purpose. Among them, thresholding, edge detection, probabilistic relaxation, mathematical morphology, texture analysis, and Markov field models appear to be valuable tools with a wide range of applications in the field of unsupervised pattern classification.
Following the same idea of adapting image processing techniques to cluster analysis, one of our other objectives is to model spatial relationships between pixels by means of other textural parameters derived from autoregressive models (Comer & Delp, 1999), Markov random fields models (Cross & Jain, 1983), Gabor filters (Jain & Farrokhnia, 1991), wavelet coefficients (Porter & Canagarajah, 1996) and fractal geometry (Keller & Crownover, 1989). We have also already started to work on the adaptation of fuzzy morphological operators to cluster analysis, by extracting the observations located in the modal regions performing an

adaptive morphological transformation of a fuzzy set, defined from the data set, with its associated mode membership function (Turpin et al., 1998). Face to these promising results, we are working on the introduction of fuzziness in other morphological operators such as fuzzy watersheds. Genetic algorithms, which have been used for image segmentation (Yin, 1999), are also powerfull tools that have to be tested.

12. References

Benslimane R., Botte Lecocq C. & Postaire J.-G. (1996) Extraction des modes en classification automatique par ligne de partage des eaux. *Journal Européen des Systèmes Automatisés*, Vol. 30, No 9, 1996, pp. 1169-1200

Botte-Lecocq C. & Postaire J.-G. (1991) Iterations of morphological transformations for cluster separation in pattern recognition, In: *Symbolic-Numeric Data Analysis and Learning*, pp. 173-185, Nova Science Pub., New York

Botte-Lecocq C. & Postaire J.-G. (1994) Mode detection and valley seeking by binary morphological analysis of connectivity for pattern classification, In: *New Approaches in Classification and Data Analysis*, pp. 194-203, Springer-Verlag, Berlin

Comer M. L. & Delp E. J. (1999) Segmentation of textured images using a multiresolution Gaussian autoregressive model. *IEEE Image Processing*, Vol. 8, 1999, pp. 408-420

Cover T. M. & Hart P. E. (1967) Nearest neighbor pattern classification. *IEEE Information Theory*, Vol. IT-13, No 1, 1967, pp. 21-27

Cross G. & Jain A. (1983) Markov random fields texture models. *IEEE Pattern Analysis and Machine Intelligence*, Vol. PAMI-5, 1983, pp. 25-39

Davis, L. S. (1975) A survey of edge detection techniques. *Computer Graphics and Image Processing*, Vol. 4, 1975, pp. 248-270

Eigen D. J., Fromm F. R. & Northouse R. A. (1974) Cluster analysis based on dimensional information with application to unsupervised pattern classification. *IEEE Pattern Analysis and Machine Intelligence*, Vol. PAMI-4, 1974, pp. 284-294

Golay A. (1969) Hexagonal pattern transform. *IEEE Trans. on Computers*, Vol. 18, No 8, 1969, pp. 733-740

Gowda K. C. & Krishna G. (1978) Agglomerative clustering using the concept of mutual nearest neighbourhood. *Pattern Recognition*, Vol. 10, 1978, pp. 105-112

Hammouche K., Diaf M. & Postaire J.-G. (2006) A clustering method based on multidimensional texture analysis. *Pattern Recognition*, Vol. 39, 2006, pp. 1265-1277

Haralick R. M., Shanmugam K., Dinstein I. (1973) Texture features for image classification, *IEEE Trans. on Systems, Man and Cybernetics*. Vol. SMC-3, No 6, 1973, pp. 610-621

Hummel R.A. & Zucker S.W. (1983). On the foundations of relaxation labeling process. *IEEE Pattern Analysis and Machine Intelligence*, Vol. PAMI-5, No 3, 1983, pp. 267-286

Jain A. K. & Farrokhnia F. (1991) Unsupervised texture segmentation using Gabor filters. *Pattern Recognition*, Vol.24, 1991, pp. 1167-1186

Keller J. M. and Crownover R. M. (1989) Texture description and segmentation through fractal geometry. *CVGIP: Graphical Models and Image Processing*, Vol. 45, 1989, pp. 150-166

Mallat S. G. (1989) Multifrequency channel decomposition of images and wavelets models, Theory for multiresolution signal decomposition: the wavelet representation, *IEEE Trans. Acoustics, Speech and Signal Processing*, Vol. 37, 1989, pp. 2091-2110.

Matheron G. (1985) *Random sets and integral geometry*, Wiley, New York

Meyer F. (1989) Skeletons and Perceptual Graphs. *Signal Processing*, Vol. 16, No 4, 1989, pp. 335-363

Meyer F. and Beucher S. (1990) Morphological segmentation. *J. Visual Communication and Image Representation*, Vol. 1, No 1, 1990, pp. 21-46

Morgenthaler D.G. & Rosenfeld A. (1981) Multidimensional edge detection by hypersurface fitting. *IEEE Pattern Analysis and Mach. Intell.*, Vol. PAMI-3, No 4, 1981, pp. 482-486

Moussa A., Sbihi A. & Postaire J.-G. (2001) Classification automatique par extraction des noyaux des classes utilisant une approche Markovienne. Journal Européen des Systèmes Automatisés, APII-JESA, Vol. 35, n° 9, 2001, pp. 1073-1087

Parzen E. (1962) On estimation of a probability density function and mode. *Ann. Math. Statist.* Vol. 33, 1962, pp. 1065-1076

Porter R. & Canagarajah N. (1996) A robust automatic clustering scheme for image segmentation using wavelets. *IEEE Image Processing*, Vol. 5,1996, pp. 662-665

Postaire J.-G. & Vasseur C. (1981) An approximate solution to normal mixture identification with application to unsupervised pattern classification. *IEEE Pattern Analysis and Machine Intelligence*, Vol. PAMI-3, No 2, 1981, pp. 163-179

Postaire J.-G. & Vasseur C. (1982). A fast algorithm for non parametric density estimation. *IEEE Pattern Analysis and Machine Intelligence*, Vol. PAMI-4, No 6, 1982, pp. 663-666

Postaire J.-G. & Touzani A. (1989) Mode boundary detection by relaxation for cluster analysis. *Pattern Recognition*, Vol. 22, No 5, 1989, pp. 477-490

Postaire J.-G. & Touzani A. (1990). A sample-based approximation of normal mixtures by mode boundary extraction for pattern classification. *Pattern Recognition Letters*, Vol. 11, No 3, 1990, pp. 153-166

Postaire J.-G., Zhang R. D. & Botte Lecocq C. (1993). Cluster analysis by binary morphology. *IEEE Pattern Analysis and Machine Intelligence*, Vol. PAMI-15, No 2, 1993, pp. 170-180

Rosenfeld A. & Smith R.C. (1981). Thresholding using relaxation. *IEEE Pattern Analysis and Machine Intelligence*, Vol. PAMI-3, No 5, 1981, pp. 598-606

Sbihi A. & Postaire J.-G. (1995) Mode extraction by Multivalue Morphology for Cluster Analysis, In: *From Data to Knowledge: Theoretical and Practical Aspects of Classification*, W. Gaul and D. Pfeifer (Ed.), pp. 212-221, Springer, Berlin

Sbihi A., Moussa A., Benmiloud B. & Postaire J.-G. (2000) A markovian approach to unsupervised multidimensional pattern classification, In: *Data Analysis, Classification and Related Method*, H.A.L. Kiers, J.-P. Rasson, P.J.F. Groenen and M. Scheder (Ed.) pp. 247-254, Springer, Berlin

Sbihi M., Moussa A., Postaire J.-G. & Sbihi A. (2005) Approche Markovienne pour la classification automatique non supervisée de données multidimensionnelles. *Journal Européen des Systèmes Automatisés*, Vol. 39, No 9-10, 2005, pp.1133-1154

Serra J. (1988) *Image analysis and mathematical morphology : theoretical advances*, Vol. 2, Academic Press, New York

Siedlecki W. & Sklansky J. (1988) On automatic feature selection. *Int. J. Pattern Recognition Artificial Intelligence*, Vol. 2, No 2, 1988, pp. 197-220

Touzani A. & Postaire J.-G. (1988). Mode detection by relaxation. *IEEE Pattern Analysis and Machine Intelligence*, Vol. PAMI-10, No 6, 1988, pp. 970-978

Touzani A. & Postaire J.-G. (1989). Clustering by mode boundary detection. *Pattern Recognition Letters*, Vol. 9, No 1, 1989, pp. 1-12

Turpin-Dhilly S. & Botte-Lecocq C. (1998) Application of fuzzy mathemetical morphology for pattern classification. *Advances in Data Science and Classification, Proceeding of the 6th Conf. of International Federation of Classification Society, Springer,* 1998, pp 125-130

Yin P.-Y. (1999) A fast scheme for optimal thresholding using genetic algorithms. *Signal Processing,* Vol. 72, 1999, pp. 85-95

26

Articulated Hand Tracking by ICA-based Hand Model and Multiple Cameras

Makoto Kato, Gang Xu & Yen-Wei Chen
Ritsumeikan University
Japan

1. Introduction

Vision has the great potential to give the computers the ability of collecting information. In this chapter we study the tracking and capturing of 3-D free hand motions by computers. The hand has no markers and no special devices and no special conditions are required.

This chapter presents three techniques for the vision-based tracking. The first one is the ICA-based motion analysis. The second is articulated hand motion tracking by multiple cameras. The third is particle filtering with prediction.

A human hand has many joints and its high dimensionality makes it difficult to model hand motions. To make things easier, it is important to represent a hand motion in a low dimensional space. Principal component analysis (PCA) has been proposed to reduce the dimensionality. However, the PCA basis vectors only represent global features, which are not optimal for representing intrinsic features. This chapter proposes an efficient representation of hand motions by independent component analysis (ICA). The ICA basis vectors represent local features, each of which corresponds to the motion of a particular finger. This representation is more efficient in modeling hand motions for tracking and recognizing hand-finger gestures in an image sequence.

This chapter also proposes a new technique to simultaneously estimate the global hand pose and the finger articulation imaged by multiple cameras. Tracking a free hand motion against a cluttered background is a difficult task. The first reason is that hand fingers are self-occluding and the second reason is the high dimensionality of the problem. In order to solve these difficulties, we propose using calibrated multiple cameras and at the same time improving search efficiency by predicted particle filtering.

The effectiveness of our methods is demonstrated by tracking free hand motions in real image sequences. The method is easily expanded for tracking human body motions in 3D.

2. Related work

Recently, recognition of hand gestures and hand motion tracking has become an important issue in the field of human-computer interaction. Many researchers tried or are trying to create a method by camera.

The hand tracking methods by camera can be divided into two categories. One is appearance-based, and the other is model-based.

In the appearance-based methods, mapping between image features and hand pose is established. Hand pose estimation is formulated as an image database indexing problem, where the closest matches for an input hand image are retrieved from a large database of synthetic hand images. Stenger et al. proposed a new framework for Bayesian tracking based on the tree representation of the large database, which is effective for tracking 3D articulated motions in front of cluttered background (Stenger et al., 2003). The problem with the appearance-based method is that it requires a very large database.

In contrast, the model-based methods use an deformable hand model. The hand pose at the current frame is estimated from the current image input and previous pose. The problem of using a hand model is the high dimensionality. The high dimensionality causes an exponentially high computational cost. Particle filtering is one of the most successful object tracking algorithms (Isard & Blake, 1998). However, to keep tracking correctness especially for rapid motions, it needs a large number of particles. Since it is infeasible to maintain dense sampling in high dimensional state spaces, two methods have been proposed to solve these problems. One is to reduce the state dimensionality and the other is to improve sampling and to make better prediction.

To reduce the dimensionality, Zhou et al. proposed an eigen dynamic analysis (EDA) method and constructed a dynamic Bayesian network based on EDA to analyze the generative sequence of natural hand motions (Zhou & Huang, 2003). Wu et al. presented a method to capture natural hand motions by PCA and showed tracking results by particle filtering (Wu et al., 2001).

This chapter proposes a new model-based method. The previous researchers (Zhou & Huang, 2003) (Wu et al., 2001) have reduced the dimensionality of hand *pose* space by PCA. Then they have learned basis motions in the PCA space. In contrast, we directly reduce the dimensionality of hand *motion* space by PCA. However, at our approach, it is impossible to use the PCA basis vectors for particle filtering, since the PCA basis vectors represent global features. To solve this problem, we propose to perform ICA to extract local features.

ICA (Hyvarinen et al., 2001) is a way of finding a linear non-orthogonal coordinate system in any multivariate data. The goal is to perform a linear transformation which makes the resulting variables as statistically independent from each other as possible. ICA has been successfully applied to many applications of image analysis and pattern recognition, such as face recognition (Bartlett et al., 2002), sign-language classification, color indexing, classification of multi-spectral images, and edge detection. In the proposed ICA-based hand motion representation, the ICA basis vectors of hand motions correspond to the motions of a particular finger and they are statistically independent. The representation is very efficient at particle filtering, since we can directly use these basis vectors. Furthermore, a linear combination of these ICA basis vectors can actually represent any hand motions.

To improve sampling efficiency, Rui et al. propose Unscented Particle Filter (UPF) (Rui & Chen, 2001). The UPF uses the unscented Kalman filter to generate sophisticated proposal distributions that seamlessly integrate the current observation, thus greatly improving the tracking performance. This method needs to establish a system dynamics model. As for our 26-DOF problem, it is even hard to establish the system dynamics model. Deutscher et al. propose annealed particle filtering which is modified for searches in high dimensional state spaces (Deutscher et al., 2000). It uses a continuation principle, based on annealing, to introduce the influence of narrow peaks in the fitness function, gradually. It is shown to be capable of recovering full articulated body motion efficiently. However, the experiment is done against a black background. Bray et al. propose smart particle filtering which combines the Stochastic Meta-Descent (SMD), based on gradient descent with particle filtering (Bray et al., 2004). Their 3D hand tracking result is robust and accurate. However, they need depth maps generated by a structured light 3D sensor, which are not available in real time.

We propose to add prediction to particle filtering. Parameters in the next frame are predicted and more particles are accordingly generated for areas of higher likelihood. The method is straightforward but proven to very effective in significantly reducing search cost.

Another problem with the model-based approach is self-occlusion. While a hand moves freely, parts of the hand change from being visible to being invisible, and then becoming visible again. Previously proposed techniques avoid this problem by restricting hand motions to only those that are frontal to the camera (Wu et al., 2001). To overcome this restriction, we propose to use multiple pre-calibrated cameras, so that parts invisible in one camera are still visible in at least another camera. While this is the right approach to the self-occlusion problem, more observations put more burdens on the already busy computer. This motivates further improvement of search efficiency. Although Rehg and Kanade (Rehg & Kanade, 1995) proposed to use multiple cameras for finger tracking, hand motion in this chapter is much more complicated and we need to design and implement more efficient method.

3. Representation of hand motions

3.1 Hand model

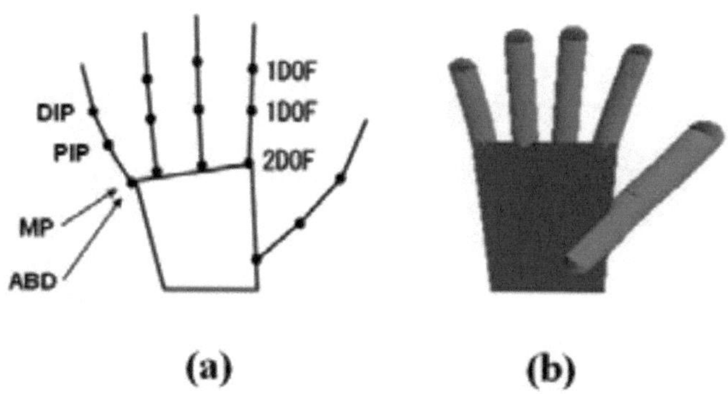

Figure 1. (a): Hand model with the name of each joint, and the degrees of freedom (DOF) for each joint. (b) Hand model rendered in OpenGL.

In our study a human hand is rendered in OpenGL using spheres, cylinders, and rectangular parallelepiped. A human hand can be described in this way: the base is a palm and five fingers are attached to the palm. Each finger has four degrees of freedom (DOF). Two of four DOF correspond to the metacarpophalangeal joint (MP) and its abduction (ABD). The other two correspond to the proximal interphalangeal joint (PIP) and the distal interphalangeal joint (DIP) (Lee & Kunii, 1995). It is shown in Fig. 1. Therefore, our hand model has 20 DOF. In addition, to represent the position and orientation of a hand, we need 6 more parameters, 3 for position and 3 for orientation. In total, the hand model has 26 DOF.

3.2 Hand motion data

The data of hand motions is captured by a data glove. It is collected starting from the open-palmed, 5-fingers extended position, with the fingers moving to various combinations of touching the palm. Since a hand consists of five fingers, 31 different hand motions are captured as:

$$ {}_5C_5 + {}_5C_4 + {}_5C_3 + {}_5C_2 + {}_5C_1 = 31 \tag{1} $$

where C means combination.

Angles of 20 DOF of 15 joints are measured. We divide the motion data of each DOF into 100 instants along the time axis. Then the motion of each DOF can be represented by a row vector of 100-dimensions. We arrange the thumb, index, middle, ring, and pinkie in order, where each finger consists of four DOF which are MP, PIP, DIP, and ABD in order as Fig. 2. We define this 2000-dimensional row vector as a hand motion vector $\mathbf{x}_i$, $i = 1, \cdots, 31$.

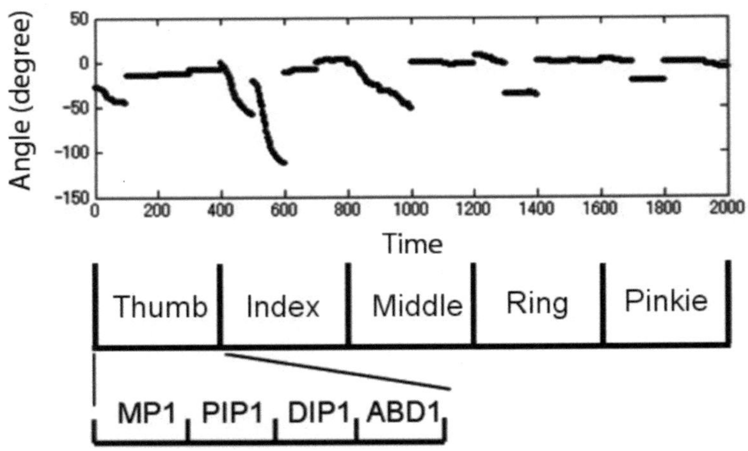

Figure 2. Example of a hand motion vector $\mathbf{x}_i$. This vector represents the hand motion, where an index finger is bended intentionally. The numbers on x-axis refer to time in each DOF. The numbers on y-axis refer to angles.

3.3 Constraints of hand motion

Analysis of hand motion is a task of high cost, because the joint angle space of hand is $\Theta \subset \Re^{20}$. Fortunately, a hand motion has certain constraints. One type of constraints is the so-called static constraints in literature (Lee & Kunii, 1995), which define limits on the ranges of finger motions such as $0^\circ \leq \theta_{MP} \leq 90^\circ$. These constraints limit hand motions within a boundary in $\Re^{20}$. However, these constraints can not be used to reduce the dimensionality.

Another type of constraints describes the correlations among different joints, and we can use this type of constraints to reduce the dimensionality of hand motions. For example, the motions of the DIP joint and PIP joint are generally not independent and they can be described as $\theta_{DIP} = \frac{2}{3}\theta_{PIP}$ from the study of biomechanics.

3.4 Dimensionality reduction by PCA

The purpose of PCA is to find a smaller set of variables with less redundancy. The redundancy is measured by correlations between data elements, i.e.

$$\mathbf{r}_i = \mathbf{P}(\mathbf{x}_i - \mathbf{x}_0)^T \tag{2}$$

where $\mathbf{P}$ is the transformation matrix. Each row of $\mathbf{P}$ corresponds to the first several basis vectors, which are calculated from the sample data set using Singular Value Decomposition (SVD). $\mathbf{x}_0 = \frac{1}{31}\sum_{k=1}^{31}\mathbf{x}_k$ is the mean of the data set.

Fig. 3 is the rendered hand motions along the PCA basis vectors. We can see that a hand motion along the PCA basis vector represents a global finger motion which means that fingers move together. Most of hand motions along the PCA basis vectors are unfeasible hand motions.

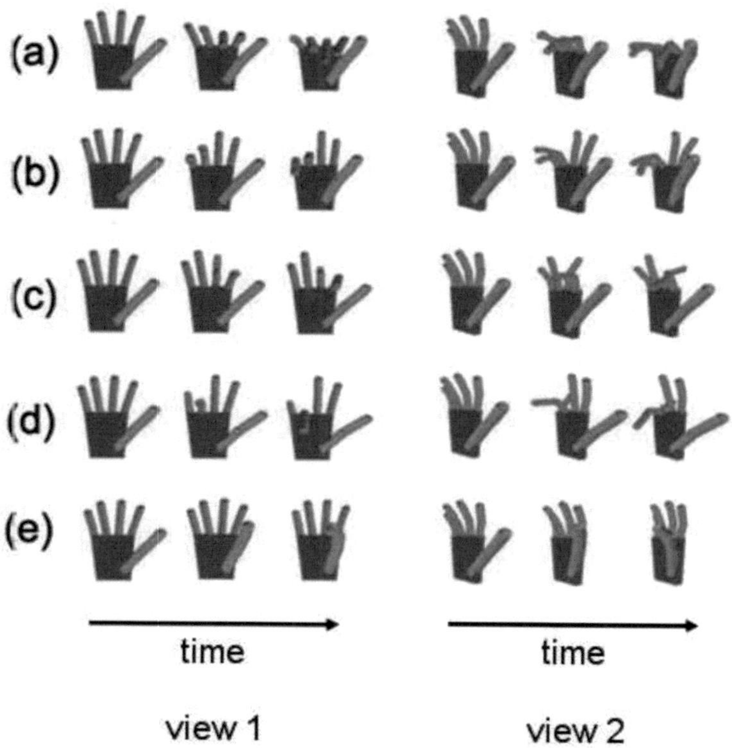

Figure 3. Rendered hand motions along the PCA basis vectors from frontal view (view1) and tilted view (view2). (a)-(e) corresponds to the first five PCA basis vectors respectively.

3.5 Representation of hand motion by ICA

Although PCA is efficient for dimensionality reduction, it has difficulty representing the intrinsic features, because its basis vectors represent global features. In order to solve this problem, we use ICA to represent hand motions. First, we perform PCA to reduce the dimensionality. Then we perform ICA to extract intrinsic features. ICA is a generalized technique of PCA and has proven to be an effective tool of feature extraction.

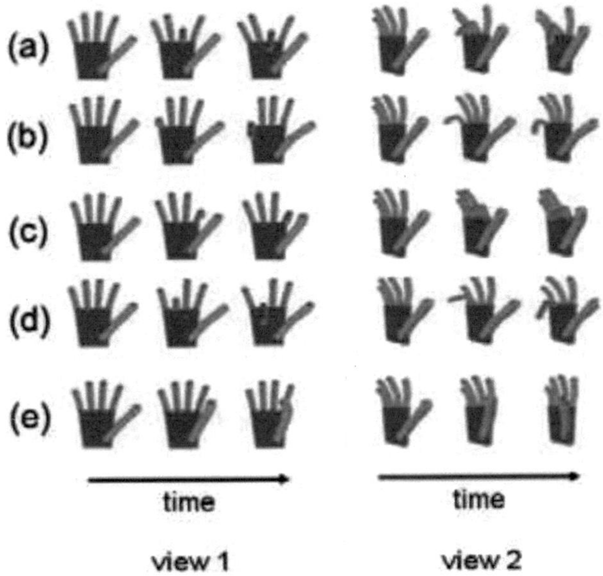

Figure 4. Rendered hand motions along the ICA basis vectors from frontal view (view1) and tilted view (view2). (a)-(e) corresponds to the five ICA basis vectors respectively.

A hand motion vector $\mathbf{x}_i$ can be represented by a linear combination of basis vectors as

$$\mathbf{x}_i = \sum_{j=1}^{N} a_{ij}\mathbf{u}_j = a_{i1}\mathbf{u}_1 + a_{i2}\mathbf{u}_2 + \cdots + a_{iN}\mathbf{u}_N \quad (3)$$

where $\mathbf{u}_j$ is the j-th independent basis vector and a_{ij} is the j-th coefficient. Equation (3) can then be written as follows in matrix form:

$$\mathbf{X} = \mathbf{AU} \quad (4)$$

where $\mathbf{A}$ is the mixing matrix, producing a matrix $\mathbf{X}$ with hand motion vectors in its row. Because we want to obtain $\mathbf{U}$ from sample hand motions $\mathbf{X}$ alone, the problem is actually the Blind Source Separation (BSS) problem, which can be solved by ICA as

$$\hat{\mathbf{U}} = \mathbf{WX} \quad (5)$$

The goal of ICA is to find the unmixing matrix $\mathbf{W}$ such that the rows of $\hat{\mathbf{U}}$ are as statistically independent as possible. Several ICA algorithms have been proposed. Here we use the infomax algorithm proposed by Bell and Sejnowski (Bell & Sejnowski, 1995), which was successfully used in face recognition (Bartlett et al., 2002). The approach is to maximize the joint entropy by using stochastic gradient ascent. The gradient update rule for the weight matrix $\mathbf{W}$ is as follow:

$$\Delta\mathbf{W} = (\mathbf{I} + g(\mathbf{U})\mathbf{U}^T)\mathbf{W} \tag{6}$$

where $\mathbf{U} = \mathbf{W}\mathbf{X}$ and $g(u) = 1 - 2/(1+e^{-u})$.

Fig. 4 is the rendered hand motions along the ICA basis vectors. Compared with PCA basis vectors as Fig. 3, a hand motion along the ICA basis vector represents a local finger motion which corresponds to a particular finger motion. We can see that only one finger moves dominantly, while other fingers move very little. Furthermore, hand motions along the ICA basis vectors are feasible hand motions.

3.6 Efficient representation of hand pose

The ICA-based model can represent a hand pose by five independent parameters, each of which corresponds to a particular finger motion at a particular time instant respectively. This is shown in Fig. 5. It can also expressed formally as follows:

$$\begin{aligned} HandPose &= ThumbMotion(t_1) + IndexMotion(t_2) + MiddleMotion(t_3) \\ &\quad + RingMotion(t_4) + PinkieMotion(t_5) \\ &= ICAbasis5(t_1) + ICAbasis3(t_2) + ICAbasis1(t_3) \\ &\quad + ICAbasis4(t_4) + ICAbasis2(t_5). \end{aligned} \tag{7}$$

Thus, any hand gesture can then be represented by 5 parameters t_1, t_2, t_3, t_4, t_5.

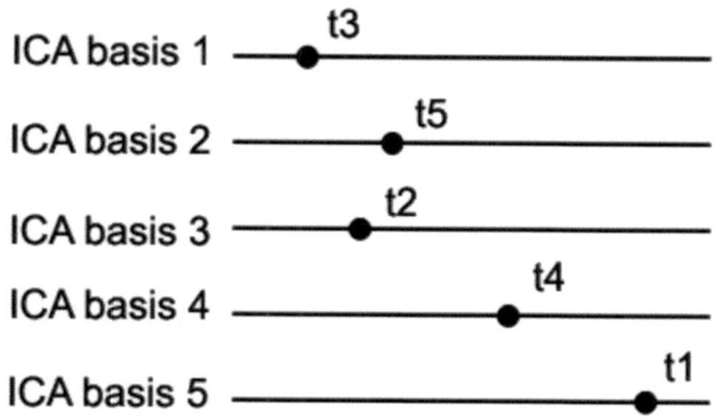

Figure 5. Each row represents the hand motion along the ICA basis vector. A hand pose is determined by five parameters t1-t5 which refer to time. The ICA basis 1 corresponds to a middle finger motion, the ICA basis 2 corresponds to a pinkie motion, the ICA basis 3

corresponds to an index finger motion, the ICA basis 4 corresponds to a ring finger motion, and the ICA basis 5 corresponds to a thumb motion.

3.7 Justification of the ICA-based hand model

When we solve the blind source separation problem, we need to know the number of source signals. To verify the 5-dimension ICA basis is sufficient to represent the finger pose and motion, we use "leave-one-out cross-validation". The result is shown in Fig. 6. In the figure, the vertical axis indicates root mean square (RMS) error, and the horizontal axis indicates the number of the ICA basis vectors used to recover a hand motion data. The average of RMS error is plotted along the vertical axis. The error bars shows maximum error and minimum error.

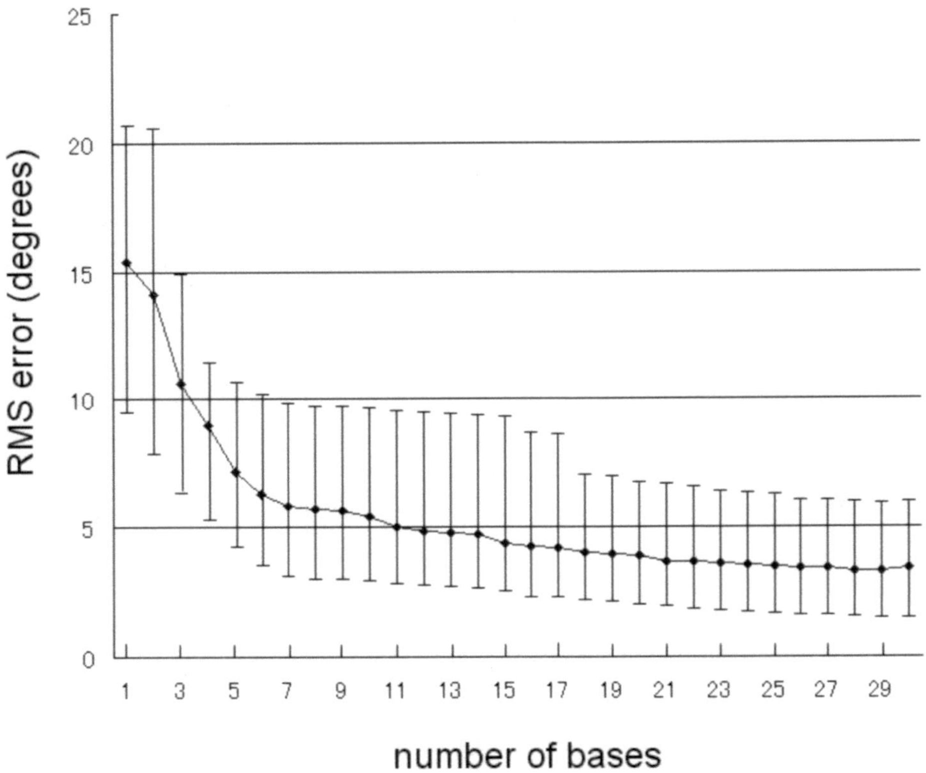

Figure 6. Leave-one-out cross-validation on the hand motion data set.

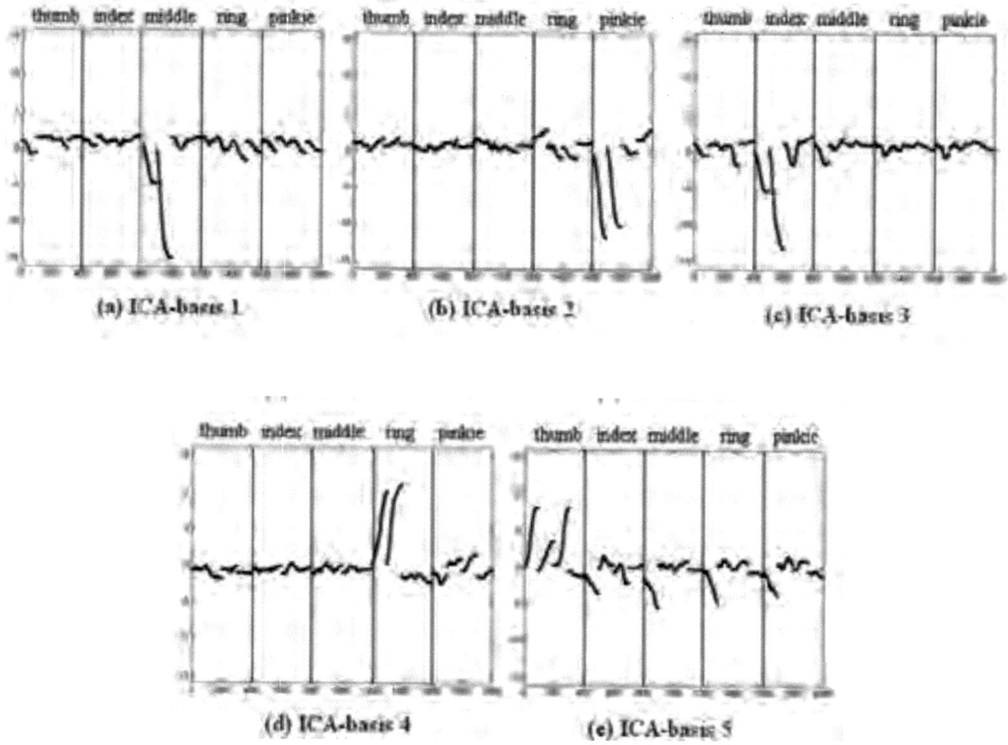

Figure 7. Five ICA basis vectors.

The five ICA basis vectors are shown in Fig. 7. ICA can be applied only if the independent components are "statistically independent" and also obey "non-gaussian" distribution. Here, the independent components are the ICA basis vectors. We calculate the covariance matrix of the independent components to verify statistically independent. The covariance matrix is

$$\begin{bmatrix} 7.6711 & -0.1993 & -0.3399 & 0.1826 & 0.162 \\ -0.1933 & 6.5648 & -0.1007 & 0.3804 & 0.3889 \\ -0.3399 & -0.1007 & 6.2993 & 0.1464 & 0.0071 \\ 0.1826 & 0.3804 & 0.1464 & 6.1052 & -0.3711 \\ 0.162 & 0.3889 & 0.0071 & -0.3711 & 4.4959 \end{bmatrix} \tag{8}$$

The covariance matrix is almost diagonal, which implies the independent components are statistically independent.

In order to measure "non-gaussianity" of the resulting independent components, we calculate the kurtosis of each independent component. Since the kurtosis of Gaussian distribution is equal to 0, we can measure "non-gaussianity" by calculating the kurtosis. The normalized kurtosis (Hyvarinen et al., 2001) is defined as

$$\frac{E\{x^4\}}{[E\{x^2\}]^2} - 3 \tag{9}$$

The normalized kurtosis of the independent components is shown in Table 1. Note that the normalized kurtosis of Gaussian distribution is equal to 0, that of Laplace distribution is 3, and that of exponential distribution is 6.

	Normalized kurtosis
ICA basis 1	16.6535
ICA basis 2	9.7997
ICA basis 3	13.1544
ICA basis 4	9.0106
ICA basis 5	4.3983

Table 1. Normalized kurtosis of each component.

4. Hand tracking by particle filtering

4.1 Particle filtering

The particle filtering algorithm (Djuric et al., 2003) is a sequential Monte Carlo method. The algorithm is powerful in approximating non-Gaussian probability distributions. Particle filtering is based on sequential importance sampling and Bayesian theory. With particle filtering, continuous distributions are approximated by discrete random sample sets, which are composed of weighted particles. The particles represent hypotheses of possible solutions and the weights represent likelihood.

There are three main steps in the algorithm: resampling, diffusion, and observation. The first step selects the particles for reproduction. In this step, particles that have heavier weights are more likely to be selected. Heavy-weight particles generate new ones, while light-weight particles are eliminated. The second step diffuses particles randomly. A part of space that is more likely to have a solution has more particles, while a part of space that is less likely to have a solution has fewer particles. The third step measures the weight of each particle according to an observation density. Fig. 8 shows a pictorial description of particle filtering.

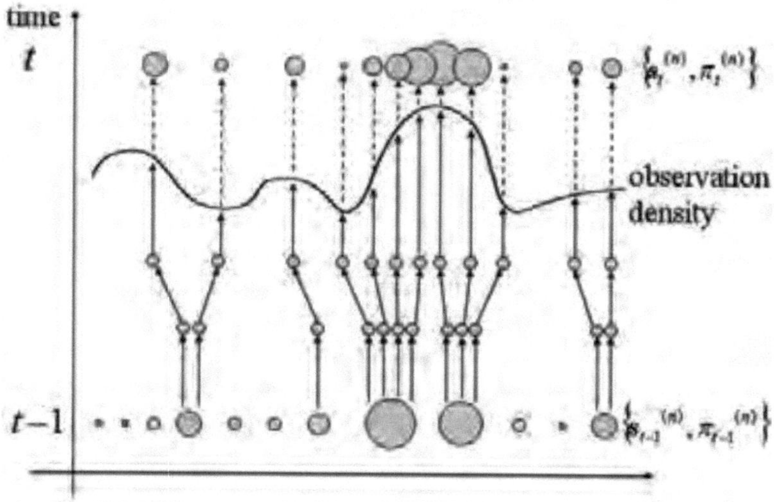

Figure 8. One time-step in particle filtering. There are 3 steps, resampling-diffusion-observation.

4.2 Generating particles

We implement particle filtering for tracking articulated hand motions. According to the Bayes rule, the hand pose of the current frame $\mathbf{x}_t$ can be estimated from the prior hand pose $\mathbf{x}_{t-1}$ as

$$p(\mathbf{x}_t \mid z_t) \propto p(z_t \mid \mathbf{x}_t) p(\mathbf{x}_t \mid z_{t-1}) \tag{10}$$

where z_t is the observation of the current frame.

The important part of particle filtering is to generate particles. In order to represent a posteriori $p(\mathbf{x}_t \mid z_t)$, we employ a time-stamped sample set, denoted $\{\mathbf{s}_t^{(n)}, n = 1, \cdots, N\}$, which is weighted by the observation density $\pi_t^{(n)} = p(z_t \mid \mathbf{x}_t = \mathbf{s}_t^{(n)})$. The weights $\pi_t^{(n)}$ are normalized so that $\sum_N \pi_t^{(n)} = 1$. Then the sample set $\{\mathbf{s}_t^{(n)}, \pi_t^{(n)}\}$ represents the posteriori $p(\mathbf{x}_t \mid z_t)$. The sample set is propagated from $\{\mathbf{s}_{t-1}^{(n)}, \pi_{t-1}^{(n)}\}$ which represents $p(\mathbf{x}_{t-1} \mid z_{t-1})$. A prior $p(\mathbf{x}_t \mid z_{t-1})$ can be represented as

$$p(\mathbf{x}_t \mid z_{t-1}) = \int_{\mathbf{x}_{t-1}} p(\mathbf{x}_t \mid \mathbf{x}_{t-1}) p(\mathbf{x}_{t-1} \mid z_{t-1}) \tag{11}$$

Then random samples are drawn along each ICA basis vector, i.e.,

$$s_t^{(n)} \sim p(s_t \mid s_{t-1}) = N(s_{t-1} \mid \sigma) \tag{12}$$

For finger motions, we can make samples along each ICA basis vector shown in Fig. 12 due to the efficient representation of hand pose by the ICA-based model. A finger motion is determined by five parameters in the ICA-based model which has five dimensions. Other parameters are position and rotation. They are presented by translation t_x, t_y, t_z and

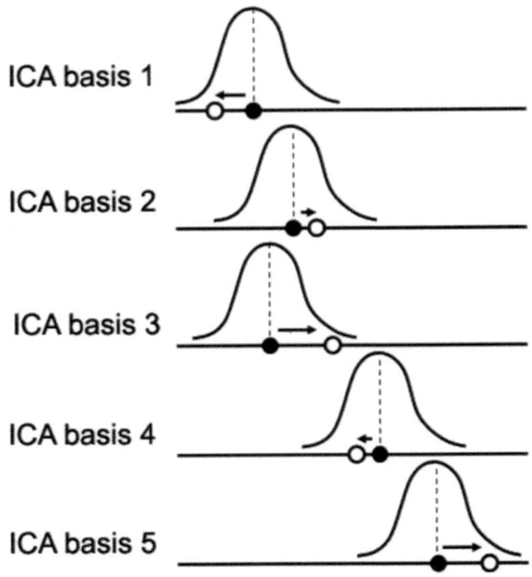

Figure 9. Generating hypotheses along each ICA basis vector. Black points indicate current sample s_t, while white circles indicate hypotheses s_{t+1}.

rotation r_x, r_y, r_z. They also propagate as

$$s_t^{(n)} \sim p(s_t \mid s_{t-1}) = N(s_{t-1} \mid \sigma_{translation}) \tag{13}$$

$$s_t^{(n)} \sim p(s_t \mid s_{t-1}) = N(s_{t-1} \mid \sigma_{rotation}) \tag{14}$$

Then the total dimensionality of $\mathbf{s}_t$ is 11, including 5 for finger motion, 3 for translation, and 3 for rotation.

5. Occlusion-free tracking by multiple cameras

5.1 Tracking by multiple cameras

We perform camera calibration so that the intrinsic parameters and positions and orientations of the cameras recovered (Zhang, 1999). Once the cameras are calibrated, a hand model is projected onto the images, and the projected images are compared with real observations so that the parameters of the hand model can be estimated. Since calibrated cameras do not increase unknown parameters, more images do not mean more parameters. They merely bring more information.

In our currently experiments, we use two cameras looking at the hand, with the two cameras separated by roughly 90 degrees. This brings a great improvement over using a single camera, and is sufficient in handling occlusions.

5.2 Relation between the hand model and two cameras

The relation between two cameras is drawn as follows. The 3D coordinate system centered at optical center of camera 1 is $\mathbf{X}$. The 3D coordinate system centered at optical center of

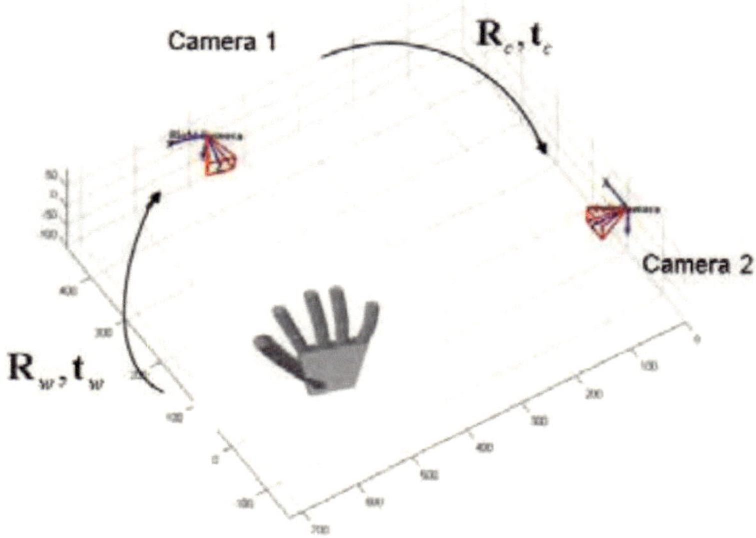

Figure 10. Relation between two cameras.

camera 2 is $\mathbf{X}'$. As depicted in Fig. 10, the rotation matrix and the translation vector from the coordinate system of camera 1 to the coordinate system of camera 2 are $\mathbf{R}_c, \mathbf{t}_c$. Then the relation between the two coordinate systems is given by

$$\mathbf{X} = \mathbf{R}_c \mathbf{X}' + \mathbf{t}_c \tag{15}$$

The 3D coordinate system of hand model is $\mathbf{X}_m$. The rotation matrix and the translation vector from the coordinate system of hand model to the coordinate system of camera 1 are $\mathbf{R}_w, \mathbf{t}_w$. Then the relation between the two coordinate systems is given by

$$\mathbf{X}_m = \mathbf{R}_w \mathbf{X} + \mathbf{t}_w \tag{16}$$

From (15) and (16), we can transform $\mathbf{X}_m$ to $\mathbf{X}$ and $\mathbf{X}'$, and then project the hand model onto the images.

5.3 Observation model

We employ edge and silhouette information to evaluate the hypotheses. For edge information, we employ the Chamfer distance function (Stenger et al., 2003). First, we perform Canny edge detection to the input image. In the result image of edge detection, the edge pixels are black and other pixels are white. Then, at each pixel, we calculate the distance from each pixel to the closest edge point by using distance transformation. If the distance is over a threshold, the distance is set to the threshold. A distance map of the input image is obtained. Fig. 11 (b) shows an example of distance map. Then we project the edge of the hand model onto the distance map. We add all distances along the edge points of the projected hand model, and calculate the average of distances. Then the likelihood from the edge information is

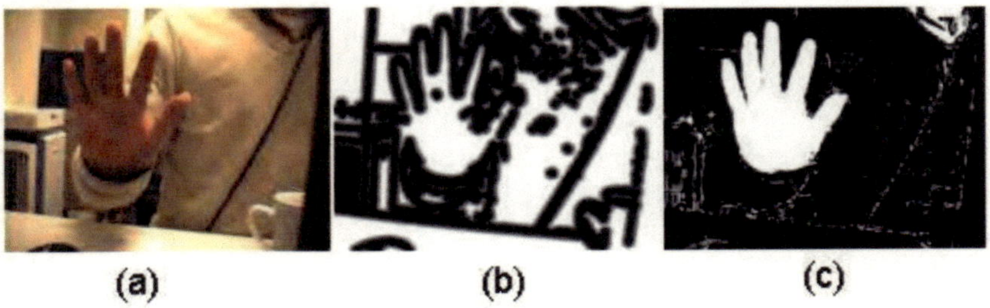

Figure 11. (a) Input image (b) Distance map of edge observation (c) Extracted silhouette

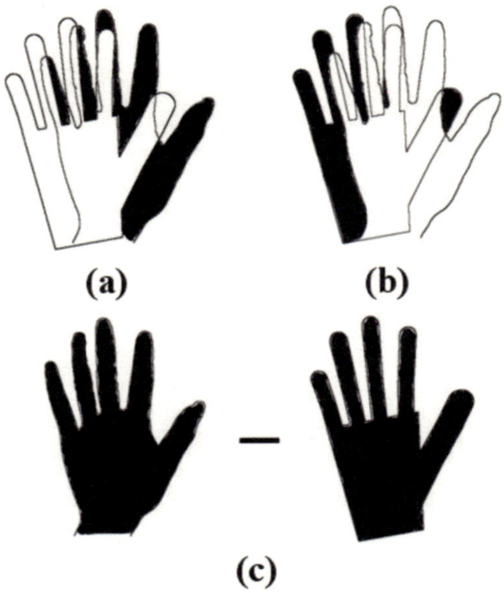

Figure 12. Areas of silhouette measurements. Black areas are the corresponding areas. (a) $a_I - a_O$, (b) $a_M - a_O$, (c) $a_I - a_M$. Note that a_I is the silhouette of input image, a_M is the silhouette of hand model, and a_O is the silhouette of overlap.

$$p_{edge}(z_t \mid \mathbf{x}_t) \propto \exp\left[-\frac{(averageDist)^2}{2\sigma_{edge}^2}\right] \quad (17)$$

where averageDist is the average of distances.
In order to extract the silhouette of a hand region, we convert image color space from RGB to HSV (hue, saturation and brightness). Then the skin color region is extracted by using a threshold. Fig. 11 (c) shows an extracted silhouette. We calculate subtractions of the area of silhouette. The three calculated subtraction results are shown in Fig. 12. The subtractions of $a_I - a_O$ and $a_M - a_O$ are used to measure the similarity of the hand position. The subtraction of $a_I - a_M$ is used to measure the similarity of hand finger pose. Then likelihoods from the silhouette information are

$$p_{sil\_IO}(z_t \mid \mathbf{x}_t) \propto \exp\left[-\frac{(a_I - a_O)^2}{2\sigma_{sil\_IO}^2}\right] \quad (18)$$

$$p_{sil\_MO}(z_t \mid \mathbf{x}_t) \propto \exp\left[-\frac{(a_M - a_O)^2}{2\sigma_{sil\_MO}^2}\right] \quad (19)$$

$$p_{sil\_IM}(z_t \mid \mathbf{x}_t) \propto \exp\left[-\frac{(a_I - a_M)^2}{2\sigma_{sil\_IM}^2}\right] \quad (20)$$

Thus the final likelihood is

$$p(z_t \mid \mathbf{x}_t) \propto p_{edge}(z_t \mid \mathbf{x}_t) p_{sil\_IO}(z_t \mid \mathbf{x}_t) p_{sil\_MO}(z_t \mid \mathbf{x}_t) p_{sil\_IM}(z_t \mid \mathbf{x}_t) \quad (21)$$

When we use multiple cameras, the likelihood is

$$p(z_t \mid \mathbf{x}_t) \propto \prod_{i=1}^{n} p_i(z_t \mid \mathbf{x}_t) \quad (22)$$

where n is the number of cameras.

5.4 Particle filtering with prediction

The classical particle filtering requires an impractically large number of particles to follow rapid motions and to keep tracking correct. It becomes a serious problem when the tracking target has a high dimensional state space like hand tracking. In order to tackle this problem, we propose using prediction to generate better proposal distributions.

According to the Bayes rule, the hand pose of the current frame $\mathbf{x}_t$ can be estimated from the prior hand pose $\mathbf{x}_{t-1}$ as

$$p(\mathbf{x}_t \mid z_{1:t}) \propto p(z_t \mid \mathbf{x}_t) p(\mathbf{x}_t \mid z_{1:t-1}) \tag{23}$$

where

$$p(\mathbf{x}_t \mid z_{1:t-1}) = \int_{\mathbf{x}_{t-1}} p(\mathbf{x}_t \mid \mathbf{x}_{t-1}) p(\mathbf{x}_{t-1} \mid z_{1:t-1}) \tag{24}$$

z_t is the observation of the current frame, $p(z_t \mid \mathbf{x}_t)$ is the likelihood distribution and $p(\mathbf{x}_t \mid \mathbf{x}_{t-1})$ is the transition probability distribution. (23) can be interpreted as the equivalent of the Bayes rule:

$$p(\mathbf{x} \mid z) \propto p(z \mid \mathbf{x}) p(\mathbf{x}) \tag{25}$$

Figure 13. Five-finger tracking with 50 particles by our method. The projection of OpenGL hand model's edge is drawn on the images

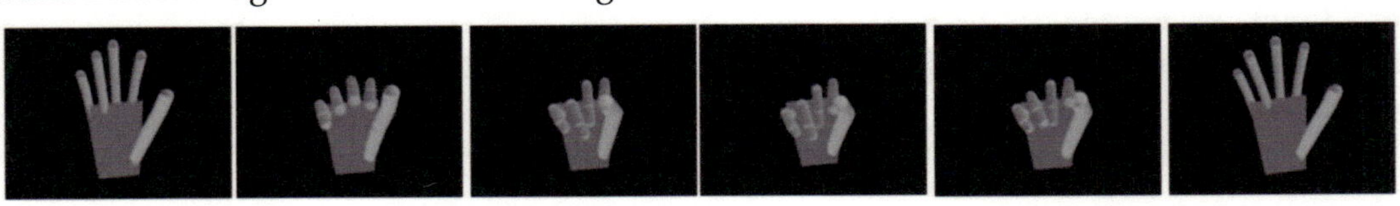

Figure 14. Examples of the corresponding OpenGL hand model of Fig. 13.

In particle filtering, the sequence of probability distributions is approximated by a large set of particles. Therefore, how to propagate the particles efficiently in areas of higher likelihood significantly affects tracking results. The particles are defined as follows: in order to represent a posteriori $p(\mathbf{x}_t \mid z_{1:t})$, we employ a time-stamped sample set, denoted $\{\mathbf{s}_t^{(n)}, n = 1, \cdots, N\}$. The sample set is weighted by the observation density $\pi_t^{(n)} = p(z_t \mid \mathbf{x}_t = \mathbf{s}_t^{(n)})$, where the weights $\pi_t^{(n)}$ are normalized so that $\sum_N \pi_t^{(n)} = 1$. Then the sample set $\{\mathbf{s}_t^{(n)}, \pi_t^{(n)}\}$ represents the posteriori $p(\mathbf{x}_t \mid z_{1:t})$. The sample set of the posteriori is propagated from $\{\mathbf{s}_{t-1}^{(n)}, \pi_{t-1}^{(n)}\}$ which represents $p(\mathbf{x}_{t-1} \mid z_{1:t-1})$ as shown in Fig. 6. The transition probability distribution $p(\mathbf{x}_t \mid \mathbf{x}_{t-1})$ affects $p(\mathbf{x}_t \mid z_{1:t-1})$, which in turn affects $p(\mathbf{x}_t \mid z_{1:t})$.

$p(\mathbf{x}_t \mid \mathbf{x}_{t-1})$ is modeled by a dynamical model. The simplest dynamical model is

$$\mathbf{s}_t^{(n)} = \mathbf{s}_{t-1}^{(n)} + \mathbf{B} \tag{26}$$

where $\mathbf{B}$ is a multivariate Gaussian distribution with covariance $\mathbf{P}$ and mean $\mathbf{0}$. However, this simple dynamical model does not propagate the particles efficiently and many particles are wasted in areas of lower likelihood.

To overcome these difficulties, we simply use the first-order approximation of Taylor series expansion for prediction:

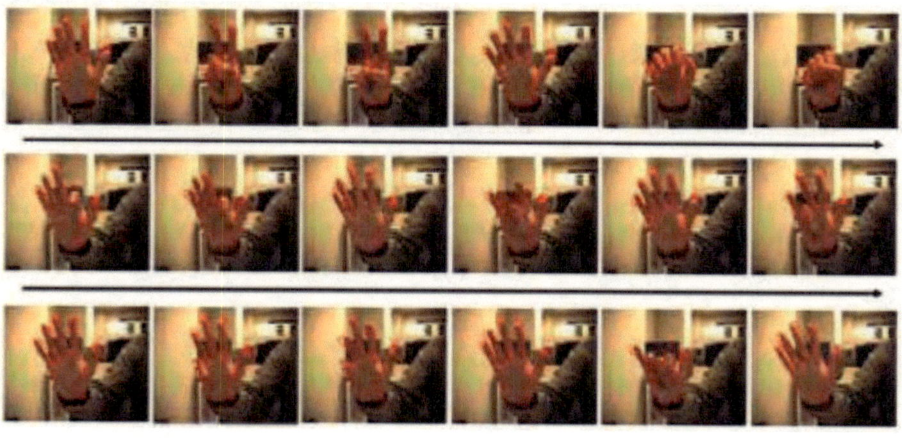

Figure 15. Demonstration of finger tracking with 200 particles. The projection of OpenGL hand model's edge is drawn on images.

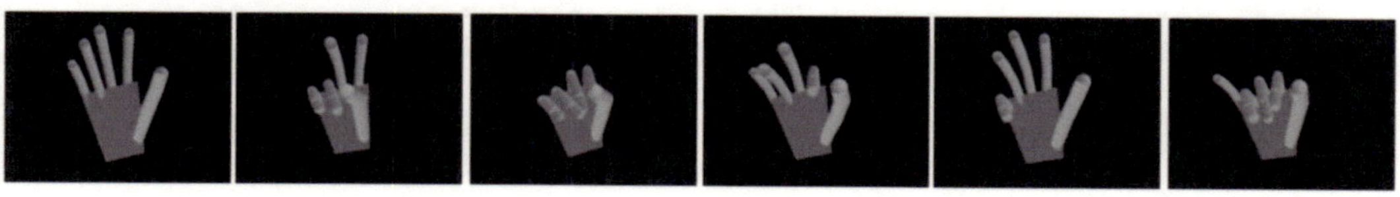

Figure 16. Examples of the corresponding OpenGL hand model of Fig. 15.

$$\mathbf{s}_t^{(n)} = \mathbf{s}_{t-1}^{(n)} + \frac{\partial \mathbf{s}_{t-1}^{(n)}}{\partial t}\Delta t + \mathbf{B} \tag{27}$$

We also tried to use the second-order approximation of Taylor series expansion

$$\mathbf{s}_t^{(n)} = \mathbf{s}_{t-1}^{(n)} + \frac{\partial \mathbf{s}_{t-1}^{(n)}}{\partial t}\Delta t + \frac{1}{2}\frac{\partial^2 \mathbf{s}_{t-1}^{(n)}}{\partial t^2}\Delta t^2 + \mathbf{B}\,. \tag{28}$$

However, the tracking gets trapped in local minima. The reason is that the second derivative cannot be estimated accurately due to noise.

6. Experimental results

The proposed algorithm has been tested on real image sequences. We collect training data using a data glove. The training data is 31 different hand motions as described in Chapter 4. At first, PCA is applied to reduce the dimensionality. Then ICA is applied to obtain the ICA basis vectors. We applied our tracking algorithm on real image sequences. In the experiment, we assume that the hand model is roughly matched with the hand at the first frame. Then our tracking algorithm automatically track hand motions. The hand model is manually initialized to fit finger length and palm size. The experimental results demonstrate the effectiveness of our method by tracking hand in real image sequences. The video sequence is available from http://www.cvg.is.ritsumei.ac.jp/~kmakoto/.

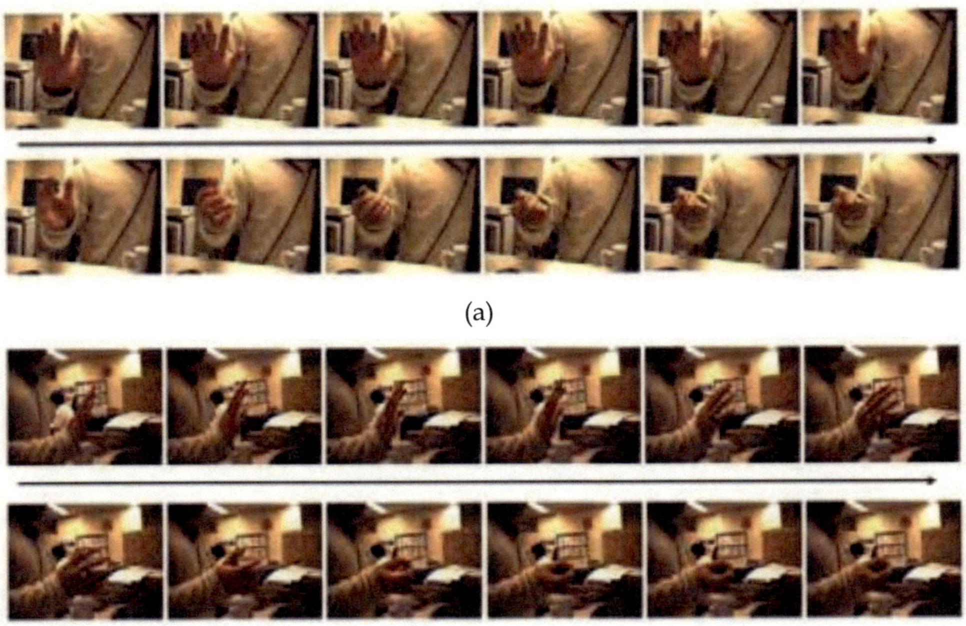

(a)

(b)

Figure 17. Two image sequences (a) and (b). (a) is taken by the left camera. (b) is taken by the right camera. The image sequences include rapid motion, large rotations angle against a camera, occlusions and a cluttered background

6.1 Tracking local motions by one camera

We did two experiments by using one camera. In the first experiment, we use 50 particles per frame. Fig. 13 shows some frames of video sequence. Fig. 14 shows some corresponding hand models. The second experiment includes some local finger motions including rock-paper-scissors. We use 200 particles per frame. Fig. 15 shows some frames of the video sequence and Fig. 16 shows some corresponding OpenGL hand models.

Experimental results show that the ICA-based model is very useful for articulated hand tracking in image sequences since all hand motions can be represented by only 5 parameters and each parameter corresponds to a particular finger motion in the ICA-based model.

6.2 Occlusion-free tracking by multiple cameras

The tracking by one camera has some limitations. One of the limitations is caused by occlusions. The other limitation is caused by extreme changes in rotation angle toward a camera. One solution to the problem is tracking by multiple cameras. The following two image sequences (Fig. 17) include rapid motion, large rotations angle against a camera, occlusions and a cluttered background.

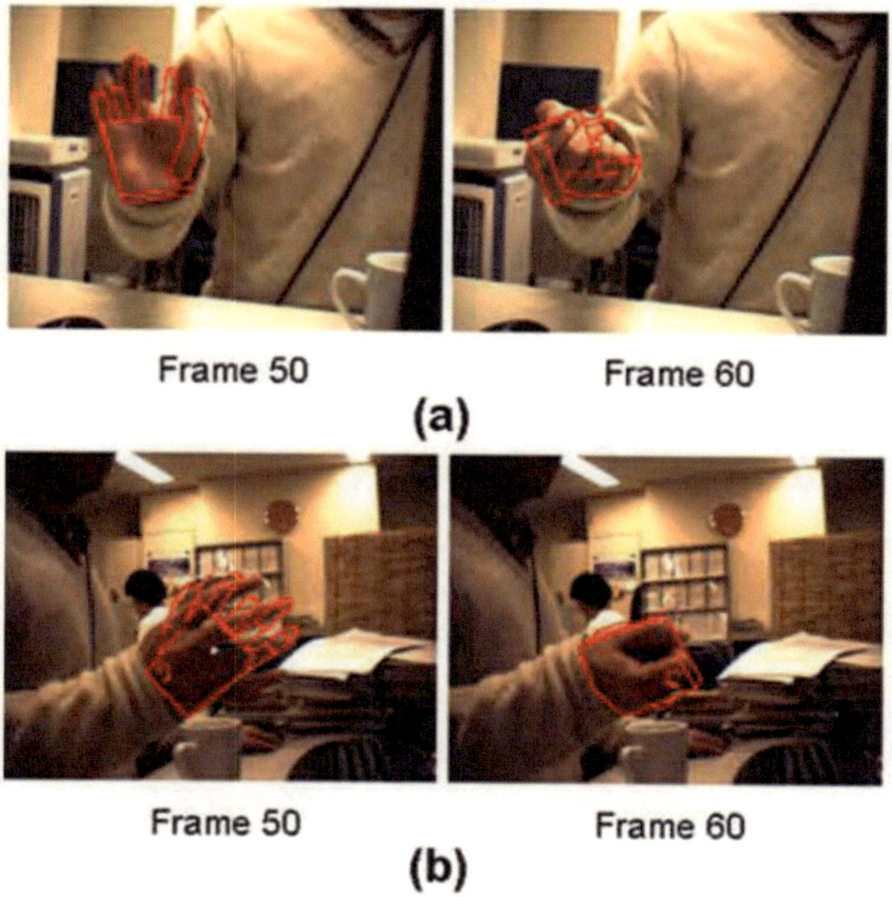

Figure 18. (a) Tracking result by the right camera only. (b) Tracking result by the left camera only.

At first, we tried the experiment by a single camera to two image sequences respectively, shown in Fig. 18 (a) and Fig. 18 (b). In Fig. 18 (a), at frame 50, the hand orientation is slightly incorrect and then the error becomes larger, finally, at frame 60, the hand orientation is completely incorrect. In Fig. 18 (b), at frame 50, the hand orientation is incorrect and then the error becomes larger, finally at frame 60, the tracking estimated that the hand fingers exist at the hand wrist position.

Fig. 19 shows the tracking result by multiple cameras. The experiment was run using 10000 particles per frame. The tracking correctly estimated hand position and motion throughout the sequence.

From the results, we can see that occlusion is a severe problem for tracking by a single camera but is not a problem for multiple cameras.

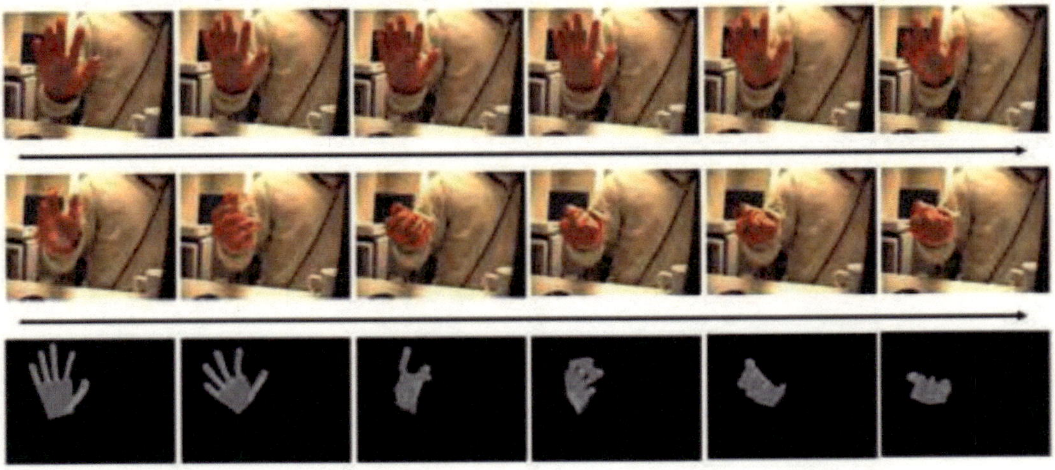

(a)

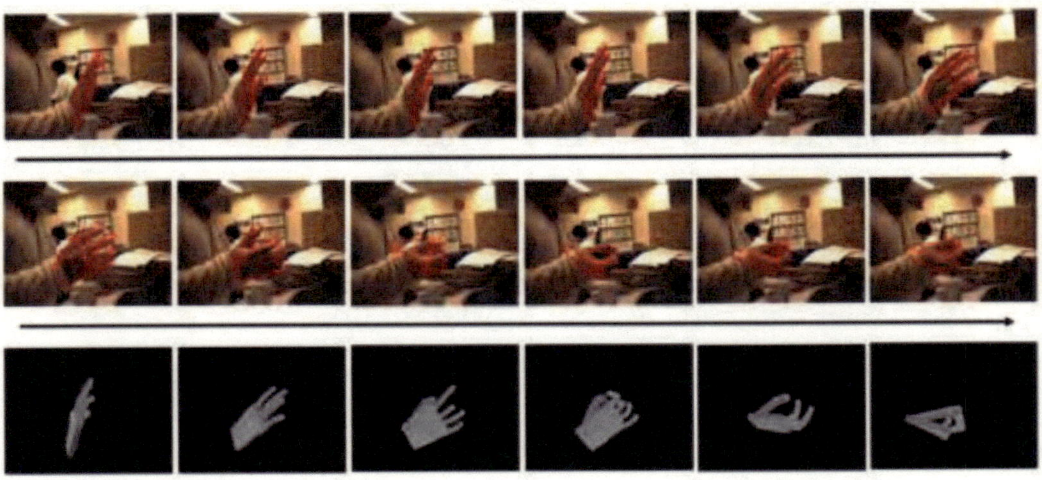

(b)

Figure 19. Tracking result by two cameras. (a) Camera 1 view. (b) Camera 2 view.

The projection of hand model's edge is drawn on the images by red lines. The CG models are examples of some corresponding hand models

6.3 Tracking with prediction

In this experiment, we compared the methods with prediction and without prediction. Fig. 20 (a) is the result without prediction and Fig. 20 (b) is that with prediction. In Fig 20 (a), at frame 50, the hand orientation is slightly incorrect, and then the error becomes larger and finally, at frame 60, the tracking estimated that the hand is upside down comparing with the real hand. While with the prediction, we can avoid such kind of error (Fig. 20 (b)).

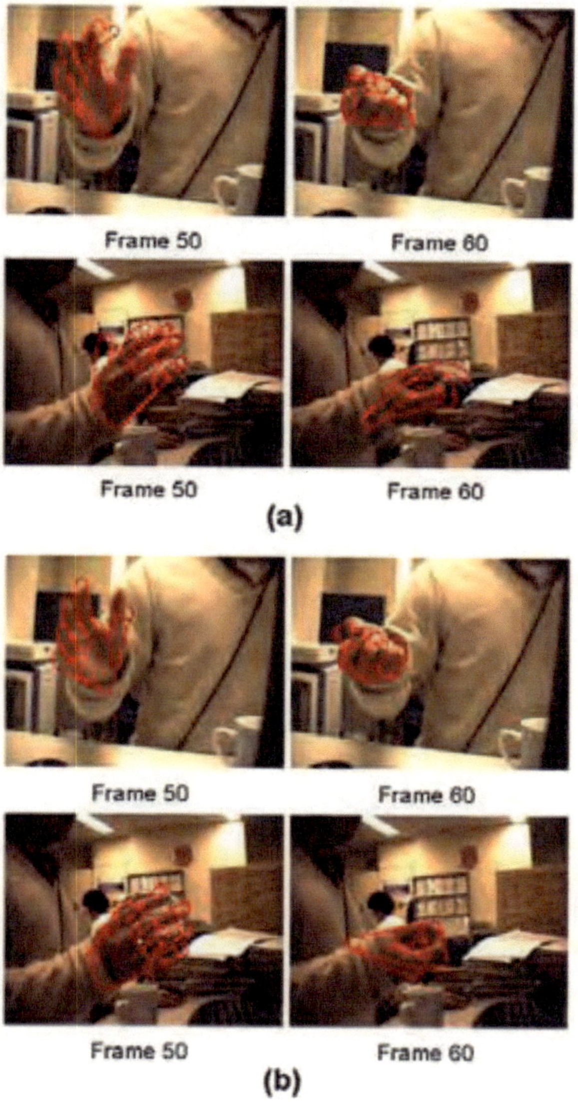

Figure 20. (a) Tracking result without prediction. (b) Tracking result with prediction.

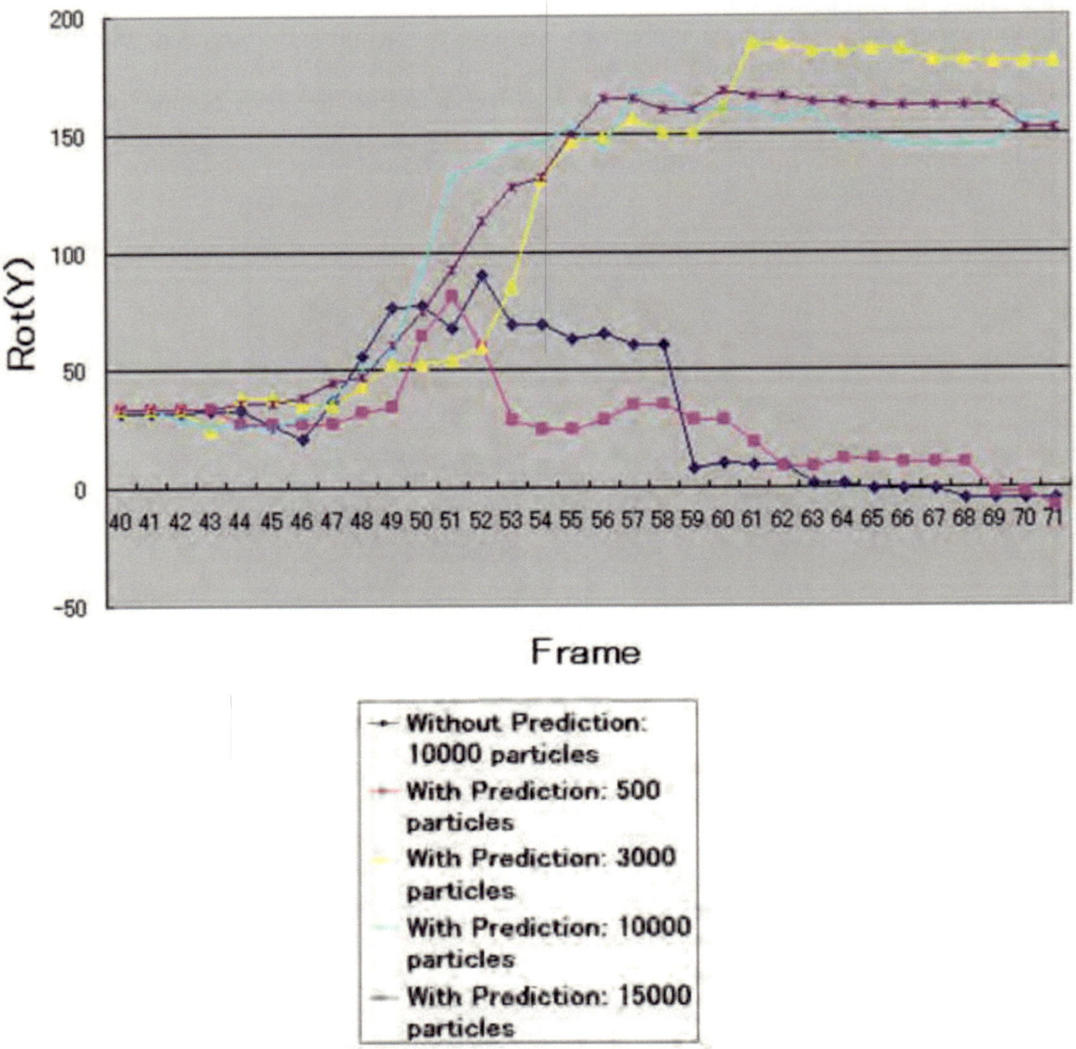

Figure 21. Trajectory of the rotation around Y axis (unit: degrees).

6.4 The number of particles

We also did experiments with different numbers of particles per frame in order to find out how many particles are suitable for the tracking. We show the trajectory of the rotation around Y axis in Fig. 21.

We did the experiment with 500 particles, 3000 particles, 10000 particles and 15000 particles. The results have dramatic change when we increase the number of particles from 500 to 10000. And the results only have slight change when we increase the number of particles from 10000 to 15000. Therefore, 10000 is the optimized number of particles for this hand motion.

7. Conclusion

In this chapter, we proposed three new approaches, the ICA-based hand model, articulated hand motion tracking by multiple cameras, and Particle filtering with prediction.
The ICA-based hand model is the ICA-based representation of hand articulation for tracking hand-finger gestures in image sequences. The dimensionality of the hand motion space is reduced by PCA and then ICA is applied to extract the local feature vectors. In the ICA-based model, each of the first five basis vectors corresponds to a particular finger motion, because the joints in each finger have stronger dependencies than the joints across different fingers. In the ICA-based model, hand poses can be represented by five parameters with each parameter corresponding to a particular finger motion. We implemented articulated hand motion tracking by particle filter using this ICA-based hand model. Experimental results show that the ICA-based model is very useful for articulated hand tracking in image sequences.
Next approach is an articulated hand motion tracking by multiple cameras. This method is useful for gesture recognition. Tracking a free hand motion against a cluttered background was unachievable in previous methods because hand fingers are self-occluding. To improve search efficiency, we proposed adding prediction to particle filtering so that more particles are generated in areas of higher likelihood. The experimental results show that our method can correctly and efficiently track the hand motion throughout the image sequences even if hand motion has large rotation against a camera.
The methods in this chapter are easily extended to many other visual motion capturing tasks.

8. References

Bartlett, M. S.; Movellan, J. R. & Sejnowski, T. J. (2002). Face Recognition by Independent Component Analysis, *IEEE Trans. Neural Networks*, vol.13, no.6, pp.1450-1464, Nov. 2002.

Bell, A. J. & Sejnowski, T. J. (1995). An information-maximization approach to blind separation and blind deconvolution, *Neural Computation*, vol.7, no.6, pp.1129-1159, 1995.

Bray, M.; Meier, E. K. & Gool, L. V. (2004). Smart Particle Filtering for 3D Hand Tracking, *Proceedings of Int'l Conf. Face and Gesture recognition*, pp. 675-680, 2004.

Deutscher, J.; Blake, A. & Reid, I. (2000). Articulated Body Motion Capture by Annealed Particle Filtering, *Proceedings of Computer Vision and Pattern Recognition*, Vol. 2, pp. 126-133, 2000.

Djuric, P. M.; Kotecha, J. H.; Zhang, J.; Huang, Y.; Ghirmai, T.; Bugallo, M. F. & Miguez, J. (2003). Particle filtering, *IEEE Signal Processing Magazine*, pp.19-38, Sept. 2003.

Hyvarinen, A.; Karhunen, J. & Oja, E. (2001). *Independent Component Analysis.* Wiley, 978-0471405405, New York.

Isard, M. & Blake, A. (1998). CONDENSATION-conditional density propagation for visual tracking, *Int. J .Computer Vision*, 1998.

Lee, J. & Kunii, T. (1995). Model-based analysis of hand posture, *IEEE Computer Graphics and Applications*, 15: pp.77-86, Sept. 1995.

Rehg, J. & Kanade, T. (1995). Model-Based Tracking of Self Occluding Articulated Objects, *Proceedings of Int'l Conf. Computer Vision*, pp. 612-617, 1995.

Rui, Y. & Chen, Y. (2001). Better Proposal Distributions: Object Tracking Using Unscented Particle Filter, *Proceedings of Computer Vision and Pattern Recognition*, Vol. 2, pp. 786-793, 2001.

Sminchisescu, C. & Triggs, B. (2001). Covariance Scaled Sampling for Monocular 3D Body Tracking, *Proceedings of Computer Vision and Pattern Recognition*, Vol. 1, pp. 447-454, 2001.

Stenger, B.; Thayananthan, A.; Torr, P. H. S. & Cipolla, R. (2003). Filtering using a tree-based estimator, *Proceedings of Int'l Conf. Computer Vision*, pp.1102-1109, Nice, France, October 2003.

Wu, Y.; Lin, J. & Huang, T. S. (2001). Capturing natural hand articulation, *Proceedings of Int'l Conf. Computer Vision*, pp.426-432, Vancouver, July 2001.

Zhang, Z. (1999). Flexible Camera Calibration by Viewing a Plane from Unknown Orientations, *Proceedings of Int'l Conf. Computer Vision*, pp.666-673, Greece, Sept 1999.

Zhou, H. & Huang, T. S. (2003). Tracking Articulated Hand Motion with Eigen Dynamics Analysis, *Proceedings of Int'l Conf. Computer Vision*, pp.1102-1109, Nice, France, October 2003.

27

Biologically Motivated Vergence Control System Based on Stereo Saliency Map Model

Sang-Woo Ban[a] & Minho Lee[b,c]
[a]Dept. of Information and Communication Engineering, Dongguk University
South Korea
[b]School of Electrical Engineering and Computer Science, Kyungpook National University
South Korea
[c]Dept. of Brain and Cognitive Science, Massachusetts Institute of Technology
USA

1. Introduction

When the human eye searches a natural scene, the left and right eyes converge on an interesting area by action of the brain and the eyeballs. This mechanism is based on two attention processes. In a top-down (or volitional) processing, the human visual system determines salient locations through perceptive processing such as understanding and recognition. On the other hand, with bottom-up (or image-based) processing, the human visual system determines salient locations obtained from features that are based on the basic information of an input image such as intensity, color, and orientation. Bottom-up processing is a function of primitive selective attention in the human vision system since humans selectively attend to a salient area according to various stimuli in the input scene (Itti et al., 1998). If we can apply the human-like vergence function considered human attention process to an active stereo vision system, an efficient and intelligent vision system can be developed. Researchers have been developing the vergence stereo system. It was known that the two major sensory drives for vergence and accommodation are disparity and blur (Krishnan & Stark, 1977; Hung & Semmlow, 1980). Krotkov organized the stereo system through waking up the camera, gross focusing, orienting the cameras, and obtaining depth information (Krotkov, 1987). Abbott and Ahuja proposed surface reconstruction by dynamic integration of the focus, camera vergence and stereo disparity (Abbott & Ahuja, 1988). These approaches give good results for a specific condition, but it is difficult to use these systems in real environment because the region extraction based on intensity information is very sensitive to luminance change. For mimicking a human vision system, Yamato implemented a layered control system for stereo vision head with vergence control function. This system utilized a search of the most similar region based on the sum of absolute difference (SAD) for tracking. The vergence module utilized a minimum SAD search for each pixel to obtain figure-ground separation in 3D space (Yamato, 1999). But these systems may not give good results when the camera is moving with background because the SAD contains much noise by moving the camera. Jian Peng et al. made that an active vision system enables the selective capture of information for a specific colored object

(Peng et al., 2000). But this system only considered the color information for the selective attention. Thus, the developed active vision only operates for a specific color object and the luminance change deteriorate performance of the system. Bernardino and Victor implemented vergence control stereo system using log-polar images (Bernardino & Santos-Victor, 1996). This work considers only the intensity information. Batista et al. made a vergence control stereo system using retinal optical flow disparity and target depth velocity (Batista et al., 2000). But this system mainly converges on the moving object because of optical flow. Thus, this system only considered the motion information of retina and do not consider intensity, edge and symmetry as retina operation. Moreover, these all approaches take a lot of computation load to get the vergence control. Therefore, we need a new method not only to sufficiently reflect information of images such as color, intensity and edge but also to reduce the computation load during vergence control. Conradt et al. proposed a stereo vision system using a biologically inspired saliency map (SM) (Conradt et al., 2002). They detected landmarks in both images with interaction between the feature detectors and the SM, and obtained their direction and distance. They considered intensity, color, and circles of different radius, and horizontal, vertical and diagonal edges as features. However, they do not consider the occlusion problem. Also their proposed model does not fully consider the operation of the brain visual signal processing mechanism because they only considered the roles of neurons in the hippocampus responding to mainly depth information. On the other hand, the selective attention mechanism allows the human vision system to process visual scenes more effectively with a higher level of complexity. The human visual system sequentially interprets not only a static monocular scene but also a stereo scene based on the selective attention mechanism. In previous research, Itti and Koch (Itti et al., 1998) introduced a brain-like model in order to generate the saliency map (SM). Koike and Saiki (Koike & Saiki, 2002) proposed that a stochastic WTA enables the saliency-based search model to vary the relative saliency in order to change search efficiency, due to stochastic shifts of attention. Timor and Brady (Kadir & Brady, 2001) proposed an attention model integrating saliency, scale selection and a content description, thus contrasting many other approaches. Ramström and Christensen (Ramstrom & Christensen, 2002) calculated saliency with respect to a given task by using a multi-scale pyramid and multiple cues. Their saliency computations were based on game theory concepts. In recent work, Itti's group proposed a new attention model that considers seven dynamic features for MTV-style video clips (Carmi & Itti, 2006) and also proposed an integrated attention scheme to detect an object, which combined bottom-up SM with top-down attention based on signal-to-noise ratio (Navalpakkam & Itti, 2006). Also, Walter and Koch proposed an object preferable attention scheme which considers the bottom-up SM results as biased weights for top-down object perception (Walther et al., 2005). Also, Lee et al. have been proposed a bottom-up SM model using symmetry information with an ICA filter (Park et al., 2002) and implemented a human-like vergence control system based on a selective attention model, in which the proposed model reflects a human's interest in an area by reinforcement and inhibition training mechanisms (Choi et al., 2006). Ouerhani and Hugli proposed a saliency map model considering depth information as a feature (Ouerhani and Hugli, 2000). They insisted that little attention has been devoted so far to scene depth as source for visual attention and also pointed that this is considered as a weakness of the previously proposed attention models because depth or 3D vision is an intrinsic component of biological vision (Ouerhani and Hugli, 2000). Ouerhani and Hugli just used range finder for getting depth information but did not consider any mechanism about how to deal with binocular vision process. None of the proposed attention models, however, consider the integration of a stereo type bottom-up SM model and a top-down selective attention scheme reflecting human's preference and refusal. In this paper, we propose a new human-like vergence control method for an active stereo vision system based on stereo visual selective attention model. The proposed system reflects the single eye alignment mechanism during an infant's development for binocular fixation, and also uses a selective attention model to localize an interesting area in each camera. The proposed method reflects the biological stereo visual signal processing mechanism from the retinal operation to the visual cortex. Thus, we use a new selective attention model for implementing a human-like vergence control system based on a selective attention mechanism not only with truly bottom-up process but also with low-level top-down attention to skip an unwanted area and/or to pay attention to a desired area for reflecting human's preference and refusal mechanism in subsequent visual search process such as the pulvinar. Moreover, the proposed selective attention model considers depth information to construct a final attention area so that the closer attention area can be easily pop-up as our binocular eyes. Using the left and right saliency maps generated by the proposed selective attention models for two input images from left and right cameras, the selected object area in the master camera is compared with that in the slave camera to identify whether the two cameras find a same landmark. If the left and right cameras successfully find a same landmark, the implemented active vision system with two cameras focuses on the landmark. To prevent it from being a repetitively attended region in the vision system, the converged region is masked by an inhibition of return (IOR) function. Then the vision system continuously searches a new converged region by the above procedure. The practical purpose of the proposed system is to get depth information for efficient robot vision by considering focusing on an interesting object only by training process. Moreover, the proposed method can give a way to solve the occlusion problem. The depth information of the developed system will operate for avoiding an obstacle in a robotic system. Based on the proposed algorithm together with an effort to reduce the computation load, we implemented a human-like active stereo vision system. Computer simulation and experimental results show that the proposed vergence control method is very effective in implementing the human-like active stereo vision system. In Section 2, we briefly discuss the biological background of the proposed model and the proposed stereo visual selective attention model. In Section 3, we explain the landmark selection algorithm in each camera, the verification of the landmarks and depth estimation using eye gaze matching. In Section 4, we explain the hardware setup and describe computer simulation and the experimental results. The discussion and conclusion will be followed in Section 5.

2. Stereo visual selective attention

2.1 Biological understanding

Fig. 1 shows the biological visual pathway from the retina to the visual cortex through the LGN for the bottom-up processing, which is extended to the extrastriate cortex and the prefrontal cortex for the top-down processing. In order to implement a human-like visual attention function, we consider the bottom-up saliency map (SM) model and top-down trainable attention model. In our approach, we reflect the functions of the retina cells, LGN and visual cortex for the bottom-up processing, and dorsolateral prefrontal, posterior parietal cortex, the anterior cingulated gyrus, and the pulvinar nucleus of the thalamus for the top-down processing (Goldstein, 1995).

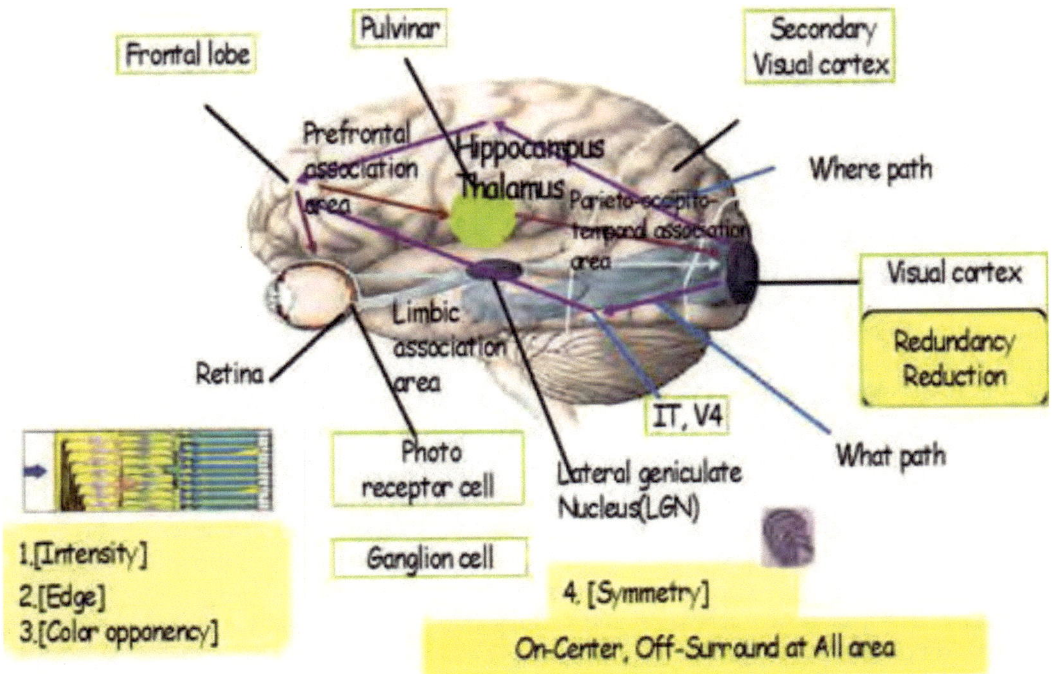

Figure 1. Biological visual pathway of bottom-up and top-down processing

Fig. 2 shows the proposed stereo saliency map model in conjunction with vergence control process based on the simulated biological visual pathway from the retina to the visual cortex through the LGN for the bottom-up processing, which is extended to the limbic system including the pulvinar for the top-down processing. In order to implement a human-like visual attention function, three processes are integrated to generate a stereo SM. One generates static saliency in terms of monocular vision. Another considers low-level top-down process for reflecting human preference and refusal, which mimics the function of the pulvinar in the limbic system. Finally, we can build stereo SM based on two monocular SMs and depth in terms of binocular vision.

2.2 Static bottom-up saliency map

Based on the Treisman's feature integration theory (Treisman & Gelde, 1980), Itti and Koch used three basis feature maps: intensity, orientation and color information (Itti et al., 1998). Extending Itti and Koch's SM model, we previously proposed SM models which include a symmetry feature map based on the generalized symmetry transformation (GST) algorithm

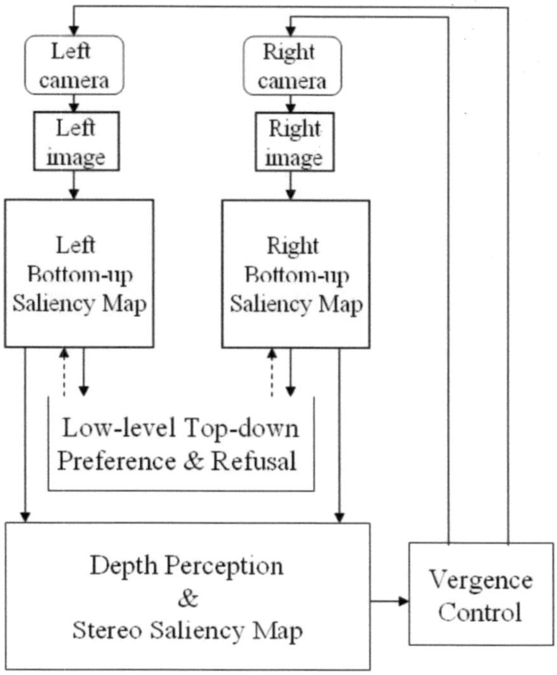

Figure 2. Stereo saliency map model including the static bottom-up SM process, the low-level top-down preference and refusal process and depth perception

and an independent component analysis (ICA) filter to integrate the feature information (Park et al., 2002; Park et al., 2000). In this paper, we investigate through intensive computer experiment how much the proposed symmetry feature map and the ICA filter are important in constructing an object preferable attention model. Also, we newly incorporate the neural network approach of Fukushima (Fukushima, 2005) to construct the symmetry feature map, which is more biologically plausible and takes less computation than the GST algorithm (Park et al., 2000). Symmetrical information is also important feature to determine the salient object, which is related with the function of LGN and primary visual cortex (Li, 2001). Symmetry information is very important in the context free search problem (Reisfeld et al., 1995).In order to implement an object preferable attention model, we emphasize using a symmetry feature map because an object with arbitrary shape contains symmetry information, and our visual pathway also includes a specific function to detect a shape in an object (Fukushima, 2005; Werblin & Roska, 2004). In order to consider symmetry information in our SM model, we modified Fukushima's neural network to describe a symmetry axis (Fukushima, 2005). Fig. 3 shows the static bottom-up saliency map model. In the course of computing the orientation feature map, we use 6 different scale images (a Gaussian pyramid) and implement the on-center and off-surround functions using the center surround and difference with normalization (CSD & N) (Itti et al., 1998; Park et al., 2002). As shown in Fig. 4, the orientation information in three successive scale images is used for obtaining the symmetry axis from Fukushima's neural network (Fukushima, 2005). By applying the CSD&N to the symmetry axes extracted in four different scales, we can obtain a symmetry feature map. This procedure mimics the higher-order analysis mechanism of complex cells and hyper-complex cells in the posterior visual cortex area,

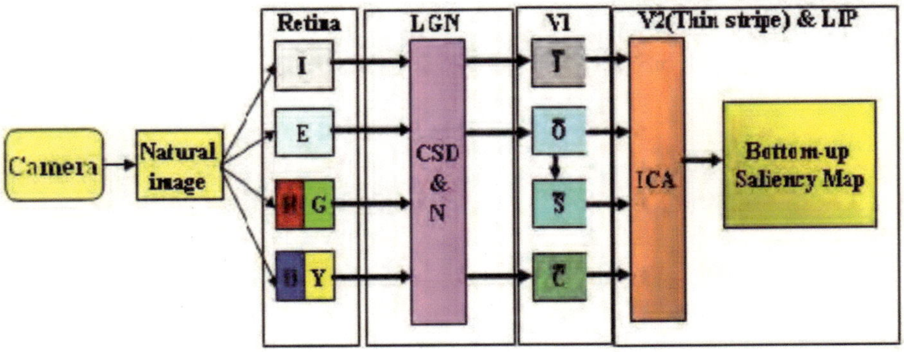

Figure 3. Static bottom-up saliency map model (I: intensity feature, E: edge feature, RG: red-green opponent coding feature, BY: blue-yellow opponent coding feature, LGN: lateral geniculate nucleus, CSD&N: center-surround difference and normalization, I : intensity feature map, O : orientation feature map, S : symmetry feature map, C : color feature map, ICA: independent component analysis)

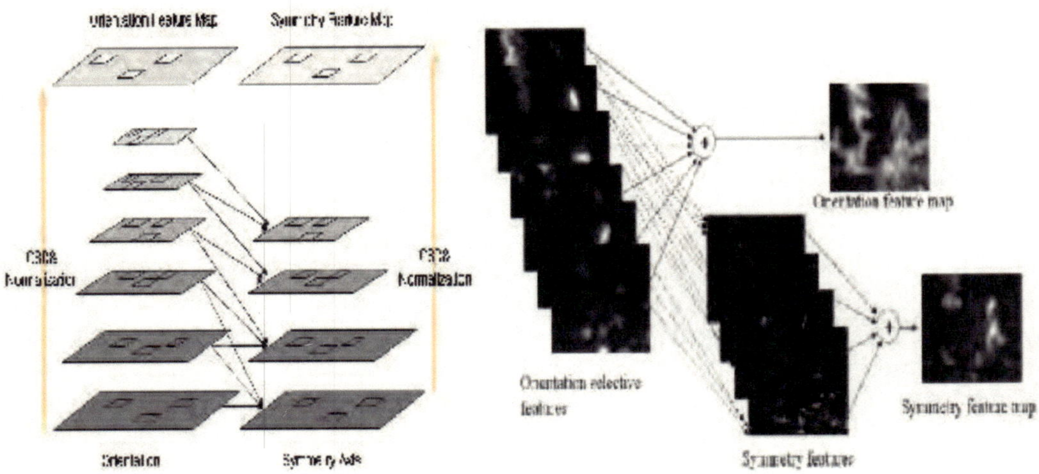

Figure 4. Symmetry feature map generation process

beyond the orientation-selective simple cells in the V1. Using CSD&N in Gaussian pyramidimages (Itti et al., 1998), we can construct the intensity (I), color (C), and orientation (O)feature maps as well as the symmetry feature map (S). Based on both Barlow's hypothesis that human visual cortical feature detectors might be the end result of a redundancy reduction process (Barlow & Tolhust, 1992)and Sejnowski's results that ICA is the best way to reduce redundancy (Bell & Sejnowski, 1997), the four constructed feature maps (*I, C, O, and S*) are then integrated by an independent componentanalysis (ICA) algorithm based on maximization of entropy (Bell & Sejnowski, 1997). Fig. 5 shows the procedure for computing the SM. In Fig. 5, S(x,y) is obtained by summation of the convolution between the r-th channel of input image(I_r) and the i-th filters(ICs_{ri}) obtained by the ICA learning [9]. A static SM is obtained by Eq. (1).

$$S(x, y) = \sum I_r * ICs_{ri} \quad \textit{for all } I \tag{1}$$

Since we obtained the independent filters by ICA learning, the convolution result shown in Eq. (1) can be regarded as a measure for the relative amount of visual information. The lateral-intra parietal cortex (LIP) plays a role in providing a retinotopic spatio-feature map that is used to control the spatial focus of attention and fixation, which is able to integrate feature information in its spatial map (Lanyon & Denham, 2004). As an integrator of spatial and feature information, the LIP provides the inhibition of return (IOR) mechanism required here to prevent the scan path returning to previously inspected sites (Lanyon & Denham, 2004).

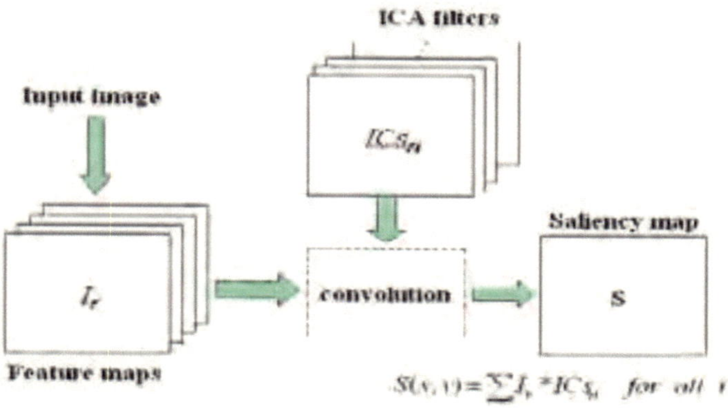

Figure 5. Saliency map generation process using ICA filter

2.3 Low-level top-down selective attention

Although the proposed bottom-up static SM model generates plausible salient areas and a scan path, the selected areas may not be an interesting area for human because the SM only uses primitive features such as intensity, color, orientation and symmetry information. In order to implement a more plausible selective attention model, we need to consider low-level top-down mechanism that can reflect human preference and refusal for visual features. Human beings ignore uninteresting areas, even if they have primitive salient features, and they can memorize the characteristics of the unwanted area. Humans do not pay attention to new areas that have characteristics similar to learned unwanted areas. In addition, human perception can focus on an interesting area, even if it does not have primitive salient features, or if it is less salient than the other areas. We propose a new selective attention model that mimics the human-like selective attention mechanism and that can consider not only primitive input features, but also interactive properties with humans in the environment. Moreover, the human brain can learn and memorize many new things without catastrophic forgetting. It is well known that a fuzzy adaptive resonance theory (ART) network can easily be trained for additional input pattern. Also, it can solve the stability-plasticity dilemma in a conventional multi-layer neural network (Carpenter et al., 1992). Therefore, as shown in Fig. 6, we use a fuzzy ART network together with a bottom-up

SM model to implement a selective attention model with preference and refusal process that can interact with a human supervisor. During the training process, the fuzzy ART network "learns" and "memorizes"the characteristics of uninteresting and/or interesting areas decided by a human supervisor. After the successful training of the fuzzy ART network, an unwanted salient area isinhibited and a desired area is reinforced by the vigilance value ρof the fuzzy ART network, as shown in Fig. 6. As shown in Fig. 6, corresponding four feature maps from the attended area obtained fromthe SM are normalized and then represented as one dimensional array X that are composedof every pixel value a_i of the four feature maps and each complement a_i^c computed by $1-a_i$, which are used as an input pattern of the fuzzy ART model. Then, the fuzzy ART model consecutively follows three processes such as a choice process, a match process and an adaptation process.

During a choice process, for every node Y_j in the F2 layer, a net activity y_j is calculated using a fuzzy conjunction operator ($\wedge$) as shown in Eq. (2), which can be seen as the degree of prototype bottom-up weight vector W_j, being a fuzzy subset of input pattern X

$$y_j = \frac{|X \wedge W_j|}{\alpha + |W_j|} \tag{2}$$

where the fuzzy conjunction $\wedge$ is computed by component wise min operator and the magnitude operator $|\cdot|$ of a vector is calculated by its L_1-norm defined by the sum of its components. And the parameter α works for avoiding a floating point overflow. Node Y_j in the F_2 layer with the highest value y_j is chosen as the winner node. After selecting the winner node for input pattern X, the fuzzy ART checks the similarity of input pattern X and the top-down weight vector W_J of the winner node Y_J as shown in Eq. (3)

$$\rho \leq \frac{|X \wedge W_J|}{|X|} \tag{3}$$

where a vigilance parameter ρ is defining the minimum similarity between input pattern and the prototype of the winner node. The synaptic top-down weight vector W_J are identical to the bottom-up weight vector W_j. If the similarity is lager than the vigilance value, then the vector W_J is adapted by moving its values toward the common MIN vector of X and W_J as shown in equation (4)

$$W_J^{(new)} = \eta(X \wedge W_J^{(old)}) + (1-\eta)W_J^{(old)} \tag{4}$$

where η is a learning rate. When Eq. (3) is satisfied, we call resonance is occurred. However, if the similarity is less than the vigilance, the current winning F2-node is removed from the competition by a reset signal. The fuzzy ART searches again a node with the next most similar weight vector with the input pattern X before an uncommitted prototype is chosen. If none of the committed nodes matches the input pattern well enough, search will end with the recruitment of an uncommitted prototype (Frank et al., 1998).

As the number of training patterns increases, however, the fuzzy ART network requires more time to reinforce or inhibit some selected areas. For faster analysis in finding an inhibition and/or reinforcement area, we employed the hierarchical structure of this network. Fig. 7 shows the modified hierarchical structure model of the fuzzy ART. The hierarchy of this network consists of a five-layer concatenated structure, in which each layer represents a different hierarchical abstract level of information. The highest level of the model stores the most abstract information that represents a highly abstract cluster. The lowest level of the model stores more detailed information. The input of the higher level in the model is generated by dimension reduction of the input of the lower level by averaging operator. For example, if the dimension of input for the lowest level is 32 by 32, the dimension of the next higher level becomes 16 by 16. The input pattern comparison with the memorized patterns of the model starts from the highest level, then the proposed model progress to the lower level according to the resonance result at the fuzzy ART module for the level. In the highest level, the input dimension is so small that it takes short time to finish the process of the fuzzy ART module. If the current input pattern has no resonance in the highest level, the hierarchical model can finish the process without considering the other lower levels, through which it can reduce the computation time. After the training process of the model is successfully finished, it memorizes the characteristics of the unwanted or desired areas in order to reflect human's preference and refusal. If a salient area selected by the bottom-up SM model of a test image has similar characteristics to the fuzzy ART memory, it is ignored by inhibiting that area in the SM or it is magnified by reinforcing that area in the SM according to human interest.

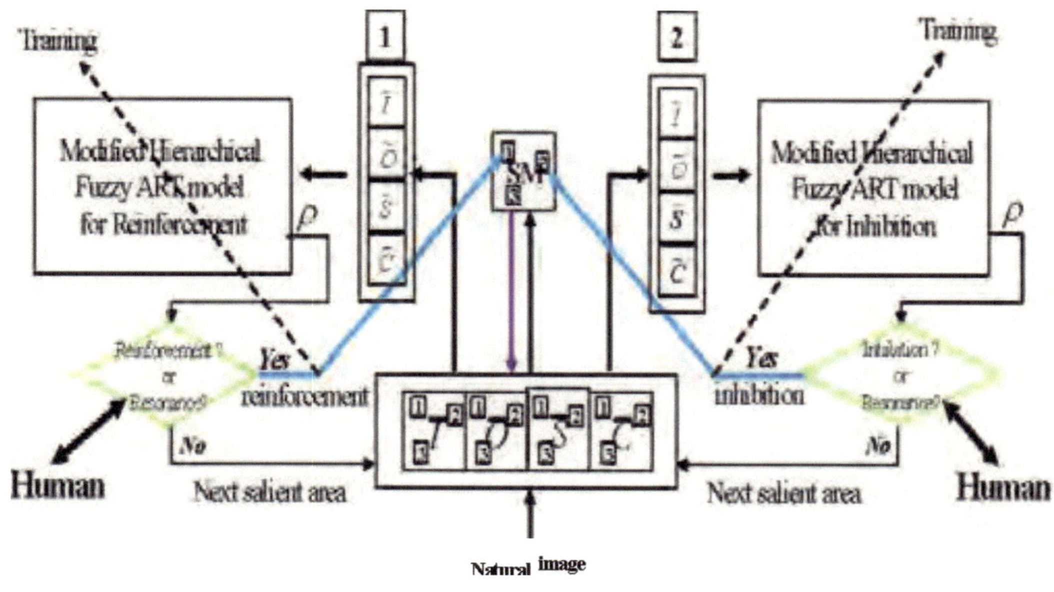

Figure 6. The architecture of the proposed low level top-down attention model with reinforcement(preference) and inhibition(refusal) property: (I : intensity feature map, O : orientation feature map, S : symmetry feature map, C : color feature map, SM: saliency map). Square block 1 in the SM is an interesting area, but block 2 is an uninteresting area

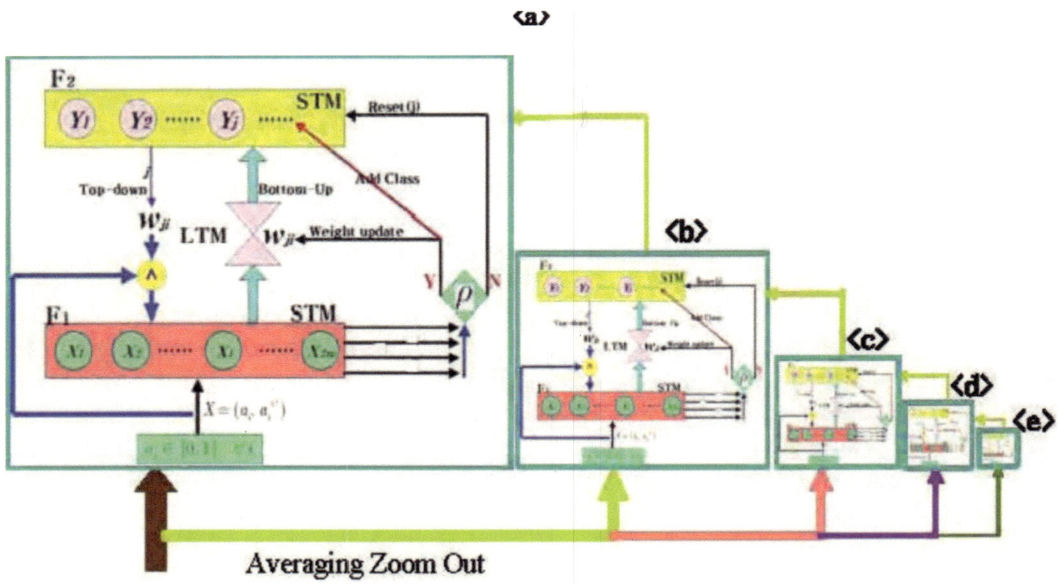

Figure 7. The modified hierarchical fuzzy ART network, where <a> represents the lowest level in fuzzy ART network and <e> does the highest level one

2.4 Stereo saliency

In this paper, we now utilize the depth information obtained by the vergence control vision system to construct the stereo saliency map model, which can then support pop-up for closer objects. In our model, the selective attention regions in each camera are obtained from static bottom-up saliency in conjunction with the low-level top-down preference and refusal, which are then used for selecting a dominant landmark. After successfully localizing corresponding landmarks on both the left image and the right image, we are able to get depth information by a simple triangular equation described in Section 3. Then, the proposed stereo SM model uses depth information as a characteristic feature in deciding saliency using a decaying exponential function. The final stereo SM is obtained by $S(x,y)\cdot \exp^{-z/\tau}$, where z is the distance between the camera and an attend region, and τ is a time constant.

3. Vergence control using the stereo selective attention model

3.1 Selection and verification of landmarks

During an infant's development, binocular disparity by binocular fixation is decomposed into three different mechanisms; alignment of eyes, convergence and sensory binocularity (Thorn et al., 1994). According to this fact, the single eye alignment should be the first factor considered regarding convergence that needs binocular fixation. In order to accomplish the single eye alignment, we use successive attention regions selected by the selective attention model in each camera image. Most of the stereo vision systems fix one of two cameras in the master eye. Humans, however, will probably not perform single eye alignment in this manner. The eye that has the dominant landmark may be considered the master eye, and the other eye is the slave eye that aligns itself to the landmark of the master eye. In our model, the trainable selective attention model generates the maximum salient value for the dominant landmark in each camera image. Comparing the maximum salient values in two camera images, we can adaptively decide the master eye that has a camera with a larger salient value. As shown in Fig. 2, the selective attention regions in each camera are obtained by the low-level top-down SM model for reflecting human's preference and refusal in conjunction with the bottom-up static SM model, which are used for selecting a dominant landmark. The low-level preference and resual SM model can reinforce an interesting object area in the bottom-up saliency map, which makes the interesting object area to be the most salient region even if it is less salient than another area in the bottom-up saliency map. Moreover it can inhibit an unwanted object area in the bottom-up saliency map, which makes the unwanted object area to be the least salient region even if it is more salient than another area in the bottom-up SM model. Therefore, the proposed attention model can have an ability to pay an attention to an interesting object area by the low-level top-down attention process together with the bottom-up SM model. Although the position of a salient region in the left and right cameras is almost the same, there exists a misalignment case due to occlusion and the luminance effect. In order to avoid this situation, we compare the difference of y coordinates between a dominant salient region in the master eye and successive salient regions in the slave eye because one of the successive salient regions in the slave eye may be in accordance with the salient region of the master eye. When the difference of the y coordinates is smaller than the threshold, we regard the salient region as a candidate for a landmark. In order to verify the candidate as a landmark, we need to compare the salient region of the master eye with that of the slave eye. The regions obtained by the IOR function, which is to avoid duplicating the selection of the most salient region, are compared in order to decide on a landmark. If the IOR region of the master eye is similar to that of the slave eye, we regard the IOR regions as a landmark to make convergence. The comparison of values of the IOR regions between the left and right cameras is used for the verification of a landmark.

3.2 Depth estimation and vergence control

After the landmark is successfully selected, we are able to get depth information. Fig. 8 shows the top view of verged cameras. First, we have to obtain the degrees of two camera angles to be moved to make a focus on a land mark. Considering the limitation of the field of view (F) in the horizontal axis and motor encoder resolution (U), we can get the total encoder value (E) to represent the limited field of view of the horizontal axis. The total encoder value (E) can be obtained by Eq. (5). As shown in Eq. (6), the total encoder value (E) is used to calculate the encoder value (x_t) of the horizontal axis motor for aligning of each camera to a landmark. In Eq. (6), R denotes the x-axis pixel resolution of the image and T denotes the relative pixel coordinate of the x-axis of a landmark from the focus position. In other words, T represents the disparity of x- axis. The x- axis encoder value (x_t) that uses to move each camera to the landmark point is translated into the angel (x_d) by Eq. (7). As a result, the angles a and b are obtained by Eq. (7) by substituting T for the x coordinates of the left and right cameras. Obtained depth information is used to generate a stereo SM. Finally, the proposed model decides the most salient area based on the obtained stereo SM and makes two cameras to focus on the same area by controlling motors of them, which is called vergence control.

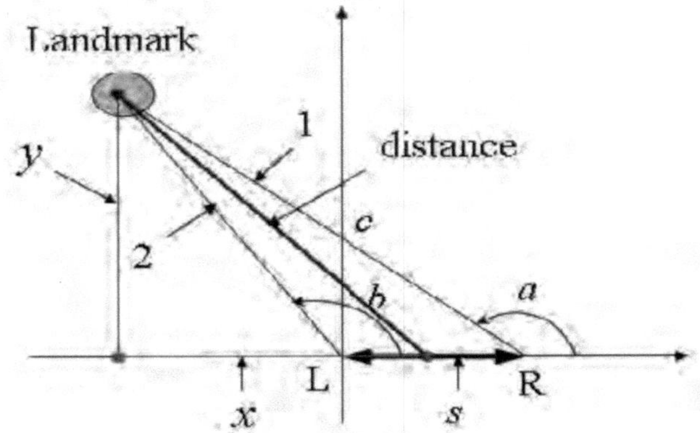

L: Left camera focus center, R : Right camera focus center, a : Right camera angle, b : Left camera angle, c : an intercept of the line 1, s : The distance between the two cameras focus, 1 and 2 : straight line from right and left cameras to a landmark

Figure 8. Top view of verged cameras

$$E = (F\times 360^\circ)/U \quad (5)$$

$$x_t = -E + (E\times T)/R \quad (6)$$

$$x_d = 90^\circ - (R\times x_t)/U \quad (7)$$

The vertical distance (y) is obtained by the following Eqs. (8-10).

$$\tan(a)\cdot x - s\cdot\tan(a) = y \quad (8)$$

$$\tan(b)\cdot x = y \quad (9)$$

$$y = \frac{\tan(a)\cdot\tan(b)}{\tan(a)-\tan(b)}\cdot s \quad (10)$$

Eqs. (8) and (9) show the equation of straight lines between the cameras and the landmark, respectively. In Eq. (8), x and y denote the disparities for x-axis and y-axis respectively between a land mark and a current focus position and s represents the distance between each focal axis of two cameras. Eq. (10) is the equation to calculate the vertical distance (y) in Fig. 8.

Fig. 9 shows three different cases for differently calculating depth information. If the angle of a and b shown in Fig. 8 are above 90° (case 1), the distance is $\sqrt{\dot{x}^2+y^2}$ because of $x = y/\tan(b)$ and $\dot{x} = |y/\tan(b)| + s/2$. If angle a is above 90° and angle b is less than 90° (case 2), the distance is almost y because the error is very small if the vergence point is not very close. If the angle of a and b are under 90° (case 3), the distance is $\sqrt{\ddot{x}^2+y^2}$ because of $x = y/\tan(b)$ and $\ddot{x} = |y/\tan(b)| - s/2$.

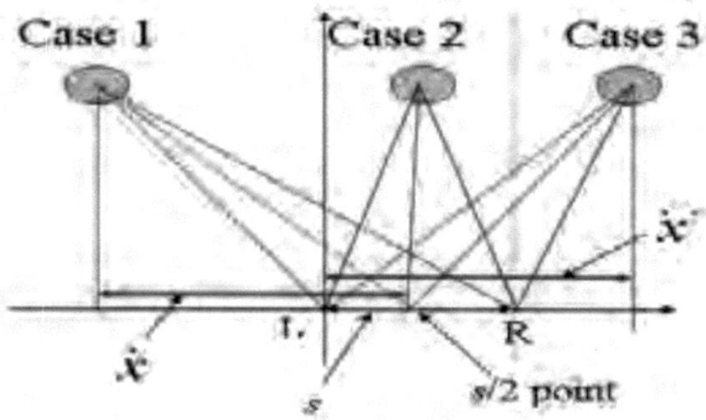

Figure 9. Three cases of obtaining the depth information

4. Implementation & Experimental results

4.1 Hardware implementation

We implemented a stereo vision robot unit for vergence control of two cameras. Fig. 10 shows the implemented system called by SMART-v1.0 (Self Motivated Artificial Robot with a Trainable selective attention model version 1.0). The SMART-v1.0 has four DOF and two 1394 CCD camera and Text to Speech module (TTS) to communicate with humans to inquire about an interesting object, and tilt sensor to set offset position before starting moving. We use the Atmega128 as the motor controller and zigbee to transmit motor command from a PC to SMART-v1.0. The SMART-v1.0 can search an interesting region by the selective attention model and vergence control which are explained in section 2 and 3.

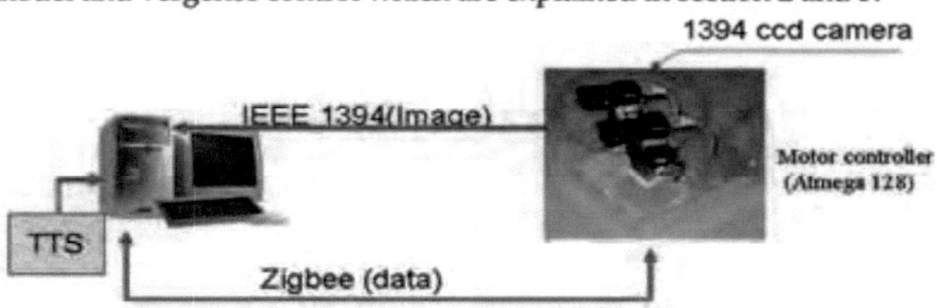

Fig. 10. SMART-v1.0 platform

4.2 Experimental results

4.2.1 Static saliency

Fig. 11 shows an example in which the proposed bottom-up SM model generates more object preferable attention by using symmetry information as an additional input feature and ICA for feature integration. The numbers in Fig. 11 represent the order of the scan path according to the degree of saliency. As shown in Fig. 11, the symmetry feature map is effective in choosing an attention area containing an object. The ICA filter successfully reduces redundant information in feature maps so that the final scan path does not pay attention to sky in the input image. Table 1 compares the object preferable performance of three different bottom-up SM models using hundreds of test images. The bottom-up SM model considering both the symmetry feature and ICA method for integrating features shows the best object preferable attention without any consideration of top-down attention.

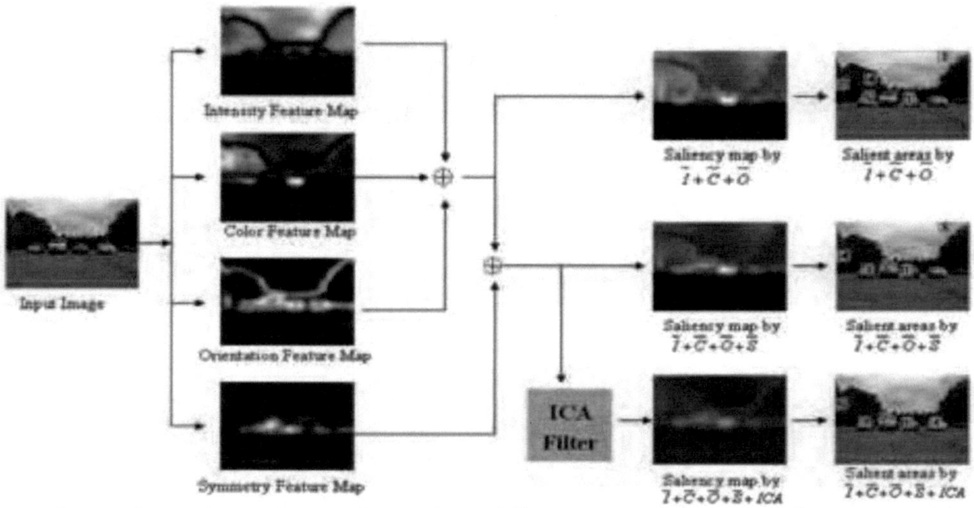

Fig. 11. Comparison of attention results by three different models for a same input scene. One is a result by $\bar{I}+\bar{C}+\bar{O}$ model. Another is a result by $\bar{I}+\bar{C}+\bar{O}+\bar{S}$ model. The other is a result by $\bar{I}+\bar{C}+\bar{O}+\bar{S}+ICA$ model

Salient area(SA)	$\bar{I}+\bar{C}+\bar{O}+\bar{S}+ICA$	$\bar{I}+\bar{C}+\bar{O}+\bar{S}$	$\bar{I}+\bar{C}+\bar{O}$
1st SA	165	150	143
2nd SA	106	104	103
3rd SA	68	77	64
4th SA	66	57	47
5th SA	46	32	28
Total	451	420	385
(%)	90.2 %	84.0 %	77.0 %

Table 1. Comparison of three different bottom-up SM models for object preferable attention

4.2.2 Low-level top-down selective attention

Fig. 12 shows the simulation results using the low-level top-down saliency component of our proposed model. Fig. 12 (a) shows the scan path generated by the static SM model, where the 3rd salient area is deemed a refusal area according to the human's preference and refusal, and it is trained by the low-level top-down SM model for refusal. Also, the 2nd salient area is changed after training the low-level SM model for preference. The bottom image shows the modified saliency map by reflecting human's preference and refusal during training process. Fig. 12 (b) shows the modified scan path by the preference and refusal low-level top-down attention process after training human's preference and refusal as shown in Fig. 12 (a). Fig. 13 shows an example for lip preferable attention, and Table 2 shows the performance comparison between the bottom-up SM model and the low-level

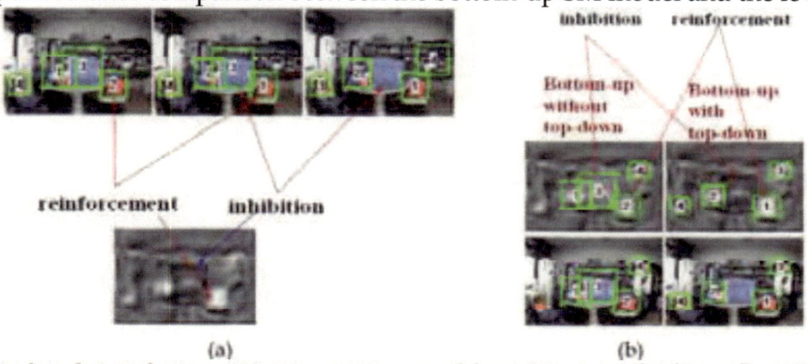

Fig. 12. Low-level top-down attention processes; (a) training mode for reflecting human's preference or refusal by reinforcing or inhibiting saliency map (b) experimental results reflecting human's preference and resual after training like (a)

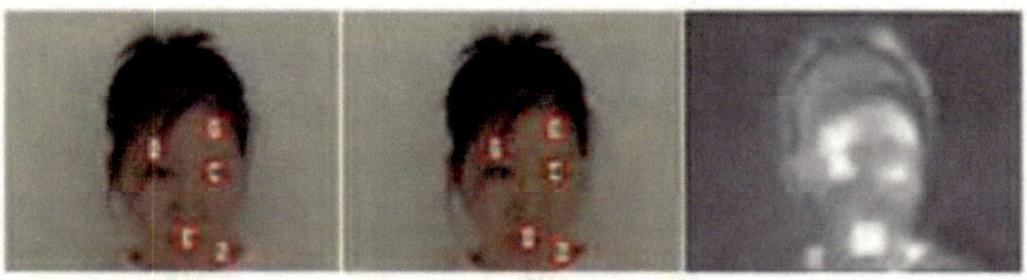

(a) (b) (c)

Fig. 13. Simulation results for lip preferable low-level top-down attention; (a) without considering the low-level top-down process, (b) considering the low-level top-down process, (c) saliency map after considering the low-level top-down process

	96 Training images	90 Test images	
		Bottom-up saliency map	Low-level top-down saliency map
# of images containing lip in 1st salient area	96	35	88
# of images containing lip in 1st salient area	0	55	2
	100%	38.9%	97.8%

Table 2. Low-level top-down attention performance

4.2.3 Stereo saliency and vergence control

Fig. 14 shows a simulation result using stereo saliency. As shown in Fig. 14, by considering the depth feature, the proposed model can make closer attened objects mostly pop out.

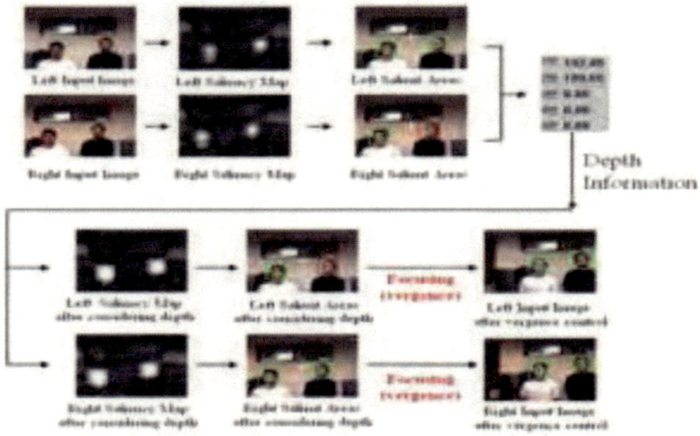

Fig. 14. Stereo saliency and vergence control experimental results

5. Conclusion

We proposed a new biologically motivated vergence control method of an active stereo vision system that mimics human-like stereo visual selective attention. We used a trainable selective attention model that can decide an interesting area by the low-level top-down mechanism implemented by Fuzzy ART training model in conjunction with the bottom-up static SM model. In the system, we proposed a landmark selection method using the low-level top-down trainable selective attention model and the IOR regions. Also, a depth estimation method was applied for reflecting stereo saliency. Based on the proposed algorithm, we implemented a human-like active stereo vision system. From the computer simulation and experimental results, we showed the effectiveness of the proposed vergence control method based on the stereo SM model. The practical purpose of the proposed system is to get depth information for robot vision with a small computation load by only considering an interesting object but by considering all the area of input image. Depth information of the developed system will operate for avoiding an obstacle in a robotic system. Also, we are considering a look-up table method to reduce the computation load of the saliency map for real-time application. In addition, as a further work, we are now developing an artificial agent system by tracking a moving person as main practical application of the proposed system.

6. Acknowledgment

This research was funded by the Brain Neuroinformatics Research Program of the Ministry of Commerce, Industry and Energy, and the sabbatical year supporting program of Kyungpook National University.

7. References

Abbott, A. L. & Ahuja, N. (1988). Surface reconstruction by dynamic integration of focus, camera vergence, and stereo, Proceedings of IEEE International Conference on Computer Vision, pp.532 -543, ISBN: 0-8186-0883-8

Barlow, H. B. & Tolhust, D. J. (1992). Why do you have edge detectors?, Optical society of America Technical Digest, Vol. 23. 172, ISBN-10: 3540244212, ISBN-13: 978-3540244219

Batista, J.; Peixoto, P. & Araujo, H. (2000). A focusing-by-vergence system controlled by retinal motion disparity, Proceedings of IEEE International Conference on Robotics and Automation, Vol. 4, pp.3209 -3214, ISBN: 0-7803-5889-9, April 2000, SanFrancisco, USA

Bell, A. J. & Sejnowski, T. J. (1997). The independent components of natural scenes are edge filters, Vision Research, Vol. 37., 3327-3338, ISSN: 0042-6989

Bernardino, A. & Santos-Victor, J. (1996). Vergence control for robotic heads using log-polar images, Proceedings of IEEE/RSJ International Conference. Intelligent Robots and Systems, Vol. 3, pp.1264 -1271, ISBN: 0-7803-3213-X, Nov. 1996, Osaka, Japan

Carpenter, G. A.; Grossberg, S.; Markuzon, N. J.; Reynolds, H. & Rosen, D. B. (1992). Fuzzy ARTMAP: A neural network architecture for incremental supervised learning of analog multidimensional maps, IEEE Trans. on Neural Networks, Vol. 3, No.5, 698-713, ISSN: 1045-9227

Carmi, R. & Itti, L. (2006). Visual causes versus correlates of attentional selection in dynamic scenes, Vision Research, Vol. 46, No.26, 4333-4345, ISSN: 0042-6989

Choi, S. B.; Jung, B. S.; Ban, S. W.; Niitsuma, H. & Lee, M. (2006). Biologically motivated vergence control system using human-like selective attention model, Neurocomputing, Vol. 69, 537-558, ISSN: 0925-2312

Conradt, J.; Pescatore, M.; Pascal, S. & Verschure, P. (2002). Saliency maps operating on stereo images detect landmarks and their distance, Proceedings of International Conference on Neural Networks, LNCS 2415, pp.795-800, ISBN-10: 3540440747, ISBN 13: 978-3540440741, Aug. 2002 , Madrid, Spain

Frank, T.; Kraiss, K. F. & Kuklen, T. (1998). Comparative analysis of Fuzzy ART and ART-2A network clustering performance. IEEE Trans. Neural Networks, Vol. 9, No. 3, May 1998, 544-559, ISSN: 1045-9227

Fukushima, K. (2005). Use of non-uniform spatial blur for image comparison: symmetry axis extraction, Neural Network, Vol. 18, 23-22, ISSN: 0893-6080

Goldstein, E. B. (1995). Sensation and perception, 4th edn., An international Thomson publishing company, ISBN-10: 0534539645, ISBN-13: 978-0534539641, USA

Hung, G. K. & Semmlow, J. L. (1980). Static behavior of accommodation and vergence: computer simulation of an interactive dual-feedback system, IEEE Trans. Biomed. Eng., Vol. 27, 439-447, ISSN: 0018-9294

Itti, L.; Koch, C. & Niebur, E. (1998). A model of saliency-based visual attention for rapid scene analysis, IEEE Trans. Patt. Anal. Mach. Intell., Vol. 20, No. 11., 1254-1259, ISSN: 0162-8828

Kadir, T. & Brady, M. (2001). Scale, saliency and image description, International Journal of Computer Vision, 83 -105, ISSN: 0920-5691 Koike, T. & Saiki, J. (2002) Stochastic guided search model for search asymmetries in visual search tasks, Lecture Notes in Computer Science, Vol. 2525, 408-417, ISSN: 0302-9743

Krishnan,V. V. & Stark,L. A. (1977). A heuristic model of the human vergence eye movement system, IEEE Trans. Biomed. Eng., Vol. 24 , 44-48, ISSN: 0018-9294

Krotkov, E. (1987). Exploratory visual sensing for determining spatial layout with an agile stereo camera system, University of Pennsylvania Ph.D. Dissertation also available as a Tech. Rep, MS-CIS-87-29

Lanyon, L. J. & Denham, S.L. (2004). A model of active visual search with object-based attention guiding scan paths, Neural Networks Special Issue: Vision & Brain, Vol. 17, No. 5-6, 873-897, ISSN: 0893-6080

Li, Z. (2001). Computational design and nonlinear dynamics of a recurrent network model of the primary visual cortex, Neural Computation, Vol.13, No.8, 1749-1780, ISSN: 0899-7667

Navalpakkam, V. & Itti, L. (2006). An integrated model of top-down and bottom-up attention for optimal object detection, Proceedings of IEEE Conference on Computer Vision and Pattern Recognition (CVPR), pp.2049-2056, ISBN: 0-7695-2597-0

Ouerhani, N. & Hugli, H. (2000). Computing visual attention from scene depth, Proceedings of 15th International Conference on Pattern Recognition, Vol. 1, pp. 375-378, ISBN: 07695-0750-6, Oct. 2000, Barcelona, Spain

Park, C. J.; Oh, W. G. S.; Cho, H. & Choi, H. M. (2000). An efficient context-free attention operator for BLU inspection of LCD production line, Proceedings of IASTED International conference on SIP, pp. 251-256

Park, S. J.; An, K. H. & Lee, M. (2002). Saliency map model with adaptive masking based on independent component analysis, Neurocomputing, Vol. 49, 417-422, ISSN: 0925-2312

Peng, J.; Srikaew, A.; Wilkes, M.; Kawamura, K. & Peters, A. (2000). An active vision system for mobile robots, Proceedings of IEEE International Conference. Systems, Man, and Cybernetics, Vol. 2, pp. 1472 - 1477, ISBN: 0-7803-6583-6, Oct. 2000, Nashville, TN, USA

Ramstrom, O. & Christensen, H. I. (2002). Visual attention using game theory, Lecture Notes in Computer Science, Vol. 2525, 462-471, ISSN: 0302-9743

Reisfeld, D.; Wolfson, H. & Yeshurun, Y. (1995). Context-free attentional operators : The generalized symmetry transform, Internatioanl Jouranl of Computer Vision, Vol. 14, 119-130, ISSN: 0920-5691

Thorn, F.; Gwiazda, J.; Cruz, A. A. V.; Bauer, J. A. & Held, R. (1994). The development of eye alignment, convergence, and sensory binocularity in young infants, Investigative Ophthalmology and Visual Science, Vol. 35, 544-553, Online ISSN: 1552-5783, Print ISSN: 0146-0404

Treisman, A. M. & Gelde, G. (1980). A feature-integration theory of attention, Cognitive Psychology, Vol. 12, No. 1, 97-136, ISSN: 0010-0285

Walther, D.; Rutishauser, U.; Koch, C. & Perona, P. (2005). Selective visual attention enables learning and recognition of multiple objects in cluttered scenes, Computer Vision and Image Processing, Vol. 100, No.1-2, 41-63, ISSN: 1077-3142

Werblin, F.S. & Roska, B. (2004). Parallel visual processing: A tutorial of retinal function, Int. J. Bifurcation and Chaos, Vol. 14, 83-852, ISSN: 0218-1274

Yamato, J. (1999). A layered control system for stereo vision head with vergence, Proceedings of IEEE International Conference on Systems, Man, and Cybernetics, Vol. 2, pp. 836 -841, ISBN: 0-7803-5731-0, Oct. 1999, Tokyo, Japan